Muck, Silk and Socialism

Muck,
Silk
and Socialism

Recollections of a Left-wing Queen's Counsel

John Platts-Mills, QC

First published posthumously in 2002 by Paper Publishing
Oldwood Cottage, Wedmore
Somerset BS28 4XW

Distributed by Gazelle Book Services Limited, Falcon House Queen
Square Lancaster, England LA1 1RN

British Library Cataloguing in Publication Data
A catalogue record for this book is available from the British Library

ISBN 0-9539949-0-2

Typeset by Amolibros, Watchet, Somerset
This book production has been managed by Amolibros
Printed and bound by T J International Ltd, Padstow, Cornwall,
England

Table of Contents

List of Illustrations

Plate section facing page 176

Plate section facing page 368

Acknowledgements

I SHOULD like to record my gratitude to Mary Dobson for her tireless and exhaustive research in an endeavour to improve the accuracy of my memory. Any failures on this score are entirely my own and must be put down to obstinacy or to later additions or amendments; also to my second son Jo for rescuing the manuscript, scanning it onto disk and generally reviving the belief that it could be published; to my eldest, Tim, for helping me bring it up to date and seeing it through the publishing process; to Tony Benn and Mike Mansfield for the Foreword and Introduction and to Barbara Cole for the jacket text. I hope that the many other people who have helped with and contributed to the writing of this book will forgive me for not mentioning them all by name. It has been nearly twenty years in gestation and during that time has taken on many different guises.

I am also pleased to thank the following for their kind courtesy in allowing me to use their photographs: Messers Gilman and Soame of Oxford for pictures of rowing at Oxford; Alexandra Sheriff for her father's caricature of the Oxford crew; Alpha for the picture of the Oxford crew at Henley and of H D Samuel's Chambers; The Tate, London for Janet's "Oriental Portrait"; Universal Pictorial Press and Agency for the picture of the wedding and Robin Smith of that agency for help finding other copyright owners; Thames and Hudson for the picture of Assington from *The Destruction of The Country House* by Roy Strong, Marcus Binny and John Harris; the *Sheffield Star* and the *Sunday Express* for the pictures of miners in Yorkshire; Mirror Syndication for pictures of campaigning in 1945; Topham Picture Point of Edenbridge for the pictures of the Finsbury meeting; Andrew Wiard/Record for the pictures of the Grunwick Strike; Ivan Lawrence QC for his caricature of the Kray Trial; The Corporation of the City of London for the picture of the Japanese Emperor.

Other illustrations are used with the permission of: *Illustrated London News* for the Sheriff cartoon; Getty Images for picture 18; Associated Press for picture 39; PA Photos for picture 40; Report for pictures 58-62; Atlantic Syndication for the Low, Vicky, Jak and Mac cartoons.

Every effort has been made to trace all copyright holders, but if any have been inadvertently overlooked, the publisher will be pleased to make the necessary arrangements at the first opportunity.

JPM
September 2001

Through the loss of a computer disk, the entire manuscript had to be scanned, which resulted in a few oddities that had to be weeded out. Sadly, Father died on 26th October 2001 just as he was completing the final proof-reading of this book. We therefore hope that readers encountering the odd error, particularly in some proper names, can 'tut' sympathetically.

Tim Platts-Mills
December 2001

Foreword by Tony Benn

THIS IS the story of a man who has devoted his life to the cause of progress, using his immense talents and boundless energy to help improve the lot of humanity.

Possessed of a phenomenal memory and a clear mind, John Platts-Mills has given his readers the opportunity to share his experience over three-quarters of a century as an activist, socialist and human rights lawyer.

Travelling all over the world, he knew many of the most significant figures of our time, and his modest account of his own work makes this a book that merits close study, and should be read by anyone who wants to understand what is happening and why.

Born into a well-to-do family in New Zealand, John came to England as a Rhodes scholar, trained for the bar, got involved in the anti-fascist movement in the 'thirties, served in the pits during the war and was elected as a Labour MP in 1945.

For those who now look back uncritically at the record of that reforming post-war government, his account comes as a healthy reminder of its less attractive side when the Cold War led to the harassment of the Left in parliament and ultimately to his own expulsion from the Labour Party and defeat in 1950.

During those years he was denounced as a fellow traveller because of his work in trying to build bridges with the Soviet Union, which, had they been encouraged by Foreign Secretary Ernest Bevin, might have changed the course of history.

Despite the witch-hunting which he experienced, John carried on with a formidable series of campaigns against imperialism, for peace and justice and supporting those who were being persecuted or tortured by repressive regimes or suffering at the hands of the judicial system in Britain.

His work with Amnesty and the National Council for Civil Liberties took him to South Africa, North Africa, Iraq, Tunisia, Chile, Libya, British Guiana, Vietnam, Aden, Ireland and Czechoslovakia.

Appearing in many high-profile cases in British courts, we also get an insight into the workings of justice here and the prejudices which exist within the legal profession.

This book is a memoir but it is so precise in its recollection that it might almost be a diary and John must be a formidable archivist to have been able to recall it all so precisely.

He was re-admitted to the Labour Party in 1964 and worked to help the miners in their historic campaign against the Thatcher attack, winning the support and admiration of many young men and women who regard him, quite correctly, as a legendary figure – modest, charming and encouraging, who has inspired them in their own work.

Unhappily, because of his great age, John Platts-Mills is not as well known to the new generation of Labour and Socialist activists as he should be, but any who take the trouble to wade through this massive book would have much to learn about what really happened and why we are where we are now.

His reflections on all these events make an important contribution to our history, and any future historian will be using this book as a guide to the years during which he has lived, and his comments on those whom he met.

If there is one lesson to be learned from it, it must be the importance of having principles and sticking with them, whatever pressures may be brought to bear to push you into silence or compliance.

John never surrendered, and kept on working for his own deeply held beliefs with remarkable success on many occasions, always inspiring those helped and assisting us as we face problems at least as difficult as those with which he had to contend.

For these reasons this is a book for this, and future generations to read and study, and we must all be grateful to him for having had the patience and application to put it all on paper so that we can read, study and use all he has learned in a life-time committed to all that is good and true, in a world still marred by so much brutality.

Tony Benn
July 17th 2001

Introduction
by Michael Mansfield QC

THE LIFE story of John Platts-Mills or JPM as he is affectionately known, straddles the major years of the twentieth century, and can truly be said to encompass a contemporary history of our times. It is a remarkable and compelling account of groundbreaking events chronicled by someone who played an active role in them; sometimes centre stage, sometimes behind the scenes, unheralded and unrecognised. Unlike him, many of the other players became household names, unlike him many are no longer alive.

The theme throughout, continuing into his ninety-fourth year, has been a singular and persistent struggle to secure justice in both the legal and political arenas. Justice for those facing intransigence, prejudice and oppression and for whom there would otherwise have been no effective voice nor support. It is a struggle not confined to domestic issues, but one that John has carried to all corners of the globe. He has been tireless in his efforts, always tempered with humour, infused with learning, and most of all imbued with courage.

He is a kaleidoscopically colourful character, a "Renaissance" man, who combines an astonishing array of talents—born in New Zealand; Oxford-educated; a miner; Labour MP; Queen's Counsel; political emissary known to a succession of world leaders. He provides a refreshing antidote to the superficiality of spin and soundbite characterised by current political celebrity, and particularly to those who feel impelled to write their diaries and biographies when they are barely beyond the cradle! This long-awaited and much overdue reminiscence has a breadth of perspective and a depth of detail rarely encountered. There are graphic descriptions of the daily grind and danger experienced by Yorkshire miners during John's time as Bevin Boy; his aspirations to be Solicitor General under the post-war Attlee government; and the tensions and drama of defending those accused of murder prior to the abolition of capital punishment.

I have been personally privileged to witness first-hand some of his inspiring exploits. They stretch from watching him rally the mass picket outside the gates of the Grunwick Print works in NW London in 1977, confronting lines of riot-clad police whilst he was immaculately dressed in bowler and pinstripes. Then working alongside him at the Old Bailey whilst he conducted a magical and masterful cross examination attacking the very fundament of the so-called forensic science of fingerprinting; and attracting as a result such judicial venom from the trial judge Mr Justice Melford 'Truncheons' Stephenson that all our fees were docked. Finally last year, 2000, accompanying him at The Guildhall in the City of London where, recently elected as one of its elder statesmen, resplendent in red robes he welcomed the Commonwealth heads of government to a dinner in their honour.

Here is a man for all seasons. A man who knows no bounds. Whether you agree or disagree with his views – no one can doubt the overall message of this book – purpose can only be promoted by passion.

Michael Mansfield

Prologue

IT IS said that history is written by the winners. Mine is a footnote to a loser's history for beginners.

Socialism is based on the belief that an honest person will want to work towards the well-being of the whole of society. Some of those who spend their lives in such a cast of thought and action become saints; others are treated as irresponsible outcasts. Many people grasp at socialism in their youth and when disillusion sets and they shed their beliefs, it is regarded as a sign of maturity. For me, the idea of socialism came late in life; I was almost thirty. Perhaps coming later it made a deeper impact.

I joined the Labour Party because it embodied Socialist principles. I parted company with Labour only when its leaders themselves moved so far from these principles that it was embarrassing to them when the gap was pointed out. When the party bureaucrats wished to end or suppress a course of conduct, they made an example of one among the malefactors and thereby silenced the others. I spent twenty-one years in the quaint artificial wasteland that Labour created for its discards. Over the years, one thinks of Stafford Cripps, G R Strauss, Nye Bevan, D N Pritt, Lester Hutchinson, Leslie Solly, Konni Zilliacus. All would have made useful cabinet ministers, and three of them did.

In 1941 Churchill gave me a wartime job encouraging support for Stalin. The Soviet Union appeared to be a genuine attempt to apply the principles of socialism, and on an enormous scale. To the astonishment of the world, the Soviet Union not only survived but shook off the attacker and finally destroyed him. Churchill required me to preach only the good stories about the Russians; he didn't care whether I believed them or not. He enjoined me not to worry about the future: it was a wartime job that could do no permanent harm, and so soon as the war was over, he would put the balance right. The holding back of the Second Front so that Germany and Russia might bleed one another white was part of that plan. I suppose one result of the highly successful propaganda was that I believed it myself. I was

1

certain that there were no Labour camps, no mass slaughters, no engineered starvation of kulaks, no decimation of military leaders in the late 'thirties. Millions of us believed all this.

The commitment to socialism took me into parliament in the 1945 draft, but almost destroyed my legal career. Our society is bound together by strict rules and even stricter prohibitions. The lawyer who is vociferously left-wing will find it hard to receive advancement at the Bar. There are no written rules but it is understood that the higher appointments are generally a reward for ability and for good behaviour. Advancement by recommendation from higher-ups creates the cosy intimacy of the gentleman's club, helping to keep out women, blacks and Asians and encouraging the otherworldliness some judges display. There are joyful signs that this has now changed, but in those days the practice was absolute. It also fosters too close a reliance on police evidence and an inability to accept that a policeman may sometimes succumb to the pressures of the job by assaulting or even framing a suspect. It is this attitude that led to the miscarriages of justice suffered by the Guildford Four and the Birmingham Six, amongst others.

Although the majority of policemen and women are honest and decent, it is the greatest folly to imagine that the police, as a whole, are incapable of committing misdemeanours. When a client offers the clearest evidence of assault while in detention, the fabrication of evidence or the procurement of a statement by the use of undue pressure, many lawyers turn away. Taking on such cases won me the unhappy reputation of a police-basher, but I had already gained a certain notoriety in the pre-war years, when the "premature anti-Fascists" – those who opposed Oswald Mosley and his blackshirts – were treated as potential traitors. In the 1950s, the same accusations of treachery were made against the Peace Movement.

In the 'thirties a guiding slogan was "If your name is in Debrett, never mention Soviet". The modern equivalent for avoiding social disgrace might refer to Gaddafi or to Arafat. Men who challenge our authority, even in their own lands, are threatening and therefore evil. Because our society regards them as a menace, the good citizen is expected to revile or at the very least ignore them. One flicker of an eyelid of recognition or of friendship and you are condemned as turncoat or traitor. I have never agreed with this view, nor accepted newspaper judgements about the character of individuals or events. The campaigns of vilification run by certain editors, in which readers are encouraged to hate some newsworthy personage, are as depraved as they are cruel. A barrister could never adopt the attitude that he must not "speak with enemies in the gate". A client must be argued for. The murderer, the child molester, the rapist: no one is so bad that he cannot be spoken with and listened to. In the same way, nothing will stop the diplomat from speaking face to face, however "unspeakable" the other may be. Every person and every nation should be guided by the example of the lawyer and the diplomat.

Taking silk brings higher fees and added kudos in public life. Any left-wing cause with which you are involved necessarily benefits from the distinction of your position and it can be helpful to have a Queen's Counsel chairing a public enquiry, especially if a controversial result is to be expected. However, a disappointingly large number of journalists hold that a QC is *ipso facto* a member of the establishment and has no right to distance himself in any way from nationally-cherished beliefs. Headlines such as "QC criticises police methods" or "QC backs Gaddafi " provoke them to outrage. I have found that the higher up one is in British society, the greater is thought to be the act of betrayal by the espousal of radical causes.

Within the family, one working title for my memoirs has been "Trout-shooting in New Zealand". The explanation is that in my youth I shot trout with a .303 rifle. The refraction of light meant that you could never be sure where to aim and the water so retarded the bullet that it soon lost its momentum, but the blow of the bullet sent a shock-wave through the water to stun any fish within yards. The fish would float belly-up and drift with the current. The trick was to get out into the rapids and catch them before they were carried downstream. I am told that my approach to politics and to life in general has been conducted in similar fashion: fire in the right direction and hope that when the smoke has cleared and the shock waves have subsided, the impact will somehow have achieved the desired effect. There is some merit in the analogy. In mitigation, I can only say that I have always tried my hardest, for what that is worth.

Chapter One

Childhood

MY POLITICAL activities and attitudes have been described as perverse and eccentric. I was brought up to think that political activity was a perfectly normal part of life. Father (Jack) took no part in such things except to be utterly conservative – a common New Zealand trait – although Mother (Daisy) was deep in public life. She skirmished on the fringe of all the political parties and groups, and took a great interest in social issues. In 1913 a general strike was called in support of the waterside workers. The sheep farmers, whose wool exports were in jeopardy, mounted their horses, acquired long police batons and came to Wellington, advancing on the strikers. Daisy established herself at the gatehead of the main wharves as doctor to the resulting bleeding crowns. At the age of seven, I carried buckets of water from a convenient tap in the Post Office Square under the noses of the horses of the police, and of the Special Constabulary whose riders had done the dirty work.

The following year, we three children waved banners outside a hansom cab in the general election. The banners read "Strike out the top line", the prohibitionist slogan for getting rid of the drink trade. From 1911 there was a compulsory vote on prohibition at each General Election. The brewers and whisky importers returned argument and persuasion with invective and opprobrium, and it seemed to us that our slogan had very few supporters. But the Women's Christian Temperance Union was one of Mother's many causes, so we waved our banners regardless. Rather than teaching us to take part on any particular side, this merely established the habit of joining in whatever might be going on, which was very much a Platts characteristic. The Platts half of my family was highly liberal in outlook with every wish for good things to be done, but the Mills half was entirely reactionary.

My paternal grandfather, Edward William Mills, had arrived in Wellington, or Port Nicholson, as it was then called, in 1842. In his teens, he went off to the Australian gold rush, where he quickly discovered that the best money was not in prospecting yourself but in providing material for those who were. He made a fortune, returned to New Zealand and became something of a potentate. He took public office, introduced to Wellington the telephone, the tram-car and the shipwright's business, and built steam ships and locomotives in a mighty foundry. The grand house on Aurora Terrace was one of Wellington's giants. E W Mills named it Sayes Court to mark his wife Louisa's descent from the English diarist John Evelyn. The five Mills daughters were married off to important men and, on the whole, the four sons followed their father in terms of initiative.

The youngest of them all was my father, Jack (John Fortescue Wright Mills), born in 1867. He ran racehorses and was active in rowing, hunting and polo, but was mostly kept at home to tend the family's horses, dogs, bits of farming and carriages, and to act as guardian and keeper to his sisters and mother. His outstanding achievement was the finding of Daisy Elizabeth Platts to be his wife. Daisy was one of New Zealand's first women doctors. My parents married in 1902, two years after Daisy graduated from the Dunedin medical school. Their three children were born at two-year intervals, and the youngest arrived on 4th October, 1906.

My older brother and sister were both quite well-built so I imagine that my mother was experienced at childbirth. But when I came along, I was very big indeed. I was well overdue and, although my mother was a doctor, the techniques of inducement were not very advanced at the time. I was still in the womb at twelve and a half pounds so, in a desperate attempt to rouse me, my mother went for a walk up a hill taking a whistle with her and telling Mr Pearce that if she blew it, he was to come with a wheelbarrow. There was a mighty view up there, it stretched for a hundred miles around. To the north, Mount Egmont a perfect, snow-capped cone rising above the sea, to the south, the rolling foothills beyond which, the fearful Cook Strait dividing the North and South Islands. And so it was that I was born on Campbells Hill, on a clear spring day at ten in the morning with the finest scenery New Zealand has to offer spread around before me. The experience was enough to persuade my mother not to have any more children but at least it cannot be said that she had nothing to look at. When the job was finally done, I was wheeled carefully home by Mr Pearce like a prize marrow fresh from the crop.

Daisy was tall for a woman, slim and energetic. She had masses of dark brown hair, which turned grey quite early in life and was piled up in a tumult with many hairpins. If she were going out, the hat was held on with pins that seemed to go clean through hat, hair and head, with a knob or ferrule screwed on the pointed end. She would do her surgery and leave something on to cook, with full written instructions, then off on her round. As a pre-school child, I very often accompanied Daisy in her buggy over the unsealed Karori roads. For six years, Mother was house physician to the children's ward at Wellington Hospital and was elected to the hospital board, topping the polls for two consecutive terms. Daisy was also a bigwig in the St John's Ambulance, serving as a lecturer and examiner, and as Wellington Divisional Surgeon for twenty years. She gave up private practice in 1915 to do special work for the Public Service Commission, finally retiring in 1933. We were very proud of her.

Daisy's father, Fred Platts, was born in India, son of a former sergeant in Her Majesty's 17th Foot. When he was sixteen and a cornet in the light cavalry, the colonel's wife advised him to go to England to get an education. In spite of his protests that he needed nothing more than he already had, he went to England to Bedford School and then on to Aberdeen University, where he won a "double first" in Classics. He was next heard of in Australia as Church of England parson in a parish in North Adelaide, which stretched 400 miles north of the city. After he had been there a year, he decided to beat the bounds of the parish. Some of the Platts family were still in India and with the cavalry and he persuaded them to send him a dozen good cross-country horses. Many horses for the Indian cavalry were born and bred in New South Wales and were called Walers as were most young living things in that colony. With five supporters and his dozen horses, he set off on his parish round. 300 miles north and still well within the parish, was the "Kingdom" of Ned Kelly, the most infamous highwayman of Australia. Fred met Ned and told him how much he needed God and soon nuggets of pure gold began to appear on the church offertory plate. On Ned complaining that the distinctive clang that his nuggets made on hitting the plate was putting his life in danger, Fred claimed to have invented the deep woollen offertory bag, which solved the problem.

The parish became rich. The parsonage was the biggest in the diocese, the parson paid the biggest subvention to the bishop and Fred was able to continue to produce what became his thirteen children. A suggestion was made, I believe from another parish, that all this money was being paid because Fred and his team, during the parish visit, had saved Ned Kelly and his gang from the police. He had five solid witnesses to the fact that he had only tried to save their souls, but the rumours persisted. In the end, the parish council made the subject taboo and agreed never to speak of it again. Shortly after that, the Bishop of Adelaide sent for him and said:

"You know, Master Platts, why I have sent for you?"

"No I do not and am unwilling to think why it could be."

"It is because of the Ned Kelly scandal."

"You know what we have decided in the parish on that topic?"

"Yes I do."

Upon this, Fred advanced two paces and punched him on the nose so that it bled. The bishop, with his nose still bleeding, at once dismissed him from his living and decreed that he was no longer a "clerk in Holy Orders". Fred appears to have challenged this hasty decision as being made in an unfit condition, but he was transferred to teach Classics at Melbourne Grammar School. All went well for a couple of years until the son of the mayor became his pupil. He was not a stupid but an indolent boy, as were so many sons of important people, and Fred found it necessary to box his ears for failing to learn his lessons. The next day Fred was walking in the new Melbourne City Park when the bishop, riding by, asked if the story was true. On Fred's confirming this, the bishop struck him with his riding crop. Fred promptly pushed him off his horse, then ran round and punched him on the nose. He appears to have been unfrocked once again and sacked from the school and would have been in a sorry state but for some little savings he had managed to accumulate. The suggestion was made in the *Melbourne Age* in March 1867 that during this period he sent his wife, my grandmother, to meet each immigrant ship and collect for the Mission to Seamen, which did not exist. My own feeling is that this must have been politically inspired.

Salvation came in the form of Bishop Neville of Dunedin, New Zealand, who was passing through Melbourne on his way to the 2nd Lambeth Conference. He sought out Fred and asked him:

"Are you the fellow who punched two bishops on the nose?"

8

"Yes I am, and do you want to be the third?"

"Oh please, no more violence, but you are the man I want for our parish at Port Chalmers in New Zealand. This is the sea port on the East Coast of South Island which is supplying the biggest Gold Rush in the history of the Southern Hemisphere. There arrive each year 10,000 souls who have suffered the perils, both physical and moral, of the Eastern Passages and are thirsty for the Word of the Lord. There are good men ready to help you build a church and a parsonage and there will be a rich life for you and your family."

And so it came to pass. There was a quarry of good building stone, ample timber and many willing and skilled hands to help. The church and the parsonage were built and the story of the "10,000 thirsty souls" can be read in the vestry today.

This is the story exactly as Daisy told it to me. I think she got the towns wrong and the Ned Kelly episode happened when they were in Victoria as he would have been only two years old when they left Adelaide.

Dad was big and strong but a bit ponderous. He was not quick in action or thought, and all was impeded by a monstrous truss – standard remedy for an inguinal hernia. This he bore from about 1912 when he gave up his polo and drag-hunting and rowing, until my sister had him stitched up by a Hampshire surgeon forty years later. That was more than half his life rendered cumbersome and tedious. He had lots of thick, dark brown hair and a full walrus moustache. He always wore a bowler hat and the raising of that hat was a minor ceremony. There was no exaggerated flourish to it but it was held on edge for a moment at shoulder level. The kissing of a female relative was always fun, and it was as though the brushing of cheeks had to be screened behind the hat. With anyone but close friends, the only greeting was, "How do you do?" and the reply was, "How do you do?" There was no sense of question or answer on either part. I used to stand back and watch with delight, wondering whether I would ever have a bowler and carry it with such aplomb.

It was fortunate that Daisy wanted to work because her salary was very much needed. We were always hard up. Jack shared all the family capacity for spending and enjoying the Mills' money, and none for making any more. He passed lightly through whatever came his way. He inherited and lost his share of his father's money, then he inherited the share of his elder brother and lost this too. Apart from these two short periods of extreme prosperity, there was never any money. It was always doom or boom. On marrying, Dad used his inheritance to buy the Karori Tea Gardens with its acres of garden and big, almost commercial greenhouses, the woods, stream and ponds. We were all born in the great, rambling wooden house. I can still place exactly the kauri tree, said to be the southernmost in the land, the totara, the graceful rimu and flaming pohutukawa, each a carefully nurtured specimen.

When Dad had gone through all the money, we suddenly moved to the smallest terraced house in Willis Street. There was no way through to the back garden except through the house, and no back garden. There was no room for buggy and horse so the pastoral share of the practice had to be run from a hired hansom cab. When I was about six we moved round the corner to a very big house at 81 Abel Smith Street. When I last visited New Zealand, it housed the headquarters of Jack Newman's nation-wide bus service. There must have been room, even then, for a few buses in the garden. We were there when World War I came.

For some years, when playing with my elder brother Bill and sister Deed (Ada) I had been made to play the German with an Uhlan helmet. Bill was the English and Deed the French. They claimed the more favourable positions by virtue of age alone, and although I stood my corner as best I could, I was always beaten in the wars that were waged between us. On 4th August 1914, I was bowling my hoop on the road. It was a big iron hoop of great power with a hooked iron handle for beating and guiding it. You could make those hoops go flying on a hard surface, though on long grass nothing much would serve. An adult voice said to me, "Little boy, we are at war with Germany," a shattering statement that threw me into total confusion. Was I now the real enemy because there was a real war? What troubles I was going to suffer from my brother and sister!

In anger I gave my hoop an almighty blow so that it went flying into Abel Smith Street just as the milk float was coming past with the daily delivery. This was an open-backed chariot bearing a large churn of milk to be ladled out to customers. On the churn was a polished brass sign with the name of the Welsh purveyor, for it seemed that all retail milk was dealt with by the Welsh as certainly as all retail greengrocery by the Chinese. To my shame, the hoop ran into the forelegs of the horse and encircled them causing the horse to fall down and the milk float to tip over. But I didn't get into any trouble. I think the milkman attributed it to the start of the war.

It was in the kitchen of the house at Abel Smith Street that we children had our operations. Daisy was a devotee of the system of child-upbringing propounded by Dr Truby King, who believed in eliminating from the body any unnecessary protuberance, making all smooth. One could remove the tonsils, adenoids and the appendix; with males, there was a further choice. (I don't know why, but my appendix was spared until I reached the age of sixteen.) A surgeon would come to the house and we were laid out in turn on the kitchen table, which had been scrubbed and pumiced until it shone, then varnished and disinfected. The smell of varnish and carbolic was a useful distraction from the horrid taste of chloroform. Being under the mask and feeling that there was no escape was frightening. The only relief was the counting and I never got beyond ten, and this gave me complete confidence in doctors.

Dad still had a sufficient interest in the Karori place for us to be able to move back there. We acquired a gardener when Daisy rescued a visiting German from Soames Island internment camp for enemy aliens. Mr von Bulow proved to be expert at every sort of gardening and the daily offering of vegetables arranged symmetrically in a trug was an exhibition piece. He must have wondered at our capacity for vegetables, for Daisy used discreetly to take the surplus to the local hospital. This skill in gardening seemed inconsistent with the man''s bearing and demeanour, for he carried himself like a guardsman. When home during the school holidays, I came to have great admiration for von Bulow. He showed me exercises, including a press-up on one arm that I could copy only ten years later. Von Bulow lived in the whare, a one-roomed house in the woods, and kept himself so much alone that the neighbours scarcely knew of him. I never heard a word of hostile comment about our having him there.

I remember in 1916 an insurance representative coming to call on us. Some bargaining was going on about a policy for me, some one hundred pounds' worth. My mother said, "John, drive the geese away from the door. Your father is going to sign his name." I cried, "Boo," to the geese; the geese ran; my father took up a freshly-shed quill, and cut and split it with a sharp knife. He stood, took off his jacket to roll up his sleeves and made threatening motions of a circular character with his right hand, then took the quill and signed. He was not a highly literate fellow. Jack had a copy of *Ewart on the Horse* and except for *The World's Hundred Best Short Stories*, which took up many volumes, it was his only book. Daisy had many more but they were all medical or on subjects of a para-medical type; and endless copies of the *British Medical Journal*, sent by post and all unopened. We children took great pleasure from the medical books, which were brightly illustrated in colour. Pictures of bits of the body were always a delight, especially if they were the richer bits.

We were brought up in a very prudish fashion. All New Zealanders were. Daisy lectured quite regularly to groups of young women about maturity and sexual problems, but nothing of the sort was discussed with us. From notes and references to books left about at home, the topic was limited to birds, bees, butterflies and flowers. Pistils and stamens figured largely. I believe that she later wrote a booklet about venereal disease, but this was certainly not seen in the house. After years in practice as a GP, Daisy was heard to use the phrase "these dreadful social diseases like clap and rape and the pox".

Then came the inheritance from Jack's eldest brother, and we moved into Sayes Court with its halls and reception rooms, the ballroom with mirrors and chandeliers, and ample stabling. Even the taps in the bathrooms seemed more powerful than any seen before and were christened "thunder taps". In New Zealand, we liked to think of ourselves as too democratic for servants. Mother had two "lady helps", Victoria and Sibyl Spiers, who lived with us and did much of the housework. They began in their teens and for the next fifteen years were with us whenever Mother could afford to pay them, and several times came back even when she could not. They left to get married, but still came back. Once, at Sayes Court, Vicky moved in with her family knowing that she wouldn't be paid for some time but determined to help us.

The family business had become that of a general importer of all sorts of hardware from machinery to brooms and brushes. As transport became easier and quicker, anyone could go to Britain and find a manufacturer of one line, import those articles, tour the country with his wares and take the whole market for himself. Such an importer could run his business from one back bedroom with no overheads. E W Mills had a great building on a prime site with enormous overheads and a big staff. They could not compete and by 1920 were in real trouble. Dad, as managing director, took the blame. He was fired by his united brothers-in-law, who made him sell all his shares in the business and retire. Brother Bill was also fired, and we were all turned out of Sayes Court. They also ordered Dad to sell his children, or at least take them away from school and let them earn their own livings. I had just started at Nelson College when we reached this lowest ebb of our family fortunes.

These upheavals left Daisy apparently unperturbed. It did not occur to me at the time that Dad's business and financial failures might have led to her saying something by way of disapproval. "Done it again" would have been the most obvious reproof, yet at no time did we hear a word of disharmony between them. Daisy was entirely devoted to Jack. She moved us back to the old house in Karori, but the cost proved too great. The estate had to be split up into building sections and sold. The sale yielded a poor result and we took from it only enough to buy a small new house in Amy Street near the trains. The house had one room like an atrium, with half-a-dozen tiny rooms no bigger than cubicles leading off. Amy Street seemed a poor sort of name so we re-christened it Marsden Avenue. This was justified by the building of a fashionable girls' school of that name at the end of the road. Bill and I made a passable attempt at a street sign, "Marsden Avenue", and nailed it to a lamppost and the name was soon adopted by the borough council.

Dad surrendered and became the houseman of the family. He would wear his dressing gown until lunch-time. He made porridge daily and would serve tea in bed to all whom he could forestall. His fried tomatoes were a dish in themselves with milk, mustard, sugar and all else besides tossed in. Dad cleaned the shoes of the whole family, but cleaning the shoes of house-guests was a problem. He could not go the round of the bedrooms to collect up footwear after hours and sometimes had to ask them to remove their shoes at breakfast. When Daisy got her first car (a Hupmobile which was, I think, the first one of its type in the country) Jack was quite out of his depth. He never sat behind the wheel and never lifted the bonnet. The side and back lamps were paraffin and these he would trim, but the grandiose brass headlamps powered by carbide with water dripping onto it were too modern for him.

Father could sense earthquakes coming. There is said to be a rumble that precedes the tremor, but the vibration is so low that the normal human ear cannot detect it. He would say, "Here's one," and it was a second or two before one felt the tremor. He was as gentle, considerate, thoughtful and unlearned as anyone could be.

The second worst rebuke he ever administered to either me or my brother was to address us as "sir" with the phrase "if you were to repeat that conduct, I don't know what I should do…" and the worst was "Sir, if such conduct were to be repeated any further, I should have to consider reporting it to your mother". It could be said that he never succeeded in anything except to arouse a wealth of extreme pleasure and sympathy. He was loved by many, and above all by his third and youngest child.

After losing his job, Dad was a quiet, home-keeping fellow unless my mother took him for an occasional outing. The fashionable thing for men was to belong to the Wellington Club and to have a spot of whisky with friends. Daisy called this "spotting" and barred Jack from going to his own club. Our Uncle Thomas got into the liquor trade and so badly did Daisy take this that we were not allowed to meet him, see him or know him. Prohibition was obviously right because Mother said it was and Father didn't demur, but the world of Tom seemed free and adventurous. He was the unseen flag-bearer of another life that was hidden from us; even his name hinted at a broader future. For many years, if faced with a difficult choice, I would think "Tom" and wonder if there might be a different approach to the problem.

My parents also differed on religion. Dad was not prejudiced against the church, merely indifferent. He went for his baptism at Mother's request immediately before their marriage, but so far as I know, attended church on no other occasion. Mother seemed quite content with this; her own zeal was sufficient. I was introduced to religion at St Mary's, the Anglican church in Karori, not on my knees at the altar but in a mechanical way from behind the organ. From the age of seven, I blew the church organ for Mother to practise. A long wooden arm went straight to the top of the bellows, and a weight on a string showed by its height the air available to the pipes. With normal music I could keep up, but when Daisy reached for a certain stop and gave it the full diapason, then even the most furious pumping could not keep the pressure full. The weight would soar up the scale as the organist plunged her legs at the pedals and hammered the keys and pulled at the stops. At ten I was promoted to the choir, so pumping was out.

In March 1910, New Zealand's most talked of criminal must have been Joe Pawelka, a young Palmerston North butcher. Remanded to Wellington on burglary charges, he escaped and went on the run in the Manawatu district. He stole to stay alive. Buildings were set on fire, people were scared to go out and scared to stay at home, armed gangs chased every reported sighting and, somehow or other, two men got themselves shot and killed. All was blamed on Pawelka. He was convicted of escaping from custody, a series of minor thefts and one count of arson, but acquitted of all other charges, including murder and armed robbery. Although he was just twenty-two years old, the cumulative sentence added up to twenty-one years imprisonment. The judge capped it by declaring Pawelka an "habitual criminal", which meant that he could never be set free.

Twenty thousand signed a petition to protest against the severity of the sentence. Every journalist must have written about Pawelka, prison and punishment, and every family talked about it. There were mixed feelings in August 1911 when he escaped from the Terrace Gaol (only a few hundred yards from our house) and was never recaptured. I was four years old and at my most impressionable. All my knowledge and all misconceptions of prisons began with Mr Pawelka. I heard older members of the family discussing the condemned man's last night in his prison cell, and wrongly thought that Pawelka had been sentenced to death. The effect on my mind was frightening.

The clearest and strongest political belief I have held is that the death penalty should be abolished everywhere and forever; that the concept of no death sentence should be written into the Charter of the United Nations as a fundamental human right; and that any departure should lead to punitive sanctions against the country and individual concerned. Its use can never be justified, not even for the worst of murderers, the war criminals. It was the imagined horror of Pawelka in his death cell that made me opposed to capital punishment. It also gave me the worst fear that I suffered in all my youth. Even at the age of ten, after evening choir practice in midwinter, during the long walk home from St Mary's down the dark country roads, when I was frightened that some man might jump out at me, there was the consolation of comparing my favourable position with the misery of Pawelka.

My education began when, at the age of six, I started at the local state school This was still in the days of learning by rote. I was good at committing things to memory and I soon began learning an incredible quantity of mainly useless stuff. To this day I can quote a good number of the formulae I was taught. I enjoyed school and did well for a time. Eventually, however, my willingness to pick up new ideas and pursue them like a terrier got me into some trouble.

At the age of about eight I joined the local boy scout troop which brother Bill had played a large part in forming. One day he came across a book which recorded all of the scouting badges. There were badges for cooking, pet-keeping, tent-making, sailing, and so forth.

They were a revelation, and I set to work to gain badges. This was the first example I can remember of a tendency "to go over the top". I was obsessive to a degree. I was soon going absent from school for a couple of days at a time. For example, to put myself to the local boot-maker, in order to make a pair of boy's boots for the boot-maker's badge and to qualify for the leatherworker's badge. And a couple of days off school to go collecting leaves for the fifty needed for the naturalist's badge. Mother showed me how to trace both Latin and Maori names and how to approach museum curators and librarians.

Then came the signalling badge. Semaphore was easy – just waving a pair of flags. But Morse had endless possibilities – I could do it with flags or with lanterns, with a pair of sticks (one short, one long) or by throwing hoops in the air, with drops of water into a bucket, by knocking on a wall or by shuffling my feet. And this was all very well. The major trouble began when I learned to do it by blinking. My mother was already disapproving of the badge business because it was affecting my schoolwork. When one day she asked me what I was doing after school and I replied, by blinking, "I'm going off to town to see the harbour master for advice about the navigator's badge," she was enraged.

"I've had enough, I'm sending you away to boarding school where there are no scouts, no badges, no wasting of time, just hard work learning. Let me not see another wink." And so in 1917 I was sent to Ocean Bay School in Marlborough Sound, which was run on roughly similar lines to Gordonstoun or Timbertops. Unless you were prepared to take on a two-day cross-mountain trek, Ocean Bay could be approached only by sea. From Wellington, it was a crossing on the Picton ferry and a short train ride to Blenheim, then four and a half hours down the Opawa river (crossing the perilous Wairau Bar) and across open sea to Ocean Bay, where Jack Crump, headmaster and retired Methodist missionary, would be waiting to row us ashore.

It was a prep school on a sheep station of 1,500 acres. It was thirty miles (two days' climb across mountains) from the nearest shop. I was to board there for two years but I didn't mind at all – as I have said, my only rule was to do whatever I was told and my mother had brought me here so that was that. Nothing shocked me but everything was new. It proved to be rather like an Outward Bound school. We worked very hard at the standard curriculum from nine till twelve. I learned to make notes for exams and to cram like mad. I got to the stage where I would begin an answer by giving a page and a half of notes before getting to the question. I did a lot of showing off. There were only sixty boys in total and we were all taught lessons by the same man. He was a dreadful chap named Pat Fitz Fitzgerald Fitzgerald Eager (the excessive quantity of Fitzes – perhaps there were more, I'm not sure – was due to his being from some Irish family of great importance). Since I was one of the best at exams, he took me aside one day and said to me, "You must work your very hardest. You mustn't let the McCormac brothers beat you. After all, they are not from the professional classes, so it wouldn't do to let them win." It had never before occurred to me to try and beat anyone in exams and neither that the professional status of one's parents made any difference to anything. And so it was that this man introduced me not only to the concept of competition, but also to that of class distinction. In New Zealand, we boasted that there were no social grades at all – we were all New Zealanders – and this was what I was brought up believing. In fact, it went further than that. Through ignorance, the name Hongi Huki Huki was to me nothing other than a New Zealand name, as was for example Cohen or Svensen. Nevertheless, regardless of Fitzgerald and bizarre as it may seem, I came to enjoy exams a great deal.

Lessons stopped at twelve and we spent the afternoons being put through our paces on all the routine of sheep management. At the age of eleven, I enucleated a young ram with my teeth. It was a very simple process. At twelve I killed, fleeced and dressed an adult sheep. This was New Zealand life; there were ninety million sheep in the country, we lived with sheep and on sheep and the killing of one was a routine part of life – I thought about it no more than the milking of a cow. I don't think vegetarianism had been heard of in the colony in my time.

Back then before about 1910, sheep stations were not bounded by anything except mountain ranges and headlands – your station would stretch from the top of the nearest range to the edge of the sea and between the nearest two headlands. Four times a year there would be a big mustering of all the sheep for special occasions – shearing, births, deaths, marriages etc. – and at school this was done, not by men on horses with dogs, but by scores of boys spread across the countryside, twenty paces between them, shouting "hey!", "hoy!", "woah!" and "come on, you brute!" (to the junior boys, that is, since it was they that had to do the real work, like going down into small gullies to ferret out hiding sheep).

We lived as much in the sea as on land. We took from the sea everything that could be used. In the bay we had our own oyster and mussel beds. During the summer, when it was dead low tide at four on a Sunday morning when no master could conceivably be about, the whole senior school would be down there sitting on the oyster beds, cracking the oysters and opening them with knives and eating them with a saline dressing as provided by the sea. We went on the water in every conceivable sailing machine – we even built a Maori canoe. We cut a great totara tree from the bush and since it was hard wood, we spent weeks chipping at it with axes and then hollowing it out using slow-burning fires. It took twenty of us a whole year of working to complete it. When it was finally finished it held thirty boys and, although it had a tendency to roll over, we paddled it a mile across the sea to Port Underwood and back. It was more stable under sail than with paddles.

My years at Ocean Bay made me content to tackle anything that life could bring me. I have a kind of maxim about it: "Once you have castrated a ram with your teeth aged eleven and made a Maori canoe, you're fit to face any activity of any kind whatever, in any medium." Not poetic, perhaps, but certainly telling.

We heard little news from outside our own isolated realm of bush, sea and mountain, and the end of the First World War was a memorable occasion. At morning assembly the headmaster declared, "Boys, the war is over. We have won. We have conquered Germany!" and I am sure we all burst out cheering. Our upbringing was jingoistic to a degree. It was an exciting school. Boys were given a quite remarkable degree of freedom and trust in the hope that it would foster both self-reliance and self-discipline, but we were not encouraged to think for ourselves.

CHAPTER TWO

New Zealand Education

AT THIRTEEN, it was off to Nelson College: a great school in its way, but suffering from an immense military and rugby tradition. We were put into the territorials, which meant two hours' drill every Friday afternoon. We had our own range for .22 firing, and access to a proper long-distance range for .303 with red flags and warning sirens, and even a few derelict 18-pounder field guns. In four of my six years we were champion cadet corps, and in 1921 winners of the *Weekly Press* Shield for small bore shooting. I was passed as a small arms instructor and became sergeant-major of the college company. Few boys had wit enough to realise what nonsense that military stuff was.

Even the younger masters, who had just come back from the war and were perhaps pacifists in intention, found themselves caught up in the general eagerness to defend New Zealand against the Yellow Peril. The Chinese were there in their millions and were longing for space; they would certainly overrun the Pacific. Nothing could have been more absurd, for who had ever caught the Chinese beyond their own borders? No one thought of the Japanese as possible attackers. Throughout the 'twenties, Japanese warships made visits of friendship to New Zealand ports. We often saw expeditions of three or four men walking over the country roads smiling and waving happily whilst taking photographs. We learned afterwards that the Japanese had deliberately collected photos of every part of New Zealand that they could reach. However, we prepared for the Chinese with some diligence.

The final joy was that we were entitled on holidays to take a gun with a handful of .303 ammunition to the mountains and rivers where deer and pig and fine trout were aplenty. Tramping was a widespread colonial habit, going over old tracks and mountain ranges. The remote bush country had sound huts, some of which we helped to build and keep in repair, which held a pot or two, a supply of salt and matches, firewood and an axe. Occupiers were expected to replace what they used. No doubt it was the combination of this military training and a normal upbringing with a gun in wild places, going cross country with others in unison, that made the New Zealand expeditionary forces so formidable.

The First World War had also had a major impact on rugby-playing at Nelson College. During the war, they had played senior rugby, contributing their members to the local provincial team. This was because all the fit young men were away in the army, and in the last couple of years the senior boys stayed on at school, their families hoping that the latest expeditionary force would be the last of all. It all changed when the soldiers came back, for boys left earlier and the strength of senior school sides was dissipated. It would have required miraculous coaching to make anything of those teams for the next six years. When I got into the senior team, we were seldom victorious. If memory serves me correctly, in 1923 we were beaten 50-0 by Inangahua Junction Rovers (second team).

Until the age of thirteen, I had neither seen nor held a rugby ball. I had twice played with a soccer ball, each time being spanked for not trying. "For not trying what?" I asked, having no idea of what ought to be done. One day in the dormitory a shorter, sturdier boy called me "spindleshanks". I decided that I was not good enough and must somehow overcome that baleful name. So I exercised and swelled until I bulged, and became the school champion athlete. I had a straight back and, through perseverance at exercise, developed big muscles and stamina. I had no sort of inborn skill, but tried very hard at everything. In the third form, one boy was upbraided for studying hard and called a swot. He burst into tears and said, "You would do the same if you wanted to come top." I think these were the first occasions on which it ever occurred to me that there was any competition to do better than others.

Brother Bill was four years older, but I was born heavier and grew bigger. Although much smaller than me, Bill had won Nelson heavyweight boxing when under ten stone and played in the rugby 1st XV. I thought he was a hell of a chap. In my third year at Nelson he was head boy: a position he achieved through personality. It never occurred to me that you could limp into the sixth form, regardless of ability, if you kept at it long enough. At university he didn't do much except play hockey for

Wellington Province, help to reduce the local deer population as a menace to sheep farmers, and establish fly fishing as permissible for New Zealanders. (Until then, freshwater fish were treated as food and caught by cruder methods. Fly fishing was, for the kiwi, an effete Pommy indulgence.) It is not that Bill was in any way stupid. He had considerable determination and vigour, while I never remember having decided anything much at all. I just did what followed on and what the next adviser suggested.

At the age of sixteen, I took part in a strike-breaking expedition. A seaman's strike in New Zealand had stopped wool shipments and passengers alike. One of my uncles (a schoolteacher who should have known better), a schoolfriend Ken Anderson and myself signed on as deckhands on the liner SS *Marama*. We slept in a steerage cabin over the propeller, but otherwise we lived with and as ordinary crew: scrubbing, painting and standing lookout watch at the ship's bow. One night I rang the alarm bell and shouted that there was a ship on fire. A weary voice from much higher up on the bridge replied, "Silly ass! It's the moon rising."

At Sydney, after unloading we went to a coaling berth. There we sealed up everything below decks and saw ourselves and the ship covered in coal dust, which then had to be scrubbed and washed down. Late in the evening, all who wished to go ashore were mustered together and ushered through lines of police and angry pickets. We were hurried into taxis and taken to the main hotel. After a couple of days' leave, we were ushered back in the same undignified fashion. It was clear enough that we were not popular, but I didn't fully understand why. On the return journey, we had fare-paying passengers: Chinese migrants, who would be shipped straight back to Australia unless they could speak English. The test was the ability to sing our national anthem and I spent many hours teaching them to sing "God save the King". I then developed appendicitis, which was sufficient punishment for scabbing.

Despite Daisy's involvement in public life, our upbringing was quite reactionary and we had no real understanding of political issues. Father accepted whatever Mother proposed, for she was the educated one, full of lofty opinions, but these opinions, however strongly held, were never discussed with the children. Mother entertained very little. Ladies would come to visit when she was "at home", arriving by buggy, swathed in veils against the Wellington wind. Although Daisy knew all the top politicians, they were never invited to our home.

My parents were not racists and I grew up entirely ignorant of racial groups. At school, we were all equally kiwis, and I was unaware that Cohen and Svenson were other than New Zealand names. At the turn of the century, there were famous Maori and half-Maori families such as the Barrons and the Graces, who took leading parts in all sectors of life: playing rugby, but also providing ministers of state, members of parliament and business men of great distinction. We went to the same schools and universities as their children, and stayed in their homes during holidays, and they with us. I remember staying with the Pomare family in the Hutt Valley. Ngaere woke me at two a.m., saying he was hungry. We went to the kitchen and cooked and ate sixteen eggs between us, with toast and butter, although in those days schoolboys ate raw eggs as readily as cooked ones.

Yet there was a profound prejudice against Catholics. Most New Zealanders were Protestant of some sort and saw Catholics as reactionary idolaters. The colonising branch of the Catholic church was the Marist Brothers. They had schools in many parts and produced good rugby teams. When Nelson College had a Marist team as opponents, we "put in the boot" as hard as we could. There was no taunting, no anticipating what we would do or gloating over it afterwards. It was a subtle influence. Our curate would not have approved. He had been a boxer at heavyweight in some school or university and was my first contact with "muscular Christianity". His attitude to the Bible and the Prayer Book was equally robust. The question of the existence of God did not arise; He was *There* for Certain. For me, this state of conviction lasted only until I reached university.

At Sunday services, it was customary to look sheepishly at the girls' crocodile on the other side of the cathedral, but that was as close as we came, with few exceptions. The Bishop of Nelson had two attractive daughters, rather older than me and both suitable for brother Bill. We were asked to tea on Sunday afternoons, but nothing came of it. Nearby lived a widow with her two daughters; again, nothing came of it. In my last year, I became friendly with Una, a doctor's daughter. Her brother Dick was a student at Nelson, so she had every excuse to attend school functions. Una hit a tennis ball as though she were a man, and drove a golf ball or a car with equal authority and strength. She was very good-looking and short enough to be petite, had she not been too strong. Una came on an expedition that climbed Mount Arthur at Christmas 1924. Mount Arthur was no great feature of a mountain, but it is the best I have done.

In 1924 I was head boy and about to become champion athlete. I was no end of a swell in the school. Training began with a morning run. They were bright mornings and I went further and further into the country until I found myself beside the first of the orchards that began within two miles of the school. The apples were glowing and ripe and it was inevitable that I should munch one on the way home. Next day two were stuffed into the bulging pockets of my running shorts. Soon I was taking a pillow case and coming back with three or four pounds of apples. The two boys with whom I shared a small dormitory were delighted; even the next dormitory had a share. I thought of my father's main recollection of the study of Latin at Wellington College. Two of the many meanings of "malo" were "a naughty boy" and "up an apple tree". But this was more than a schoolboy up an apple tree, this was highly thought-out theft.

The consequences of being caught were fairly obvious: disaster and disgrace. The head of school would be sent down for stealing apples and appearing before the magistrates. It might even mean jail, for borstal was not yet invented. Disaster for myself and for the college. But the headmaster could not allow that to happen. Surely he would have to protect me for the sake of the school? I took added precautions. The pillowcase never appeared on the outward journey but was tucked safe in a pocket. I went earlier, I spread the area of my depredations, moved to another orchard, went well away from the road to prevent the owner from coming upon gaps in his crop. I made innocent runs on alternate days and kept a scrupulous look out. Indeed, no one appeared; no milkman, or postman, or irate orchardist. I perfected my technique and "cased the joint" so well that, like any Old Bailey client, I had complete confidence. The only explanation I can offer is that I enjoyed the tingle of apprehension and the popularity that came from dishing out the spoils.

In my eight years at boarding school, Dad came to a school function only once. That was for sports day in my last term. Daisy was busy and he came alone. Everyone knew that I was likely to be Dux Ludorum, not to say Morrison Memorial Cup-holder, and the principal master concerned with sport told my father this at the beginning of the afternoon. Dad spent the rest of the day in a sort of euphoria. He bowed in stately manner to all, shook most graciously every hand that was offered, congratulated the headmaster, Charlie Broad, on the excellence of the arrangements, the splendid standard, et cetera. Jack was in top form. He had not looked so distinguished since he was managing director of the family business.

Brother Bill had started in the family firm, for he was E W Mills after his grandfather, but Deed and I were both Platts-Mills and felt that we owed it to Daisy to become doctors. We entered Victoria University College in 1925 and started reading medicine on the same morning. I lasted for less than a month, then changed to the law. Almost every middle-class boy in the colony became a lawyer or a doctor, unless he stood to inherit a sheep station. If I were to change from medicine, there seemed no alternative but to be the other of those two. Looking back now, I am quite unsure whether I dropped medicine for fear of competition from Deed in our joint classes, or for fear of exposing her to competition. We had each done a bit of science, but my university scholarship was based primarily on chemistry and physics and maths, while Deed had read zoology and biology for years and was full of knowledge. There was room for dodging on either hand. Deed followed in Daisy's footsteps by completing her studies at Dunedin Medical School and becoming a general practitioner.

As we lived within walking distance of Kelburn, I could walk or run from Karori for the eight a.m. lecture, then a day at university before the five p.m. lecture. Most of the students in the law school worked as law clerks or in insurance companies, fitting in lectures before and after work. I had a number of scholarships and supplemented them with manual labour in the summer vacations. It was either with axe and cross-cut saw in raw bush, or with claw hammer and barbed wire and fence posts along the boundaries of sheep stations. The money wasn't much, but it was needed and was proudly earned.

I was no sooner established at university than Una came and set up halfway on the route between Karori and Kelburn. I could not understand that anyone should move the distance from Nelson to Wellington without a job, or the excuse of further schooling, just to read books and listen to music and wait. In these days, no doubt, I would have stopped my journey halfway, moved in with Una and ceased to trouble my family anymore. I was too stupid or shy or backward.

When there was no eight a.m. lecture, on a clear morning I would run up Campbell's Hill and there to the north-west at 130 miles distance see the perfect cone of Mount Egmont above the sea. If it were not so clear a day I would run at a lower level round the perimeter fence of the local reservoir, perhaps seven miles. On weekends I often went tramping in the Tararuas, the great range visible from Wellington some twenty-five miles away. One fellow student and tramper was A E Beaglehole. Many years later, he earned New Zealand its second Order of Merit for his work on the diaries and log-books of Captain Cook. There was always some sporting event coming up and I was in constant training.

Almost everyone at Victoria played rugby and I was put into the university third team as wing-forward. Dennis Blundell and I found ourselves playing together at Upper Hutt. We enjoyed the game and afterwards, in the changing room, he commented that it was cheating of me to be playing in that grade. He rang the captain of the university 1st XV and lodged a "complaint". There followed an inquiry into where I had played before. In my first year away from Nelson the rugby team came under new guidance and, when the season was halfway through, they had beaten everyone in sight. Someone mistakenly concluded that, as an old boy of the school, I must be a distinguished player and moved me up into the university side.

Dad began to take an active part in my sporting activities. On a Saturday he would produce the boots, which in those days were minor fighting machines with strengthened toes and heels and a yard of laces. He had washed and dried them the night before and now they were oiled and the laces whitened and ironed. Four hours before the game he cooked a big steak with extras, then had me asleep again with three hours to go. At two hours the music started. This was loud enough to wake any sleeper and of a martial sort to lift a player's spirits. At first Dad tried to take the gramophone with us in Daisy's car but it jumped so that you had to give the needle a push and it scratched the record. Daisy had to come because Dad insisted that I should be driven to any rugby games in town. She would drive us there, then get straight back to the kitchen for her weekly baking session, leaving us to come home by tram or bus. Setting out time varied, for there were several rugby grounds as far away as Petone, but arrival had to be by Dad's reckoning just half-an-hour before kick-off.

Many of the great 1924 All-Blacks team played for Wellington clubs and we saw Athletic Park as the very hub of World Rugby. The Invincibles had come home entirely victorious; they even won at Twickenham with fourteen players after Cyril Brownlie had been ordered off for violence. Their captain, Cliff Porter, captained Athletic, and the university side played them five times one season. At the end of that season, I was selected for the Provincial team. We played against most of the other Invincibles, including the Brownlie brothers. And so I came to have a quite spurious reputation as a rugby player although, after those two seasons in Wellington, I hardly played again.

Then there was boating. I would take a small yacht round the Pelorous and Queen Charlotte Sounds, and also trained a team of sea scouts for Canon Fielden Taylor. I had learned the basics of rowing at Ocean Bay, and in 1925 Hartley Ferrar, who had rowed in some Cambridge boat, put me through the rudiments of what might be called classical rowing, but on dry land in his back garden at Karori. (He accompanied Captain Scott to the Antarctic on what became known as "the farthest South expedition", weathering two winters in their ship frozen up in the ice.) In 1926, my father, who had rowed for the Star Boating Club on Wellington Harbour in the 1890s, said, "If you haven't much on this summer, why don't you go and join the Star?" I did, and got into a Youth Four with Diehl, Cummerford and Mullins. We were launched into the regatta world at Picton, where the boats lined up nine or ten abreast. We won, and repeated our success at every regatta that had a race for Youth Four, including Christchurch, Wanganui, Taumaranui and the national championships, nine in all.

There was even one regatta at the confluence of two rivers – was it Taumaranui? We rowed the first half down one river, then across a T-junction, and the other half straight on into the other river, and therefore upstream. There were Maori canoe hurdle races first, and we hoped that the hurdles would be taken out before our race. At the national university, of which Victoria was one college, there had never been an inter-varsity boat race and we introduced it for the first time at the Auckland Tournament at Easter 1927. Victoria won.

Since I was interested in sports, it seemed obvious that I should take a more active part than those who were busy earning their living. If there was no one else offering, then I was put in to represent Victoria. We had a most skilled exponent in the art of the mile walk. He urged me to take up this remarkably contorted game in which the backward toe must not leave the ground until the forward heel had landed. We practised in local races, then were ready for the university contest. There were eight entrants, two from each college. The course was four rounds of a football pitch, and by the time I had reached the middle of the last round, the others were just about to cross the finishing line. It would have been immodest of me to mince home a full minute later. I was just about to stop when a messenger came flying across the field, crying, "Don't stop, don't stop! All the rest are disqualified." I reduced my pace to an even more stately measure, strutted the rest of the way in my best style and came home the unchallenged winner. I regard this as my only real athletic triumph.

Manual work in the holidays helped to keep me fit. One summer vacation was ten weeks in a bush camp with a dozen other men cutting a track through thick bush in the Tararua ranges. Our food and gear were shipped in by packhorse. After leaving the train, we slept the first night in a barn where sheepdogs had been and carried into camp the rarest crop of hairy great fleas. They beset us for two and a half months. The trees we were to clear were tall and thick. Trunks stood sixty feet high and the soil was six feet below the bed of rotting trunks and coils of supplejack and fern. We surveyed a track more or less straight and then clawed our way through the rank undergrowth; along hillsides, over streams with an occasional rough but strong bridge. The tools were the long two-handed cross-cut saw, the axe and the mattock. We learned to squat over the axe to hold it rigid and to cut and hone the blade to a fine edge with a steel rasp. One competition amongst us was to shave with an axe. Most of us grew beards.

I had brought a .303 rifle and took a few hours off at weekends to fill the pot, for we were surrounded by wild pig, deer and trout. This was such a success that for four weeks I was elected camp cook. Each day we had fresh venison steaks, roast pork or trout spitted and turned over an open fire. Breakfast was sourdough pancakes and meat, toast and jam. We had a fifty-gallon water tank that took fifty pounds of flour. It soured and fermented, providing its own rising. The mixture was stirred from on top with a pole and was fed on to a sizzling pan by tap. My best act of butchery was two sucking pigs with one shot, and a third pig so frightened by the same shot that he ended up in a small pond and was drowned. At the Masterton summer fair, we were so brash that we had entries in the vertical and horizontal chops and in the giant cross-cut classes. We ended with places in each and winner of the vertical, to the vexation of the locals who saw us as callow youths from town. It was a splendid course of training for sports, and yielded something modest towards the family's bills.

In Michaelmas 1925 I was bidden to a dance and there found Nell Blair. She was feminine and dainty, but as strong and determined a driver as Una was. Being a painter, she decided to attend art classes attached to Victoria. It was obvious, at least to her, that I needed taking in hand. This was the year I got five blues and every minute was precious. She arranged my timetable, decided what I was to do outside university and warded off all interference. She would, as often as not, provide a car, with herself as chauffeur. Nell decreed that I would attend only such social functions as I could spare time for and gave Una a polite but prompt dismissal. When, in my third year, I worked as a law clerk, it was with the distinguished firm of Chapman, Tripp, Blair, Cooke and Watson, of which her father was head. (I was later called to the New Zealand Bar by Archie Blair, who had been made a judge just in time.)

Victoria had a reputation as the most radical meeting place in New Zealand and offered every opportunity for an involvement in politics. Walter Nash, who was to become our first Labour prime minister, had a son studying at Victoria and offered classes to discuss socialism. They were held on Sundays somewhere near the foot of the Kelburn cable car. He had a key to a side door and we went upstairs. About a dozen students came to what we called Walter's Sunday School. I attended, but remained unconvinced. Today I regard E D Morel, one of the first MPs at the beginning of the move from Lib-Lab to Labour and the Social Democratic Federation, as a hero. When I first met his son in 1928, I told him that his father was "a fire-brand". It is unthinkable that I should use that term today of anyone and, least of all, of anyone on the left. I have since learned that people need to be inflamed. New Zealanders were too complacent, too concerned with convention.

My enthusiasm for the cadet corps had been so great that I carried on into the Territorials proper at university and reached the rank of captain in the 1st Battalion Wellington Infantry Regiment. In 1926 or '27 the battalion did an exercise in entraining and travelling some distance inland, then crossing ten miles of open country to the sea. We were about 1,000 strong, in thick uniforms and carrying guns. It was a hot day and when we reached the shore, the order came, "All into the water". Five minutes later across the sand dunes appeared two men on horseback. They produced notebooks and began taking our names for bathing without neck-to-knee costumes, although there was no dwelling or other human within five miles of us. I insisted that we were under military orders and not under their jurisdiction. They demanded to see the colonel, and I brought him naked from the sea. The colonel shouted at them and swore and proclaimed the freedom of New Zealanders to bathe on their own shore. He demanded their names, rank and authority. In short, he was absolutely splendid.

Nell Blair and several of the professors urged me to apply for a Rhodes Scholarship. This was supposed to be given to very worthy people, instinct with a desire to sacrifice themselves or found an empire, or to follow Rhodes from Cape to Cairo. You were also meant to be hot at your books and at sport. Exams were easy enough and I was coated with "Blues". As for high purpose and nobility of character, I was as mean and grasping as the next fellow. The idea of a trip to England and three years at Oxford was quite attractive. Indeed, in New Zealand the scholars were treated with much higher regard than they deserved.

It was a rough sort of selection. You put yourself up for it on the suggestion of various professors and arranged the best testimonials that you could. One Wellington professor (Tommy Hunter, Philosophy) told me that although he had voted for me, I shouldn't have got the scholarship. I was too ambitious and could manage without. Geoff Sceats (a good athlete and of a most grave and serious disposition) should have had the job, for he would return to New Zealand to teach or do something else useful; I would probably stay in England, and expect to be Lord Chancellor, which was not what Rhodes intended.

At Oxford, Rhodes scholars competed to see who could produce the most overblown commendation. I was placed well up in the lists with this passage from Charlie Broad, headmaster of Nelson, who wrote, "What he has done for his college he will do at no very distant date for New Zealand and for the Empire." None of us had any notion how near we were to the demise of the Empire, nor how interested I would become in its replacement by something better. As for New Zealand, although I love everything about it, I have been, as a Kiwi would express it, "a fat lot of use" to the country. The contest was won by Derryberry of Tennessee and St Johns who was clear winner with "He was King of the

Campus, secretary of the YMCA, he heeled the All American and was of a poifectly Christ-like disposition."

At selection time, the half-dozen or so nominated went to Government House, where the governor-general presided. I already had a smart suit for, to celebrate some special event in the previous year, Daisy had told me to get "a good address" from Father and go and buy myself the best bespoke suit the colony could provide. He, poor fellow, hadn't been allowed to think of any address save his own since he was married. He thought that Daisy had taken leave of her senses and pointed out that I had plenty of nice girl-friends and what possible use could "an address" be to me? When he realised that it was only a tailor that was wanted, he was filled with ideas. He had long since stopped buying tailor-made but got his suits off the peg at the big store. He would go to "the club", where he was still a member, and find some old fellows who would know. The search for a tailor was sufficient excuse, the suit was created – and is still worn today, seventy years later.

Andrew Sharp, who went on to establish the real history of the Maori voyages to Aotearoa, was the fellow scholar for the year. He came to stay with us for a week or so at Karori that we might become acquainted. Andrew played a lot of tennis, but he didn't have to pretend that he had flashed down the wing and crashed over in the corner, or snatched victory with the final over. He was most advanced in the social graces that enhance university life, the salon Rhodes Scholar rather than the muddied oaf, and proved to be a most comfortable travelling companion. How does an aspirant at thousands of miles distance decide to what Oxford college he should apply? Andrew selected St John's, but John Evelyn had entered Balliol in 1637 and that was good enough for me. Oxford colleges couldn't meet their Rhodes Scholar applicants before accepting them. I never heard of an applicant having to take his second choice of college. If they had seen us before, acceptance might have been different.

When I was selected, Archie and Rose Blair, Nell's parents, took us to Rotorua on holiday, and there was nothing more obvious than that we should be engaged. We were not, but decided that she would come to England as soon as she could. Nell came before I finished Oxford and we lived in London in some vacations and Paris when she worked at a studio there. By 1931, it was clear that I would not return to New Zealand and would have no security in Britain for some years, and Nell wisely retired. She soon became engaged to a wealthy sheep farmer, but eventually married the outstanding glass-engraver of the day, John Hutton. The judge sent a message that I should write a definitive work on contributory negligence.

For New Zealanders of my day, England was called "home". "We've been home" meant, in those days, only "We have been to England". Every friend and neighbour offered introductions. My parents knew the Prime Minister, Bill Massey, and I suppose it did me no harm that he was one of the selection committee for Rhodes scholars for my year. He didn't really know anybody in England so gave me an introduction to Billy Hughes, Prime Minister of Australia in the First World War.

In June 1928, Andrew and I set off for Oxford at a tempo fit for a luxurious world cruise with long stopovers in Australia, Ceylon, Cairo and Malta. In Sydney, I produced my letter to Billy Hughes. He insisted that we stay at the Hotel Australia in the heart of Sydney; Australia had funds available for just such a purpose and we must not pay a penny. He then took us the rounds of Sydney, showing us parliament, Government House and the governor, and all of the tourist sights. Then he sent us off through the Blue Mountains to the Jenolan Caves. Billy Hughes must have owed something to Bill Massey, but we never discovered what it was. We were certainly entertained on a prime ministerial scale.

From Melbourne we went fifty miles east through Fern Tree Gully and Emerald to Jembrook, where my father's sister, Alice, and her husband, Jack Russell, had reared a family of sons and helped lay waste the jarrah forests of Australian hardwood. Aunt Alice had been there for thirty years. The milling had gone on since 1880 and replanting with comparable timber had barely begun. The compelling question of what to do when the timber runs out had only just come into the mainstream of the family's thinking. It was my first contact with the "green" notion that we should all plant more than we use and perhaps leave behind us fewer and wiser users than we ourselves have been.

After a stop at Perth, it was on to Ceylon, where we stayed for two weeks and were most happily received by the family of Bishop Sadlier of Nelson, from whom we carried introductions. This is one of the most beautiful countries on earth, and it was here that Andrew and I met our first experience of colonial ways. If a man driving his cows on the highway was rather slow in moving them aside so that our car could pass, the driver leaned out and struck the man violently on the head. Our introduction to the true character of British colonial life was completed when we met the language used by Tamil workers in Colombo and on the tea plantations. The language, and the phrase-book used by the masters, was called Ingi-Var, which is translated as "Come here"; in general use, another word is added meaning "boy".

CHAPTER THREE

Starting at Oxford

ANDREW AND I entered London by train, our ship having berthed at Liverpool. A cabman took us to a small hotel in Russell Square, but even a cheap hotel was prohibitive for we had not yet drawn any of our Rhodes money. After a few days, we set off through the town in search of cheaper lodgings. Across Waterloo Bridge and beyond the station, a boarding house offered rooms at half the price; that night we met bedbugs for the first time. I have not encountered these creatures since, except in the regal sheets of post-war Bucharest.

We arrived at our colleges a few days before term began: Andrew at St Johns and myself at Balliol. I was allotted rooms in the south-east corner of the front Scottish Baronial quad. There was no carpet on the narrow, winding stone stairs that ascended a slim tower. They were known as the weeping stairs, for already by the autumn term, they dripped water. My sitting room or "sitter" was almost bare, except for a table and chair, a piece of carpet and a couch that was harder and less inviting than any ever seen; a barren couch, meant for scholars exhausted by study. There was also a small bedroom.

Now the same space seems to accommodate three undergraduates. There is no personal servant of the kind that the scout was seventy years ago. If there were an agreed waking time then he knocked you up with a small can of very hot water for shaving. He had a primitive gas ring on a ledge on the landing. There was a large earthenware pitcher or jug full of cold water. Scouts of Scottish origin called it an ewer. This stood in a large earthenware basin. There was also a large earthenware bedroom pot, a chamber pot. There was no heating in the bedroom and in the sitting room the heating was from a small coal fire. The scout's job of carrying up fair water and coals and taking down slops and ash was quite arduous.

The retiring age for a scout was when he could no longer do this carrying or no longer get a younger man to help him.

The only lavatories were underground next to the east wall of the quadrangle against the Trinity Wall. They were fifty yards from the nearest bedroom, had no heating and were lit by feeble gas flames They were named Lady Perriam after the charitable donor of the century before last. The bathrooms were under staircase 22 and 100 yards across an open quadrangle from the furthest bedroom. There was a hot shower in the barge and in the OUBC boathouse, so that if you rowed you were well provided for.

There were a great many bookshelves in the sitting room, empty save for the Bible and *Excerpta et Statutis* and half a dozen minor text books left over by previous occupants: a Latin text, a history of Macedonia in Roman times, and the like, but very rarely anything to do with science of any sort. In the 1920s, the college was still dominated by the idea, inherited from Jowett and Milner, that the empire must be ruled by scholars who had read Classics at Balliol. Law had by 1928 become a cheap and timid alternative.

There was little in New Zealand student life that prepared one for Oxford and it was a relief to get away to call upon my tutor, Theo Tylor, whose scout had been monitoring the arrivals. Tylor looked older than expected. He was still in his twenties but wore heavy glasses rather to shield his eyes than to enlarge their competence, which was then very little. Being almost blind, he offered a hesitant handshake, but at the moment he perceived a response, there was a warm greeting. I was christened Platts and invited to call him Theo.

He offered a game of chess; we spent three years considering this game but never played it. He played regularly in the British Championship at Hastings and on occasions when he had won several games, the better moves would be in the paper. I had hoped to sit for LLM in London that term. Theo Tylor encouraged this, but was more interested in whether I wanted to get a first in Oxford or to get a blue, and in what game. "No one can get a double first and a blue. What do you think of that?" I hadn't even considered it. He challenged me to bet that I could do it. I didn't accept, but would have lost.

To see whether I was capable of taking a research degree, he sent me off to Professor Holdsworth, who lived just below Folly Bridge in a house built into the river. My first session was with two others, one of whom was John Foot, one of the distinguished Sons of Isaac of Plymouth. Holdsworth had a walrus moustache and spoke like a machine-gun. He addressed me: "You are the biggest, you answer first. What do you know about Bushell's case, and when was it?"

That was the case where, in 1674, the independence of the jury was first established. Bushell was the foreman of a jury that refused to decide the facts of a case as the Old Bailey judge directed, and he locked them up and starved them and kept them without light or water for two days and nights. Someone got their plight before a high court judge and he granted Habeas Corpus. In the course of the trial, the Lord Mayor said that the defendant William Penn deserved to have his tongue cut out and he would cut Bushell's throat as soon as he could, while the recorder expressed his admiration for the Spanish Inquisition. I answered, "About the seventeenth...the sixteenth...the eighteenth century?"

"I see you have a vague idea about it within a century or two, and even that it might come in a book on constitutional law. You have a fortnight before we meet again. Perhaps you would care to read a little and write an essay on it. You will find it dealt with in a rather summary and casual fashion in the *History* by Sir James Fitzjames Stephen and more thoroughly in the first volume of my, if I may say, definitive work on the subject." By definitive, he meant illustrious. The others were asked similar questions about other leading cases and sent off to write their essays.

So I read about Bushell's case. I followed the movement of the Quaker people who were hoping to join the *Mayflower* at London or at Plymouth and were having their meeting in Gracechurch Street. I researched the trial. In the Old Bailey records, I checked the families of each juror. I went to the town halls of various boroughs and, in one case, to the address where it seemed from voters' lists that a family of the same name might now live. The occupants in 1928 professed ignorance of the name and were startled and ashamed that anyone from their house should have been associated with the Old Bailey, even as a juror. It did not matter that he was a part of history and a part of the structure of our inalienable rights. I wrote the essay and handed it in.

At the next meeting, Holdsworth said, "I've not yet read your essay, but what do you think about Bushell's case?" What did I think? I knew, for I had studied every detail of the case. I had visited the address of every juror and had probably met the descendants of one. I told him, "No one has ever before asked me what I think about anything. I've come here to find what you think." My education had been devoted to learning by rote; to hearing what other people had to say, then memorising and reproducing it. With the exception of Professor Brown, who took a course in Aristotelian Logic, all the lecturers at Victoria had followed that pattern. I was obsessive about enquiry, without any overall thought, but my parents were delighted that I did well in exams and were quite satisfied. Was education really about understanding?

My answer outraged Holdsworth. "If that's what you think, you have no right to be here. Had you not better go back to the place whence you came and not trouble Oxford any further? What is your college? I know the Master and I am sure he would release you and rusticate you. Oxford doesn't need you, Sir." I limped back to Tylor with my sorry tale and he drew the conclusion that I certainly needed Oxford. He decided reluctantly that I'd better try for an ordinary BA in Law. I wrote him an essay a week and we debated them. I went to such lectures as he prescribed from other law dons, including Cheshire of Exeter, Fifoot of Hertford and Jolowicz of All Souls. Tylor took a friendly and encouraging interest in every aspect of his students' lives. He well deserved the knighthood he later received. I would have made him a baron or at least a baronet.

It was Theo Tylor who had the idea of reviving the undergraduates' law society that had originally been formed in 1923, with myself as secretary. This was long before the days of voting for any such office – it was "you and you shall volunteer". But what to do for a name? One of the college's more recent high-fliers was Lord Blanesburgh. He had done the Chancery Bar, the High Court and the Court of Appeal as Bob Younger, and was now a Lord in Ordinary of Appeal. I was given an appointment at his room in the House of Lords, where I addressed him as "My Lord Blanesburgh". He replied with a burst like a machine-gun, each word clipped and fired out: "Don't call me Lord Blanesburgh, don't you 'My Lord' me; if you don't know me and you are a barrister, call me Younger; if you know me, call me Bob. Bob's my name. They all call me Bob. You call me Bob." He allowed his name to be used and the Younger Society has survived for more than seventy years. Its Michaelmas-term dinner is an occasion in Oxford legal life.

Every Balliol undergraduate in his first year had to produce an essay each alternate Saturday and read it to the Master. Scholars of the college were expected to set an example to the rest, but Rhodes Scholars were excused. They were not expected to be literate. If they could write, that was a bonus; to produce an original notion on any topic was impossible. I had learned a trick about essays from Ken Saxon, English master at Nelson. Take the time allowed for writing the essay, devote half to framing the opening sentence, then go for it. The beginning passage was meant to make the reader open his eyes and then his mouth, shutting his mind to the emptiness and lack of knowledge shown by the body of the piece. I asked Sandy Lindsay, the Master of Balliol, whether I might be allowed to write the essays. He did so allow.

From home, I was armed with introductions to several survivors of the suffragette movement, including Frederick Pethick-Lawrence of Old Square, Lincoln's Inn, an eminent barrister who was in the House of Lords for Labour when I entered the Commons. Because of Mother's beliefs, I was introduced as a young man very much interested in politics, prohibition, and social reform. Votes for women in 1895 – for all women in all types of elections – put us ahead of other nations. Any New Zealand visitor to the Lawrences was expected to know all about the movement, but it had not occurred to us for years that women could be without the vote.

Several of the letters came from Anna Stout, wife of the retired Chief Justice and former Prime Minister, Sir Robert. In the 1890s, Lady Stout had been an active suffragette. She provided introductions to the lady queen of the women police of London and to the lady commander of some unit of women soldiers. I hope to be forgiven for not remembering their names or very much detail except that each was a powerful and determined person and I felt that women's rugby and tug-of-war perhaps had a future. Anna Stout also gave me a letter of introduction to Nancy Astor, whom she had joined with two soldier sons in uniform in the first march of British suffragettes after the war. As tended to happen with Nancy, the acquaintance had blossomed.

On seeing me off from New Zealand, father had presented a brown trilby with a stiff sort of brim, a malacca cane with a silver top, and a pair of lemon kid gloves. "All the young men will wear this kind of gear when they go up to London or away from the university. Put it on top of your cupboard until you need it." One of my first social acts in Oxford was to put the hat, stick and gloves on top of the cupboard and to send off the letter to Cliveden, not far down the Thames, to Nancy Astor. (I had also foolishly carried the full uniform of Captain in the 1st Battalion Wellington Infantry Regiment, including great coat and ceremonial sword, to Oxford, then had the extreme embarrassment and expense of being called on to return it.)

Nancy's reply came almost by return of post. "You shall attend for lunch on Sunday, you shall catch this train, and change here, and will be met at Twyford. If you can possibly go to early church, then come straight after that and we will have plenty of time for a good long talk." I was duly met at Twyford by two distinguished fellows in uniform. I was expected to sit in the back of the vehicle (a Landaulette-de-ville, as I recall) but insisted on sitting in the front and learning all about it. After a slight hesitation and even demur, this was conceded and we set off to Cliveden. The under-footman sat in the back. Cliveden was indeed imposing. As we drew up, a young footman came out to greet the arriving guest. He ushered me in and took my belongings as if it were quite normal. This gave me a bit of confidence, for it is fair to say that nothing in my experience had prepared me in the slightest degree for what I might expect, or be expected to do.

Inside the house, a man rather older and less resplendent in his sober costume announced gravely that her Ladyship was expecting me. There inside the great hall stood this diminutive little creature dressed more for a summer picnic than a grey winter's day. In an instant, she was down on her hands and knees with her forehead touching the carpet. Not knowing what to make of this, I cried, "Arise, Lady Astor!" She looked up and said, "Nancy," whereupon I repeated, "Arise, Nancy!" She got to her feet and advanced with both arms extended. By then I had my jacket off and was preparing to throw it in front of her, meaning to live up to the occasion. Nancy explained, "Only thus can one welcome a person sent by Anna Stout."

She said, "You are a Rhodes scholar and so must be a great athlete." I admitted only to the mile walk. The answer came, "No walking until just before tea. I'll entertain you now for a while, but then I have to talk my head off to all manner of people, and you can do the same. Later, if you're very quick, I'll take you for a two-mile walk and we shall see the river and back." In the meantime, she offered a choice of indoor tennis with her or outside football with her boys when they got back from church. I chose both. She was strong and played a vigorous game, skipping nimbly about the court. Afterwards, playing football with the boys, I saw a number of cars arrive and it looked as though there would be a large gathering for lunch. When we went in, my muddy shoes were yielded to the footman in exchange for a pair of his Lordship's.

The footman ushered us into a room where twenty or more people were gathered, all deep in talk. This was November 1928, under a Conservative government, but Ramsay MacDonald would be in within the year. I have no doubt that all the intrigue for which Cliveden later became world-famous was then going on. It was the very core of possibility of prospective English aristocratic Fascism; it was the beginning of the gathering of the Men of Munich, who later tried to ally the United Kingdom with Hitler. I was introduced to quite a few of them and for all I know they were the chaps who would eventually bring Ramsay's government down, and drag him in to social circles where he didn't belong.

My companion at lunch proved to be a young lady of the Lyttelton family. We were put at one end of an enormous table where we needn't interrupt our elders. She at once started a severe interrogation. Her great grandfather had helped to organise the main settlements of our colony through the New Zealand Company. Were the founding fathers still remembered? Had I come to write the history of the company or the colony, or at least to learn how to write it? How had the Maoris fared after the Maori Wars, and was their earlier history reasonably dealt with? And so it went on. My slight and only skill was the ability to summon up in an instant such few facts as I possessed and to dress them up as superficially suitable for the occasion. I had lived in two streets named after founders, two other names had been adopted for the main streets of the capital city, and I had rowed on a harbour that bore her own name.

In the following spring, I went to the Astors' twice more, but no young Lyttelton turned up. I asked Nancy how I could get her to come to Eights' Week to have strawberries on the barge. "Ask her, of course, you silly! Look up her dad in *Who's Who* and write a polite but business-like letter saying, 'You're expected, and the whole crew will be inspired by you.' If you can't get her to come, I'll get her for you and I shall come, too." Clearly, help was needed. David Gordon was our first Balliol undergraduate ever to read Agriculture, although he later "ploughed" in the subject (Oxfordese for failure). He was due to be both an earl and a marquess and seemed to be the sort of calibre to deal with their two ladyships. They were met, conveyed to the barge and set up in a choice position, but I doubt whether I ever saw the girl again. It was rumoured at one time that David would marry her.

In Sydney, Billy Hughes gave me a letter of introduction to General Sir Ernest Swinton, Chichele Professor of Military History at All Souls. This also brought a luncheon invitation. The repast consisted of a bottle of gin and a plate of wafer biscuits. The general was a big man, slightly peppery and very talkative. He spoke of Billy Hughes as though he knew him well, but could not really distinguish between New Zealand and Australia. After a few minutes he turned to the tank and, without any helping questions from me, continued for a steady half-hour. He was the inventor of the tank and had been an adviser to the Imperial War Cabinet of Lloyd George. It only required the slightest mention of another aspect of the question "What did Lloyd George think of it? What did the cabinet think was the future of it?" and off he went again. Balliol lodge was alerted and asked to send out a rescue party and, at about four in the afternoon, I was accompanied from the All Souls lodge up the High and along the Turl to the college. I was just capable of putting myself to bed.

Tylor said that I must ask the general to lunch in my rooms with two or three of the other students. My scout was delighted to help with the food and it was no impediment that he spilled the chops on the stairs, for we shovelled them all up and got them back in the dish. We had gin and wafers for the main visitor, who talked for two hours about the tank, to the delight of everyone. Every term thereafter, I was invited to All Souls for lunch and he was invited back to Balliol or, in my last year, to lodgings. The subject of the tank always came up, but the general was knowledgeable and full of other talk. He was a rarity amongst military men in that he wrote a comic book about one of his own military operations in South Africa. In *The Defence of Duffer's Drift*, he described the same events from half-a-dozen viewpoints, including the Boer's-eye view. It may have been this book rather than the invention of the tank that gained him his fellowship at All Souls.

Oxford was more than good to me, and one don was particularly so. Kenneth Bell, the Dean of Balliol, was an overgrown schoolboy of a well-established Oxford-don type. He had the mustachios of a First World War field officer and gave entertaining and provocative lectures on European history. He was sober, diligent and devoted to the young men of the college. His family life seemed as correct and normal as could be. Shortly after our lot had gone down, however, he abandoned his dear wife, Essie, and their family and set up with his secretary in a remote part of England. He eventually gave up the secretary and took holy orders as a Church of England parson before returning to Essie in South Parks Road. Some of his children, unfortunately, were as irresponsible as their father.

When I was newly arrived, Kenneth Bell decided that uncouth and country cousin that I was, I might still be worth an attempt at salvation. Accordingly, he set Terence Bird the task of showing me Oxford and trying to deck out a gauche colonial hulk in some new rigging and attire. The younger students were rather cautious of Rhodes Scholars, who tended to be both older and bigger. Terence and I were the same age, for he had spent four years at university in Rhodesia, where he had been brought up by his father, and by his mother in London. He was an extraordinary mixture of his mother's London correctness and politeness and the varied talents of his father, Freddie. Terence and I walked about Oxford most afternoons, inspecting everything. We decided, on his proposal, that as we didn't know the people in college, we would invite ourselves to tea with everyone in turn. None refused, and some we even managed to repay.

Freddie Bird was a short and bustling Irishman with some skill at everything, and a slight willingness to show more than he possessed. He had been a major in Regents Park in the First World War and was known by his neighbours as Major Bird. Freddie had designed and built the "Great Dipper", the switchback railway at the British Empire Exhibition at Wembley in about 1923, which had made him a lot of money. He backed the show to continue for two years more and put all his takings into a renewed and improved dipper. Nothing came of it and all was lost. His brother-in-law bought a farm called Moorlands near Colchester in Essex and set Freddie up there in his truly Irish style. It was the first home I visited away from Balliol, and Freddie was my host that first Christmas in England.

At Moorlands, Freddie had everything and nothing and it was a joy to behold all the new things he would produce constantly from nowhere. In his drawing room, he kept all of his plans, drawing boards and instruments and, since he could do anything with engines, one found retired vehicles tucked away in various barns. Freddie grew and dried his own tobacco and, from odd corners of a dilapidated garden, produced vegetables and fruit of various kinds, as well as wines made from such things as parsnips, cowslips, and the elder (both flower and berry). He kept hens and geese, and made butter and cheese from his own goats. Every part of his house was a sorry mess, yet at regular intervals he brought forth from that chaos the most remarkable meals.

In the second term, Terence allowed me to accompany him to the Oxford University Air Squadron which was, I believe, with the Cambridge Squadron, the foundation of the Royal Air Force Reserve. It was said that they were intended for the young English gentleman who had flying room at home, and perhaps a string of horses, that he might be lured away from his bloodstock into the air for at least part of the time. In fact, the positions were quickly hogged by eager young colonials, who were tough and inclined to elbow people out of the way when there was something available free.

We learned to fly in the Avro trainer, which was the simplest two-winged aerofoil construction and an uncrashable plane for beginners. You could fly three or four days a week and in summer you could have two weeks' daily instruction at Manston aerodrome, including a bit of night-flying. Everyone had the experience of spending almost an hour grinding round and round gaining height over Manston and then from 10,000 feet doing a power dive towards Calais in a Hineidi bomber. We reached the speed of 100 mph, but only with a following wind. Air traffic control did not exist. You would announce your intention to arrive at an aerodrome only for the purpose of making sure there would be lunch available, usually at the RAF mess. It was as though anyone sailing a small boat could draw up beside any stationary man-of-war, board it, and have lunch in the ward-room with the senior officers.

College life was very mixed. Undergraduates who frequented the home of the Bells were referred to as the Belfry people. Their main gathering was a Sunday walk that took in, in turn, every attractive village in the neighbourhood for a pub lunch. They were not the "hearties" of the college, nor yet the over-elegants. These latter tended to congregate round Sligger Urquhart. Those who went to the Sligger chalet in Switzerland for summer reading seldom took part in sports except for a little light fencing and sometimes the arduous work of the Poetry Club. In the time of my second son they were known to the hearties as "readers"; only to be seen out after dark and then moving very slowly. It was almost impossible to bridge the gap between the two dons, but I fell somewhere in between.

"Sligger" Urquhart not only made much of every Catholic boy in the college, and over a wider field, but spread his charms to many others. At Balliol we had our own Anglican parson and chapel. Parson Barrie was deaf, but in due course became a bishop. He treated colonials as so likely to be barbarians that it was not worth the missionary effort and risk of approaching us. We rather resented his attitude and in my second term I took this up with Dick Ashburner from Sydney and Terence Bird. We decided that we were entitled to be recognised as souls, even if lost souls. We recruited a couple of other colonials and launched a 'Mission to Barrie', bearding him in his rooms. Barrie accepted our argument and set a special communion table. Thereafter at least two of us kept up our attendance, although I had lost my religious faith at Victoria. Law was supposedly all logic and reason. The only need for faith was the belief that if you worked hard enough you would find the right answer. (Later there came the equally strong conviction that if your opponent were to apply himself diligently, he would find an answer that the judge might think to be even more satisfying.)

I was contemporary with Henry D'Avigdor-Goldsmid and with Edouard Roditi. The first was extremely wealthy and inherited one of the loveliest houses in Kent. At Balliol he had a grand piano in his rooms. Some of the rougher young gentlemen, for all colleges tend to have their share of them, poured beer into his piano. He was moved onto my staircase and was not troubled again. Roditi was an aesthete, the kind of person more usually found in Wadham or Hertford. He had jonquils in season in his room which he scented, and arum lilies out of season, which he gilded. He was not religious but had on the wall at his bedhead a sheet of black velvet with a silver crucifix on it. A similar group of young men invaded Roditi's room and debagged him. He, too, was moved by the college to my staircase, where peace was said to prevail. I'm not sure whether this was because I was older and perhaps more mature, or because I was a heavyweight boxer. Despite this, he was soon bullied into leaving the college.

I did not come across Roditi again but D'Avigdor eventually became Lord Lieutenant of Kent and on the rare occasions when I "went special" to Maidstone Assizes, for I was not on the South Eastern Circuit but on the Western, he put me up in the greatest comfort.

In 1930, when I resumed boxing after a break, certain muscles had become stiff and I developed a shoulder strain. Someone recommended a masseur in North Oxford. He smelt of hartshorn and other embrocation, his room smelt of it, and for fifty yards in either direction along the Woodstock Road you could smell it. In the course of my treatment, he asked was I a mason? I was not. He said that if I wanted to stay on in England, the easiest way to make friends was through the masons. There were plenty of lawyers and judges who belonged. Did I know Lord Valentia? I did not. Would I care to meet him? Well, I do not rightly know what I answered, but probably out of politeness said that I would if Mr Liniment recommended it. I never did meet his lordship.

Instead there came a note from John Foster, Fellow of All Souls, inviting me to lunch in the college. He urged that I should let him nominate me for membership of the Apollo University Lodge of Freemasons, and I did. I went to several meetings and took instruction and underwent various processes. The whole of Oxford life was still after two years rather dreamlike so that the fantasy of masonic life was no great extension. I came by and still possess an apron unsuitable for kitchen work: an elegant ceremonial apron of soft white chamois leather with triangular flap, bound with wide moiré braid of brilliant sky blue, trimmed with braid rosettes, hanging pendants and metal chains. I rolled up one or both trouser legs and grappled with a fellow member in a ritualistic manner, but as though for life and death, and left the lodge shortly after.

Despite this, John Foster remained most friendly to me. He was the noisiest of our group and extremely entertaining. He shared with Quintin Hogg being the only two men who have come to London from Oxford in my time, saying from the outset that they intended to be high court judges. Neither succeeded, although both became Tory MPs. Quintin renounced his peerage to remain an MP and went on to become Lord Chancellor, Chairman of his Party and as a life peer, Lord Hailsham.

They say once a mason, always a mason, but that was more than seventy years ago and since that time no one has asked me: Are you a mason?

Were you a mason? Would you be a mason? No one has shaken hands in a peculiar way or given a sign of any kind.

Rugby was even more quickly abandoned. Although the Rhodes Scholarship was given partly for my Provincial games, I rarely played again after leaving Wellington. For the few college matches in which I did play, Terence Bird provided transport on his Brough Superior motorcycle. This was one of many remaining treasures of equipment from the days when his father had designed the big dipper at Wembley. The Brough Superior was described by the Rolls Royce designers as the only machine built in Britain with machinery equal to theirs.

Chapter Four

Oxford Ends

FROM THE summer term of 1929, I concentrated on rowing. The Balliol VIII were about fourteenth in the First Division and in three years of summer eights we went up six places. When summer approached, the crew was taken off to comfortable digs at Marlow, Henley, Kingston or even Putney. It was astonishing to find what financial support went into the activities of quite a modest crew, but that was as nothing compared to the massive sums spent on training for the boat race.

I rowed with Lewis Clive, he on stroke side and me at bow, for a couple of weeks in trials in the 1929 Michaelmas term, the 1930 trials and, when we got into the crew, throughout boat race training in 1931. We shared lodgings for a month or so and came to know one another well. Lewis was very strong. He insisted on a run up Henley Hill after training. This was quite consistent with my idea that in the ordinary course of preparation you trained incessantly until you were bust and only tailed off in the last few days before the contest. The coach was Archie Campbell-Douglas, a Guards officer. When he learned what was going on, he complained that if you could still run up a hill after rowing, you were not trying hard, and the running had to be stopped.

I rowed with the crew from the 1st January until ten days before the race, then had to be pulled out with a minor injury. The crew had plenty of female admirers and it wasn't unusual for macho young chaps to pull themselves up to the lintel above the door on entering or leaving the boat-house. I showed off by demonstrating that it could be done with one arm and strained a hand muscle. It was a bitter disappointment, all the more so for being self-inflicted. Our training routine eschewed smoking and spirits, and called for the fullest concentration of physical efforts on the sport in hand. The lighter sports of dalliance, so favoured of the poets

Sheriff's Cartoon of the Oxford crew that appeared in The Sketch *in March 1931. W L Garstang rowed in my place on the day.*

(at back, l. to r.) C. M. Johnston; L. Clive; J. F. Platts-Mills, (next row, l. to r.) W. D. C. Erskine-Crum; D. E. Tinné; R. W. G. Holdsworth; (next row, l. to r.) G. M. L. Smith; R. A. J. Poole; (in front) E. R. Edmett, the cox.

for spring, were shunned. When we were billeted at Leander, Zita Baker wrote asking, "When, oh name the day, when I can follow you down the winding road to Henley?" I raised the possibility of female company with the crew as a general topic and so far as it was possible to get a serious response, we all agreed: No Zita by request.

Zita was the wife of John Baker, a cytologist whose pioneering studies into chemical contraception helped to lay the foundation of Oxford's scientific empire. I met him at the OU Exploration Society, not long after his return from the New Hebrides. The Bakers were in all respects a very modern and "progressive" family, a thing to which I was unaccustomed. They talked freely about sexual aspects of their life. For example, their daughter Venice was named after the place of her conception, as they explained to me. But in her general character, Zita was as unlike her husband as could be. She was a tramp with a vivid and alarming spark. Though no great beauty, Zita knew how to make herself attractive. She treated herself as entitled to the attentions of any young man she fancied, and usually gained them.

I believe that Zita was set on to me by Mrs Enid Shawyer, an Oxford widow who showed outstanding hospitality to many students from the Commonwealth. Mrs Shawyer assumed that I had come to the university to find a wife and provided every opportunity for me to discuss this with her daughter, Nicolette. Nicolette was gentle, charming and highly marriageable, but we were not for marrying. Her mother decided that this was solely because I was gauche and backward. To remedy this, she arranged a short course of guidance from Zita Baker.

In the Michaelmas term of 1930, Zita's technique was to invite me to Sunday tea, to Sunday lunch, or to an evening meal. She would then send me from the living room on errands to fetch some trifle from one room or another, where she would occasionally follow. Finally it was to the bedroom to fetch a shawl. There Zita followed and said she had bought some shirts for her husband but they were too big for him and I must try them on. In a moment she had me part undressed and into John's shirt and she was in like state and trying to smuggle herself into the same shirt. It was certainly a step forward in my education.

The Oxford Union Society provided the real heroes for the university. Douglas Woodruff was reputed to be the most entertaining union speaker between the wars. His only rival was Brian MacKenna, who had had rather a chequered educational life. He was trained by Jesuits and went to more than one university abroad before ending up at Oxford. The contrast between these two was that Woodruff brought rejoicing to all sides at the expense of his opponents, but always ended on a profound note of sincerity. MacKenna presented some outrageous thesis and maintained it right to the end. The result was that Woodruff became president and MacKenna, a few years later, held every other office but was several times defeated for the presidency. The union voter was as wayward as any other.

I joined the union in my first year and spoke a few times. When Quintin Hogg was president, he put me "on the paper" for some quite unremembered topic. The debates were so ephemeral that there was neither chance nor merit in remembering them. I know that in 1929 I spoke in defence of the motion "That this House regrets the alliance between Trade Unions and the Labour Party", but the only one I remember in any detail was the Eights' Week debate in 1931 when Geoffrey Wilson as president wrote, offering me a supporting role with G K Chesterton, speaking for the motion 'that the Law is an Ass", Woodruff and Lord Darling to oppose. (The alternative offer was a debate against Cambridge on the motion "that this House believes in Ghosts", on whichever side I chose.)

Darling was supposed to be the most amusing person on the High Court Bench. In fact, he had very little to commend him except for his absurd misuse of the notion of judicial ignorance. The joke of universal and irremediable judicial ignorance is a very limited affair on such lines as "What is a vacuum cleaner? And why would anyone want to clean a vacuum, anyway?" He was a godfather to Lewis Clive, an office he shared with the prime minister, Neville Chamberlain. I was switched from supporting the motion to opposing it, and Darling worked out our plan of defence: it seemed heavy and ponderous. By contrast, the movers of the motion, neither being a lawyer, were dextrous and gay and scandalous.

Chesterton's physical girth proved to exceed his height. Woodruff said of him that he had "been to America and looked round". They made such fun of the law and lawyers and judges that poor Darling was almost in tears. He made some pawky joke about his Mistress the Law, and the audience doubted whether he had ever, even when much younger, enticed any mistress for any purpose. My unfortunate contribution was to comment that "many an ass had entered Jerusalem", which greatly upset Woodruff. He and Chesterton were Catholics.

At supper, Woodruff denounced me as a bloody and sacrilegious colonial who had dared to soil the whole evening with monstrous blasphemy. Father Ronald Knox, who was the outstanding Jesuit of his time and the senior member responsible for the union, replied, "My dear Douglas, you are so young you haven't heard anything yet." I thought it was only a quotation from Chesterton and said so, but that did not seem to placate Woodruff. When I came to the Bar, Woodruff's editorial work for the *Universe* and the *Tablet*, the two leading Catholic periodicals, was conducted in Fleet Street, just at the entrance to the Inner Temple. He never failed to show his disapproval of my conduct and applied the same judgement to all that I did publicly thereafter, sustaining an attitude of constant hostility throughout his life.

My tutor had made it clear that he expected me to get a good degree. I was a determined taker of notes and last-minute crammer, and in that sense was well prepared. Shortly before the final exams for the BA degree, I was pressed into a college water polo team. They knew that I could swim and throw a ball, and was not averse to pushing opponents under when needed. The only trouble was that I got pinkeye from some infection in the baths. With a week to go, I was more or less blinded and couldn't read my notes. Tylor had an instant remedy. His reader was crammed with Tylor's notes and we had an intense six hours of cramming each day. I was so filled with dates and references and cases and propositions and arguments that I was chewing them over hour after hour. I couldn't sleep and was getting exhausted. Rupert Reynell, a Harley Street consultant who had been at Balliol as a Rhodes Scholar, provided sleeping pills and I worked myself even harder right up to the exams. The result was at least satisfactory.

In the summer term of 1931 there were the Finals of BCL (nominally, the Oxford research degree in law). It was a bad year for the college academically. Our leading scholar suffered a poor third in Greats. The twice-termly luncheons with General Swinton encouraged the dons in the belief that there might be support in All Souls for some sporting candidate, that perhaps there was some "hearty" vote to be exploited. It was insisted that I must put myself up. Another of the false steps that led to this egregious mistake was my having volunteered for the master's essay.

Every sensible entrant for the September exam must have spent the summer term reading and becoming up to date not only in his own subject but in general matters about politics, philosophy and life. I went to America on a free trip with a combined debating team of the British Universities League of Nations Society to go the round of the summer schools from New York all the way to Ann Arbor in Michigan. The main topic was whether the United States should join the League of Nations. She never had, and this had broken the heart of Woodrow Wilson, the Democrat from Virginia, for he was one of its founders. I had joined the OU League of Nations Society in my first term, for in the 1920s world peace seemed to be a very real possibility.

When we arrived in New York, Eric Price Holmes and I looked round for a court to visit. It was long vacation and all the courts were shut except for one, where a number of prostitutes (we were told up to 1,000) were being tried for corruption in paying four dollars each to a police officer. That was dull stuff. But there was a judicial inquiry conducted by His Honour Judge Seebury into the malpractices of Jimmy Walker when he was Mayor of New York City. One or other of his innumerable relatives had been put on the governing body connected with every service or commodity supplied to the city authority, and each one then drew an extraordinary fee or salary. Some pretence was made to qualify some of these useful relatives. It may have been that an aunt studied the coal and oil supplies of the city and when a new co-ordinating board for the supply of fuel was set up, she was a most suitable lay-person to be vice-president of the relevant body.

Eric and I found ourselves at a press conference given by the judge to report on some of the innumerable topics covered by the 'Seebury Probe'. We introduced ourselves to the press room. It was rumoured to be so well supplied with free liquor and food and easy chairs that journalists had there established the longest running poker school in New York history. Eric introduced us as "the London *Times*" and when this was announced to the assembly, a very American voice came from its deep chair, "If you are the London *Times*, then what do you think I have been this last three years?" – "Did someone say *The Times*? Oh no, that's quite wrong. The London *Telegraph*. We are the *Telegraph*." We were welcomed and offered breakfast, for it was nine a.m. and taken in to the press conference: a thirty-foot-long table with journalists each side.

At nine-thirty he appeared: a large, red-faced, grey-haired man, every kilo a judge, with a diminutive woman on his arm. This, we learned, was

Dorothy Thompson of the *Herald-Tribune* and doyenne of American scribes. She had quizzed him in his private room. There was a chorus of questions before they sat down. The judge had an enormous open box of cigars which he sent spinning down the table. It seemed as if each newsman snatched one out as the box passed; it was empty when it reached the end. The last man, next to where we sat, raised the box and cried, "Missed, Jedge." The judge took a cigar from his breast pocket and threw it to the man. "Take it, boy."

The questions were of the type: "What's breaking on timber, Jedge?" – "Timber will be next week." – "Anything yet on Aunt Jane and the sewers?" – "There's smelly stuff coming up on that but not for a while; it's still maturing. It's cement this morning; now that's a story you can make stick hard." So the corny exchange went on as they launched into the detail of the cement racket. Five minutes was enough and we bowed out.

I then went with members of the Knox family from New York up to Vermont, meeting a summer colony of the editorial staff of the *New Yorker* on the way and seeing New England life. At Camden, Maine, I stayed with the family of Joyce Borden-Turner in a great house with many servants and Duzenbergs (the American Rolls Royce of the day) and a yacht or two standing in the cold water off the house. We crossed to Cold Harbor to call on Nicholas Murray Butler, Head of Columbia University and a veteran of liberal education, but apart from that I made no further preparation for the forthcoming exam.

The Borden household was highly religious and there were always hymns and prayers before breakfast. Table talk was meant to be only of state and church and if any personal matter arose, you were expected to call on Granny in the library after breakfast. At dinner-time, I told a story about Stephen Murray and the Oxford Movement. He was the son of Gilbert Murray, Classics professor at Oxford and one of those who had founded the League of Nations. Stephen was an idle fellow except when it came to racing motor cars. He founded the University Motor Club and went rallying, but did nothing by way of study or passing exams.

Stephen had asked me to go with him to a cocoa party for Oxford Group supporters at Somerville where, on a special occasion, the young ladies would be allowed to stay up until nine o'clock. We heard a number of girls make confessions, on their knees in the centre of the room, tearfully and prayerfully. The confessions were about the most humdrum little things like being late for something or forgetting something. This was too much for us. Stephen devised a number of horrible-sounding vices with Greek names, crawled into the middle of the room, and there knelt and confessed. Some were so moved by this that they, in turn, said that if Stephen could confess such horrible things, then they too could confess. There followed disclosures of matters really no graver than those we had already heard. Stephen was so touched by this response that, as he said himself, he was "converted". He made a genuine confession about misleading us all, and about his truly idle life. He joined the Oxford Group, married an attractive Quaker girl named Margaret, raised a substantial family, and later came to the Bar in Admiralty Chambers.

It was rather a scurrilous story and in derogation of the movement, but in the account of it I used the word "converted". The outcome was a summons to the library after breakfast next day. Granny was almost in ecstasy at the description of Stephen Murray's conversion. She wished me to choose the hymns for the next breakfast time and read a passage from the Bible. I could even choose the passage. My story at the Borden table was a ribald one, but it was not for me to explain that to Grandmother.

I suppose I really made the trip to see Joyce Borden-Turner, who was spending the summer with her elders. I was much attached to Joyce, but she wanted children now and no delay, and no question of the future and getting established had any importance by comparison. I was far too immature for this and hadn't even started at the Bar. Joyce had of her own a worth of £400 a year, which might have been enough to keep us both, but I had no understanding of what that could mean. In short, it was a misconceived visit.

Even if I had spent the summer preparing for the All Souls' exam, it would have made no difference to the result because I lacked the basic training in Latin and Greek and never made it up by years of dog Latin and Roman law. It might, however, have led to a respectable rather than a disreputable result. Fortunately, I was so little known outside Oxford that it affected nobody except the Master, the Balliol dons and the examining Fellows of All Souls. An aspirant presented himself at the college in full academic gear with robes and mortar board and explained his degrees. I was unaware that I'd gained a Double First in New Zealand, but knew that I had a second in BCL. The warden answered, "Many a Lord Justice of my acquaintance has done no better."

The exams ran for several days, and it became increasingly obvious that I was doing worse and worse. There were free translations in Greek and German and conversations in both languages, not to mention free translations in Latin and half-a-dozen papers on other topics. With a little more courage, I would have retired from the scene with apologies for ever having entered. I was too cowardly for that and went on right through to the cherry pie dinner given by the college to the aspirants. When it came to All Souls' Day, the new Fellows were Quintin Hogg and Morgan Goronwy Rees. It was explained that I was not really expected to stay another year for the sake of sitting it again. Only Richard Wilberforce had this honour bestowed upon him, and he became a Fellow in the following year.

Looking back I can see that two things were axiomatic in my youth: whatever was to hand I would do with the utmost vigour, with planned and scheming vigour, and that if any person who seemed to be in authority made any suggestion as to what I should do, I at once did it without question. My good fortune was that people suggested actions that at that time and on the other side of the world were quite sensible as "kick this, hit that, push here, pull there. Read more, get up at four. Have three hours' study and one hour's run. Dry or muddy, four hours done (before any others were up)." I recently discussed our respective youths with Quintin. He said he had observed that all his contemporaries at school and at university spent half their working time playing games. He resolved that he would not waste his time playing any game, ever, on any pretext, and so he would gain 1,000 hours or more over his contemporaries that he would devote to reading but which they would never make up. When it came to sitting for All Souls in September 1931 he thought that, as I was put up by Balliol and as in addition to the possible "hearty" vote Balliol had a strong bloc in All Souls, I was a possible runner. He did not allow for the 1,000 hours. Moreover, if I had not kicked and hit, pulled and pushed for 1,000 hours as advised to do, I would never have been in Oxford to sit for All Souls. What made it possible to be there and to sit for All Souls also made it impossible to succeed. I do not suppose any Rhodes Scholar has ever become a fellow of All Souls or ever will. The difference between the all-rounder and the all-straight-and-narrower. I refer, of course, to the fourth year immediate post-grad September exam fellows: I believe a Rhodes Scholar has recently become a more senior sort of fellow.

Because of this disaster, I did not dare go near Balliol again until October 1938 when Sandy Lindsay was standing in a by-election against Quintin Hogg and I went back to canvas for Lindsay as an Independent Labour candidate. I nearly met the master as we approached one another walking in the middle of the great quad. He saw me, stopped ten paces away and said in a loud voice, "Damn you, Mills!" He then turned his back and marched away. When we were both in parliament a decade later, we became quite close friends. I have often proclaimed the putting up for All Souls as the pinnacle of my academic career. It has always been accompanied by an account of the actual outcome. But to have sat for All Souls at the instigation of Balliol was, I thought, really something.

When I first came to Oxford, the world was about to plunge into the Great Depression. At the university we were so protected and secure that in spite of Balliol's radical tradition, I remained unaware of all this. In 1929 I went with a coach-load of fellow students to deliver parcels of food and clothing to unemployed miners at Riska, just up the Ebbw Vale from Newport. We poured out friendliness and help and played a bit of football with them, but even with that visit, I didn't understand what it was all about. I didn't see that there were politics in all this, that the pits were privately owned and the men, out of work, were long since out of money and the whole village near to starving.

Lady Frances Ryder and Celia MacDonald of the Isles were the leaders of a group who gave hospitality to colonials at Oxford. They organised entertainment on a lavish scale. There were invitations to London balls in the high season, during vacation, and in London Week there were tremendous House of Commons parties at which we were introduced to MPs and cabinet ministers and entertained at their expense. The group also organised weekends as family guests in stately homes. If you wished, you could have a whole vacation as personal guest of the family in a succession of large country houses, and I spent a week at a time in several such places.

The object of the Rhodes Trust was to bring to Oxford some of the brighter young men from the remoter outposts of empire in the hope that they would take back a grounding of British ideas and values to spread amongst government and executive posts in the Commonwealth and the United States. While at Oxford, we were introduced to the fullest enjoyment of the rich life, and it was made clear that these were some of the perks for adherence to what is really a reactionary way of life and of thought.

At Michaelmas 1931 I had to decide whether or not to return to New Zealand. Since the Rhodes idea was that the chosen ones should carry back to their homeland the ineffable benefit that flows from an Oxford education, there was neither necessity nor room for a Rhodes Scholar to stay in England. At Theo Tylor's insistence, I went to consult Bob Younger, Lord Blanesburgh. He would have none of this and insisted that England could not afford to lose such "pearls". It was immensely flattering and I agreed to stay on.

CHAPTER FIVE

Pupillage

AFTER THE All Souls Exams, in September 1931, there came looking for me in college a man who insisted that he be allowed to drive me to London. It seemed that Bryant Goodman Irvine had given him this transport idea, and I think the connection came through the Apollo University Lodge. He had a long-nosed Bentley with a strap around the bonnet to hold it together. We came by the High Wycombe route, and all the way he talked about the sacred character of Kingship, and of Service to the Monarch and the People. He made it appear very normal and natural.

He took me to William Sanderson at Old Square in Lincoln's Inn. Sanderson was a barrister who before the start of the First World War had gathered around him an active group of extremely Royalist and Loyalist young men. A number of them had been connected with the Chambers of F E Smith, Lord Birkenhead and a high proportion were killed in France. Sanderson maintained a certain momentum with a new generation of young men, who met under the title of "The English Mistery". This was meant to represent an old English word relating to service, and so service to the State and Crown. (The word is also related to an occupation or calling as in "the mistery or craft of goldsmith, or of beggarman or thief".)

The English Mistery had the beginning of theories about race and breed, primogeniture and male dominance underlying its constitution. England's salvation required that it be led by men of good breeding and of good taste, and freemasonry held out the best hope of finding them. Sanderson was in favour of religion, but only if the church was kept firmly under the control of the king. He was particularly incensed by arguments that God had an especial care for the lowliest of men: "The Church says any soul is good enough for God, but the statesman must consider quality."

Sanderson held a weekly soirée to which came his supporters, mainly young barristers and sometimes young women of his or their acquaintance. His supporters in 1931 included John de Rutzen, whose grandfather under the title Baron de Rutzen had been senior stipendiary magistrate at Bow Street; the grandson inherited the same title, under which he practised. There were also John Davenport, Bryant Irvine, and John Green, who soon joined the BBC.

The more businesslike gatherings were, I believe, on Thursdays. Over a gentlemanly drink of sherry, we talked about personal matters at the Bar and then at some stage we sat on the front of our chairs bolt upright with our hands on our knees. We then contributed a short paper on some aspect of the Mistery. It was one paper per evening, and each lasting about fifteen minutes. On the subject of kingship, the topics might be: the King and the State, King and Parliament, King and People, King and what-you-like, King and Nonsense. They really were trivial little papers written by well-intentioned but dim little people.

I contributed a paper on the attitude of the Mistery to women; it was not meant to be entirely serious. It developed their notions of male predominance and of family and breed, and what I saw as the obvious consequence: that human procreation should be reduced or, it may be, restored to the herd system. One good man with the right stature, and of the right stock, should undertake as many women as he could manage. (I now know that a man is unlikely to be able to manage one, let alone more than one woman.) To my surprise, this effort was taken as a serious contribution and aroused a lively discussion from a full house. Some even asked whether there was not growing a certain measure of equality between the sexes, and perhaps Sanderson's theories should take account of this.

Ill-health was another subject on which Sanderson had strong views. Those who became ill through no fault of their own might have some call on our sympathy, but the majority of invalids, whose suffering sprang from self-inflicted causes, deserved only condemnation, their suffering merely serving to denote their innate inferiority. One of his more unusual sayings was to the effect that "People never become ill without cause, and they ought to be ashamed of it". Yet Sanderson, who was very small and extremely short-sighted, was himself handicapped. Two mature ladies cared for him at Old Square and he seldom left his chair. We didn't like to speculate on the causes of his disablement. Curiously, for an invalid, he believed in living dangerously. He thought that the safety net of pensions, insurance companies and public health measures stifled character, which could only grow by facing danger.

William used to say that anyone who could speak two languages was a rascal; he claimed it was an old proverb. It took me a month or two to realise that notions about purity of blood and nobility of race could lead to peculiar points of view about people of other races. At about the same time, I realised that some of our number would try to choose a cab with a driver who wasn't Jewish, and the opinions of Adolf Hitler began to appear in the English newspapers. I excused myself from further attendance and wrote a long, argumentative letter explaining my position. I thanked William, but said Good Day to them all. The movement did not suffer from my departure and indeed seems to have prospered, producing three or four MPs, despite Sanderson's condemnation of parliament as "a mob-house". He equated democracy with degeneracy, and regarded the secret ballot as a most cowardly thing.

At Balliol I had joined the Oxford University Carlton Club. This was the Conservative centre and most who joined were real Tories, but my interest was in the excellent dining room on the corner of George Street opposite Balliol. Bryant Irvine was also a member of the club, and in 1932 he introduced me to Miss Flora Fardell of 9 Gerald Row, London. She was of mature years, tall and elegant and fair. Her gatherings were, I think, on a Wednesday evening and included supper. Although she put me on to a group which provided aid for young men newly out of prison, her politics were nearer to the sharp edge of the Tory Party. In return, I asked our hostess to dine at the Royal Empire Society. We were invited to visit parliament and took tea on the terrace. It became easy to believe that if this was noble service, there was also some gilt and fun that went with it.

In April a man came to call and introduced himself as the agent of the Duke of Devonshire. The Duke took a close interest in Eastbourne and neighbouring parts of Sussex. He wondered whether I would care to become the MP for Eastbourne. Their member, a barrister named Edward Marjoribanks, had just died at the age of thirty-two. They were unprepared for this, and had to produce his replacement at once. It was an extraordinary idea. I had no connection with Eastbourne and was not even a member of their party. Furthermore, I had just been accepted as a pupil at 5 Essex Court and was trying to get established at the Bar.

His Grace had thought of all that. He knew many solicitors with good briefs to spare, there was a rich living to be won in politics if you had the right backing, and the Duke was in a position to decide who should be the MP. Perhaps I would consider it? He would call on me in four days. The next day I was invited to meet a man at the Carlton Club, where he gave me dinner. Did I know his brother, a solicitor? Did I know the firm of which he was a partner? I had heard of the firm, a most distinguished and large one that had my host's name firmly in the title of the partnership. Had I room for any more briefs? He knew Mr Armstrong-Jones, and had known Branson, the previous head of my chambers.

I took all this information to No 9 Gerald Row for advice but was told, "You must decide for yourself, but do consider the advantages." I decided, and rejected the proposal. When I next called on Miss Fardell, she delivered the majestic judgement, "No doubt the hour will bring forth the man." What she meant was, "You are a fool, but if you're lucky, you may get another chance." Several of those in the group went on to become MPs, including Bryant Irvine, who became Tory MP for Rye, which he represented for many years, ultimately holding a round dozen of the most junior offices known to man.

William Sanderson's group held the view that the government should not introduce conscription, even in wartime, because the only men and women fit to fight were those who volunteered. The volunteer was the genuine patriot fighter. A conscript, in the extreme reckoning of this ideology, was on the verge of being a traitor because he wouldn't have fought to defend his country unless he had been forced. Sanderson held himself responsible for all those who had died, as it were, under his aegis.

I met Janet at one of Sanderson's soirées. Her father was A T C Cree, a barrister-turned-lieutenant in the Durham Light Infantry, who was killed in the second battle of Ypres in May 1915. Janet was the second of his three daughters. She shone for stature and beauty and elegance. (I suppose there were several others who shone at the same time, but I didn't actually notice them.) But what in the world to do about it? To approach a girl and say "Come to the flicks", you needed the price of two tickets and a mug of something in the meantime and in those months I really was penniless. A New Zealander with little money comes to the Bar feeling very bare indeed. A three-year scholarship awarded by the Inner Temple, worth £200 a year, was about to run out. The first two years' worth had been spent at Oxford to make up to a reasonable sum the Rhodes money of £400 a year. Only £200 remained; one hundred guineas were needed for the call fee to the Bar and the same amount as a pupil fee to join chambers. At that time, the pupil fee was regarded as compulsory. I did not hear of any pupil who did not pay it, and all pupil-masters exacted it as a matter of form.

If I was not to be an MP, how to live? The opportunity came from L C Graham-Dixon. who had recently started his own coaching school at ancient Clifford's Inn. He guaranteed to get one through Bar Finals with the greatest ease, but had a surplus of pupils he could not cope with. There was a very short time to go and he needed help. I found myself lodging in his back room, studying for my own exams while tutoring for a fee during the day, and was at once launched. A number of men who became distinguished judges joined in our self-teaching for the Finals, and I was kept alive.

All Graham-Dixon's lot passed. He prescribed twenty questions only for each paper and he and his tutors crammed the aspirants with those questions and no others. Always enough of them were asked by the examiners to enable the student to pass. The Chairman of the Bar-teaching organisation at that time was a retired silk named Langdon. There is no reason whatever to suppose that Langdon knew what questions his examiners were likely to set, but he was a close friend of LC, so we all made jokes at their expense about the sources of the twenty questions.

I dared to find Janet's address and asked her out to supper, which meant Schmidt in Charlotte Street or thereabouts at, say, half-a-crown a head, including a glass of wine. I learnt that Janet was a painter; there was a picture recently bought for the Tate Gallery by the Chantry Bequest from the Royal Academy exhibition, and there was tempera. I had heard of tempera as a pre-oil medium of the ancients and knew that some part of an egg came into it, but I had not previously met tempera as a way of life. The artist lived in the studio and the day-to-day affairs of the studio were uniquely and exclusively devoted to tempera.

There was the manufacture of the boards, with layer after layer of whatever was required. I had already made close acquaintance with an ancient Bentley of Rolls Royce extraction and had found that it had as many as seventeen layers of paint, each fully hardened and baked on before the next one arrived. The foundation board to carry a tempera painting had just such a succession of layers to strengthen and confirm it and make it smooth enough to take the next stage. Bits of parchment obtained from the lampshade shop were boiled for hours on end, rendering the studio no longer tenable as a dwelling place, and the parchment a sticky mess.

This stewing of the parchment was necessary to create a medium fit to carry the gesso, or plaster of Paris, which came next. This had to be absolutely neutral, and slaked lime was slaked again and dried and slaked again in small balls in muslin bags. It had to be more neutral than zero-minus-minus. This, in its turn, was smoothed on to the board. Then the earth was searched for new additions to the raw colours. Or, rather the raw earths of the earth were searched. One met the actual powdered earth from Umbria and Sienna in person and saw them concocted and mixed to make what seemed like ever-new ranges of colour.

No doubt this work of preparing the board and then the paint played some part in preparing the mind and soul of the painter for the work. This was not required to be neutral. On the contrary, it had to be passionate and hot beyond boiling. But it had to be pure heat like nuclear heat, rather than gas or electric or thermal. The surroundings of the painter had to be a bit like that, too. It had to be flooded with classical music. It was lived in the simplest home-made clothes, like those usual in the past for a coachman or even a boatman. The shoes tended to be flat-bottomed and with a low profile; the profile would probably be observed only if they were upside down and seen on the horizon.

I was hopelessly in love with the girl but offering nothing of what usually went to make a prospective husband in middle-class circles in the early 'thirties. What I needed was an adjournment. If only the whole procedure could be stayed for, say, four years. I had been accepted for pupillage, and this seemed to hold out every kind of promise. What I needed was a formal document to be drawn up to bind all parties in most solemn form, but then to be kept in escrow for the necessary period. I had no courage even to hint at, let alone to make such an absurd proposal. All my love, all my devotion, yours forever, and postponed for four years?

During the following four years, I attended upon Janet regularly and frequently as my practice developed. By late in 1935 I was beginning to feel that I might be able to support her as I felt she had a right to expect and, more importantly, it appeared that competition from other and better placed men was becoming severe. In December I proposed and was accepted and in May 1936, the wedding was solemnised.

In the meantime, I continued with my studies, tutoring most days before breakfast, after breakfast before court, at lunchtime and again in the evening. Weekends likewise, so that the time seemed to be fully occupied. I went on diligently tutoring well into my second year at the Bar. Brian MacKenna, of Oxford Union fame, proposed that we should share lodgings and our kitchen soon became a meeting place for many who were called in 1932. Kenneth Diplock was amongst them, and Joe Stephenson, Harry Phillimore, Jack Ramsay Willis, Noel Hutton (who became Parliamentary Draughtsman) and a host of other eager young barristers. Ours were a bright enough lot, but we didn2't manage a first-class amongst us at the Bar finals. One evening shortly after the results were declared, Cheshire of Exeter College came to dine in the Inn and, being an examiner, declared what a poor shot we had all made at the papers. He said, "Then we came to this smart Oxford crew," and he reeled off some of the names, "now we'll see some good marks." And then "Flop," said he, "not a one amongst them."

As his promise from the beginning had indicated, Brian MacKenna was one of the earliest of his year of call to take silk and to go on the High Court Bench. His Irish origins stood to his disadvantage and barred him from any further promotion to a higher judgeship and he retired from the High Court Bench earlier than he need have done. He also withdrew from activities and attendance at the Bench of the Inner Temple, but this was through the intolerable manners and malevolent tongue of High Court Judge Melford- Stephenson.

I tutored no more at weekends after August 1932, which was when Arthur Wilson of Sydney, my fellow pupil to H D Samuels, joined with me to buy a boat. (Arthur had a bit of money and a fast car. He was probably the first on our side killed in the war in Europe, having been machine-gunned on a minesweeper in the North Sea before our troops were landed in France for the Phoney War.) We paid thirty pounds at sight for the Hawk as she lay in Chichester harbour, buying her from Harold Payton, who was somewhat senior to us in chambers. He was already Commodore of the Pin Mill Sailing Club on the Orwell and was about to take delivery of a brand-new boat built on the Isle of Wight.

The Hawk was a thirty-foot clinker-built and cutter rigged boat, a converted ship's lifeboat, fully rigged and found. There was ropeage and cordage, four sails, a compass, and fathoms of chain to the anchor, and tinned food to last us for six months of weekends, plus an outboard motor that could be slung onto a rig over the back. We took her and sailed straight out of Chichester harbour eastward, round the Owers and into Littlehampton, and were so pleased with our success that every weekend thereafter we left the boat at some new mooring and sailed into every port and inlet from Land's End to Harwich that could carry our three-foot draught. There were perhaps three weekends in mid-winter when we tried to get out of port against a head wind and were driven back.

When Arthur left chambers at the end of 1932, he to some extent took the boat with him, and I sailed less for a while. After a year or so, Brian MacKenna and I had to leave Clifford's Inn when it was to be pulled down. We took lodging in the basement of 1 Paper Building, and Brian stayed there for several years.

CHAPTER SIX

First Law Cases

FRANK SOSKICE, who tutored Terence Bird for admission to Balliol, had got me a pupillage in his chambers at 5 Essex Court, where Branson had served as Treasury junior during the First World War before he became a Puisne (High Court) judge. The head of chambers was now H D Samuels. Sammy's chambers were known as "the factory" not only because we churned out work as from a conveyor, but also because a good deal of it depended on the Factories Act, under which injured workmen could recover damages. Defective machinery and improper methods of work were our stock in trade.

Sammy was a Western circuiteer and indeed became leader of the circuit. During the war he had found himself in Aldershot, where he became friends with William Charles Crocker. Between them, they helped to get the law relating to motor car insurance into the books. There were plenty of running down actions or "runners", as they are known – a name that has been popular since the first days of stage coaches. When I came into chambers, the first Road Traffic Act of 1931 had just come fully into fruit. The Act made insurance for motor cars compulsory so that anyone who was injured or whose property suffered as the result of an accident could now claim compensation if the driver had been careless. For the first years, every insurance company gave the maximum service to its insured persons and most claims were fought. Underwriters were still feeling their way and had not learned the merits of settling hostile claims.

Likewise, they were checking every pin-pricking point on the meaning of their policies. Every policy had an arbitration clause and every possible point of argument was taken to arbitration. We would sometimes end up with two arbitrators and an umpire, all barristers, with two advocates on each side, making seven in all to help settle the plainest points of the meaning of English words in the Policy. I write Policy with a capital P because in the eyes of the insurance company their policy was sacred writ. For example, "limited to private and domestic purposes" could be a three-afternoon argument. Arbitrations were held after court, beginning at four-thirty p.m. and going on until seven. It was all done in private, which gave the advantage that the tendency of Lloyds' underwriters and companies to resist claims was not exposed to public gaze.

An extraordinary blockage of "runners" had arisen from compulsory road insurance. There were so many that a new court was set up and a new procedure list to clear the backlog of work in the high court. You could serve your writ, which had to have statement of claim with it, after fourteen days. Within fourteen days after that, you would appear before Mr Justice Horridge or Mr Justice Swift, with a summons for directions in open court. From then, the trial could easily be on within a month. Nothing would excuse you from an early trial except complicated injuries, the future of which was not yet clear. In short, the case would be over within three months of the road accident whereas now it is a steady three to five years.

The bottom end of the running-down trade was the inquest, at which counsel appeared for the company to express deep regret and perhaps just hint at the possibility that it was the poor victim's own silly fault. Harold, Sammy's senior clerk, would be at chambers at nine a.m. and, shortly after that, a number of large cars would purr up Middle Temple Lane on their way to various coroners' courts. For me in 1932, the fee was £1.3s.6d in Greater London; £1.1.0 for the barrister, 2s.6d. the clerk's fee. For anywhere in the home counties, it would be £2.4s.6d.

I remember my first appearance in the high court. During my first fortnight of pupillage, Harold said to me, "Go into Rigby Swift's court and tell him Sammy is coming." I knew the formal beginning, "If your Lordship pleases, may I mention the case of Smith against Jones," but then went on to say, "Will you please adjourn for a moment? My master is coming." With a broad smile, Rigby replied to that informal approach, "Oh, your master is coming, is he? And pray what manner of master is he?" Before I could say a word, he rolled on. "Is he by chance a master of this honourable court of the King's Bench Division, or a master in Chancery? Or could it be more appropriately that he is a master in Lunacy?"

I began to reply, "If your Lordship pleases..." but was interrupted. He was away again. "Oh, he cometh, cometh he? Tell me, young gentleman, is this his second coming, by chance?" After this sublime piece of sacrilege, he was leaning forward muttering to his clerk, obviously asking, "Who is this stupid young man?" Sammy then came, and all was well as he shuffled into his seat. On circuit at a later date, Rigby's marshal told me that he had said to him after lunch, "Come, marshal. Let's go back into court and give old Sammy a bit of a hammering." Rigby Swift is famous for stories of his observations in court. They must all be true because mine is true. (I also heard Rigby say, in speechmaking at a Temple wedding, "Remember, dear friends, matches are made in heaven, but they are impregnated on earth, and they are not always of the safety variety.")

Harold, the senior clerk, had a facial scar from gas in the First World War, and a tendency to exhibit a boxing style of sharp, straight blows delivered with a snort and a grunt and a stamp of the foot, a style he had learned as an army divisional lightweight champion. He had come as junior war hero into the chambers of Barrington-Ward, and then into the chambers of Branson, the Treasury junior. He never tired of telling the stories first of Barrington-Ward, that having stayed in the chambers throughout the war when every young man had left, he ended up with the biggest common law practice in the Temple. Shortly after the war, he had fourteen cases of one sort or another in the high court on one day, and fourteen leaders. He dared not leave his chambers for fear that the clerks of one of his leaders or his solicitors might catch him.

Of Branson, Harold could not withhold the story of when it became his turn to become a high court judge. It was the time when F E Smith, whose clerk he was, as Lord Birkenhead, went onto the Woolsack. As he could not take his clerk, he hoped to find him a position with a high court judge. Smith hit on the dodge of elevating a county court judge who had no clerk. He knew Acton from Wadham days. If Acton would take Smith's clerk, he would be appointed to the next judgeship. No, he would not. Besides, Branson's turn had come, and he claimed it by right. The issue was fought out with the Lord Chancellor's department, with all existing former Treasury juniors expressing their views, even with the chairman of the Bar and the Dean of the Barristers' Clerks Association. Branson won. Acton, and Smith's clerk, had to stand back for the next vacancy, so Harold became senior clerk at 5 Essex Court to Sammy.

Harold was, for me, the source of such phrases as: "Is it quite suitable for a young gentleman in your position to live in such a part of London?" or "to have a shabby old car like that?" and "I can recommend a tailor of good taste" or "a car that my friend Tom has for sale". But I suppose that every senior clerk has used such words. He was so close in with underwriters and tariff companies that if Sammy was going to be free for a day, Harold would ring a few assessors and, like as not, the answer from someone would be "I have just sent one to—" naming one of the London solicitors, "and will ring them and say that Sammy is free". Harold would not, of course, ring the solicitors as that would be touting, but to ring his friends the assessors was another matter.

I had the utmost good luck in that my Balliol tutor, Theo Tylor, sent me to London with introductions to four of the leading solicitors of the day. I don't suppose they much minded whether or not you had firsts, but wanted to know if you could stand up in court. Certainly, after a few years, instructions of all kinds began to come in. We were rather the lower end of the near-commercial, insurance, common law business and it was a great surprise when, on a tutor's introduction, firms like Linklaters, Farrers, Sharp Pritchard and Theo Goddard started sending in briefs that had nothing whatever to do with running down.

Often I was to be the junior to one of the leading figures in the chancery division, of whom Wilfred Greene and Gavin Simonds were typical; or, on the common law side, Porter, Somervell and others, and attending upon them while they advised on the most abstruse questions. There were Privy Council opinions and appearances, high court opinions and appearances, and chancery matters, and there seemed no end to it. At the same time, the busy young barrister in knock-about common law chambers was off to inquests and magistrates' court and county courts, and having those two or three appearances a day that call for every spare minute of work and every ounce of vigour.

5 Essex Court was saved from being the commonest running-down chambers only by the mass of minor commercial work that arose through the arbitrations over "policy points", and by the presence as second in command of Ronnie Armstrong-Jones and third in command Frank Soskice, who was to become Attlee's first solicitor general, then second attorney general, home secretary and, as Lord Stow Hill, a Labour peer. Ronnie Armstrong-Jones had been to Eton and then to Oxford, where

he rowed in the Magdalen crew – in effect, the first post-war Oxford crew, which won the Grand Challenge Cup at Henley. He was quite a fellow. Ronnie inherited some of Sammy s common law practice but would touch no part of it, or of any other law, except running down cases. By the end of the 1930s, he was in court even more than Sammy himself. It was "runners" every day, and endless defences to be settled in between.

He earned a name for probity over Groom v Crocker. Crocker had sent instructions to Ronnie for Groom with a plain back sheet saying: "Settle defence admitting negligence and denying liability." This meant that insurers had decided to settle and wished their pleadings to make this clear, but also to deny the plaintiff the right to sign judgement. You could deny liability on the basis that, even though the man had lost an arm or a leg, you had not admitted any loss. Negligence without loss was no action at all. When it came to the trial, or at any time in between, you could settle.

Mr Groom, the defendant in the running-down action, did not admit negligence and indeed was asserting that he was innocent. When he discovered that his solicitors had caused the defence to be signed and put into court admitting that he was negligent, he was outraged. He sued Crocker; Crocker instructed Armstrong-Jones to accept the blame by saying that he had considered the papers and the case and had advised that there should be an admission of negligence. This was far from the truth and Ronnie declined. Crocker withdrew his work from chambers, but, fortunately, there were twenty other solicitors from insurance companies who poured in their work.

Ronnie had a "place" in Wales, inherited from his father, Sir Robert, the first appointed First Visitor in Lunacy for the whole country. He had several wives, one of whom was the attractive Australian actress, Carol Coombe. Visiting the Welsh "place" on a sporting occasion, she shot a great-crested grebe in full plumage. Ronnie decided that the bird should be stuffed and set in a glass cage with gold binding. This required the best taxidermist in all England, who was reputed to be at the Army & Navy. Off went the bird with proper instructions. After some weeks without reply, there were telephone calls and enquiries, then a letter. Eventually the bird was returned duly stuffed, but also plucked. It had gone to the game department. There was a wide sense of dismay.

Now Ronnie had never had an account at the Army & Navy. For all we knew, friends of his had not either. He declared in the most minatory form that unless a great-crested grebe in full plumage was produced duly set up in a glass case with golden binding and free of charge, then both he and all his friends would withdraw their accounts from the store. That great firm would be ruined. A & N then scoured the markets of England and Wales, produced a bird and in no time had it mounted in a glass cage with gold edges, and all free of charge. Honour was satisfied. To make a little more of the story, Ronnie always described it as a golden-crested grebe. This was to justify the gold edges of the case. There is no such bird.

My first jury trial was defending a ladder, carried by a painter in central London, that had unwisely poked its nose through a large shop window. It was tried at Westminster County Court before his Honour Judge Alfred Tobin. The ladder won, on the ground that its unoffending end had been given a sharp push by a casual stranger who had every opportunity of seeing what he was doing and was solely responsible for the damage. He had escaped, pursued by an angry crowd.

The learned Judge Alfred Tobin was famous for that a rather junior counsel, Henry Bensley Wells, for some years had appeared before him on behalf of the London General Omnibus Company in runners and had invariably been successful. The LGOC moved all their cases into his court. The Bar Council went into the question of the consistent winning and decreed that young Mr Bensley Wells should not appear in that court any more, on any occasion, for any kind of case. We might assume he was an excellent advocate and that the LGOC prepared their cases with extreme care; always was too often. Besides, the two assumptions were unfounded. Bensley Wells was a famous rowing man. If anyone known to have been in any Oxford boat appeared before him when he later became a county court judge, he would give them tea and recount the names of one particular crew from bow all the way to number seven. He would stop there and so omit both stroke and cox. One was left to assume that he was stroke; it was not so, because he was cox. That was no discredit because he was very successful.

My next jury case was before Mr Justice Goddard and a jury at Taunton. I was for the plaintiff, widow of a man who had been knocked down in the street by a car. She lost. We had reached the point in cross-examination where it was apparent that the defendant driver was fairly close behind the pedestrian, the pedestrian appeared not to have heard him, and the driver had given no warning. That should have been a strong enough position to enable the merest beginner to win for the plaintiff. I was still in my first year at the English Bar and I added in the most boyish and fatuous fashion, "The effect of it was that you sneaked up behind him."

Goddard groaned loudly. It was almost a roar: a combination of anger and amazement at my folly. "So that's how you put your case," he said. No amount of withdrawing and apologising to the witness and the court had any effect and the jury threw us out. Here was the widow denied even the modest compensation that she might have been awarded for loss of her husband. Here was the judge who felt that it was more important to teach me a lesson than to put right by one sentence in summing up the imbalance caused by my misjudgement. It was an early lesson in being discreet.

Mr Justice (Jimmy) Cassels, father of Frank Cassels, added his own case of one question too many. He cross-examined the police sergeant in a drunken-driving case on the lines: "He gave his name? His address? His telephone number? His business address? His office number? His car number? His birthday? He gave you all these correctly?" – All answered by "Yes, sir." – "He gave you all these correctly and yet you charge him with being drunk?" "Yes, sir. He gave me all these with his arms tight round my neck."

One member of Sammy's chambers was Edward Duke, or "Dukie", whose father was Lord Merrivale, President of the Divorce Division and called the "Duke with the Port Wine voice". Edward was not particularly bright at the law. He had, however, two solicitors who were most faithful to him for their cases before the Registrar of the Lambeth County Court, where Dukie became the "Attorney General". He had promised that when his father died, he would retire from the Bar. It would be unseemly and derogatory of his father's fame if the Lord Merrivale were to appear in minor debt-collecting cases. In the meantime, he undertook no case of any kind except before that registrar.

In my pupil year, there came to him an appeal case in workmen's compensation from that very neighbourhood on the Western circuit whence his family came. On no account would he undertake the appeal. He was satisfied that he was quite incompetent to do it, and the job was allotted to me. It came on before Lord Hanworth, Master of the Rolls, whose court had decided a somewhat similar appeal the previous year and had found against my present contention. I set off to prove that the present case was different in such an important respect that our case did not have to follow the recent authority. It was about some aspect of "when is a man at work": for example, on the journey to his place of work, crossing a neighbouring railway yard, or the public street. In preparation, I had explored every possible angle from which the matter might be seen.

I had barely begun to outline the facts of the case when the court called upon my opponent, Martin O'Connor, who was known for taking on any case on a speculative basis, a practice forbidden by the Bar but well recognised as existing. He said that he thought he had the advantage, for their lordships had decided the very facts of this case a year ago, and entirely in his favour. "No," said Hanworth. "Is that quite right? Perhaps you have not read your *Times* of two days ago where it is reported that their lordships in the House of Lords reversed our decision of a year ago." I, of course, looked very wise, pretending to bow appreciatively, as much as to say I was just about to produce the copy of the paper in my support.

In fact, I was as much unaware of it as was my opponent. Fortunately, Harold was in court and I managed to pass him an urgent note without drawing attention to the fact and in a moment he was upstairs in the Bar library and came back with the very cutting, which he slipped to me unseen by the court. I won the appeal without having to do more than ask for costs and bow politely, and learned the rule that it is worthwhile reading *The Times* every day. Since then I have gained distinct advantage on a number of occasions from reading the daily Law Reports. Nowadays, as like as not you will meet the judge at lunch-time who was reported in *The Times* from the day before. (The other matter in *The Times* of personal interest at my age is the obituary column; many old acquaintances come forward to lend their names in this area.)

By the beginning of the war, underwriters had begun to learn the merits of settling their cases, which were in the main "runners", and the field of industrial injuries was minute. It was reduced almost to nothing, this field of claims by injured workmen, by the rule of "Common Employment". If the employer could show that an injury was due in part to the fault of a fellow employee, then that was one of the risks that a workman was assumed to take. The first Attlee government got rid of the rule in 1945, just in time to save the Common Law Bar. At the same time, we got rid of workmen's compensation, and now industrial injuries have not only replaced the "runners" but far outstripped them in number, in amount of damages, and in fees.

When I started in London, Dr John Baker, husband of Zita, gave me an introduction to Mary Adams, who ran BBC Talks at Savoy Hill and, from its beginning, the similar department of television at Alexandra Palace. Mary (First Class Honours at Newnham) was a magnet that drew many exceptional women to London and to her salon. The first person to whom Mary introduced me was Harriet Cohen, just back from representing Britain (on the piano) at the Geneva Disarmament Conference in 1932 and preparing to set off on another tour. My only duty was to help her pack. Mary later introduced me to Ellen Wilkinson, Margaret Lloyd, Monica Felton and the Russians Olga Chechotkina and Ekaterina Chevalova: all powerful and determined women.

Mary's husband was Vyvyan Adams, a reform-minded Conservative MP and one of the few who remained loyal to Winston Churchill throughout the 1930s. We became close friends. Mary gave much of her time to backing up Vyvyan in his parliamentary work – every MP regards that as the main job of a spouse. In 1951, Vyvyan drowned at Gunwalloe in Cornwall, despite the bravest efforts of his young daughter Sally, who succeeded only in rescuing her mother. It was a needless tragedy, but it set free in Mary an extraordinary gift for discerning and using the talents of other women. She blossomed and became a world centre of womanpower.

Mary did her best for me with a mock murder trial at Savoy Hill in 1932. Our judge was the Irish Silk Maurice Healey, one of the few, including Sergeant Sullivan, who came to the English Bar from Dublin. Morris was very Irish and brought so many unscripted witticisms into the trial that the only possible response was for us all to laugh. We had no jury to join the merriment and no canned laughter to make up for their absence. The prosecutor was Arthur Vivian, who shortly after that became Clerk of the Skinners' Company. He remained close to chambers and we enjoyed his hospitality at the Skinners. The ratings for our mock trial entertainment reached an all-time low and I have not been heard on the BBC in the seventy years that followed. Their judgement is probably as sound now as it was then.

Thanks to my family and the speech of the parson at Port Chalmers, I had what was regarded in New Zealand as an English accent, but after three years at Oxford I still could not cope with the OU diphthong. Boots were pronounced as in the phrase "a beaut pair of beutes". The judges and the Bar together regard themselves as guardians of the language: conservative guardians who insist upon the Queen's enunciation or accent. It was Vyvyan Adams who polished off the roughest kiwi edges to render my accent fit for the dainty English ear:

> Any hounds found scrounging or bounding around these grounds or arousing the owls, fowls, mouses, or even the brown mountain trout, will be impounded by the County Council and found a thousand pounds.

I thought I had mastered this, but not with full confidence.

On the first occasion when I had a claim for a thousand pounds, it was before Mr Justice Hilberry without a jury. I overlooked the fact that he was the most ill-educated and affected man on the Bench and opened the case: "My claim is for ten times a hundred in units of sterling currency." Hilberry had a handkerchief sticking out of his jacket pocket. He fluffed this in front of his nose rather as Kenneth Kaunda did, and said, "Eauw, you mean a theusand peunds." I had sat and listened to him in court, and as a pupil in various cases, but had not noticed that he had the same problem. He was regarded as the leading old boy of University College School up on Hampstead Hill and they, like Balliol with Ted Heath, had failed to cure this lapse in pronunciation.

Everyone from New Zealand was expected to play or to have played rugby. So, finding myself at Llanelli on my first case in Wales, I was opposed in a hire-purchase case by Rowe-Harding. He had been captain of Cambridge and captain of Wales and was a distinguished three-quarter, as well as being a champion sprinter. He knew that I was from New Zealand and assumed that I played rugby, so after the case we were invited to take tea with the judge. His Honour Judge Frank Roberts began by saying, "I was there, man. I saw it all!" It was nearly thirty years after the game at Cardiff Arms Park in 1905, and almost every Welshman made the like claim when he met a New Zealander.

The judge then gave his account of Rhys Gobe thundering down the line and, faced with the full back, flashing the ball to Teddy Morgan who plunged over the line. I reminded him that by then the touch judge was waving his flag vehemently because Rhys Gobe had carried the ball out of play. "Oh no, man, not at all! He was waving his flag not in execution of his duty, but with jubilation at the result." It was in the course of this recital that the judge took the green book from his table and threw it across the room at Rowe-Harding, crying, "Take it, man, take it!" I am not sure that the cups went flying, but they may well have done.

My first real brief concerned the gold clause in American bonds. All North American bond issues (whether state, city, federal or corporation) seemed to be based on this clause, which declared that one dollar by bond shall be worth so much fine gold, or so many bushels of Minnesota wheat, pounds weight of Ohio hooves, flagons of best beer from Utah and so on, giving up to as many as a dozen different measures of one ounce of gold. This guaranteed the stability of the dollar and that there would be no inflation in America or, for that matter, in almost any other country. The English tariff companies (the insurance companies who joined the big league) had bought American gold bonds in great quantity and insured them with Lloyds. No one could imagine that a gold bond would ever go wrong, so the premiums were low and the insurances and re-insurances were multitudinous. In short, you didn't have to pay much to insure a gold bond.

President Roosevelt was trying to shake the world out of its slump and hoped to do it without taking part in a world war. One of the first steps was to declare illegal the gold clause, the object being to restart American business by creating inflation. In England, the tariff companies sued Lloyds and, through the lordly Linklaters, I had the luck of getting the junior brief for Lloyds. It was on the strength of my getting the instructions to advise that Janet and I married and got going with a family. Without any payment of fees and merely on the prospect, we were launched.

So much was involved that all the main leaders of the Bar participated in one way or another, whether as arbitrators, or leading for the defence or for the claimants. Among them were Wilfred Green, Gavin Simons, Porter, Tucker and Raymond Evershed. All five ended up in the Lords, but four of them were translated during the running of the case. Evershed was a fairly junior silk at the Chancery Bar, and this was the first case where he attracted a fee of 1,000 guineas. In commemoration, Harry Cohen of Linklaters gave him a golden guinea mounted in silver and duly inscribed. Evershed had been regularly at Balliol in the early 'thirties, and through this case I came to know him better. Years later, when he was retired, he asked me where we first really got to know one another. I said I thought it was this gold bond case that really gave us our introduction. He said, "I don't remember that one." Life at the Bar is a bit like that.

My first Privy Council case came in about 1934, on appeal from the Maori Lands Court. As a New Zealand lawyer, it was thought that I was bound to know Maori land law, but I knew no more about the subject than did my leader, Owly Stable. He, at least, was quite at home in the Privy Council. I have no recollection of whether or not we won. The point about being a lawyer for a long time is that it is not the law you remember but the people. If you've been called in New Zealand in 1928 as a barrister and solicitor, and then in London in 1932, and with any normal Bar experience, you've met a lot of people and heard a lot of stories. All barristers have their share of entertaining cases and any one of us could write a book about them.

The barrister's trade leads to the wildest uncertainties and irregularities. You're way up at some stages with work piling in and the solicitors appearing to adore you. Shortly after you are down in the dumps, desperate for a brief and wondering what the chances are of going on at all. Suddenly it all comes again: a new line of solicitors, a new type of work and everything opens up afresh. What possible calling can give more freedom and independence? Where else can you go into parliament and into high, or low, politics and yet carry on with your practice unaltered? In some ways, it is rather like the life of an actor on a provincial circuit, who meets his agent only at Crewe or Bletchley or Bodmin Road, where he changes trains. For thirty years, I had cases over a large part of England and some part of the Commonwealth so that Sunday was given up to travelling. In the 1930s, main-line trains on Sunday were largely occupied by players changing post and by the stray barrister looking for Monday's brief.

CHAPTER SEVEN

Clive

IN 1932 when I was just beginning in chambers, Lewis Clive came up to London. He invited me to join him to row pair-oared for a term and to enter for the Goblets at Henley. Lewis was doing his law finals and had to be protected from travelling. I was solely dependent on tutoring fees and on a few guineas earned from briefs, mostly at the rate of one guinea each, and had no other place to work save the Temple. Perhaps my tutor or the college would have got me some tutorial job in Oxford. Tylor was approached and was prepared to help. The master was willing, and suggested that I could do some lecturing and have lodging in the college. I might even have joined the Oxford Circuit and organised a brief or two. I had not courage or flair enough to rise to this.

In fact, Lewis joined with H R A Edwards (known as Pinkers or Jumbo) with whom he had already had success and together they won the Goblets for pairs at Henley in July, and the Gold Medal at the 1932 Olympics the following month. If I had joined Lewis, his chances would have been gravely diminished, but he was so good that he might have overcame the burden of pulling me along. Theirs was the last British Olympic Rowing Gold for many years. Edwards was probably the only man in the history of the Boat Race who actually stopped rowing in mid-race. This was in about 1926. He was very young and it was all too much for him, but he at once left the university. However, he came up a few years later and in 1932 rowed again in the crew. As a coach, he became a famous figure in Oxford rowing.

Lewis Clive was in many ways an exceptional man. He was born and bred at his mother's home at Whitfield, Allensmore, a few miles south-west of Hereford. The house was large, dignified and Georgian and the views from it were spectacular. His father was a lieutenant colonel in the

Grenadier Guards, killed in action in France, and had also been Tory MP for South Herefordshire. It was my impression that, throughout her widowhood, Mrs Clive helped to rule the county from Whitfield. If it were not Mrs Clive who owned or influenced something, then it was the Bulmers, as I was to discover some years later in reviewing the constitution and conduct of the magistrates of Hereford.

In 1933, Lewis took part in an expedition that explored and mapped land in Canada's desolate North-Western Territories. And when he came to London, he added to his many distinctions that of being apprentice to the family bank, Glyn Mills, generally known as being the treasury to the armament industry. He found lodging in Bedford Street between the Strand and Covent Garden and asked me to join him there. After the war, the whole building was taken over by the Communist Party. At the time we were there, I daresay neither of us had ever heard of the organisation. But it was there that the politics of the harsh world caught up with and engulfed us.

In 1934 and 1935 we had a prolonged London social season when Lewis's sisters engaged in "coming out". During the vital period we were in white ties and tails for two or three nights a week. There were debs and dowagers to supper in Covent Garden and to the cinema or even to the opera or a play. If the ladies were still there in the early hours, we would visit Covent Garden market. We fixed them all up with rather homely fare, for Mother Clive was a great producer of home-tinned fruit from Hereford and the cider was from her neighbours, the Bulmers. During our short summer social whirls, Lewis regularly asked that he might bring his friend and there were parties all over Mayfair and Belgravia. He took part in all the great social occasions of the season and this went on until he became a Labour councillor and gave full time to his work.

Living in London gave the chance of taking one's holidays in Europe. At first, it was just across to Paris for the opera or the cabaret, but soon there were more ambitious ventures. In 1934 a New Zealand lawyer friend and I made a walking tour of parts of Austria and Germany. After a walk over the Steineres Meer from Austria, we came uphill from Koenigsee and passed Hitler's mountain retreat at Berchtesgaden. As we approached, a crowd of people were gathering on the hillside and we joined them. Hitler, of whom we had scarcely heard, came out from what seemed to be quite a small house. He spoke slowly and quietly in an unemotional voice; to us, it was incomprehensible. At first, one didn't notice the gradual increase of pace and sound and the raising of the pitch, which continued until it was almost a shout. We heard "volk" more than once, and long dramatic pauses. It was Hitler in full flood, and those next to us were in tears.

It was a harsh, cracked voice, which became savage and fierce as he shook his head and snarled and stamped, thrusting out his arms in a foretaste of the final salute. Hitler ended in a state near hysteria and the silent audience seemed shocked. Then came a final shout and stamp, and the victory greeting and arm salute, Sieg Heil, given once only, and greeted by a roar of approval. He stood for a moment, turned in military style and marched away with the half-dozen supporters who had come out with him. It was the lowest order of demagogy, but meant nothing to us except that we had been present at a spectacle.

During the long vacation in that same year, Frank Soskice and I planned to row down the Danube from Vienna to Budapest with Laszlo Gombos, a London solicitor with the firm of Theodore Goddard. Laszlo was to bring his rowing boat by the paddlewheel steamer from Budapest, his native city, and we would row it back downstream; it was no great feat, but about 160 miles. While waiting in Vienna, Frank and I put up at the Hotel Sacher, which was still run by Frau Ed Sacher, famous for having "whipped the canaille from the door" in troublesome times. The hotel was as grand and as opulent as its history. Our suite was no exception – no one could have less than a suite. The bath was of marble with gilt taps, and was sunk in the floor of an oversized bathroom. We visited the opera and picture galleries, in particular the Kunsthistorisches Museum, where we discovered Pieter Breughel the Elder and fell in love with his myriad of Dutchmen and women.

Vienna in the 1920s and 1930s was the envy and admiration of the Socialist world. The city council raised very heavy taxes and built the Karl Marx Hof, the Reaman Hof and the Goethe Hof, great blocks of flats that housed a quarter of a million people, let at nominal rents. Gas, electricity and water were supplied at cost. By law, the council required employers to provide holidays with pay; domestic servants were awarded overtime rates and were to be fed the same food as their employers. This was perhaps overdone because there were taxes on the having of servants and many wealthy families sacked them all or retreated with them to the country.

In Austria, private armies were illegal, but here were two: the Schutzbund, a part-time armed workers' militia, and the Heimwehr, the force led by Prince Starhemberg, the wealthy Fascist aristocrat. Starhemberg's Heimwehr had bombarded with cannon the Karl Marx Hof and the Goethe Hof six months before, so this was a necessary point of pilgrimage for Frank, who was already edging towards the idea of being a Labour politician. (He was a thoughtful and progressive chap and neither of us suspected that his devotion to Hugh Gaitskill would carry him to the extreme right of the party.) The buildings had been much restored but still bore scars of the three-day siege. We were told that perhaps 300 had died in the buildings when the families came under attack, and nearly a thousand had been injured, so it was a worthy point of pilgrimage. The concept of a workers' militia was at that time a bit difficult for us to imagine. It was before Spain, which was to open our eyes.

Laszlo arrived with his boat, which was partway to being a racing skiff. It was clinker-built but fairly fine, with sliding seats and comfortable room for three plus baggage. It sizzled along, with the water bubbling around it. We set off with great confidence and, with the flow under us, did fifty miles on the first day. We had overlooked that our hands and bottoms and muscles were soft, and that evening we were considering taking the next day off. In fact, we set off well bound up with sticking plasters and did only twenty miles.

We soon settled down to a steady routine, which gave us time to enjoy the few great cathedrals and palaces and even fewer cities, and learned, we thought, to take advantage by proper coxing of the better currents. On several occasions shots were fired across the river between Hungary and Czechoslovakia — not really near us, but close enough to be uncomfortable. They came equally from either side and two or three times we drew ashore while the protagonists exhausted themselves.

As we arrived in Budapest, that late summer Friday was a special holiday given to water festivals. The river was afloat shore to shore with pleasure boats. We gathered that Laszlo belonged to several sporting clubs, all with boating interests, and that he had persuaded their members to arrange a ceremonial welcome with boats and flowers. A message had been sent from Ujpest, just north of the city, and the welcoming flotilla came out to meet us. Hungary was no longer part of the Austro-Hungarian Empire under Emperor Franz Josef, but ours was an imperial welcome. We came home across Europe on the Grand Orient Express.

At Balliol, Soskice, Cecil Binnie and their friend Haws were known as "the World, the Flesh and the Devil", although no one knew which was meant to be which. They made a pretence of living a highly indulgent life, but were in fact ordinary undergraduates. Haws's nickname was based on the expletive with which he introduced every observation, as in "Haws! Isn't it time we stopped for lunch?" Later in the 'thirties, Janet and I went by car up the Loire and on to Paris with Frank and Haws. We saw many fine chateaux and a few churches, one of which had tombs of our Plantagenet kings – this was in a part once England.

Haws took us to another church that was part of his own history. He had married in Oxford the princess of that village and was taken to be introduced to his parents-in-law, a very proper French family. After Sunday lunch, they went to climb the church tower to view the countryside. Haws couldn't manage the climb and when they came down he was sitting on the altar drumming his heels against the altar cloth declaiming, "So did they enthrone the Harlot of Paris in the Revolution." His marriage did not survive very long.

In Paris we joined company with Alexander Kerensky. At thirty-six, he had been liberal premier of all Russia and so governed the country for a few months in 1917. Our connection with him was that Frank's father, David Vladimir Soskice, was secretary to his cabinet. He had come to Britain many years before and married a Miss Ford Madox Hueffer, than which nothing could take him deeper into Bloomsbury life, and thus had an open line of retreat when the Bolsheviks took over. At the Soskice home, all the surviving members of Kerensky's cabinet turned up at one time or another. (Their other natural resorts were Estoril and Long Island, both havens for ex-Royals.)

The French World Exhibition was on and, in the Soviet pavilion, Kerensky, with his monocle and haughty demeanour, was at his grandest. His hair was iron-grey but still stood vertical *en brosse*. At every photo of a revolutionary speech, he exclaimed in a loud voice, "This is a forgery and I have the original. It was not he, 'that Stalin', or 'that Lenin', it was I. I made that great speech, I held the people in the palm of my hand, I was their leader." It was aimed at drawing the attention of the Soviet wardens of the show but had no effect. Equally fruitless was his constant interest in any young woman that passed. He would follow at once with his monocle and occasionally with his feet, the monocle directed roughly toward their knees. He would exclaim, "Ah, very fine. Magnificent. Most promising." No response came. We all enjoyed the spectacle; only Janet was too polite to laugh aloud. We returned home from there to the forebodings of war.

Lewis Clive had not sailed very much before we set up together but in August 1935 he joined in a longish trip in the good ship *Altair* from Christchurch, Hampshire to the Scillies. On the way back, we were becalmed for two days off the Eddystone Lighthouse. Being late for an appointment in Scotland, he insisted on being rowed some miles to shore, somewhere just to the west of Bigbury Bay, and set off to climb the cliff and, for all I knew, to walk all the way to Scotland. His was the direct route in most things.

He left the bank, the Grenadier Guards, and the Bar to which he was a student. His mother was delighted and said, "Now we shall put you into the business itself." That was to be either Guest, Keen and Nettlefold, or Armstrong Whitworth. Lewis was not having this and put himself to work first in the Fabian Society and then in civil liberties, before launching into the Labour Party. To each of these three, he gave large sums of money from his substantial possessions. The Fabian Society was run by the absurd John Parker, who had been president of the Oxford Union, and was probably the first president officially a member of the Labour Party. He was MP for Dagenham from 1945 until 1983, but had no real notion of socialism and scarcely spoke in parliament. Lewis also joined Chatham House, the Royal Institute of International Affairs.

Lewis was a founder member of the National Council for Civil Liberties, which was run by Ronald Kidd and Sylvia Crowther-Smith, urged on by a group of left-wing lawyers of whom Binford Hole, Dudley Collard, Geoffrey Bing and Neil Lawson were the leading figures. When the hunger marchers of the National Unemployed Workers Movement came to London in 1932, Kidd had seen plainclothes policemen amongst the marchers, trying to foment trouble and then drawing their truncheons to make arrests. He set up the NCCL in February 1934,[1] days before another hunger march was due to reach London, and sent observers to Hyde Park in case these violent and provocative tactics were repeated. Lewis and I went as observers. Although I don't recall any sort of clash with the police, I do remember seeing Red Ellen Wilkinson at the head of the march.

Before the NCCL was officially established, Lewis took me to a meeting in Caxton Hall at which Lord Marley was chairman. Marley had been Minister for War in Ramsay MacDonald's second government and so was out of a job when Ramsay sided with the Tories in the National Government of 1932. I think the meeting was about the Encitement to Disaffection Act, but certainly Lewis had taken some part on behalf of Kidd in organising the meeting. These activities were, for both of us, a great leap into social thought and action.

The Incitement to Disaffection Act of 1934 was brought to Kidd in its embryonic form by some Tory MP, possibly by Vyvyan Adams. When Kidd asked his lawyer supporters to help with criticising the Bill, the minor part as message boy was allotted to me. I took it to the biggest names in the law that I knew namely, William Holdsworth, Vinerian Professor of English Law at All Souls, and J L Brierly, who held a similar position in International Law. I had been to them both for lectures and tutorials. Holdsworth was so pleased with his formula that he said he'd better put it in writing. I then said I thought it so important that he ought to sign it, and he did. Holdsworth's actual phrase – that the bill was a "most daring encroachment upon the liberty of the subject" – was so widely canvassed that it went into a leading textbook on constitutional law.

Kidd made the best possible use of the two learned professors and raised such a campaign against the bill that major amendments had to be made. He kept Holdsworth's original signed manuscript, but it was probably lost on one of several moves. The Socialist lawyers' group, the Haldane Society, realised how outstanding Kidd was as a propagandist and campaigner and gave him the maximum support in all his campaigns. It was my first excursion into "fixing" or arranging things behind the political scenes, and helped me to the mistaken and foolish idea that, with sufficient effort, there was nothing that couldn't be altered.

The line we were taking was that young soldiers should not be liable to challenge for being unwilling to fight against their fellow countrymen in their own country; for example, Irishmen in Ireland. The Act said that it was a crime to suggest this to a soldier. It was aimed at preventing and punishing attempts to seduce members of the armed forces from their duty or allegiance. It was intended to replace the Incitement to Mutiny Act

---

1 An earlier National Council for Civil Liberties had been set up in 1916 but soon disappeared without trace. George Lansbury was on the executive committee.

1797, which had been enacted to block libertarian ideas that came from the French Revolution and the Mutiny of the Nore. Under the Mutiny Act, a crime could not be proved unless it were shown that the wrong-doer tried to persuade the soldier to disobey an order as well as to be disloyal to the Crown.

It was only a crime if an attempt had been made to persuade the soldier to depart both from his duty and from his allegiance: allegiance being the duty that a serviceman owes nominally to Her Majesty. I say "nominally" because the average person would probably think of his duty of loyalty as owed to the country rather than to the head of state as symbol of the nation. A citizen might have profound republican views and think that we would all be better off if the head of state were elected. At the same time, he might be content to continue in an attitude of complete loyalty to the existing hereditary head of state.

The 1934 Act made the two heads of complaint alternative and not cumulative. To establish a crime, one need now only show an attempt to persuade a member of the services to refuse to obey an order. There need not be the slightest sense of disloyalty. For example, it would be an offence to say "Don't return to barracks tonight; stay with me instead", although this referred only to the man's duty. Before the 1934 Act, both duty and allegiance had to be threatened, as in "Don't return to barracks tonight. Stay with me instead and so avoid going abroad tomorrow morning on active service", where both duty and loyalty would be involved.

Our progress leftwards was aided greatly by reading *The Times* each morning. We read the serious politics and soon learnt, we thought, to assess the politicians, even to tell truth from falsehood. Typical of the decline of our confidence in governments was the Hoare-Laval fiasco. In October 1935, Mussolini invaded Abyssinia (now Ethiopia) with a full modern army and airforce. The Abyssinians, who had only the most primitive equipment, fought back for seven months. This invasion was in defiance of the Covenant of the League of Nations, which provided for collective action by way of sanctions against any law-breaker. All acts of aggression were breaches.

Sammy Hoare was foreign minister and at the general election in mid-November 1935, he solemnly declared that, if re-elected, the British government would enforce every sanction necessary to drive the Italians out of Africa. The invasion force was dependent on imports for every need, and even a denial of their water supply would have sent them all home. By December, no sanctions had been imposed, and we then learnt of the Hoare-Laval Pact, which ceded to the Italians as large a slice of Abyssinia as they had ever hoped to gain by invasion.

I had continued to see Nancy Astor each term for a weekend on the Thames. After coming down at the end of my three years at Balliol, there was a feast in St James' Square, off the famous gold plates, then a return visit to our rooms in Covent Garden. My own political change from conceivably Tory to left-wing Labour was aided somewhat by Nancy's right-wing attitudes, but the Hoare-Laval Pact brought it to a head. Lewis and I decided that there was nothing for it but that our worthy efforts should be devoted to something a bit more honest than that. I went to the House of Commons and told Nancy of my decision. She was sure I would some day come back to her way of thinking.

Although we had not yet joined the Labour Party and did not know the candidate, we canvassed together for Sydney Silkin in the 1936 by-election for Peckham. He got in and founded a whole dynasty of Labour Silkins, both in the Lords and in the House of Commons. Lewis then joined the Labour Party and was quickly elected as a councillor for North Kensington, becoming Kensington's first Labour councillor. I took a fancy to canvassing. It remains today the one means of influencing individuals to stand against the current swing of political feeling or, if the swing is on your side, to get people interested in furthering it, although it takes an inordinate amount of time.

Gilbert Harding joined in canvassing for Lewis, and I suppose I should say, too, that I took a fancy to Gilbert Harding. He was the chap with the large mustachios and pretence of gruffness who lorded it over the *Brains Trust*. In several political activities with Harding, so unobservant was I that I didn't realise that he was an established homosexual. He was already capable of drinking his share, especially of gin, and when after an interval I met him again at the height of his prowess, I found him with a houseful of young men of very distinctive character who seemed to run every aspect of his life.

In the 1930s, Oswald Mosley held constant provocative meetings in the East End of London and particularly in Jewish areas. He would march in with his Blackshirts and union jacks and with drums beating, and often with a full police escort. A crowd would collect, and in a short time someone in the audience would protest against the Fascists' horrible abuse. The speaker, usually Mosley himself, would point in his haughty and imperious manner to the offender and the police would move in.

If he did not get away fast enough, the protestor would be arrested and charged with causing a disturbance or some other offence under the newly created Public Order Act of 1936. We called it the Mosley Protection Act, but it was nominally aimed at preventing his marching in the streets with uniformed men. After the meeting was over and Mosley had left in triumph, the crowd would stand about discussing what he had said. The police would again advance and any who might complain would be arrested for obstruction. This was a pattern as predictable as were Mosley's meetings at Ridley Road night after night.

The Bar as a whole was not particularly anxious to defend anti-Mosley protesters, who were generally regarded as Communists. I had no such objections. The NCCL arranged for defences in some hundreds of these cases and every young barrister in the Haldane Society who did criminal work was called upon to lend a hand. Many lawyers took the view that Mosley should not be given a speaking platform if it could be prevented, although none of us went so far as to disrupt meetings. This was against complete freedom of speech, but I still believe that it was right. The principle of freedom of speech cannot be used as an excuse to insult and bully people, or to create disorder.

Jews were called "vermin", "venereal-ridden vagrants", and worse. At one meeting in Victoria Park, in the heart of the East End, a speaker from the British Union of Fascists had said, "The Jews among us are a cancer and every foul disease…We will extirpate them thoroughly from our public life." This was quoted in the House of Commons in March 1936, yet the government still permitted Fascist rallies while anti-Fascist meetings were either banned or broken up.

I defended dozens of young men and women who had publicly protested against the vile speeches of Mosley and his thugs and found themselves prosecuted for "insulting words and behaviour" under the Public Order Act, which carried a fine of up to £50, and three months' imprisonment. These arrests took place at meetings in which Fascists had called for the persecution of the Jews. One was prosecuted for shaking his fist at the speaker, another for whistling. One chap had been sent by his wife to fetch home their little daughter in case there was any trouble. As he neared the meeting, he was arrested for "blowing his nose as an offensive gesture".

The police were always present at these meetings and seemed to be well in with Mosley's guards. Apart from arresting hecklers, they paid no attention to what was said and concentrated their efforts on dispersing the audience afterwards, a process which usually involved further arrests. I was aware of only one prosecution against a Fascist speaker. The police had been willing to let him continue, but were pressed into taking action by outraged local citizens. Although convicted at the Thames Police Court, he appealed to the London Sessions and was acquitted, bringing in police shorthand-writers to prove that he had said nothing provocative; at least, they "had not written down anything provocative". It was even said that senior policemen found it difficult preventing some of their young constables from joining the Fascists.

If two practising barristers could join Mosley's party and wear their uniform, then why not a few practising police? The barristers were Fred Lawton, later Lord Justice of the Court of Appeal, and a colleague of his in chambers – Barry Hudson, I think. I am probably the last one alive who saw them in uniform in 1936 in Middle Temple Lane. I had just joined the Labour Party and was greatly shocked at seeing them in this menacing attire. Years later, I was junior to Fred in a few cases at Leeds during my Kingston-upon-Hull period. He discussed his Fascism as an aberration. He was clearly very upset at it, and apologised for having done anything so stupid. He remembered our meeting in the Temple and told me how hot and heavy and uncomfortable were the jackboots that he was expected to wear.

He knew what troubles I had had in public life and in a professional way through being an anti-Fascist and then a Stalinist. I was, in effect, standing common law junior in civil matters to Linklaters until they dropped me after I had been advertised as speaking at a public meeting about the Soviet Union. The next time I appeared in a case where Linklaters were concerned, they were instructing Fred Lawton as their junior. He had inherited my trade.

I have a note reminding me that on the day that Singapore fell, I travelled from London to Colchester in the company of a distinguished magistrate who had presided at a court in one of the main centres of Fascist activity. I had appeared before him dozens of times, but in almost every case my clients were convicted and sentenced. He said to me:

"In all those years when you appeared before me, you were always on the same side. I was satisfied that it was the wrong side. Yours were always the hooligans, the breakers of the peace, the poorly dressed local 'boys'. The police evidence was always consistent and clear; the defendants had set out deliberately to interrupt the meetings and to destroy the freedom of speech of perfectly respectable visiting political speakers. They even tried most shabbily to blame the uproar on the political speakers. I know now that you were right and I was wrong. I see now that the Fascists were seeking to do in our country not merely what Hitler had done, but something much more likely and attainable with us. They were seeking to betray the country just as Petain and the rest of the quislings throughout the world are doing today."

His last words were, "Thank God we rounded them up in time."

All the magistrates in that area adopted the same point of view. They had not thought of the possibility that the police could lie on oath in open court. Consider the state of mind of the late Lord Denning, Master of the Rolls, who said that it would not have been possible for any Court of Appeal to have accepted that the police lied on oath, fabricated statements and gave false evidence.

The highest fees and the best chances of advancement at the Bar are in the civil rather than the criminal side of the law. The cream of civil chambers were called commercial chambers, and insurance was the bottom end of commerce. I had started in civil chambers, devoted to insurance matters, and had every chance of a good career. Defending Mosley's victims relegated me to the bottom end of all barristers' work and I was in the magistrates' courts of London three or four days a week, which would be sufficient to guarantee the end of all expectations of a high court practice.

My clerk Harold was at pains to see that the litigation clerks were quite unaware of my close connections with the magistrates' courts. The clients of the big solicitors (the banks and giant corporations) are like other mortals and in due course I appeared half-a-dozen times in City or East End courts instructed by Linklaters on trifling police court charges for great corporations. The familiarity showed by magistrates and their clerks was put down by Linklaters to the excellent work of my own clerk in PR.

A disadvantage of graver importance in these Mosley cases was that a shorthand writer from the Special Branch took a careful record of what was said in court and noted the names of all defending lawyers and of the witnesses they called. In some cases, they took the names and addresses of everyone in the public gallery. Although there is nothing wrong with any person attending a public court and taking notes, when it is for the Special Branch it is plainly *in terrorem*. It is saying to the defence lawyer, "Take heed, we have our eye on you. We are an official organ concerned with traitors and sedition, and you are on the list."

For a minor case in the magistrates' court, the prosecutor would be a police officer or solicitors clerk. In Mosley's cases, a barrister was usually brought in to prosecute. There was nothing wrong with this except that it made the costs for the defendant very much higher if he were convicted and if the magistrate ordered that the costs of the prosecutor be added to a penalty. One barrister serving as prosecutor told me who the special note-taker represented. From the anti-Fascist defences, my Special Branch file went back to 1932 or thereabouts.

There had been several occasions in magistrates' courts where Mosley's men, present as witnesses, had murmured imprecations and threats against myself, but I had never taken them seriously. I always carried that admirable defence weapon, a rolled umbrella, and wore a baton-proof helmet – a hard bowler bat. When the warnings were uttered, there were so many police about that there could be no cause for alarm. It is not that I am particularly brave, but I can recall only one occasion on which I was terrified.

One night Terence Bird and I were travelling from north London through Essex, aiming at Morelands in the midst of the Colnes. We drove through the Ongars, the Rodings, and the Easters. The curious thing about these villages is that they come in groups, such as Earls Colne, White Colne, Wakes Colne and Colne Engaine; there are three Ongars, seven Rodings and two Easters. It was dark and the country roads and crossings were unlit. All the signposts were arranged for horse-drawn traffic, with which you didn't need to read the notice until you got there. We were in an ancient Lancia with big headlights that had to be aimed at the sky to read the directions, and at each junction we had to stop and look at the signpost from different angles.

The police must have seen the lights and their antics from several miles away and had their suspicions aroused. We were quite unaware of any local interest at all. Terence had his nose in the map, which he was reading with the aid of a torch. I was looking out for notices and, like every driver with a pilot, wanting at the same time to check every direction that I was given. As we emerged into a broad cross-roads junction, headlights showed up from three entry roads ahead, all pointing straight at us. They were plainly up to no good.

I had never been taken unawares like that before but had sometimes thought of it and had worked out that the sensible thing would be to withdraw as fast as possible – not by turning and retreating, but by going hard backwards. If you are assailed from behind, your assailant will be so surprised that he will fall over, with you on top of him. Your assailants in front will also be surprised and they, too, may not be ready for the next step. On this night, I stopped the car and instantly reversed. We crashed into the front of another car, unlit and fortunately so close behind that I had not got up speed. It was not merely a hold-up, but an effective one. We were trapped with no way out.

Sitting in the dark in our stationary car, I was suddenly conscious that my knees were rattling together quite uncontrollably. I tried to stop it. I put one hand between my knees and it was battered from both sides. I shouted to Terence, "Look, my knees are knocking."

He said, "How can I see? It's too dark."

I said, "Put your hand down and feel it."

The reply came, "My dear John, I wouldn't think of touching your knees, and it's the police coming."

From all four cars came the policemen: eight of them, with four torches and four notebooks at the ready. We had to explain who, where, whence and why all the stoppages at crossroads. We raised a laugh when Terence explained that I was a simple colonial from a territory where there were no signposts and nowhere to go, anyway.

At Mosley's meeting at the Carfax Assembly Rooms in Oxford in May 1936, Frank Pakenham (later Lord Longford) and Dick Crossman were thrown out and landed in the road. Frank promptly joined the Labour Party, of which Dick was already a member. It was said that this was because Frank landed on his head. A better explanation was that he had landed on his feet. In 1934, I'd been to one of Mosley's great rallies at the Albert Hall, where there were similar incidents. I was too far from any one of them to be involved and, I suppose, had not courage enough to make a commotion myself. I sat in a sharply sloping side-section that led up to the boxes. The seats were narrow, and the rows so close together that you had to stand to let someone pass. In the aisles were the uniformed brigade in their grey trousers, black shirts, buckled belts and knee-high boots.

As Mosley spoke, questions were shouted. He would stop, hands on hips, and shout back, "I didn't hear. Will you stand up and repeat the question louder?" If the questioner responded and if it were a hostile question, then half-a-dozen stewards would force their way in. If necessary, they walked on the knees of the man's neighbours. He was then punched and seized and dragged out of the hall. A few such incidents were enough to inhibit interruptions. There were scuffles in the upper galleries, but one could not see the detail from where we sat.

On one occasion in about 1936, when Mosley's activities were at their height, the police cordoned off Trafalgar Square. In the centre stood supporters of a civil liberties march from Hyde Park, surrounded by Mosley's band of opposed marchers. Both groups were surrounded by the police, but separated from the mass of onlookers, who had been pressed back into the various side streets. Lewis and I were done up in our best, with bowler hats and umbrellas, and came through the police ranks as though we were senior officers or perhaps from the Home Office. We believed that the Home Office would send along persons who would be able to say whether anything untoward, particularly in the way of violence, had taken place, enabling the appropriate minister to answer in parliament, "What, violence! At Trafalgar Square last Saturday? I can assure the Honourable Member there was none! Why, we had people there."

Our aim was to invigilate the conduct of the police towards the two groups at the plinth. We were looked at with surprise by a number of uniformed officers, but on the occasion of two or three actual challenges, which were on the lines of "Excuse me, sir, but ...", Lewis replied, "It's all right, officer," and boldly reached into his inside pocket and half-drew out something that might have been a document of authority. We were thus able to walk about undisturbed and speak to people and generally keep an eye on things.

I also joined the Haldane Society, which not only fought Fascism but pushed into all manner of action at home and abroad. For this, Neil Lawson and the secretary Dudley Collard were mostly responsible. They insisted that everyone join the Labour Party and a trade union. Dudley also tried to get them into the Co-op. The Haldane was the first of the independent Bar societies and was founded in late 1929 as a lawyers' protest group against Ramsay MacDonald's moves towards the right. In 1924, MacDonald took the place of Baldwin as prime minister and had nobody suitable to make Lord Chancellor. They had enough difficulty getting law officers to join the cabinet. Labour chose as Lord Chancellor the Liberal MP and former Secretary for War Viscount Haldane, and for that purpose he had to change parties. He had to endure the ill-wishes of many of his former friends. Lloyd-George said of him, "Many a man has taken that course [that is, across the floor of the House] but none has left such a slimy trail of hypocrisy." I was told of this by his daughter Megan who had it direct from her father. He said that after the debate he had second thoughts and felt he had gone too far. He went to the Hansard room and had them delete the whole of it.

Before monthly meetings of the executive committee of the National Council for Civil Liberties, Binford-Hole held a meeting of interested Haldane lawyers to discuss the agenda. We usually had several EC members there, and two of them were to become high court judges. We thought of it as an efficient way of getting through the business rather than as a secret caucus aimed at controlling the public decisions of the council, but it certainly went a long way towards usurping the functions of the EC. At one stage, when Harry Thompson was chairman of the NCCL, he too attended. After a few visits, Thompson pointed out the undesirable features of what we were doing. "We have notable figures from the broad liberal world such as Henry Nevinson and E M Forster. We parade than as fairly representing the movement, and yet here you are going about in secret and rigging things behind their backs." We abandoned the practice.

Geoffrey Bing played an important role in both the NCCL and the Haldane. For the latter, he visited a number of countries that had turned Fascist and got himself into the principal prisons, as in Rome, Helsinki and Berlin, to bring comfort to anti-Nazi prisoners. He was always trying to find some legal process that might be applied to get them defended and, if possible, released. Bing was a splendid conspirator. He often spoke in riddles, and always rather softly. It was assumed that you knew all of today's affairs in any quarter of the globe. He would tell a story in so discreet a fashion that one had very little notion of what it was about, and all punctuated by knowing glances and a pursing of the lips and a pleased, giggling laugh so that you were prevailed on to agree that you understood it all.

In the autumn of 1936, Bing came to me and said that he needed a seconder for a resolution at the League of Nations. I explained that I wasn't actually a member of the League of Nations, but how could I help? The League of Nations case was clear enough; there was to be a seconder. Bing's argument was along the following lines:

> "The point is that your High Commissioner is the first Labour representative for New Zealand. We understand that he is a strong and progressive-minded man, and he will love the chance of playing an important part at Geneva, especially in a good cause. We want you to see him and get him to agree to second the speech of Litvinov in a motion about collective security. No one else will second the Russian and unless he is seconded, his motion cannot be debated or even moved. It will be one of the great speeches in the history of the League."

In the winter of 1934-5, Litvinov had produced the wonderful phrase "Peace is indivisible". He had used it in several speeches around the world and was about to produce the Geneva version, and with reference to the situation in Spain. The Spanish government appealed to the league for help against the armed intervention of Germany and Italy, but Britain wanted strict application of the Non-Intervention Agreement. New Zealand was a member of the League with its own vote, yet we had never played any part in great affairs save as an acolyte of Britain. Now here was Bill Jordan, our high commissioner, about to step out on the world stage to speak for New Zealand with an independent voice. It was a chance to unite Europe against the Fascists and head off a world war.

Bing added that Ivor Montague already had a copy of the Russian's speech and wanted to discuss it with Jordan. I looked forward to meeting Ivor, who was a leading theoretician and writer of the British Communist Party as well as a film director. He had brought back from Spain notable pictures of the British Battalion of the International Brigade. I was already in full agreement with collective security, and the whole idea appealed to me. I went to New Zealand House, which was then in the Strand, and was welcomed by Bill Jordan. (Walter Nash had introduced us while I was yet a student at Victoria.)

Bill Jordan grew up in London and some years later he was to take me to his school in Old Street and introduce me as prospective Labour candidate. As a policeman, he had involved himself in early murmurings of democratic representation for the police, but had retired in 1904 and gone to New Zealand. There he had been secretary of the Labour Party from its foundation in 1907, later becoming president. When Labour won the general election in 1935, he was given the important post of high commissioner to London. All New Zealanders resident in London were invited to call on him when he first arrived.

I went to New Zealand House and put the proposal to Jordan: namely, that New Zealand should go to the League of Nations and sign herself up as supporting the motion for collective security and asked that we, all three, might call upon him. Ivor would send a copy of the speech in advance, and we would follow. Ivor's idea was that Jordan should make his speech as a genuine empire man, but seeing world peace as he thought the empire should see it. Jordan was immediately attracted by the idea and thought that Nash would be also. It was necessary to get direct authority from his government and he would put up the idea. In a few days, he obtained general approval.

Ivor and I then prepared a speech for him, based on our assessment of Jordan's own approach to the League and New Zealand as its smallest member. We had to get him to work himself up to the point where he would "appeal to mankind" and "denounce aggression". It was done with appropriate gestures and rehearsed several times in front of a full-sized mirror. Bill co-operated fully and prepared thoroughly. He did his job in a manful fashion and put New Zealand on the map at the League of Nations. We had hoped to be present in Geneva but in the end Ivor and I were kept by other commitments.

The announcement that New Zealand would join in full sanctions against Italy was the first time that we had ever taken a stand in any sense against Britain, and the new line undoubtedly shocked Conservatives in both countries. Anthony Eden complained that Jordan was the least helpful dominion representative he had ever been sent. Bill was thought to be unduly susceptible to flattery from "certain left-wing sources". I was already a member of the British Labour Party and Ivor Montague was a prominent Communist; Eden would have been horrified to think that any speech written by us could be adopted by New Zealand.

Lord Cranborne, Under-Secretary of State for Foreign Affairs, took Jordan on one side and, according to Foreign Office files, unsuccessfully "adduced every argument he could think of to bring him to assume a moderate and reasonable attitude", but found Jordan "impossible to influence and entirely impenetrable to argument". The Dominions Office warned that "by his irresponsible utterances he creates a serious danger to peace". Poor Bill was only trying to persuade the League of Nations to apply its own sanctions, something that they were too cowardly to do. I thought he was a hero, and told him so.

If Britain had not wanted New Zealand to interfere with her exclusive right to speak for the whole Commonwealth in international affairs, she should not have placed us in a position to do so. Britain carried New Zealand into the League and anyone who could read could see that we were bound by our signature to the covenant. As Bill Jordan said at Geneva, "We are deeply concerned that the spirit of the covenant, to which we have all attached our signatures, shall be made into a living thing." Experience seemed to have taught Eden and the British government not to read their obligations when they were asked to abide by them, but what rights had "little Belgium" in 1914 that little Abyssinia had lost in 1936?

We boasted that we were Britain's first ally at least for the last ten minutes of Britain's history. In the Boer War and the First World War, we took our full share. We were to do so again in the Second World War. Indeed, by geophysical accident, we were at war with Germany before Britain came in. It had been agreed that we would both declare war at the same time, but, because of New Zealand's proximity to the date-line, officially we declared first and stood alone against the might of Hitler's army for all of twelve hours.

New Zealanders knew that if another war came, we would be involved, and had every reason for seeing that it didn't come. There was a strong feeling for peace and a willingness to work for it. The Wesleyan Youth Movement proposed that the government should hire a big ship, load it with typical New Zealand families and exhibits, and send it to meet the peoples of the Pacific in the hope of persuading them that peace was within the reach of all. This proposal was forwarded by Harry Atmore, Member for Nelson, and one of the very few MPs I had met before leaving the country. He came to Nelson College several times, and we had also met him while tramping on high walks in the mountains and over old mining railway roads. He was of more open mind than many of his fellows.

Walter Nash offered to put New Zealand's armed forces under the control of any League of Nations force that might come into being. We had no standing army but only a few officers and instructors who were a regular backbone to the territorial army. It was not a question of New Zealand taking on the world. We were reminding the members of the League that all were pledged to take on aggressors: in this case, Franco, Mussolini and Hitler. We did not want war, but if all had expressed their determination to stand by the covenant, there would have been no need for war.

I wrote to Gilbert Murray for his advice as a founder of the League. He was delighted with the thought that New Zealand might take a lead on Spain. "The great danger now, as it seems to me, is that for the sake of a quiet life we allow, first, small breaches of the Covenant, then larger and larger breaches." The prospect of a direct war so terrified the other European nations that Italy and Germany had every chance of taking Spain without in any way endangering themselves. Any action Bill Jordan took "would be warmly applauded and backed up by the chief supporters of the League of Nations movement in this country". Bill greatly enjoyed his time at the League and in 1938 became president. He continued to speak out against Fascism, but could do little to help Spain.

Grotius, a lawyer of the low countries, the most precocious of young men ever born, held that nations in the wider community should behave towards one another as individuals do in their own state. Through the law on contracts, I learned that a man was bound to stand by his agreement; a breach was a civil wrong, and therefore a breach of contract. If citizens were liable for breach of contract, why not nations? A citizen can be held to a contract not only by damages to pay for the harm done by a breach but sometimes also by an injunction backed by a court order and a policeman standing by to insist that it be carried out: a mandatory injunction. The rule is clear enough: if the evil results of a breach would be such that an order for damages after the event would not readily compensate for the harm likely to be done, then compulsion may be used.

Between nations, the supreme offence that needs restraining is the resort to violence, and the results of this are so incalculable and so likely to result in many deaths that it must be stopped. The policeman at hand is the sanction introduced by the covenant of the League of Nations at Versailles in 1918, and by the charter of the United Nations at San Francisco in 1945. Sanctions must be developed to the point where their force equals that of a policeman. Sanctions against Mussolini over Abyssinia in 1935 were abandoned; those against Hitler and Mussolini over Spain in 1936 were never tried.

Despite the anti-Fascist defences, no barrister had a better start than I. By the mid 1930s, I was as well launched at the Bar as anyone of my call, thanks to Tylor's introductions in London, and the combined efforts of Tom Inskip and his sister-in-law, Lady Alice Fergusson. She was daughter to the Earl of Glasgow, New Zealand's first governor-general rather than simply governor, and was married to Charles Fergusson, chairman of the Rhodes selectors for my year, who finished his stint as governor-general just about the time I came to Oxford. At Lady Alice's invitation, I stayed with them at Kilkerran in Ayrshire for holidays. I was a contemporary of their sons; Bernard went on to become governor-general of New Zealand in his turn. I remember how at the start of lunch Charles Fergusson would cut the cake and put a piece for each of the boys on the end of his knife and throw it to them across the room. This was the cue for taking their places.

In about 1935, Lady Alice invited me to dinner and introduced me to her sister, Lady Augusta Inskip, with the intention of advancing my legal and political career. The Lady Augusta was a marvellous hostess and through her I met Mary Best and Christian Maxwell, two women deeply involved in liberal causes. Christian later went on to become a painting companion to my wife Janet, and a dear friend to us both. It was Christian's brother, the author Gavin Maxwell, who introduced me to smoking tyres in a Cooper Cup Austin 7 at Brooklands, the world's first specially built motor-racing circuit.

The fame of the Lady Augusta as a fixer on the British political scene was shown by the fact that her husband, the quietest and gentlest and perhaps the most unlearned attorney general of the century, was also made lord chancellor and lord chief justice. In addition, she arranged that Baldwin should be prime minister and later, in due course, Neville Chamberlain likewise. Ramsay Macdonald had one short innings for Labour and then got in again only in such a way that he held office at the whim of the Tories. It was said that Baldwin and Chamberlain took the advice of Augusta Inskip, who told the Tories to promote Ramsay as PM of a "National" government.

Tom Inskip was the most easy-going and accommodating person, big and round and red-faced like a Somerset apple. He did me enormous good. He was also the most stupid man ever to hold the highest judicial office. When he went to the Court of Appeal as Master of the Rolls, Scrutton, speaking for his brethren, said that it was not possible. When he went to the Lords, Lord Thankerton said the same. The only thing possible was that he should go back to being Lord Chief Justice, where it was thought he could do the minimum of harm and be helped in any difficulty by two supporting judges.

In those days, all jobs to prosecute murder or arson on circuit were in the gift or nomination of the attorney general. It was usual for him to scatter these prosecutions about to new silks who came to his attention. I was given this chance in my fourth year as a junior, supporting James Tucker, KC, for the prosecution at Wells Assizes of a boy just old enough to be within reach of the gallows. It was the most sordid case of child abuse. At puberty he was sent by the local authority into the care of a mature but childless couple who had a small farm. On his first afternoon there, he was introduced to unsavoury practices with a nanny goat, and with his foster father. After some months, the foster mother discovered what was going on and decided to comfort the lad herself by taking him into her own bed whenever the husband was away. This occurred several times a week, and for some years. As it was combined with arduous farm work, he grew into a weedy, meagre fellow.

The killing came when Mum dressed and went downstairs after one of her ministrations to the boy. He, still naked, took Dad's shotgun meaning to use it on him and fired, taking the top off her skull and the whole of its contents. The charge had to be murder or nothing. There was no room for accident. Josh Caswell, KC, defended him, supported by an eminent psychiatrist – something of a novelty in those days – and it appeared that the boy was emotionally in a torment. He loved Mum and had a deep hatred for Dad. His own crucial evidence was that in the six months between arrest and trial he had put on three stone in weight. "I have at last begun to grow."

The trial ended on a Saturday, market day. The town was crowded and the case notorious. The jury was sent out at three-thirty to consider their verdict. At seven-thirty they came back with a question, "Could it be manslaughter?" The judge was Travers Humphries, the outstanding criminal judge of the day, and this put him in a tizzy. He said that well, it couldn't really be manslaughter, but perhaps it could, but really it couldn't, but well, perhaps. It took the jury another two hours. By then the square outside the court was packed; mainly, it seemed, by women. The verdict was not guilty and the roar of delight from the square that greeted the news could not have been greater if the price of Somerset lambs had doubled. I hope the lad has since had a long and fruitful life. After Wells, there followed murder prosecutions almost in profusion. Most, if not all, were convicted, then got off in the Court of Criminal Appeal as it was then called; none were hanged. I believe that all were commuted to life imprisonment by the home secretary.

CHAPTER EIGHT

Marriage

DAISY SAW the early appearance of success at the Bar and decided that her place was here in London to take charge and direct it all. I suppose I was her favourite. Deed, who had come over in about 1933 and was in practice at Christchurch, Hampshire, went back to fetch our parents. They returned late in 1935 and for a while we lived together in a quiet Paddington square. Now, as the time for the wedding approached, everyone had to be told. Daisy was not very strong and spent a little time in hospital at Greenwich and at Clapham, but was then well enough to be told that I was to be married. She was, I believe, deeply jealous. She was capable of summoning up an illness on a whim and now encountered frequent whims. Mother took herself to Christchurch and decided to be too ill for the wedding.

Janet had an introduction to the Bishop of Chichester to do with murals for Sussex churches, and we had become good friends. We boldly asked him to marry us, which he agreed to do. Rayner Goddard was Chairman of the joint Inner Temple and Middle Temple Church committee and I asked for leave to use the Temple Church and Hall. He replied, "It's no use, my boy, the Temple isn't a Registered Marriage House. It's not a real wedding, you can't get properly 'done'. You might as well not get married at all as come here. It's illegal, that's all there is to it."

He added, "Of course, you could do what we did with our girl Peggy and Eric Sachs. We took them along to Caxton Hall on a Friday and had the legal bit; that was £5. Then on the Saturday we fetched them to the Temple and had them done properly with the full church business. Of course, we didn't let them meet between the Friday and the Saturday. The only other way is to pay thirty-two guineas to the Archbishop of Canterbury for a special licence because with that, if the parson will do it, you can marry anywhere — you can do it in the coal cellar or the attic or out in Fleet Street itself — but I know you can't afford that, so that is out of the question."

We got leave for the church and hall for the afternoon of Saturday, 30th May. Bishop Bell of Chichester officiated, assisted by Anson, Master of the Temple and Janet's cousin, Claud Wood. The organist was Thorburn Ball who, with two others, was to score a total of 150 years running Temple music. Jack was not to be put off by Daisy's illness and came up to London for the occasion. Encouraged by Lewis Clive, he flirted with all Janet's grand-aunts and aunts and was a great success.

Janet's mother, Ivy, was descended from the family Grout who, earlier in the nineteenth century, had swathed the nation in black crepe or "grouts" as compulsory mourning wear and decoration, following Queen Victoria after Prince Albert died and as compulsory contribution to the wealth and distinction of the Grout and then the Williams families. It was obvious, and indeed traditional, that the bride's mother should pay for the feast. I contended strongly for that, but was defeated. I got it ordered in her name and the bill was sent to her, but she was adamant.

Lewis did the job of best man to perfection. It was as though he had spent his whole life preparing for the occasion. Lewis made all the speeches, dealing with representing the father of the bride (who, after all, had been dead since 1915); he made a speech responding for the bride and groom, because he knew I wasn't any good at speeches; he proposed the health of the bridesmaids and responded for them; then he proposed his own health, which was a great success, and made a suitable response.

The honeymoon was arranged likewise by Lewis. When the time came, there was the biggest possible Rolls Royce waiting, and so off to Waterloo station where we were met by the deputy station master in a bowler hat. He ushered us, with a guard of honour of porters, onto our reserved compartment in the train for Bournemouth. We were off to Christchurch, to visit Daisy. On the following day, we travelled to Salcombe. A five-masted barquentine, the *Koenigen-Cecile*, lay on a reef just outside Salcombe Heads, where we saw her last cargo busily floating off.

One idea for the honeymoon was to sail the good ship *Altair* to France. After two days of local nibbling such as going westward far enough to see Eddystone lighthouse in the distance and eastward to make acquaintance with Start Point, we set off for France. It was the most ill-judged voyage, but fortunately a mighty north wind came and after ten minutes running before it, we realised that the whole adventure was going to be far too much. We put about and got the engine going and after two hours of hard bashing into the wind, we were safe in the shelter of Brixham harbour. The wind kept up, I got toothache, and we'd had enough of a sailing honeymoon. Within two days, we were at home.

We married, as it were, into Finsbury and had a small Regency house just behind Kings Cross Magistrates' Court. A few days after the wedding, I joined the Labour Party, through the St Philip's ward. In 1934, Labour had taken over the majority from the Tories at Finsbury and so ruled at the town hall. I soon became committee member, secretary and delegate to the general management committee at the town hall and, as an active local party member, was sent to the party's annual conference as delegate for the Haldane Society.

It wasn't long before I came into conflict with Alderman Harold Riley who, since 1934, had been leader of the Labour and Cooperative party on the council. He ruled Finsbury with exceptional skill and cunning. Every action of the party seemed to be in furtherance of some scheme of Riley's. All nominees for any post, whether alderman, councillor, chairman or member of committee, were his nominees. The intended future mayors and aldermen were bespoken for some years ahead, and each was beholden to Riley for the prospect. A substantial number of the councillors were council employees and the position of all local government officers was dependent upon their personal relations with, and complete subservience to Riley. They were continually placed in positions in which a conflict arose between their public and professional duties and Riley's personal wishes.

Riley was a born intriguer with the "lean and hungry look" of one who did not sleep "o' nights". He could be found every working evening after eleven p.m. in a teashop opposite Kings Cross Station. There he and his faithful supporter, Nelly, who also sat on the executive, held court. When I first started in the ward and was making a slight stir, he said, "You know we want to work with you but you must not upset things too much." When I learned about the late night tea parties, I started getting the council agenda and joining Riley and Nelly at Kings Cross. There I saw who would take the trouble to come and call. I chatted gaily about their evening's work and so impeded whatever scheming talk was intended.

An agent could offer to his councillors financial inducements by way of fees for inspections. If the borough had a lot of building going on, there were visits to the site to meet the architect, the planners, the engineers, and to view progress. These visits were arranged nominally by the appropriate subcommittee. Riley would invite those whom he favoured. If you were not invited, you would probably not learn of them. If he were not in a meeting himself or represented by one of his fully trusted supporters, then he would have an observer just outside the door. The listener would happen to move away as the first committee member emerged. At a council meeting, Riley would arrange in advance who would propose or second what resolution, who would thank or congratulate whom.

His behaviour was sometimes close to manic. Among my papers, I have a note that on the evening of 13th July 1939 at a meeting of our political council in Finsbury Town Hall, he actually threw an inkwell at Mr Newanson, who then struck him a blow across the table so hard as to knock Riley and his chair backwards onto the floor. Two nights earlier, at the executive meeting, Riley said that his first ground of complaint against a councillor whom we may call Mrs Jo was that she was not on the register as she was living in sin. He added that as he could not prove what he had just said, he would proceed only on the basis that she was a cow. I refrained from hitting Riley. The charm of this scene was that Riley was at that time living in unmarried bliss with Nelly.

On the Sunday nearest to 1st May, Socialists from North East London would collect at St Pancras Gas Works and march to Hyde Park. In 1937, Riley decreed that this march was nothing to do with us. No part of it was in the borough and we had no money for any such things, therefore the Finsbury Labour Party would not take part. It took very little organisation by the St Philip's Ward Committee to alter all that. When we marched off from the gas works, Riley was in the front row with Nelly. Red Ellen Wilkinson was with us, a band played, and the whole of the party that could walk turned out. Ellen was almost a local as she lived in Guilford Street just outside our boundaries, and Jarrow had marched on the genuine 1st May.

I came to know Ellen through her Hire Purchase Act. She had first obtained permission to introduce a Private Member's Bill in the 1931 parliament but had then lost her seat. Ernest Watkins drafted the bill and

I assisted on secondment from the Haldane Society. We had a number of sessions with Ellen at the House of Commons, and various places at supper. Her bill went through in 1938 and, when it came to the second reading, I had the fun of sitting under the wings, as it were, under the gallery usually reserved for civil servants advising the minister in a debate.

The theory behind the Hire Purchase Act was that the dealer or shopkeeper entered into an agreement with the buyer to sell the goods. The dealer then sold the whole transaction and the goods to a finance company, who let the goods on hire purchase to the buyer. Only when the last penny was paid did ownership pass to the buyer. If before that time the buyer were to dispose of the goods, the finance company could recover them from the new owner. It led to an enormous increase in retail sales. On the face of things, this narrow economic measure was most remote from the flame-thrower Ellen: champion of the unemployed, supporter of refugees from every harassed minority and a determined aide to democracy in Spain. This is to overlook the fact that at an early age Ellen had been a national organiser of the Co-operative Society workers and then of the Shopworkers Union.

Ellen also intervened in parliament to protect home film-makers. Movies for public showing were made on flammable film and so, because of their danger, had attracted the control of the Home Office. This had led, unintentionally but directly, to film censorship. The question was whether the "non-flam" acetate used by private film-makers should be subject to the same controls. Since films of a progressive or non-commercial character tended to be made on non-flam, this became a civil liberties issue.

Sidney Bernstein of Granada Films was a leading radical director and already a power in the cinema. He took up the cause of the amateurs and gained Ellen's support. I had the chance of entertaining all concerned in my nearest approach to a club – the Royal Empire Society at Northumberland Avenue, to which all Rhodes Scholars were elected members – to get Bernstein's guidance on the main points. The NCCL made their submissions to the advisory committee that had been set up by the Home Office, and lobbied Members of Parliament. The Home Office accepted the Bernstein point of view and non-flam films were protected from censorship.

Guilford Street was just across Greys Inn Road from Janet and me. Ellen's flat was a very modest, ill-lit affair. Parts of it were coloured black, including the seductive boudoir. To entertain evening guests, the hostess usually wore a sort of black, trousered garment rather like pyjamas, and it must have been difficult to find her in the boudoir when so attired. It was common knowledge that Ellen was in extremely close relations with Herbert Morrison. Indeed, Ellen assumed that we knew of this for she made some comment about the flat being handy for parliament, and even handier for Lambeth. There must have been something about Herbert Morrison but it was a bit difficult to understand her attraction to him.

In the last few years of the 1930s, Ellen was seldom at home in the evening. Night after night she did public meetings in all corners of London. It was part of a campaign to reinvigorate local constituency parties after the early 1930s' disasters of MacDonald and Chamberlain. Her hire purchase aides provided a supporter, and I must have done twenty or more meetings with her in those few years. If Ellen couldn't come, then we did them on our own. In the weeks leading up to the 1945 election I spoke in many London boroughs. Most local parties remembered that their last public meeting was one of Ellen's before the war. Her concentrated series of meetings laid the foundation for Labour's clean sweep of London in 1945.

Ellen's speech-making was quite electric. She had developed the technique of any good essay writer: a startling opening phrase followed by an explanatory passage; a bit of history, both national and local; and then came today's solution. She introduced me to the idea that a busy politician should be jack of all trades and ready to speak on a different topic every night of the week. Ellen was a real leftie and an outstanding politician. She was splendid to see, for although hers was rather a homely face, there was the flaming red hair and a jolly good figure. In parliament, Ellen was treated as a personal friend by most Tories, to say nothing of her party colleagues. She could, and did, get on with everybody and she was into everything.

In 1935, I took up with Krishna Menon, who ran the India League, the London branch of the Congress Party. To me, India was the outstanding problem of our whole empire system. Its people suffered most and must be given the chance to try and solve things for themselves. Krishna's intention was to inform the ordinary British voter of the need for Indian liberation, so he himself became a councillor – for the neighbouring borough of St Pancras. We spoke on the same platform at meetings all over the country, arguing the case for the liberation of India, and for a good part of that year I was doing two a week. One regular meeting was at Whitestone Pond on Hampstead Heath, midday Saturday.

We had first met in 1931 when Gandhi was staying with Sandy Lindsay, the Master of Balliol. Our second meeting was at India Club in the Strand, before Gandhi finally set off for India in December of that year. Krishna came from the Malabar Coast, the place of the first European settlement and of the first Catholic schools. He was exceptionally well educated, had degrees in different subjects and came to London to carry them further. He was a barrister and a member of the Middle Temple. Krishna was halt in one leg and leaned heavily on an ornate stick. He worked hard and pushed others equally hard. Some found him too demanding and were, I believe, driven out by this. I had no difficulties because I laid down strict limits as to how much time he could have, and within that there were no limits. Whether it was Aberdeen or Lord Soper's chapel in Kingsway made no difference to me.

Krishna was the India League. Two women helped with secretarial work, but anyone who belonged was pressed into action to organise a meeting or to make a speech. It might be said that there was a general and many NCOs, but no rank and file. Each Wednesday he met some supporters late at night in a small cafe in a back street at St Giles, at the foot of Tottenham Court Road. He was very slim and severely abstinent. He would take tea and no more than one biscuit as we reviewed the course of the meetings and laid plans for the next week's affairs. Amongst his supporters whom I came to know later in different circumstances was Roland "Tiny" Rowland, who then was bigger and broader than he later seemed to be. Perhaps we have all begun to shrink a bit.

Most people at that time gave little thought to the evils of colonialism. The main political issues of the decade were Fascism and racism: the very core of working-class politics. At first, these issues were excluded from the performing arts. The theatre was dominated by the upper middle class: plays were about that class, and any workers were caricatures. Writers and critics and publishers were much the same. Real political issues were mentioned only with apologies, and working-class politics not at all. The Unity Theatre turned all this upside down by presenting Socialist material in an entertaining and dramatic way. They set up a theatre school, and none would do but the best. Among the tutors they had Paul Robeson,

Sybil Thorndyke and Flora Robson, and Alan Bush for music. Their objectives were to encourage and develop writers, producers and players, and then to provide a forum.

It was a brave attempt to make plays by and for working people, and through touring productions, to carry those plays to places where workers could see them. Most Unity members were amateurs, and any professionals who worked for them did it for nothing. It is impossible to exaggerate the enthusiasm and vigour with which they set about their tasks. Before the Second World War, opening nights and gala performances at Unity were always graced by diplomatic representatives of the Soviet Union. In the heady days after the war, they came from at least seven countries and even the Far East began to pay homage.

Unity began in an old upstairs hall at Britannia Street in February 1936, then moved to Goldington Street until the theatre was burned down in 1975. It was practically just around the corner from our home in Finsbury and Janet and I went to as many productions as we could. I remember a topical production (a "living newspaper") called *Busmen*, which described the Coronation Bus Strike of May 1937. It was a co-operative effort in which Bert Papworth and Bill Jones lent a hand with the writing, and Alan Bush wrote the music. (Alan developed from highly regarded musician to champion of workers' music, and we became close friends on the way.)

At that time, the most militant section of the Transport and General Workers' Union was that which represented London Transport drivers. The leaders of their branch of the union were Bert Papworth and Bill Jones. Bert Papworth had come to speak at a meeting of Finsbury Labour Party before the strike took place. General Secretary of the whole union was Ernie Bevin, the most reactionary man in the trade unions; a man who was most strongly opposed to any rank and file movement and thought that the leadership from top to bottom should be appointed and controlled by him. He was Labour in name only.

At the time of the coronation of George VI, the bus drivers' branch organised a strike in London. The stopping of London buses was a powerful weapon and it looked as though it would soon bring LGOC (the London General Omnibus Company) to terms. Then Bevin stepped in. He settled the strike for a minute and nominal improvement in conditions, then claimed it as a great victory. The busmen got nothing from it at all and went back to work discomforted and with their confidence in their own union gravely dented.

In short, he cheated and betrayed his own members. Bevin made sure that Bert Papworth and the other strike-leaders were thrown out of the union as soon as the strike was over. He had no power to keep them out forever, but when they did get back, they were excluded from office for some years. This was probably my first experience at close quarters of what the right wing of the movement can do by way of harm to its members.

Bevin had many enemies but was called "Ernie" even when they were abusing him. I thought him a horrible fellow, and this dislike was based as much on his personal attitudes as on his sponsoring of the Cold War. He regarded the left of the party as evil, as if it were a sort of breakaway unit from the TGWU, which he had founded at the end of the First World War. Indeed, the Soviet Union was seen as a sort of dissident group of his own union, and so to be condemned. Any kind of association with the Soviet Union was treated as the most evil transaction imaginable. The Coronation Bus Strike provided only the first of many examples of the devious behaviour of which he was capable.

Herbert Morrison was another devious politician, but, in the 1930s, it was a happy experience when travelling to courts on the outskirts of London to see in every direction Morrison's London County Council houses springing up. They were houses for those most in need. It is not wise to leave the provision of all the services for a tightly packed community to the good offices of the private dealer, whose aim must be the maximum profit. This is at the expense of the users, and ancillary services suffer. I believe that libraries, recreation facilities, housing for the poor, and overall supervision of transport must be answerable to the public voice through local elections.

Finsbury Labour Party engaged in what might be called very progressive actions. Through the borough council, the party engaged in municipal activities of a quite novel character. The Finsbury Health Centre, which opened in 1938, was carefully devised to make best use of natural light and ventilation. Glass bricks were employed for many of the external walls and the building was heated by hot water pipes embedded in the ceilings. The centre was so built as to make any future extensions or internal restructuring as simple as possible. It was designed by Berthold Lubetkin, who had already made his name with the penguin pool at Regent's Park Zoo and the Highpoint flats in Highgate. His watchwords were Simplicity, Reticence, and Common-sense – qualities amply shown by his buildings, which can still repay a visit.

London was threatened with heavy bombing as soon as war might begin. Finsbury hired Lubetkin to devise deep shelters that could be built for the whole of our community and, for that matter, for the whole of London. They were to be built at the minimum of cost and with the maximum of advantage, and with every clever dodge that could satisfy these two requirements. I think the first one was devised to be sunk under Finsbury Square at the very southern end of our borough. It was intended to serve city workers during the day and our southernmost borough dwellers when they were there. Other inner London boroughs took up the idea but, in fact, no deep shelter was built. When bombing started, it was so ferocious that there was no chance of doing any building. The London population was saved partly by evacuation to the countryside and partly by use of the tubes, and by Anderson and Morrison surface shelters. When the bombing stopped, never to start again, it was pretty apparent that there was no longer scope for deep shelters.

It was obvious that Lubetkin had taken considerable inspiration from the achievements of the Socialist city authorities in Vienna. He was bursting with new ideas about workers' dwellings and after the war he devised for Finsbury a modern block of council flats. We had Nye Bevan declare it open. It had to be high-rise because there was no space for houses, but he foresaw the worst of the evils that would follow: that families would become isolated, that lifts would be fouled, and that gangs of youths might tyrannise the block. He required that we as councillors should win the support of the young people who lived there and run for them special courses in local history, the elements of architecture, health and fitness, and social welfare. For example, they soon learned to tell the difference between Peabody Buildings and those belonging to the Guinness Trust – both first class tenements from the last century.

Our best developments for organised sports were with swimming pools. It was not difficult to encourage the setting up of the Spa Fields Swimming Club, which satisfied one requirement of Lubetkin. To satisfy another, we tried to persuade the swimmers to make a canvass of flats to see who was ailing or in need and to co-operate with the welfare services. This was the least successful of our social efforts, and probably for the reason that tenants were carefully hand-picked so were not usually in need. The housing officer was persuaded to include in each block a councillor or two as leaven, but it always led to criticism that they were taking unfair advantage. We thought that councillors should be on the spot to deal with problems as they arose; they should also set an example of how to be good tenants.

Lubetkin's flats contained many novel contrivances for convenience and comfort in living: central heating; corridors tapered so that remoter flats could be slightly larger; several lifts to every floor, and each lift large enough for prams; every flat provided with a ground-floor store room big enough for pram, bicycles and spare furniture, and a strong lock; gardens and fountains all about. Buildings were so positioned and roofs so designed that the prevailing wind whipped through a covered space on the top floor, drying clothes straight from the most modern of washing machines housed on the same floor.

Lubetkin gained praise enough for himself, and for us his equal has not followed him. After making a great name, he retired from architecture and went off to farm dairy cows in the Cotswolds and died in 1990. In honour of his achievements, the Royal Academy in the Summer Exhibition of 1991 showed several of his plans and drawings, including Finsbury Health Centre. At the RA Dinner I had the pleasure of meeting his daughter, Sasha. It was ironic that Berthold Lubetkin and his design partnership Tecton were introduced to the borough by Harold Riley, tyrant of Finsbury, in one of his few worthwhile acts.

The Spanish Civil War had begun a few days after our marriage. As a married man, I was barred from going; and then our son Tim arrived before it was decreed that a child was a bar. Ellen took in anti-Nazi refugees from several European countries and passed some on to us. We were living in a most curious house of four stories, but with only about a room and a half on each floor. Ellen showed us that even the smallest house or flat could hold one temporary refugee for each twelve square feet of living space. We had quite a number of young men from the International Brigade moving through London. They were on their way to join or on the way home. Some were discharged, some were wounded and convalescent. There was really no provision in those early days for dealing with them.

Most stayed only a day or two but one Glaswegian boy whom Janet and I particularly remembered stayed longer than most. He was still shell-shocked. He was so disorientated that he had lost contact with normal domestic usages and we had to teach him as from the beginning about what happened in the dining room and the bathroom. It was as though he had had a stroke of the kind that causes one to start all over again. We were ill-equipped for this, but were able to point out that in the lavatory the throne was actually made for sitting on and not to support you as you squatted beside it. He had lost touch with his family in Glasgow and we guided him in enquiring how to find then again.

Another Scottish boy, Jack Brent, was a war hero and the most joyful person one could meet. Though more or less paralysed from the waist down, he was mobile in the sense that he could, with the aid of sticks, balance on his entirely stiff legs and swing each forward in turn. Christian Maxwell provided him with transport, and others with a flat in Eton Place, just by Chalk Farm. The flat was always busy with visitors, and all were organised. One group was to get him a set of bagpipes, for his lungs were in good shape and he was skirmishing with lessons. Another group provided his team of editors and encouraged him to put today's ideas into words. Until his death in 1951, Jack was a bright star.

The Spanish people had rejected their king and voted in a moderately progressive government. For the army and for General Franco, this was too much of a move towards radicalism and they started a right-wing revolution and war. Hitler and Mussolini poured in planes and guns, and later sent troops. The Soviet Union sent supplies direct from the Black Sea until one of the ships was sunk by an Italian submarine. The great hope was that the Popular Front government of Leon Blum in France would boldly support the legitimate government of Spain. It was not to be. Blum was scared of his own right wing in France, who were only too willing to respond to Hitler's siren voice. He introduced the idea of non-intervention and included in that was the denial of the right of the Spanish government to buy what and where it wished. For the rest of the world, the choice was between "Arms for Spain" and "Non Intervention".

Anthony Eden did not want to be seen opposing a government that was faithful to the League of Nations but if non-intervention was good enough for the left-wing French government, it could certainly be adopted by the British Conservatives. What was good enough for Eden was good enough for Clem Attlee. He at once showed his well-known inability to work out and to stick to any principle. When Chamberlain later made his trip to Bad Godesberg to meet Hitler, and then his further trip to Berchtesgaden, to bring home the fruits of the two visits on a piece of white paper to be waved at the crowd from the aeroplane door, Attlee praised the first visit and abused the second. As he was to do later over Marshall Aid and the partition of India, so he did now over Spain. In the course of a couple of days he was capable of changing from supporting no right to buy in England, to demanding the right of Spain to buy.

Ernie Bevin, utterly reliable in his adherence to an evil principle, did not change. He went on supporting the full notion of non-intervention. Late in 1937, we learnt that the NEC of the Labour Party would consider sending a deputation to Spain to visit the British contingent of the International Brigade. An approach was made to Bevin to see whether, if asked, he would participate. In no circumstances would he go. Attlee's visit to Spain with Philip Noel-Baker, Ellen Wilkinson and John Dugdale was greeted with the utmost enthusiasm both there and within the party, but had no effect on the inevitable result of the war. By early in 1937, in spite of heroic determination on the part of all those on the government side, it seemed clear enough that Franco must win.

Our ward was deeply involved in trying to organise home support for Spain, although Riley opposed all this. Most of his plans seemed intended to ensure that the party never took the slightest action over anything that was not strictly within its local business. With the support of the ward committee, I procured a shed just opposite Rowton House, the bob-a-night dossers' bed and breakfast place, and canvassed the streets of Finsbury with a barrow collecting warm clothes and tinned food for the International Brigade.

When Lewis Clive set off for Spain I started a series of weekly meetings in the Chapel Street marketplace. Support was mixed but a lot of people stopped to listen and there was always a crowd. I had a small stepladder with a good, bold poster "Arms for Spain" stuck on the front, and I stood well up the ladder and harangued them from over the top of the poster. This all ended after the collapse of the republic, but I resumed the same sort of weekly meetings years later as the Finsbury MP.

In February 1938, Lewis summoned me to take a Sunday walk with him. We went by train to Seaford, then walked over Beachy Head to

Eastbourne. He told me that he was off to Spain as he thought it was the best thing he could do. We discussed the likelihood that he would find himself one Labour adherent among several Communists. At twenty-seven, it was most likely that he would be older than his comrades and might even be lecturing them on the political position that he held. It did not occur to either of us that his companions might be as well informed as, and even more eager and authoritative than he was.

He came to stay with us in Kings Cross for his last night in England. I helped him pack his gear, persuading him not to take the pair of wooden boot-lasts, weighing at least six pounds, which he was packing in his best cross-country boots to take with him across the mountains. It was almost as though he would take his formal dress and top hat. He would obviously be an excellent soldier in any medium. I saw him off from Victoria for a short, private walking tour in the Pyrenees, the current euphemism for joining the Spanish government forces as a member of the International Brigade. It was a matter of the utmost secrecy because it seemed pretty clear that his family, supported by Neville Chamberlain, would have done their best to prevent him from ever reaching Spain.

Before going, Lewis wrote for the New Fabian Research Bureau a book called *The People's Army*. In this he criticised social injustices in the British Army; in a democracy the armed forces should be run on democratic lines. He also proposed a minimum wage of twenty-one shillings per week, and that more soldiers be commissioned from the ranks. Major Attlee contributed a foreword to the book.

Lewis arrived in time to take part in the first retreat over the Ebro and, in early summer, in the glorious advance, then to suffer the slowing down and frustration of that advance. There were reports from Spain of his startling feats of endurance and strength. Being cut off with a Welsh mining chap on the first retreat across the Ebro, Lewis spent several days carrying a heavy machine-gun and sometimes his not-too-well comrade, and finally crossed the river with the same burden. He swam the river in the dark more than once to spy out landing places for the re-crossing. He did not engage in the final retreat after the triumphal re-crossing because on a hill near Gandessa on 4th August 1938 he was shot in the head.

We had taken Tim on holiday to Walberswick on the Suffolk Coast. There I read in the *Express* that Lewis had been killed. Probably most people have lost a well-loved companion at the height of their friendship and have not foreseen such a summary end. War involves killing, but that could not be for us. He had so much to give to the future; surely it could not really be denied to us. The report must be a mistake. Perhaps this reaction saved me from the heaviest shock of the news. I remember sitting on the sandhills with tussock blowing about me and feeling rather dazed. "Dead ere his prime" and I certainly knew of no peer for him.

I received his last letter a few days later. It was written from hospital in Barcelona, where he says he was not gloriously wounded, "simply suffering from the homely complaint of jaundice". They were reliant on ten-day-old newspapers and had "a positive thirst for news … For instance, what is happening on the Labour Party Executive? Is it gradually being won over by force of circumstances?" Lewis expressed the confident hope that in two or three years time he would be "back in England, this war happily won.

"As a matter of fact, I have a faint but even more ambitious hope. There are now three other Labour Councillors in our Battalion. The other day we were sent for by a high authority, Comrade Andre Marti to wit, to discuss ways and means, and they all three with one accord said that in their opinion their constituencies demanded their presence for a brief visit some time this autumn. I gasped. But if three then for Heaven's sake four."

He fancied a week in a farmhouse in Snowdonia or the Lake District; a bit of rain and mist after the Spanish sun; "much food and much exercise". I was to join him. "And please bring Elizabeth." This was Elizabeth Wilkinson, to whom he was devoted.

Lewis had been very impressed by Marti, the French Communist leader, and had promptly joined the party. Ever since 1938 I have suffered from a tendency to treat members of the Communist Party not as potential traitors and enemies of the working class, as well-behaved Labour Party members seem expected to do, but rather as slightly over-eager fellow workers. I regarded them as working for the same cause as Labour but with a zeal that put ordinary workers to shame, and that on occasions made them heedless of the personal well-being of individuals, even of their own immediate associates. Anything else would have seemed a betrayal of Lewis Clive.

By his will, I was heir to the Clive umbrella. This was born in 1926 with a cherry stick and Fox frame, and a silver band with the boyish slogan "Stolen from Lewis Clive, Whitfield". I added "By J P-M". It was lost at Maidstone in the early 'eighties when I hung it on some railings leading down to the railway entrance and walked away and left it. Perhaps it had served its term with me and it should go on to serve mankind in general, or at least one man other than me.

There were memorial services for Lewis at St Martin-in-the-Fields and at the Inner Temple. During the service at St Martin's, I sat between Harry Pollitt, Secretary of the Communist Party, and Jim Middleton, then Secretary of the Labour Party. The only comment I heard between them was when Jim said, "I hope you are not going to try to make political capital out of this, Harry."

Lewis's mother, for whom I had great affection and who had shown some patience with me, announced that she was sure I had lured him into going to Spain, and even organised his death, for the sake of making propaganda for the government cause. I was so shocked by this story that I broke off all connection with the Clive family. It was monstrous conduct on my part. I should have challenged that idea in the strongest possible way and sought to explain it all to her. I knew Meysey and Judith, the elder brother and sister, well enough and should have made sure that they understood. I failed even to try. There was never a word until Tom, our third son, met a son of Judith, married to a Lyttelton and living near the top of Highgate Hill. He visited there and brought a most welcome greeting from them. (Meysey married Elizabeth Pakenham, sister to Frank, and was killed in the Second World War.)

Why were all the thoughtful young men caught up with the Spanish Civil War? The International Brigade was an attempt to stop Hitler and Mussolini in Spain, and so to prevent a future war that would certainly take the rest of our young men and perhaps alter the whole future of the United Kingdom. In Spain, Hitler had an opportunity to rehearse his military and murderous dreams and to display his skill at foreign invasion. After Spain came the Rhineland and Alsace, where no other country opposed him. Hitler was the menacing power for all the world. He was capable of winning the support of the Chamberlain government, egged on as they were by the Cliveden group. The folly of Neville Chamberlain was that he believed that Hitler would never make war on the West. He knew how eager Hitler was for an accommodation, and how ready were France and Britain. The dishonesty of Chamberlain was in pretending that he thought it was "peace in our time" when he was confident that it would be war by Nazi Germany direct to the east against the Soviet Union.

It is not really presumption to discuss this in a personal way because our group of lawyers, on the left of the Haldane Society and the Labour Party, followed every move in the utmost detail and took part in organising opposition to it. And, since Chamberlain was a godfather to Lewis and was closely associated with the Clive family, we all felt we really were parties to what was happening. Once Chamberlain was in Downing Street, Lewis would now and then send a polite note setting out our harshest interpretations of his activities. He would respond by inviting us to No 10 or to his room in the House of Commons, although I am not sure which venue impressed us most. He assumed that we were entirely on his side and merely needed enlightening. Although Chamberlain did his best and spoke frankly, we regarded ourselves as being quite past learning anything fundamental from him.

In the years leading up to the Second World War, Chamberlain saw Nazi Germany as the strongest rival of the Soviet Union. He wished to ensure that the Germans should expand eastward in preparation for war against the Soviet Union, and that they should arrive in the buffer countries free from opposition. He then gave guarantees to those countries that, on condition that they would reject any proposal for Soviet support, Britain would ensure that they would not be invaded. These guarantees were quite useless. We could do nothing whatever to help them. We could not get a man or a gun or an aeroplane even to Poland, let alone to Romania or Bulgaria.

Joseph Kennedy, American Ambassador in London, reported to the US Secretary of State that Chamberlain had described the Polish Guarantee as "futile" and had admitted that it could not possibly help the Poles. All these guarantees were as openly invitations to Hitler as was the successful mission of Lord Runciman on behalf of Chamberlain to persuade the Czechs to hand over control of the Sudetenland. It was a term of this persuasion that the Czechs should not allow the Russians to enter their country to defend them. Just as a defeat for Hitler's forces in Spain might have ended him, so could his adventure in Czechoslovakia.

Between Berlin and Prague stood the Sudeten mountains, a splendid natural fortification and heavily defended by the Czech army, an army thought to be as powerful as any in Europe. The evidence at Nuremburg showed that if the Czechs had remained in control of the Sudetenland and if Hitler had sought to attack Prague, then probably the first city to have been occupied in the resulting battle would have been Berlin. The Czechs were well prepared and were entirely united, but their resulting enormous strength was shattered by the betrayal to Hitler forced upon Benes by the British government and its Western supporters.

In the Tory Party, this diabolical work of the betrayal of Europe to Hitler was sponsored by the Right wing, with Halifax and the Astors in the lead. The only one to make a real stand against it was Winston Churchill, with his small handful of supporters. When the war began the Labour Party was faced with the question of whether to back those Tories in the Commons who wanted to replace Chamberlain with Halifax. The Labour Right wing plainly would have preferred Halifax. The turning point came in April 1941 at Bournemouth when the Labour Party resolved that we would support Churchill. In response to Czechoslovakia, the Haldane Society organised a meeting to which we invited Churchill, Lloyd George and others. Churchill answered, "In this crisis of man's affairs, I cannot serve you," but Lloyd George did. I believe that he had not spoken in public for some years, and his speech was disappointing. It lacked the Welsh *hywl* or spirit we had been led to expect.

The Haldane also organised 250 signatures of practising barristers and solicitors demanding "Hands off Czechoslovakia", although in rather more pompous and academic terms. In September 1938 I had the job (with a barrister named Colonel Grey and shepherded by Dudley Collard) of taking these to Downing Street and presenting them to the fellow who came to the door. This gesture made no difference to the fate of Czechoslovakia, for Hitler was there within a few months with all the grisly consequences, but it satisfied our vanity and made us feel that we were taking a part in world affairs. It was my first action in connection with Czechoslovakia, but by no means the last.

I was to learn the effect on myself almost immediately. Terence O'Connor was Solicitor General. He complained that it was most unbecoming for a young barrister to take part in political affairs. Indeed, that we should set off for Downing Street and make a fuss against the government was something of an outrage. I tried to assert that it was well intended and aimed at saving the world from Hitler. Besides, it was no more than ordinary politics. His response was that a young barrister should keep out of politics when starting at the Bar.

I knew him quite well socially through Hugh Farmer and his family and protested that he himself was deep in politics and it had not done him any harm. He was the Solicitor General, had a good practice, plenty of money and high-standing in the land, and all resulting from politics. He replied that that was quite different. If you went into parliament, then you could do as you liked. But unless you intended to enter parliament, then you had no right at all.

We, on the left of the Haldane Society, foresaw that Hitler would soon be in Prague. This meant that we should try to establish escape routes for Czech lawyers and academics who would be in danger. In the name of Lord Rutherford, but under the chairmanship of Binford-Hole, a committee of young English lawyers had set going a similar scheme in Germany. My main job was to get Rutherford of Cavendish Laboratory to sign whatever we wanted by way of requests or assurances or protests. I made two or three trips to Cambridge to the Cavendish Laboratory and there he introduced me to Peter Kapitsa, who later was a leading figure in Soviet atomic research.

Binford-Hole then sent me to Prague to explore setting up escape routes for Czech academics against the day when Hitler would arrive in the city. Two young Englishwomen, Christian Maxwell and, I believe, Sheila Grant-Duff, followed on to organise and conduct escapes. Their reception was not very good as a number of the expected Czech victims, no doubt learned professors and skilled lawyers, were not worried enough or were simply too loyal to their own people to take advantage of such opportunities as we could offer. Life in Prague had been so secure that people did not foresee the peril in which they stood. Likewise, there appeared to have been no Hitler-like movement that would give any foreshadowing of what was to come. When such people later came under intense pressure (for many of them were of progressive tendency and liberal outlook) their escape was helter-skelter.

In 1938 the fees for the gold clause case were paid. Mine for the whole of the work came to £900, which was several hundred times greater than my normal fee, and so Janet and I bought Moorlands at Chappel and Wakes Colne in North Essex. £800 for fifty acres and a house, an ancient thatched barn, and sheds, garages, pigsties and outhouses of all kinds round the pond. Geese and goats were in possession and the farming had been abandoned. Our part of Essex was at the end of the longest fetch of the south-west wind across land after leaving the Atlantic. It was thus the driest corner of England and seed ripened there quicker and more surely. In Roman times, our rail junction (Marks Tey) was the site of a main seed-growing area for the Roman empire and has been famous for seed-growing ever since. Freddie Bird was living at Moorlands. He stayed on, but we brought in Peter Gregory to run the farm for us. Peter was recommended as a good Socialist and a first-class farmer by Dudley Collard's brother, who had been with him at Reading University. He was certainly a willing worker.

In cultivating a twenty-acre field that had not been worked since 1925, we followed local advice to plough a half-inch deeper to get the lower soil moving. We ploughed and before we planted anything up came the brightest crop of yellow. It shone across the valley. Half the parish said, "It's sharlock. Plough it in as green manure." Others said, "No, it is mustard. That field hasn't grown mustard since the early 1920s." Before we could decide what to do there came a man from Reckitt and Colman in Norwich. He offered an excellent price for the mustard, and they brought in their own machines and harvested it themselves. We next sowed the field with seed supplied by Reckitt and Colman but had so little success that we went back to the local routine. I knew Eva Reckitt as part-owner of Central Books, first in Charing Cross Road and later in Grays Inn Road. I now learned something of the source of her money, which she poured so freely into left-wing literature.

When the war came, it was our wish that the farm should lend full support. Peter was soon on the local War Agricultural Executive Committee and carried out every experiment that authority suggested. He grew rape with its vivid yellow flower, linseed and flax, malting samples of barley, rye for thatching, and wheat, oats and rye for seed. Whatever new crop was wanted, he would take it up at great expense and with some success, but with no profit: throughout the war, not a penny of profit, and enough livestock only to keep the place going. Peter was an excellent farmer. If, in 1945, instead of railing at him, I had suggested a change of policy and that the aim should be the maximum profit, he would have done it admirably. Instead we had a long-winded and inconclusive arbitration, then separated. We did not meet again until Lysenko appeared in Russia with his outrageous claim to have bred coloured cotton.

CHAPTER NINE

Assington

WHEN CHAMBERLAIN came back from Munich in September 1938 and said there was "peace in our time" Denis Dobson, whom I had met in the Haldane Society, said to me, "That means war within six months. I think that we should get our families out of London." We had two children apiece and decided to buy a house big enough to hold them all. As I already had the small farm in north Essex we looked in that direction. The hall at a neighbouring village, Assington, was for sale: a large Elizabethan mansion with Tudor chimneys and onion domes on pillars. There was an enormous hall where you could stand up in the fireplace, a giant empty library, and a dining room in proportion. A whole wing was devoted to cookery and servants' quarters. There were probably seven bedrooms on the first floor and a round dozen on the top, but a total insufficiency of bathrooms.

In the early summer of 1939 we bought the hall with eighty acres of garden and park, two cottages, a large stable and an old walled garden with every kind of plum and soft fruit, all for around £3,000. The fact is that Denis put up all the money but I took some responsibility. He was good enough to treat me as half-owner when, at the end of the war, he sold it for £6,000. We signalled war preparations by making something approaching six hundred pounds of conserves, preserves and the like, and installing bees and a cow. Freddy Bird came to run the place as bailiff. He at once began to order things suited to a manor and a large estate, none of which we wanted, and we decided sadly that he would have to go. Freddy promoted himself back to Tiger Hill, an establishment that he maintained in a condition even more like Moorlands than Moorlands itself.

Assington was too big for our little families; Denis and I would have to find reinforcements. Most young lawyers had a family home or other retreat in the country, so would not be interested in our idea. New Zealanders were a much better prospect. Nell, the judge's daughter from Wellington, and her husband John Hutton were about to have twins and I thought they would want to be out of London. John later became famous as a glass engraver and has windows in many noted places such as Coventry Cathedral, New Zealand House and many Cunarder ships. He was then a painter, a good hand at bricklaying, and a strong fellow fit to be exploited. (In due course, he went off as a camouflage officer in the 8th Army. Denis Dobson became an officer in the RAF and lost a lung for his trouble, and ended up stationed near John Hutton in the Middle East.)

Nell suggested another New Zealander, Monica, who arrived with a child, and nominally bringing her husband, Trevor Williams. He had been a history don at Merton, but was now a cavalry officer in an armoured machine and destined to be Montgomery's Chief of Staff, Intelligence. It was said that Montgomery would complain if Williams couldn't tell him the name of the next German to be captured the other side of the sand hill. He was a very young brigadier and brought great distinction to Assington.

The only other lawyer in our group, Bertie Lewis, was part-German and part-Chinese. He was in Pritt's chambers and the Haldane and was a leader in tenants' defence work. He arrived with his beautiful Swedish wife, Klaris, and their daughter, Karin Ann. Another, Kirsty, was born later. Bertie was very able and fairly wise. He had a pistol and a revolver and, what with a twelve bore shotgun and a .22 Winchester repeater bought by me the year before to go farming, that was the total of our armament. (The armament was of some significance during the phoniest period of the phoney war.)

I suppose we were all middle-class. It was usual for such families to have assistance in looking after the children and we all arrived with one or more "nannies". Thelma Dobson came with a professional child nurse and a cleaning lady, Mrs Winyard, who brought her husband and two children, and finally took on the cooking for the entire household while Janet did the housekeeping. Our contribution was two German girls, Irene and Connie, and a Czech boy: all refugees. In about April 1940, terror spread in official quarters about refugees from Central Europe. Ours were instructed to appear before the County Court Judge at Colchester, His Honour Judge Hildersley, and were asked many questions. For example,

Mrs Fox, who often visited us, was asked how she dared to change her name from Fuchs. Was it because she wished to conceal her German identity? Was she a spy, by chance? She answered that it was, as she thought, undesirable for her boy to have to go to an English school when his name was Fuchs.

She did not know enough of English history to ask the learned judge why he had changed his name from Hildersheim to Hildersley. Of his earlier history I know little, except that at the beginning of the First World War he had gone to that famous pupil master, wit and author of *Forensic Fables*, Theo Matthew, and asked him whether it was wise to change his name. Matthew answered, "My dear Hildersheim, I'm sure you will decide what is right, and whichever you do, it will be most courageous."

We worked hard at redecorating the whole of Assington and wired up all those parts of the house that were limited to paraffin lamps. One of the cellars contained an engine that drove a generator, and a battery system. We had perhaps forty large batteries that could retain electric power for many days but, with us, required charging at least twice a week. Before the wiring, there had been two carbon overkills on the top floor when paraffin lamps had smoked so badly that a room had been filled and festooned with black. Our amateurish wiring gave freedom from that disaster, but when the place burned down in 1957, the suspected cause was defective wiring. (The V&A later mounted an exhibition on the decline of the country house, and the front page of the programme showed Assington Hall in flames.)

We had an Aga stove, and also a giant boiler where five-foot logs could be thrown in. In autumn we hired a circular saw and learned how to reduce a great pile of timber to burnable logs. There was also a game cellar in which we hung anything we could acquire from home or away, although we were not particularly successful with anything except pigeons and rabbits. We borrowed a tractor and plough and had up to two acres of parkland pressed into service for vegetables. The neighbouring farmer sent a man to milk our cow regularly, but several of the women learned how to do that and took the burden from him. There were also calves in due course, as there were hens, eggs and chicks, geese and goslings, and beehives.

In the park was an ancient dam that had formed a stew pond in its day, when the foundation of the house was thought to have been as a minor religious attachment to the monastery in Bury St Edmunds. The trees reflected the fashions of the eighteenth and early nineteenth century. As a result, we had a redwood, a monkey puzzle and two giant cedars; the older cedar had been heavily chained to support the lower, horizontal branches. Assington was near enough to Colchester to have taken some Roman influence. When the biggest elm in the park blew over in an east wind straight from the Urals, several pieces of Roman tessellated pavement were found amongst the roots.

The church was a stone's throw from the house. I believe the living was in the gift of the owner, which meant Denis. He was never called upon to exercise any rights, although we did occasionally read a lesson in church. Stephen Murray shot a hole in the weathervane on the church tower and, just under that, in the body of the tower we took and destroyed a hornets' nest and recovered their beautiful papier-mâché home. Hornets are so rare in these days that one ought to preserve them, even at the risk of being stung, and I am sorry that I ever took a hand at reducing their population.

Ronnie Armstrong-Jones gave us his old racehorse and Tishy the polo pony to look after. Later in the war, a man called The Major arrived to stay for a short time. He was an ex-cavalry sergeant major and we learned every aspect of horse management, including dressage. Tishy was a genuine "waler" bred in Australia and trained in India. I had spent days on end riding in New Zealand but had never learned the simplest aid, save to kick and to pull and cajole, and had never jumped more than a three-foot stream. The Major made horsemen of some of us.

At Assington everything was proposed to be run as a sort of collective, but it was the most ill-organised collective imaginable. We did not think of it as a commune, or a Socialist experiment. Ralph Milner was, I believe, the only Communist. We were simply a group of families trying to live together and doing our best to share. It was understood that each family would put what it could to the running of the place, in terms of rent and labour, but there was no formal agreement and nothing in writing as to how we would share and what contribution each should make. The women supposedly took it in turns, a week at a time, to run the kitchen, although it quickly fell to Janet and Win Winyard.

After a few months, Mr Steward, a skilled gardener with experience in large vegetable garden management, responded to an advertisement and brought his family to live in the gardener's cottage. He was soon producing a trug basket each morning with the vegetables washed and trimmed and laid out like a Flemish still-life. It took a resolution from the general meeting of the household to persuade him not to waste his and our time with this gaiety. I now see that that was a mistake. A skilled man should be allowed to demonstrate his skill by showing off a bit. Besides, soil washes off far more easily when damp from the ground than after it has dried. Mr Steward also organised rat-hunting in stables and garden buildings. He taught us how to handle and breed ferrets, and their use for bolting rabbits out of warrens. This is not meant to be a ferret keeper's *vade mecum*, but the trick in carrying a ferret is to get a firm grip on the back of its neck before it can get a firm grip on your finger. You then carry it as a cat carries kittens, except that you don't do it with your mouth.

Later in the war there was built within two miles of us a large but entirely bogus aircraft base; presumably part of the successful campaign to convince the Germans that the invasion was to be by the Pas de Calais, not Normandy. Perhaps twenty pairs of scrim panels painted to look like bomber wings were set round a big pasture field. It was near to the Colchester coast and on a straight line from North Holland to London. The Germans bombed the field and scored two direct hits, scattering wings about. Although quickly restored, the field was then ignored by the Germans until the last days of the occupation of Holland, when it is said that a single plane made a last visit and dropped an enormous log of wood dressed up like a bomb and tied with red ribbon. And once a genuine bomber, limping home from Germany, could reach no further and ended up in the far hedge. I believe that only the hedge suffered.

Despite our proximity to "the base", Assington was a very safe place during the war except for the danger of such things as the bees. With the aid of a book, Janet soon became adept. She would approach the bees quite uninhibited, unhelmeted, unveiled and ungloved. They crawled all over her and never an angry sound or act. With me it was different. I was extremely vulnerable and when armed from top to toe still attracted dive-bombing attacks the minute I was within reach of the hive.

We soon learned that they have guards on station twenty feet up, at quite a distance from the hive. When an enemy approaches, they start their power-dive from full height straight at the offender. When I was scented or sighted, the angry buzz began and they would dive bang onto the helmet, which was really an old straw hat with a veil. They would crowd round my neck and try to find a way in, and round the top of my boots. One Christmas I suffered four stings and spent four days in bed. In short, I was susceptible and the bees seemed to know it instinctively.

Some children were brought by families we knew whose work kept them in London. The children stayed, and at one stage there were between twenty and thirty altogether. Young Demi Demetriou, whose father had a restaurant in Great Queen Street off Kingsway and was a retired Cypriot politician, was completely unaffected by bees. He kicked a hive over and was stung in fifty places. Next day he kicked it over again with a similar result. The effect on him was nil. On another occasion he fell from a first-floor window, a full twenty feet high, and it was no worse than the bees. A number of those who had care of him saw him pass the dining room window and they all suffered more than he did.

We really needed a schoolteacher, so Elsa Elliott came with her husband Maurice and their two children, Judith and Brett. She had an infant class of twenty or more. Toward the end of the war, when the two eldest boys at Assington were seven, our Tim went to join Karin Ann at A S Neill's Summerhill, which was then at Blaenau Ffestiniog in North Wales, while Denis's son Roger went off to another prep school, and later rowed for Cambridge. Maurice Elliott went into army education where he helped, no doubt, to win the 1945 election. It was much complained by the Tories that the whole of army education was supporting Labour. One hoped that all education would do that, but it has since proved that it is not always the case.

Assington was better for the men than the women, for we had the advantage that we were often away. The wives were stuck there with babes and nannies. Squabbles were unavoidable, with the result that the common nursery and kitchen became highly avoidable. The assistants seemed unable to realise that they were being paid, in part, to co-operate. And so it went on until nearly all the nannies had left and the refugees were interned. After Hitler's invasion of Russia it finally became clear to authority who we were fighting, and we were able to get most of our refugees released as desirable, rather than undesirable aliens. Among their number was Ludwig Koch's family. He had been in England for some time pioneering wildlife recording with the BBC but his wife and daughter only left at the last minute. On arrival, they were promptly interned on the Isle of Man.

Several of our warriors helped win the war but lost their wives – some temporarily, and some permanently – as the price of their absence. The lot of the man left behind is probably worse than that of the wronged husband. His sense of guilt probably outweighs the modest quiver of triumph at his conquest or her surrender.

One way or another, a dozen families in addition to the unaccompanied children joined in at Assington. Some went back to London when the bombing of 1941 was over and did not come back when the V1 and V2 weapons began. By that time, the Allies were advancing in every corner of Europe and there was never enough of the V2 to excite people into moving their homes. The whole thing began with two families seeking wartime protection. It ended as a notable effort by a group of women to make a richer than rationing life for a large number of children. This they did by hard work and common country sense, and they succeeded, it might be said, in spite of the help of their menfolk.

In October 1939 I tried to join the RAF, but was denounced as too old and with too little training. I was told that the pilot age would lower much faster than my age would advance; if I would be patient for a while, they would have me very soon. Then I applied for an appointment in the Judge Advocate General's Department dealing with the RAF. They had no room, either. The JAG was the legal, disciplinary and court martial department of each of the services. Many barristers who served in the war ended up there.

I stayed in the Temple and occupied my evenings with volunteer work in the London River Police. This consisted of rehearsing the knots with rope-ends under Waterloo Station, or trips in an open motorboat downstream through the Port of London and round the docks. It was always downstream because it was thought that there was no possibility of crime in Kensington and Chelsea. We wore steel helmets to show that we meant business, but, unless the weather was rough, it was pretty quiet. It was obvious that, once bombing started, the river would be the only free way for the emergency services and I seriously thought of offering myself for a full-time job in the River Police, if no more active service turned up.

In May 1940, the RAF Volunteer Reserve offered an administrative post. At an interview with the selection committee, the chairman told me that I was wanted not for legal duties but for "a special job in one of our operational rooms at Fighter Command Headquarters near Stanmore". It was understood that the ops rooms were a vital step in the assessment of information from the whole country. Radar had only been invented in 1935 and the Radio Direction Finding reports all came through Fighter Command Filter Room, to which I would be posted. If you weren't to fly, there couldn't have been a more exciting job. On 4th June, I received my appointment as Pilot Officer, the most junior thing you can be, and instructions to report to Loughborough for an officers' training course.

Before I could get there – indeed, the very next day – came the Invasion of Assington Hall. We were descended upon by twenty policemen. A handful were locals, including the Chief Constable of Suffolk, and a dozen came from some higher echelon in London presumed to be M15. Most of our menfolk were lingering on with their London jobs before disappearing into military service. I was also absent, but Denis Dobson was at home and he had to bear the brunt of it. The police ransacked the house and produced my shotgun and rifle, putting them proudly on the dining room table, but failed to spot Bertie's handguns left lying in his room.

They dug every corner of the place where there was any sign of the earth being turned. By then, the whole of the walled garden and beyond had been brought into subjection and there was plenty of probing for them to do. Timothy, aged three, is said to have told one policeman at the raid, "I'm not frightened of you, there's a much bigger one round the corner." Every child was asked where their mother's safe was, as though all were mine.

Plainly, the raid was the result of local gossip based on our being a co-operative household with six families, some of rather left-wing views, and a number of refugees from Germany and Czechoslovakia. The whole thing was really like a charade. It appeared that what was being sought was guns or money or both, illicitly obtained and there for no good purpose. Donald Somervell was attorney general and so leader of the Bar, and I asked him to find out what was happening. He reported back that the information on which the police relied had "turned out to be inaccurate". But once a rumour is launched, there's no catching it up, and it soon became apparent that others were by no means satisfied.

Roy Robinson, sub-treasurer of the Inner Temple, later heard of the raid through some official quarters and turned my furniture out of the flat in the basement of No 1 Paper Buildings and left it standing in the rain. I got special leave from the RAF and went down to London to accost him in his lair and he was greatly shamed by my gallant attire. He volunteered that his workmen should put the furniture back. (The rent at that time was almost nothing; even I could afford it out of a pilot officer's pay, particularly as Brian McKenna was living there and paying it.)

I duly reported at Loughborough on 7th June and arrived with a group of about fifteen other chaps, all training for the next echelon of entrants to the "deep hole" that contained Fighter Command Headquarters. We had a bit of physical training suitable for men in their mid-thirties and some old-fashioned drill. There were foundation lectures in overhead tactics between defending fighters and attacking bombers, and we were taught to decipher a secret code. The first such genuine message that I had to deal with read as follows:

"The underside of fighter aircraft wings which have heretofore been coloured sky blue will for the future be duck egg green STOP As duck egg green is not yet available the colouring will remain sky blue STOP".

The few senior officers at Loughborough dined regularly in mess. They wore "mess kit" and some day we might aspire to such outfits. We were to learn to behave as gentlemen and not as sergeants, who had their own mess, or as other ranks, whose eating habits and resorts would be inspected. We should learn the appropriate address to batmen and to mess orderlies, and how to deal with those senior to ourselves. The idea was to introduce us to the traditions of the RAF, although being so newly born, the service had not amassed a great adhesion of flummery. The RAF seemed to have acquired a short handbook of instant traditions and we were learning them by heart.

The officer in charge of the camp was Geoffrey Bing's uncle, a group captain past his normal "use-by" date and recycled because of the war. He understood Geoffrey's outspoken views and actions against the Nazis and gave no sign of disapproval. He was quite close to Geoffrey and introduced himself in a most friendly fashion. It seemed that he knew a lot about my politics, untried as they were, and I assumed that Geoffrey had told him I was coming.

When training was completed, we had written exams. I showed off as usual and gave full answers. We were told to leave so soon as we were finished and most were packed up and gone by half-time. Only two of us remained; we had both been writing steadily until the end. We wondered whether our fellow students were out of practice with exams or had given brilliant short answers. The CO was there and said that he had glanced at some of the papers and our first guess was more accurate. My companion suggested that the CO should not mark the papers but just pass us all and say what a high level had been achieved. He insisted on marking the papers but agreed to stifle the marks.

The final stage was showing that we could conduct the parade through minor drill manoeuvres. A marker was stood at a distance and we were lined up. "Now march the parade on the marker. Come on, Platts-Mills, show us how to do it!" I took command. A few smart orders "about turn, quick march, left wheel" etc. It was quite simple. In fact, after a few more orders we were in a hopeless muddle. The file had somehow got into three ranks instead of two, the marker was in the middle and was facing the opposite way. I gave up and they all burst out laughing. The CO laughed loudest. He said, in an ordinary conversational tone, "Excuse me, Mr Marker. Would you mind stepping out of the ranks and walking round to your proper position at the right-hand side of the front rank? Now, who's next?"

We were all confident that this first stage of training had been completed satisfactorily and were looking forward to the next. At the end of the course, we were posted in two groups: one half to Stanmore, and the other, including me, to Yatesbury on the Marlborough Downs. On the last day we were held back for several hours and told that Air Ministry confirmation had not come through. When the instructions arrived, all were to proceed on the next stage towards Fighter Command – all except myself. I was to go to Uxbridge forthwith, where I found myself in a somewhat anomalous position. I was not posted to any duty and was not, so far as I could understand, there "for posting". The officers appeared completely at a loss to know what I was to do.

While at Uxbridge I met Jim Cooper. He was a psychiatrist in that part of Regents Park professionally nearest to Harley Street. He had become a psychiatrist in the RAF with a duty of persuading pilots who were fed-up with flying that they ought to try again. His success at this had come to the attention of Higher Command and he was asked to look into the problem of the balloon girls on the Merseyside. He had an enormous American car that did nine miles to the gallon and endless coupons. We drove to Liverpool and visited eight main barrage balloon sites and Jim addressed meetings of the girls. They had had enough. They had kept up the balloons for six months night and day. No Germans had come near them or looked as though they ever would come; their boys were away at the war. There were no local boys, they had had no home leave, they all voted for taking down the balloons and going home. Jim argued with them in their hundreds. He cajoled them. He warned and threatened them. If the balloons came down, then the next night the German bombs would wipe out Merseyside. But they would not be convinced and soon the balloons came down and the girls went home. The balloons had been so successful that there was little AA defence within miles. All that day the skies of Merseyside were untroubled and Jim and I withdrew to the neighbourhood of Ilkley Moor. So it continued the next night and the next day and on the third night from every Nazi bomber base in north-west Europe they came at 20,000 feet. The familiar drone. The bombs rained down on Liverpool and Runcorn, Bootle and Birkenhead, Wallasey and Widness. Merseyside was a waste. Women from every balloon site in the UK were brought to Merseyside and told the sorry history and saw the outcome. Balloons of Britain were saved and Jim's reputation was made.

Then came Hulavingdon Aerodrome just north of Chippenham in Wilts. I had flown there with the OU Air Squadron in August 1930. It was a nicely disguised aerodrome on the rolling plains of Wiltshire. There were enormous hangers with sloping sides all roofed over with turf. The "apron" in front of the hangars was of course well-groomed turf. The turf on the hangers had been neglected and small bushes were growing all over them. The remedy was obvious and Jim advised that the bushes should be eliminated and the turf mowed until it was as neat as the surrounding fields. Later, Jim also advised on the state of affairs in Inner Temple.

At No 1 Depot there was no flying because there was no aerodrome. I was supposed to be a warrior, so had best equip myself in some way for fighting; if not in the air, then on the land. Here was a chance to polish up the skills learnt as a musketry instructor and captain in the 1st Battalion Wellington Infantry Regiment. Before leaving Loughborough we were all issued with standard Webley and Scott revolvers, big heavy six-shooters, and with ammunition. Uxbridge had a splendid small arms range and sufficient of an assault course for bayonet drill. I spent three days on intensive assault course work and bayoneted and butted everything in sight. Then came seven days on the range with an armoury sergeant, who became a good friend. He turned the key to Pandora's box and I must have fired 2,000 rounds of pistol and small arms ammunition. My shoulder was bruised black and my right arm was in tatters. (This was before the days of the two-armed crouch for a pistol; the body was half-turned and one arm held at full length.)

At the beginning of July came notification that I was to be posted to Aden. Again, we were given no indication as to my duties. It wasn't until a week later that we learnt that they were to be "administrative". In May, it was Fighter Command Filter Room, and I had successfully completed a training course for those duties. Yet I was now to be sent to Aden to perform work for which I was unqualified and unprepared. It was a puzzle. A responsible officer at Uxbridge remarked, "How can you hope for any but a supernumerary posting at Aden or anywhere else in your position?" This was the first even partial explanation I had been offered. I asked him, "What on earth is my position?" The fellow must have lost his nerve because he wouldn't say any more.

I was left with the inescapable conclusion that it was connected with the Assington raid. In spite of the attorney general's assurances that the chief constable was content, plainly Sir Archibald Sinclair, Minister for Air, was not. I had been judged and found guilty of some undefined potentiality towards disloyalty. I asked for an opportunity to clarify the situation, to have the chance of at least knowing the evidence against me, but this was denied. Quite apart from any political question involved, I had been personally recommended to the RAF by Bill Jordan, the High Commissioner for New Zealand. He gave me a letter that I took when I first volunteered. If I failed to challenge this discrimination, how could I explain it to him?

I wrote to the under secretary of state, setting out the sequence of events and again requested an interview with some appropriate official. In conclusion, I stated that as a New Zealander, I was not accustomed to having my integrity challenged. Perhaps this was being a bit grand about it, but anyone would have been angry. Although willing to be judged by the views of the commanding officers under whom I had served in the RAF and elsewhere, I could not accept being condemned by someone who did not know me, and on indirect evidence that I was not permitted to know of or to challenge. I had been appointed to Aden under suspicion, and was therefore reluctant to accept the posting. This was getting pretty serious because refusal of orders in wartime could be a court martial job. Legal advice was called for.

Harry (W H) Thompson had moved his firm from Chancery Lane to High Wycombe, so was conveniently placed for Uxbridge. He was the first solicitor to set himself up in business as willing to represent and to advise only workmen, trade unions and tenants. His principle was that the most wretched and dishonest worker must be better than the most noble and lofty employer, and the tenants always better than landlords. He at once moved me out of Uxbridge and into his own house, and there we launched our campaign against Sir Archibald Sinclair and Ernie Bevin.

By this stage, we had a coalition government, so I could pick on a good supply of Labour cabinet ministers to back my request that I be allowed to serve in some useful and appropriate position. (Apparently, I was now too old to be a pilot and probably too tall to serve as a rear gunner.) Ellen Wilkinson was very suspicious of the posting and advised that I should not accept it. Ellen was my champion in the cabinet, and with Bevin in charge of recruitment for everything, one needed a fairly determined combatant.

Ellen was then at the Ministry of Home Security and, in the course of her inquiries, learned that there was a file at MI5. She approached the junior minister and asked to be allowed to see it. Although in Churchill's cabinet, she was told that it was not the practice to show MI5 minutes and dossiers to Labour ministers, even to Labour prime ministers, junior Tories were allowed to see them, and possibly it would have been so with Liberals in their day.

However, the junior minister told her that in his opinion the files were quite useless. He had once had occasion to read through a great number on men and women who were known to be favourable to Russia. The majority had one identical phrase: "He arrived late at the meeting and stood at the back with his mistress and left early." Apart from such a phrase, scattered like confetti through the files, there was no reason to suppose that any of them had a mistress at all. It was put in purely as a make-weight and all the agents had learnt its use.

Ellen warned that the Aden posting might have the direct purpose of removing me from the scene – on a permanent rather than a temporary basis. She foresaw the danger of a fatal accident. I thought this was fanciful and even absurd. I joked about having just fired 2,000 rounds of small arms ammunition at Uxbridge and boasted that I would give a good account of myself. She was quite serious, however, and gave her opinion after ringing up in my presence two unknown colleagues and telling them a short outline of the story. I decided to follow her advice.

No commanding officer would have dreamt of carrying out such an extraordinary order as Ellen anticipated, but no one thought that Aden could become involved in hostilities from any quarter and I wanted a posting that offered the chance of useful service. On reflection, I really ought to have gone to Aden. I should have brought my civilian pilot's licence, long out of date, up to RAF standards, learned the local tongue and made acquaintance with the anti-colonial movement; unless, of course, Ellen's fears had been proved correct.

Instead, I was kept on extended leave. In the autumn, while ploughing in a longish field, I heard an aeroplane coming in fast. In a moment there was a German plane straight ahead. Somehow I learned that he was firing his guns, but at the same time I knew that I was in the ditch. The tractor went on alone and stopped in the hedge just where the aeroplane had crossed. It had all happened in an instant. The only damage was the slightest dent in one wheel guard. The pilot probably reported another kill, and I decided to carry a shotgun on the tractor.

While the Battle of Britain was on, I had occasion to travel towards Maidstone. It was a cloudless and windless day and the sky over Kent was wreathed with vapour trails. They wove circles, spirals and loops and long straight lines, several of which dived vertically towards the ground, but not a plane to be seen. In general, aeroplanes had not previously flown fast enough or high enough to leave vapour trails. It was an extraordinary sight and I thought of Crusoe's wonder at finding the footprint of Man Friday. I also thought of the Filter Room, and the role that I might have played.

I supposed I must have been at fault somewhere, but couldn't see how; everything had gone so well at Loughborough. Janet suggested a possible answer. At one point we were given a two-day pass and she came up to visit. We went out for the evening with two other trainees. One of them had become very friendly and was seldom out of my company; he probably bought me a drink more often that I did him. Janet told me later that she had felt uneasy in his company. He was always asking questions and was a most attentive listener. Janet wondered whether perhaps he was set up to do this and had made a critical report. I said, "But I didn't say anything controversial, and I didn't talk about politics." Janet said, "You didn't talk about anything else."

Many lefties who had served in Spain were called up or were accepted when they volunteered. Several more got in only after a tussle with the authorities. Always near the recruitment office there was someone with the attitude of Archibald Sinclair or Ernie Bevin, and they had to be overridden. We used to advise the would-be servicemen to get testimonials of honesty, decency and loyalty from such people as D N Pritt or Ivor Montague. Pritt was in parliament and so had impressive notepaper; Ivor wrote as a film director with an address in Dean Street. Here were two people whom the armed forces would not have tolerated in their ranks, but a letter from either was enough to get someone else in.

So far as I know, Ivor Montague and I were the only two who were excluded from any form of normal war service by the stupidities of Bevin. Archibald Sinclair thought it quite treasonable that anybody on the left should dare to infiltrate himself into the RAF under his command. My "infiltration" had begun with the University Air Squadron in 1929, when I was a political babe-in-arms and had given no thought to the left, the right, nor any position in between. But we later became eager anti-Nazis. An anti-Nazi history was of no help, and to have been prematurely anti-Nazi was a positive hindrance. Geoffrey Bing's uncle was the first person I had met outside the Haldane who was aware of the incongruous position of the premature anti-Nazi. We were condemned throughout most of the 1930s on the grounds that only Communists were against the Nazis and this hostility carried over into the war years.

Geoffrey Bing spent his first days in the army occupied with preparing potatoes and it looked as though this was his price for being on the left. Those who could joined in a major campaign for the recognition of his talents. It succeeded and he went to an officer training centre at Aldershot. He was awarded the baton of honour for his group and was next at the

Airborne Forces Development Centre. There his extreme ingenuity was put to full use and he contributed to new developments with parachutes and the towed-glider carrier plane used by the thousand in the invasion of Europe. He ended up a staff major.

As Ellen found out, my hostile record began with the anti-Mosley defences and included the visit to Downing Street in September 1938 to present the petition in defence of Czechoslovakia. It was undoubtedly the view of the government that although working chaps could be on the left, it was most menacing if a middle-class person held the same views. He might be better educated and might influence others. The RAF invited me to retire, and I accepted. I continued to press for an inquiry, but was told that my case had already been fully considered. Asking where, when and by whom it had been considered brought no response.

It was several months later, when I was driving a tractor in a muddy East Anglian field, that I received the most glamorous document that ever went through the post. In copperplate, on semi-parchment, and bearing the sign-manual of the sovereign himself, came my commission as a pilot officer. I was addressed as "Trusty and well beloved" and told that "especial Trust and Confidence" were reposed in my "Loyalty, Courage, and Good Conduct". I thought these commendations fully justified.

A similar irony arose over my relations with foreign governments in exile. A fellow Western circuiteer, G R F Morris, approached me in Pump Court quadrangle during the war and said that one of the great Cyrils was a member of M15 and had the job of keeping an eye on me. Morris proposed that I should meet Cyril Harvey each month, dining at his expense and telling him all that I knew. Wherever I might be and whatever I was doing, I should use any excuse and get to London to make my report. This seemed somewhat improbable, given MI5's hostile file on me, their exploits at Assington, and their interference with my attempts to serve with the RAF. However, I had great confidence in Morris. He was a Welshman of rather aristocratic bearing, utterance and connections, and he and his first wife were both active in the Conservative Party.

For some years, he entertained the circuit mess with stories that referred to his recent contact with members of the royal family or other bigwigs in the social order. This practice later reached its height at the Bar Hotel in Bodmin, where the telephone was in the dining room. Gwyn was heard to say, "What, the palace? Do you mean Hammersmith Palais? I don't understand. Oh, The Palace. I beg your pardon. Of course. Yes," and a pause. "Yes, I could advise on that at once, just as I stand here. Yes, the procedure is the same and the succession is immediate at the moment of death, just as with a male heir. The formula will be: 'The King is dead; long live the Queen'. Yes, thank you very much. Please mention it to my clerk." This is thought by many to be apocryphal, but it was not so.

I agreed to meet Cyril Harvey, at least to hear him out, and a splendid black-market dinner resulted. I had become quite at home at several addresses in Lowndes Square, Little Europe of the governments in exile, and at its extension on the north side of Knightsbridge. All of these governments had left-wing members amongst them. Right-wingers had hived off with the Nazis and remained friends with the occupying forces, or were in quisling or Petainist regimes. As one of the few active young lefties still in London, I was sought out by exiles with progressive ideas. It was easy to attach each of them to a Labour or Liberal MP, who would do lesser parliamentary jobs for their countries: asking a question in the house; arranging an introduction to an under-secretary or even to a minister; or fixing up a visit from abroad.

Cyril explained that he wanted to know not just the matters that were common form in Britain's relations with governments in exile, but also anything that might seem relevant in the personal lives of their leaders. He gave a discreet and very slight indication of interest in any aberrations in the social conduct of embassy members, and sought information about other British Socialists. I made it clear that I was not willing to try my hand at spying on people's private lives. I would not betray political confidences or engage in surveillance of the sexual habits or delights of others, least of all with my own colleagues. That was reason enough for rejecting the commission, but I argued that if even one example were observed, it would prejudice my chances of ever getting further help from any of these countries or individuals.

There was still plenty to do. It wasn't unusual to find a middle-rank representative of a visiting government who was trying to live up to what he regarded as a standard appropriate to his position and the good fame of his country, but without the means of doing so. He would soon be getting into debt and in danger of having to resort to unsatisfactory steps to bridge the gap. This was the kind of material that Cyril could use. A word to him enabled our government to give discreet assistance, or to require his own government to do what was needed. Not only did I feel justified in doing this, but insofar as it helped to smooth relations with these governments, it was a bit of a contribution towards the war effort. The black market dinners could be excused.

The "Great Cyrils" were Harvey, Asquith and Radcliffe. Cyril Radcliffe was perhaps the ablest lawyer of our day. He and the Scottish lawyer James Scott Cumberland Reid were the only two in the last century to go straight from the Bar to the Lords, excluding those who become lord chancellor. Cyril Asquith, son of the prime minister, went through all the run of judgeships to the Lords. And the third was Cyril Harvey. In their early days at the Bar, it was thought that all three would go to the Lords together, but when Harvey continued as a somewhat aged silk doing run-of-the-mill defences at the Old Bailey, he must have appeared as odd as I myself did in my later years.

I also did a brief spell of fire-watching at the Temple, at the height of the London blitz. When not on fire duty, I sometimes stayed at Eton to dodge the bombs and try to get a good night's sleep. I was invited there by Grizel, wife of Hubert Hartley, an Eton housemaster. He had three times stroked Cambridge winning crews in the early 'twenties and so turned the tide in a long succession of Oxford wins. She was a commanding figure and a great beauty, as well as being filled with charm and knowledge, and the betrothal of these two at Cambridge was one of the events of the year. Grizel's father was the noted surgeon Horton Smith, who was killed by a horse bus as he was crossing Parliament Square with his umbrella raised and shouting, "They must give way to eminence."

Grizel put me up with the parson next door to her house. One evening we had an elderly bishop to stay. He was to confirm the college boys on the coming Sunday and we took him to the chapel to check the necessary arrangements. A large throne-like chair would be placed in the transept facing down into the nave and there he would sit when it came to the actual confirmation, the laying-on of hands. The school parson and I set the chair in the middle with its back to the altar. The bishop was old and had a fine head of silver grey hair and an enormous grey beard like unto pictures of the Almighty. He moved the throne slightly to one side saying, "Not in the middle, I pray. The young gentlemen are impressionable and might mistake me for a much more Illustrious Personage."

On one occasion I met at Grizel's a chap named Anthony Bevir who worked closely with Churchill. After dinner he told me privately, "I wish I had known that you knew Grizel when we were considering in Cabinet the question of your internment." He further said that he would have asked leave of Churchill to ask Grizel, which would have simplified matters, and thus would have ended it all. It had not occurred to me that Churchill and his inner cabinet might have thought of internment, and I was too astonished to ask Bevir for any elaboration. When I returned to London I checked and found that he was Churchill's Private Secretary for Home Affairs.

It was quite a change: being offered the safe Tory seat of Eastbourne only ten years earlier, with all the advantages His Grace's man had claimed would accompany it, to being considered for internment as a potential traitor. Perhaps it said more about the British system than it did about my character. All that I had done was to show my extreme loyalty by denouncing the intentions of Hitler before it was polite or socially acceptable to do so.

CHAPTER TEN

War Years

I SPENT most of the war years in London, getting on with work of one kind or another. In June 1940, while still in pilot officer's uniform, I was briefed to defend Canon Morris and other members of his Peace Pledge Union at their trial at Bow Street over the poster "Wars will cease when men refuse to fight. What are you going to do about it?" The prosecution pressed this as an attempt to create disaffection amongst servicemen. The trial was noted for the appearance of Sir Donald Somervell. This was said to be the only occasion in history when the attorney general had come in person to prosecute at Bow Street. If a case called for the personal attention of the attorney general, he would normally be represented by the senior one of the Crown prosecuting team at the Old Bailey, or even by the solicitor general, his immediate junior.

Mary Adams came to court as an intermediary and it was she who helped to settle the trial. The weakest of our defences was that the poster had been devised and published two years before. During the hearing with Somervell, we offered to withdraw the poster at once. At his suggestion, I told the magistrate of it in open court before our final addresses. The more sensible defence was that we were in the war to defend the right, amongst other things, to free expression of opinions and we should not willingly reject that principle. I cited a statement of Mr Justice "Owlie" Stable from a case in the King's Bench Division earlier in the month:

"The expression of views, no matter how unpopular, how fantastic or how wrong-headed they may appear to the majority, is a right, and a right which I, among others, am paid to see observed... It is those views which are held by only a few, those views which are unpopular, those views which do run counter

139

to the views of the great majority of mankind, particularly in times of national emotional crisis, such as war – it is those views which this court should be particularly zealous to protect."

Sir Robert Dummett, the Chief Magistrate, adopted this in his judgement and dismissed the case.

Although legislation decreeing compulsory military service made allowance for pacifists, the official view was that they were cowards and shirkers. I had had no previous contact with pacifism but found conscientious objectors to be men and women of principle. I certainly never had the feeling that I was dealing with a client who was really a cheat or a fraud. One pacifist I remember was Victor Rose, a member of the Independent Labour Party, who was rejected by the conscientious objectors' tribunal, and so appeared at the Brentford Magistrates' Court. He chose to go to trial, which came on at the Middlesex Quarter Sessions before Mr Thorpe, KC. I think this was in May 1942. Thorpe opposed the calling of witnesses to the character, integrity and sincerity of Rose and argued that as the tribunal had rejected him, he was not genuine and there could be no diminution of the sentence from the maximum of two years. Finally, twelve months' sentence was imposed, which he saw as lenient.

When I returned to the Bar after my brief interlude with the RAF, Donald Somervell told me that he had followed in the cabinet all that had gone on about my case. He said that he wasn't going to allow any of that sort of persecution; "friend Ernie" had no influence over any aspect of Bar life and never would have. He knew that I had had many nominations for prosecutions on the Western Circuit when Tom Inskip was A-G and promised that I would have some from him. Somervell was true to his word and I was soon doing trials from Bodmin to Bristol to Winchester, both at circuit towns and at quarter sessions.

The war brought a great reduction in the work of all courts. Young males were called up, and convictions were no bar to military service so long as you kept quiet about them. Other civilians were too busy as volunteers in the ARP and similar forms of service and had no time to squabble in the civil courts. Occasionally men turned up in the Temple in uniform on leave and fitted in a case or two. You were entitled to appear in court in uniform without wig or gown. Those still at the Bar took briefs marked "Mr (Still-here) for Mr (Hero-absent-on-War-Service)". You took half-fees for that and hoped that your clerk would mark it a bit higher to make up.

However, the government introduced a weight of wartime Emergency Legislation by Order in council with the minimum reference to parliament and corresponding to the Defence of the Realm Acts of the First World War. These led to very little litigation but to much advising. For example, the government wished to take rights over all real property and passed decrees accordingly. The London estates such as Portman, Westminster and Russell held their lands on a variety of titles and subtitles, the complexity of which could not be known to the draughtsmen of the rules. Their solicitors (Linklaters, Farrer & Co, Theo Goddard, and such firms) came to me with their ducal estates.

Members of chambers distinguished themselves in various ways. Frank Soskice served as a soldier in East Africa. Michael Lee became a sailor and was highly decorated. His main feat was to capture a submarine by jumping onto the deck from a small naval boat, armed only with a cutlass. (After I went to Stalin's funeral, Michael insisted that Soskice should not keep me in chambers as my being there would impede his promotion and that of everyone else. He went on to become His Honour Judge Michael Lee and earned an honourable retirement.)

Tommy (TNC) Burrows was a handsome young man and doing well at the Bar. He flew with the RAF and made all the outings and bombings needed to gain promotion and to earn a distinguished medal. He committed the error of taking advantage of the wife of a most superior officer. All this he told me on what proved to be his final leave. The only remedy against a certain amount of future disquiet on his RAF station was death or glory. He expected to come back next time with a VC or better. He gave me a short manuscript with his views about the future organisation of social and political life in England. It was lost when we were blown out of our chambers at 5 Essex Court. Tommy likewise was lost. He held on too long over a factory on the Baltic coast of Germany and was shot down.

The Inner Temple was very heavily bombed. Fire-watching was compulsory for city workers but we sorted it out so that it was not usually more than one night a week. Those who dwelt in the Inn were mostly older people and retired judges or their widows, who had moved out of

London for the duration. As a result, residents were not available as fire watchers or air raid wardens. Most of those who guarded the Temple slept in chambers for their one night. Our Wednesday shift usually practised climbing somewhere or squirting with a stirrup pump before we dispersed. For a long period there was an alarm every night until eventually the rule was that we took no action until we heard a bomb fall in our neighbourhood. In the city we were surrounded by firemen and professional air-raid wardens and, to tell the truth, they were so efficient and ready that our most useful job was to find the easiest way for their equipment to come in and to guide them to the scene of the incident.

Bert Brooks was Chief Fire Warden for the Inn and he would take me up on the roof of Middle Temple Hall to check that the water buckets and sand buckets were full. We had a forty-rung ladder, the longest I have climbed. I pretended to be quite "at home" on ladders and if there were no wind I would go up comfortably, but I was always a bit scared of any commotion. One night I saw a succession of fire-bombs strike from east to west on the South Bank from Blackfriars Bridge to Westminster Hall perhaps half-a-dozen times. The whole was ablaze for hours. It prepared the way for the Festival of Britain Building in 1951 and for all the development that has now followed it.

One explanation of the bombing of the Temple and of the South Bank opposite was that we had an exceptional target in Inner Temple Gardens. This was an enclosed practice range for air gunners, built of corrugated iron sheets and shining like the sun. It was the most curious shape, a sort of rhomboid. The north wall must have been ten feet by ten, and twenty feet away was the south wall of forty feet by forty. Air-gunners fired from the small part at the image of an attacking aircraft that could appear at any point on the enormous screen opposite. Guns were aimed and pressed, and an electronic process at once recorded where the imaginary bullets would have gone. We heard that of the many thousands of gunners who trained there, none had ever scored an inner on the target. There were no bomb-hits on the practice range for it was protected by a barrage balloon operated by a score of young women. On seeing this, Jim Cooper recognised that the German High Command would understand the importance of this target while the pilots would equally understand the importance of the barrage balloon and so would veer to left or right of it. Foreseeing the result, Jim Cooper had recommended that the library be emptied and the more delicate parts of Temple Church be protected with sandbags. He had also suggested that the wharfingers on the South Bank should be advised to keep their warehouses as empty as possible. The books were saved but sandbags could not help against direct hits.

A hundred yards north of the balloon, bombs and fires cut a swathe from Middle Temple Lane to Kings Bench Walk. It was wide enough to demolish the Inner Temple Hall and Library, Crown Office Row, the Master's House and what is now Francis Taylor Building, and to gut the Temple Church. With Janet and the children safe in the country, we had no house of our own in town and I put up wherever I could. One morning I arrived from safe hiding halfway up Hampstead Hill with Stephen Murray to find Brick Court destroyed and the quadrangle occupied by a pile of smoking brick rubble. The ground-floor entry to 5 Essex Court was filled with rubble and I climbed up over the pile that led conveniently into a window of my room on the first floor. Chambers were intact except that some windows were blown in and a few small hurricanes had muddled up the papers; few were lost. On the same night, at least one fire-bomb landed on Middle Temple Hall. It came through the east end and broke the wonderful screen into a thousand fragments. Earlier in the week, I had been on fire-watch duty on the roof of that hall.

Many Haldane Society members were away in the war and, for want of anyone else, I took over as chairman. We were anxious to help with every piece of war effort that we could. To give an example of the range of work, according to the minutes for October 1941, at one meeting the executive committee wrote to the war cabinet offering the services of our Law and Reconstruction Subcommittee; offered to the Fabian Society our pamphlets on police, on prostitution, and on a proposed Ministry of Justice; discussed the publication of guides to military law for soldiers and airmen;[2] arranged for the benchers of Gray's Inn to entertain the Soviet Ambassador Ivan Maisky; organised members who were fluent in the appropriate languages to provide lectures for refugee lawyers; set up a joint conference with the NCCL; elected delegates to the National Peace Council; agreed to subscribe a guinea to Finsbury's Lenin Memorial Fund; and accepted Clem

---

2 The companion work, a guide to the law for sailors, was written by me and, I think, had already been adopted by the navy and was circulated in many thousands. I wrote it during the first of the London bombings.

Attlee's resignation as vice-president. He didn't tell us why he resigned, but we thought it was because we had praised the Russian war effort.

We set up through the Haldane an international group aimed at bringing together refugee lawyers from various European countries and helping them to establish themselves in London. T Tylor, a young solicitor with Coward Chance, and I were joint secretaries. We ran free classes in the Temple, giving foundation courses in the common law, and covering such topics as company law, contract and tort and crime. We then discovered, as should have been obvious, that one of their main needs was private international law, being the rules by which ordinary dealings of men are continued or integrated across foreign borders (for example, in marriage, divorce, inheritance and business affairs). By 1943, our members were all foreseeing the day of their return home. This activity went on busily enough until I went to the pits, and by the time I came back, had completely died. I hope it was of use to someone.

In the late summer of 1940, Otto Sling sought me out in London. He claimed acquaintance with Christian Maxwell, who had helped organise escape routes from Prague. Otto was a fair-haired chap with a determined manner. As a young medical student, he had gone to Spain in support of the Czechoslovak contingent. At the front he was twice buried alive and went home with a bullet in the lung. He'd had to leave Czechoslovakia just before the German occupation of 15th March 1939 because he was a member of the Communist Party and Jewish. Otto was enthusiastic and indefatigable, a powerful organiser. He demanded premises and furniture in central London for setting up Young Czechoslovakia, a left-wing youth club for young Czechs and Slovaks in London. Premises were two a penny, and many friends had furniture that they were bound to lose if it were just left about. Lists were kept, but whether anything was ever returned is most doubtful. Next, he wanted money to finance the club. There was a news-sheet, lectures, cinema, English lessons. Then money was needed to finance some publication of Czech writings, and so it went on. I agreed to be a sponsor of the Czechoslovak-British Friendship Club, and later served as Treasurer.

Otto was a real inspiration to many young Britons. He recruited a team to back him, one of whom was a lovely girl named Marian, who worked with youth groups and then for civil liberties. As Marian Slingova, she later became a Czech patriot of high standing. I came to know them both as good friends. I shared lodgings with Otto at times in at least three different places in London. One such lodging was with Jack Brent, whom Otto helped to nurse. They were both heroes from Spain. Otto's wound was used to keep him out of the Czech army which was as much to the right of centre as was Benes and his government. By 1944, the bulk of them were based in Moscow and were firmly on the left, and a prime contributor to this change was Otto Sling. He was accepted into a medical contingent and set out for the territories liberated by the advancing Soviet army.

The Yugoslav government-in-exile had also set up in London. Their Minister of War, General Mihailovic, led the Chetnik forces, which were thought to be the centre of resistance to Germany but were so busy fighting the Communist leader, Tito, that Hitler gave them some co-operation. In Britain, we heard only jumbled reports of Tito and his partisans, who were fighting in the mountains for the Allied cause. In the middle of the war, Mrs Margaret Lloyd set up the Yugoslavia Emergency Committee and became its secretary; I was messenger-boy and letter-writer. We published all we could find about Tito and got his stories into the press and on the radio.

Margaret was a friend and neighbour of Mary Adams and, as one of the Russells of Woburn, she had connections and competence to organise anything. Margaret also had sufficient money to aid the causes she backed. Her husband, Dick, was a leading civil servant and seemed to keep her fully informed over matters wider than his own department. Margaret brought in as sponsors a gallant array of knights and ladies, and politicians both left and right. It might be expected that she would approach the Lords and Ladies and that I would deal with the politicians, particularly the hard left such as Pritt and Gallacher. It was not so, for she knew them better than I did.

Tito sent to Britain Leo Mattes, a young journalist but also a warrior from the mountains. From a single room, he provided an embryo embassy. He and Mrs Lloyd summoned me with their plan already in outline. Fitzroy Maclean had brought to England a brilliant young partisan leader named Vlatko Velebit from the mountains of the same name. He was a lawyer from Belgrade and a powerful advocate. Maclean had introduced him to General Eisenhower and the British military leaders with great success. Margaret was concerned that Churchill had not yet seen Velebit and told me to organise a meeting of MPs, preferably Tories, which would fill the gap. So much was Tito in the news with his successes that within the week we had forty Tory and a few Labour MPs gathered at the Royal Empire Society in Northumberland Avenue.

Vlatko Velebit, who had an excellent command of English and was obviously very well-educated, told them what was happening and what was needed. He then asked why Tito was not receiving tanks from Churchill. (A partial explanation is that when Tito's men were fighting in the mountains and woods, they had little use for heavy equipment; now they had come down into open country.) It was rumoured (and very much hoped) that within a week of the meeting with Velebit, the tanks were rumbling towards Bari on the way to Dubrovnik.

In about October 1941, Peggy Cripps summoned me with a message from her father. I knew Stafford Cripps quite well through the party and through chambers' life. The message was, "The Old Man wants to see you. I've recommended you for a job that he wants done." And so I went along to parliament to see Churchill. He said, "Cripps says you can do this job for me. It's the following. If English people believe what I've been teaching since 1918 there'll be no War Effort. And now is when we want a War Effort. I've been teaching them the Russians are monsters, they're devils from Hell. They eat their own children, they teach their children to eat their children. But how the children survive to eat their children..." says the Old Stupid to me, but he was in that sort of mood. "Now I've got to change all that. Cripps says you can do it."

I said, "All right. If you want that done, I'll have a go."

He said, "After the war, you won't want people to know that you spent a substantial part of your war effort in pro-Soviet propaganda, and I won't want people to know that I set you on to it, so we'd better keep it quiet. It may take you a couple of years, but you must start at once. You may choose your own team. Make them work hard and you can have all the money you want from Williams." (He was the Minister of Information.) "Now, get on with it! And come and tell me how you're getting on." There was no more formality than that, and such a truce isn't made forever. There was a bit of a debate as to which outfits we should approach. It was decreed that the Dean of Canterbury and Churchill's wife Clementine would lead their team in an attack on the adult population, backed by the newspapers. I was to take on the senior schools of England. So we set up an outfit appropriately named the Anglo-Soviet Youth Friendship Alliance for Understanding and Goodwill.

Our team was mostly young women whom I had met in the peace groups that attracted progressive-minded young people before the war. Kootie Hookham became the leader of the team, with Helen Guiterman as deputy. In the youth anti-Fascist peace movement, they had aimed at cementing peace by organising anti-Nazi co-operation on a world scale; now they threw themselves into the present activity with enormous vigour. They were as war-like as could be. Part-time workers came from the trade union movement such as the Engineers' Union and the staff association of the London County Council, as it was then, and youth groups including the Scouts, Guides and the YWCA. We soon had a national council to which came representatives not only of all the main youth organisations in the land, but of many local bodies besides.

We met at such places as the House of Commons or the LCC and held monthly meetings that really did inspire the work. Our office was a minute house at 12b St George Street, Hanover Square and we burst the walls with activity. We determined to do some propaganda amongst all grades of schools but, above all, amongst the senior classes, which were the immediate feeding-ground for the factories and for the services for the next few years. The Ministry of Information gave us every support we asked for. We could send anything sensible to Russia, and could eventually bring anyone or anything from Russia that was worth having by way of propaganda. We were, in effect, given a blank cheque on the Ministry.

We had some success. For example, with our first appeal for English youngsters to send parcels to the Red Army. We contacted the secondary schools in half-a-dozen main education areas such as the LCC and the West Riding of Yorkshire. The invitation was to send a small parcel of knitted goods, or something useful to a soldier such as stationery for him to write home, a toothbrush and toothpaste, and one or more of the half-dozen items that a member of the Red Army was allowed to take as his travelling companions. There was also to be a letter addressed to "Dear Ivan" in Russian, if possible. We would forward the parcels, and printed on the appeal in scarlet letters was the firm instruction: "Send no money. Parcels only, postage prepaid." Many tons of goods arrived, and £16,000 in cash. The children were eager and enthusiastic because by the end of

1941 the Russians had started to reverse the German advance, administering to the Nazis their first set-back. This was near Rostock, where Russian cavalry were able to attack the Germans from behind.

In the course of such appeals, many hundreds of tons of modest parcels were received at the office and crated up for carriage on the Murmansk convoys. I suppose most of them were lost in those bitter seas, but a great many got through because hundreds of letters came back from "Dear Ivans" in reply, leading to further work for our volunteers. Additionally, there were essay competitions on such themes as "What I will say when I next meet Stalin". We usually took age-ranges from fourteen to eighteen, or sixteen to eighteen, and had many thousands of essays. It seemed as if every literate person in England who wasn't in the services was reading essays and judging them. The final judging between half-a-dozen essays would be by chaps like Arthur Mee, editor of the *Children's Encyclopaedia*, with prizes presented by literary giants.

We organised teams of speakers who lectured in schools throughout the country, often going out night after night. We brought over young Russian heroes and heroines, including Lyudmila Pavlichenko, a young sniper from the Red Army who shot 309 Germans in the defence of Odessa and Sevastopol; although wounded four times, she had refused to leave the battlefield. Later arrivals included the youngest admiral in the Red Navy, aged perhaps twenty-eight, with his epaulettes and his golden dagger; the youngest Red Army general, equally young and covered with gold; and the first woman to breed a thousand pigs. These and other startling young figures were paraded round the country and, through interpreters, we presented them to thousands of young people at schools and at public meetings. They amply performed the work that Churchill wanted.

Early in 1942, we held a public meeting in Sudbury, Suffolk. The organisation in which Mrs Churchill took an active part sent Tom Driberg as one of the speakers. He had been elected independent member for Maldon, Essex where in 1945 he was to be re-elected for Labour. Before going to the meeting, Tom came to Assington for high tea. He arrived sitting in the back of a large chauffeur-driven car and made no move towards getting out until the chauffeur came round and opened the door for him. He did not enquire whether the driver was fed or rested, or what he could do during the meeting. It upset me to see with what contempt he treated the man.

Soon after this, I attended the Labour Party annual conference, representing the Haldane Society. At the opening meeting, George Oliver, Chairman of the Conference Arrangement Committee, expressed doubt as to whether I had a right to vote "in view of reports of what had been happening at Sudbury". I asked him later what caused this extraordinary outburst. He was a barrister and owed a sort of fraternal duty of good faith. At first he declined to answer on the "You know quite well" basis. Finally, he complained that we had been raided by the police in the presence of the chief constable of the county, that we held a Russian friendship meeting in Sudbury, and that we had entertained an MP who had just beaten a Labour candidate at Maldon. George was MP for Ilkeston, Derby for forty years. Poor Ilkeston and poor old George and, for that matter, under George's irrational tutelage, poor Labour Party.

Kotie Hookham had enlisted her sister Margot Fonteyn as one of the vice-presidents of the ASYFA; others included the actor John Mills and the renowned pianist Moura Lympany. Our sponsors were equally eminent, including Dr Julian Huxley, Michael Foot and Megan Lloyd George, MP. We thought of ourselves as a perfectly respectable group, but it was clear that many others did not share that view. At the Caxton Hall in March 1942, Stafford Cripps had addressed one of our earliest meetings with the warning, "We must not make our outlook on the future too narrow by over-concentration on Anglo-Soviet friendship." This was an extraordinary statement, when Anglo-Soviet friendship was the sole purpose of the organisation.

At a point when there was serious shortage of men for vessels on the Atlantic crossings, I volunteered for the navy. I attended a medical examination, at which the other men were skinny, aged gentlemen, all either retired or nearly retired merchant marine seamen, but needed for their long sea experience. Physically, I suppose the contrast was fairly striking and, as with the other tests and exams, it would be silly to deny that I had advantages. After an intelligence test, there was an interview with three bright young women officers. A great fuss to find my papers. Why were they not there? Where had they gone to? But then it was discovered that they had been ceded in a shortlist of their own. Where had you been to school? "Ah, yes. Nelson, of course. No doubt connected with the Admiral." Nelson, New Zealand was as much connected with that gentleman as Wellington, Marlborough and Blenheim were connected with their namesakes.

However, with the disclosure of a certain measure of contact with landborne military forces and the experience of sailing out of and into every inlet in the south and south-east coast of England where a cockleshell could safely berth, the demand was, "We shall want you next week at Dartmouth, at the officers training school for the navy. Can you make yourself free?" I replied that I understood that no one was promoted to any officer's position unless he had first served his time in the ranks. "We haven't any time for that sort of thing now. You shall get your orders at once." If urgency and need had shortened the time for action in that service, so Ernie Bevin's technique which had kept me out of the air force acted within days to protect the navy from me. I wrote asking where my orders had got to and saying that my address had not changed, but there came no response. I wrote again, complaining without making any specially smart points, but again no response, then dropped the matter.

At least there was still work in the courts. A major case in 1943 was the Hereford Birched Boy Scandal, when the whole nation debated the quality of the unpaid and unqualified persons who served on the local Bench. Three such magistrates, sitting as a juvenile court, ruled that as punishment for theft, William Payne, aged thirteen, and Dennis Craddock, aged eleven, be removed from their homes and handed over to the local education authority until they reached the age of eighteen. Each was also to suffer four strokes of the birch, and as soon as possible. The birching was carried out within minutes, before the respective parents had been given time to appeal. Mr Payne pronounced himself quite satisfied with his son's treatment and played no further part in the matter. Mr Craddock did lodge an appeal, but found that it was too late to save his boy from the beating.

Father Craddock was a special constable and knew his legal rights. He invoked the process of Certiorari, which moved the Divisional Court to bring up and quash the verdict and sentence, and somehow to rehabilitate the suffering bottom. The case was heard by Lord Chief Justice Caldecote, who thought the whole process monstrous; Mr Justice Charles, who thought it hilarious; and Mr Justice Hallett, who simply followed on. Between them, they quashed the conviction and expressed outrage at the clear incompetence of the magistrates. Tom Inskip said that their actions had gone so far beyond irregularity of procedure that they amounted to a denial of natural justice; "everything had been done wrong that could be done wrong." Mr Justice Charles agreed that the actions of the magistrates were "absolutely outrageous", adding that the affidavit in which the chairman, Mrs Bentley-Taylor, attempted to explain what had happened "had an air of satisfaction and really made the matter worse".

Because this was at a point in the war when there was virtually no domestic news, the press was delighted with the Craddock case. Questions were asked in parliament and a motion was tabled in the Commons, asking that the magistrates concerned be removed from the Bench. Lord Morris added to the quality of the debate by declaring that "the type of men they wanted were qualified magistrates, not retired old dodderers of either sex". The Craddocks took out a writ against the magistrates and against the police officer who had carried out the birching, claiming damages for wrongfully taking away, false imprisonment, causing physical harm, and loss of the boy's services; and the three beleaguered Hereford worthies came down to London to plead their case before the lord chancellor.

The NCCL gave Mr Craddock every assistance. His son's case was an excellent example of the incompetence and prejudice the working classes felt they habitually received from the middle-class meddlers who ran these courts. Herbert Morrison, fearing that there might be some undermining of the war effort if people thought that their civil rights were in jeopardy, went to Claude Schuster of the Lord Chancellor's Department, who recommended that he take advice from Rayner Goddard. Goddard was of outstanding brilliance and had gone to the Court of Appeal in October 1938 as Lord Justice. He is said to have advised that Whitehall instruct an appropriate junior to present the case for the Crown and give him, Goddard, the biggest bucket of whitewash that they could find. He would then go to Hereford, hold an inquiry and put all matters to rights.

Hubert Parker, then Treasury Junior, later Lord chief Justice, was sent for the Crown and I was hired by the Crown to represent the Craddocks, and there followed in Hereford a week of the Birched Boy Inquiry. Hereford was a quiet cathedral town, run by the white-faced Hereford cattle and the Bulmer cider family. We held our sessions at the local Assembly Hall, where there was ample room for thirty or more representatives of the press. Hubert Parker and I held a press conference each morning before we began, and very often again after court, setting out the course we intended to take and what evidence would be presented. The reporters and the nation relished every word of it. I do not now remember — or even understand — how we came to abandon every rule for the proper conduct of English barristers by holding these American-style press conferences.

It became apparent that the proceedings before the juvenile court had been of a most informal and improper character. The boys had been charged with breaking and entering certain premises, stealing pencils and other small items valued at 11s. 6d from a school, theft from a furniture store of articles valued at £36, and with malicious damage on an extensive scale to other goods in the store. From the start, it was presumed that they were guilty of all charges. Chief Inspector Wheatley, who was prosecuting, offered no real evidence and before the question of guilt or innocence had been formally determined, made a most biased and untruthful statement — namely, that Dennis Craddock had asked for other charges to be taken into consideration.

Although Dennis Craddock admitted stealing from the school, at both the remand hearing and the trial he had consistently pleaded "Not Guilty" to the other charges so that the requirement of proof should have been of a most strict sort. Mrs Bentley-Turner seemed genuinely surprised when we pointed out the pleas of "Not Guilty" in the court register. "I can only assure you I listened to the case in the belief that the pleas had been ones of 'Guilty'. I can only suppose it was carelessness on my part." Of her colleagues, Mrs Ainslie had thought the pleas were "Guilty to all three charges except breaking and entering", and Mr Bufton claimed not to have realised that, from the point of view of an affidavit, it mattered how the boys had pleaded; he conceded that that might be an admission of crass ignorance.

The question arose as to how long it took for the chief inspector to drag the boy from the court to the police station. Mr Craddock said it was about ten minutes' walk. Finally, Goddard disclosed that during the luncheon adjournment he, too, had gone and tested himself with a stopwatch. "At an ordinary pace", it had taken him just under three minutes. I challenged that he had run the distance, knowing that in his youth Goddard had been a notable sprinter at the college that Balliol men addressed as Bloody Trinity and had won the 100 yards race for Oxford in the university sports. He denied having run to the police station and insisted that he had moved only at the shuffling sort of pace that a bulky policeman might adopt when pulling a reluctant boy.

The main aim of Goddard and of Hubert Parker (aside from his desire to become lord chief justice) was to show the innocence of the magistrates. It meant the most absurd and perverse rendering of the proceedings and of all the entries in the books of the court. The outcome was as Goddard had forecast. He wrote a report establishing that the boys had denied only breaking and entering; those charges were at once dropped. The boy Craddock had admitted his guilt from the beginning. Every record that he had pleaded "Not Guilty" was entered in error by the junior clerk and not noticed by the chairman of the court, who had signed the register as correct without troubling to read it. (Mrs Bentley-Turner promptly resigned from the Bench but was succeeded as chairman by the self-confessed "crassly ignorant" Mr Bufton, on the unanimous vote of all the other Hereford magistrates.)

After this case, Goddard went whizzing ahead. In July 1944, he went to the Lords as a Lord of Appeal in Ordinary and in 1946 became Lord Chief Justice. After his retirement in 1958, Goddard lived in the Temple and came regularly to lunch in a wheelchair. (The same wheelchair still waits for his successor just inside the main door of the Benchers' department of the Inner Temple.) When I first became a Member of the Bench, Goddard vexed everybody at lunch by saying that he wanted to die and insisting that no one was willing to sit next to him. I had that honour and when he looked round and saw that it was me, he said, "Mills, you know very well I didn't run. I only walked and shuffled to the police station." He habitually addressed me as Mills, taking his lead from Brian McKenna, who had introduced us in 1932.

Another important case in 1943 was the prosecution of Dave Springhall. This was my only real spy trial. Len White was Secretary of the Civil Service Clerical Association, the biggest of the civil service trade unions. He was an active supporter of the NCCL and was at times a member of the executive committee. Len was a short, dapper, business-like fellow, whom we called the Napoleon of Whitehall. He told me in late 1942 that a member of his, Mrs Sheehan, who was a clerk in the air ministry, had been charged with sedition. Prosecuting counsel had told him that the hearing would be before a magistrate and *in camera*, with a guarantee of no publicity. The case would be presented as a trifling one in which Mrs

Sheehan had revealed a secret about some detail of jet propulsion, but almost accidentally and certainly not maliciously; the penalty would be the slightest possible.

On this information he had decided, with the Clerical Association's solicitor, that they ought not to have Mrs Sheehan defended. I knew prosecuting counsel and was sure that Len could have complete confidence in him. Mrs Sheehan pleaded guilty and was awarded a three months' sentence. What Len White was not told was that this leniency had been purchased by Mrs Sheehan's promise to give evidence against Dave Springhall, were he to be prosecuted. If she had been defended, she would not have given any such promise. Indeed, she would have pleaded not guilty and might have been acquitted, for the evidence against her was very slight indeed.

In June 1943, Springhall, under his given name, Douglas, was tried *in camera* at the Old Bailey for disclosing secrets to an enemy. He had been a political commissar with the British Battalion of the International Brigade in Spain. In his current role as national organiser of the Communist Party, Springhall was in touch with all Communist civil servants and so learned any secrets that they had. He applied his skills particularly to the junior edge of the civil service. From Mrs Sheehan he had obtained details of a method of deflecting or confusing the radar of an opponent by releasing a handful of shreds of foil. As the pieces fluttered slowly to the ground, each bit reflected the radar and gave the effect of a rainstorm. Under this cover, an aeroplane might escape detection. Springhall handed details of this and of an advance in jet propulsion straight to an officer at the Soviet Embassy.

Maxwell Fyfe, the solicitor general, prosecuted. The material witnesses were Mrs Sheehan and a senior airforce person to show the importance of the information disclosed. Part of our defence was that it was well known that we had shared all our military secrets with the United States when they were not even in the war. It was perverse to treat the Soviets as enemies when they were bearing and breaking the heaviest Nazi attack. Springhall was convicted and sentenced to seven years' imprisonment. The Communist Party expelled him from membership for the ignominy of being caught.

It has since been claimed that, in the early 1930s, Springhall was involved in the recruitment of the Cambridge Apostles to the Soviet cause. If he did help the Cambridge spies, he was the only member of that group to have spent time inside a British jail. There is no saying what a haul might have been made, had a Springhall been loose in Oxford. If he really had such a success at Cambridge, I find it surprising, for he was most indiscreet. He was forever telling all and sundry that he had given the Russians every new invention he could find. Perhaps he was trying to create an atmosphere in which his Russian indiscretions might seem like American ones, for while our American ally had full access to everything, our Soviet ally was systematically frozen out.

The British authorities may have looked down on the Russians as second-best, but the workers didn't agree. Many of our students from 1941–2 were now in the factories. It had reached the point where almost every big gun produced had written on it in red letters GUNS FOR JOE. And tanks were labelled TANKS FOR JOE, or sometimes T'ANKS FOR JOE (i.e. thanks). I went to Churchill every six months and told him how much the ASYFA had spent, how many essays had been written, and reported on our other successes. Then, in 1944, he summoned me to his room at the House of Commons quite out of turn and said, "Look at these pictures in the newspapers. This is what you've done. 'Tanks for Joe'. Why not tanks for me? Why not 'Tanks for Winnie'? Aren't I any good? You've gone too far. You had better go and do something else. What do you want to do?" Churchill always spoke in this entertaining, gruff voice as though he were very grave and serious, always making a great joke of it all.

I had been chairman of the Anglo-Soviet Youth Friendship Alliance for two and a half years. I had run all over the country, delivering perhaps a hundred lectures, and my reputation as a hardened left-winger with a tendency towards approval for Russia meant that the family had gone a bit short of money. When the pro-Russian activities were at their height, it all became too much for the leading city solicitors, who had made my first eight years at the English Bar so entertaining and lucrative, and they politely disappeared. What could I do next?

I told Churchill that if he was fed up with me, I'd go to the mines. He said, "Well, you'll never get another chance, so you'd better go and do that if you want to," then slyly added, "Ernie can't chuck you out of that." He expressed his certainty that we would meet again. (We did, after the war – looking over the shoulder in the House of Commons urinals, which are placed near to the Commons chamber, handy for old men in a hurry.) Few had volunteered for the coal-mines before. Every sensible person seemed to have preferred the services to the pits. I had no experience of underground matters, but thought it was probably safer there than on top. It was ironic that Bevin had inadvertently provided me with a way of giving some war service, and that he had blessed it with his own name, but getting into mining as a Bevin Boy took some months to sort out.

After my disappointments with the RAF and the navy, I had lost all enthusiasm for military service and certainly didn't wish to have the same humiliation again. When the army began making tentative approaches and expressed interest in my availability, I was somewhat wary. I applied for and received several postponements, but was eventually instructed to report to a named unit at Colchester on 20th April 1944. They also sent a travel warrant and subsistence money for the journey from London. Before I could use these bounties, a letter arrived demanding their immediate return and countermanding the instruction to report. I replied that I would consider returning the money and the warrant if I were given a fair report as to why the army had rejected me. There was no reply, and therefore no return of money.

Chapter Eleven

Yorkshire Main

IN JULY 1944 I received a voucher for a third-class train fare to Doncaster, a few shillings for food, and instructions to report to Askern Colliery, the Bevin Boys' camp north of Doncaster. Askern was a smallish pit. One shaft was working coal while the other had been converted into a training centre.

Bevin was a chap to be despised on principle, but the idea of forcing people into the pits was a sensible one because we were dependant on coal. I was a volunteer because it seemed to me a wonderful chance of seeing more of English working-class life, on which score I was a bit short. After all, I came from a colony that had rejected the idea of classes and class distinction. I had seen it very actively in Oxford and in my first days at the Bar, but wanted a better understanding.

Mining families didn't want their sons to go into the pits in wartime since the services were thought to offer the chance of a safer and better life. The Bevin Boy system was aimed at getting a selection of young men from all classes in order to placate the miners and their sons, to persuade them that they weren't to be isolated and kept in the pits. One met in training camp young farmers, city workers, seamen, students from public schools, and some who had already got into university but were now short-circuited for a while. One who died as the result of a pit accident was a member of a ducal family.

The older Bevin Boys and those who came from the forces often arrived with a desire to help the miners, but most of the younger men resented the compulsion. During the six weeks' training, they began to take an interest in the novelty of the work. They realised its importance from the national point of view, and eventually most were won to willing co-operation.

The general reaction of miners to the Bevin scheme was that it had at least one advantage: when he returned to his ordinary life, each Bevin Boy would be an ambassador to carry the miners' case to an ill-informed and bewildered public. In a dormitory of twelve Bevin Boys, we had three with broken bones in the hand in a fortnight. With the exception of myself, every boy in that dormitory ultimately proved unable to carry on in the mine, or remained and suffered some severe injury. That they were proud of these injuries is of some importance when considering the overall success of the scheme.

The first week's training was conducted above ground. In the second week, we were sent underground to get used to the dark and the heat. One of the first coal-mining crimes named in the appropriate Acts of Parliament is going to sleep below ground. On the first day, at the first invitation to sit and rest for a moment, every one of us was sound asleep. The warmth can be oppressive, but I felt at home there where it's dark and warm and comfortable.

During the rest period on my first day above ground, one of the instructors asked if I knew Frank Cousins, then insisted that I must go and meet him. Frank was a Doncaster man through and through and was in his first TGWU job, based on the town. There had not been a volunteer there before nor, to use the modern term, a yuppy amongst the Bevin Boys, and so the training staff had probably been at pains to find out what my interests might be.

I had visited Doncaster on two previous occasions for meetings about Russia and the war. Both were crowded and excited gatherings in the Labour Hall; one presided over by the chairman of the Labour Party, and the other by the president of the Donny Co-Op – Alderman Judd, father of Frank Cousins' wife Annie. That evening I went unannounced and introduced myself, becoming a regular, if not frequent, visitor to the Cousins' house in that quarter of Doncaster called Downcast. It had been named after the shaft of some ancient pit, but was an inappropriate name for a distinctly upmarket neighbourhood.

After training, I was sent to the village of Edlington to work in the great Yorkshire Main colliery three miles south of Doncaster. In its time, just before the war, it is said to have been the greatest producer in England with 28,000 tons a week. A regiment of 3,000 worked at the pit; a village of 11,000 depended on it. Before nationalisation, it was one of the Big

Six, the property of Doncaster Amalgamated Collieries, and, from it, Mr Charles Markham, its previous owner, once boasted that he had drawn a cubic yard of gold.

Yorkshire Main was like a great ship. From every part of Edlington you could see the chimney or its smoke. In a quiet time, you could hear the pit-top machinery and the hooting and whistles. However, the smoke was the thing that really dominated the village. It poured up with the solid flocculence of new-shorn wool tumbling on the shearing floor. The column was so high that there seemed always to be a slight drift in it even when the air was still in the pit yard. To see the setting sun light up the rolls of billowing smoke with the wind arching over the plume at the chimney top was fascinating. And at all times it poured its load of foul soot on the land underneath.

The pit was sunk 3,000 feet in the Barnsley bed: hard bitumen coal, the finest steam coal in the world. At Edlington, the seam was about three feet six inches thick and was sandwiched between two other seams, making six feet or more of good coal. When Yorkshire Main was sunk round about 1911, miners came from every coal-field in Britain, and some from Europe. When the Doncaster pits were being sunk, it was common for a notice to be displayed: "No Yorkshiremen need apply." There grew in these villages a cosmopolitan community that lacked even the slight point of cohesion that comes from a common tradition.

While working at Yorkshire Main I lodged with Percy Wardle, President of the Pit Committee, and was made very much at home. Janet came up to visit on an occasional weekend, staying at the Cousins' house. I joined in whatever was going on in my pit village and in the union. Percy had some influence and we got it passed through the union that a penny a week should be deducted from everyone's pay for the Miners' Welfare Fund. The fund had a large building with a dance hall, a gym and so on, but it was hardly used except as a boozer on Friday and Saturday night and Sunday lunchtime, when it was filled.

In no time, we had PT classes arranged with an army instructor and boxing classes, which the boys loved. Bruce Woodcock, the British professional heavyweight champion, lived in Warmsworth, one village away from Edlington, so we got him to open the club. I had to spar two rounds with him. I wasn't much good at boxing but I was very good at running backwards. I could hit chaps and then get away from them. I couldn't hit hard enough to hurt, except to make noses bleed. Since I was quite good at that, I often won.

On the day shift, we had to report for duty by six a.m. at the pit-bottom. As it took some time to get the whole shift below ground, the carriage of men in cages (man-winding or man-turning) began at five-thirty. Any man who had not got his lamp from the lamp-cabin by five-fifty, when the buzzer went, was counted as "buzzed" and listed as an absentee. If he arrived at the lamp-cabin one minute late, he went home without pay. I came close to being buzzed on several occasions, but never missed the last drop; Percy never missed the first one.

On the day shift, we got up about four-thirty or five a.m. We went in our shifting clothes – tidy enough to see us home again through the streets in daylight – and wearing great hobnailed boots which could be heard like the clogs of Lancashire clumping down the streets. At first in the back streets one clumped along alone. Then a neighbouring door opened and a warm ray of light barred the street. The supporting clatter of the neighbour's boots gave you confidence. As you turned into the main street near the pit gate, there were shadowy figures all around, and all clattering. And, as you turned into the pit gate, you found yourself in a flood of men, all making for the baths.

Those coming on shift entered on the clean side where there were something over 2,000 lockers. The miner, clad only in his boots, went through the showers into the dirty side, where he had another locker containing his working clothes. This naked parade was one of the things that gave young miners their great respect for physical development and prowess. As they were undernourished and overworked in youth, their bodies were usually small, but often beautifully muscled as though by intensive physical culture.

The lockers were steam-heated so that all contents were thoroughly dried between shifts. The heat was almost sufficient to destroy and, I should think, would certainly have embarrassed any of the minor forms of life that might have been present. As you opened the dirty locker, the stench of clothes and socks puffed out. Putting on the foul working clothes we called "getting into your mook" (muck) and was the worst moment in the whole day.

In every part of the pit were edges that clutched at one's clothes like evil spirits in the legendary forest, tearing triangular nicks down the sleeves and the outside of trousers. Bit by bit, one or another developed until finally a jacket ended up with the back or arm torn completely out and held on only by a safety pin, and the trousers quite unsuitable for conventional wear. Before the pit-head baths were introduced, no miner could be seen walking through the streets with such tears and his wife was required to mend them all.

Last out of the locker came the helmet and the Dudley, a half-gallon metal water-bottle on a shoulder strap. Our lamps weighed eleven pounds, were a foot high and could be hung by their hook from a leather belt around the miner's waist. The miner thus burdened walked with his stomach thrust out to give the lamp a good forward carriage, his knees bent and pointed outwards so that the lamp bounced against the inner thigh rather than the bony knees, and he jogged along for all the world like a pregnant woman.

No one must take below anything that could make a light. Every old miner I have met has a story of a pit explosion, of dead bodies found and examined by their mates who must by law leave them exactly as they are found, and of the management later finding some smoking material beside the corpses where their mates happened not to see it. By planting evidence, the blame for the explosion could be passed on to deceased men.

(Readers may wish to skip some of the following pages which give detailed descriptions of coal-mining.)

In each shaft there were two cages counterbalanced. They started off so gently that you scarcely noticed they were moving. The cages accelerated until they passed in the middle so fast that the lights of the lamps in the opposite cage were not seen and there was only a slight flutter in the wind as they passed. This was a 3,000 feet drop, yet the cage slowed up so gently that you scarcely felt the change and the cage sometimes stopped half an inch above the bottom without hitting it at all. The only point at which one felt pressure was on the soles of the feet.

The winding rope was a steel cable strong enough to carry 100 tons. The end of the cable was pushed through a hole on top of the cage. The hundreds of separate steel strands were unravelled and spread out, then molten metal was poured over. In theory, once the metal had solidified, the cable could not be pulled out, although every miner had private visions of the winding rope tearing out of the cap in the case of an over-wind.

All pits have at least two shafts: one, open to the sky, down which the fresh air is drawn; and the second, up which the foul air is drawn by fans. If the way were open between the bottom of the shafts, fresh air would come down one shaft and be sucked straight up the other. To prevent this, the second shaft was sealed completely at the top (except for a hole through which the winding ropes passed) by a series of doors that opened against the wind pressure.

If you went in at the number two shaft, you were met with a sound like the rushing of a violent stream as the air sucked in through every crevice between the doors. The same sound was encountered at many points underground where the passage of air was barred by doors making an air lock. Every coal-face needed open airways at opposite ends; fresh air flowed to the face, while returning hot air flowed back to the pit bottom. By manipulating the doors and partial obstructions at different points, it was possible to regulate the precise speed and volume of air at any point on the face.

The great heat increased every smell. Break the skin of an orange and the smell would carry a hundred yards in a return airway. On the morning shift, with men who have been drinking a lot of beer the night before, the situation can be imagined. I never saw any toilet in Yorkshire Main but two thousand men each day used the pit for their ordinary purposes. So great is the drying effect of the wind that all excreta were quickly desiccated and the only problem was that of paper supply. We used instead a piece of stone or coal.

There was a great deal of explosive and poisonous gas. Where the coal is mined by machine, much dust is created, and it is not only the gas that is explosive, but also the very coal dust itself. The only remedy is to dilute the dust with finely ground limestone. This was scattered in the air-stream so that in every part of the mine coal-dust and stone-dust, intimately mixed and black-grey in colour, settled deep. Travelling by foot, the cloud became almost impenetrable. At the face, it was like an old-fashioned London fog with police flares showing through. Within half an hour, we were fouled from head to foot, blackened under our clothes, in our boots, and under our helmets. The only part clean was where a river of sweat had washed it off.

At the pit bottom, we waited until the foreman arrived with the routine of work for the shift, then set off for the coal-face. The men had to walk in along the roads where moving ropes and tubs added to the danger. Sometimes a special roadway was cut and a man-carrying tram was put in but this, too, was not entirely safe. In Yorkshire Main, one part of such a carriage became detached from the rope and was pushed up and jammed against the roof of the roadway so that one man was killed and several injured. On another occasion, a wheel came off the car and, as the carriage lurched over, one rider jumped off. He landed on the return rope running in the opposite direction and was bounced back under the wheels and killed.

The form of extraction adopted in Yorkshire Main was the long wall advancing method, then almost universally used in Britain. The coal-face was anything up to two hundred yards long, with roadways leading to the middle and to either end. This face did not advance its ends in either direction but might best be described as a tunnel that advanced sideways. It was necessarily exactly the height of the coal-seam being taken out, thus for a seam three feet thick, the face could be only three feet high.

For safety's sake, it is necessary to have above the coal-face a natural roof which will not break easily. If there are several seams of coal and the strata above the top one is of material which does not form a strong roof, it is customary for the top strata of coal to be left. It was claimed at the time that in British mines ninety-eight per cent to a hundred per cent of coal was extracted, but at Yorkshire Main we left behind and buried forever almost as much coal as we drew out.

The miners lined up side by side, facing the coal-wall and working into it with picks and shovels, a conveyor belt running behind them. If the face were worked properly, the coal would have been undercut by the cutter on the previous shift. The cutter was like a great steel box five feet long, three feet broad and two feet high. It was operated by compressed air and it moved along the whole face with a chainsaw running round a long arm, tearing out a cut four inches thick and four and a half feet into the coal at any prearranged height.

Then came the borer with a machine into which an enormous five-foot corkscrew was fitted. This bored into the coal towards the top of the face. Next came the cardox men with their thirty-pound weight steel shells (four feet long and of two-inch diameter) to be thrust into the holes. Each shell contained solid carbon dioxide at a pressure of many thousands of pounds to the square inch.

Once the face had been cleared, the men crouched at about twenty yards' distance. The shells burst with a muffled roar, leaving a foul and lingering smell. If this procedure had been carried out correctly, the colliers who came on the next shift would find about ten tons of coal per stint, so shaken that it could be readily detached from the coal-face and broken into a size convenient for loading onto the belt.

One difficulty was that as soon as the cutter had passed, the front of the face began to flake off and topple over, making it unsafe for the borer to do his work. Chocks or wedges knocked into the cut would uphold the face, but the cutter man was fully occupied in manipulating his clumsy giant and the management would not pay a separate man to do the chocking up. As a result, the boring was usually left until the coal-face had settled down. By then, it had been squashed down by the roof and the whole of the cut had closed up.

A coal-seam contains gas that collects between the vertical layers and when one layer is peeled off, the pressure is released and gas pushes the next layer out ready for falling. Cutting through all the layers causes the gas to ooze out. The miners then say that the "nature" or "virtue" has gone out of the coal. Coal that had settled down was more difficult to break off than if it had never been cut; it was lifeless and jammed hard by the roof. It was because the virtue had gone out of the coal that the Bevin Boys working on machine-got coal never bore the blue face-scars of their seniors.

When coal is being hand-got, if it is on the proper angle and has all its virtue in it, as one layer is peeled off along the line of cleavage, the roof pressure is shifted on to the next layer; the gas within begins to splutter and burst through the coal all up and down the face; overhead there are cracks and groans, with each one of which the roof and the coal-face shudder and rain down small bits of coal, and the face itself veritably boils. The collier rushes at it with his pick in a frenzy of joy and belts into it, leaping back as the great slabs come crashing down. It is then, when the gas bursts through the coal, that he gets the face wounds and the lifelong blue scars.

This working of the coal with its own innate energy is the true joy of hand-getting and the collier responds to it with delight at seeing his skill bring such results. There is nothing a miner loves better than to see the coal piling up along the belt and knowing that it is thundering into the tubs. I have cried with exhaustion and satisfaction, leaning against the coal-wall at the end of a shift when my whole stint was cleared off.

On 4 West each man's stint was four and a half yards wide and the distance we were expected to move forward each day (the "web") was four and a half feet. To prevent the roof falling in above the face, steel props were erected every four feet, with steel bars jammed in on top of them. The open space where coal had been extracted was called the "waste" or "gob", with millions of tons of rock above it. Unless packed tight with something as solid as the coal that had been taken out, this space was bound to close in. Props would be shattered and buried.

The roof must be of strong material if it is to protect the face. If strong, however, it tends to remain as an unbroken roof even when pressed down. It is like a giant lever whose fulcrum is just at the face, and it is here that the roof is most likely to break. To take the pressure off the face, we drew off the props, pulling them forward and forcing the roof to break off over the waste area. Removing the props and bringing the belt one web further forward was the job of the coal-face workers on the bye-shifts between coaling shifts.

Although the coal-turning shift with its row of gleaming lights, dense coal dust, sweating naked bodies shining through the gloom, the rush and bustle of the drive for coal, and then the river of the precious stuff that flows along the belt, was the most interesting shift, the most dramatic was the drawing-off shift. The steel props back in the waste were already under immense pressure. A strong chain was attached to the bottom of one, then drawn tight with a powerful ratchet and lever. As the chain tightened, the men crouched down, wondering if the whole roof would collapse with it.

Once it had fallen, they must decide if it was safe to fetch the half-hundred-weight steel prop back into safety. They judged by sounds. Unless the cutter or the borer was about or the belt was creaking along, they had a chance of hearing, for the roof and the coal talk incessantly. The groans and the creaks, the sharp cracks and shaking of roof, the rustle and slither of small stuff slipping down from a break away back in the dark hinterland in the waste enable them to tell what is coming next.

These conditions of roof breaking-in would still be operative during the coaling shift, and the breaking roof in the waste continued to flow down onto the belt itself. The miner had two objectives: to press forward into the coal as fast as he could, and to break off the roof behind him equally fast. As coal toppled down in front of him, the roof was falling in behind. This is called the advancing long wall system. I called it the living tomb system.

A variant of this was followed in most of the faces of Yorkshire Main. The roof was forced to break off, but was eased down by building a series of packs or hollow rock walls at intervals along the face. They helped to control the fall but could not alter the amount of collapsing necessary to fill up the waste, or the amount of subsidence that would continue, strata after strata, for hundreds of yards above the coal-seam. The breaking-in of the strata above can be felt and heard for as long as two years after the face has moved away, until finally it settles down in some stable condition.

The contractor and his mates had the job of keeping open the roads needed for servicing each face. They moved along about two metres a day, cutting the rock to enlarge the road, extracting mangled steel rings for recycling, and then setting in strong steel arches which were bolted at the top. In this founderous and shifting land, the floor rose, the walls and roof crushed in, warping and bursting the rings with their breaking-strain of sixty tons. The floor of the road, level at the beginning of the shift, might be heaved up at an angle by the end so that the roadway would soon be completely closed without this never-ending repair work. They were "forever climbing up the ever-climbing wave". It was like painting the Forth Bridge; the workers might have moved a mile in two years, but would be back in the same place.

Mice lived in the packs, particularly at junctions where the haulage lads had their snap. (This usually consisted of bread and dripping, called Yorkshire marmalade, and was carried in a small tin that snapped shut to keep out the coal dust.) It was quite common for a family of mice to get trapped inside a pack by the sudden shifting of weight downwards, resulting in a hideous squealing which could continue for hours. Mice were the most numerous animals below ground. They came down in the horses' food supplies, and the cats waiting for them would jump on to every tub of food as it left the pit bottom.

The heat and the difficulty gave many excuses for "having a minute" (a very good Yorkshire minute was five minutes), squatting in small groups at the side of the tunnel, having a bite to eat or at least a brief rest. The warmth and the dark were too much for the trainee Bevin Boys, and at meal-times we would nod with a sandwich part-eaten. The mice would run out and pick up the morsel that dropped out of our mouths and we would be woken by excited squeaks.

We had about forty pit ponies, permanently stabled underground. Jock, a highly skilled and devoted horseman, kept them in remarkable condition. Since the stables were permanently lit, none showed any sign of blindness. They came up only once a year, and a special field was kept empty for that one week in August. Horse-riding was forbidden, but the pony drivers rode whenever they felt safe from discovery. It was desperately dangerous, especially on the return airways which varied greatly in height and width.

In my days at Yorkshire Main, the endless rope system was almost universally employed. A steel cable ran over rollers along the floor of the roadway in between steel rails. The rope was stretched tight and, because of the great tension, would only operate satisfactorily in a straight roadway so a new system was required for each change of direction. Since the rope ground on steadily at around three miles per hour, it seemed harmless and innocent.

Sometimes tubs were accidentally loosed and would set off down a slope. A full tub held about fifteen hundredweight, and five to nine tubs made up a "run". An escape of tubs was the most dangerous occurrence on the haulage system, but it was one of the few pit dangers of which there could be some warning. You would hear the rumble of their gathering speed, or even see them break away.

The boys on the roads had little respect for anything, human or divine, but had a healthy regard for runaway tubs. There were lads in the pit pointed to with awe who had been under a run of coal and survived. The most frequent cause of death amongst our Bevin Boys was through runaway tubs. The recognised alarm was a scream or a piercing whistle. I heard this only once.

It was a minor affair on an air return, a back road which didn't carry coal. We were working at the bottom of a steep incline. For protection, we had stuck a heavy wooden sprag in the middle of the track halfway down the slope and positioned a partly-filled tub above us with the wheels secured. We had taken every precaution. Suddenly I heard a scream of such a frightening character that I dropped my shovel and looked up. Herbert, with his five pints a night and eight at weekends and enormous girth, who served his time on the roads and had worked in every job in the pit and was now a contractor, had grabbed his lamp and was off down the road, shouting to us as he went.

All I remember is throwing out my arms wildly to push off and thinking of nothing but moving as fast as I could. What I pushed against was the face of a fellow Bevin Boy, a music student. I had planted my fingers neatly in his eyes. It may not have helped me forward very much, but it certainly delayed him. I was not conscious of anything until fifty yards down the roadway. The low roof kept Herbert bent forward like a sprinter at the start of a race, and he went like the rabbit in Wonderland. When we returned we found that nothing had happened. The tub had started to run but was stopped by some loose stuff on the rail. Thus even a newcomer learnt respect for runaway tubs.

My own accident came on the day I was sent to work with the haulage lads. The empty tubs were drawn inbye at the loader end, and it was my job to unhook the ninth tub from the tenth so that they could be switched over to the main belt to be filled. When the whole line of tubs was being pulled on the endless rope, it was impossible to detach the chain on one tub from the hook of the tub in front because the chain was too tight. When they were not under pressure, the tubs bumped back together and you couldn't get your hand in to release the chain. But if the boy at the front undid his clip so that the tubs began to run back, there came a moment when the chain was loose enough to be unhooked, and with the tubs not so close as to trap your hand.

The boy let the tubs run back. I tried and missed. There was a lot of delay and shouting; he clipped on and drew gently forward again. I tried again and missed. Back and forward, and again I missed each time. In my anxiety, I got my head down between the two tubs. The next I knew was to feel my helmet gripped between the back of one and the front of the other. I had missed again, and backed out violently like an old cow coming out of a bail. My helmet was caught between the tubs, and squashed in flat. My only injury was a bruise on the behind where I hit a rock in the wall. The lads promoted me to some simple and less responsible job.

Four men died in accidents in Yorkshire Main in 1945. I saw a stretcher go out with the boot placed neatly on the stomach of the injured man — it had been taken off to enable the foot to be dressed. I saw another boot placed neatly on the stomach of a man with the foot still inside it. Those were only the accidents I happened to see. The great majority of the men working on the coal drew blood in some way or another on every shift. Their knuckles and arms and backs were notched and grazed day after day, and they bore the scars of the deeper ones for life. This was mainly due to the desperate dark.

As soon as you got away from the pit bottom, all was darkness. There, where everyone was surrounded by moving things, heavy and dangerous tackle, irregular floors and projecting head traps, there was no light. Except at road junctions, the dark was relieved only by the lamp carried by the miner himself. On the coal-face these were hung up in a line and gave a tolerable light, but at all other points the lighting was insufficient.

When travelling, each miner shaded his lamp by putting a piece of thick paper behind it to avoid dazzling the man walking behind. As soon as we sat down, we took off our helmets and placed them over the top of our lamps – after first looking at the roof overhead to check that it was safe. Anyone leaving his lamp uncovered in company would be reminded of it: "Doest tha' want to take a photograph, lad?" Pit language was not normally so polite.

Friendly greetings were often couched in terms of horrible abuse. It was a debauched language, adopted by wide sections of the community. Pit lad to dog: "Fook off, tha' fooking fooker". Chapel lay-reader to pit lad: "Nay lad, tha' must not say 'fook off'. Thee wave thy hands and say 'Shoo, go home' and dog will fook off all right." Emphasis had to be given by a louder voice, which was also needed to overcome the constant noise of machinery.

The grinding and clattering of machines and the hissing of compressed air was magnified by the confined space of the pit. Yet at the same time, it was the worst place for transmitting sound. The irregular walls and obstructions muffled it so that even at a quite short distance nothing was heard. At an official enquiry into the cause of an explosion the evidence of the nearest witness might well be: "I felt a sudden puff of wind. Something out of the ordinary. I decided to go and see." It was just so at an enquiry I attended.

At one time, accidents were frequent at Seven South in Yorkshire Main. There was a fatal accident on the first day on which one newcomer was working at the face. He said, "Rag up, boys, and let's get out." His mates said, "There's no hurry—we'll have a tub full by knock-off." Miners showed a curious mixture of toughness and sentiment. Pit-owners were miserly over compensation and the miner who was injured was likely to lose his wages for the day on which he went for a medical to support his claim.

We have the story of the man who had his ankle smashed and his leg broken early in the shift, who got his mates to rag him up and put him in the gob till knock-off to make sure of his money. Will Lawther says that the Bevin Boys soon exceeded the toughness of their fellows. When some miners walking in came upon two dead bodies in the pit and wanted to shift them out, it was a Bevin Boy who is supposed to have said, "Hide one in the gob. We'll get a holiday on this one today, and another on that tomorrow."

At Yorkshire Main there was shortage of material and tools and, since each group was responsible for its own, we had almost constant friction and minor bickerings between the different groups. There was nothing more exciting than a piratical expedition to a different part of the pit by a gang armed to the teeth with spanners and crowbars for the purpose of secretly ravaging and pillaging someone else's supplies.

The pits were dangerous but I rejoiced in the work, although it was the most arduous I have ever tackled. The experienced miner on the face loves coal-getting. If the coal was properly prepared and the machinery was going well, the gang would fling into their work with zest. It was only when there were interruptions and unnecessary stoppages that our working morale was weakened.

Normal working required that the face should advance every twenty-four hours, one web further into the coal. If one collier failed to fill off his stint, the next phase of turning over the belt could not take place until an extra man had come on and cleaned off what remained. Of the ten long wall advancing faces in Yorkshire Main in my day, not a single one was on a twenty-four-hour turnover, and most were worked on a seventy-two-hour cycle. For nearly one third of the time, the belt was stood through some mechanical defect. For a further third of the working time, the men were dealing with coal that was not properly prepared. The faces were hopelessly undermanned and desperately under-supervised.

For the miners, the pit was the tyrant of their lives. They feared and hated it, yet it held them economically – because they could get no other job – and emotionally. The most common talk was of the desire to get out of the pit, but they did not take the first step. They attributed their hostility and bitterness to the bad treatment received through the years between the wars. "They have thrashed us for twenty years past and are preparing to do it again." The miners had no confidence either in government or management or, in some respects, even their own powers to better their conditions.

Pit talk was mostly of politics, horse-racing, and mining stories: about the struggles against the owners, the General Strike of 1926, unemployment and the bad days of the early 'thirties, and starvation in the village. We really learned what the miners had been up against. A constant feature was the conflict with the "gaffer". This was not usually about the great industrial issues, but over a hundred trifling things.

One example would be the pit-top canteens, which provided the underground miner with extra food. Their ration was less than that provided for old-age pensioners, prisoners-of-war and ex-enemy workers. Except for the weekly addition of some extra cheese, they received the same as a typist or other sedentary worker. I never heard of any other country under rationing where the miners got only the same as the ordinary civilian. The New Zealand government enquired as to what rations the English miner received and said that they could not understand how the miners produced any coal at all.

The miners rationalised their refusal to use the canteen. They blamed the cooking, the food, the service, although these were quite tolerable. They said that the canteen robbed the miner's wife and family of food – if the supplies did not go to the canteen, there would have been more available for the domestic ration. They felt that if they went to the canteen, they were robbing their own children. Obviously, the reverse was the case.

I have never known more conscientious or diligent workers. Bearing in mind the poor lighting and the difficulty of supervision, it would have been the easiest thing to idle, if one were disposed to do so. Their attitude towards the work was best shown by the difficulty in which Bevin Boys repeatedly found themselves. The lads were willing to prove that they understood the miners' attitude of hostility towards the management and showed this by a casual approach to the work. The minute that a Bevin Boy showed how well he could slack, he was exposed to ridicule. It was at first careful and moderate, but soon developed into real hostility. If a Bevin Boy persisted in idleness for longer than a week, the miners would get him shifted and he would end up working by himself or working in one of the rottenest jobs in the pit.

After serving my time in stone as a repairer's mate I was anxious to get onto the face itself. David and Dai, the checkers on 4 West, made enquiries and I mentioned it to the manager, who said that he would consider it. Nothing further was heard. Several weeks later, we learned that the under-manager was leaving. David and I saw him just before he left and made formal application that I should be allowed to start on 4 West the following Monday. He could not say whether this would be acceptable, but I started then, anyway.

On Tuesday, the safety-man who was concerned with the welfare of the Bevin Boys came and gave David the formal paper making him responsible for my welfare for the first month. By Wednesday the management had discovered that I was there and I was ordered off. I must give them credit for fighting hard, but we fought harder and I stayed put. There seemed to be some technical or tactical objection to my going to the face, and though it was widely discussed in the pit, we never discovered exactly what it was.

While working on the face, I hoisted eagerly my stint of ten tons a day onto the belt. This greatly amused the regular chaps, who found my eagerness for Ernie Bevin's need for coal quite misplaced. I would finish my stint, then help the fellow next to me. The older miners who had finished at half a stint stood round to watch the scene with amusement and a typical greeting would be, "Would'st tha' like little brush and pan to sweep up dust and put on t'belt? Leave a bit for us when tha's gone back to tha' cushy job in London."

CHAPTER TWELVE

1945 Election

I WAS happy to stay in the pits until the war came to an end, but then hoped to go to Westminster. We were all very hopeful of a Labour victory in the next election and Frank Soskice, home early from the war, had been promised the job of solicitor general in Attlee's government. Soskice wanted me to go into the House too, so he could keep an eye on me. In March 1944, I applied to the party to be placed on the list of candidates. A leading Quaker – I think it was Seebohm Rowntree – learned that I was on the list and sent me to the King's Norton constituency with his blessing. I took a weekend off to go to the nomination conference, but a Bevin Boy cut little ice compared with a captain in uniform. Raymond Blackburn appeared in military array with ribbons and won the nomination easily. He had come with a letter of recommendation to the local management committee from Harold Laski, chairman of the Labour Party.

Then Krishna Menon summoned me from Yorkshire. He was only ten years older than me but seemed to be prematurely ageing. We met at India Club, where he promptly announced that he had a seat for me in parliament. I was to be the "Member for India" and my overriding job was to see that India was made independent. Krishna had decided that I would represent Finsbury, and he had great influence. I was willing to stand, but how was this to be done? The situation in Finsbury was, to quote Ellen Wilkinson, quite a considerable mess. Harold Riley had consolidated his hold on the borough and was now mayor.

In 1941, Deputy ARP controller Riley became involved in a dispute with Henry Davey, the acting town clerk. Riley rented a property from the Worshipful Company of Skinners but for some time had not paid rent or rates. When the owners sued Riley, he pressed Davey to requisition the place. Davey declined. Riley ordered the health authorities to examine all of the Skinners' properties in the borough "with a comb" in the hope of finding inadequacies. He then got the council to pass a resolution ordering the requisition of the disputed property, telling Davey, "If you don't requisition, you will never be town clerk." The Co-operative Party sacked Riley, there was no requisitioning and the Labour Party Branch that Riley operated as his base was disaffiliated. Although he represented only some disaffected former members of a political party, Riley remained in control. Whenever his dictatorship appeared threatened, the majority was retained by co-opting his own nominees onto the council. No one could get Riley out of the town hall, where he lived on a permanent basis.

John Fishwick was appointed town clerk and proved to be an excellent administrator. (Throughout my time as MP and councillor, one couldn't have asked for a better guide.) Riley had Davey dismissed. The dismissal was considered late at night, without the full story being told and with the council "in committee" so that the press and public were excluded. The item had not been on the agenda and Davey was not there to defend himself. NALGO, Davey's union, suggested arbitration but the council wanted the matter dealt with by their car parks committee. This was a committee of Riley's own creation, composed of his friends and Gilbertian in the fullest sense. Finsbury was full of bomb-sites and car-parks were not a problem. At a hearing in January 1944, the National Arbitration Tribunal was told that under Riley's regime, any matter could be referred to any committee, though it had nothing to do with the topic.

In the previous eight years, the council had had five town clerks or acting town clerks, three borough engineers, three borough treasurers, and three medical officers of health. John Fishwick told the tribunal how senior officers in positions of responsibility worked in "a very definite atmosphere of fear". Alderman Charlie Simmons, chairman of the No 1 branch of ASLEF at Kings Cross, who led the local Labour Party branch formed after the disaffiliation of Riley's section, testified that council decisions had depended "almost 100 per cent on Mr Riley's wishes". The tribunal found for Davey and ordered his reinstatement as deputy town clerk. They condemned Riley on every point and his improper behaviour was fully exposed. Sacked by the Co-op and expelled from the Labour Party, yet he remained mayor. The people of Finsbury could do nothing about it until the end of the war when there would be an election. Questions were asked in parliament, but the minister was powerless.

Finally, the district auditor made an extraordinary audit of the borough's finances. He raised a surcharge of over £1,000 on Riley and the former town clerk, who had been the first officer to be subjected to Riley's wilful demands such as "House me, feed me, humour me, obey me". I thought that was rather unfair. According to the district auditor, the sixty-odd council members appeared to have completely surrendered their functions to Riley. Even the top post was in his gift as he had arranged a treadmill for the succession of mayors.

Mayor in 1938-39 was Dr C L Katial, a close friend of Krishna Menon. Dr Katial ran a busy private medical practice in Aldersgate and was part-owner of a famous jewellery store. He was a man of some substance and he aimed at having the Finsbury seat for himself. Krishna and I called on him and, after insistence on one side and the other, the doctor asked what he would get in return if he yielded up his place. "When India is independent, I will make you Minister of Health for all India." I'm not sure that he ever achieved this ambition but the doctor yielded. Krishna further demanded that he accompany us on a tour of the other ex-mayors, who thought that they were in the running for the job.

First was Alderman Simmons, who said, "I thought the position was rightly mine!" After the arguments had been considered, he also asked, "What do I get in return for yielding up?" Krishna promised to make him chairman of the Metropolitan Water Board, which was seen as one of the most important public jobs in the borough. Simmons joined the bandwagon and we went to call upon Charlie Allen. He lived in my own ward of St Philip and was more amenable, but none the less needed persuasion. He was promised the most luxurious trip to India and a meeting with the president of the state.

Krishna was fully confident about the future. India would be free, he would take part in its governance and would have such access to national funds that he could make reasonable promises for the future. He was so free from doubt that his certainty spread to anyone who knew him. Krishna kept his promises to the Finsbury hopefuls, although Charlie Simmons got only a seat on the Water Board and went no higher. Dr Katial became something very authoritative on matters of health in some part of India. The job was a bit beyond him and in due course he was back in Aldersgate.

It seemed that the real force behind the idea of my being MP came from Miah (Michael) Cliffe, a big, jovial, easy-going fellow and a formidable organiser. He was a presser, equally at home working the great trouser-press or wielding the oversized hissing steam-iron – the weasel of "Pop goes the weasel". Finsbury had become a great centre of the rag trade and produced uniforms in innumerable factories. Every factory or garment shop of any size had its own union group, and Miah organised them all into the Union of Tailors and Garment Workers. This was the foundation of the Finsbury Trades Council, which represented 8,000 trade unionists, mostly in printing, gin distilling, transport and clothing manufacture. As its Secretary, Miah was able to give considerable support to the London Trades Council, one of the most powerful industrial bodies in the country during World War II.

When my proposed candidacy came to the knowledge of Herbert Morrison, he determined that I was not to be the MP on any terms. Morrison had run the LCC from 1934 with outstanding success and had brought distinction to the party and its work. He re-housed so many people so well as to give the assurance of a great Labour majority in London for years to come. He held the rather narrow view that the Labour Party was the preserve of the working class and the way to tell whether a person was a member of that class, and so qualified for party membership, was the way he spoke. If the sound of a person's voice did not appear somewhat similar to Morrison's own, then he was not likely to be a valid member of the party and least of all a Member of Parliament.

My first contact with Morrison was in 1941 at the party conference at Central Hall in London. I was the sole delegate from the Haldane Society and had been nominated for the National Executive Committee. There was only one seat on the NEC to represent the interests of all the Socialist organisations affiliated to the party. These organisations, each having one vote per thousand members, were:

Socialist Medical Association	1 vote
Haldane Society	1 vote
Histadruth (Jewish Labour Party)	1 vote
Arsenal Co-Op	5 votes

The only other candidate on that occasion was Joe Reeves, a long-time member of the NEC, and the delegate and nominee of Arsenal Co-Op. The result of the election was Joe Reeves, 7; and me, 1. Morrison, as

*1 1880: Converting timber from virgin forest with machinery supplied by
E W Mills & Co.*

*2 1890 The Star rowing club coxed IV; top left: my father J F W Mills, bow. Middle:
G Elliott, 2. Right: G Pearce 3. Seated:G Richardson, stroke.*

3 1900: *My parents' wedding. Most of the women are still in part mourning for grandfather E W Mills' death three months earlier.*

4 1918: *Mother elected "The Tramway boys' Queen" at the Wellington Victory carnival.*

5 1925: *My father J F W Mills.*

6 1921/22 Summer: "Tramping" from Nelson College. My cousin Trevor Fisher at the back. I am on the left.

7 1922: Strike-breakers moving the wool crop to Australia. I am on the right.

8 1922: Nelson College senior 'A' team. We won the New Zealand section of the Imperial Challenge Shield run by Beaverbrook Press.

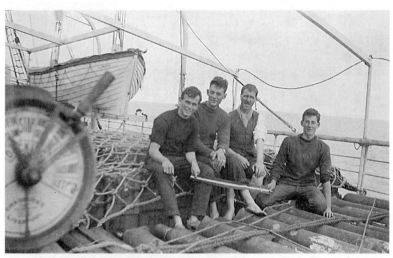

9 1924: Nelson College in my time. It was damaged by an earthquake in 1929 and later rebuilt.

10 1923: Nelson College First XV.

11 1924: Cross-gartered as Malvolio in Twelfth Night.

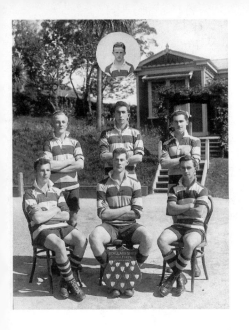

12 1924: Nelson College first seven-a-side rugby team.

13 1924: Nelson College Cadet Corps being presented with competition prizes. We almost swept the board. I am Sergeant Major on far left.

14 1927: Victoria University College amateur athletics team. We won the Inter-University shield.

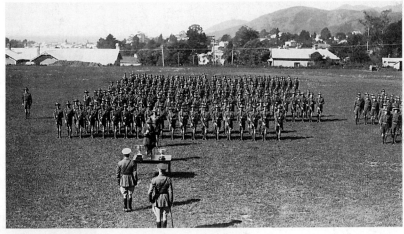

15 1927: *North Island v South Island at Athletic Park. The grandstand is at the back! I'm in striped socks.*

16 1927: *In the First Battalion Wellington Infantry Regiment at Victoria College. Colonel Greenish seated fourth from left.*

17 1927: *Photo to accompany Rhodes Scholarship submission.*

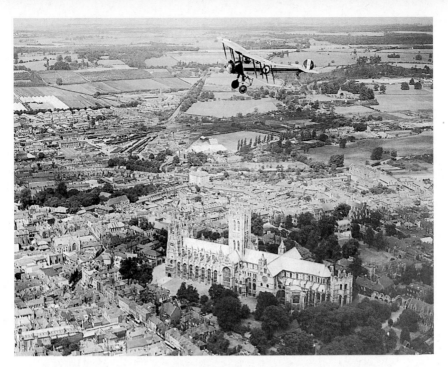

18 1930: Over Canterbury Cathedral in an Avro trainer out of Manston airfield on the day my First in Law was announced.

19 Summer 1930: The Balliol IV at Henley.

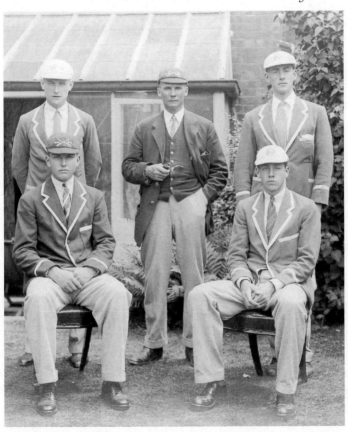

20 May 1930:
Eights Week.
About to make a
bump at the
barges.
21 Pursuing
Lincoln down the
Barges. I think
we bumped them
next day.

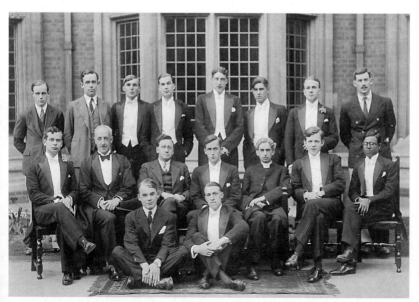

22 May 1931:
The Oxford
Union Eights
Week debate:
"The law is an
ass". Father
Ronnie Knox, J
Boyd-Carpenter,
Herbert Morrison,
and Bryant Irving
took part.

23 February 1931: The Oxford crew at Henley. I am fourth from the left and Lewis Clive sixth.

24 February 1931: The Oxford crew training at Henley. Lewis Clive and I are in the "engine room" at 6 and 5 respectively.

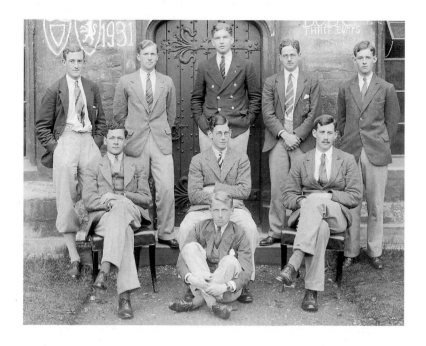

25 May 1931: *The Balliol Eights Week crew. We made three bumps. In May 1930 we had made four.*

26 1932: *Janet's "Oriental portrait" bought for the Tate Gallery by the Chantry Bequest while she was still a student.*

27 1934: In H D Samuel's Chambers, 5 Essex Court.

28 May 1936: The wedding. Leaving the church. Janet's sister Eleanor is replacing a shoe.

29 1938/39: Officers training for "The deep hole", Fighter Command. I am sixth from the left, middle row.

30 1936: Assington Hall where we hid our families for the duration.

31 Summer 1936: With sister Deede to the royal garden party given for colonials. I seem to have forgotten how to wear a top hat!

32 1940: RAF identity card as a Pilot Officer.

33 1944: In my muck.

34 July 1944: The barracks at Askern training pit.

35 July 1944: Coming off shift at Askern training pit. I am the tall one.

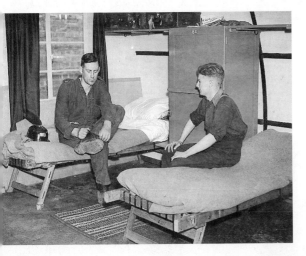

FINSBURY PARLIAMENTARY ELECTION 1945

VOTE LABOUR

JOHN PLATTS·MILLS
LABOUR CANDIDATE

36 June 1945: General Election poster.

37 June 1945: Campaigning in Islington market.

38 June 1945: An eager young MP!

Who Is?

Is he really trying to tell them that it's he —who's Very Tasty, Very Sweet? No, surely not, although he's pretty good, of course. It's J. F. Platt - Mills, Labour candidate for Finsbury, canvassing in an Islington market.

'VERY TASTY VERY SWEET.'

<u>Opposite</u>

39 November 1945: With a party of parliamentarians going to Yugoslavia to invigilate Tito's election.

40 March 1946: Returning from taking part in a Youth delegation to Russia. Being met by Janet with nos 3 and 4, Tom and Barney.

41 1947: *A Russian underground station! Janet came with me this time.*

42 1948: *A bit of farming at Morelands.*

43 1947: *The Rumanian Embassy. Being invited to visit the country. Janet and I went later that year. D N Pritt is on the right.*

chairman of the Conference Arrangements Committee, announced the results. He gave the name of the winner, and then was at pains to add, "I'd like to announce the vote for the loser in that contest: Platts-Mills one vote, for he voted for himself." The winner had also plainly voted for himself, but this was not mentioned.

Morrison sent the London Labour Party organiser, Hinley Atkinson, to meet one by one with every person on the Finsbury management committee. There were eighty or more, and it was reckoned that he had made seventy visits. He warned each of them that the party would not stand for it; that I was likely to be another Pritt (a most flattering impossibility) and it was their duty to Finsbury and to the party to vote against me. (Morrison's later statement that "we didn't want any more Crippses and Pritts in the Party" came at a time when Cripps was a senior member of the cabinet.)

Poor Hinley had an injured hip and his movements were slow. All meetings were duly reported – more particularly as the majority of those approached were trade unionists of Miah Cliffe's persuasion. Cliffe and Joe Trotter both insisted that I should stand firm. Trotter was a carpenter and a power in the Trades Council, as well as being chairman of the Finsbury Labour Party General Management Committee.

Each of the ex-mayors came to me in turn and said that it was grossly unfair: Morrison was behaving badly, Hinley was behaving badly, but I hadn't a chance. As a result, I had to release them from their assurances and each declared that he would stand. The ex-mayors were all members of the GMC, and all four of us were nominated. Each had a vote in his own right, and each of the three received only the one vote. There were, I think, ninety-eight delegates present. Joe Trotter said, "Well, comrades, let's make it unanimous. We'll have another vote." This was duly done. On the 20th November, 1944, I was adopted as prospective parliamentary Labour candidate and unanimously recommended to the NEC for endorsement. Adoption as official candidate came on 28th May, on the motion of Alderman Dr Katial.

To start the beginnings of a campaign while I was away in Doncaster, we needed someone to set up an office and act as secretary. Our good friend Thora Silverthorn was the principal organiser for women in the main Civil Service Trades Union, and formerly married to Dr Sinclair-Loutit, Medical Officer for Finsbury. He had been one of the first British doctors in the Spanish Civil War, to which she had gone as a nurse. Thora recommended Mrs Edith Green, whose husband was away at the war. Mrs Green had just had her babe, Anne, and so was off work for the time being. She was delighted to join in the prospective battle and lent herself to acquiring an office: the back room of Nat Gould's tailor shop was contributed on behalf of the party. I was on the underground minimum salary for a miner of £5 a week, and I think I probably paid her £2 a week for this part-time work. We made Nat Gould an alderman at the next opportunity.

From underground in Yorkshire it was not easy to keep abreast in any detail with current affairs. Edith Green became my lifeline, sending a weekly note with cuttings. From these, I learned that Churchill had invaded Greece. Edith's husband was posted to Greece and his letters had a regular section on the army's actions and his own opinion of the politics involved; Edith sent copies on to me. The officers knew that for a good part of the war Britain had housed the Greek king, who was not popular with his people. In 1917, his pro-German feelings had resulted in the then Crown Prince George's removal from the succession and his voluntary exile in Switzerland. Now, as king, he resisted the appointment of the Archbishop Damaskinos as regent.

The British troops also knew that EAM-ELAS, the Communist/Socialist coalition, had held down and badly mauled many German divisions before finally driving them out. ELAS held at least three-quarters of Greece and were likely to take the rest from the small minority of monarchists. In every occupied country of Europe, the people preferred those who had fought the Nazis. In Greece, Churchill set the British army to defeat them. Young Captain Green vividly described the general feeling of revulsion amongst officers and men alike against what they were required to do. He described, too, the delicate change from friendship between locals and British, united in finishing off the Nazis, to hostility when the locals realised that our army was there to destroy them. We had invaded Greece, and the Greeks dared to defend themselves. The British Army, having been attacked, fired on ELAS forces and, as Seymour Cox put it in parliament, "British soldiers and Greek patriots were lying dead in Athens, each with an allied bullet in his heart."

Labour Party members followed this closely because our leaders in the united wartime government had to take joint responsibility for what

Churchill was doing, however much the rank and file might disapprove of it. The annual conference was held at the Central Hall, Westminster, in mid-December – while Athens was under constant shelling. Bevin had the job of justifying the shootings. He described what was going on in Greece as though he regretted it, but then excused himself as being required to accept it as a member of the government. He demanded loyalty to the Labour cabinet ministers who, he said, were parties to the decision.

This was untrue, as Churchill showed in his *History of the Second World War* (Vol VI, p 251) which records that he alone took the decision to order the shooting. "There was no time for the Cabinet to be called," he wrote. The telegram to General Scobie, which was sent at four-fifty a.m. on 5th December, was in the terms: "Do not hesitate to act as if you were in a conquered city where a local rebellion is in progress…with bloodshed, if necessary." It is not regarded as polite or proper to lie deliberately, but here was Bevin, put up by Attlee to lie to party conference. The handling of Greek independence badly shook Churchill's prestige and Bevin's lie went a long way to restoring it. This was one of his experiences with Bevin that led Churchill to believe that Ernie was the man best suited to carry out his policies in the event of a Labour victory.

There was an emergency resolution put forward by the executive committee of the patching and bodging kind habitually used when it is in a fix:

> "This conference deeply regrets the tragic situation which has arisen in Greece and calls upon the British Government most urgently to take all necessary steps to facilitate an armistice without delay… . This conference looks forward to the establishment of a strong democratic system which will bring peace, happiness and reconciliation to our generous and heroic Greek allies."

It went on to foresee an armistice, negotiations and a conference, and a provisional government followed by free elections. The hinge phrases sounded like Herbert Morrison's work. "Give them a bit of 'deeply regrets' 'calls upon the Government most urgently to take all necessary steps', 'looks forward to establishment of a strong democratic system', 'peace, happiness and reconciliation', 'generous and heroic allies'." He would add,

'Fill in with any words you like, provided you have these phrases." What the conference wanted was, "Stop the monstrous invasion, withdraw the British Army, stop pressing the king upon them."

And how did Bevin deal with that? He condemned emotionalism and melodrama. He said:

> "The steps which have been taken in Greece are not the decision of Churchill, they are the decision of the Cabinet. ... I took part with my Labour colleagues in the whole of these discussions, going on for nearly four years ... I am a party to the decisions that have been taken. ... I cannot bring it to my conscience that any one of the decisions was wrong."

In the inter-war years, Greece had had fifty governments. Bevin admitted that the Greeks hated the Metaxas dictatorship and had divided feelings about the monarchy. He continued, "No excuse as to how it started can wash out the fact that the British have been attacked," but this was thoroughly dishonest. We had not declared war on Greece. We were there determined to kill or at least to drive out into Bulgaria those Greeks who controlled the greater part of the country. Bevin was at pains not to explain what we were doing there – trying to force back an unwanted king and, in the meantime, impose an archbishop as regent – and he did not explain why a Socialist party should encourage such actions.

The miners' delegate declared that his federation would support the resolution "out of loyalty" but expressed their regret at the "bankruptcy" of the Labour leadership. "If the tactics which the Party had exhibited continue, some of us will have to leave the Party." Aneurin Bevan said it would be deplorable if the world regarded the unanimous carrying of the resolution as an endorsement of Bevin's speech. In full-blooded Nye fashion, he declared that Bevin had only three bodies of supporters: Fascist Spain, Fascist Portugal and the majority of Tory MPs. He described Bevin's statement as "garbled and inadequate where it was not unveracious". Our representatives in the Churchill government must "exercise a more decisive influence on the conduct of affairs or leave the Tories to do their own dirty work".

Jim Griffiths replied to the debate for the executive and argued that a vote of no confidence in the conduct of the government in Greece would be an indication to the Labour members that they should at once withdraw from Churchill's government. We would then lose all credit for having taken a part in winning the war, we would lose the manna that dropped from Churchill upon us. This argument finally carried the day and the resolution of "deep regret" and "necessary steps to facilitate" was adopted.

A second resolution on Greece was then passed unanimously; it was the only one truly reflecting conference feeling:

> "This conference expresses its admiration of the Resistance movements which have proved their value to the Allied cause. It demands that the Government shall give an immediate pledge that, as territories are cleared of the enemy, their administration shall be left to the democratic control of their own inhabitants with no attempt at interference or dictation by outside forces, political or military."

In June 1945, I took two weeks off work for the election campaign. We filled the biggest room in each schoolhouse and had two grand meetings in the town hall: one in the first week, and the second on the last night before the election. There was some competition to get the town hall for the last night and also to prevent the Tory rival from getting it. Ours was a straight Labour/Tory fight. We had no intervening candidate, although in other constituencies there were several Nationalists about (those who were left over from the National Government of Ramsay Macdonald, as it was called, and then of Chamberlain) and there were still National Liberals and the like.

It was expected that a diligent candidate would go door-to-door in the constituency. In Finsbury, we worked out a system for speeding this up by having a number of canvassers who worked each side of the street, having the doors already open so that no time was spent by the candidate waiting for the knock to be responded to. I assume others did the same. For the last week, four leading miners from my own shift at Yorkshire Main came down. They were put up in the borough by some supporters in the party and were quite happy to go the round of all the public houses, at lunchtime and in the evening, and talk. I am sure that they were much more valuable and more comfortable there than on the knocker.

On 1st April, the *Sunday Dispatch* had run a lurid report of a supposed interview claiming that I'd issued a challenge to every miner in England that I was the tallest man working on the coal-face. The "interview" implied that I was still shooting up as a growing lad of thirty-eight. The Bar takes a dim view of any kind of boastfulness and this rubbish was reported to the Business Meeting of the Western Circuit at Winchester. I was called upon to explain. A reporter had phoned and asked my height, but that was the nearest we came to his story. The Bar was satisfied, but it had been an embarrassment at the pit.

Will Lawther, President of the NUM, agreed to speak at one meeting and Frank Cousins, settled in London after being promoted to his job as a national officer in the T&G, spoke at two. Herbert Morrison insisted on his right to address the meetings. I had to agree with my closest advisers that he had done no real harm to my selection chances and having him repeat the same sort of nonsense at the election would help to expose him in his true character. When Frank spoke in rather fulsome terms of personal support and added some stuff about the distinguished career in coal-mining, Morrison took it upon himself to try to restore the balance.

The general theme of his final comments was on the lines: "You may find him quite a smart young fellow but we know that the average London constituency doesn't take terribly well to such people, and when you get tired of him, then you can throw him out next time." When Morrison learned that Frank was coming to speak at the eve of poll meeting, he volunteered himself to come again. He was the big London name for Labour, so it was impossible to reject his offer and he was, after all, merely reiterating and emphasising the demand he had made at nomination time the year before – namely, that I should not become the candidate.

As their contribution to election expenses, the London Labour Party allotted to me Will Webster, an experienced, professional parliamentary agent. He was former chairman of the Bethnal Green Labour Party and had spent ten years on their borough council. He had also been Labour Agent for North Islington. He knew the routine and, in spite of being eighteen stone and rather sluggish and prone to sleep at any hour, he carried through all that was needed. As he told me after, he was allotted one extra task and that was to spend so much money that my election was plainly illegal, keeping careful books to show the overspending. A great excess of leaflets and the like had been printed and we had giant posters on all the best sites. There was much goodwill in the borough and I assumed that the printing and the sites were either free or given at very low prices. I went personally to thank the shopkeepers who ran their businesses below the posters. There was no basis on which I could have known that Will was overspending. I was never shown any receipts and it never occurred to me to ask for them.

Will kept genuine books showing this overspending, but he also kept a separate set that he disclosed to me after the election, and which proved me comfortably within the limits. He and I were friends by then and after disclosing the accurate and condemning books to me, he destroyed them. At the joyful celebration lunch the day after the election, Will went fast asleep at the table. I did not dare breathe a word of this and have no idea whether it happened to any other MP. Morrison and Hinley Atkinson relied on the innocence and trustfulness of a first-time candidate. If it had not been for the happy chance of Will and I becoming friends, I would have been disqualified as a member and possibly faced grievous charges in the magistrates' court. Watergate and more recent "dirty tricks" campaigns had nothing to teach the London Labour Party under Herbert Morrison.

In the big cities, with many constituencies close to one another, there was much cross-visiting between candidates. The party encouraged this and invited candidates to give lists of dates when they would be available to speak in neighbouring constituencies. It was thought that we might give two evenings a week, but it was a matter of fitting in with the neighbours' open nights. I had Elwyn Jones from East Ham, Edith Summerskill and Lord Nathan, Geoffrey Bing from Hornchurch, a lame colonel from East Anglia and, I think, three others all come to speak. In return, I went to East Ham, Shoreditch, Islington and St Pancras.

Most London candidates were already well established in their various constituencies through being borough councillors or having stood at earlier elections and were well known to one another. I came as something of an outsider. All of us, through our agents, were drilled in the recording of canvassing results so that in the last two weeks we had a good idea that the sentiment was strongly on our side. Not only did we feel confident at home, but most of us thought of all England as being the same. I don't remember applying my mind to the difference between county and town in the veneration in which Winston Churchill was held. Tory candidates in country constituencies probably had the same confidence in their own chances that we had. Churchill expected his war success to carry the day. Indeed, Attlee seemed a poor little thing by comparison.

At some stage in the election, Churchill made a return trip from Westminster to his new constituency of Woodford. It was intended to yield two triumphal rides through London. The return route brought him in an open car from the Angel down Rosebery Avenue, past Finsbury Town Hall and along Greys Inn Road; in fact, clean through the borough. The routes were well publicised in advance and exact times given. We decided to make his journey something of a test. We gave maximum publicity to it and urged people to turn out. The Tory canvassers also worked hard to get their supporters onto the streets. There was a splendid response and the route was well-lined from the Angel. At the town hall, there was a particularly good muster. I stood by the senior police officer, who talked of the need to get a reinforcement from Kings Cross Road police station to make sure of getting Churchill through.

When Churchill arrived, he was in an open car. Seeing the great press of people, he stood up at about Sadler's Wells. With the roar that greeted him, he raised his hat and waved it. He then realised that it was a hostile sound and he looked round, amazed. Further on, the uproar began again. He tried another wave, but no luck. We could see how, from a standing position, he slumped down in the seat and buried his head in his chest. I think there is a rule that any MP at all times, and any aspirant in election times, gives a welcome to any visiting MP, however opposed. I tried to live up to this and gave Churchill a little private wave to which he responded.

We were at the time the smallest constituency in London and one of the smallest in the country. The pre-war population had been much reduced by bombing and evacuation, so that the total of those registered to vote numbered a little over 20,000. My Tory opponent was a thirty-nine-year-old squadron-leader, F A Burden, whose main claim to fame was as British Schools Boxing Champion in 1921-22. Nearly 14,000 votes were cast, and Labour took 9,786. The vote took place on 5th July, but the count and declaration were postponed until the 26th so that the forces' votes from overseas could be brought to England. By mid-afternoon we knew it was a Labour landslide. At Transport House, Attlee received Churchill's letter of congratulations and the information that Churchill would hand in his resignation to the King at 7 p.m. Herbert Morrison at once made another of his bids for power. He said that Attlee ought not to accept the invitation to form a government until the Parliamentary Labour Party had the chance to elect a leader. It was typical of Morrison.

That evening, the Labour MPs for Greater London joined in a victory rally at Central Hall, Westminster. All seemed to have heard about Morrison's behaviour. Even at the hall, he openly canvassed for a PLP vote on the leadership. He must have felt that he still had a good chance because he was as smiling and as chirpy as could be until Attlee walked in – straight from the palace, to announce that he had agreed to form a government. It was a public meeting that packed the hall. There was great excitement which, at Attlee's speech, approached the ecstatic. We sang the great traditional songs such as "Jerusalem" and "England Arise", and the old community favourites. Elwyn Jones and I were asked to speak for the new members, but I have no notion of why we were chosen.

In the course of the evening, we began to realise what an extraordinary victory it was. No more coalitions, no minority government; the fullest opportunity to enact the whole of our programme. The country had been steeped in the manifesto "Let Us Face the Future", which fairly set out our proposals. This vote made it clear that Britain wanted decent housing, proper health treatment, equal chance of education, and something approaching fair shares for all. The speeches that night were received by what one could only describe as rapturous cheers.

Then came Ernie Bevin. We all assumed that Hugh Dalton, the man with most experience in the field, was to be Foreign Secretary and that Ernie was to be Chancellor of the Exchequer. Those were the jobs they wanted and had asked for. At Central Hall, Ernie certainly spoke as if that were his job. He explained what an extraordinary opportunity he would have to discharge the debt that we owed to all the groups and supporters and even individuals who had, from the depths of occupied Europe, helped in the destruction of Hitler. Britain had probably suffered less than any other part of Europe, and our modest financial power was to be at the service, through him, of those who deserved it most. Even the Communists were to be included. This really was socialism. The audience gave him an ovation.

Bevin then waddled back to his seat, and in so doing, he turned away from the audience and gave a great wink to those on the platform, as much as to say, "That's the way to bring them to their feet; give them a few words and ideas of the kind they like, and you can get away with murder." Ernest Millington, the Commonwealth MP and included as a Labour supporter, also saw this display of sly insincerity and I'm sure many others did, too. Looking back, I can only think of Ernie's wink in those terms – that he didn't mean a word of it.

As a newcomer, I had no special knowledge of who would form the cabinet. Cripps was the only leading figure in the party with whom I had more than mere acquaintance, but he was not likely to ring up and tell me the inside story. I really had no idea of the tussle that was going on, except for the general rumours that we all knew. On the following day, Friday the 27th, Attlee changed his mind more than once. Before lunch, he told Dalton that he would "almost certainly" be Foreign Secretary; shortly after four p.m., he told Dalton that he would probably be going to the Exchequer. Bevin could not have learned of the change before then, which would account for his confident speech the night before, of how he would deal with the country's finances.

On Saturday the 28th, Attlee took his first half-dozen senior ministers to the palace to kiss the monarch's hand and to receive their seals of office. By then, the rest of the Parliamentary Labour Party had collected at Beaver Hall, the city home of the Hudson Bay Company. I believe that one of our number was away ill. We were all talking, exchanging stories of what happened and congratulating one another. The feeling of elation was even more intense than at Central Hall because now we were at full strength and we knew we were in power.

Attlee and his team arrived from the palace and were received with the expected rapture. William Whiteley, the Chief Whip, then called, "The Foreign Secretary". We all looked expectantly to Dalton, but Ernie Bevin stood up. This was probably the biggest surprise of my life; this experience, too, was shared with others. Ernie moved a vote of confidence in "the new Prime Minister". This was seconded by Arthur Greenwood and supported by George Isaacs, Chairman of the TUC. This was the quietus for Morrison. Attlee had carried us through to a splendid victory and the PLP didn't need a leadership vote. Our demonstration of support was clear enough, even for Morrison. Attlee spoke only a short time. He promised to carry through the election programme, then set off for Potsdam to help wind up the war.

Hector McNeil was a real Bevin man, and most reactionary in foreign politics. He was to succeed Philip Noel-Baker as Bevin's Minister of State in October 1946. I asked him why the switch took place between Foreign Office and Exchequer. McNeil told me that Churchill and Attlee had met, probably over lunch, and that Churchill had objected to the choice of Dalton as Foreign Secretary, saying, "You can't have him. It's got to be Bevin. He is the only one I can trust to carry out my policy towards Russia." I had no difficulty in believing this story at the time, but McNeil was less well informed than I thought. Other explanations were canvassed. One that held the floor for some time was that the King's influence carried the day. Dalton's father had been a tutor to the Royal Family and George VI had come to hate Hugh Dalton. He didn't hesitate to express this view. However, the more likely explanation was that later given by Attlee himself.

The best place for Morrison, as Attlee saw it, was as Leader of the House and Deputy Prime-Minister, where he would not have a ministry behind him on which to build a power-base. That, in effect, put him in charge on the home front. In that case, Bevin could not be Chancellor of the Exchequer because he would then have to work in close co-operation with Morrison. Bevin's hostility to Morrison went to extremes; for example, he referred to him as "a little bugger" and "a scheming little bastard". We all heard of this because civil servants are excellent broadcasters. Morrison and Bevin had to be kept apart, else Attlee would have had a full-time job keeping the peace.

Amongst my telegrams and letters of congratulation were several from those shocked by my choice of party. Flora Fardell, who would have had me in twelve years earlier as a Tory for Eastbourne with a safe seat for life, wrote:

> "You will know that, in some ways, your Parliamentary candidature has been a surprise! I did not know you had ceased to be eligible for the office of Vice-president of the Young Conservative Union!! I shall hope however that you will be of value to the best of your colleagues."

She meant, no doubt, those that were well to the right and close in with the Tories. These were the very people who would later force me out of the party and out of parliament altogether.

CHAPTER THIRTEEN

Starting in Parliament

ON 15TH AUGUST, parliament formally reopened and the speaker led us to a victory thanksgiving service in St Margaret's. We began with the National Anthem, everyone except the choir petering out after the first verse, and they struggling on to the end. The hymns must have been chosen as likely to be known even to the atheists in our party. Then followed the King's Speech, read by His Majesty himself in the House of Lords. The Speaker, Black Rod and senior members from both sides had automatic admittance, but there certainly wasn't room for us all. Only a few of the most junior backbenchers were allowed in just behind the Lord Chancellor's woolsack and they perched on the pediment of the throne within a few feet of the monarch.

The Commons Chamber was still damaged from being hit by a bomb and the Lords lent their Chamber. In our borrowed home, the Speaker offered a most curious formula:

> "I have to acquaint the House that the House has this day attended His Majesty in the House of Peers, and His Majesty was pleased to make a Most Gracious Speech from the Throne to both Houses of Parliament, of which, I have, for greater accuracy, obtained a copy, which is as followeth"

The House hadn't, in fact, attended at all, but only that tiny number.

The King's Speech, which was the first statement by the government of its proposals, was a good piece of prose and well read. It dealt with the expected topics, including the establishment of a National Health Service, a house-building programme, public ownership of the Bank of England, nationalisation of the coal industry and repeal of the Trades

Disputes and Trade Union Act 1927. It also referred to the Charter of the United Nations, which I regard as the greatest achievement of mankind, far ahead of splitting the atom or the moon-landing.

The first misuse of the Most Gracious Speech carried a fraud that Attlee and Bevin were to practise on the House and on the World:

> "In the Far East my Ministers will make it their most immediate concern to ensure that all prisoners in Japanese hands are cared for and returned to their homes with all speed. The bringing of relief to those who have suffered under Japanese tyranny and the disarmament and control of the enemy will continue to impose heavy demands on My Forces."

While the Labour government were putting these words in the mouth of the King, they were preparing to use Japanese troops to re-impose colonial rule on French Indo-China and on Dutch Indonesia (the East Indies). Those two countries had been occupied by Japan and, as Japan fell back across the Pacific under American pressure, had liberated themselves. Attlee and Bevin became self-appointed gods of the Far East. They used Japanese troops, re-armed for the purpose, to subjugate two independent nations. Far from bringing relief to those who had suffered, Attlee's government re-imposed that very tyranny. Mere backbenchers had no notion that Japanese troops and restored collaborators were in action against the wartime heroes, and I don't believe the cabinet was fully informed.

The final intention of the government as set out in the King's Speech was to "press on with the development of My Colonial Empire and the welfare of its peoples". Our colonial empire had to wait nearly twenty years before Macmillan's Wind of Change blew through Africa, and the French colonies fought a long and bitter war before defeating the French. The contribution of Attlee and Bevin to the development of the empire was slight. Also promised was the early realisation of full self-government for My Indian peoples, and a call for the blessing of Almighty God, which we greatly needed.

The King's Speech was followed by the Humble Address, the Prime Minister's reply to the King's Speech which he himself had just drafted. Attlee was, in effect, having a public talk with himself. The Labour Party was determined to do everything by the book. Colonel Douglas Clifton Brown, the Conservative Speaker from the coalition government, had been pressed to continue in his post. He was the obvious and excellent choice, and was always more than fair to me. By tradition, Members petitioned the King for our ancient rights and privileges. The new boys muttered, "It would be more than his job is worth to refuse."

To the Tories, parliament "used to be the finest club in Europe"; this was before we arrived and spoilt things for them. They were still trying to come to terms with the shock of losing power, having seen themselves as natural rulers, as the party with a right to govern. There were on our side of the House many professionals: managers, scientists, doctors, lawyers, and the like. Older Tories were heard to say, "We have always understood the real Labour man, the trade union leaders, the working fellows, but these sleek-haired newcomers in their hundreds are cuckoos – not the genuine thing." During the election, Churchill declared that a Socialist state would prove itself an oppressive dictator; he even threatened a Labour Gestapo. Some Tory MPs must have thought of that when, on the first day of the new parliament, the whole body of Labour joined in singing the Red Flag.

In the debate on the Address, Mr Attlee told us that two of our main problems were housing and coal. He suggested a partial remedy for the first in the requisitioning of empty houses. (When the leaders of the squatters' movement were later prosecuted for conspiracy, their defence used this assertion of Attlee's.) Of the second, he said:

> "All the liberated countries in Western Europe need coal, and without it there is bound to be unemployment. If industry cannot work, railways cannot function, and badly needed food will be lost for want of processing facilities. We must get coal."

Bevin's first important speech as Secretary of State for Foreign Affairs, delivered on the third day of the Debate on the Address, carried the support of the Foreign Office itself, and of the cabinet and of party headquarters. Much care and thought must have gone into this speech. Yet it was a rather bewildering muddle, and my colleagues began to wonder from where Bevin drew his confused and mistaken ideas. It was also taken by us to be an open declaration of war on the left.

The very first topic with which he dealt was the close union between the Chiefs of Staff of America and Britain, of "the great allies who have had to fight this war". This last phrase could have included the Soviet Union, but it plainly does not. There was no indication throughout the war of joint planning between Eisenhower and Voroshilov or any other Russian, and precious little planning between the fleets. The speech ended on the same theme, "I cannot close this statement without again paying a tribute to the United States. It has been a marvellous partnership. I shall never forget the dark days of 1940..." Again it was made clear that it was to America alone that his opening statement had referred. The whole world knew of the twenty million Russian dead, so there was the conventional one cheer for "that marvellous Red Army". Even Churchill did better than that.

Bevin thought that the worst situation he had to deal with came from the state of mind of the mass of ordinary people in the countries that had been occupied by the Nazis. They had been taught to disobey and oppose authority, to work slowly and reluctantly. It would be difficult for them to acquire discipline, energy, and the habits of work. There is neither sense nor reality in this conclusion, for people under merciless occupation are more than likely to react by sullen disobedience, as Bevin saw. Once free and running their own countries, there is no question of undermining their leaders and they turn with some joy to rebuilding and resurrection.

Bevin won our sympathy by speaking of the millions of displaced persons and prisoners-of-war scattered widely across Europe. Then he turned to the forthcoming European elections and tried to show that although they would not be up to the standards of independence and freedom required in Britain, we must accept them, provided that the result was not the "substitution of one form of totalitarianism for another". Towards the end of the speech, he spoke of the only election actually coming up, that in Bulgaria, warning, "We shall not be able to regard as representative any Government resulting from such elections." My understanding was that the Bulgarian electoral law excluded from standing or voting only members of the Nazi party that had run the country for Hitler during the war. It was an unfortunate choice for Bevin as his forbidden system.

"The Fascists and Nazis are so detested by everybody that there is a tendency, at the moment, to extend these names to groups of people and parties who are neither Nazi nor Fascist, but simply people who want to be represented, and are disliked by the majority party but who see the possibility of winning power, and therefore would like to deny these parties the opportunity to express their views in the elections."

Bevin was really as muddled as he appears in this passage.

Bevin's argument was that if the bulk of people in a lately occupied country call some new party Fascist, we should not accept that stricture. If their electoral law says that for this first election, known Fascists who openly backed the Nazi occupation should not be allowed to play a part, then the resulting vote would be contrary to our conception of a free election. The contrast is between the majority party and those they denounce as Nazis. But there has been no election and "majority party" means only the party that has obvious mass backing. That must refer to the leadership who had opposed the Nazis throughout the occupation. The people who had suffered under the Nazis should be best able to spot a minority group of right-wing politicians who were really Fascists at heart but were for the moment presenting themselves as "simply people who want to be represented". The horrible possibility is that Bevin felt that in Eastern Europe, the further away from any Russian nominees, the better. Even old Fascists would serve, provided you did not call them by that name.

Towards the end of his speech, we heard "Peace is indivisible", but Bevin borrowed nothing else from the great Russian statesman, Litvinov. On the subject of Greece, we had the usual phrases about establishing a stable democratic government and restoring law and order. More informed comment came from Major Lyall Wilkes, Member for Newcastle-upon-Tyne (Central), who had spent more than four months in ELAS territory in the last stages of the German occupation. In his maiden speech, Wilkes told the House that more than 20,000 Greeks were detained for political reasons. The Greek army was controlled by a Royalist clique, who made no secret of their hatred of the other Balkan regimes. British troops, sent in to prevent excesses and political reprisals, were not now fulfilling that role.

In a powerful speech, Michael Foot told us that no true democrat could applaud the direction Greece was taking. Their foreign secretary had recently resigned in disgust at the "trend of events" and at preparations "for a terror and for faked elections". Foot urged the cabinet not to work for continuity in foreign policy; "so many people in Europe remember the shameful record of Toryism in our foreign politics ... they hope that when they look to London in the future they will hear no more kind words for the dictators". This was true not only of Europe. The whole world had changed and, as Jim Callaghan put it, the foreign secretary would have to find "new men and new methods" for the future.

I had thought that delivering the maiden speech would be no more intimidating than speaking before any other tribunal to which one was not accustomed. My speech was carefully prepared and although it dealt with solemn matters, it also made jocular mention of class distinctions in Britain and in New Zealand, and this part was to be delivered with changes of accent. I remember that at some point I thought it would be appropriate to look round the chamber in a friendly manner. I did so, but saw nothing. It was a frightening experience and I was thankful for the fact that by tradition maiden speakers are given a kindly and indulgent reception.

The speech began with messages of goodwill from New Zealand. Because of my wartime activities, it was probable that I would soon be involved in Russian affairs and it was wiser not to raise the subject in a maiden speech. It seemed to me that the next crucial topic of our time was bound to be atomic energy. Two Japanese cities were still smoking from the bomb, which gave a passable excuse for stepping in and pontificating about it. I said that we ought to share our knowledge of the atom and its activities with all the world, and to make use of the powers available in the idea for the benefit of the future. I also said that Lord Rutherford would have been delighted to see this extension of his work used to defeat Fascism. We had just heard of the ill-treatment in the POW camps and were delighted that these special bombs had ended the war within days; that was enough to unsettle the judgement of anyone. On reflection, mine was an arrogant statement, for Rutherford would have been horrified by the depth of suffering at Hiroshima and Nagasaki.

It was inevitable that some complaint about the campaign in Greece would be included. Edith Green's husband had just died there, of diphtheria caught while bathing in the Mediterranean. He was probably one of the last casualties of the war. In July, four former prime ministers of Greece denounced the government, the administration and the police as being infested with royalists, Fascists and quislings, and the former commander-in-chief of the army demanded that the military be purged of traitors. It was not practicable to hold elections while the people lived in terror.

The independence of India also came in, with a call for the release of imprisoned political leaders. I had kept Krishna Menon's declared purposes quiet, but when parliament assembled I made an immediate approach with Krishna to Pethick-Lawrence, who was already in the Lords as Secretary of State for India. He re-assured us that there was nothing to worry about because he, Attlee and Cripps were all quite satisfied that "we could not hold India down any longer". Krishna was far too cautious to be satisfied with that and I took part in a couple of deputations that waited upon Pethick-Lawrence. India was freed in 1947. (Krishna became High Commissioner in London, and for a short time he flooded me with Indian Privy Council murder appeals.) No one of us had the slightest idea of the carnage that would follow between Hindu and Moslem, and of the millions of lives that would be lost as the groups withdrew one from the other.

My maiden speech had not needed "tidying up", but in those days you could edit your own speech in Hansard. Herbert Morrison was famous for doing it, for he sometimes got in a muddle about the use of words, and it was soon put right. No one was averse to it. The ministers usually had their PPS do it for them. I can vouch for the Morrison story for I often saw him there when I was rendering my own outbursts a little more elegant. It was in no way treated as a criticism of the Hansard reporters, who wrote faithfully what they heard. If I made any real alteration, I would find the reporter and get his agreement that there was no change in meaning.

Attlee and Bevin had both appealed to the miners for extra tons of coal to help resettle Europe and to keep it warm. Bevin had asked, "help us, not for profit, not for the capitalists, but in the task of building peace, and bringing succour, help and warmth to millions of your fellow workers at home and abroad". Philip Noel-Baker, Bevin's minister of state, now repeated the call, asking for up to 100 million tons to keep the factories working, and to prevent old people and babies from dying of cold. I knew

Noel-Baker well through his actions in favour of Republican Spain, when he had spoken at public meetings at the Albert Hall and elsewhere. He was reasonably liberal in outlook. I left parliament and went straight back to Doncaster and was turning coal on the next afternoon shift at No 9 South. It was too much for me and, with a slightly crushed finger, on the 19th September I was relegated to light work in the Temple where I have been ever since.

I thought of myself as a cross between a miner and a barrister. Because of the bomb damage, Westminster Hall was occupied by scaffolding that came at its lowest point to about eight feet above the floor. Upon entering the Great Hall, I used to inspect the scaffolding roof just above my head and even tap it with my umbrella before taking off my bowler hat. I suppose this was carried over from the pit, where we would always check the safety of the roof with our pick-handle before taking off our helmets. When I was sacked from the party, the first expression of regret and protest came borne by a deputation from the Senior Wood Repair Group of the Office of Works. I always wore a bowler and carried a rolled umbrella because demob-dress predominated at the Bar. On leaving the forces, the wartime officer was issued with a grey flannel suit with a dark stripe, a bowler and an umbrella. Every young barrister would like to have been thought of as being an officer during the war, so he dressed in the same style. I did the same and probably continued longer than anyone in the Temple.

We were made much of by the servants of the House, as the staff were called. Many took the trouble to learn the names of members and addressed them so. You could get service in almost any part of the House, short of taking a meal in the chamber itself. At a moment's notice, a comfortable bed could be provided, or a shorthand writer or whatever else was needed. We had lockers rather like boys at school. I remember meeting Dick Crossman at our respective lockers early in the term and he said, "Just like first day back at school." On another occasion, Quintin Hogg came upon me drafting a speech. I had my feet up on a book on the polished table, a cup of coffee, and papers strewn on every level surface. He said, "Nelson, NZ, must have been just like Eton," meaning that they, too, had learnt to spread themselves about and work in comfort.

There was no London practice left, although our set were busy enough and, with any luck, it would soon be re-established. In the meantime, I had little to do. I approached our Labour whips and they pointed out that most members found their own spare time work but that if they attended to their parliamentary duties assiduously, they could be in the chamber from two-thirty until ten at night, and that was enough work for anyone. In fact, as I soon learned, no one was in the chamber for any occasion except Question Time and high-level speeches, or occasions that promised some excitement, or matters of his own particular interest.

It was clear that I was extremely critical of the Foreign Office. As a result, I was approached by representatives of various of the smaller countries anxious to arm me with details of their problems. Resulting contributions to debate related to Indonesia, French Indochina, Germany, Romania and the Carinthian people as typical cases. There were other such international situations about which I was fully armed with detail but did not speak. The problems of the bigger countries and of the larger domestic interests were put in the hands of more distinguished parliamentary personalities, usually Tories, and they seemed to be run in a somewhat commercial fashion. It was strictly contrary to parliamentary practice and, I assume, all parliamentary law, for members to be paid in any way for actions they might take in the House and I was warned of this by the Home Secretary, Mr Chuter Ede, on the first occasion that I approached him.

It was the very beginning of injection-moulding for the mass production of plastics. A constituent, with his solicitor, had approached me and explained some question of licensing and of the difficulties and delays. There was no suggestion of payment to me, though the solicitor was obviously paid for the job. I was able to tell Chuter Ede with a quiet mind that I was in no real danger. In late 1945, I was approached by the Showmen's Guild, who asked that I might represent them in parliament. They were the organisation for circuses and other public and open-air shows of all kinds. I did not feel able to give the attention to their job and requirements that their proposal called for. Later they were probably glad that I declined. Nowadays, I gather that it is not difficult to find published advertisements from MPs asking to be employed as consultants and even indicating the general line of their skills and interests.

The whips offered to put me on the all-party Select Committee on Statutory Instruments, which had been set up in 1944 to protect the citizen against bureaucratic encroachment. We were to read the Orders in Council and other regulations and matters of subordinate legislation made by government departments or ministers. These ^"lay on the table" for a certain length of time so that interested members could study them and it was our duty to spot anything that might lead to an abuse of power. Since we were given the job of being interested, we read and discussed them, then raised points of amendment or comment that we thought proper.

On that committee I made some acquaintance with James Scott Cumberland Reid, KG, Member for Glasgow, Hillhead, and found that he was pretty quick at seeing obscure points. I believe the only Orders in Council that we overthrew altogether were spotted by Reid as being *ultra vires*. Reid, who was one of the most brilliant men of the century, went from the Scottish Bar straight to the Lords in 1948. Only one other man in the last century has gone to the Lords direct, and that was Cyril Radcliffe.

At annual conference, there had been frequent discussions of the idea that backbenchers should have some formal and constitutional means of expressing their views to ministers. Herbert Morrison took the initiative and set up seventeen consultative committees. Each group should consist of up to a score of members who had special interest in a particular topic. No Member was required to serve on any group, but all were asked by the whips to give their preference. I applied to be put on the Foreign Affairs and on the Fuel and Power groups, and found myself on both. The latter was to be a miners' advisory centre, greatly concerned with nationalisation. Unfortunately, that change was not aimed at giving any improved conditions to the miners but merely giving them a new master.

Except for myself, I think the members were all ex-miners and so were from mining constituencies. They treated it as rather freakish that I should go back to the pits, not only in the weeks between the taking of the poll and the declaration of the results, but also after that result was declared. (The difference was that they returned each weekend to their villages and so kept in constant touch with their own pits.) A seat in the House had become almost a traditional way of pensioning off a miner who had given long service to his union, so it was hardly surprising that most of the mining MPs were reactionary men who showed less interest in parliamentary work than in the drinking facilities the House offered. Even so, nothing could be more flattering than that they accepted me as one of their members. I was invited to speak at the dinner given by the miner MPs to the government at the Russell Hotel in the first year of our parliamentary life, and welcomed in every way. They expected me to drink with them every evening at whichever bar they were then frequenting. Yet, with the exception of the Miners' Charter, I did not take a single sensible step to try and recruit them into any sort of progressive activity.

Before the election, the Miners' Charter had been handed out at all our Yorkshire pits. It had been compiled by a group of working miners including Bill Kelleher of Brodsworth Main. The charter set out a list of improved conditions for miners on the basis of which it would be possible to demand from them the millions of extra tons of coal that the government needed. The argument was that other groups of workers were not being asked specifically to work harder; it was only miners. Very well; give them some incentives. The Miners' Charter seemed to offer the very thing. Let them have the best supplies of restricted foods. With most things being rationed, it would be easy to give extra to groups or to individuals. Why not the best schoolmasters to the pit village school, or a gardening instructor for the pit allotment gardens?

The government would have nothing to do with the charter. They argued, why shouldn't the more numerous farm workers, factory workers, or the better organised electricity workers have the same advantages? What of the railwaymen? Everyone else would want more, too. In spite of this, I made so much fuss over the charter that some on the Fuel and Power Committee began to take it up and we even passed resolutions that were sent forward to various ministries. A change was made in the composition of the group: new faces appeared, even more lumpen and reactionary miners, and their job was to say "no". It was in vain, for we persevered.

Then the group began to miss a meeting or two. It was not summoned by the whips. At first, there were apologies and explanations, and then just wide gaps between meetings. Arthur Horner, Secretary of the NUM, and Manny Shinwell worked out a new Miners' Charter that standardised wages and gave a five-day week. Our group was ended, with the whips declaring that it was for want of interest since nationalisation went through. In fact, we caused the government so much bother that this modest forum was removed. The group was butchered because it had too much to say. This was the first great bloomer of my parliamentary career. If I had given some thought to the matter and been sensibly advised, I should have devoted more care to explaining my point of view to the miners' group and less to making a general nuisance of myself.

Whatever may have since happened in Eastern European countries, they were then newly liberated from Nazi occupation and were a ferment of new ideas as to how they should govern themselves and how their economies should be organised and exploited. The miners I met were full of progressive plans. I visited each of these countries and think there was not one in which I did not go down a coal mine. In Yugoslavia, it was the Srem; in Poland, I attempted to work a shift down a pit in Silesia; in the Soviet Union, it was at Stalino; and in Romania it was at Resita. I recite these experiences not with the object of showing to what degree I was willing to pretend I was a genuine coal miner, but rather to show what extraordinary opportunities were missed with miners who were also British MPs. If I had taken my fellow MPs to share in the experiences, perhaps we could have bred a block that might have influenced the character of the Attlee government.

There is still reason to believe that if workers have a direct financial interest in the success of their industry and a say in its management, then that industry is likely to be more successful than if the only nexus between worker and management is wages for work and obedience. After the setting up of the National Coal Board in January 1947, I went back to Doncaster to see what changes had been made. I was no longer fit for anything on the coal-face and precious little use even for quiet work on the roads. Except for my own inability, nothing was changed. There were the same men in charge with the same positions. The same men did the same work at the same level of eagerness – that is, eagerness to be out of the pit and home. The tools were the same and breakdowns the same.

The various nationalisation acts provided for the appointment of "experts". The Labour Party has for a long time had in mind the picture of an impartial and emotionless figure filled with knowledge of a particular calling, perhaps with a university degree, certainly with years of practical experience and with high qualities of management. He was already in place, in the factory or the pit. You had only to take over the trade and you took over him as well. In the pit, he was the deputy, the overman or the gaffer. In the factory, he was the manager or foreman. In each case, he went straight on with his job. But he was not impartial; he was almost invariably Tory in make-up and practice. He was an in-built Tory, opposed to the trades unions and experienced at bossing the labour force.

One might have expected Labour to take steps towards implanting some workers in management but such few trade union members as did come on to directors' boards were there as managers or directors, and in no sense as representing the workers' point of view. Each of the national boards was to be headed by a distinguished personage. A typical example of these appointments was Lord Hyndley, Chairman of the National Coal Board. He did indeed come from the right quarters, except that he was boss of the biggest coal company in the land and could only fully represent the owners. Here was the chance to have some outstanding man represent the trade union side, yet the government made no attempt to train Labour men for the higher jobs in industry.

Nationalisation was not aimed at any shift in power between the owners and the workers. The basic industries were to be more efficient through scale and were to give cheaper services to all who were dependent upon them, but the public would have no say in their control. Each of the nationalised industries was needed for the profitable running of some aspect of private industry so that by taking them over and introducing new capital, we strengthened private capitalism. Coal and rail required immediate heavy investments. Some of the other undertakings were inefficient and called for the sacking of surplus labour. Invariably, the most successful businesses were left in private hands.

In Finsbury we produced more gin than the rest of England and had a famous brewery. I had debates with delegations of distillery owners and brewers and visited each of their works. The debate took the form "our principles" on one side, and "our survival" on the other. I never had to face a request to urge the government not to nationalise the distillers and brewers because there was never the slightest sign that Attlee's Cabinet had thought of it. If in 1947 we had nationalised brewing and distilling, and the import, refining and distribution of petroleum, it would have made a great change in our budgets for the last fifty years.

While I was still in the pits, Donald Bruce and Barbara Castle got the Foreign Affairs Group going and set it alight over Greece. This was the most vigorous backbenchers' committee and the only one likely to be of any real use. We met on a weekly basis, under the chairmanship of Seymour Cocks of the Union of Democratic Control. Other members included Kenneth Younger, Leslie Solley, William Warbey, and Konni Zilliacus. The foreign secretary did not normally attend, even when under sustained criticism; he sent Carol Johnson, secretary of the special interest groups' liaison committee, on his behalf. Bevin paid little attention to the Foreign Affairs Group, beyond treating us with open contempt. He regarded us as so many Communists, but we were the full strength of the Labour left. At one of our meetings, he called me a traitor; I do not recall the circumstances but it might have been because of the work I did for Churchill during the war.

From the start, we raised criticism about Bevin's behaviour in Greece. British forces set up in government those who had collaborated with the Nazis. The running of the country was to a great extent influenced by our police and our military missions, who acted as overseers while the Greek government carried on a major tyranny. Bevin wanted things to be as they had been before the war: the king must return and elections would be faked. The group asked Bevin to attend our meeting to satisfy me about Greece, but he declined. Instead, he offered to receive a small deputation to hear our point of view. I missed out, being back in the pit.

When Bevin accepted an invitation to visit Moscow in December to meet the foreign ministers of America, China and France, all guests of Stalin, we applauded and asked him to recognise Romania and Bulgaria, to support the Soviet proposal for a Four Power Council to control Japan, and to invite the Soviet Union to be a sponsor of the UN Commission on Atomic Energy. All were pro-Soviet ideas, but so many of Ernie's declared intentions were in defiance of our election policy to maintain the wartime friendship with the Soviet Union. There was a full house on 26th March 1946 when Ernie gave a long-winded twenty-seven-point rejection to criticisms of Labour foreign policy. The meeting was confidential but a full report of it appeared in a Toronto paper and from there was reprinted throughout the world. In mid-1947, certain Members pressed to have our special interest groups closed down in favour of regional groupings.

The government departed from a number of our election pledges and at first little was achieved. The explanation was that although we had made promises, there was no full detail of the legislation that would be needed. No ministry had been asked to approve a blueprint of what these new acts would contain, let alone the small print. Policies of the former government had developed their own momentum and were difficult to halt, and this was particularly so where civil servants disapproved of the change in direction. I began to judge everything that I was asked to do or to support strictly on the basis of the pledges to which I was party. I did not adopt this basis of judgement in the least bit suspiciously as expecting departures from the blueprint, but merely as a guide to myself. Like any barrister, I looked to my brief to see what I was supposed to be doing. There was the manifesto on which the Labour Party had fought; there was my own election address, which had been composed strictly on the basis of the proposals and promises in that manifesto; and there were the resolutions of the last party conference at Blackpool, just before the election.

Denis Healey had appeared in uniform and made a startlingly aggressive and attractive speech, laying down the future foreign policy of the party. He demanded that Britain use its surviving economic power and prestige as a victor to aid those in Europe who had helped in the overthrow of Hitler. Yet Bevin's international policy was to seek out and support in every country whichever party was certain to oppose the Communists. For example, he wanted a Monarchist-Right Wing Socialist coalition in Spain. We were told that Bevin's policy must continue because, were it to end, the Soviet Union would triumph. The people of Europe had made it quite clear that they didn't want these parties, but wherever Bevin lent a hand, the old reactionary and Fascist-leaning parties advanced in power.

In Yugoslavia, Tito called a general election for 11th November. The Communists were already being criticised for supposed dictatorial methods and Tito was anxious to impress upon the West that he was introducing a democratic system. The Yugoslav government broadcast an invitation for American congressmen and British MPs to invigilate the general elections, called for 11th November. No one replied to this, so they approached Konni Zilliacus and asked him to get together an all-party group of MPs and journalists. They knew Zilly well through his pre-war life as an official of the League of Nations and his known support for the left. Zilly approached several members and, when he had a few names, asked me to help.

Fitzroy Maclean had been sent to the partisans in September 1943 as Churchill's liaison officer and stayed there for eighteen months before coming back to the House of Commons. He seemed the ideal person to approach for help in organising the delegation, but would have no part in it. When he had been stationed with Tito in the mountains, it was on behalf of the allied armies and was a respectable duty. He reacted as if to be invited now when the war was over – and by me – must be a Communist plot. He seemed determined to shatter the idea that he had had any contact with the Communists, although he was already regarded as something of a world figure for just that reason. It is in keeping with this change that he later supported the infiltration of anti-Communist saboteurs into the Balkans. Fitzroy was one of my early introductions to the bitter distaste that the right has for the left. However, he did give me a letter for Tito.

Tito had aroused great interest and we soon got together some twenty-one names, including one or more members of the National Liberals (a most recondite group) and two Tories. Then Fitzroy persuaded the Tories not to go so that we were the weaker by this. We finally set off with one Liberal, one National Liberal and nine Labour MPs, including Lester Hutchinson, who was to continue on to Albania as personal guest of Enver Hoxha. Journalists were well represented. Lieutenant Colonel Basil Davidson, MC, of *The Times*, Ken Syers of the *News Chronicle* and Major John Ennals of the *Daily Herald* had fought with the partisans so were already popular with the Yugoslav government. We also had Miss McClurg for the BBC and Kingsley Martin of the *New Statesman*. Margaret Lloyd and Leo Mattes came too for the BBC.

Just as we were leaving, Flight Lieutenant William Teeling of Brighton launched a scurrilous attack upon the visit: he didn't approve of our going at all; transport was in short supply and what right had we to preference? We were obviously going to take part in the election on Tito's side. He asserted that I had read in *Reynold's News* (the left-wing Sunday paper) that Tito wanted British visitors and that I had volunteered and had gone round collecting names. Tom Driberg gave the truthful explanation, which showed that all Teeling's points were wrong. The fact was that the Yugoslavs provided the transport, and we had been at pains to ensure that our visit would not be publicised in Yugoslavia until after the election to forestall any allegations that we were there to help Tito.

I thought it strange that Teeling should set upon me. I had played little part in parliament and had no acquaintance with him. His story was pure guesswork, and an erroneous guess at that. Though I was only the office boy, he had me down as a busybody and the organiser of the whole thing. Teeling did not look like a flight lieutenant, or certainly not like a dashing young one. It would have been hard for him to squeeze into the cockpit of an aeroplane.

Another Tory MP, Sir Thomas Moore, spread the lie that our expenses were met from the Yugoslav Relief Fund, a charity to help relieve war suffering. It was an extremely nasty thing to say and a measure of his hatred of the left. He had joined the regular army in 1908 – and behaved as though he had. It was a curious coincidence that both he and Zilly had fought with Churchill's interventionary army in Russia against the Bolsheviks. Hector McNeil for the Foreign Office said that he was "disturbed and puzzled" by the arguments of the Tories, who were losing their sense of proportion. We were not really a delegation and were never official in any way. The high point of criticism was reached with the Tory MP Beverley Baxter: "I prefer to use the word 'delegation' because, having watched the corpse-like obedience of the party opposite, I do not believe that eleven Members of it would blow their noses without the permission of their party."

Our trip was on a Dakota. The only seat was a narrow metal ledge right the way round, which gave maximum space for cargo or for soldiers but meant that it was pretty uncomfortable. It was a great relief to break the journey at Paris for half-an-hour. This was a long flight and it was after midnight when we reached the unlit partisan landing ground near Zagreb, our descent guided only by Very lights fired from a pistol. Yugoslavia was the most powerful and important country in the Balkans but had suffered terribly in the war. The whole country was like the worst of the Ruhr. We saw villages razed to the ground. 7,000 bridges and miles of railway track were destroyed. The Germans had a mobile device that inserted explosive between the ends of each pair of rails; to finish the job, each sleeper was smashed. Ministers of the old regime used to boast that although their army was not much good, their defences were impregnable because they had never repaired the roads; they were now worse than usual.

The countryside bore the mark of feudal times and centuries of oppression. We saw miles of land intensively cultivated, but few farmhouses; all the people lived in protective villages. Although the whole country was poor, our delegation was entertained lavishly. On our first day in Zagreb we talked with members of the Croatian government, inspected a prison, then spent the evening at a reception given by the prime minister. In Belgrade, for some days in a hungry land, we were feted by every embassy in turn. It was medieval: sucking pigs, each with an apple in its mouth; the largest sturgeon I have ever seen; and wine and *slivovic* with everything. We were all somewhat surprised at the lavish provision made for us but took this as a measure of their desire to establish confidence between our two peoples. Whenever we saw a pig in the countryside after that, we saluted him with the cry "He's booked for the Diplomatic Corps".

The voting age was reduced to eighteen and, for the first time, women had the vote. The Communists formed a National Front to fight the election in coalition with the smaller parties of the left. The right-wing opposition parties felt that without access to the press, which was controlled by the National Front, they couldn't compete fairly, so boycotted the elections. If there were several candidates in a constituency, it was because they were rivals in the coalition. Alternatively, one could cast a vote against the government altogether. In their election campaigns, the national leaders did not demand a vote for their particular party in the Front. The Democrat leader toured the country for a month; he did not say "Vote for the Democrat in your constituency". We were told that the Communists wouldn't let him say it, but found that Tito himself, whose election campaign had been the most sustained, at no time argued "Vote for the Communist", but only "Vote for the best man to carry out our policy and to represent your area".

By the reforms, every landholder was reduced to a maximum of forty hectares; in the best land, thirty. This applied to every working landlord, though the non-worker lost his whole estate. The church got the maximum in each parish, and while we were there, the Archbishop of Croatia was in trouble because he had decided to divide as many parishes as possible in two so as to double his land holding. The government made no effort at collectivisation. UNRRA was producing the latest American row-crop tractors, and those and its lorries and food had already saved the people for the coming winter. There was a high degree of co-operation in re-building, harvesting and marketing, and UNRRA described it as the country in Europe where co-operation was most developed. In the part recently liberated, the previous winter battles had interrupted the wheat-sowing, and a great effort was made to put in maize at the last minute over the whole area.

We saw this campaign neatly reflected in one election contest in the Srem, a coal-mining area north-west of Belgrade. At Vrdnik in Voivodina, a strong Communist party led the reconstruction and production effort in the local pits and their candidate had gathered the 150 signatures necessary for nomination. He was a miner and had fought in the hills with the partisans. His opponent was a rich farmer who had carried on in comfort with the Germans; not collaborating, but fitting in and making decent money. Yet the miners were voting for him to emphasise the importance of food supplies. This rich farmer had led the drive for the late sowing of the empty wheat land and had organised not only the village and the neighbourhood, but even the peasants who had been allotted his own land, taken from him by the agrarian reform. The miners were satisfied that the pit would work all right and were anxious to see that in an agricultural area, the best man to lead the peasants should be their representative. There was a lively contest and the farmer won.

Our hosts asked each of us whether there was anything we would especially like to do. I asked to go down a coal-mine and that is why I was taken to the Srem. The pit lads were working with rather primitive tackle in a mine that had been damaged by the enemy, yet were already producing more than pre-war. I thought they were magnificent. I met one working barefoot and others who had only felt slippers – two working on the face, so desperate was their shortage. I worked with them, but not for long. Like all miners, they accepted any reasonable opportunity to squat on the coal in the gloom to talk and take a rest. Wherever I went in the pit, they sent greetings to British miners. They were all eager to know whether we would nationalise the pits as they had done. They also asked if there were any chance that some of them might come to England to learn how to apply modern methods and modern machinery. I raised this with our embassy in Belgrade and also with the NUM, but nothing came of it. They also produced a list of machinery parts that were needed. I tried this on the same authorities and on our Foreign Office and the British Council, but with no luck.

On the day I left the Srem, I rejoined our delegation at Belgrade. We then attended a party at Tito's White Palace, which had been taken over from his royal predecessors. The palace was heavily guarded. I remember that there was more than one set of outside gates and our coach-load was handed on by telephone and outrider from one set to the other. Inside the palace, each gallery and grand stairway had its share of armed guards. It was decorated in fine style. The reception room in which we were entertained had a number of great chandeliers that sparkled as though every bead of glass had been taken down and given an individual shine. Before leaving the mines, I had been given a red rose for Tito and presented it to him that evening as "A red rose from your miners in the Srem".

Tito was a decorative chap and wore a white or very light-coloured uniform with several rows of military decorations. His complexion was as though straight from a summer tan, but in fact done rather inexpertly so that it looked as if it was painted on. He was built on a powerful mould and gave the impression that at any moment he might thrust one hand in his jacket front in a Napoleonic stance. He was constantly striking a pose and seemed rather vain. I think Tito was smoking Russian papyrosi cigarettes, with their own cardboard holder attached at one end, and each cigarette standing upright in the mouth of a right-angled holder. It was quite absurd and I had not seen the like before. It was certainly the first time I ever saw someone followed about by an aide-de-camp to hold the ashtray.

Tito asked me, "What have you done with Winston Churchill?" "What should we have done?" "Well, you beat him in the election. If it had been here, we would have shot him, or at least we would have driven him into the woods." This may have been a genuine Yugoslav preoccupation, but I'm sure that Tito's remark was an attempt at humour. As comrades in arms, they had got on well together. I thought of Churchill, now too heavy to climb from the kerbside onto the crown of Downing Street, and too portly to hide behind the biggest tree in the Dinaric Alps. They took their politics seriously in the Balkans, as Churchill said in parliament on 16th August:

> "A friend of mine, an officer, was in Zagreb, when the results of the late General Election came in. An old lady said to him, 'Poor Mr Churchill. I suppose now he will be shot.' My friend was able to reassure her. He said the sentence might be mitigated to one of the various forms of hard labour which are always open to His Majesty's subjects."

We all remarked on Tito's apparent vanity and self-indulgence. The contrast between the state of the country and the extravagant provision made for us was so acute that it could not be put down to traditional hospitality. It showed some error of judgement that must have begun at the centre and was now established. We considered whether this lavish style of life with palaces and cars and decorative uniforms and flunkies was in any way justified. Should the new rulers be imitating those whom they had so rightly displaced, and what kind of example was Yugoslavia setting for other countries moving towards a new way of life? During the partisan days he had lived as rough in the mountains as any other man, and it seemed extraordinary that he should now affect a pose of exaggerated elegance. Could he be wishing to show the change from the coarse homely figure of Stalin to some imagined image of a Western statesman?

Tito's large dog developed an immodest passion for one of the sucking piglets. When he raised his sights and nose to table level, Tito bade the dog withdraw. It did so, but with great reluctance. The evening was a remarkable mixture of informality and ostentation. Zilly sought to engage Tito in conversation in his own tongue but was cut short and urged to speak in English so that all could understand. On the question of his greatest success and satisfaction, Tito answered that it was the unity of all Yugoslavian provinces and the end of warring between them. He would have been broken-hearted today at the bitterness of civil war that has brought the total dismemberment of Yugoslavia.

Coming back, the weather was too bad for air travel so we had to return through Trieste. The future of this area was in dispute; was it to be Italian or Yugoslav? For us it was clear that the people of Trieste were for Yugoslavia. The villages and the town itself were ablaze with flags and with posters of Tito. There was a grand reception and banquet, delegations of workers and anti-Fascist groups, and all supporting Tito. We reported accordingly. Hector McNeil had made it clear in parliament that our visit was nothing to do with the government and they were not interested in any conclusions we might form. Like as not, however, Mr Stevenson (the Minister in Belgrade) or one of his officers came to any functions we attended. We wrote a unanimous report on what we had seen and filed a copy with parliament. Margaret Lloyd sent copies to the Foreign Office and to Mr Stevenson.

Kenneth Younger was the nearest to the left you could get and still be "in with" the establishment. Attlee thought him very promising. Kenneth sometimes tipped us off as to what was being said in high places and we learnt from him that the Foreign Office found our report sensible and well-balanced. Our conclusions were the same as theirs. They raised one exception, pointing out that we had been misled over Trieste. The local Communist Party distributed some thousands of flags and posters and organised the deputations. In short, the whole thing had been rigged.

The new Yugoslavia had every cause for wanting friendship with the Soviet Union. Help to them had come first from the East, and that help had established Tito as the certain victor. The restoration of the cities, of transport and of food supplies began from Russia before UNRRA came in, and the two countries were establishing, they believed, the same system of government. However, the Yugoslavs did not want to be too close to Stalin; they wanted equally to be friendly with the West. Tito had told our little group:

> "You need not worry about our friendship for it is always there waiting for a chance to show itself. What you have to do is to restore the confidence of our people in your good intentions. Once you do that you will be surprised at how much friendship we have for you."

But the Yugoslavs had not seen any continuing friendship similar to the military help of the war. Instead, there were now signs of hostility, further stimulated by our visit.

CHAPTER FOURTEEN

First Visit to Russia

DURING THE war, we saw in England the harm caused by the lack of a united movement among young people. Evacuation of children to the countryside severely disrupted their education, and juvenile delinquency reached its highest peak. Although we desperately needed fuel, our lads were reluctant to work in the mines. It wasn't that they lacked patriotism, but that they could not see the desirability of working for the benefit of the whole community. It was generally agreed that a wide organisation for young people was needed. I suppose its general purpose was to try to inspire them with some of the self-sacrificing attitudes so usual in the teaching of the scouts and guides, Christian organisations such as the YWCA and YMCA, and their East European counterparts, the Young Communists.

The World Federation of Democratic Youth was established in London in November 1945 at the World Youth Conference, attended by young people from all the allied countries. The preliminary meeting was a packed affair at the Royal Albert Hall on 29th October with Stafford Cripps presiding. There followed a reception at some grand hotel, and meetings continued for the next fortnight. The headquarters would be in Paris, and our Kutti Hookham of the ASYFA was elected one of the three secretaries.

For me, the most interesting visitor was N A Mikhailov, First Secretary of the Central Committee of the Soviet Komsomols. (Through most of the war years, his assistant had been Yuri Andropov.) Mikhailov was no longer young, but it seemed that senior officers could go on even into their thirties. He was impressive in a number of ways: he was calm, and always moved and spoke moderately slowly; he was well-briefed and knew something in advance of everyone with whom he spoke and seemed always

210

to have something prepared to say to each person; he mixed serious questions and proposals with a bit of light-hearted banter; he confirmed my belief that the job of the person speaking through an interpreter is to address himself to the person to whom he is speaking as though ignoring the translator.

It was not yet a self-harming action to join in a group that had Russians amongst them, but there was still considerable prejudice. In July the ASYFA had launched an appeal to raise £50,000 for a youth centre in Stalingrad. We had in mind a hostel for a thousand, plus a library, restaurants, theatre, sports facilities, and so forth. This would not only commemorate the great victory at Stalingrad and serve as a memorial to their war dead, it would also consolidate friendship between the young people of our countries. We had kept in close contact with the Soviet Anti-Fascist Youth Committee. This was led by Lieutenant General Evgeny Fyodorov, the young scientist who had accompanied Papanin on the North Polar Drift Expedition, and by Olga Lepeshinskaya, prima ballerina of the Bolshoi.

When the Russians decided to bring over a delegation of young Britons to learn the truth about their system and to report on the situation of children and young people in those parts of Russia recently liberated from the Nazis, the invitation came through the Anti-Fascist Committee. The ASYFA allotted places in proportion to the relative strength and importance of the main youth organisations, such as the Boy Scouts and the Girl Guides and the National Union of Students, each of whom was invited to appoint a delegate. We also included the main groups outside the youth bodies, such as the forces, miners, engineers and young farmers. Thirty or more were shortlisted and came to London for a selection contest.

The seventeen chosen formed a broad cross-section from different walks of life. They included Lawrence Daly, a young Scottish miner who went on to become General Secretary of the NUM; Harry Rea, a teacher who had parachuted into France with the SOE and became a resistance hero; and, from Equity, Gordon Jackson, who later played Hudson, the butler in *Upstairs, Downstairs*. Jim Callaghan, MP, representing the navy, was our most distinguished fellow traveller, but did not join us until January. There had been no requirement that they read or speak Russian. I mastered it enough to make speeches on radio in Moscow and Leningrad, though it is now long since gone.

Our trip had the blessing of the Foreign Office and the Ministry of

Information, yet we still found ourselves obstructed by Whitehall. Several delegates were of an age to be called up for military service, so needed written permission from the Ministry of Labour before they could leave the country; all were refused. We appealed, but in vain. It was a throwback to the pre-war attitude of no friendship with the Soviet Union. We found plenty of backbenchers to support us. The matter was raised with the Minister, George Isaacs, and soon put to rights. As VIPs, we were to travel by air. Just before Christmas, we gathered at St James Street by five-thirty a.m., travelled by coach to Croydon Airport (then on its last wheels as a civil flying place), and returned to London at noon as the flight was postponed because of the weather. This happened repeatedly. In the 'forties, those who travelled by air in winter accurately described it as "Gone today, here tomorrow".

After several false starts, our big breakthrough came when ten set off one morning. Only ten could be accommodated, as the plane had to be prepared with extra petrol for a non-stop flight to Berlin in case the weather at Hamburg should be bad. Those who were going ahead were to spend three or four days in Berlin, waiting for the others. The most striking thing about Berlin was the spate of anti-Soviet stories amongst the British soldiers. There was no Red Army; they hadn't beaten the Germans because they couldn't have; "Look, they haven't got a single motor car." It was true that the only cars were a few commandeered German ones used by senior officers and officials. For the rest, transport was by primitive peasant carts that had accompanied the army from the steppe years before. Women were not safe after dark in the English zone, while the Russian zone was prohibited. "We always go armed," they said.

The explanation for these stories lay in the fact that the German people were riddled with anti-Soviet propaganda. In addition, the girls with whom our soldiers associated had guilty consciences about the way in which they treated Russian prisoners and the way in which their menfolk treated the Russians at home. They feared that the Russian occupying troops might take revenge for the atrocities of the past and were busy describing the things that they were expecting. A third factor was that the Red Army sacrificed everything to fighting efficiency. In Berlin, the Russians did not care whether it took three hours or three days for a load of supplies to cross the city, or to cross from one zone to another. The Soviet soldiers who stood guard were their youngest recruits and many looked unkempt and woolly. The fighting troops were long since back home, leading the work of reconstruction and industry.

On Boxing Day we flew to Moscow by Russian-built Dakota, bedded down in all our warm clothes. Many of our immediate hosts were known from the World Youth Conference and at the airport we got a great reception. There were greetings and toasts with vodka and champagne, and chocolates and great rosy apples. The press wrote down every word, then demanded personal statements about our first impressions of Moscow, still sixteen miles away. We drove in a convoy of limousines to the Moscow Hotel, the biggest and most modern in the capital. Dinner was ready, itself a great meal, then off to bed to prepare for the reception banquet at eleven p.m.. The typical breakfast was at eleven a.m., dinner at four-thirty or five p.m., and supper at eleven p.m. We got used to this by our sixth week. I qualified by age as the leader, perhaps even as the father of the expedition and soon learnt the responsibilities attached to the role. At every gathering there were speeches of greetings, of thanks and farewell. But it had its compensations. "Where is the leader? Will you come this way, please? Here is your suite." Four rooms for the leader, and only one each for the others.

We saw all the great sights: the museums and galleries, the opera, the ballet and Red Square. The main streets were broader than anything I had ever seen before and any city would be envious of the central hill crowned by the Kremlin and the river flowing beside it. It is as though the Tower of London, Windsor Castle and Hampton Court were all combined and set on a slight hill, with immense wide spaces all around. I think what struck us most sharply were the shops and the rationing system. Everything was rationed. The essentials of life such as butter, bread and soap, were controlled by a quantity system. The less essential were on a points system so that if you bought a hair-drier, you couldn't have a new bicycle for a year or so. Shop windows and shelves were bare, but whenever there was anything to buy, there were long queues. It was so in the Soviet Union from the beginning and continued so until the break-up in 1991, but in every town one saw markets where country people sold private produce. Nearly sixty per cent of Soviet citizens worked on collective farms, where there was no rationing of food.

While we were in Moscow, the temperature was twenty-five below zero centigrade. I had Daisy's 1900 buggy coat in green Irish frieze, from the first year of her marriage when she had her own buggy and horse for pastoral rounds. When it was known that I was to visit Russia in mid-winter, the tailor from Chapel Market at the Angel added a fulsome musquash collar. Our Soviet hosts held that it was the coat of a burglar from Berlin and ordered immediate replacement by a padded coat with astrakhan collar, commissar third class, and bearskin hat, as they did for all our delegation. (I still have Daisy's coat. It is the greatest coat in the Temple and is never allowed out save when there is snow on the ground.)

The Moscow Metro stations were beautifully decorated with marble, mosaics and symbolic statuary, but they were always crowded. I never saw an escalator that you could walk down; people stood two abreast all the way. A girl at each carriage door of the trains helped passengers in and closed the doors. So great was the crowding that one was physically helped in with a knee in the back and the doors then snapped to before one could rebound. The trains, which are by tradition a battleground for Soviet people, were so crowded that several might pass a small crowd at a stopping place and not one passenger able to board, though all tried. There were no queues for public transport; Muscovites had the independence of which we boasted in London before the forerunner of London Transport taught us how mistaken we were and made us all queue.

Our delegation was kept busy in Moscow, but this packing of the programme seemed a subterfuge to prevent us going about alone. We had all heard stories that we would only be able to go where taken and would see only what they wanted us to see, and we began to think that we could not even leave the hotel without permission. After all, our photos had been taken for Soviet internal passports, which we were never given. Could we dare go out without them? By the fifth day, a number of the delegates began to think of themselves as prisoners in the hotel. To test this, four or five put on their coats, fur hats and snow boots. Sure enough, Tamara appeared at the head of the stairs. She called out, "Please, not now. You can't go out; Moscow radio are just arriving. Where are you going?" One answered, "We can't wait. We're just going out to the lavatory." And down we ran.

This was an immense hotel and the whole of Moscow seemed to be pouring in through the doors. We still had to pass the enormous doorman in braided uniform. Astonishingly, he took no notice; we were outside and free. We ran up the street waving at the hotel and shouting in the gathering dusk, poking out our tongues at the windows. After that, no one thought that we were in any way limited. If there was time to spare in the programme (and we arranged whole days free) then we were all over the place, as inquisitive and impertinent as ferrets. In fairness, I think that the nervousness of the guides was at least in part due to their desire to save us from collision with the host of bylaws, rules and regulations to which they were accustomed. Later in the tour, two of our members, out on a private foray, took photos of a railway station without permission. They were brought back to the hotel by the militia, but only after some delay.

A further reason for our not being able to go about in small groups was that none of us spoke the Russian language. As official interpreters were in short supply, it was almost impossible to have serious talks with our hosts for want of translation. Mr Broomfield and Miss Seton Watson, two young members of staff at the British Embassy who spoke fluent Russian, were allotted to help us in Moscow and Leningrad. They were a comfort and were heavily overworked by us. We tried to get them joined up for the whole of the tour but the logistics did not extend so far.

The general plan of the visit was worked out with our Soviet hosts. We were given our own plane and crew, we decided what institutions we would visit and what persons we would invite to meet us. After Moscow and Leningrad, we mapped out a tour from Kiev and the Don Basin in the south-west, across to the Volga and Stalingrad, south to Georgia and Azerbaijan, by the Caspian oil route to Samarkand, and then north to Sverdlovsk in the Urals. We weren't able to fit it all in, but every ambassador in Moscow was envious of our freedom to travel.

We were determined to go into private homes and were greatly helped by Paddy Costello, a junior military attaché at the British Embassy, who willingly shared with us his extensive knowledge of Russian domestic life.

The New Zealand Ambassador in Moscow described him to us as an excellent and most reliable diplomat, well-informed about Russia. Costello had been a guards officer before joining the diplomatic corps and later became a university lecturer. In 1981, Chapman Pincher named him as a spy for the Soviet Union. I find it impossible to believe this suggestion, but you can say anything about a person when he's dead.

New Year was the main winter festival. Many squares had gaily lit trees and decorated booths. Grandfather Frost was everywhere, and every family we visited seemed to have a tree with lights and presents on it. In the

Slav countries there is no phrase that corresponds to taking "pot luck". If you are a guest, then everything is on the table and every bottle is uncorked. In days of rationing and food shortages, this tradition must be a real impediment to entertaining. Every meal with guests, even in a private house, started with a toast drunk in vodka. It would invariably be followed by another and another. We had been warned of this by John Dugdale, a junior minister in the admiralty, who had been with a government wartime mission to Moscow. He was late appointing a young representative, but announced that he was sending Jim Callaghan, a genuine navy man. He thought we would need him to support our drinking power because none of us were used to vodka; Jim would drink enough to float a battleship.

John Dugdale was right about the drinking power. After the first week, we had to fight a main political battle to free ourselves from vodka for breakfast. It was not only available, it was pressed at each meal, although our hosts themselves tried to hold back. Our young women complained to the British Embassy that at feasts they would be plied with great quantities of alcohol while the hostesses limited themselves to fruit juice; was it genuine hospitality, or something more sinister? When Mary Robinson of the YWCA first drank with us, she declared it was her only alcohol since a glass of sherry on her twenty-first birthday. She ran the YWCA hostel in Great Russell Street and thousands of girls had passed under her guidance and care, although she was not yet thirty. I remember some big occasion where Mary was called on to propose the nineteenth toast. She rose, firmly unsteady, and swayed forward on her toes until we feared the worst. But then, by a miracle, back on her heels to a similar degree. Then forward again across the table, with the words, "If only my organisation could see me now. Whoops to the YW!" We certainly needed Jim's support.

On the night of his arrival, we took him to the theatre and then to the usual eleven o'clock supper, but this time a special celebration. I sat between Jim and a young Soviet admiral in full uniform and covered with medals. Any Soviet serviceman had medals galore and wore them at supper with us because it was always a state occasion. We knew Jim had plenty of medals, yet he wore only the dark blue and light blue ribbons of the defence medal. Any eager fire-watcher could have got that. In short, he was extremely modest. We had no sooner assembled than the admiral rose and proposed a toast to "Ze Royal Navy". We all stood up and Jim, a glass of vodka in hand, whispered to me, "I don't drink." The whisper was loud enough for others to hear and we all cried, "You must, Jim! The honour of the Royal Navy is at stake." He swallowed it down manfully. But then there had to be the toast to the Red Navy and no one but Jim could propose it. After this, Jim's defences were down and he drank his way round the circuit like a hero. I believe that from the moment we staggered back to England, liquor seldom passed his lips.

A young Orthodox priest accompanied us on several of our Moscow visits. He took us to three churches, including his own parish church on the outskirts of the city, where we heard him preach. Every service was crowded. All the congregation stood, except when kneeling. There were strong male voice choirs with accent on the bass, and the vestments of the priests and their regalia were gorgeous. We went to a synagogue and to a Free Church service as well; they were equally crowded. In each case, the worshippers were mainly old women. Our official Christian representative was Penry Jones of the British Council of Churches. He was a member of the Ionian Community and had lived on that island for some statutory period. He led our forays into churches and himself preached at one Orthodox service where most of us were present. Friendship came into his sermon a good deal, and he included the passage from Luke "Friend, go up higher". It was easy to develop the idea of friendship in those surroundings and company.

However, Dr Eric Taylor, an agronomist from Cambridge, was profoundly dissatisfied with everything that we saw, and equally whether it was a farm, a factory crèche or a school. About the farms, he really came alight. Eric gave us the most intimate detail of each beast, its breeding and qualities and foibles, and the same detail of the conduct, demeanour and skills of each farm girl and each manager. Even when praising something, he presented it in such a way that it was shrouded in gloom. Mr Broomfield at the British Embassy said it was as though Eric saw everything only through a Russian midwinter fog. If they noticed his hostility, our hosts said nothing.

Leningrad, for all its grace and beauty, seemed to be a provincial town living in the past. The rebuilding was to be exactly as before. On a visit to Warsaw in 1949, Janet and I were told that when that city was destroyed, the Poles turned to Stalin for advice. They had two factions equally divided.

One wished to begin again on open ground, which would be cheaper than clearing the rubble. The other wished to build as before to preserve history and memories. Stalin said, "You are likely to change so many things. If you can keep the city, it will make the changes easier." Kiev was also being new-built from ruins, but in a very modern way. All the services of water, gas, electricity and the like ran underground in large working tunnels. There was to be no more digging up the street to get at the gas leak. All the main buildings were designed on a central plan, and the city transport likewise. Jim Callaghan and I asked whether Britain should not have separate representation in the Ukraine, although none of our hosts raised this with us.

The Russians are a proud people. They clearly felt a sense of achievement for having overcome the tremendous difficulties against which they had had to battle. I understood this, remembering the feeling on any day after a night of bombing in London, and our strange sense of pride when returning servicemen saw the ruins where their homes used to be. It was a feeling that we, too, had taken our share of the hardships. The Russians didn't boast about their suffering, but if people were genuinely interested, then they spoke freely. When I commented to one young worker on the way that people put up with the shortage of housing and clothing for the sake of getting the cities rebuilt, he said, "You must realise this is not easy. These results are not obtained without great efforts. All our leading young people will live shorter lives because of the efforts we are making and they know this, but they think it worthwhile."

Young people made tremendous contributions to overcoming major difficulties such as the war against illiteracy, the building of the Dneiper Dam and of Komsomolsk, the reconstruction of the Donbas mines and of Stalingrad. We spent four days in Stalingrad and saw that the reconstruction was mainly in the hands of some 25,000 young workers who had come from all parts of the nation, representing every trade and profession, to rebuild the city that they so prized. Almost all, whatever their previous calling, were pressed into service as bricklayers. When we returned to Moscow, the British minister invited us for dinner. He wished to introduce us to a very distinguished Soviet citizen, an outstanding person who held the highest order in the land, the Order of Lenin. We were delighted. "Order of Lenin? Why, that's nothing. We had six of them to dinner last night, and all under twenty-five, and all bricklayers."

The rebuilding of schools always took priority. In Stalingrad, the school building programme was complete, with fifty-six modern schools built before a single permanent house had gone up. There were 200,000 people in temporary houses and another 100,000 living in any kind of shelter that they had managed to adapt: an upturned tram, a derelict tank, a large-calibre water pipe or an unused water tank, and almost every basement left in the ruins. Everything possible was pressed into service; for example, we saw a tram on rails being towed by a camel in the snow.

In Kiev we heard that students were rebuilding the university. We found the place full of activity. As it was about thirty below, the favourite jobs were repairing inside. We were introduced to a number of young men who had a smattering of Russian but were plainly German. They were prisoners of war who lived in a nearby POW camp and were trucked in to work; from then on, all was changed. We were told that they were treated as ordinary Russian workers, with trade union rates and normal working conditions. There was plenty of larking and joking between Russian girls and the German boys; an occasional slap by a German hand on the behind of the girl bending down to paint the wainscot. One of the Germans said, "We think the Russians are a bit soft the way they treat us." They were very young, so must have been a recent intake to the Nazi Army and this may have led to lenient treatment.

Students in higher education were paid sufficient to make them independent of their families so that they would not have to work their way through college. Every university and technical institute had a crèche for the children of students, something that was unheard of in Britain. In every town were Pioneer Palaces and Houses of Culture where young people could develop their physical, mental and cultural capacity. The adult equivalent was the House of Rest and Culture, christened by some Russians the House of Rest from Culture. These were not just large empty buildings. So eager were the people to use them that the shift system had been introduced, and this applied even to swimming pools, schools and hobby circles.

We spent three days in Stalino, the central town of the coal-mining area, the Don Basin. The pits had been destroyed either by the miners before the Germans arrived, or by the Germans before they withdrew. The Nazis had tried to get some coal out but met with extreme resistance, and the story of one pit was that obstruction was so determined that many people were killed and the Nazis finally filled up a shaft with dead bodies. The Russians took the chance of rebuilding the pits, which were now being re-equipped. The two and a half miners in our delegation (Dilwyn Evans from the Rhondda, Lawrence Daly and myself) went down one of the biggest pits and found that because it was very wet, it was dust-free and miners suffered from rheumatism rather than chest complaints. Work on the face was done by the usual continental practice of hand-got with air picks. Women worked underground, but only to tend the motors. Lawrence was so impressed with the set-up and the standard of machinery, both on the roads and at the coal-face, that he said he wanted to come and work there.

The "leading young people" of the nation were treated with great respect and because we were their guests, we were given the finest treatment. At any place we visited, we were shown round by the director or manager. If there were some question on which there was doubt or misunderstanding, a university professor would come and stay until we were satisfied. Great prominence was given to leaders, such as the Secretary of the local Komsomols, and they naturally took charge. Those doing the most important or most successful work were well rewarded. One might find the director of a factory receiving 3,000 roubles per month while the old-age-pensioner working part-time as a cleaner or guard was paid only 150 roubles. We also met miners who earned more than the director of the mine, and factory workers on higher pay than their managers. Wages had a wide range, depending entirely on the type of work. The Russians aimed at equality of opportunity, but there was no pretence at equality of earnings.

It seemed to us that the efficiency of Soviet administration and industrial work was due to the fact that every individual was held to immediate personal responsibility for the job he or she was doing. For example, you could not get into the building housing the Moscow Radio Committee unless you had a pass, however distinguished the person who took you. On one occasion I was rushed past the doorman by the director herself, who shouted that we were late to record a broadcast and that it was a matter of great urgency. The doorman followed up the stairs, but too late. I got in all right, but was not allowed out until the pass was obtained.

In Leningrad, I went to a German War Criminals trial. We sat in a box right against the stage with the best view of the prosecutor, who was summing up for the state. During the interval, we wished to go across the stage to the other side. I was accompanied by the Secretary of the Leningrad Komsomols, who was known throughout the city for having played an outstanding role during the siege. We went to the back of the stage with a major who was one of the officers responsible for the arrangements of the court. At the door into the wings, we were stopped by a young soldier. The major produced his pass, but it had no effect. Explanations had no effect. The colonel had to be fetched to issue the pass and usher us through. There was no getting round the rules, however important you might be. In all places, we found a blending of respectful discipline and friendly familiarity between senior and junior grades of workers. Parallel with that was the extent to which all grades of workers mixed in public. In the best seats at the theatre, where we always found ourselves, we rubbed shoulders with admirals, railway workers, woodcutters, factory workers, students.

Ernie Bevin came to Moscow and we were all invited to the embassy to meet him. We knew he had been to the Bolshoi the evening before and that he had seen *Cinderella*. We were to make our first visit that evening, to see *Don Quixote*. We crowded round Bevin demanding, "What was it like, Ernie? Tell us about the Bolshoi." He replied, "Yes, I went. I saw them. I saw the Russian people. There was I in the Royal Box and there they were below me, packed in, all dressed the same. Frightened people; frightened to look beside them, frightened to look behind them, almost too frightened to look in front of them, like so many civil servants." Olga Lepeshinskaya, the principal ballerina, later told us, "It was one of our proudest nights. Stalin was there, and all the allied foreign ministers, and the auditorium was packed with the staffs of visiting embassies. We all decided to dance our very best for them." When we told her of Bevin's error, she said she wished he had seen *Don Quixote*. They played that for its true political story: the struggle of a stupid old man who tried to maintain the practices and modes of the past, refusing to yield to modern ideas and ways.

We thought of ourselves as without prejudice, but had the skin of cynicism that comes from reading English newspapers. For about a fortnight, any sight of militiamen speaking to civilians brought out such questions as: "I wonder which station they go from for Siberia? and "Who holds the key for the local salt mine?" Then we stopped, for such ideas bore no relation to what we saw. There was no indication of terror or pressure. People spoke of Stalin as if he were someone they knew, but one for whom they had tremendous regard for his heroic leadership during the war. The up-to-date idea is that Stalin had no military strategy; that he declined to consider the advice that Chamberlain gave him through his emissary, Stafford Cripps; that he gravely weakened his own forces by wanton and barbarous slaughter of his officers; that he was saved only by the brilliance of the generals that remained and by the magnificent sacrifices of the Russian people.

With two MPs on the team, Jim and I had the slight expectation that some or all of us might have the chance to meet Stalin, although we did not like to ask. Jim had the gift of a pipe sent by his constituents, but that was scarcely enough to justify a request. Each time we came back to Moscow we thought that this might be it, and when we made a visit to the Kremlin we couldn't believe that it was to be limited to the museums and cathedrals. In 1951, I saw Stalin's corpse lying in state, but that was our only meeting. I feel sure that no one of us in the delegation had any idea of the true character of the man.

The night before the election of Deputies to the Supreme Council, we heard the broadcast of Stalin's final speech. Although our Russian translators couldn't understand it very well, they told us of the homely phrases, the simple, direct and positive approach and the stirring call to co-operation in the work outlined. They complained that this was not Stalin. They had heard their leader on the radio many times and he had a most attractive voice. This was the coarse voice of an uneducated peasant, probably from Azerbaijan. After some argument, we had the explanation that throughout the war the Moscow evening news had been given by a very beautiful voice, that of a professional broadcaster, which many people had assumed to be Stalin's. It was like the BBC Nine o'clock news bulletin which was introduced by "This is the Nine o'clock news and this is Alvar Liddell reading it". We knew the voice and had confidence that no paratroopers had captured the BBC. So it was in Moscow. Now, hearing Stalin for the first time, our Russian companions said, "That's not Stalin. It's a frightful accent."

In Moscow during the election, we divided up into small groups and went off to inspect the polling booths. I think that Lawrence Daly and I were with Keith Moore of the AEU. After we had seen a certain amount of the voting and talked with the scrutineers and militia and with some voters, there chanced to come a rather distinguished person. He was introduced as the only holder of the Order of Lenin in the constituency. It was a bit difficult to follow exactly his calling. He wrote a lot, but was not a writer or journalist; he published without being a publisher. He had organised writers and publishers and printers to come together in a collective that encouraged more writers and publishers and printers so that they covered the whole city. His plan had been extended to the other cities and now was nationwide.

It was about one o'clock, so he asked us to come home for lunch. With three grown children, he had more than the usual supply of rooms; in fact, it was two adjoining flats with a door opened between. When we accepted, he asked whether we would mind if he invited some neighbours to call. They came, and they turned out to be the party secretary, local mayor, town clerk, manager of the biggest factory in the borough, and so forth. The joined flats and the landing outside were bursting with people and, as we arrived, we saw extra tables and chairs being brought in and food by the hamper. An ample supply of bottles was already in position and it wasn't long before we were in for the first speech of welcome and the first toast.

Every toast was for us or directed towards us and we had to drink them all. After half-an-hour of vodka with a slight sifting of caviar, we moved to the serious antidote to the drink — many rounds of heavily buttered items with bits of meats and savoury attachments. Every one of our eighteen or more hosts made a speech of sorts and proposed more drinks until we could no longer stand for our toasts but took them sitting, and then even lolling. It went on to five o'clock and there was much singing and further drinking. We had had several weeks of heavy drinking and thought we had learned to manage; we had to be helped home to bed.

Back at the hotel, we learned that each group had had a comparable lunch invitation: a similar bigwig, a chance meeting, a spontaneous gathering of famous friends, the plentiful food, the drink and the talk. It was all carefully laid on. It was apparent that the ample food came from our hotel and we joked that we remembered the precise pattern of the holes in the cheese that we'd had the day before. We thought at first that it was reprehensible to make such preparation and that we had been tricked, but although it would have been better if our hosts said that they had arranged for us to meet leading figures in each constituency, they were most interesting people and excellent lunches. When we got home, I wrote a report about the election and our general impression, saying that there was free expression of opinion and a secret vote and that the churches were free from interference. Knowing what Russians now say about the state of affairs forty-five years ago, there must be a doubt whether there was anything we then saw that justified my statement.

The press conference at the end of the visit was a great affair and went on for three hours. The whole foreign press corps were there and all the local papers. Throughout our stay, it was clear that the Russians had a high regard for the British, not only because of our joint struggle against the Nazis, but also for our industrial power and high standard of living. It had seemed obvious to us that the Soviet authorities wished this regard to continue, yet questions at the conference were aimed largely to embarrass the British government, and the Russian papers published only those answers that were of that character. One questioner wanted to know why we had re-armed the defeated Japanese troops and were using them to restore French and Dutch colonial rule in Indochina and in Indonesia. It was a question impossible to answer without reflecting discredit on our own Labour government.

For the return to London, we were escorted to Moscow Airport. A customs official, fifth class, came into the room and announced that he would inspect our baggage. One of our hosts objected. She was a powerful woman who could order up an aeroplane at very short notice. She explained that we were guests of the Soviet Union, going home with all the honours and gifts that they could bestow. There could be no question of undoing our baggage. In response, he invited our distinguished hosts to leave the room. They left very promptly. It was agreed that Members of the British Parliament were exempt from inspection. Jim and I quickly picked up "our baggage", which seemed to be considerably more than half the total, and moved it outside. Our delegates were busy reminding us that that bag was full of bottles, and the one with caviar must necessarily be ours.

The search that followed was very thorough. Even books and notebooks were ruffled through, but nothing was interfered with and we brought out thirty or forty undeveloped films. Pauline's medal was the only thing that aroused interest. She was the Women's Land Army representative from Spalding, Lincolnshire, and the medal was an Iron Cross with oak leaves, a souvenir from Berlin. Finally, Pauline explained that she had bought it for two cigarettes from a German policeman in the shambles of Hitler's Chancellery. The Customs officer said she had been cheated and should have had one cigarette change.

When we were leaving Russia, Ekaterina Chevalova, one of the guardians who had accompanied us throughout, had discreetly said, "When you get back, please write to me about your visit, about our country and about Stalin. Please write how wonderful he is, and how all the people love him." Ekaterina was an extremely wise woman, educated and informed. She deserved every protection she asked for and I willingly gave it, although I didn't really believe it was necessary. When the great Ulanova danced at Covent Garden, Ekaterina came as personal companion; her standing was such that she could add herself to any delegation. It was no surprise when she turned up at one of Mary Adams's Salons. Jim and I both kept in contact with her until quite recently.

Chapter Fifteen

Colonialism, Etc.

THE RUSSIANS were not alone in questioning the morality of our behaviour in Indonesia and Indochina, but facts were hard to come by. The Labour government had moved with vigour to restore the French and Dutch colonies, but Attlee and Bevin kept very quiet about their adventures in that part of the world. Perhaps a sufficient reason for secrecy was that the first released British prisoners from Japanese camps were then arriving home in England and stories of Japanese atrocities were front-page news. The country would have been horrified to think that we were using the same murderous troops to suppress the heroes of the resistance.

When Hitler seized France in the summer of 1940, Vichy France ruled in Saigon. The colonists collaborated with the Japanese and were left in control throughout the war. The resistance movement, the Vietminh, won over the country people and when the Japanese surrendered in 1945, they took over Hanoi and Saigon and promptly put the French administrators in jail. British troops, mainly Indians and Gurkhas, moved in and were welcomed. We opened the jails, re-armed the collaborators and some of the Japanese, levered out the Vietminh and summoned the French to come post-haste from Europe. Most of the French troops were brought out by American ships, supplied with American weapons, and supported by armed Japanese. The bitterness and hostility of the people of Vietnam towards the French and the west generally was shown in their later successful wars against France and then against America.

For a short time in 1945, J J Lawson was Secretary of State for War. On 29th September, he was reported as saying "Britain will not fight for the French against the Indo-Chinese or for the Dutch against the people of Java". He can't have known what his prime minister and foreign secretary were up to. The British troops withdrawn from Vietnam were shipped to the Dutch East Indies to wrest control from the Indonesian provisional government that Dr Sukarno had set up in August. Bevin declared that Britain had an agreement to help the Netherland Indies government regain control of her territories and, to prepare the way, our troops blasted the villages and occupied the main towns. The Dutch had no forces available and we helped them get together such soldiery as they could and trained them at York Racecourse into an army of colonial occupation. In 1946, 10,000 Dutch servicemen trained in Britain.

Backbenchers first heard of this on 11th December 1945, when the American reporter Ed Morrow disclosed that we were using the Japanese to wage war. On the adjournment, Tom Driberg raised the question of Indonesia and expressed deep concern and disapproval that our troops were being used to hand back other nations' colonies, and that we were acting in concert with the Japanese. No one of us realised that these tactics had first been employed in Indochina. Bevin insisted that our soldiers were there to disarm the Japanese, to free British prisoners of war, and to release foreigners, including British citizens interned by the Japanese. However, Indonesian representatives gave me precise information that each of these statements was untrue. The British prisoners of war had all been released some two months before we got there. Those who remained in the country did so of their own free will in the hope that they might be used as witnesses to identify certain Japanese whom it was hoped to try for war crimes. We were actually engaged in re-arming Japanese soldiers to protect Dutch interests, although we passed this off as "preserving law and order".

Year by year at party conference, Labour had supported the idea of colonial freedom. Representatives of independence movements addressed conference; debates and resolutions followed, and our determination grew more settled. In our manifesto for 1945, "Let us Face the Future", the party's accumulated wisdom about the colonies was watered down to a promise to promote "the planned progress of our Colonial Dependencies". For me (and, I should have thought, for every first-time candidate) this was election shorthand for all that had gone before. I expanded it in my own election address to:

"The Old World – A Starving and Enslaved Empire

Tories will never develop the Empire for the benefit of all its people. In African colonies ninety-seven per cent of the people are illiterate; India the average length of life is twenty-seven years; two million starved to death in Bengal."

and contrasted our hope for:

"The New World – Free the Peoples of the Empire

Give Burma its independence. Lift the colour bar in Africa. Release the Indian political prisoners. Let India decide its own future."

Our new Secretary of State for the Colonies was George Henry Hall. Under -Secretary was Arthur Creech Jones, a middle-of-the-road parliamentarian but a great Fabian and free-thinker. In the 'thirties, the NCCL had had the advantage of his efforts in taking up not only cases about the civil rights of people in the UK, but all manner of colonial issues. The NCCL was the main resort for victims without money who had been wronged in the colonies. Creech Jones seemed just the man to preside over the liberation. We were no sooner in power than all of this was thrown to the wolves. We would hold on to "our possessions". "We are great friends of the jolly old Empire and are going to stick to it," Herbert Morrison said in January 1946.

Now that Attlee's private papers have become available in the Public Record Office, we learn that he was personally in favour of releasing the colonies from bondage. He argued for this with Bevin, yet he kept it secret and remained bound to the wheels of Juggernaut – Bevin, the uncouth idol.

Their debate was carried on so quietly that even the cabinet was not aware of it; ordinary backbenchers had no idea. It is only now that his weakness of character and even duplicity in this matter have been disclosed. On 1st September 1945, Attlee produced a memorandum for the government and Foreign Office rejecting the demand of the latter that the UK should take over the Italian African colonies of eastern Libya, Cyrenaica and Italian Somaliland. He summed up a full argument with the words:

"Cyrenacia (sic) will saddle us with an expense that we can ill afford. Why should we have to bear it? Why should it be assumed that only a few Great Powers can be entrusted with backward peoples? Why should not one or other of the Scandinavian countries have a try? They are quite as fitted to bear rule as ourselves. Why not the United States?"

In parliament, Attlee spoke of the colonies as though we were in the days of Chamberlain, yet in this memorandum he argued with some eloquence that perhaps their day was past. It may be that having unveiled this point of view, he expected Creech Jones to pick up some shreds of it. Creech Jones was a great disappointment to those of us on the left and I believe to Attlee as well. He could have anticipated Macmillan's "wind of change" by ten years. But why should a Socialist think that a colonial people should be handed to anyone? What business was it of ours, of the other great powers, or of anyone else to run colonies? Attlee should have asked, "Why not free the colonies now?" and "What should we be doing to start preparing them for independence?" Those questions were not even within our understanding.

To question the right of France, Holland or any other nation to keep colonies would be to invite argument against the principles of colonialism. If the UK were to remain an imperial power, it was essential to maintain a united front with other imperialists. India would be granted independence because she could no longer be kept captive, but on the understanding that she would continue to provide British military bases and a market for our goods. The new Labour government had no intention of helping any other colony to independence or self-sufficiency; it was to be exploitation as before. The colonial peoples rightly demanded social, economic and political freedom; all they got was a sheaf of ten-year development schemes aimed at improving each colony as a producer of cheap raw materials and a buyer of expensive finished products. In parliament, we had to live through the grandiose pretensions of the Groundnut Scheme and its sad failure.

The UK had been driven into a corner by the war. Our foreign investments were sold off, yet we were still massively in debt. The Labour leadership fell in with Tory arguments that we could not manage without the money we drained from the colonies. In February 1946, Bevin told the Commons, "I know that if the British Empire fell it would mean the standard of life of our constituents would fall considerably." Their parliamentary equivalents would have said the same over the Slave Trade Act, and, no doubt, the standard of living of some people fell with the ending of feudalism. As an argument, it was dishonest and dishonourable.

The greed of the Labour Cabinet would lead, in 1948, to a sustained and horrible jungle war. The Malayan resistance (Malays and Chinese) liberated their country from the Japanese before our troops landed there in September 1945. The British overthrew the independent Malayan administration and resumed power. Early in 1946, Chin Peng was honoured by the UK as a resistance leader and marched through the city and past Westminster in our Victory Day parade. I was introduced to him before the march and we had supper afterwards at the Royal Empire Society. Two years later, he was again leading the movement for national liberation in Malaya, but against British troops and their Japanese allies. As the leader of the Communists, he was now called a traitor and a renegade and had a price on his head of £27,000, dead or alive.

Thousands of Malayan patriots were killed, deported or forced into detention camps. Trade union activities were outlawed, and anyone who gave food to the resistance fighters risked execution. Air raids rained bombs onto the jungle and our troops went in for the Nazi practice of razing villages as collective punishment. All this was done by our Socialist government to the Malayans, who then numbered fewer than six million, in order that we might keep control of their tin mines and their rubber plantations. In the six years of the Attlee government, we drew from their country £460 million.

Burma was a great exporter of rice, minerals and timber, especially teak, but the main industry was petroleum. The Dutch East Indies was rich in rubber, tin, oil and coffee. Although most of that money went to Holland, Britain did have some financial interests. Vietnam had oil, rice, rubber, tea, coffee and coal. Such storehouses must be kept as colonies to replenish the wealth of their "home" countries. Without colonies, could France and Holland be restored as European powers able to contribute to the defence against the USSR? The setting of the sun on one empire might pass to another, and who knows what the Soviets would do in the gloaming? Without our depredations, these lands would have been rich. Left to themselves, they may well have become staunchly independent and found some form of democratic representation. Oppression encouraged the colonies to turn to Communism, but Attlee and Bevin could not see this for themselves.

Other pledges in the party manifesto were ignored, including:

> "Now that victory has been won, at so great a cost of life and material destruction, we must make sure that Germany and Japan are deprived of all power to make war again. We must consolidate in peace the great war-time association of the British Commonwealth with the USA and the USSR. Let it not be forgotten that in the years leading up to the war the Tories were so scared of Russia that they missed the chance to establish a partnership which might well have prevented the war."

We were shocked to learn that our government deployed Japanese soldiers in south-east Asia; the discovery that their predecessors had considered using Nazi troops in Germany was equally abhorrent. In November 1954, Churchill boasted to his Woodford constituents:

> "Even before the war had ended and while the Germans were surrendering by hundreds of thousands, I telegraphed to Lord Montgomery, telling him to be careful in collecting the German arms, to stack them so that they could easily be issued again to the German soldiers whom we should have to work with if the Soviet advance continued."

While our own soldiers were liberating Belsen and other extermination camps, Churchill was contemplating making use of the Nazis. The mass graves, the gas chambers, the Gestapo torturers: all these were as nothing. Our real enemy was the Soviet Union. Churchill's project that we should beat Germany, after Germany and Russia had bled one another white, had been achieved only in part; Russia remained strong. The Tories, the Labour cabinet and the American administration were united in wanting Germany re-armed and, as a preliminary, the heavy industries of the Rühr would be restored to full vigour and placed under appropriate ownership. The same men that had first put Hitler in power and had run his war industries were to be re-established in power by us.

Labour had pledged to put an end to Nazism, to establish democracy, and to bring the Rühr under public ownership; each of these aims was abandoned on American orders. The left of the party challenged every Nazi appointment, but with a complete lack of success. The German industrialists were so pleased at getting back into power and profit through the Allies' denazification' that they coined the phrase "Let us have 1,000 years of denazification" as the obverse of the Nazis' 1,000 year reich.

My view was that Bevin's actions in international matters were likely to damage the interests and well-being of my constituents by launching us into expenses and dangers which could bear harmfully upon us. Why should our lads be sent to Indonesia to hold the fort until the Dutch were ready to put down the new republic? Why should we re-arm Germany when we had just made enormous sacrifices in getting her disarmed? Wasn't it morally wrong that Germany should be rebuilt before the nations she had devastated? I attributed all this to American influence. America was dominating the UK for her own purposes.

At the end of the war, Churchill and the coalition government stood very high in American esteem. The UK had received enormous credits under lend-lease, mainly for war materials of all sorts, both military and civilian. We had assumed that this beneficence would continue after the war. When Attlee took Churchill's place, all was changed. In American eyes, the Labour Party was well over halfway to Communism, that most dreaded feature of human existence. Lend-lease was cancelled by President Truman on the 2nd September 1945, the day that Japan was officially declared to be defeated, and repayment was summarily demanded. There was nothing in Labour's election programme that foresaw that the kingdom would come into our hands as a bankrupt. The UK had borrowed over £4 billion from abroad at a time before inflation had begun. Our so-called "invisible earnings" had been halved, as had exports, one third of our ships were gone and government spending abroad was five times that of pre-war.

We tried to bridge the gap between imports and exports with loans. The first was a giant $3.75 billion borrowed from America before the end of 1945 and largely devoted to buying US goods, and $1.25 billion from Canada. Unfortunately, the rising price of goods in America rather lessened the value of both loans. I blamed the government for not having a clause that the American loan should keep its value by a percentage increase equivalent to the percentage increase in their prices. The austere Stafford Cripps was Chancellor of the Exchequer and I challenged him that he was partly to blame, and would now be forced to devalue sterling. He replied, "Over my dead body!" Apart from the delight of hearing this phrase used in public life, there was the sadness of the devaluation of thirty per cent against the dollar in 1949, Cripps being very much alive.

The first big revolt against government policy came in December 1945, when Labour backbenchers protested against the terms of the American loan which would, it was feared, give Washington a measure of control over British policy-making. We were already dependent upon their money. When it came to the vote, forty-four Labour MPs abstained. The twenty-three who voted against the loan included Michael Foot, Jennie Lee, Jim Callaghan and Barbara Castle. Jim was so strongly opposed that he resigned his job as PPS at the Dominions Office in order to vote against the loan. The odd thing about this revolt was that the "hard left" were not involved. Willie Gallacher, Phil Piratin, Zilly, Pritt, S O Davies, Leslie Solley, William Warbey and myself all voted with the government. The interest rate of 1.6 per cent was fair, and we needed the money.

In March 1946, Bevin gave the Foreign Affairs Group his personal promise that British troops would be out of Greece immediately after the elections of that month. The Americans ordered otherwise, and so they stayed on. We grew increasingly angry. In that same month, Labour MPs sent a message conveying our greetings to the unity meeting in Berlin between the German Social Democrats and the German Communist Party. I do not now remember who organised it. The whips were upset by this but were so considerate of my position that they called on Sandy Lindsay of Birker, formerly Master of Balliol, to reprimand me. He summoned me to take tea with him in the House of Lords Library and said, "You know how upset the Whips are about this. Do you have to do it? I know how much the Germans have suffered and that there are good grounds for thinking that the division between the working-class parties let Hitler in, but the Whips want you to stop."

He then introduced me to the librarian and to their excellent law library, and invited me to use it for any legal work that I was doing at the House. I not only used it for reading, but also took tea and held legal conferences there. My clerk brought along the solicitors and they thought it really was a great thing to have tea in the House of Lords Library.

The group of Labour MPs opposed to Bevin's policies grew quickly in 1946. At a public meeting, Zilly reportedly said that seventy Members were prepared to break with the party on foreign policy. He was roundly condemned for this assertion. In October, Bevin threatened that his critics would be expelled. Almost at once he received a letter demanding that the UK play a mediating role between the free enterprise system of America, and the totalitarianism of the Soviet Union, and warning against infection by "the anti-red virus which is cultivated in the US". The letter was signed by twenty-one Members. I was not amongst them.

Donald Bruce was said to have drafted the letter. As he was PPS to Nye Bevan, and Jennie Lee was a signatory, it was most prestigious. Other signatories included Jim Callaghan, Michael Foot, Lyall Wilkes, Dick Crossman, Joe Reeves, Woodrow Wyatt and Sidney Silverman. Dick Crossman then tabled an amendment to the Address in Reply to the King's Speech, which called on the cabinet to change its attitude. We wanted a "democratic and constructive Socialist alternative to an otherwise inevitable conflict between American Capitalism and Soviet Communism in which all hope of World Government would be destroyed".

This was followed by a bumper meeting of the PLP, at which Attlee and Morrison spent over two hours trying to persuade us that loyalty came before policy. Attlee insisted that it was improper for backbenchers from the ruling party to offer amendments to the Address from the Throne. The Speaker and the Table Office did not agree and Erskine May was innocent of any such ruling. Morrison threatened us with the re-imposition of standing orders to maintain party discipline and demanded that signatories should withdraw their names. Morrison moved a resolution to this effect and it was carried 126 – 33, but there were plainly up to 100 abstentions.

This amendment was signed by fifty-seven backbenchers, including five PPSs; Joe Reeves and Barbara Gould risked their seats on the NEC to sign. Although the government imposed a three-line whip, some of the Members actually proposed to vote against the government. At the end of the debate, the two ILP members called for a division. The government won the vote by 353 to none, for the Tories voted with the government and the ILP members acted as tellers. The bravest Labour MPs dared only to abstain.

In a second amendment, 45 Labour Members voted against peacetime national conscription, while 132 abstained. We had not had conscription in peace-time for centuries, since the days of feudal levies. Now it was to be introduced by Labour. Pacifism had been a particular strength of the party and there were in the House, Members who had been active thirty years earlier as young men in "no conscription" campaigns. On the second reading of the conscription Bill, in April 1947, we mustered seventy-two votes against. The result was that the government accepted this as a rebuke and reduced the period of conscription from eighteen months to a year. It was the nearest we ever reached to victory, and was easily scuttled by Ernie when we tried again at the party conference in Margate later in the year. He complained that we had conspired to "stab him in the back".

Bevin was in New York at a meeting of the Council of Foreign Ministers when he heard of the amendments. He was outraged. His cable trumpeted, "Am I not entitled to know where Parliament and the Cabinet stand, and is not the world entitled to know by a vote?" He resented any form of criticism and began to display signs of a highly advanced state of paranoia. When the Yiewsley and West Drayton constituency party wrote to Bevin expressing their serious concern about his foreign policies, Bevin replied that his policies had the unanimous support of the cabinet. He complained of "inspired criticism", for he had received "a whole host of resolutions all couched in similar terms, obviously all inspired and not the real feeling of the people of this country".

Letters of objection to Bevin include the whole range of disapprobation. His policy is "distasteful business", leaves the writer "disillusioned" or "disgusted" and has led to a group of "backbenchers with worried consciences" and "those who have courage enough to voice their alarm". "Your foreign policy will bring down the Labour Government"; "I watch very often in anger"; "if you are pleasing Churchill in foreign affairs, can you possibly be pursuing a correct policy?" These quotations are from personal letters to Bevin in his capacity as Foreign Secretary so that they were necessarily preserved in files at the Public Record Office. There are few letters of praise and satisfaction. Bevin's files are well worth browsing through.

On 27th February 1946, Bevin dismissed a section of official Labour policy that related to his actions as "merely a pledge given in the enthusiasm of a conference". A month later he sent to all ambassadors and other heads of missions an account of a score or more of criticisms of his behaviour raised at meetings and of his answers to them. To Point 18 he wrote of himself:

> "Mr Bevin said he was anxious to get the Mediterranean as near to an international waterway as possible and thus end 3,000 years of struggle. This could not be done by transferring power from one country to another and that is what he meant by saying that we should grow together and try to understand each other."

Ernie's statement was incoherent. The last sentence must have caused hilarity in every British Embassy and certainly led to many jokes. The quaint biological reference gave rise to conjectures as to development of Siamese twins on an international scale, and it is said that the word symbiosis came into more general use as the result of that "direction".

Sir Alexander Cadogan was our senior diplomat and Permanent Representative at the UN in New York. During Bevin's time as Foreign Secretary, he felt the pressure from the left in the Commons as bearing more heavily upon himself than it ever did upon Bevin. We find him complaining that the criticism in parliament "amounted to a censure of our foreign policy which I represent to the UN and to the US", and

> "the policy I stand for is all agreed by the Cabinet; there is no vote taken in the House and yet 40 out of 600 are allowed to raise an objection against the Government as a whole. Their objections encourage every opponent both in the UN and in the Council of Ministers to use them against me."

He asked Bevin to arrange that foreign affairs debates should result in a vote; everyone would then know how slight was the opposition. He added, "The element of treachery ought to be brought to a head." On 15th April 1946, Cadogan reported to Bevin, and Bevin to Attlee, a complaint that "we are being dragged at the heels of America". I have only recently found in the Public Records Office the detail of the Cadogan-Bevin mutual commiseration. If I had known that the fellow used the word treachery, I should at least have threatened to sue him and perhaps even used the word of him – but only under the protection of parliament.

Other members of the cabinet show themselves as equally sensitive. For example, the Attorney General Hartley Shawcross, in New York at the UN with the British delegation, on 15th November 1946, wrote to his younger brother Christopher (who was, I thought, even more able than Hartley):

"I am concerned to see that you have joined in a letter to the PM on foreign policy. Present criticisms of Government policy seriously weaken our position here and I urge you not to join in them. ... I have always strongly urged the importance of friendship with the Soviets and the desirability of supporting a social democratic policy for Europe midway between Soviet and American extremes. But I am convinced that Soviet policy is more subtle and sinister than is commonly realised and that a policy of mere appeasement and acquiescence is dangerous. I hope you will use your influence in this sense."

In the same way, Hector McNeil explained on 13th November 1946 by telegram to the Ambassador in Washington what he saw as the limited effect of the vote on Dick Crossman's critical amendment:

1 The number of deliberate abstentions by Labour Members is exaggerated. There were not more than 80 and may have been less than 70. Of the amendment's 57 signatories, a very high proportion were young and inexperienced "intellectual" MPs. It is skilfully worded and undoubtedly brought in several MPs who did not fully realise the significance of what they were doing.

2 The original sponsors of the amendment deliberately excluded "cryptos" and fellow travellers, who signed later. Critics generally were anxious not to align themselves with current Moscow-inspired attacks on the Government. Crossman's strictures on Communism and the anti-British diplomatic and propaganda offensive of the Soviet Union, though unpalatable to a very small section of the party, undoubtedly reflect the views of an ever-growing majority

of Labour MPs. Perhaps for this very reason some of them feel that they must emphasise their left-wing position, and the outcome is a demand for a doctrinaire Socialist foreign policy, combined with outspoken criticism of the USA.

3   Apparently, they will try to form an opposition group. Indeed, it is impossible for such men as Foot and Crossman to cohere with Zilliacus, Platts-Mills and others of the extreme left. The two wings are already publicly attacking each other. The majority opinion, especially amongst TU MPs, shows considerable resentment against these critics. Rotherhithe and North Paddington by-election successes confirm that the policy of the government receives steady and overwhelming support from public opinion.

4   The foregoing will enable you to put political developments in perspective. Please inform consular staff of this.

McNeil advised Attlee to dissociate Labour publicly from any idea of collaboration with Churchill; to make plain that he was not sacrificing any Socialist principles to America, but to show it as inevitable that our path should frequently run parallel to theirs. He was right about the chances of the two left-wing blocks uniting, or even collaborating. The Foreign Policy amendments to the Address in Reply were one of the few occasions when those of us on the far left joined forces with the larger, more moderate group that had coalesced around Dick Crossman, Michael Foot, Ian Mikardo and Tom Driberg. In April 1947, fifteen of Crossman's group formed "Keep Left", a group which promoted Socialist policies at home and anti-Communism abroad. Naturally, they brushed us aside.

Ernie Bevin was not entirely evil and there is in the Public Records Office an example of his acting with exemplary good sense. In July 1948, the Foreign Office was arranging a visit of British miners to the Swedish mines. They proposed to exclude Arthur Horner because he was a Communist. Bevin said please to treat him as Secretary of the NUM and forget the point of his being a Communist.

CHAPTER SIXTEEN

Post-War at the Bar

ALTHOUGH I did my best to follow international issues, local constituency matters always had priority. I took them very seriously, recognising that the main reason for my being in parliament was to serve the needs of the constituents. In Attlee's first government, the main problem was housing. The situation was particularly bad in Finsbury, which had suffered heavy bomb damage. We had 14,000 families living in only 5,000 houses. It was for the local authority to find accommodation and an MP could only refer an enquirer back to his borough housing department. Even a councillor could do no better.

Just after the general election, I got on to the Finsbury Borough Council and there sat with an overwhelming majority of Labour Councillors. Harold Riley, in spite of set-backs over one legal process and another, persisted in fielding a rival ticket for the council and the Labour Party pressed into service anyone capable of standing against his "Genuine Labour" ticket.

Only two of Riley's group were elected, while our party took forty-seven of the sixty seats. At first, the council was very busy. My first public task as an MP had been the opening of another building designed by Lubetkin. We tried to keep up the pre-war building activity but it was almost impossible to get new houses built.

With other fields of enquiry, it was possible to make more progress. Demobilisation was one that was worth pursuing. Service people were abroad in many places and their local officers were unlikely to make allowance for special circumstances. Ministers in any department are habitually anxious to help MPs of any hue, since there is nothing a minister wants more than to have friends in all parts of the House. A little attention to the minister's PPS and a polite note to the minister himself, setting out the exceptional merits of the particular case, would yield results in perhaps eighty per cent of serious issues.

I sent to the *Islington Gazette* as a matter of routine anything that I came upon in Hansard that touched Finsbury or Islington. James Campbell, the editor, started sending me readers' questions to raise in the House. These were usually of a parochial kind. As I turned to foreign policy, so the paper followed. James arranged that when I was to raise a point on foreign affairs, he would lead it in by an article or news report the week before so it appeared that I was always in touch with what a conscientious reader might think was the latest matter of importance. James Campbell was the most valuable ally anyone could have had. He wrote approving editorials, suggested articles that I might contribute, and even paid the occasional fee. After a year of this we met and had lunch at his local, then exchanged family visits. He grew an assortment of soft fruit, including white currants that I had long fancied. Within a season, Janet was growing in our own garden black, red and white currants from his cuttings.

Janet and I had taken a house in St John's Wood. At 13 Cavendish Avenue, the Eyre Estate offered at a pre-war rental a magnificent Victorian family house (with slight war damage) and a substantial garden with a great row of pear trees that reached up thirty feet.

Our boys had been brought up in a remote Suffolk village and it was important to find somewhere quiet where they could safely play and ride their tricycles. There were children in most of the houses on the west side and some on the east. The walls between the back gardens on the west were fairly low and, where they were not, they were pushed over to make them lower still. Games ranged over the gardens from one end of the street to the other, sometimes accompanied by the playing of Myra Hess, whose practice in quiet weather came welcome by the hour from Cavendish Close.

The Avenue, which backed onto Lords Cricket Ground, had some claim to fame:

Sir Thomas Beauchamp lived at the end; Brian Johnson, the cricket commentator, had a house somewhere in the middle; and round the corner near Myra Hess lived Sir Andrew McFadyean, a senior figure in the Liberal Party and formerly an outstanding civil servant. We also had as near neighbour Lord Hunt, who set up the Royal College of General Practitioners, following the Balliol tradition of never belonging to a club unless you have founded it yourself. At the top of Cavendish Avenue was the hospital of St John & St Elizabeth. After the Spanish Civil War I had no good opinion of Catholics and was sure that the nuns would make a hopeless fist at being nurses. I saw their black dress as a symbol of ignorance and backwardness. They proved to be our First Aid and Rescue Centre because each of the boys had occasion to present himself there after taking a tumble. The nuns proved to be the most wonderful nurses. Any being they could get as a babe they cosseted and cuddled; one arrived at thirteen months and we could scarcely get him away. The boys fell in love with the nuns and were much at home at St John & St Elizabeth.

I was well housed, with a booming family of four boys and two yet to come. There was every possibility of getting a legal practice together again. I went into chambers in Mitre Court with Frank Soskice, then Solicitor General, and one or two others. One of the more entertaining cases was Cutler vs Wandsworth Stadium in 1946. At one stage, before the trial at first instance, Sir David Patrick Maxwell Fyfe was to lead. David was one of the more ambitious men at the Bar, having gone up to Balliol hoping to meet Tory politicians of influence, amongst whom he could make his way, and expecting to be prime minister or at least Lord Chancellor. He was rather a dour Scot and very devout; it was thought by some that he had never laughed in his life and he was never heard to make a joke. In his last year at Balliol, there was left as his memorial a couplet in the Junior Common Room commonplace book:

"There is nothing nearer death in life
than David Patrick Maxwell Fyfe."

This did him less than justice because he was a sharp enough lawyer and a most amiable fellow in ordinary life, although his persecution of homosexuals can in no way be condoned. In 1945, he had been appointed Attorney-General – a position he lost after the Labour victory. In 1954, as Viscount Kilmuir, he succeeded in becoming Lord Chancellor.

Alfred Cutler, chairman of the local bookmakers' organisation, was suing the owners of Wandsworth Greyhound Stadium. During the war, dog racing was encouraged. There must be some outlet to enable the well-paid factory workers to lose their money by gambling and so relieve the upward pressure on prices in the shops. It became extremely popular and was the essential laundering place for black-market money. In those days, one was embarrassed to be in possession of a £5 note, which was regarded as the plainest proof of the black market. But "I won it at the dogs" was ample cover, even for the Inland Revenue.

At Wandsworth, the bookmakers had the advantage of a stand in a most convenient position, accessible to the whole gambling and viewing public, where they themselves could see one another and the races and the stadium as a whole and from which, I dare say, they could retreat hurriedly when needed. An official tote was run by the stadium in competition with the bookmakers, and in 1945 the managing director of the stadium had personally taken an income of £430,000. He decided to increase his share of the betting by moving his competitors, the independent bookmakers, to a position behind the totalisator buildings, out of sight of the racing and the stadium and with a miserable approach for the punters. This new position heavily decreased the bookmakers' income.

David Fyfe and I decided that we should know something about the subject at first hand. The bookmakers invited us to an evening meeting. It was dinner in the directors' suite, and an inspection of all the relevant sites. Further to arouse our interest, we were each given a £5 ticket on a treble. This was a bet on one dog in each of three races, with a probable fortune to be won if all three dogs came home, but nothing if one were to fail. We scarcely noticed the first of the three races, but by the second race we had two winners already and our interest was very real. If the third dog were to win at anything like the odds of the first two, then the total would have been several thousands, a small fortune for the time. But in the third race, our dog started tardily and took little interest in the hare. We urged it on with coarse shouts of excitement, and when it failed lamentably, it was deep disaster. However, we were now better versed in the ways of dog racing and the course, and the practices of the bookmakers. David then left the case because he had other work needing attention.

The plaintiffs relied upon Section 11 of the Betting and Lotteries Act, 1934, that was thought to regulate their affairs. The statute prescribed that on such dog tracks, bookmakers would be allowed a position for carrying on their trade that gave them a fair chance of doing business. As a matter of common sense and bookmakers' lore, this required at least that they should be in a place where they could see the race, and where the punters should have ready access to them, and where they should be in view of the punters at all times. The defendants argued that even if they had committed a breach of Section 11 (which they denied), the breach gave the plaintiff no civil remedy.

On at least six occasions, we obtained injunctions restraining the stadium from moving them, and, on six occasions, the Court of Appeal upset the injunctions. We had the luck of coming on habitually before 'Owly' Stable or Roland Oliver, each of whom was a betting man. They were as good supporters of bookmakers as any judges could be, and, by chance, they were available when the applications were made. With them, we couldn't go wrong and so when it came to the trial, we succeeded. The defence won in the Court of Appeal on the argument that the section which gave the advantage of a good position to the bookmakers was not intended for the protection of the bookmakers but was in the Act only for the convenient administration of the dog track, or for the regulation of the conduct of the sport. As a consequence, bookmakers could not rely upon it for supporting any civil rights. I, being unskilled at legal reasoning, still think that this was an unsound conclusion. The House of Lords upheld it and we lost in the end.

It is possible to apply to High Court judges, and indeed other judges, too, to "move them", as we say, for a prompt and summary remedy in cases of emergency. This is fairly common now in family cases, but was perhaps less so forty years ago. When counsel is well enough known to the judge, it is possible to get an injunction by telephone, and without papers, provided the proper undertakings are given. In the Wandsworth Stadium case, Fergus Morton, as a Lord Justice, once sat for the whole Court of Appeal at nine o'clock at night on the edge of his bed, overlooking South Kensington tube station, on the last day of term, and reversed a judgement given by his own court earlier in the afternoon. This restored the bookmakers to their prime position in the stadium on the ground, which the defendants seemed quite unable to confute, that we were all in danger of race course riots if the bookmakers were pushed out of sight for the coming Bank Holiday Monday afternoon meeting.

The same judge once granted me an injunction on the golf course at Rye during the Bench and Bar golf match. Other typical examples of the gaining of such impromptu services would be Mr Justice Lewis, in his flat at midnight at Notting Hill Gate; Mr Justice Jenkins, as vacation judge on his farm in Kent at night on Christmas Eve; and Mr Justice Birkett, at the lunch table of the Connaught Rooms, the freemasons' restaurant. Frederick Nicholson was a very good clerk (he later became quite a figure at the Bar) and there was a time when we knew who was the judge and where he was available on any day of the week for immediate application.

My other clerk or secretary, Mrs Green, stayed on for a while but the constituency work eventually proved a bit much and she retired. Hymie Berger came and offered himself. I remembered him from the pre-war British Youth Peace Assembly hearings and he seemed an ideal person for the job. Finsbury took a special interest in the hearings, which were set up by John Gollan in 1939 to enquire into working conditions amongst young people. We were particularly concerned because we had many youths coming into our area to work. John was an eager, hungry Scot: always terribly determined, always diligent and informed and active. Mr Comyns Carr, KC, served as Chairman, I was Secretary, and Hymie Berger proved to be a capable and business-like member of the panel.

I was beginning to earn enough at the Bar to keep the family. My parliamentary salary was, I suppose, surplus to requirement and Hymie appropriated it to himself. It was a modest £1,000 a year, but princely compared with the wage of £5 that I had been paid for lifting by hand sixty tons of coal a week. Until Hymie's arrival, my career as an MP had been a quiet business. He increased by tenfold my work. He was master of everything that a clerk in parliament could do. He knew exactly the places that he could go, the steps that he could take, and the documents that he could file in my name.

Hymie exploited the full limits of his access to such places as the Question Office, the Black Rod's Office and the Whips' Office, and he organised the secretaries of those MPs who were friendly to us and insisted that they should learn his techniques. But this assistance was not limited to Labour Party clerks; Hymie organised a branch of the T&G devoted to MP's secretaries and he treated them all as common clerk-fodder. Many young Tory women found themselves in his branch of the Union. Hymie and I christened them "the Priglets". They all approved of him.

We had a large room to ourselves, he and I, whereas most Members had to share – sometimes with three secretaries in one room. We were straight opposite parliament and next to the Abbey in a big building rather set back from the road. We had so much activity going on and made such a commotion that no one wished to share it. Hymie had a most elaborate filing system with everything alphabetically and instantly available. With any speech coming on, he would make me rehearse to him and even, I think, to a mirror, and sometimes we shouted at each other. He was so helpful to the other clerks that they stifled any possible complaints about the noise.

I should say that a good test of how active a Member may be is provided by the length of inches of his index in Hansard. You could exclude the ministers who were forever answering questions and the like, and the leaders of the Opposition, but for ordinary private Members there was quite a busy sweep conducted between some of the secretaries as to who would clock up the longest record in the index. Hymie claimed that he had won several shillings on this basis from rival clerks. The page on which my name appeared was quite near to those on which came Piratin and Pritt, who were my close rivals as well as friends.

When I was expelled from the party, Mrs Zilliacus commented that the trouble was not that I was a crypto-Communist but that Hymie was a crypto-Member of Parliament. I knew that he was a member of the Finsbury Communist Party, but what mattered was that he was fully informed by constant assiduous reading. In fact, he was always ahead of the normal run of information because he read the American papers as well as our own. He would draw attention to the debates that were either due or likely to come on, and to the Late Night adjournment debates and suggest that I might take part in them. Hymie kept the agenda constantly under review. He framed innumerable questions and would so arrange them that they were frequently first in the list for that minister on his particular day. I found in Hymie the fullest support and encouragement for my beliefs. On Foreign Affairs particularly, our views were very consistent and he had an entirely free hand to draft questions, although he could not put them down until I had checked them with him.

Our normal routine would take the following course: I would be in court in the morning and, if I were free by lunch-time or by Question Time, would arrive in the inner lobby, just outside what is now the Lords' Chamber. Hymie would be waiting with all my questions set out, and for each question he would have a supplementary question prepared, and sometimes a whole series of supplementaries, according to whether the answer of the minister was Yes or No, or of a positive or a negative flavour.

Perhaps the peak was reached on 24th September 1948, when we had eighteen written answers – meaning that I had not called for an oral answer in the open chamber at Question Time. Looking back now and seeing how much disturbance we caused by way of my questions and interventions, I can well see that I was regarded as a real nuisance by Ernie Bevin and Attlee in particular, and the leaders of the party in general.

A minor feature of parliamentary life was the debate that took place every day, except Friday, at the adjournment. You obtained the right to move on any subject for a maximum of half-an-hour, in which time you must leave the necessary period for a short reply by the government and, if you were willing to allow it, for one or more other Members to join in. Any Member could put his name down on the list and then there was a draw. There were not very many people wishing to occupy the House late at night so that if you kept on putting your name down, you were bound to get a chance. You did not notify the subject until after you had won a place. Both the fixture and the subject were open to negotiation; that is to say, you could exchange any date with any other person of any party. In the same way, you could notify the junior minister whom you were expecting might reply and give him any amount of detail in advance so that he might collect material on the very point that you were anxious to raise.

Throughout the Attlee first period of 1945-50, the government made a point of showing that we were very busy making new laws, and each day at the end of Question Time we had a vote "to suspend standing orders". The effect of this was that the House was then free to continue after the normal ten p.m. closing time, and we usually did go on. I recall a debate on 3rd March 1947, which, according to Hansard, did not begin until twelve-fourteen a.m. As usual when I was going to speak, a number of extreme right-wing Tories had gathered to make a demonstration. The topic that I had chosen to debate was the question whether the southern-most parts of Austria should not now join Yugoslavia. The Tories made such an uproar that order was not restored for several minutes and then they sustained objections for further precious minutes so that several valuable points had to be omitted. The Tories wanted Carinthia to go back to pro-Nazi Austria rather than to anti-Nazi Yugoslavia. Sadly, our government backed the Tories. It was a typical adjournment debate and served to ventilate the question.

If Hymie was active in international matters, when it came to the affairs of the constituency he was a whirlwind. I don't suppose I ever signed fewer than twenty letters a working day, specifically about individual constituents' enquiries and complaints and rights. I approached a number of our new ministers, asking what was going to happen to requisitioned buildings in their control, and wondering if there was any chance of their being used for temporary occupation by those who were in most urgent need. There was no response. I did not see that there was a very simple remedy, but others thought of this. One morning in September 1946, Hymie rang at about seven and said that an important new political crisis had arisen. I must go at once to a rather high-class sweet shop at the foot of Gower Street. I got on my bicycle and went to the appointed place and there was Hymie, all eagerness. Squatters had moved into the Ivanhoe Hotel and were occupying it for want of any better place. This incursion seemed to me to be a very good idea, and I gathered that Hymie had played some part in helping to organise it.

We went to the hotel and there found a group of about ten families, many of whom were my constituents. They had been lodging in overcrowded places with families or friends and had tried in vain to get help from the council. They had brought necessary gear such as mattresses and bedding, as well as food and provisions for cooking it, and seemed to have settled in. Police were on guard with the vague idea that some wrong had been done, but not knowing what. Steps were already underway to get water, gas and electricity switched on. Within days, the authorities began trying to get the supply cut off again, and there were several submissions and deputations to local authorities and the power companies.

Shortly after that, Abbey Lodge was occupied. This was a very big block of flats just south of the church. In support of the squatters, crowds of up to two thousand gathered in the road outside. There were police horses aplenty, and marbles were rolled under their hooves. It was frightening enough to be sitting down, with the horses slipping about over our heads; the horses were terrified. Their rolling eyes and flared nostrils reminded me of the pictures of equestrian battles where horses shared the "shot and shell" of their riders, and particularly of Lady Elizabeth Butler's "Scotland for ever, the Charge of the Scots Greys at Waterloo".

The movement then spread to Regents Park, where the government was de-requisitioning scores of empty houses. Local authorities varied in their treatment of the movement, and the police reflected their views. In Kensington, they were far more liberal. Those occupying Fountain Court in Buckingham Palace Road and Duchess of Bedford House seemed fairly free to come and go. At Abbey Lodge and the Ivanhoe there were near-siege conditions as supporters tried to pass in food and other necessities. Baskets were lowered and raised by rope and parcels were thrown in at the windows. At Abbey Lodge, a way was found in at the back from Regents Park. The police had not noticed this. I climbed over a wall and went in because some Finsbury families were there. It was only a few hundred yards from my home at Cavendish Avenue.

Collections were taken up for money, food, blankets and the like, and petitions were circulated in support. There were also opponents of the whole scheme and scuffles inevitably arose, leading to arrests and court appearances. No support came from the government, and even Ellen Wilkinson denounced the seizure of possession as anarchy. I suppose she was right in a sense, but only in a very limited sense because I am sure the squatting movement helped to urge on local authorities and government departments to increase their activities and relieve the housing problem.

The main judicial process resulted from the arrest in mid-September of five Communists thought to be ringleaders of the movement, including Councillor Tubby Rosen of Stepney, who was known for organising tenants' movements and rent strikes. I arranged that Sir Walter Monckton, KC, the outstanding leader at the Common Law Bar, should represent them. They pleaded not guilty and were tried at the Old Bailey for conspiracy. The defendants were convicted and bound over for two years. Mr Justice Stable told them that, had he thought that they were exploiting the miseries of the homeless for their own vain purposes or for a political party, he would have imprisoned them. He was satisfied that they were genuinely distressed by the suffering of the squatters and had wanted to find them homes. The judge then informed Monckton that since he was not fully confident of his own interpretation of the law on the matter, he would provide the relevant certificate should Monckton wish to appeal the case.

When conspiracy proceedings were imminent, Professor Constantinescu-Jass decided that I was likely to be arrested and insisted that Janet and I should set off at once for a holiday in Bucharest. He was Minister of Information in the Romanian government and the leading world authority on Orthodox churches (both decoration and ecclesiastical procedure). He had been sent to London to establish diplomatic representation for Romania; we met at Westminster and became friends. The politics of Romania during the Second World War had become extraordinarily confused. At the beginning of the war, the Iron Guard, a Fascist organisation, took power and sided with Hitler. Britain declared war on Romania. In August 1944, the left-wing parties overthrew the government and declared war on Hitler. The change in general attitude and relative strengths was not uninfluenced by the advance of the Red Army from the North and East.

Janet and I flew to Paris and there remained for several days, trying to get clearance for a flight across Europe. The problem was that the Americans controlled the airways of Europe from Frankfurt. Romania was so unimportant to them that any cross flight took priority. There followed a six-hour flight to Bucharest. The Douglas Dakota was not pressurised so had to be flown low, which was very hot but gave a wonderful view of the Hungarian Plain and the Transylvanian Alps. In Bucharest, we were installed in the rather grand Athenee Palace Hotel. The next day produced a gigantic Moscow-style parade of the soldiery and the populace, reviewed by King Michael. He was still reigning, nominally as an absolute monarch, but in fact with all the panoply of parliament and ministers and constitutional government. The Russians were so pleased with the king for going along with this farce that they presented him with the order of Lenin done in diamonds. It was not many months before he left the country with two train-loads: one of his supporters, and one loaded with his possessions or spoil – pictures, furniture, gold and all.

On the night of the parade, Janet and I went to a play put on in the Railway Workers' Theatre. We sat in the front row with Gheorghe Gheorghiu-Dej, General Secretary of the Communist Party and a former railwayman. On learning that we would spend the next day sightseeing in Bucharest, he said, "That's no good. You must see the whole of Romania for sights. Charles must take you." Charles Kormas became our guide and constant companion. For part of the journey, we drove in the prime minister's car with an armed guard. In two remarkable weeks we visited most corners of the country: to the Black Sea on the East, to the Russian borders in the North, and Transylvania with Cluj on the North-West, and down the valley of the Jiu from Petrosan to Craiova.

I even managed a shift down a pit when we visited a coal mine at Resita, near the Yugoslav border. Two women working machines underground boasted that they were more advanced than their Soviet sisters who had not yet won this right. Some of the other high occasions were dinner with Mr le Riche, the coal miner whose distant ancestor had been a member of Napoleon's grand army and had lost his way on the retreat from Moscow, ending up thousands of miles from his intended route; inspecting the magnificent woven rugs for which Romania is famed; and a visit to the Iron Gate: vertical cliff walls 300 feet apart and running for nearly a mile where the Danube bursts through the mountains and Hadrian began his bridge which was finished by the Emperor Trajan.

Ana Pauker, the Foreign Secretary, was getting quite old but still had striking looks. She was said to have had her husband executed as a traitor, but we never learned the whole story. When she entertained us to dinner at her house, we were somewhat circumspect. I thought of her as a preying mantis. Later we read *The Balkan Trilogy* by Olivia Manning. All the immediate pre-war characters whom she describes were still there in 1946 and behaving just as she had expected they would. (We had long since met Olivia Manning – yet another of those talented women who floated naturally in the orbit of Mary Adams.)

A general election was due soon. The story in London was that the Communists were not allowing the opposition to organise their voters. I sought out the leaders of the opposition groups: the Peasant Party, the Liberals and the dissident Socialists. Each claimed to be the equivalent of our Labour Party. The leaders of the Peasant and Liberal parties both admitted that they had no policy or programme of their own. Their only real "policy" was to complain about everything the government did. Almost daily, there was a letter of complaint, with a copy to the British minister. Bevin and Attlee were openly hostile to the Romanian government, although Stefan Voitec, leader of the Social Democratic party, had as many members in parliament as had the Communists, and shared in power.

The job of British Minister is to build and maintain friendly relations with the government to which he is accredited. In Romania, the effect of the stream of letters was to make him appear as a conspirator with the opposition and, for that matter, with Bevin and Attlee against the

Romanian leadership. I had several talks with our minister in Bucharest and he expressed the hope that I might be able to help him to explain his position to Bevin. He had never before represented a government that seemed to be goading him into betrayal of the very job for which he was brought up and trained and employed.

The opposition leaders said that they were prevented from campaigning freely. Janet and I met them in various ways in public and in private. They had their own newspapers, both national and local, and held their meetings without any difficulty. This was certainly true in Bucharest. Yet it was equally true that they could not hold meetings at all in some areas. That was because each of the two main opposition parties, when in power, had been responsible for what can only be described as massacres. In 1907 was the classic example of war between artillery and unarmed peasants: 11,000 were killed in one barrage. The Liberals were in power at the time. In 1933, the Peasants Party was in power: 480 railway workers were shot dead at Trevitza in Bucharest. Dr Maniu, the current leader, felt that should not be held against him, for he was not in the government at the time; he was merely party president. Similar slaughters took place in Timisoara and Petroshan. It was no wonder that they were hated.

Romania was in the second year of a desperate drought. Because of this, many of the peasants were in real difficulties. Collectivisation had not begun; they were still farming their own smallholdings and had no larger body on whom they could fall back. Worthy churchmen were teaching that, as all believers knew, the last ungodly government on earth led to a seven-years' drought. They asked the peasants, "What will you feel like when we reach the seventh year?" This was the kind of nonsense that the priests were preaching. I thought it blasphemous. In the cities, the main signs of the drought were the numbers in peasant dress who were looking for jobs, and the overflow of meat at low prices in the butchers' shops as peasants were forced to sell their hungry stock.

In the country, most roads were unsealed and the few vehicles were followed by a cloud of dust that could be seen for miles. When travelling by car, dust got not only into the boot but into the suitcases and covered every bit of the contents. Our faces, hands and clothes were grey, and sometimes red, with it. We saw trainloads of peasants on open flatcars, all making for the Danube Delta. Since the smaller rivers had dried up, they were in search of food for their animals, and reeds for bedding to replace the straw that had all been used. Many seemed to be carrying some small object with them, such as a vase or a picture, which might be sold or exchanged for food. We thought it was getting late for the main harvest but it was all hand-done so began earlier and lasted longer than in the UK.

The government was trying to help the peasants by confiscating land from the big holders and redistributing it to those who actually worked it. Janet and I went to an open-air meeting at Alba Iulia where the Prime Minister, Petru Groza, was to present land deeds to peasants. There came whole families in horse-drawn carts, bringing food for the day and settling down in the great square. The meeting didn't break up till after dark. This speech by Groza lasted for six hours under the hot sun, if you count two hours of presentation of land certificates to the peasants. We found in Eastern Europe that people were accustomed in country areas to all-day meetings and long speeches. This was, I think, based on centuries of experience of market day.

As in all peasant societies, there was often great resistance to change. I recall a dinner at Resita, after a short stint in the pit and a visit to the great steel works. The chairman of the local trade union branch boasted that in bringing together fifty leading workers in the plant and the village, he had managed to exclude every Communist except one: he was secretary of the branch, so could not be kept out. Resita was the traditional heartland of social democracy. It might just as easily have been some deep Labour stronghold in the Midlands, standing firm against change.

CHAPTER SEVENTEEN

Further Policy Criticisms

WHEN VARIOUS crowned heads came to London in 1947 to join in celebrations for the Royal Wedding, they were housed in the Savoy Hotel. The weather was very cold. Fuel was in short supply and rationed. The Savoy procured a large tonnage of fuel-oil from 200 miles away and had it brought to London in tankers. Arthur Lewis was MP for West Ham and organiser for London catering workers in the General and Municipal Workers Union. Some of his members worked in the Savoy and drew his attention to this use of oil. The government said that the honour of England was at stake; crowned heads must lie cosy and warm. Arthur said the honour of the NUGMW was at stake; crowned heads must share the discomforts of the common people.

Arthur led his members out on strike and they marched and picketed in the route of the lorries. The drivers arrived at the front door in the Strand, not knowing the area. The carriageway there is laid out like a small mushroom flattened on its side. Once tankers got in, there was no getting out. It took half a day to get them down Savoy Hill at the side, and every minute of that was pure joy for the BBC reporting staff. Not a driver or striker could be kept out of a broadcasting studio. On the following day, lorries arrived at the service doors on the Embankment and Arthur and his dozens of supporters mounted the tankers. The police thought it more important to have the pickets off, before ensuring the delivery. The whole operation took many hours.

I was in debt to Arthur for a useful note he had provided, and was asked to come to the Savoy as he hoped to get the strikers to lie down. On the night of 11th November, Arthur lay in the road with a number of other strikers, arms linked, in front of a tanker and delayed it for some time. It was so successful that I lay down beside him. When the police began picking up the prostrate bodies and arresting their owners, I thought that, as a barrister, I had gone far enough and was on my feet and away. Fully 200 supporters paraded outside the hotel, shouting, "Squeeze the rich" and "Support the strikers". It was the first legal strike since 1939. On the next night, three MPs joined the pickets on night duty. They were Lester Hutchinson and Captain Hugh Delargy from Manchester, and Wing Commander Millington from Chelmsford. Arthur and I tried to get some London MPs in, but they were a disappointing lot and it was difficult to get a radical squeak from any of them outside the House.

Arthur was arrested on the 17th, not for lying in the road but for jumping on a tanker. He made a great fuss and struggled, shouting out, "Fetch the press. Where are the reporters? Look what they are doing to me. I am an MP. They are twisting my arms and hurting my wrists." This is a tactic that sometimes succeeds. Whether the police respond by abandoning their project or by twisting a bit harder depends on their snap judgement of whether the balance of feeling is for them or against. Both Arthur and the policeman in charge, Police Superintendent Rowlerson, were experienced campaigners; it could be said that by crying aloud Arthur "tried it on" and, by holding on a bit tighter, the police "got away with it".

I appeared for Arthur at Bow Street on a charge of obstructing the highway and obstructing the police. He was a great size and caused more obstruction by standing in the street than by standing on a tanker. I think we established that the hotel paid the police a fee for attending in force at the scene, which would not be an unusual procedure. On this, we tried to base the argument that they had ceased to be policemen and were private employees of the hotel, as though they were modern security guards. This did not succeed and it cost Arthur a £5 fine and £10 costs. His elder brother Jim, another union official, was charged with obstructing the constable who had arrested Arthur, but was discharged. I defended most of the thirty pickets on trial; the others were fined twenty shillings, with twenty shillings costs.

David Weitzman, Labour MP for Stoke Newington, got into far more serious trouble. Late in 1947, he and his three brothers were prosecuted for offences against wartime restrictions. I thought that the one I represented was possibly guilty, as were two others, but against David there was not a shred of evidence. It was one of Lord Denning's first trial cases at the Old Bailey. David was a silk with a very large mixed practice; before Denning became a judge, he had probably had more leading briefs with David as his junior than with any other junior counsel.

After the death of their father in 1924, David had assumed sole responsibility for his poverty-stricken family. He educated his brothers and loaned them sufficient money to start up a small supply company. The four brothers, along with two accountants employed by the firm, were charged with a conspiracy to misuse wartime regulations relating to the manufacture and supply of toiletries. By these regulations, one was allowed to produce in wartime only a proportion of what one had produced before the war. The prosecution claimed that there was no pre-war manufacture and the firm was therefore not entitled to any quota. The defendants produced evidence of very substantial production in different parts of London before the war; much evidence was devoted to this, and much time to challenging it. Although David knew that his brothers made cosmetics, he had no involvement with the firm. One of the prosecution's own witnesses, a receiver named Mr Davis, stated that he was "quite satisfied not only that Mr David Weitzman had had nothing to do with the running of the company but that he had no control over its business".

Five of the six defendants were found guilty and sentenced to prison. The summing up was extremely severe upon David, and he was awarded twelve months' imprisonment and a £500 fine. It had been a long trial and the transcript would not be ready for several months. As a result, the hearing of the appeal before Goddard and others had to stand over until March. The delay was really nothing as compared with that which now takes place so often, both in the hearing of cases at first instance and in the hearing of appeals. It was allegedly because of this long delay that the Lord Chief Justice granted bail pending the appeal. Probably the true explanation was that the Chief Justice realised that all would have to be acquitted because of that summing up against the one.

The appeal was led on by Archie Marshall, and he and his junior, Sheldon, presented the argument on the basis that you could not reasonably have one conspiracy to act in breach of whatever laws might be made relating to cosmetics; that for the proceedings to go ahead with any sort of fairness or balance, there would have to be several separate conspiracies alleged. For example: one to pretend that there was a pre-war quota, or that it was much larger than it actually was; another to produce much greater quantities of cosmetics than their quota, if any, allowed. All of the convictions were quashed. The principle that you cannot have a rolled-up conspiracy of different kinds all in one has since been fully accepted.

In the course of the appeal, it was not possible to avoid critical reference to Denning's summing up, and this summing up played its full part in securing the acquittals. The court complained that the trial judge had not put before the jury the main points in David's defence, and declared that "there was no case against Mr David Weitzman and there never had been. "…In the opinion of the Court, the case against Mr David Weitzman ought to have been stopped at the close of the case for the prosecution."

Just after his retirement from the Bar, I saw a television programme in which Lord Denning reminisced about his career. In the course of this programme, the interviewer asked Denning whether he had ever been reversed in the Court of Appeal. Denning replied that he remembered one case shortly after the war where four brothers were tried in his court by jury. All were quite obviously guilty, and all were properly convicted. They got off, simply through a legal trick or technicality. The only "trick" was the exposing to the Court of Appeal of Denning's unfair summing up. What the Bar had said at the time was that Denning should be promoted to the Court of Appeal as fast as possible because it was quite unsafe to leave him to try any criminal case. At that time, his law was regarded as splendid, and the Court of Appeal could well do with him. Seven months after the appeal, at the age of forty-nine, he was there as Lord Justice Denning.

As his counsel told the court, David Weitzman was a man of honour and no member of the Bar was more beloved. I could not imagine anyone less like a black marketeer. I recall one well-known MP who, wishing to have the Left on his side, asked three of us to supper at a restaurant near Piccadilly Circus. The permitted maximum charge for any meal taken at a public restaurant had at that stage been raised to 12s. 6d. We had no notion of the cost until after the meal, when he paid for us £6. 5s. each. Being somewhat unworldly, we were all deeply shocked; we did not walk out, but broke into a chorus of disapproval. It was too late for anything else.

Another Labour Member, John Lewis, was thought to have made a lot of money from rubber. He asked fellow MPs to a party in his big modern house near the top of Finchley Road. We found there half-a-dozen footmen in gold uniforms with what appeared to be tigerskin lapels, and fine, soft mink-like covers on the lavatory seats. This was just after the war and food was heavily rationed, yet he had caviar in plenty. Harold Wilson later banned him from the offices of the Board of Trade for corrupt behaviour. It was no great surprise when John Lewis turned up in the Profumo affair as the man who reported Dr Stephen Ward as running a call girl service.

Some say that a rich man has no place in the Labour Party but there is the greatest difference between a man like John Lewis and the millionaire George Strauss, who represented Lambeth North and was probably the wealthiest man in parliament in my day. Strauss had been one of the leading British supporters of the Spanish republican government. He inherited some sort of broking business in the City and lived in an appropriate mansion at 1 Kensington Palace Gardens, where every other mansion housed an embassy or an Arab oil prince. Attlee made him Minister of Supply. He was always the most unassuming, modest and generous man, who would give subs discreetly to leftish causes. He and his wife would always house a couple of visiting Russians or East European delegates.

Most Britons were poor. Although we had won the war, life was hard. Some foods were controlled, others were rationed. A world-wide shortage of wheat led to problems with bread supplies. A popular little rhyme ran:

> "Rule, Sir Bensmith,
> Sir Bensmith rules the bread;
> Britons never, never, never
> Shall be fed."

Sir Ben Smith was Attlee's Minister of Food. He disagreed with Bevin over sending food to Germany and had to resign in May 1946. One month later, because of the threat of riots, bread rationing was introduced – something that had never been needed during the war.

Then came the worst winter for a century and the longest cold spell I have ever known. A curious phenomenon developed on London roads. Many became coated with ice that settled in ripples so that if you drove a car, it bumped all the way. If you drove fast enough to override the bumps, you were liable to skid. Because of the weather, it was often impossible to shift coal supplies and most of us burned wood blocks which councils had been tearing up to replace with tarmac: these had been laid in Victorian times as the ideal non-skid surface for horses' hooves. In Lisson Grove, there was a council yard and the able-bodied men of Marylebone paraded with wheelbarrows to collect their share. The blocks were impregnated with tar; they were splendid burners but, in their turn, impregnated every chimney with sticky soot.

Lack of coal impeded the supply of electricity. The petrol ration was reduced, and the government launched an austerity programme that was to include a £12 million reduction in food imports. Michael Foot called for a great Socialist offensive and Dick Crossman wanted the establishment of a Ministry of Production. For my part, I returned to Yorkshire Main and put in a spell working down the pit. I was on the same coal-face I had left in September '45, but after eighteen months of soft life, I couldn't manage it and was relegated to the back roads, where I stayed for only a couple of weeks before returning to parliament.

There was an urgent need for new houses, schools and hospitals, but little money could be spared. We had been beggared by the war, and by the exactions of our American allies. What of the new homes, schools and hospitals we had promised to build? What of our commitment to a new health system? From its inception, I was an eager supporter of the NHS. New Zealand's first Labour government established a fairly complete national health service and I wanted something similar for the UK. I grew up believing that poor people should have free medical care, and that those with some means should not be bankrupted to meet the bills. Daisy had never earned much from medical practice: her charges were very low and she was no good at getting them in. She regarded her services as public property that people could claim of right.

The Socialist Medical Association was treated by the Haldane as a sister body. We were both affiliated to the Labour Party and the SMA pressed consistently at party conference for the addition to its policy of a national health service. When it came to drafting the necessary Acts and Regulations to put it into effect, the SMA offered the help of the considerable work they had already done in preparation. Nye Bevan would have none of it. He would not even receive the officers of the SMA. He wanted no dealings with the left. He would not willingly be seen with them, and discouraged his lieutenants from doing so. We were at pains to distinguish Bevan from Bevin. Ernie Bevin, the traducer of labour virtue; Nye Bevan, who was giving reality to our most romantic dreams. Bevin and Bevan, however, were at one in treating with disdain respectively the hostile squeaking or the adulation of the left.

I feared that Ernie Bevin's foreign adventuring would destroy all that we had achieved during the war. He was destroying the goodwill we had built with Russia, and he was encouraging the resurgence of Germany. In October 1946 and again in August 1947, Bevin assured the House that heavy industry in the Rühr would be nationalised. Later he changed this to a promise that the German people would decide the issue. The ordinary German played no part in the decision to reinstate the old industrialists. In some cases, quite infamous Nazis were installed as managers. If Nazis were back in charge of the Rühr, what troubles were we not storing up for the future? Food was another problem. The best agricultural land was in the East German zone, but a large part of its produce was allegedly being taken by the Soviet Union. Britons had to share their food supplies with the citizens of Berlin, and Germany was seen as a drain on our taxpayers. It had been agreed that Germany should make reparations to compensate the Soviet Union for her massive wartime losses. However, Germany was all but ruined and the UK, America and France found themselves providing the goods sent as reparations from the zones they controlled. There were frequent disagreements about the Russians' insistence upon their legal right to reparations. Anything of value in their sector was dismantled and sent back to the Soviet Union.

The UK also received some items from the Germans. I know that Davy United, a Sheffield firm famed for building steel rolling mills, received from Krupps a machine that could work a single piece of steel weighing 100 tons. This had been the latest American product of 1936. Immediately after the delivery, Krupps received the newest American model, improved by a decade of the most intense development. Theirs was a much more powerful machine with even finer tolerances. Such acts of "reparation" placed Germany a long way ahead of the UK in steelworks plant manufacture. To me, it was obvious that Germany would again be economically the most powerful force in Europe. America had decided that the best way to keep Communism away from our side of the continent was to have a strong German state. Germany was to be rebuilt as a battle tank against Russia in the world-wide crusade against Communism.

Churchill's celebrated speech at Fulton, Missouri in March 1946 included the following:

"From Stettin in the Baltic to Trieste in the Adriatic an iron curtain has descended across the Continent. Behind that line lie all the capitals of the ancient states of Central and Eastern Europe: Warsaw, Berlin, Prague, Vienna, Budapest, Belgrade, Bucharest, and Sofia. All these famous cities and the populations around them lie in the Soviet sphere, and all are subject, in one form or another, not only to Soviet influence, but to a very high and increasing control from Moscow. Athens alone, with its immortal glories, is free to decide its future at an election under British, American and French observation."

Greece was the supreme example of the Churchill/Bevin policy in action. The "free" Greek government behaved in a horrifying fashion towards its own people. They tried to suppress the left, not by any normal political means but with savagery. Death sentences were handed out in scores at a time. In the years immediately after the war, 1,200 alleged Communists were executed. Girls of twenty and boys as young as fifteen and sixteen were on trial for their lives. It was an open Fascist terror, comparable only to that of Franco and the blood was on Bevin's hands. We called him "Bevin the Kingmaker"; Spain, Greece and Jordan were typical of his successes. By the summer of 1948, Truman could report to Congress that Britain had spent $138,000 000 in maintaining troops in Greece, where they contributed greatly to the furtherance of American aims.

Greece had suffered occupation and repression during the war, and we on the left believed that it deserved better than this narrow treatment at our hands. In my view, a true Socialist government would seek the friendship of all nations and trade fairly with all; it would bring home the troops; end colonialism; and actively involve the workers in the running of industry. Attlee's government wasn't interested in any of these things, whatever demands might come from the party rank and file.

Bevin controlled the block votes at Labour Party Conference and at trade union congresses so that the Labour view was necessarily falsified. He excelled himself at the Bournemouth conference in 1946. In what was meant to be a debate on foreign affairs, sixty per cent of the time was given over to ministerial speeches, twenty-five per cent to procedural matters such as the moving and seconding of resolutions, and the remaining time (less than half-an-hour) was given to the general debate. Bevin called it "a great example of the democratic movement in action". This sort of manoeuvring left Bevin free to force on the party a foreign policy that was the opposite of what we had pledged.

It had once seemed that Attlee understood the need for a fundamental difference between Labour and the capitalist parties. When he wrote "The Labour Party in Perspective" for the Left Book Club, he declared that there could be "no agreement on foreign policy". We could not have the foreign policy of the Tories. Yet so soon as Labour was in power, he changed his mind. The Potsdam conference on German reunification was the test. The conference was adjourned for our elections. When Labour took over from Churchill's coalition government, the policies continued unchanged. Civil servants are a powerful force for inertia. They remained unchanged and no attempt was made to set them in a new direction.

In the same book, Attlee expressed the view that foreign policy must necessarily reflect the character of the home policies of a government. It was not so with his administration. Socialism at home was, in a sense, paid for by anti-socialism abroad. He knew that we could not afford the promised social reforms without American dollars, which would have to be voted by Congress. American congressmen were (and are) generally opposed to such policies as free health care and the nationalisation of industry. Their support was won by anti-Soviet actions abroad. Our foreign policy was based on three requirements: the attacking of socialism, and especially the Soviet Union; the preservation of capitalism; the exploitation and, if necessary, suppression of colonial peoples. In changed world conditions, it was only with American assistance that such a policy could be continued. The UK was reduced to client status in exchange for American dollars. It was ironic that much of our poverty was caused by expensive interference, on American instructions, in such places as Greece.

In June 1947 George Marshall, Byrne's replacement as US Secretary of State, offered his suggestions of how to help restore the European economies. Marshall Aid corresponded closely to Roosevelt's pre-war New Deal. It was intended to give up to $13 billion for the rebuilding of devastated Europe, including, it was claimed, the Soviet Union. However, the first proposals required an open market and no planning; in short, unrestrained competition. It forbade national planning, whether of industry, commerce, transport or distribution; forbade government control of banking; and violated national sovereignty in economic matters. Bevin brought together in Paris all the European nations, with the object of framing a united response to the offer. Molotov came and at once denounced the proposal; the Soviet Union could not accept aid on such terms. We believed that Marshall Aid would split Europe: the recovery of the Western half being supported with US dollars ad lib, and the Eastern half continuing with the scars and burdens of war for many years. Bevin expressed overwhelming delight in Marshall Aid, and that in itself was sufficient to turn me against it, but Molotov's arguments were conclusive.

To me, the main purpose was to provide wider markets for American industry, with all the colonies of the world thrown open to their exploitation. America's big businessmen had no interest in helping Britain, so there could be no altruism involved. Steel was essential for our reconstruction, yet under the Marshall Plan we were told that in the first year of operation we would receive not one pennyworth. We were to buy whatever they most wanted to sell. Furthermore, we were told that commodities imported under the Marshall Plan could not be used in the production of any goods that might be re-delivered to any non-participating country. The main effect of this would be to place major restrictions on trade with the Communist nations. We owed great sums of money to America, and the Soviet Union offered the only market that could take our goods without dollars and send us food and raw materials in return. I wanted Attlee's government to make strenuous efforts to increase multilateral trade around the world.

Seventeen countries gained from Marshall Aid, and I suppose the UK gained most. I was not opposed to our having the goods, some of which were outright gifts to the beneficiaries, and I realised that it was a most generous gesture. At the same time, I really believed that the offer had been formulated specifically to exclude the Soviet Union. Perhaps they should have offered a cautious acceptance and at least tried to negotiate more appropriate terms. How would the Americans have responded? The Russians declined enormous sums of money partly from foolish pride, and partly from wanting to demonstrate against US interference. I suppose my vote against Marshall Aid was for the same reasons.

CHAPTER EIGHTEEN

Visits to Romania and Prague

THE SOVIET Union responded to the Marshall Plan by keeping a closer watch on the nations of Eastern Europe. In the West, Communist parties were supposedly told not to co-operate with non-Communists. The result was that anyone with whom they did collaborate fell under suspicion of being a member of their party. I rejected the rumour that a person was a Communist unless he said it himself. It was easy enough to spread such rumours. Once they got into print, the papers responsible were likely to refuse the right of reply, or so to garble any denial that it was presented as an admission, or as plainly a false denial. The Labour leadership appeared to hold the view that Communists the world over were traitors, and that British Communists played their role fully in trying to undermine the government and the state. I dismissed such assertions out of hand.

I do not believe in blacklisting. Hymie Berger was the best clerk of any that I knew. The fact that he was a Communist made no difference to my opinion of his work. I was concerned with his capacity to represent my views; I was not concerned with his views, as long as they were very broadly in sympathy with mine. The Communists I knew were devoted workers for the ordinary man or woman. By now, the Labour group on Finsbury Council had lost all their enthusiasm, and was neutral, if not entirely negative. Kay Beauchamp was the only councillor with any bright ideas. She seemed to be trying to encourage the continuation of the Socialist policies that had already brought us great reclaim, so the fact that she was a Communist was no adequate ground for not supporting her. Labour councillors opposed on principle everything that she might suggest, and it was a principle we were all supposed to adopt.

Anyone who leaned to the left in parliament was taunted as a "fellow traveller". If he or she could not be proven to be Communist, then the term used was "crypto-Communist". Sometimes this was offensive, but often we treated it as a joke. Parliament has its own Anglican parson, the speaker's chaplain, who accompanies Black Rod and the speaker into the chamber and conducts the opening prayers. He was always available at the appropriate fee for Christian sacrament and was willing to baptise Members' babies in the crypt, a small and very attractive chapel at Westminster Hall. This was not a Tory usage because their Members preferred their own village churches, but a left-wing function. There were some in the broad left who were not profound Christians, but thought that to have their babies christened by the speaker's chaplain in the crypt was the height of fashion. We called the temporary adherents crypto-Christians.

I doubt whether the leadership of the Labour Party had any understanding of the vigour and enthusiasm with which their own foreign secretary would embrace anti-Sovietism. They realised only when it was in full swing and they were being carried along. Some Members said quite openly that, compared with domestic matters such as nationalisation and social security, at which we were having great success, foreign affairs was a rather unimportant and esoteric subject; it was not a subject that Labour people really understood. If we were seen to succeed – even with a Tory policy – was that not enough?

If Labour Members now rebelled against the government, it was likely to be on some domestic issue. The Whips had to be brought in on what was supposedly a conscience vote when an amendment of Sydney Silverman's was thwarted by the House of Lords and backbenchers threatened to revolt. Silverman's amendment to the Criminal Justice Bill would have suspended capital punishment for five years. We approved it by 245 to 222 votes. Rayner Goddard, Lord Chief Justice, was implacably opposed to any interference with capital punishment and ensured that the Lords struck out the amendment. (The vote was 181 to 28.) We tried a compromise: a government amendment that would have divided murder into two categories, with life-imprisonment for the less serious cases of "non-capital" murder. This went through the Commons with a majority of ninety-eight. Again Goddard fought and the Lords threw it out; their majority this time was reduced to eighty. The Criminal Justice Bill went through unamended.

The concern of the party leaders was how to make sure that our measures would pass the Lords, who were then in full panoply and power.

The nationalisation of the mines, steel, transport and doctors was far-reaching stuff and we knew it would lead to determined opposition. In 1949, the powers of the House of Lords were reduced so it would be able to delay bills it disliked by one year only, instead of two. Parliament needs a second chamber to revise and amend, but it must not be a rival to the Commons. It should be elected; hereditary peers and bishops are not a necessary part. (The other great improvement of 1949 was the removal of the extra votes granted to university graduates and businessmen. From then on, it really was "one citizen, one vote".)

The large numbers of Labour backbenchers who had once spoken out against Bevin's foreign policies now dwindled and shrank away from us. Many became quite openly anti-Soviet. There was a depressingly large measure of ill-will towards all things Russian, and much mutual misunderstanding. Even with Ernie Bevin around, the Russians were sometimes their own worst enemy. A good deal of support was lost by unreasonable behaviour such as the refusal to grant exit permits for Soviet women who had married foreigners.

I have always thought that the best way to prevent ill-will between nations was to foster positive relations through friendship societies, cultural groups, exchange visits, international organisations and conferences and the like. A number of societies promoting friendship with East European countries had been set up in London during the war years, and I had some form of involvement with many of them. Once the war was over, these societies were associated no longer with the government in exile but with the government in being in those respective countries. They were instantly added to the list of organisations to which Labour Party members were not allowed to belong.

An exception was made only for those "friendship clubs" that were set up with the Fitzroy Macleans of this world as their British leaders. He led the official British Soviet Society into the most hostile attitudes when the propaganda war had taken a turn against Russia, and equally was willing for the most friendly contacts when the climate had substantially changed. Any Labour MP who had belonged to a proscribed organisation withdrew at the moment of its being added to the list and would not have dared do otherwise.

I did not return to membership of any of the East European friendship societies until after my expulsion from the party. The proscribed list was treated with as much gravity as was the Catholic Index of banned books and carried the same risk of hellfire.

The NCCL and the Haldane were routinely criticised for being too far on the left, but the International Association of Democratic Lawyers, which I joined as soon as it started up, was even more radical. The main aims were to resist Fascism, to follow progressive principles, and to increase understanding amongst jurists. While Paris was still occupied by the Germans, the French Court of Appeal resolved to set up after the war an international organisation of lawyers aimed at preserving world peace. In all countries that were subjected to Fascism, the appeal courts had tended to remain the last bastions of freedom, and the lawyers supported their courts in such attitudes. In response to this appeal, in 1946 a first gathering was held towards founding the IADL. D N Pritt took a leading part in this. Joe Nordmann, the Paris-based Secretary of the IADL, represented Albania in one of the earliest wrangles of the Cold War.

In October 1946 two British destroyers, *Saumarez* and *Volage*, were mined in the approaches to the Corfu Channel and forty-four sailors were killed. Albania denied all knowledge of the mines. Several months later Britain complained to the UN Security Council, who found Albania guilty. The Russians applied their right of veto and the case was then handed on to the International Court of Justice at The Hague, where it was heard in 1948. Frank Soskice was on the British team, and I worked on the papers for him; with Joe Nordmann for the respondents, I had the pick of stories from both sides. The best one vouched for by each concerned the log-book of one of the destroyers.

A main issue was whether the ship was within three miles of the Corfu shore, or was in international waters, or was in Albanian national waters. Joe demanded that the log-book be produced, on the basis of a report that the log of one destroyer had survived. The British said that the book was irrelevant; anyway, it could not be found. The French, for Albania, argued that the Royal Navy was internationally famed for its log-books and, once reported salvaged, it was inconceivable that the log could have been lost. Demands, refusals and searches followed until eventually it was produced. There was the position immediately before the explosion, duly recorded in degrees, minutes and seconds, and attested by the officer of the watch and by the navigating officer. Then came the test, which showed that the boat's position lay not on the water at all but some miles inland on the lower foothills of the Pindus Mountains.

The case was not decided until April 1949, when Albania was ordered to pay Britain £843,947 damages for negligence in safeguarding her territorial waters. The Albanians refused to accept the judgement or, indeed, the competence of the court, so our government seized Albanian gold reserves held in London banks and diplomatic links were severed. At the time, Albania had neither the knowledge nor the equipment necessary for laying mines in deep waters and it was widely believed that Yugoslavia had carried out the act. I was certain that both countries were innocent of any wrong-doing; at least, nothing had been proved to a lawyer's satisfaction.

Early in 1948, I was invited by Stefan Voitec, General Secretary of the Romanian Social Democratic Party, to attend the formative conference of the new United Workers Party. Communist and Labour were joining to form a single party to represent all Romanian workers. On Thursday 19th February I went to Bucharest, via Prague, with Bert Papworth of the TGWU. We were guests of Gheorghiu-Dej and of the Foreign Minister, Ana Pauker. Bert and I had rooms in Ana's house, and our accommodation was noted for sheets with the royal crest and with bedbugs. The monarchy had just been abolished and it seemed to us that all Romania gave a mighty sigh of relief that the king had gone. We danced in the Royal Palace from seven in the evening to seven in the morning, rejoicing at its new ownership.

The chairman of the Resita trade union branch, whom I had first met in September 1946, came to Bucharest to urge the joining of the two parties. He had been militantly anti-Communist, but this was all changed. Now he was almost in tears as he spoke to me:

> "You will think me a traitor to the movement. You may think I have betrayed our Labour friends, but we are all convinced that we are right. For years we have fought this insane battle that only splits our working people, but the minute the king went it was possible for us to see that the old tradition was only doing us harm. Resita is unanimous for this change."

I was not suspicious of this *volte-face*, nor of the emotional way in which he sought to justify his change of heart. Delegates of the Social

Democratic parties of Eastern Europe sometimes attended meetings of the Socialist International organised in England by Hugh Dalton. My chief recollection of these meetings is of our party leaders abusing the East Europeans for not standing up to the Communists. The general line of their answer was that during the Nazi occupation, which all had undergone to one degree or another, every honest patriot had worked in harmony in the resistance movement to the degree that his courage allowed him and there really was no want of confidence between the Social Democrats and the Communists. All were now working together, and they were quite likely to join in some closer association. The Labour Party leadership insisted that the Communists had brought about this closeness by intimidation and fear. I was certain that they were wrong, for I had visited many of the East European nations and had talked with the politicians concerned.

In a speech at the Romanian Trade Centre, I warned that Bevin was about to disrupt the WFTU, the World Federation of Trade Unions. My statement was reported in London as a grave abuse of Bevin and of the TUC, and well worthy of punishment. How could the foreign secretary possibly do such a thing? Yet within three months of my expulsion, Arthur Deakin, on Bevin's orders, had withdrawn British workers from the WFTU. The United States and all the other anti-Soviet countries withdrew as well.

When the war was nearly won, the allies encouraged their trade union bodies to form a world-wide federation. By then, I was the lowest form of trade union life: a repairer's mate in a back road in Yorkshire Main. We had just voted in the National Union of Mineworkers to take the place of the Yorkshire Miners' Association and the many other independent miners' unions. In February 1945, I persuaded Arthur Horner, newly elected first secretary of the NUM, to smuggle me in to the formative conference of the WFTU in London. The organisation has since flourished. When we reached the fortieth anniversary gathering, only three attended who had been present at the formation: Gordon Schaffer was there as a journalist; Andreas Theotakis, then a Cypriot trade union leader, and later vice-president of the WFTU; and myself.

In passing through Prague, Bert and I had been entertained to supper by Dr Jiri Hajek, the leading Foreign Affairs expert of the Czechoslovak Social Democratic Party, and by the editor of Rude Pravo, the Communist

Party paper of Prague. Jiri came to London in the autumn of 1945 to represent the Czech Social Democratic Party at the founding of the World Federation of Democratic Youth. I met him there, and twice acted as his host when he later came to meetings of the Socialist International. He had spent five years in Nazi concentration camps. While in Prague, we were told of the extraordinary tension in the cabinet, which was due to the fact that for two months past, twelve right-wing ministers of various parties had obstructed all legislation and rendered normal government administration impossible. A shop-stewards' gathering of the previous week had created a powerful reaction, and a meeting of the nation's peasant leaders was due to take place the next day. We were warned that there would soon be major developments.

We left Prague by train that night, and although it was clear that an unhealthy situation was brewing, we had no idea that the very next morning those twelve ministers were to resign in the hope of precipitating a constitutional crisis. Each evening in Bucharest we heard on the BBC of the developments in Prague. Hymie phoned from London and demanded, "Get back to Prague as fast as you can. That's where things are happening." I caught a plane back to the Czech capital early on Wednesday morning, 25th February, the day on which Klement Gottwald, the Communist premier, was to announce the acceptance by President Benes of his new cabinet.

On arrival at one o'clock, I was greeted by the airport director, whom I knew. Just twenty-six years old, he was an active worker in the Czech Social Democratic Party and a close associate of Dr Hajek. In greeting me he exclaimed, "Look what we have done—isn't it wonderful?!" But all I knew was that there was to be a two-hour stoppage in the afternoon and that the crisis was coming to its peak. Quickly he told me of the latest events and added, "I have given the whole airport the afternoon off so that they can go on strike without any difficulty. You must be in town to see the demonstration."

As we drove some eight miles into Prague, the roads were filling with people from every factory and every housing estate, walking and riding into the city. By three-thirty, Wenceslas Square was packed for nearly all its length. More than 200,000 people had gathered in a most orderly and stationary demonstration. I suppose this is the biggest crowd I've ever seen. I seemed to be one of the few persons moving about as I pushed my way through the crowds, studying the people, but so thick was the press that in many places it was quite impossible to squeeze through. Relayed through loudspeakers were numerous and lengthy speeches about the crisis, and when it was announced that President Eduard Benes had accepted Gottwald's new government, there was tumultuous applause that continued for perhaps five minutes. Although the crowds were carried away with unrestrained fervour, I did not see any sign of an artificial or hysterical attitude.

When the prime minister himself appeared to announce his cabinet, proceedings had to be held up for ten minutes while the cheers rolled from end to end of the square. The names of the ministers who had not resigned were given an ovation, and almost equally cheered were those of the well-known leaders of the other parties who had now come into the cabinet. In addition to the Communists and Social Democrats, it included famous non-party men like Masaryk and General Svoboda, together with leaders of the Catholic Party, the Czech Socialist Party (the new name for the old Benes Party) and the Slovaks. In the streets leading to the square were armed police in groups of two or three. In the great demonstration itself, so immense were the crowds that I didn't notice a single policeman until the whole thing was over.

As the police formed up in order to march away, they were cheered and women started setting about them and kissing them. Respectable policemen had to push their tommy-guns aside so as to deal with this novel situation. That evening, five hours after the acceptance of the government, I saw the march of armed militiamen which aroused such furious denunciation in the Western press. Some thousands strong, they marched through Prague from every large factory in the neighbourhood, for every government factory had a home guard and an armoury. To me, this gesture showed the confidence and strength of the workers.

The next day, the Secretary-General of the Czech House of Parliament gave me the use of his office and introduced me to a number of ministers and members of different parties. They told me that those workers who were members of President Benes' National Socialist Party (now renamed the Czech Socialist Party) had practically all deserted it and joined the Communists or the Social Democrats instead. They had come to see that there was nothing "Socialist" about their own party except its title and were turning elsewhere for leadership. It was this turning away from the old and the increase in the membership of the workers' movement that so frightened the right wing of all parties.

Their only chance was to precipitate an immediate election and, at the same time, manoeuvre the Communists and Social Democrats into a position of appearing to be against President Benes, whose personal prestige was immense. The right-wingers were confident that when they had resigned, President Benes would dismiss the whole cabinet and call for a new general election. This was a fairly obvious dodge and deceived nobody. For what then happened was that the Communists, with thirty-eight per cent of the national electorate, the Social Democrats, with fifteen per cent in Bohemia and Moravia, and the powerful trade union movement drew even closer together, and, in unity, called on the people to demonstrate their will. Action committees, a novel and historic feature of the Czech revolution, were set up.

It was an unparalleled manifestation of solidarity throughout the country that showed, even to the most casual observer, the isolation of the right-wing politicians of all parties within the National Front. The tremendous demonstrations of unity led by the workers and the action committees had immediate consequences. They convinced President Benes that the left had the confidence of the people. Secondly, they gave new strength to the progressive elements in all parties to clear out of office all compromising and right-wing leaders. Mr Mayer, the principal obstacle to working-class unity in the Social Democratic Party, was swept aside and replaced by Mr Fierlinger, who, until recently, had been a vice-premier.

The Minister of Health, Dr Plojhar, a famous and high-ranking Catholic priest who had spent thirty years in the Catholic Party and six years in a concentration camp, spoke to me about the resignation of the right-wing ministers of his party. He said they had been pledged to the programme that the government had been carrying out, but by first obstructing legislation and then resigning, they had betrayed not only the government and their own party, but their own personal pledges and honour. He was satisfied that the party as a whole supported his attitude and from many districts had come messages to him thanking him for saving the honour of the Catholic Party by going into the cabinet.

I also met the Foreign Minister, Jan Masaryk, son of Tomas Masaryk who had founded Czechoslovakia after the First World War. So far as I could see, the rest of the Cabinet were overjoyed to have him in their team. Masaryk had just read reports of the denunciation by British Labour leaders, and particularly by Ernie Bevin, of all non-Communists who had joined the Gottwald government. Above all, Bevin condemned the Social Democrats and Jan Masaryk as having betrayed his father's memory throughout Europe. Masaryk described this as the most hurtful public experience he had ever suffered and said that it really was intolerable.

Very soon after that, Jan Masaryk fell to his death from a high window. Historically, there have been many examples of men prominent in Czech public life adopting defenestration as a means to render themselves – or others – martyrs. Some asserted that Masaryk had been assassinated, but even now it seems quite inconceivable to me that anyone could have thought of killing him. The suicide of Masaryk had been preceded by that of Ellen Wilkinson. Rendered distraught by what she regarded as Bevin's betrayal of everything that she and her supporters in the Labour Party and, indeed, in Attlee's cabinet stood for, Ellen took the contents of a large bottle of drugs and died from that. Bevin's policy had many victims.

Before leaving Prague, I gave an interview to the local press in which I told them my impressions of this tremendous working-class victory and wished them the success that I was sure they would have. As I set off on the Friday morning from Prague airport, my friend the director said, "I knew you would think that our people have had a triumph, and I only hope that all the British people will understand it." I am afraid he was over optimistic. On 8th March, the House of Commons voted to investigate, as a breach of parliamentary privilege, a *Daily Mail* interview with Colin Brogan, described as an "author and editor". Brogan had declared:

> "I know that any defence information will be given to the Russians. The secret supporters of the Communist party are a danger, not the open ones. ... I understand that there are twenty-nine of these secret supporters in the House."

Francis Bowles, Member for Nuneaton and Vice Chairman of the PLP, complained that this was tantamount to saying that these MPs were traitors or spies. On 12th March the *New York Times* reported that, according to an unidentified "official source", the Labour Party had decided to act against MPs who followed the Communist line:

"The Labor party's endorsement will be withheld from half-a-dozen members of Parliament in the next general election should they continue to echo Communist doctrine while sitting as Laborites ... There is a strong possibility that even earlier action will be taken, according to a source close to the executive committee of the Trades Union Congress. The pro-Communist activity of these MP's, and perhaps half-a-dozen more, will be raised at the next meeting of the executive of the Labor Party on March 24.

"In the action against the parliamentary 'crypto-Communists' the line will be drawn on the Czechoslovak issue. Those MPs who endorse the Communist victory there will be considered opponents of Labor and will not receive endorsement in the next elections. Every effort will be made to avoid the appearance of a 'purge' or measures that would enable those concerned to don the 'cloak of martyrdom.' "

My report on events in Prague placed me firmly on the wrong side of their line. Matters were not improved when the government announced new security measures. The prime minister said that Communists and Fascists would be removed from jobs involving national security. I heard this spoken as I arrived at the Bar of the chamber and walked forward to my place. As Attlee sat down, I reached the front bench and said in a loud voice, "You creatures!" It was meant to be as offensive as I could make it sound. Herbert Morrison jumped to his feet, speechless with anger, his absurd quiff all aquiver. The speaker's attention was drawn to the incident and when I reached my place, I stood as though to ask a question and was at once called. I asked, "In view of the Prime Minister's beginning of a purge of Communists, is there any reason why he should not go on to Jews and Socialists?" Attlee replied, "Jews and Socialists have a loyalty to this country. That is not so with many Communists, and some fellow travellers." It could be said that Attlee had scored on that one.

CHAPTER NINETEEN

Nenni Telegram and Expulsion

IN 1944 the British Labour Party officially recognised the Italian Socialist Party, led by Pietro Nenni, as the legitimate successor of the pre-war party of the same name which had been destroyed by Mussolini. Nenni's party was accepted as a member of the consultative association of Social Democratic Parties, which had its Information and Liaison Office at Transport House. Labour sent a message to the Italian Socialists, expressing the hope that "our two Parties may look forward with confidence to a long period of mutual and fruitful collaboration". In October the NEC sent a message to the resistance movement and to Nerini's party, expressing "pride and gratitude" at the heroism of "the workers, the railwaymen, the peasants, the partisans" who were aiding the Allied advance:

> "By your courage and endurance, under conditions of bitter mental and physical suffering, you have earned the trust, confidence, and admiration of your fellow Democrats throughout Europe ... The British Labour Party is looking forward with particular eagerness and pleasure to the time when they can renew contact with their Italian comrades."

The NEC knew perfectly well that the heroic resistance they so strongly praised was led by Communists as well as Socialists. The two parties had co-operated, openly and officially and with great success, throughout the war and for many years previously in the fight against Mussolini's Fascist dictatorship. This alliance was continued in the first post-war general election when the two parties agreed that each would withdraw where the other might prove to be stronger in order to prevent splitting the working-class vote. The elections were due to start on the 18th April 1948, and there seemed an excellent chance that the Communists might win, whether alone or in coalition with the Socialists.

The Americans, fearing that the Taranto naval base and other Mediterranean ports could be lost to the Russians, set to work to prevent such an outcome. The CIA poured money into anti-Communist and anti-labour organisations throughout Italy, and voters were offered Marshall Aid and the return of Trieste, should an "acceptable" government be returned. What the wrong choice might entail was hinted at by the intimidatory presence of British and American naval units in Mediterranean waters, war planes which flew over almost every city and town and even remote country villages, and threats to cut off imported food supplies.

This plain intimidation angered many in our parliamentary party and the idea of sending some message of encouragement to our own colleagues in the Italian Socialist Party arose in several minds. Maurice Orbach, MP for East Willesden, gathered perhaps as many as a dozen names of Members willing to lend support. He was a chess addict and in the chess room at parliament he introduced me to three young Italian journalists representing their Social Democratic Press. I think that they may have started the idea amongst MPs. Orbach asked whether I would help him with the telegram, or take responsibility for it. I agreed to take over the collecting of names and mobilised some four or five helpers to canvas fellow-Members. Most wanted to be sure that there would be quite a number of names before definitely committing themselves. I think the figure was of the order of twenty-five to thirty and we soon exceeded that comfortably.

Some contributed a few shillings to the cost of the telegram, but they were not asked for this. We devised the simple formula of "Greetings to our Italian Socialist comrades and warm hope for your triumph in the elections", and by Friday 16th we had thirty-eight names attached to the message: thirty-seven Labour Members, plus one Independent Labour, Pritt. We had collected forty-eight signatures, but several Members came to me before the telegram was sent and said that, for personal reasons, they would prefer not to have their names published in Britain, and so I withdrew them.

As Hymie and I were at the telephone in parliament trying to send the telegram early on Friday evening, there came to us Geoffrey Bing. By some extraordinary mistake he had been made a junior unpaid whip

News Chronicle, 20th April 1948

In the background right-wingers are off to the Hague for the Conference of European Social Democratic Parties.

for the first nine months of parliament, but had now happily been relieved from that absurd position. (It was widely assumed that Attlee and his advisers had mistaken Bing for Joseph Binns, Member for the Gillingham division of Rochester, who was as much on the right as Geoffrey was on the left.) Geoffrey said, "The whips know what we are up to and if anyone puts his name to the telegram he will be at once expelled from the party." We all knew that the whips had no power to expel anyone or even to withdraw the whip, and this was a gross exaggeration. Geoffrey agreed that that was so but he seemed deeply worried and asked whether I really meant to send it.

Everyone in the party and many amongst the Tories knew that I had been canvassing for signatures and there had been several refusals. As a result, I was fairly cautious and to several Members with whom I discussed it, I said, "I am not asking you because you might be hesitant." The Labour Party had sent greetings to Nenni from the last annual conference. Every Member who read the papers knew that Nenni had made an electoral pact with the Communists that they should endeavour to divide up the seats according to which of the two parties was likely to succeed best in any particular constituency. Likewise, every Member knew as well as I did whether or not the whips were likely to make a fuss. Even Geoffrey Bing, that Friday evening, did not suggest his own withdrawal. On the other hand, if we had had any idea of the uproar the whips were going to raise, I'm sure none of us would have supported the telegram.

When Bing had gone, I decided to postpone the sending. The House had long since risen and there was nobody about. Hymie and I retired to my room across the road from parliament, worked a bit and had some supper, and discussed the telegram. We weighed up the suggested threat to ourselves, and the possible chance of helping defeat the extreme right-wing government threatened for Italy. On balance, we thought we might just do some good. At about nine o'clock we decided that it should go and we set off in my brand new Daimler to what was then the all-night post office at King Edward Street in the city, where we sent the telegram with thirty-eight names attached to it. We gave the story to every news agency and directly to several main papers. They all published it next morning. The *Daily Herald* described it as an "action wholly unrepresentative of the Labour movement" and in direct conflict with the attitude of the executive.

Although no name was sent in the telegram save with the agreement of the Member himself, it is only right to say that there were two possible exceptions that I know of – namely, Mrs E A Wills and Charles Royle. Mrs Wills, whom we all spoke of and addressed as Helen, after the famous American tennis player, not only gave her assent but signed a piece of paper carrying the broad proposal that we would send a greeting for success in the election to Comrade Nenni. She was not a very active Labour Member. Most issues of Hansard passed without her name appearing in the index as having taken any part, even by mere written question, or having played any role at all except in having voted with absolute regularity, as indeed she should, on whichever side our whips required. Such votes did not get in the index.

Early in the last week of our collecting when we had well over forty names, I met Mrs Wills and S O Davies, Member for Merthyr Tydfil and Chairman of the Welsh Parliamentary Party. It was after "who goes home" and the corridors were almost in the dark. Davies asked whether I had her agreement to the telegram. I said no, whereupon he cried, "I'll get it for you," and, in the same breath, "Come along now, Helen, my dear. You will be signing this important telegram, won't you?" I had a piece of paper handy and he took it from me. He pursued her along the corridor and got her in a corner and gave her no chance of refusing. With many Welsh imprecations and such cries as "Come along, my dear. It's very important, you know. We will all be doing this", he hustled her into signing. It could be said that he should have known better, and perhaps I should, too.

I later received a note from Helen, stating, "I have been informed that you intend to send that message of good wishes to the Italian Communist Party, if this is so I hereby refuse you permission to add my name to it." I replied at once:

"I hope you don't really believe … that S O Davies and I would stoop to so paltry a trick as wilfully to mislead you. The message was to Nenni – our own colleague. … If Bevin likes to support an individual … who is working with the Italian Tories, that is his affair, but he has no power to commit us."

Helen, with her mousiness and gentleness and general quietness in parliament, was treated by all of us as great fun and I could not understand who would have so maliciously misled her. On the same day Charles Royle, Member for West Salford, wrote asking to retract his signature. Since

Evening Standard, *20th April 1948*

"Autograph Hunter in Downing Street?"

promising his support, he had "given the matter a great deal of thought" and was now "convinced that it would accomplish no useful purpose in any way, but may do more harm than good". His letter arrived too late, the telegram having already been sent.

Our action in sending the message to Nenni was immediately repudiated in the House by Hector McNeil, Minister of State, and by Morgan Phillips. The Labour Party now claimed to have withdrawn its support from Nenni and was endorsing the so-called Unity Socialists, a small group of right-wing middle-class politicians who had broken away from the Italian Socialist Party, seemingly in response to American calls for the elimination of Communist influence. The Unity Socialists, led by Saragat and Lombardo, abandoned their Socialist policies and joined de Gasperi's Christian Democratic Coalition, the right-centre party supported by the Catholic church, the big industrialists who had backed Mussolini, landowners, bankers, black-marketeers and the United States. On the 22nd March, in the House of Commons, thirty MPs had met three delegates of the Nenni Party, in London to attend an international Socialist conference as guests of the British Labour Party. Yet declarations that the NEC had disowned Nenni, and even that they had done so some time earlier, were believable in the light of their paranoid anti-Communism. It was not within belief that they could ever adhere to such characters as Saragat and Lombardo.

By Monday morning, the *Herald* had a number of quotations said to be by six of the named signatories. Herbert Morrison undoubtedly brought real pressure to bear on these MPs, who were named by Oliver Stanley at the opening of the debate in parliament, and persuaded each to say that he had not signed the telegram. This was, in fact, quite easy to say because, except at the very end, nobody signed it. They merely gave their assent to the idea and supported it. Except for the later few, when I spoke of "signatures" I meant "adherence" intended by them to result in their names being added to the telegram. One does not sign a telegram in ordinary terms. A number of them kept to this idea of swearing by the book and saying quite truly: "I did not sign." Insofar as some were timid and more scared of Morrison, or a bit more ambitious and said that they refused to have anything to do with it, then found their names listed on the telegram, it is no job of mine to speculate on the reasoning that led to their respective errors of recollection.

A few days later I received a hurried and angry letter from Charles Robertson, a doctor. He knew John Baird, MP for East Wolverhampton, as a colleague in his own profession and as a member of the Socialist Medical Association, and was both 'flabbergasted and very annoyed" to read in his morning paper that Baird had denied all knowledge of the telegram: "So far from signing it, I've never even seen it." Robertson continued, "Yet on the evening of Tuesday, April 13th, when my wife and I saw him in the House of Commons he jubilantly informed us he had just been speaking to you and that he was collecting signatures for the Nenni telegram." Baird came to me and explained that Herbert Morrison had addressed a meeting in his constituency on the Saturday. He had driven Morrison to the meeting. On the way, Morrison, who already knew the names of the signatories, had expressed the hope that he had not got mixed up with this monstrous telegram. Baird replied that although he had given his name, it was some sort of misunderstanding and he did not really mean it. Baird explained to me that he had felt forced to do this because, with Morrison coming to speak in his constituency, it would have made the whole thing intolerable if he had not adopted that view.

George Jeger, Member for Winchester, was well established as a progressive worker. I thought that George was trying to earn favour with the government so did not press him when he declined to sign the telegram. At a public meeting, when his constituents asked why he did not sign, George gave an answer that was very critical of me. Apparently, I had given him the impression that there was only one group of Socialists in Italy. It was an attempt to trick him into telling an untruth. The same trick – and he would not call it the action of a responsible man – was tried on everybody else, and that was how I had obtained the signatures. For a long time, I had been doing similar actions for other groups of Communists.

His local paper, the *Hampshire Observer*, published a verbatim report of this and was fully protected in law. I told George that if he did not withdraw his comments by an oral statement in the House, he would certainly withdraw them in open court at great cost to himself. George assured me that he had made no such statement. He would make the newspaper correct its erroneous story, and he would report that to the House. He accused the *Hampshire Observer* of "a shocking distortion". That, too, was a mistake on George's part, for the newspaper proprietors produced the reporter's notebook and insisted that George withdraw his abuse of them, not only in their paper but also in the House. Poor George. "Oh, what a tangled web we weave." The speaker came into action and saw the matter satisfactorily disposed of.

Another who opted for expediency was Walter Monslow of the railway workers. He had felt the need to protect his position in the party, and in his trade union, and begged that I should understand. It was all too easy to understand because a sense of real panic seemed to have been engendered in the hearts of many of those who signed. The newspapers took up the story day after day. The cartoonists and the radio joined in and it became a most notorious affair. We were the "Nenni goats", as compared with Attlee's sheep. Raymond Blackburn, our fellow Member for King's Norton who had started healthily on the left but turned full circle, now called us "traitors to the cause of the Labour Party and to the cause of freedom and democracy". He tabled a motion calling for a Committee of Privileges to be appointed to investigate the circumstances in which names "were allegedly appended without their approval". It was further suggested that some signatures had been forged or obtained by fraud, although Zilly correctly declared that more MPs would have adhered to the telegram, had there been time to collect their names.

Blackburn's call for a Select Committee was rejected, but the day after the Italian election Morgan Phillips, General Secretary of the Labour Party, sent out a number of letters marked "Personal and Urgent". All who were listed as signatories were asked to state whether or not they had signed the telegram, which had been sent "contrary to the policy of the NEC". His letter to me made no mention of the telegram or of Signor Nenni. Instead, I was informed that:

> "A Sub-Committee of the National Executive Committee has had its attention drawn to a series of statements made by you which appear to them to be subversive of Party policy. In these circumstances, I have been directed to invite you to attend a special meeting of the Sub-Committee at Transport House on Wednesday morning next … in order to discuss the matter."

This particular Sub-Committee proved to be the "Special Sub-Committee of Officers and chairmen of Sub-Committees of the National

Executive Committee" and was presided over by Manny Shinwell, Party Chairman. Among those present were Attlee, Morrison, Phillips, Dalton, James Griffiths, P T Heady and Sam Watson, the extreme right-wing leader of the Durham miners. Morrison knew that none of the MPs whom he had persuaded to complain would assert either in the NEC at the hearing or in the House or in public any complaint against myself. No one of them did any of these things. None would repeat in my presence what he had said to Morrison, which is why that ground of complaint failed to appear in the indictment. I was given a four-page document going back over two years and listing quotations from speeches, articles or press interviews, which were held up as evidence that I was "devoting a good deal of (my) time to propaganda that was subversive of Party policy". After two hours, I was permitted to leave but asked to submit a written statement. My "considered comments" were to be received within five days, if possible.

To give a few examples, in the *Sunday Express* of 29th February 1948 it was reported of me: "When asked why he did not come out openly as a Communist, he replied, 'I have never supported the Communist Party'." This was considered to be subversive of Labour Party policy. Also contrary to policy were: "Platts-Mills said that the new Government in Prague had the support of the great majority of the people", and a reported quote from the director of the airport in Prague, who had said, "I have given the whole airport the afternoon off so that they can go on strike without any difficulty". I found it hard to understand how such statements of fact could be in breach of policy. My comments on the situation in Czechoslovakia were supported by reports compiled by Crossman, Wigg, and Fletcher; in fact, by every Labour Member who had visited that land, although not all had liked what they saw there.

In September 1947 I had complained of "the restoration of a discredited monarchy in Greece and the propping up, with British troops, of an open Fascist terror comparable only to that of Franco." When I wrote that article for the *Islington Gazette* more than 490 persons, including eight women, had already been executed by the Greek government. On 18th August, eighty-six Labour MPs had sent a cable to King Paul, begging him to save the lives of 1,300 former resistance fighters who were under suspended sentence of death.

At the 1946 Labour Party Conference Harold Laski, then party president, had said,

"For us, as Socialists, the return of the King would be a sorry end to the brave struggle of a nation which first taught the world the significance of freedom; and I desire to say with blunt emphasis that we should place no confidence in a regime led by a King who has not only already broken the constitution he was pledged to observe, but behind whom also crouched old and evil vested interests whose sole concern is to equate their private enrichment with the public welfare."

In May 1948, in an article in *Forward*, Laski stated:

"Mr Bevin's policy is a dreadful failure. He has stained the great name of Britain all over the world by mean acts and utterances; he has been rough and brutal in negotiation; he has sought to club his critics into silence."

I could not see that my comments were worse than those of Professor Laski, or of so many others. On the following day, I received my copy of a form letter sent out by Morgan Phillips, in which he asked whether those Nenni signatories "whose names were included with their consent wish to withdraw their signatures and to undertake not to engage in similar activities in the future". Anyone failing to furnish a satisfactory reply could expect to face disciplinary action on the 28th of the month.

I answered the NEC's list of subversive quotations with a five-page defence, rebutting their arguments to the best of my ability and stressing my loyalty to the party and to its constitution. The way in which signatures were collected for the Nenni telegram was explained and I offered the only guarantee I felt able to give for the future – namely, "I willingly offer to the NEC a solemn undertaking to exercise the right of criticism accorded to minorities in the Party with scrupulous regard for the constitution and practice of the Party." The response came, as promised, on the 28th when Morgan Phillips informed me that I was to be excluded from membership of the Labour Party for my "general political conduct". The official statement on the expulsion admitted that the NEC had considered my activities in March, then remitted the matter for further consideration. On 13th April, three days before the telegram was sent, they had decided to "invite" me to appear before them – and, presumably, to expel me.

News Chronicle, *29th April 1948*

Left, right, left, right, right, right…

It was reported in the press that I had been repeatedly warned in the past. Yet prior to the meeting with the sub-committee on 21st April, the NEC had made no previous complaint about my conduct and given no warning that they objected to what I was doing. I was not permitted to defend myself except before a small caucus of the extreme right-wing party leadership. I announced an intention to appeal the decision to the conference at Scarborough, but was told by Phillips that there was no constitutional right for an individual to do this. Pritt concurred:

> "With regard to appealing against the decision of the NEC to expel you, the constitution of this highly democratic party admits of nothing of the sort. The only thing that can possibly be done is for somebody at the Conference either to move the suspension of Standing Orders to permit of the matter being discussed, or alternatively move the reference back of that part of the report of the NEC dealing with your expulsion (if they don't cunningly omit it!) The former happened in Cripps' case and he was actually given permission by the vote of Conference to address the Conference – at which he made one of the worst speeches of his life. In my case, in the hysteria of May 1948, it was on the reference back, and although I got over a million votes for the proposition that I be heard, a million was not enough ..."

On dealing with Tory calls for a Select Committee, Pritt offered the following:

1 Remember

(a) that the Tories wilt crush you utterly if they can, for they are swine, they hate ability, and they hate Socialists.
(b) that the Labour Government will not in the least mind if you are crushed, for they hate independence, courage, honesty, revolt, and Socialists.

2 Resolve, therefore, that you will defend yourself regardless of what happens to "runaways".

Early in 1946, ninety-five MPs wrote to the EC in support of Pritt's request for readmission. Since Cripps had once been in the same position but now held an important cabinet job, I asked him what we should do to get Pritt back in. He said he would do nothing. Pritt and Cripps were radical QCs who had together defended Ho Chi Minh in the Privy Council and I assumed they had much in common. There was nothing except mutual dislike.

Attlee's May Day speech in Plymouth condemned the "busy little people" who went round collecting signatures to send best wishes to the Nenni Socialists in Italy. "They wanted to sabotage the foreign policy of the Government which they were returned to support." But, as S O Davies commented, "The pressure to speak as the Prime Minister did came not from the Labour Party executive or the Cabinet. He responded to the panic and the nightmarish conditions laid down by the American Embassy in London."

Despite threats of expulsions, twenty-one Members stood by their signatures and refused to recant. It was decided to meet these demands with a common front. Tom Braddock and Geoffrey Bing took a leading part in this and they invited me to their gatherings. The response was so general that these were held in the Grand Committee Room. A letter in rejection of the complaint and in my support was agreed; the Members individually wrote to Morgan Phillips pointing out that at the time of signing the telegram, they were not aware that the NEC had formally withdrawn recognition from the Italian Socialist Party; "nor do we see how we could have known, since we can find no report of this decision in the Press nor was it communicated to the Parliamentary Labour Party". It is a fact that the NEC was quite unable to prove that it had ever withdrawn recognition from Nenni's party, and no such proof has been forthcoming up to today. The united defence incurred a slight secretarial expense for duplicating, postage and the like, and Tom Braddock sent round a bill splitting the cost between us. I paid my 4s.2d. happily. I was very grateful for their support.

To William Warbey, Member for Luton, the Italian Socialist Party had offered workers the only acceptable alternative to the "ramshackle capitalism of the de Gasperi Government" and to the neo-Fascism of the extreme right:

"I still hold the view that there was no offence against Labour Party loyalty in sending a telegram to a brother Socialist party with which the Labour Party has not formally broken off relations and which has neither resigned from nor been expelled from the International Conference of Socialist Parties."

The twenty-one were all old members of the party, and some were foundation members. Emrys Hughes, son-in-law to Keir Hardie, said: "If they throw me out, I shall go. I object to totalitarian discipline of any kind. I would like to remind Mr Attlee that he is not Stalin … . We who signed the message totally deny that we stand in any way as a subversive movement in this country.

Charles Royle, who had had second thoughts about the wisdom of the telegram and tried to retract his name, now stood firm, telling his constituents, "I am not going to be accused of ratting; that is why I took a stand with the 21 MPs. I make no apology." He received the unanimous support of his committee. "If I were expelled on this issue, there would be no West Salford Labour Party," he told the press.

My own committee showed less courage. The day after my expulsion from the Labour Party, the Finsbury management committee voted that I be excluded from membership of the local party; again, because of my "general political conduct". Just twelve months previously they had carried unanimously a resolution denouncing Bevin's foreign policy. I believe that this expulsion was on the direct instructions of Herbert Morrison, delivered, as at the time of my selection as candidate, by Hinley Atkinson. However, earlier in the year the leader of the Labour group on the council had noticed that letters from me about constituents and their housing problems were written on the same typewriter as that used by Hymie on behalf of the local Communist Party. This discovery was reported to us by Hymie's girlfriend, who was secretary to the Mayor. This caused the utmost consternation in the local party and must have contributed to their decision not to back me.

I was not invited to the meeting, but was kept fully informed of all that went on by Miah Cliffe, president of the management committee. He showed great loyalty to me whenever he could and continued a good friend. He was Mayor of Finsbury in 1956-57 and later took my position in parliament, serving as Member for Shoreditch and Finsbury from 1958 until his death in 1964. All were not so consistent. Charlie Simmons, chairman of the No 1 Branch of ASLEF, represented them on the management committee. The branch voted to support me; he, representing them, attacked me and voted against. Twenty-seven Labour members of the council sent me a letter of support that ended, "We shall spare no effort to get you back into the Party." They demanded that a full meeting of the party membership review my exclusion. The local party, now entirely under head office instruction, summoned them to a special meeting on 10th May, where they were ordered to refrain from supporting me, or be expelled. Only one councillor wavered, and so the wording of the promise was modified. Support could be given within the party, provided it was not expressed publicly. Fourteen accepted this. Miah Cliffe then resigned his position as president and walked out.

I had been expelled from the party, but not from parliament itself. The Labour Whip was withdrawn and then the question was: should I go on as a Member, or did democratic principles require that I should withdraw? The sensible thing seemed to be to consult the electorate. I hired the town hall and advertised a meeting for the 13th May and told the police rather boldly that they might expect an overflow outside. When the evening came, the hall was packed and loudspeakers were set up in the big open space of Garnault Place. The police reckoned there were 800 people outside, who stayed on for the full two hours of the meeting. Eight councillors, who continued to give public support, acted as stewards.

In Finsbury, the two prime issues were peace and housing. I was acutely aware of the fact that on neither count had the Party kept its election promises. The better life we had promised to the ordinary workers had been abandoned as too expensive. In our borough, thousands of families were in inadequate housing and they had now been deprived of even the hope of a decent home. There were plenty of sites, but because of capital cuts we had been denied permission to start readying them for construction. There were chronic shortages of building workers, bricks, steel and cement. Wages were frozen, but prices continued to rise; even on utility clothing, increases were up to forty per cent. It would have been a violation of the faith of any Socialist to have seen this and not fought against it. We had promised a safer world, yet Bevin's foreign adventuring was leading us closer to war while wasting millions of pounds per year. Our manpower and our resources should have been devoted to the needs of the people, not placed at Bevin's disposal. If we cut the armed forces and the expenditure on armaments, we could build more houses and fill the factories to produce the goods so urgently needed.

I would never have gone to the people of Finsbury and campaigned for Labour had I not believed in the pledges set out in our manifesto. When the party leaders said that they would put those pledges into practice, I trusted them. The pity is that we have never yet found a way of requiring the leaders of the party to conform to official policy. I was expelled not for departing from our policy but for trying to get it implemented. I urged my Labour friends not to resign, but to stay and work to rescue the party from the mistaken leadership that would destroy it. At the end of the meeting a motion was passed declaring, "We have every faith in our MP. We do not want anyone else to represent us and we want him back in the Labour Party." Out of some five hundred present in the hall, only a dozen dissented.

There was only one sour note to the evening. Councillor Franklin of Finsbury Borough Council had written from Southend-on-Sea: "Sorry I cannot attend being on holiday. I wish, if you will convey to the citizens of Finsbury that I am wholeheartedly in support of stand you have taken especially against the foreign policy of a 'Labour government' ".

I read the letter at the meeting and gave a copy to the *Islington Gazette*. This seemed a good way of "conveying to the citizens". The worthy councillor, through the town clerk, then complained that he had not meant his letter to reach the paper; it should only have been read out at the meeting. The town clerk, who gave me lunch on the strength of it, said it was the most curious message he had ever had to relay. That record was not to stand for long. He was next asked to report that the councillor had not written the letter at all. James Campbell, editor of the *Gazette*, wanted the complaint in writing. The town clerk naively asked, "Surely you wouldn't put him to so much trouble?" Nothing further was heard about it from anyone, except that James Campbell told me all. He was a nice fellow.

When I first learned of my expulsion from the Labour Party, I was very distressed. Yet the most heartening messages of support came from all over England, from Europe, from America, and from New Zealand. I tried to answer, in some form or other, something like 800 letters that came during those first few weeks. In addition, there were deputations and petitions and people stopping me in the street, all urging me to stay on as MP, to go on helping with their problems, and equally anxious that I should continue to work for peace. I gauged this to be an adequate response to the question of whether to go on in parliament, and I did.

When it came to the party conference at Scarborough, Edgar Duchin, a lawyer and delegate for the Haldane Society, moved the suspension of standing orders that I might address the conference. I was there, but only on a visitor's ticket as no longer a member. Morgan Phillips recommended that the motion be rejected, and so it was. On a card vote, the result was 2,563,000 against my being heard and 1,403,000 for. According to Emrys Hughes, John Wood, the Scots miners' delegate, had protested vehemently that the Miners' Union card representing 600,000 had been held up for the vote against me, whereas their delegates were mandated to vote for me. Had the delegates voted according to the instruction of their union, it would have been 1,963,000 to 2,003,000 and I would have been permitted to state my case. Having failed in the only possible appeal against the NEC decision, I was out of the party. (When I was finally restored to membership in 1969, the chairman of the NEC committee that decided in my favour was Joe Gormley, NUM President. Frank Cousins had assured him that I was "a good pit lad for whom he could vouch".)

Frank was a dear and good friend, who agreed that the future success of the Labour Party depended upon the achievement of a broad Left unity. In the week before the Nenni telegram, we had had tea together in a small tea-shop just off Smith Square. He approved of the canvassing for the telegram but thought that I ought to get myself made a TGWU-supported MP. This was something that I had first tried to arrange in 1944. Frank proposed that we should each approach the secretaries of the several T&G branches affiliated to my constituency party and get them to move the proposition. I had barely begun when the party moved to expel me.

Many of my colleagues were kind enough to wonder why Bevin had chosen me for expulsion. Probably the true explanation was given to me by Bessie Braddock, the Liverpool MP who, with her husband, played a great part in the local government of that area and had been a strong left-winger. By then she was deep on the inside of the right-wing grouping of the party and had ceased to have any connection with the left in parliament, whatever may have continued to happen in Liverpool. Ernie Bevin had told her that he had received a complaint from George Marshall, the American Secretary of State, who said that he could no longer tolerate my actions in the House of Commons in continuing to criticise United States foreign policy and Bevin's adherence to it. Bessie's words were that Marshall said to Bevin, "You've got to get rid of him." Bevin had replied: "I've no power to turn him out of parliament. But what I can do is get him turned out of the Party and then we are not going to go on letting him have his own constituency. Next time we'll join him up with a much bigger Labour constituency. They'll get him out."

All this is exactly what happened, and I'm sure that what Bessie said was correct.

On 27th May when the Tories moved for a select committee to consider the Nenni telegram, Harold Roberts, Member for Handsworth, Birmingham, said: "The Hon Member for Finsbury was carefully selected as the scapegoat. He happened to represent a division which will expire shortly. There is therefore no danger whatever of his seeking the confidence of the electorate at the General Election and inflicting a blow on the party caucus. It is perfectly safe to take him aside and assassinate him ..."

Herbert Morrison purported not to understand why an inquiry was sought, referring to the rancorous debates (and, presumably, also to my expulsion) as "a perfectly quiet and gentle discussion…settled with a speed and in an atmosphere of sweetness and light that was a positive example to Parliament itself." This was accompanied by a display of the giggling and wriggling in which he sometimes indulged. Earl Winterton said of the performance that it had done "deep discredit to the House of Commons and to his own Party". Quintin Hogg criticised Morrison's "wholly tawdry and hypocritical excuses" and his "childish and babyish piece of hypocritical rubbish", describing the speech as "a piece of mixed irrelevance, buffoonery and partisanship" which had marred his whole leadership of the House. I had known Quintin since Oxford, when he had gained an All Souls Fellowship and I had so miserably failed. In the House, he very generously said that if and in so far as there was any conflict of evidence between myself and the six cited by Morrison, he would unhesitatingly accept mine. Quintin went on to become lord chancellor and chairman of his party. If the Tories had had wit enough to make him prime minister, he would have kept them in power for a generation.

At about this time, Winston Churchill was deeply concerned with his "United Europe" movement and was about to hold a congress at the Hague over which he would preside. The whole campaign had been denounced at the previous year's Labour Party conference, and with good reason. For example, N van Zeeland of Belgium, who headed a financial commission of the movement, had before the war tried to get finances for Hitler and Mussolini. A large number of right-wing Labour MPs announced that they would go to the Hague. In spite of warnings from head office, more than fifty attended. They were later rebuked by the NEC, but were not penalised in any way.

The Nenni affair was really a trifling incident, although it had considerable effect on my own position. Morrison, for his own purposes, inflated it beyond all recognition.

In Italy, it passed virtually unobserved. According to the *Sunday Pictorial*, one Nenni Socialist, when asked for his opinion of Platts-Mills, asked, "Are they in Lancashire, perhaps?" Nenni's party was defeated in the polls. De Gasperi's victory was rightly considered a triumph of reaction; the *Economist* asserted that it would "encourage the move towards non-Socialist policies that is taking place all over Europe". This was applauded by the NEC. The day after my expulsion, I received the following telegram:

> "The Italian Socialist Party sends an expression of real gratitude and solidarity to you and other Members who signed the telegram. It considers as a sad sign of the times measures taken against Socialists for having desired the victory of the Italian democratic working classes. It trusts in the sense of justice of the English working masses against this unjust action."

It was signed by Nenni, and by Basso, the party secretary.

In 1948, Sir Victor Mallet was British Ambassador in Rome. On 19th March he sent a message marked "Important Confidential Personal for the Private Secretary to the Secretary of State":

> "I have reason to believe that Saragat would be pleased if Morgan Phillips would see his way to send him a personal message of regret at not having had an opportunity to meet him during his visit to Rome. This would remove any impression that the Labour Party are personally hostile to Saragat and trying to leave him

out. In view of his present very satisfactory attitude I venture
to hope that this message might be sent."

This is the acknowledgement that our party secretary had visited Rome
and ignored Saragat of the right wing. At that time, our expressed devotion
was to Nenni. Could Bevin please get Morgan Phillips to switch party
allegiance and make friends with poor rejected Saragat?

I came upon this information in the Public Record Office in 1991. I
should like to have known of it when I was trying to defend myself in
parliament and before the party kangaroo death squad. "Does the single
voice of Sir Victor, Winchester and Balliol, carry the day against the
unanimous voice of the Party?"

CHAPTER TWENTY

Start of the Cold War

IN NEW ZEALAND, the reaction to my being fired was mixed. From some quarters, it was quite as hostile and savage as anything in England. Newspaper editorials implied that I was a traitor with a twisted mind. Mother wrote me anguished letters but continued to give moral support, even though not understanding the issues involved. It was, of course, a great relief to learn some time later that Nelson College Old Boys' Association had decided not to expel me from membership. From sympathisers, I learnt that some kind of ban had been imposed on attempts to publicise my opinions in New Zealand. An article I had written on Czechoslovakia had been offered to the one Labour daily, the *Southern Cross*, which refused to touch it. However, the Socialist Club at Victoria University then cyclo-styled and distributed the article and it was later reprinted by the journal of the Wellington Teachers' Training College. These and other gestures of support were greatly appreciated.

My opposition to the Cold War had its worst effects at home. Some of our neighbours in St John's Wood showed coolness. It did not affect me as I was seldom at home, but it was rather distressing for Janet. The neighbours would come to visit if invited, as though it were a matter of curiosity, but they ceased to invite us back. Brian Johnson and Basil Davidson and their wives were notable exceptions, remaining as friendly as ever. At various schools, boys were asked foolish questions. A little later, Tim rang from school and asked, "What have you done to Cardinal Mindszenty, and who is he, anyway?" Tim had a maths master who was a source of constant provocation.

In 1947 my clerk Frederick insisted that I should take silk in a year's time. I would then have been aged forty-one, of sixteen years' call and six years behind, as were all my contemporaries by reason of the war.

We felt pretty sure that with being so busy and with Tom Inskip (Lord Caldecote) as Lord Chancellor, I couldn't very well have missed. However, Tom Inskip died, my clerk lost his nerve and so did I. Every barrister faces the taking of silk with the utmost apprehension. The silk is no longer permitted to do the work of a junior but must wait for the briefs appropriate to his new status, however long that might take. With my large family at home, Frederick decided that we should put off the application for one year.

One month before my expulsion, when I was laying waste all about me and earning my expulsion from the Party, Denis Dobson (of Assington and the RAF) called me to the Commons tea-room. He was now secretary to the Lord Chancellor's Department, successor to Claude Schuster. In this role, he advised the Lord Chancellor as to most of the appointments in the law, from taking silk to the highest judicial office. Over a pot of tea, Denis complained of my headstrong behaviour:

"After all that's been going on, with you abusing Ernie and Ernie abusing you, I couldn't appoint you to anything now. I couldn't appoint Ernie, either; he's even worse than you."

I told him that I might some day ask him to give me silk. He replied, "Oh yes, that's easy enough. I could see you got Silk next time, if you apply." My practice collapsed and I had to wait sixteen years. Silks must be above reproach and appear to be leading blameless lives. In 1948, I was submerged in opprobrium. To be expelled from your own party was blame indeed. My high court practice disappeared. Every brief was withdrawn and for two years no new one came. The solicitors reportedly said, "If his own party doesn't trust him, how can the judges do so?" and "It is not our doing, of course. We would gladly brief him, but it is our clients who are saying that."

Both Cripps and Pritt were towering figures at the Bar and in parliament and any comparison between myself and them would be somewhat immodest. However, according to Geoffrey Wilson, Cripps went without a brief for two years after commenting in 1931 that there were "evil forces around the Palace", with reference to Lord Halifax and the like. Having survived that setback, Cripps was then expelled from the Labour Party in about 1939 and again he lost work heavily. Pritt's fault was that he wrote a short book entitled *Must the War Spread*, in which he urged that we should not go to war against Russia over Finland. Pritt in his turn went without work at the Bar for a similar length of time.

I retired as fast as could be to winter quarters. We sold up all the family's possessions: the two small farms in North Essex with a few hundred acres of heavy clay, the new Daimler, one lesser car and a sailing boat. My most foolish sacrifice, my least well-judged decision, was the leaving of that secure retreat, that place of places, 13 Cavendish Avenue. The house belonged to the Eyre Estate but we kept the lease for many years, letting it to a rich American lady until she and her children had ruined it, then some of our boys took it over with friends. We finally sold the lease to Leo Abse, the MP and solicitor from South Wales. Within months, the house was portrayed in some high society magazine and we saw that he had made many changes.

I was virtually ruined, we had an unsecured debt of perhaps £11,000 with Hoare and Co of Fleet Street who were about the only people who would trust me, perhaps through lack of judgement. In spite of this no boys had to be sold and all got an education. In 1949 it came time for Tim, the eldest, to go to secondary school. He had always had something special imposed on him, as when he went to school at A S Neill's. At the insistence of Lewis Clive, Michael Milne-Watson and Grizel Hartley, our two pre-war boys, Tim and Jo, had been put down for Eton in the general list. I had met the appropriate masters and urged the merits of the boys. Eton seemed the most liberal school, the nearest thing to a big New Zealand school. It had a lot of music, not too much football, and produced exam results as well, and that was good enough for us. However, I was as hostile to Bevin as I could possibly be and such an anti-American attitude was quite hideous in the eye of Hubert Hartley. When I approached him, he said that no son of mine would go to Eton except over his dead body. I had no time or energy to engage in the battle foreshadowed by that assertion. It could probably have been won, but at the expense of my own dead body.

Hubert was distinguished for that in the early 1920s he had stroked the Cambridge boat to victory in three successive years after a long period of Oxford wins. His three years were followed by renewed Oxford victories. Grizel was a red-headed beauty and their marriage was the event of the year in Cambridge in 1923.

The position in which I had put myself and then found myself in public life made it plain that the boys would face a great deal of criticism on my account. Janet and I decided that they should have the best education that England could provide to prepare them for it. We tried every LCC school within reach and joined every parent-teacher group that was open to us and researched them in every way we could. We were prepared to move house to make ourselves eligible but could find none that offered the breadth of education that we were looking for in terms of wider development beyond formal schooling and without the soldiering or veneration of the Crown.

Hampstead and its lower foot-hills was teeming with Prep schools and some with first-class reputations. None of them seemed to lead anywhere so we decided to begin at secondary school and work backwards. We considered and visited several and finally lit upon the most modern of them, Bryanston, as responding to many of the requirements. The head master, Mr Coad, sent us to Mr Pooley at Dane Court prep school near Woking. At Bryanston there was no beating, a lot of music, drama and the like and some adaptation of the Dalton system of schooling. This we understood to mean a certain measure of choice among the pupils as to what they would read and when. Generally we gave it high marks and Coad agreed to have the boys. With one exception, all the boys followed Tim to Dane Court and went on to Bryanston and we were delighted.

Every student had to do Pioneering on one afternoon a week, which meant anything from building a new music school or a Greek-style theatre to widening and straightening the upper reaches of the river and clearing a path so that the runners could follow the boats through the woods. If he did not choose to play some form of sport, he could do Pioneering on five days a week. One of our boys took to forestry through Pioneering and later made a career of it. Generally, they took an agreeable enough part in school life and were helped to grow up in a rather sheltered way. They emerged as not entirely unsophisticated young men. The parents enjoyed the trips to Dorset and, as my practice recovered, were even encouraged to have fast cars for cross-country rides.

The Bar is deeply conservative and anyone who supports Communism, or is himself a Communist, can expect criticism. When I was in the newspapers for having said something in praise of Russia, G D (Khaki) Roberts wrote a letter of complaint to *The Times*, then summoned me to attend upon him at his flat in Kings Bench Walk. He was a notable figure at the Bar and had been pugnacious in dealing with the beginnings of heavy frauds in the mid-thirties when appearing at the Old Bailey. He was a Bencher of the Inner Temple so that he spoke with some authority. My views were an outrage. If I was set on holding them, I must not publish them, and it would be better that I should leave parliament and give up public life altogether than go about talking such nonsense.

When he learned that I was a New Zealander, this seemed to make up for my weakness of character. In 1905, at the age of nineteen, he had gone to Oxford and played in the university team. One of their first matches was against the All Blacks and he had been so mauled by their forwards that he retired hurt and did not play again for a year. He went on to be a great forward and to captain England. (In 1964, when I belatedly took silk, he gave me all his gear. The jacket and waistcoat were heavy with detritus and snuff but responded well to modern methods of cleaning.)

The Haldane Society of Socialist Lawyers accepted anyone on the left. Although we had a few Communists, most of our members were in the Labour Party. In the 1945 parliament, nine Haldane lawyers were in Attlee's extended cabinet. When the 1948 witch-hunt began our chairman, Gerald Gardiner, took upon himself the task of driving out the Communists. He wrote to the secretary:

> "I do not shut my eyes to the fact that our few Communist or Communist inclined members are about the most active and helpful members we have. I should be the first to oppose any attempt by Transport House to get us to exclude them … . But things must be done regularly, and if I am supposed to be persuading people that we are not Communist run, my job must not be made an impossible one."

After a year of agitation, he called a meeting to vote on limiting membership to accredited members of the Labour Party. When the bulk of the membership rejected his plans, he formed the breakaway Society of Labour Lawyers and tore the Haldane in two. Our group was then disaffiliated and banned from the Labour Party. It has never been the case that anybody on the left has quit the party because of its sustained right wing stance. It is the left who have persevered and tried to keep it as a broad church. The right has always tried to narrow it and to exclude anyone who has progressive ideas.

Prejudice against the International Association of Democratic Lawyers was also growing. In September 1948, I accompanied a small British group, which included Pritt and solicitor Bob George, to Prague for its third congress, one of the first of many international gatherings, and thence followed many inspiring conferences. Countries were generally represented according to the degree to which their governments were under American domination. Countries that asserted their independence would send chief justices, attorneys-general and illustrious academics and advocates. From jurisdictions where allegiance to the United States was not well established, would come retired chief justices and lesser academics, and fewer delegates. From Britain, we usually had Pritt, who could alone constitute a powerful group; the rest of us were modest performers.

In July 1948, the Olympic Games were held in London. The Russians brought an athlete, Irena Ponomayeva, a woman of considerable power and record performance. She must have weighed eighteen stone and was clearly destined for a gold medal. She went out shopping and found herself inside C&A. There were no assistants about and, in a moment, she had nine hats stuffed up the front of her copious jumper. With instant acceleration, she was back in Oxford Street. When caught, Irena offered the explanation that she had found herself in this treasure house surrounded by such a wealth of ladies' attire as she had never imagined. Here was not a single dress on show but scores. There was not just one hat, but hundreds on a tray; and all, so far as she could tell, quite free. There was no sign of a rouble mark anywhere. And she loved hats. But why were they up her jumper? Because that was the easiest way to carry them. She was arrested and ordered to appear at Great Marlborough Street. The expected gold medallist was on bail for shoplifting.

The Soviet ambassador called me to meet the lady and her advisers, who were numerous and varied. The advisers asked many questions, but all received the same answer: NO. Could we claim diplomatic immunity or Olympic privilege? Could she flee the jurisdiction and jump bail? Could she go to ground in the embassy? Could we get it adjourned until the games were over? Ought we to advise the Soviet government to withdraw the whole team? Could we plead that the hats were planted on her? Was it that C&A was connected with any foreign country or any religion hostile to the Soviet Union? There never was such a flurry. The answer would have been obvious to any schoolboy: let everything take its course. On

Tuesday afternoon next, the regular time for petty West End shoplifting, she will come up at Bow Street Magistrates Court. She will plead guilty, you say she is very, very sorry and explain about the new shopping experience and she will be fined £10, with £2 costs.

The ambassador agreed and said that he would consult Moscow. But could I not ask the Lord Chancellor to intervene, perhaps himself to go to Bow Street? After all, Irena was one of their brightest stars. I went to Sir Hartley Shawcross, the Attorney General, and he said, "For heaven's sake, don't you defend her. Let us get Mervyn Griffiths Jones, the best man in the business, to do the job." I had no intention myself of appearing. Griffiths Jones, Senior Crown Prosecutor at the Old Bailey, took it on and did the case free as his contribution to Olympic harmony. The offender was bound over and we all had free tickets to some part of the athletics competition. The magistrate wished Madame Ponomayeva good luck, adding, "I am not wishing luck to your whole team."

Griffiths Jones' son, Robin is now in the year 2000 Master of the Temple, that is the senior parson of our Temple Church.

Sir Hartley Shawcross became known as Sir Shortly Floorcross, for his general political approach was more Tory than Labour. In the 1950s, Hartley told me, "I should like some day to prosecute you." It was quite uncalled for. I asked him, "For which party do you think that observation would qualify you? And if you were to have no more than your usual success, do you really think that would put me in any danger?" The exchange became known at the Bar.

My other concern at the Olympic Games was the Romanian lady high-jumper, Iolanda Balas. She had already set a new world record and the question was could she do it again. This was in the days before the Western Roll or the Fosbury Flop, which so improved the performance of every jumper. She jumped bolt upright so that her centre of gravity was nearly two feet above the bar when her scissors kick took her over it. The Ambassador wondered how she could be helped to win. I know only one rule for the last minutes before a summer athletic contest. The performer must lie flat on his or her back in the shade, feet resting higher than the body. Mademoiselle Balas, who stood six feet tall and was slim and elegant, came from the changing room and stood in the boiling sun. She bent over and started to put her shoes on. I manoeuvred her into the shade, where she sat and eventually lay down with her feet up, putting her shoes on in the most restful position. She won and, I think, set a new record. I like to think that my intervention played its part.

Although I was away from the courts, it was still possible to ventilate an issue in parliament. In that same month, a young Polish Jew came to me with a problem. As a survivor of Auschwitz, he knew that safety comes only from constant vigilance. In 1946, he had warned me of the dangers of making a fuss about Oswald Mosley, who was trying to re-establish himself in the East End. Now he reported that a Polish doctor working in North London had experimented on prisoners in Auschwitz and must be sent back to Poland for trial as a war criminal. I made enquiries and found that Dr Wladislaw Dering had already been many months in custody while the Home Office investigated. Poland, Czechoslovakia and France all wanted to prosecute Dering, who had been listed as a war criminal by the United Nations.

A number of us asked Chuter Ede why proceedings were taking so long, and when Dering would be deported. The information I was given was that he had been responsible for the selection of Allied Personnel for the gas chambers and had carried out many barbarous experiments. To our surprise, Dering was released. The Home Office had not been able to establish a *prima facie* case. A complainant had been brought from Poland, saying that he could identify Dering as the man who had castrated him. When brought face to face, he realised that it was the wrong man. Chuter Ede conducted the most thorough investigation and well deserved the high compliments paid to him by Members for his "meticulous care and impartiality".

After his release from Brixton, Dering offered himself to the Colonial Medical Service and served for ten years in Somaliland as a surgeon. In 1960, he returned to Britain to receive his OBE, no doubt thinking that the page was wiped clean and he could start afresh. On the contrary, he found himself named in the best-selling novel, *Exodus*, as having performed 17,000 experimental operations without anaesthetic. The whole story came out in 1964, when Dering's libel suit against the publisher and the author reached court. It was said that some of these operations had been to sterilise teenage Jews. The opposed story was that Dering had fought in the Polish resistance, had been arrested by the Gestapo and imprisoned in Auschwitz. When they learnt that he was a surgeon, he was forced to work in the medical block. It was true that he had performed this extraordinary number of operations, but all were necessary and were performed under anaesthetic.

The jury showed the effect of the conflict of evidence by finding for Dering, but awarding one halfpenny damages and ordering him to pay the costs, which were quite enough to ruin him. Dering's case shows that it is hard enough to sort out the truth twenty years after the event. At fifty years, it's likely to prove impossible.

It is right that we do not generally recognise a time within which a murder charge must be brought, and in these cases we may have multiple murders. But what occurred in the concentration camps was not ordinary murder. It was a state affair, a world affair. The world suffered for it, and the world has now almost healed its wounds. We recognise in Britain the defence of coercion and of duress, but in limited circumstances. This defence is still open to anyone who acted on the orders of Hitler, if his own life was at risk. The fact that such excuses did not prevail when Hartley Shawcross prosecuted Hitler's senior collaborators fifty-five years ago is not conclusive. I believe that the Lords were right to reject in 1991 the Bill for renewed trials. The government, in passing the Bill a third time in the Commons, acted out of vanity and not statesmanship.

From 1950, I began to get back a certain amount of law work, but it was in the lesser courts, particularly in police and county court. I suppose until May 1948 my clerk would not have accepted it. At the Bar, any publicity is good publicity unless you are actually convicted of an heinous offence or, as in my own case, get mixed up with the left in politics. When my two years of purdah came to a close, solicitors would come bringing a new type of case in which I had not had much experience: a libel suit, for example. "Weren't you recently in a big libel action?" or "Didn't you win that last medical case?" or some other type of common law claim. A self-deprecatory smile, or "Well…"or "One gets involved", et cetera. No explicit answer was called for.

Things were easier in parliament. The MP trying to get help for a constituent finds that every minister is anxious to be of assistance, even if only through a letter from his department. I took advantage of this service even more after being sacked from the party, knowing that constituency work was essential to my survival in the next election. Ministers and their departments are so prepared to answer questions raised by Members that they have no reverse gear, and the same applied in the constituency. Borough employees regarded themselves as civil servants, entirely independent of party, and they would treat an inquiry from a member of an opposition group as fairly as they would one from the majority. As Finsbury Town Clerk, John Fishwick was a model of independence and treated me in exile as freely as he did when I sat as a councillor on the front bench of the controlling party.

For a constituent with housing problems, my standard response was to send a letter referring the complainant back to the borough housing department. Hymie and I tended to do this with a letter explaining the great efforts being made at the local level and blaming it to some extent on the government. I tried to bring home to Finsbury people that preparations for war against Russia were depriving us of the houses we needed. For example, the continuation of universal military conscription in peace-time took enough money to have built several housing estates. The money needed for new bricks was being spent on new mortars. We always sent a copy of each such letter to the borough housing department, and our local party leaders then sent them on to the London party. This undoubtedly angered the party, even before they spotted the distinctive typeface of Hymie's machine.

A greater problem was not having the use of the party rooms. Expulsion meant fending for oneself. There were still many bombed premises for which war-damage claims were outstanding. My supporters soon found convenient rooms in a derelict bomb-damaged building and set to work to do them up. Labour carpenters led by Joe Trotter, chairman of the General Management Committee at the time of my selection as candidate, soon refurbished them. We had the best carpenters in the borough. There was so much friendly aid that volunteers formed the John Platts-Mills Supporters' Club with membership cards and subscriptions, and fifty or more members paid each week for the joy of having me placed in suitable rooms. Some had dual membership of the club and the party, which needed a certain amount of discretion. I was in the borough for at least two days a week and continued to speak every Sunday morning at Chapel Street Market near the Angel. This fixture was a constant throughout my five years in parliament.

When it came to the Soviet Union, those on either side had fixed attitudes and made unthinking judgements about one another. In the 1930s, many voices had boldly asserted that evil things were abroad in Russia. I did not believe them. It was said that Stalin was murdering the best of his generals; that many people had gone to concentration camps; that millions of peasants and kulaks had been liquidated or transported to far away places. Not believed. Pritt and Dudley Collard wrote books explaining that the show trials were genuine trials, and I believed them. Then Churchill hired me to preach only the good stories about the Russians. He didn't care whether or not I believed them. He enjoined me not to worry about the future: it was a wartime job that could do no permanent harm, and so soon as the war was over, he would put the balance right. I suppose one result of the highly successful propaganda was that I believed it myself.

Richard Stokes, MP for Ipswich, in what I regarded as a blackguardly attack on a gallant ally, claimed in the House that seventeen million people were held in Soviet concentration camps. Michael Foot condemned the Soviet Union as a country terrorised by the Kremlin and run by the secret police. In January 1948, the Foreign Office had set up its own special department to manufacture and distribute anti-Communist propaganda, and I assumed that every anti-Soviet assertion came from an equally unreliable source. I challenged them as an automatic response. On the other side, the attitudes were corresponding. Any criticism of America tended to elicit an angry reply, and the most innocent statement could provoke howls of indignation if it came from the "wrong" side. If I spoke, it was "with the voice of Russia", I was "the Member for Moscow" and told to get back to Russia.

To me, Ernie Bevin was the great buffoon who was fomenting the Cold War and bringing Britain into contempt wherever world peace was revered. I tried to stop him, and in that absurd attempt, I made every conceivable error. I hurled myself at him like a clenched fist whenever he appeared to be acting in a sense more abjectly servile than usual to United States foreign policy. This was each time he answered questions in the House, usually one day a week. And his usual answer was to shout abuse almost louder than did the questioner. It meant that I was faced with great notoriety.

A typical lunchtime on Foreign Secretary question day produced an appearance before a high court master at one-thirty, the putting off of something before the judge at two, or leaving it to a leader or dodging in some way, racing to parliament by car, parking at the very door of St Stephen's entrance or in the main yard by the door of Westminster Hall itself, running all the way through the central lobby and into the passage leading to what is now the House of Lords and was then serving as the House of Commons. There was Hymie, waiting with his budget of questions: "Ask this one for the first supplementary. Then try this and this or, if he dodges, try this." Rather breathless into the chamber and taking my seat on the government side above the gangway and below the first aisle, and having the first question, and possibly the second as well, ready for Ernie.

My closest friend in parliament was Konni Zilliacus. He was much my senior; I was more an acolyte. Zilly was brought up to foreign affairs. He was born in Japan, the son of a Finnish-Swedish father and a Scottish-American mother. His education came in Brooklyn, Finland, Sweden, at Bedales in Hampshire, and then at Yale University. He spent the First World War in the Royal Flying Corps and on Churchill's Military Mission to Siberia where he lost a foot (whether in heat of battle or cold of winter he didn't disclose). This was followed by twenty years as a civil servant for the League of Nations, and in 1939 he moved to the Ministry of Information. In the House of Commons he could not bear to think of the party going wrong in his sphere and had to set us right.

We found good allies in the Communists Willie Gallacher of West Fife and Phil Piratin of Mile End. Willie had been in parliament since 1935. He was greatly loved and won many friends on both sides of the House. Phil was in the 1945 intake and, like the rest of us, was still finding his feet. Janet and I came to know his little daughter Lizzie, who was so delightful that I offered to swap two sons for her. Phil demanded three and the business broke down.

In December 1946, he intervened in a debate on the independence of India and was interrupted by Earl Winterton with the impertinent comment, "We do not want the views of foreign Communists." Winterton was a mature, rather emaciated Tory, given to boisterous interruptions. Piratin was upset by this uncalled-for remark, which he took as racist verging on anti-Semitic. He pointed out that although his father had come as a Russian refugee, he himself was British born. A week later, Piratin repeated this as a personal statement in the House, and we thought that was the end of it.

That same afternoon, Piratin was standing in the cafeteria queue in front of the well-known political correspondent from the *Daily Telegraph*. The journalist foolishly asked Piratin whether he was ashamed of his race and pushed him quite hard. He obviously didn't know that Piratin was a skilled boxer. Piratin turned and with one punch the *Daily Telegraph* was, as it were, full page spread on the cafe floor. The journalist did not give up and later assaulted Piratin and this led, after great procedural complexity, to severe reprimands for both.

1948 saw the Berlin blockade and airlift. In part, the severance of the city came because we imposed on our three zones of Berlin a single currency and excluded the East from that arrangement. Berlin lay 120 miles into East Germany and, in June, the Russians closed the city's road and railway links with the West. Nye Bevan astounded us by talking of relieving Berlin by tank thrust, if necessary. Eventually, the UK and America airlifted provisions to their zones. This was massively expensive and continued until the following May, when the Russians lifted the blockade.

To counter all this we were given the Atlantic Pact, designed to bring the nations of Western Europe under American "guidance". We were told that there was no special military significance in the fact that the weapons of Britain and the other countries involved were to be standardised on the American pattern. It was also coincidental that the headquarters of the American Eastern Atlantic and Mediterranean Fleets had been set up in London. Never before in peace-time had London housed a foreign naval headquarters. American expenditure on the armed forces was fourteen times greater than in the pre-war years and she maintained more than 400 bases outside her own territory.

It seemed clear enough to me that the Pentagon intended to use Britain as a base from which to wage nuclear war. From July 1948, I began a sustained questioning about American intentions in the UK. Two B-29 Medium Bomb Groups of the US Strategic Air Command had taken over a substantial part of East Anglia; I queried the purpose of the visit and asked Bevin to tell the House whether the occupation was to be permanent or temporary. He answered quite confidently that they were here for training purposes and the duration was not known.

Cabinet papers recently released show that the cabinet itself were quite unaware of the reasons for the visit and when some months later Attlee was in the US, he was still asking the American authorities what the bombers were doing in Britain and how long they proposed to stay. He received no answer, but could have been given the truth: that they were there to face the Soviet Union with nuclear war. I put a newspaper cutting in my Finsbury office window showing Attlee, bent double, emerging from under the wing of a US plane. It had the caption "How low can he bend". His supporters broke my window.

Churchill thought the atmosphere was right to propose to America that we should attack the Soviet Union with the atomic bomb. He suggested to Attlee privately that he should insist on a Russian withdrawal from Berlin and from East Germany. If they refused – as of course they would – we should obliterate their principal cities. Churchill spoke of "the limited time during which the atomic bomb would be in safe hands". Attlee rejected his proposals. Leftish lawyers denounced the bomb and any service of it as a crime against humanity. The defence of "higher orders" would be of no greater use in such a case than it was to the Nazis at Nuremburg.

Britain was being betrayed by putting us straight into the camp of war. The British people did not want a war, and they particularly did not want to go to war against one of their recent allies. Therefore, the British must be made to hate the Russians. A number of senior military men made public declarations that the Soviet Union was our potential enemy and was preparing for aggressive war. In a speech at the Guildhall, Attlee said, "There comes from the Soviet press a constant stream of abuse of the people of Britain." Though I repeatedly asked him to give me one single example of this, he couldn't, for the Soviet press did not publish such things. At the United Nations, Bevin derided Soviet proposals for disarmament. Zilly once wrote that "the jungle of international politics is cruel, stupid and treacherous almost beyond belief". Bevin was at home in this jungle.

In April 1949 the Atlantic Pact was superseded by NATO, the North Atlantic Treaty Organisation, which put ten West European states and Canada under the control of the Pentagon. John Foster Dulles, emissary for the White House, tried to persuade the members of the NATO group that it would be open to the United States or any other member to invade any one of their number whose territory was likely to be the victim of internal aggression. This was defined as including, for example, a parliamentary election whose result was not approved of by Dulles. This was the notion of collective defence against internal aggression. It was, and still is, one of the most threatening notions in the International Community.

The founding of NATO put the Tories in a difficult position. They recognised it as an anti-Soviet measure and had no wish to vote against Labour, who were so neatly implementing their policy, but to vote with the government would be equally embarrassing. The problem was solved by abstaining. The result was that the vote was 333 – 6. This vote showed a greater than usual abstention of Labour voters and a miserable eight on our side, meaning six plus two tellers. (I think it was on this occasion that Emrys Hughes, Tom Braddock and Ronald Chamberlain crossed the floor to vote against party instructions. All were allowed to continue as Labour candidates at the 1950 election.)

There were several groups on the left that established some sort of formal organisation to co-ordinate their efforts. None was recognised by the whips, but some had an informal whip of their own. By the middle of 1949, Zilly and Leslie Solley had been sacked from the party. With Pritt, we set up a Labour Independent Group, announcing our intention to give general support to the government, but to oppose it whenever "the Group regards it as abandoning a Socialist policy and collaborating with the Conservatives". We were soon joined by Lester Hutchinson, who was famous as being one of the first Englishman put into jail in India by the British Raj for a political offence; the "crime" was an attempt to form Indian trade unions under Indian leadership. We had a regular weekly meeting, sometimes at Zilly's house in Maida Vale. An essential link in our non-organisation was that I drove Zilly home most nights.

I did not usually see him until Question Time, and then only on Prime Minister's and Foreign Office days, when Hymie had set down some oral questions for me. On any day that Zilly was to make a speech in Foreign Affairs debates, we had dinner together in the House and "polished up his wisecracks". Pritt, however, was highly unorganised. Mavis Hill, his secretary, was busy establishing for him a world position as a radical lawyer and he was in court most days, either in the Privy Council or the House of Lords. He could spare us little time, but he obeyed our whip on the rare occasions we asked him to do something.

We could only muster three votes, since two of us were required to be the tellers on a division and, by convention, tellers do not vote. There was little opposition from the Tory side of the House when it came to foreign affairs debates and we sometimes managed so to arrange things that they joined with Labour, giving a vote, I suppose, of the order of

500 to 3. Alexander Cadwallader Mainwaring Spearman made the point that I had "a strange talent for uniting the views of hon. Members on either side of the House". Spearman had a long and illustrious career in parliament, being Conservative Member for Scarborough and Whitby for an uninterrupted twenty-five years. In this time, he achieved the high office of Parliamentary Private Secretary to the President of the Board of Trade, 1951-52.

I suggested that the allocation of speakers "might very well be, instead of between one side and the other, between those who support and those who oppose the foreign policy". Colonel Clifton Brown replied that it was "a delightful theory", but he declined to implement it. Although he was a Conservative, Clifton Brown was especially good to me. On being sworn in as Speaker in 1945, he promised free speech, fair play and absolute impartiality, but he had also promised special help for the backbencher:

"I have been a backbencher for a long time, and when we saw the two Front Benches, Government and Opposition, putting their heads together, we always used to say, 'Well, the backbencher is going to get a dirty deal.' As Speaker … I am the House of Commons' man, and I believe, above all, the backbenchers' man. When that happens I can assure you that my ear will be very sharp, and my eye will be sharp, too."

He was true to his word. When I was in extreme opposition, he treated me almost as though I were a party on my own and let me speak whenever I asked.

Zilly was much involved with Tito and with Yugoslavia. Tito would not accept that the Soviet Union had the only true Socialism. He ignored the Soviet advisers stationed in Belgrade and in June 1948 the Yugoslav Communist Party was expelled from the Cominform. Tito was denounced as anti-Soviet and anti-Marxist, and "Titoism" became a heresy. Zilly was himself excommunicated by the Cominform countries. Tito then took economic and military aid from the West. It was said that his very existence undermined and endangered Soviet power. The whole leadership of the Western World joined in praising him. They made Tito a pillar of the Cold War, which was never his intention. As his speech to us in November 1945 showed, he was the personification of the non-aligned movement, but was so buffeted from either side that he could not maintain his middle station.

Our narrow group on the left in parliament had encouraged Tito's close relations with the Soviet Union. When he broke with Stalin, we treated it as a dreadful act of betrayal. Zilly and the rest of Britain regarded it as a most common-sense thing to do, and undoubtedly all were wiser than I. I now wish that Czechoslovakia had done it, too, and had done it before they executed Otto Sling. I upbraided Zilly in harsh terms and it was some years before I realised that he was right. Khrushchev's denunciation of Stalin in 1952 was not enough to persuade me, but a few years later I became convinced. I sought out Zilly and made a suitable obeisance. He laughed, put an arm round my shoulder and said, "My dear boy, we all learn in time and it is never too late."

CHAPTER TWENTY-ONE

End of Parliamentary Career

AT CONFERENCE, the Labour Party voted for the recognition of the new state of Israel, but the government refused to comply. I asked that the British delegation at the UN support Israel's application for admission, but was told that the application was "premature and hard to accept". Norman Smith, a fellow Labour backbencher, reflected Bevin's views when he said that the State of Israel was "obnoxious and odious to most British working men". Bevin was profoundly anti-Semitic. This was shown in part by his behaviour over the Palestine Mandate. He was as unwilling to give up and let the Jewish people have it as Balfour, all those years ago, had been anxious that it should become a Jewish state. Bevin's close friends in parliament would talk of the "Jew boys" who were our fellow Members, and that correctly mirrored his own attitude. He openly encouraged the Arabs to plan for war against Israel in the hope that Britain might keep a military base in the Middle East and so protect the great oil companies.

In the winter of 1948/9, Israeli and Egyptian forces were fighting in Palestine. When Egyptian planes flew over the disputed territory, our planes flew alongside to give them cover; the information gained from high-level reconnaissance flights was given by the RAF to Egyptian officers. Why was the Labour Government hostile to the point of intervention against the Israelis? The answer was reasoned thus: many of the new settlers in Israel are Russian Jews, therefore Israel will be Communist and a tool of the Soviet Union. This faulty reasoning was well set out by the newspaper, *The People*, in its issue of 9th January 1949, which alleged that Israel was dominated by Soviet-armed Communists, who were continually attacking Egyptian territory on Soviet orders with the intention of seizing the Suez Canal. Pritt asked the attorney-general to take criminal proceedings for libel against those responsible for the paper, but nothing was done.

Communists were on the march everywhere. On 1st October 1949, news reached Europe that Mao Tse Tung had set up his government in Peking, after years of battle with Chiang Kai Shek. I learned of this while sitting in Stockholm, chairing a conference organised by supporters of Bertrand Russell on some aspect of World Peace. Our five dissident MPs sent "ardent" greetings to Mao. I think the adjective was Zilly's contribution. In April 1949, we had begun sounding out the possibilities of starting a friendship society for Communist China. I convened the meeting and found myself as chairman. In December, we held a rather grandly named National Conference at Beaver Hall. There were 403 delegates and observers. Dr Otto Kahn-Freund, a Professor of Law at London University, moved that if I were to remain as chairman it would be "the kiss of death" for the new-born infant society. I promptly resigned.

Almost every difficult situation that arose anywhere in the world was blamed on the "Red Menace". Attlee set up a Committee on Subversive Activities, but it in no way rivalled its American equivalent. If troops were sent in to break up dock strikes, the fault lay with "Communist agitators", not with the Cabinet. The London Docks dispute in the summer of 1949 arose over refusals to work two Canadian ships. Canadian waterside workers were on strike and these two ships had somehow been loaded and serviced in defiance of the strike. Accordingly, the ships were blacked in London and in every other British port. When I tried to raise the subject in the House, George Isaacs challenged me, saying that Platts-Mills "ought to be ashamed of the lead he has given to cause the trouble and confusion which is being caused". Isaacs was Secretary of NATSOPA for forty years, Member for various London boroughs (with short interruptions) from 1922 to 1959, Minister of Labour and National Service in Attlee's first government, but a curiously ill-educated man.

My only part in the docks dispute was that, when it was well forward, I was asked to address their meeting in Trafalgar Square and to join them at Stepney on the march from Beckton. Through the work of Alan Hutt, I was so versed in the early history of British trade unions that I pictured this dockers' march as taking the same route as that of the gas-workers of Beckton in their historic strike of 1889. That dispute was the basis for the formation of the first gas-workers' union and it inspired the dockers likewise to strike and to found their own union. These two led, respectively, to the General Municipal Workers and to the Transport and General Workers' Unions. The dock strike of 1949 was really a lockout because the men were willing to work every ship except these two. When I called for an urgent debate on a proposal for ending the dispute, Herbert Morrison replied, "I think it a rather quaint procedure that those who provoke strikes should require time to debate how to stop them." I protested because I had really kept clear of industrial troubles, and lawyers have never had a stoppage themselves. However, on each side our rooted hostility carried our imagination along.

Attlee's government was supremely pragmatic. Almost any principle could be sacrificed. Consider the cases of Seretse Khama and Gerhard Eisler.

Seretse Khama was heir to the chiefdom of a large tribe, the Bamangwato of Bechuanaland, on the northern border of South Africa. He read politics, philosophy and economics at Balliol but later switched to law, thinking that would be more useful to his people at home. He also joined the Inner Temple to be called to the Bar. At Balliol, Seretse became a close friend of Fraser Murray. When Fraser was sent by Theo Tylor to be a pupil in my Chambers, he and Murray rented our top floor in Cavendish Avenue, and so I came to know about Seretse's troubles with the Attlee government. Seretse himself did not put on regal airs. He spoke like any undergraduate and behaved as the well-brought-up young man should.

In 1948, he married Ruth Williams. She was daughter to a Croydon businessman and was in every way a suitable wife to a man of distinction such as Seretse. In South Africa, the government was just working out the doctrines of apartheid. A mixed marriage for an important neighbouring chieftain was something of a slur cast upon the new formulations and no one was quicker to see this than Attlee, who tried in every possible way to stop the marriage. His treatment of Ruth and Seretse was probably as horrible and anti-Socialist as anything he did in his life.

The Protectorate of the Bamangwato was run under British tutelage, as it were, by a district commissioner. Seretse's uncle Tshekedi had been regent since the death of Seretse's father. When Seretse told his uncle that his bride-to-be was an English girl, uncle demanded that the district commissioner stop the marriage; it would, in his opinion, lead to Seretse's being deposed. The London church the couple had chosen refused to marry them, but they succeeded in a registry office. The marriage was rejected by the tribe and by Ruth's father. Seretse went home and argued his case before thousands of people, and in June 1949 the Bamangwato meeting voted by 4,000 voices to 40 to accept Seretse and Ruth and to defy South Africa.

The South African government passed apartheid laws making interracial marriage or sexual intercourse illegal and told Britain that Seretse must not be confirmed as chief of the tribe. Attlee was anxious to break the American monopoly of atomic weapons and saw South Africa as his supplier of uranium, the essential raw material, but he also worried that South Africa would withdraw from the newly-formed Commonwealth. The cabinet considered the politically undesirable marriage, then set up a judicial inquiry into the question whether Seretse was a fit person to be chief. It was a thoroughly dishonest procedure, carried through without any reference to Ruth, and the decision that he was unfit to be chief was again given without any reference to the marriage.

Philip Noel-Baker, Secretary of State for Commonwealth Relations, set the junior minister, Patrick Gordon Walker, to supervise the planning of the enquiry. I addressed a question to Gordon Walker, asking for an assurance that the attitude of the enquiring judge would not be prejudiced by the marriage and adding some uncomplimentary but fully deserved observations about the South African government. It was one of the softest questions I ever asked, when something quite savage was called for. An attempt was then made to bribe Seretse into giving up the chieftainship. When this failed, Attlee refused to confirm him as chief. After our election of February 1950, Attlee's government banned Ruth and Seretse from going back to Bechuanaland.

I saw them again in June 1951 at Tom Driberg's wedding. Tom was a good ally in parliament, and Janet and I were invited. It wasn't unusual for people in Tom's position to marry as a sort of cover, but Tom had made no pretence of not being homosexual. He married Ena Binfield, who for years had run his constituency. She must have been very lonely. To us, it seemed likely that after the wedding she would go on being lonely. The ceremony was the highest of High Anglican that one could imagine, with much incense, and bells and a choir, and the organ played a modified rendering of the Red Flag. I thought the whole thing rather grotesque.

In 1956, Seretse renounced his rights as chief and Churchill permitted him to return to his homeland as a "private person". In 1966, the country was granted independence under the aegis of Macmillan's "wind of change blowing through Africa". Seretse became first Prime Minister of Botswana and was later knighted by Her Majesty. He died in 1980 but his widow, Lady Ruth, lives on. Botswana is still a multi-party democracy, but no thanks to Attlee or the Labour government.

Gerhard Eisler was a German journalist who spent the war in New York and was known to be a Communist. In 1949, he set off on the Polish ship *Batory* to travel home via Southampton and Gdynia. The American military in London regarded themselves as still operating Supreme Allied Command Headquarters, but now against world communism. The approach of the *Batory* was fully charted and on the 14th May, on arrival at the Solent, she was boarded by British police accompanied by immigration officials and by diplomatic representatives of both America and Poland. The British police arrested Eisler on a warrant under the Extradition Act of 1870. The Poles protested, Eisler refused to leave the ship and it took four men to carry him down the gangway to a tender, and so ashore. He appeared at Southampton Magistrates' Court and was remanded in custody to Bow Street. The only magistrates in Britain empowered to deal with matters of extradition are the stipendiaries at Bow Street.

The first outrage committed by the United States was the sending of American representatives onto the ship in British waters. The second was the sending of a telegram from the State Department saying that if Eisler were not surrendered, the United States intended to seize the *Batory* if she were to return to American waters and to take other measures which would, in effect, close the Gdynia-America line. Reg Paget, Labour MP for Northampton, took up the case. This was unexpected, for he was in general as reactionary as any Labour man could be, but here he was onto a good legal point. The Home Secretary, Chuter Ede, said wrongly that Eisler had been convicted of perjury, which was an extraditable offence. He had not been convicted of anything so grave. It was then said that Eisler had broken his bail, which was also untrue. In fact, Eisler had been convicted in Washington DC of contempt of Congress and of passport offences. As Paget pointed out, these were offences of a political character and were not the subject of extradition by any of our laws.

The Americans then changed their story from "convicted of perjury" to convicted of making false statements in an application to leave the United States. They added that a bail-bond was posted on behalf of Eisler for $20,000 in the Washington District Court. He was not in breach of bail until he failed to appear on the appropriate date, which had not yet arrived. On 27th May, Pritt appeared for Eisler, leading Dudley Collard and me, before Sir Laurence Dunne at Bow Street. The Chief Magistrate discharged Eisler, ruling that the offence of which he had been convicted could not be classed as perjury. (It was, to use Pritt's expression, "100 miles from perjury".) Eisler would be free to continue his journey. Although there was no right of appeal against the court's ruling, the Americans announced that they would find some way of getting him back.

Pritt told me that if the Americans could trace Eisler, they would shoot down any plane or sink any ship to get him. "Go to Chuter Ede and tell him that he must get Eisler a changed name, a new passport and identity, and out of the country by this evening". On Pritt's instruction, I asked Ede to have Eisler out of the country before the Americans could harm him. In his best schoolmasterly manner Ede replied, "I hope you are not suggesting that the Home Office is not capable of faking a passport and engaging in a little forgery. You are quite wrong. We are adept when needed." I don't think the Home Office used their "necessary arts", but Eisler was soon in Prague, en route to East Berlin. He had already been elected in his absence to the Council of the People's Congress of East Germany and to a chair at Leipzig University.

I assumed that there was a plot between the CIA and MI5 and put this to Ede in Question Time. He denied this saying that M15 was not involved. I asked, "How do you know?" I didn't expect any reply but to my delight he answered, "Because I have enquired." It showed that the Home Secretary had the same suspicion, but had enquired from those who would be the least likely to give an honest answer. In the House he said, "This case has given me the greatest personal anxiety, and continues to give me the greatest personal anxiety." His statement showed what happened to any one of Attlee's ministers when the US State Department put pressure on them. The Americans behaved with pettiness and spite. They had Eisler's wife in detention and now refused to let her leave voluntarily. She was kept on Ellis Island for a further month before being deported to Poland.

The Intelligence Services monitored parliament quite closely. It was widely understood that George Wigg was in the House to watch people for M15. He had been a lieutenant-colonel in the army, but had a surprising degree of hatred for the Tories. Wigg took a great interest in the horses and had ready access to a bookmaker at any hour of the day or night. On Derby Day and the Grand National we all got him to put on our bets.

When I was fairly new to parliament and first made a sound friendly to the Soviet Union, Paul Gore-Booth of the Foreign Office invited me to lunch. We had been strict contemporaries at Balliol. We went to an upstairs room in the Bag O' Nails, Buckingham Palace Road. He and his colleagues were always interested in what people said on Foreign Affairs; they briefed government speakers and sat "under the gallery" during debates. Several of them had noticed what I said about Russia, and he was able to speak for them in saying that they thought I must be mistaken. There was so much about Russia: its relations with other countries, its industrial and agricultural development, its military and economic strength. Was there really any need to go into the political questions at all? Was there not a danger of ruining one's reputation in the House by taking up these matters?

If I would care to take advantage of it, he and his friends would be most happy to give me some of the information on present-day events there that normally they gave only to the government or to Members on the government side who were taking part in a debate. In short, his friends in the Foreign Office were on my side and wanted to help, but also to protect me – above all, from myself. Gore-Booth later became permanent head of the Foreign Office, and of M15, so he knew what he was talking about. Any new MP of my time had before him the example of Ramsay MacDonald as the radical young MP given the social treatment in London. One touch of the duchess's fingertips and he was effectively neutralised – dehorned, defanged and declawed. The boat is more comfortable if it is not rocked, and it is easy enough to learn to keep it steady. I was not likely to attract any such attention but, in its way, Gore-Booth's behaviour was a benign example of this seduction.

Equally well-intentioned advice was offered by Harold Macmillan and Anthony Eden after my expulsion from the party. When I was no longer allowed any talk with the Labour leaders, I happened to speak in a debate on affairs in Italy. I thought I was particularly well briefed and expressed my view with confidence. I waited after my speech for at least two others to speak, as is the practice, then retired to the urinal. As I stood at my station, there arrived on either side Macmillan and Eden. They had followed me out. Both started talking at once, then sorted out who should speak first. The effect was as follows: I was quite mistaken in my idea of the events we were debating and it was so important that they felt they had a duty to explain it to me. They were both particularly well informed in Italian matters. During the war, Macmillan had been in charge of that part of the Mediterranean from a civilian position, with Eden as his immediate understudy. Each had ample personal contact with British representatives on the scene.

The point of the recollection is that I was at the nadir of disrepute in my own party and no one in the cabinet, with perhaps three exceptions, would have spent a moment to try to correct me on a matter of information or opinion. Here were numbers two and three in the Tory hierarchy in most friendly manner trying to set me right. I felt that perhaps I was not such an abandoned vagrant. Later, after much talk, they insisted on taking me for a drink in the Lords Bar, where at the time a number of Yorkshire mining MPs were having a drink. A chorus came from them, "Hi up, Jack lad. Thou art in good company, thou knows."

The CIA also expressed a kindly interest in my welfare. It began with Mr Brown, who arrived at Westminster in the last year of Mr Attlee's first government. He made quite frequent attendance in the public approaches to the chamber and its various galleries, even "under the gallery" with the Ministry Men. He introduced himself to Labour Members as Mr Brown of some American journal, but Tory Members who dined with him learned the truth and reported to us. He appeared everywhere and became known as "ubiquitous Brown of the CIA". So far as one could tell, his job was to find out on the spot how left-wing Members were faring with their criticism of America and of Attlee's acceptance of US foreign policy. We had several talks together over tea and biscuits. He didn't argue in terms of facts or opinions, but only in terms of personal consequences. He urged me to notice how all the House had turned against me and that on issues that I raised, I had united Labour and Tory. This could be altered by conceding that perhaps I was mistaken.

Through gerrymandering, my constituency had greatly changed. The Electoral Boundaries Commission in about 1948 decreed that Finsbury should join with the city. I made a quick canvass and found very few voters. Most of them were old soldiers who were unavailable on their top floors where they were guarding the building, but always available in the course of the evening at some local place. They were easy to get on with, and it looked a most promising combination. Morrison realised what this meant and at once decreed further consideration, with the outcome that the commissioners decided that the city should join with Westminster and Finsbury with Shoreditch. In Shoreditch, there was a Labour majority of about 25,000. Ernest Thurtle had sat there from 1923 to 1931, and then from 1935. He was a somewhat reactionary fellow, well-known for the most pawky article in all journalism – namely, a column about politics in the *Sunday Express*. He had married Dorothy, daughter of George Lansbury, and so, for all his dimness, had retained a certain position in the party.

During the run up to the February 1950 election, Brown of the CIA appeared in the constituency with a team of his own. He told me his enquiry showed that I was certainly losing. This was at a time when my supporters were inclined to think that we were doing well. He wasn't there to discourage me by his pessimistic outlook but plainly on a genuine mission of enquiry. The circulation and so the writ of the *Islington Gazette* did not run with such authority in the extended constituency as it did in the old one; I maintained my Finsbury votes but made no impact in Shoreditch. Thurtle won with a vote of 22,510 and a reduced majority of 14,000 plus. I polled 7,602, which was 277 less than Geoffrey Rippon, the Conservative candidate. I never saw Brown again, so was not able to acknowledge that he was right.

The Labour Independents and the two Communist MPs all failed hopelessly. After 1950, Pritt never got back to parliament. Lester Hutchinson went teaching near Dover. Zilly went back to the House in 1955. Solley eventually rejoined his local party and was accepted without demur. He went back to his practice at the Bar, which was to some degree re-established, but died of cancer prematurely. He was a courageous and dear companion.

The Labour Party's achievements in power have to be recognised. Throughout Attlee's first five-year term, there was virtually no unemployment. This was an extraordinary achievement, but was forwarded by the fact that many women from factories retired back to family life (although sometimes reluctantly) and many women from the forces achieved family life for the first time. Some servicemen saw the advantage of overseas countries they had visited and returned there. Demobilisation was phased until the market was ready to absorb them. We largely succeeded in implementing the Beveridge Plan for social security, which was the greatest step in British social life since the National Insurance Act of 1911. We carried out all the acts of nationalising promised in "Let's Face the Future" and the complaint of the Hard Left, as we later came to be called, against Bevin was that he jeopardised the advantage of these actions. He certainly spent a lot of the money that flowed from them.

One of my better political forecasts was made to Attlee at the meeting of the NEC committee that decided on my expulsion. I said that if he persisted in this narrow view and even meaner course of conduct, then the people would be so fed up with him that he'd lose his whole majority by the next election. I was not quite accurate; he merely dropped from an overall majority of 146 in 1945 to a majority of 5. That left Attlee with so narrow a hold on affairs that the Conservatives were able to force a new general election in 1951, and Churchill was in again. It was obvious that Morrison was prepared to use any tactic to make sure I didn't return to parliament; I hadn't time or energy to get into any more battles and so decided not to stand. During my five years in the House, I had taken up over 4,000 cases for constituents, written approximately 25,000 letters, asked 678 parliamentary questions and taken part in 45 principal debates. Now it was time to move on.

CHAPTER TWENTY-TWO

Peace Movement

THE 1950S were noted for the development of the peace movement, which was so reviled by the right that "peace" came to be a dirty word. After the bombing of Hiroshima and Nagasaki, it was thought that the Americans would keep a monopoly of atomic weaponry and that the Western nations would all shelter under their protective umbrella. In my maiden speech I had tried to show that America's determination to keep hold of the secret knowledge of this, the most destructive force ever known, was casting a threatening shadow across negotiations for world peace. In the same debate, Churchill told us, "there are three years before the progress made in the United States can be overtaken. In these three years we must remould the relationships of all men wherever they may dwell in all nations." He meant that America, aided by Britain, should use this knowledge to bully the rest of the world into conforming with American wishes. It was the plainest of threats.

What was overlooked was that scientists from Yugoslavia and the Soviet Union were in the team that perfected the invention, the basic material requirements of which could readily be carried about the world. At the Cavendish Laboratory in Cambridge, Lord Rutherford had introduced me to his "outstanding pupil", Peter Kapitsa, who later returned to Russia and became one of the founders of Soviet nuclear science. It was obvious to many of us that the Russians would soon have their own version of the bomb. The alleged theft of nuclear secrets was soon a feature of arrests in Canada, the UK and in America. The first Russian atomic bomb test in August 1949 caused the West to panic. Attlee ordered that the creation of a British bomb be speeded up, and witch-hunts against suspected Communists with access to sensitive military information gained a new impetus.

When Julius Rosenberg and his wife Ethel were tried in America for stealing nuclear secrets, I wrote to the prosecutor and argued that so trivial a little sketch as was alleged to have been stolen was only a schoolboy's guess, useless to anyone when the Russians had experts of their own trained by Rutherford and Madame Curie. There was no reply. The Rosenbergs were found guilty of conspiring to steal classified government information. By law, the maximum penalty should have been two years' imprisonment and a fine of $10,000. Because the offence was allegedly committed in wartime, they were sentenced to death. That the Soviet Union had, at the time, been an American ally was dismissed as a mere technicality. When giving sentence the judge said, "I believe your conduct has already caused the Communist aggression in Korea, with resulting casualties exceeding 50,000 Americans." The Rosenbergs spent two years on Death Row. While they were awaiting the electric chair, protests came from all round the world. Des (J D) Bernal, leading crystallographer and polymath, one of Churchill's wartime think-tank, generally regarded as the "all wise", hence the nickname "Sage" Bernal, shared a platform with me at Hyde Park to argue against the convictions. We kept it going for a couple of hours each evening for a fortnight on end, but to no avail.

I had already had some involvement with the early stages of the world peace movement, although hopes for peace were little more than a murmur when wise men gathered at Wroclaw, Poland in August 1948 for the World Congress of Intellectuals for Peace and gave those hopes expression. I was flattered with an invitation, but was not free to go. I would have been the bag carrier amongst Sir John Boyd Orr, J B S Haldane, Bernal and other luminaries. The first international peace meeting I attended ran for six days at Salle Pleyelle in Paris in April 1949, with a culminatory public meeting at the Buffalo Stadium. We drew some 1,700 delegates and called ourselves the Partisans for Peace. Picasso contributed as our logo his drawing of the traditional white dove. The British contingent numbered about eighty, including Des Bernal, J G Crowther, Hewlett Johnson, popularly known as the "Red Dean" of Canterbury, and three MPs: Pritt, Zilly and myself. Others said to have attended, but not personally sighted, were Louis Aragon, Pablo Neruda, Sean O'Casey, Heinrich Mann, Marc Chagall, Henri Matisse and Charlie Chaplin. One whom I did meet was Jean Boulier, the Parisian Abbé who was to become a good friend.

The name Partisans for Peace was sometimes also translated from the French as "Defenders of Peace". President was Frederic Joliot-Curie, son-in-law and former assistant of Marie Curie. He and his wife Irene were joint Nobel Prize Winners for Chemistry in 1935. He helped form the National Front of resistance in Nazi-occupied France and in 1944 was made Commander of the Legion d'Honneur and awarded the Croix de Guerre with palms. In 1946 the French government appointed him head of the Commissariat for Atomic Energy, which was founded on his initiative, but, by the time we met up with him in Paris, he had been expelled from this position for making statements against atomic weaponry. Even then, no one would run the risk of disarming first. As Edouard Herriot wrote, " 'To disarm' appears to be an irregular verb with no first person singular and only a future tense."

We set ourselves the task of approaching as many governments as would receive us and convincing them of the need for peace. I went with a group of five or six to Bonn, Paris, Brussels, Helsinki and Stockholm with the object of putting our modest suggestions, namely that the various governments should undertake to abide by the Charter of the United Nations and not to set on any warlike act unless it were on the instructions of the Security Council. We adopted a formula in keeping with the Charter. On each visit, we were received by an appropriate cabinet minister, and each gave us comforting assurances. It was no use sending me as a delegate to Attlee and Bevin, for they had just sent me packing. Almost as soon as the British Peace Committee (the BPC) was launched, it was placed on the Labour Party's proscribed list. The delegation that did come to the UK was received by a Third Under-Secretary at the Foreign Office and was told, with all politeness, that our government regarded them as warmongers. From America came the same response.

The Soviet Union took a leading part in the peace movement. Finance was never a problem because at every meeting of more than a dozen people there appeared a woman whom we might call Comrade Largessova. From a leather bag slung in front of her came a flood of the local currency to recoup delegates their expenses, or to pay in advance for the next outing. In February 1950, I attended meetings in Moscow, where we were received by the government in the Trade Union Hall of Columns, and in Helsinki, where the government seemed friendly enough but, we were told, were rather strongly under Russian influence. Then it was on to Stockholm in

March for our most successful meeting and the drafting of the Stockholm Peace Appeal.

This was addressed rather boldly "to all mankind" and demanded the absolute banning of atomic weaponry and the establishment of strict international control to ensure the implementation of this ban. Any nation making first use of atomic weapons was to be regarded as a war criminal. We called upon all people of good will to sign the appeal. One journalist wrote: "It is very difficult to find anything wrong with the drafting of that appeal if one takes it at its face value.... . It is one of the cleverest political documents this century has seen." We certainly expected that honest men and women would take it at face value, for that was its real value. I agree that it was one of the great political documents of the century.

The collection of signatures was organised most carefully and, so far as England was concerned, we brought together representatives from many areas and arranged lessons on the right procedure. We took whole boroughs as testing beds and found out how many signatures could be expected in a set time. I helped draft an instruction leaflet on "doing a street" and tried to bring into it the results of my own experience. Out of parliament, out of the party and having a fairly idle time at the Bar, I had plenty of spare time and most of it was given to the peace movement. I spoke in all the main cities. At one meeting, Pritt asked me who wrote my speeches. I didn't dare ask whether he thought they were trumpery rubbish or noble and uplifting.

When collecting was under way, the press gave us immense publicity. It was mostly hostile, but served to alert our potential supporters. Amongst our signatories were Dylan Thomas, Compton Mackenzie, Sybil Thorndyke and Jacob Epstein. One young soldier collected the signatures of 475 other young conscripts. We set ourselves the target of five million signatures but ended up with about one million. Several Western countries returned much higher figures: Italy and France delivered about fifteen million apiece. There was no sensible way of checking with any accuracy, but the organisers put the final total at 500 million. So far as I know, it was the nearest there has ever been to a world-wide referendum.

The demands of the world peace movement were not solely related to atomic weaponry. They included support for a general reduction of every form of armament and the banning of all propaganda in favour of war. We expressed our abhorrence of aggression, wherever it might occur, and condemned foreign intervention by force of arms in the internal affairs of any people. Our resolve was greatly strengthened by the Korean War, which began on 25th June 1950. The BPC called for an end to the bombardment of civilian populations, cessation of hostilities, withdrawal of foreign troops, and a public hearing for both sides to try to sort out a peace agreement. On 22nd July at the Holborn Hall, the BPC held its first public meeting. Our guests included the Russian poet Ilya Ehrenberg, who could always be relied upon for a remarkable speech, and we followed this up with a rally in Trafalgar Square. I asked Ehrenberg about Korea. He said, "If we had been concerned in this, don't you think we should have been at the Security Council to veto any action by them? If the Russians had sent their troops into Korea as the Americans did, there would already be war. But our people don't want war."

It was said that the Korean War was part of a plot by Stalin and Mao with Kim Il Sung to take the West unawares and enlarge Communist territory. If this was so, I thought it singularly ill-timed for the Russians were boycotting the United Nations Security Council in protest at the exclusion of Mao Tse-Tung and the UN's thoroughly foolish behaviour in keeping Chiang Kai-Shek on an offshore island and pretending that he represented, and indeed was, China. The absence of the Russians was taken advantage of by America, who voted the Security Council into immediate war on North Korea on behalf of the UN. The Americans and the British had constantly involved themselves in wars since 1945, but no one could provide evidence of Russian soldiers fighting anywhere in the world.

It is generally accepted that North Korea started the war by invading the South. Syngman Rhee, the Fascist dictator of South Korea, was so evil a monster and treated his citizens so badly that this might well have been a justification for the North to come to the rescue of their fellows. They were divided only by the whim of the Russians and Americans and the 38th Parallel of latitude; they spoke the same language, rode the same donkeys, wore the same straw hats. The armies of both sides had been well equipped by their advisors. It was said at the time that the ease with which the North Koreans overran the South showed the whole world that America wasn't much use as an ally and military trainer. That the North fought with greater success was probably because they were fighting against the invading Americans, while the South was fighting with the Americans.

I was genuinely surprised to learn from Khrushchev's memoirs that the invasion had been planned in advance by the North Koreans and was entirely the idea of Kim Il Sung. At the time I was quite sure that the South had begun the war and that the whole world acknowledged this. A picture widely published in left-wing newspapers showed John Foster Dulles visiting the front line at Uijongbu just days before the start of the war, and we believed that he had been sent to Korea to set it all up. Dulles was a self-righteous zealot who took upon himself the task of isolating the Communist countries. He led the opposition to Red China's claim to a UN seat and is rightly regarded as one of the main architects of the Cold War. Dulles addressed the South Korean Parliament and promised them the fullest American support although Syngman Rhee was preventing the holding of elections. Syngman Rhee may have been notoriously corrupt and repressive, but he was also a Christian gentleman and a graduate of Princeton University, as was Dulles.

When the Korean War began, Dulles had already moved on to Tokyo to draft a peace treaty with Japan. The Americans wanted to set up a military base there and were willing to offer concessions that could not fail to upset America's Pacific allies. Dulles had the further task of persuading the allied nations to accept whatever terms he chose to offer. He had immense power. Although officially "special bipartisan consultant" to the American government, he acted as though he were Secretary of State, the position he would have held had his protege Thomas Dewey not lost the presidential race in 1948. By autumn, the Americans had nearly reached the Yalu River and were threatening to invade China itself. 200,000 Chinese troops crossed the river and stopped them. General Douglas MacArthur refused to retreat. He spread his forces along an immense front 300 miles wide and impossible to defend. Within months, the Americans had been forced back to a line below Seoul. For his folly, MacArthur was dismissed the following April. Out of a pre-war population of twenty-six million, perhaps one million Koreans had now died. Peace propagandists were greatly needed, but with British troops fighting in Korea, accusations of treachery multiplied.

At Stockholm, Britain had been granted the honour of hosting the Second World Congress of Partisans for Peace. This gathering would serve as the climax to world-wide protest against the atom bomb. The intention was to strike a major blow at the Cold War and to do it here in England, which was as near as we could hope to get to Washington DC. More than 2,500 delegates from seventy countries were expected to attend from 13th to 19th November. Ivor Montague was principal organiser of preparations on behalf of the BPC and I was given the job of understudy. At first it was intended to hold the conference in London, but every serviceable hall in the centre of the city was closed to us, some even after firm booking. We looked to the provinces and found that Sheffield Town Hall was available. Ivor and I made several trips to the north. After our first visit, Ivor said that he wondered whether he could keep up the pace. He churned out new ideas and I demanded action, and our full achievement was restrained only by Ivor's insistence that each day there must be one meal at which one's skill and originality in choosing an excellent dish was tested.

Our main task in Sheffield was to gain support from local persons of influence such as the Lord Mayor, aldermen and councillors, churchmen, the Master Cutlers, the Steel-makers, Master Scissor-makers, and so forth. Many were enthusiastic and all were interested. The only hostility we met came from the Master Cutler himself, who was prepared for us with his best steel blade well sharpened. He learned of the conference from the Lord Mayor and had taken advice from Whitehall. If there were anything that he could do to obstruct our purposes, he would. Ivor and I teased him that no wars would mean fewer swords, and Sheffield steel could not readily convert to ploughshares. We did not expect him to come in person to open the conference, but his delegate could sit in a prominent place and we would give him a puff: "The Master Cutler represented by Colonel Ploughshare." I had in mind innumerable memorial services where the first twenty persons in the land are "in attendance by Lord So-and-So and Colonel Such-and-Such". The Master Cutler would not attend even by proxy, but he showed us the disparaging statement he had intended to issue and agreed to stifle it.

On 3rd August the Secretary of the BPC courteously wrote to Attlee to inform him that we wished to hold a World Congress for Peace in Britain and asked for an assurance that there would be no bureaucratic obstructions. The Prime Minister's Department did not reply until 13th September, when we were informed:

"The Prime Minister has asked me to say that in this free country there is no power to prohibit the proposed Congress provided

328

that it is conducted in such a way as not to infringe the law regarding the holding of public meetings. Applications from foreigners to attend the Congress will be dealt with on their individual merits and His Majesty's Government must reserve the right to refuse admission to any foreigner who is *persona non grata*. His Majesty's Government are however not prepared in any event to allow foreigners to come to the United Kingdom for the purpose of organising the Congress."

The preparatory commission, charged with settling the agenda and choosing resolutions for the congress, was due to meet in London on 2nd October. It included representatives from the national peace movements of America, France, Italy, China and the USSR. Jean Laffitte, General Secretary of the permanent committee of the Partisans for Peace, was already in London when we learned that he would be expelled forthwith. Laffitte was a novelist of renown and had never been troubled on previous visits to the UK. I knew Geoffrey de Freitas at the Foreign Office and sent an urgent appeal on behalf of Laffitte. The best that Geoffrey could do was to delay the expulsion. I asked him to help us clarify who would be allowed in to help with preparations but the FO took exception and I was obliged to apologise.

Although Attlee had previously confirmed that he had no power to prevent the congress, his government abused its powers and obstructed us in every way. Apart from blocking attendance by members of the preparatory commission, the Home Office now refused to let prospective delegates ascertain, before leaving home, whether or not they would be permitted to enter the UK. It was made clear to us that even citizens from countries which do not normally require visas to visit Britain might be declared *persona non grata* and turned back. They must present themselves at a British port or airport and take their chances. International travel was then considerably slower and proportionately more expensive. Delegates were expected from places as distant and as diverse as Indonesia, Libya, Guinea, Gambia, Kashmir, San Domingo, Mauritania and the Upper Volta. It was typical Bevin meanness.

The BPC had in the past entertained many prominent foreign peace-workers without running into official objections. We protested most strongly against this sudden and very foolish discourtesy and urged fairer treatment for our guests, some of whom were most distinguished. It was thought that up to 150 members of foreign parliaments would attend. How could we risk their being turned away at the last minute? We asked for permission to submit names of delegates to check whether or not they would be accepted. The Home Office (Aliens Department) was adamant:

> "As regards persons from countries whose nationals require no visas, I have to explain that arrangements cannot be made to conduct in advance and by correspondence the examination which is necessary before leave to land can be given. I have to add that the grant of a visa does not carry with it a guarantee that leave to land will be given."

We went ahead with arrangements for Sheffield, knowing that the congress would be sabotaged but unable to determine to what extent. One of the first delegates to arrive from overseas was Pablo Picasso. Janet and I had the job of greeting him at Victoria Station, thence to deliver him to the home of his English friend, Mr Penrose. We let the time of Picasso's arrival be known and advised the station-master. As the time approached, the crowds gathered. The train arrived and disgorged its load, who simply added to the congestion, for there was no way out. Picasso was obviously used to such scenes and held back for a moment. The station-master had paraded in uniform and bowler hat in honour of the illustrious guest. When urged forward, he raised his hat and shook hands with Picasso. The crowds cheered and clapped. Picasso was too famous to be turned back.

More than 270 delegates were refused visitors' visas, and the number who had not previously needed visas, yet were still turned away, exceeded 100. Even Frederic Joliot-Curie, President of the Partisans for Peace, was kept out. The congress had to be abandoned, with delegates diverted to Warsaw. The numbers were about 700 down on what we had expected for Sheffield. I missed Warsaw but believe that it was successful. Out of this congress came the World Peace Council, with Joliot-Curie as first president. I was elected to the WPC, along with sixteen other English delegates. A great, but not a singular honour.

The Australian government, even more reactionary than our own, decided to make an example of those who had attended Warsaw. They instructed British immigration officials to confiscate the passports of any

330

Australian delegates returning through the UK. Norman Freehill, journalist husband of the author Dymphna Cusack, had been at Warsaw but returned safely to their home in Belgravia through the possession of a passport somewhat different from the bulk of his compatriots. Dymphna was a great civil libertarian and she leapt into action. She forced the Australian High Commission to admit that they were in fact banning the passports of anyone visiting Communist countries for activities connected with world peace. Dymphna took them to court and won.

Attlee's excuse for attacking us was that the world peace movement was "an instrument of the Politbureau". From one of his press statements about us, came the following torrent of abuse:

> "It is a common device of disturbers of the peace to profess peaceful sentiments and to proclaim loudly that they themselves are in danger of attack. Hitler and Goebbels were adept at this. It is not, therefore, surprising to find that adherents of the Cominform whose activities are causing bloodshed and disturbance all over the world should proclaim themselves peace makers, should promote peace petitions, and should call a bogus peace conference."

Dear Clem was likening us to Hitler and Goebbels. I despised him more for this than I had even for his promoting me into the wilderness. At the start of the Korean War, Attlee decided that the Third World War was upon us. He massively increased the defence budget and this was enough to end the economic boom created by devaluation of the pound. Attlee snatched at the chance of war against Russia, but somewhat restored himself in my eyes by flying the Atlantic to persuade Truman not to use the atom bomb on North Korea. Russia and America had handfuls of atom bombs and anti-Soviet frenzy had reached a pitch where they might have been used. This was the most worthy act in Attlee's career and was all the more effective and more seemly for being done in secret.

We on the left considered parallels between Korea and Republican Spain and wondered whether an International Brigade could be raised. The difference here was that the Security Council had called upon the world to make war against Russia, as it was supposed, in North Korea. Many nations had answered the call and sent their armed forces. Nationals from any one of those countries who chose to fight for North Korea would have been regarded as fully treasonous and liable to a death sentence once they returned home. Certainly, any Briton who spoke out against the Korean War was called a traitor. It seemed that all we could do was to encourage the widest possible spread of information on what was really happening in the war.

The Women's International Democratic Federation, founded in Paris in December 1945 and co-sponsors of the peace movement, decided to send a representative delegation to North Korea to find out what was going on. I don't know who suggested Monica Felton, President of the British National Assembly of Women, as a delegate but she was an excellent choice. Monica had established her reputation as an organiser and administrator of modern housing development on the Hertfordshire County Council and the LCC and was chairman of the Development Corporations of Peterlee in County Durham and then Stevenage New Town. Monica was so marked with distinction that she was well on the way to her damehood. We all knew that this was at stake if she were to tell the truth about the war. Mary Adams had introduced us many years previously and I took a small part in persuading Monica to chance her reputation and her life by going to Korea.

The delegation set off in May 1951, with long delays at Prague and Moscow. Monica was determined that the fact-finding mission be conducted to the most stringent standards. She was criticised by other delegates for a too-cautious attitude, which they interpreted as callousness. Monica insisted that they would learn nothing if blinded by preconceptions; the aim of the mission must be "not political but humanitarian". Monica and a Danish colleague raised a protest against what they saw as political propagandising by the Communist delegates and were pilloried by the other women, who called them cold and heartless, lacking in intellectual honesty and moral courage. Yet Monica was a real heroine of the peace movement, a woman who took great risks in Korea and at home.

While the women's delegation was in North Korea, they witnessed air raids and low-flying planes raking the survivors with machine-gun fire. The Americans used incendiary bombs and, for the first time, napalm bombs made of jellied petroleum that stuck to the body and burnt in through the skin. Almost every important building in Pyong-Yang, the capital city, had been razed. American bombers had already ruined most of the towns and villages; even the countryside was devastated. On the way back to England, Monica gave a recorded talk from Moscow in which she detailed some of the atrocities that she believed had occurred. She spoke of torture, rape, summary execution; of whole families having been shot, burned to death or buried alive; and she attributed these atrocities to the Americans.

I was still in chambers with Frank Soskice, Labour's Attorney General. After Monica had come back and was about to hold her first public meeting Frank threatened me that if she repeated in England the report she had already made, he would charge her with treason. I told him that he would do better to stop his government from associating with another that was behaving so monstrously as the Americans. It was two more years before Frank turned me out of his chambers, and then only after many more provocations. Monica held a series of meetings at which she described the behaviour of the American armed services as "a calculated savagery that can only be compared with that of Hitler and the Gestapo against the Jews". Tory MPs demanded that Monica be tried for high treason for "giving aid and comfort to the King's enemies". They cheered Frank Soskice's statement that he had referred her activities to the Director of Public Prosecutions. The DPP's department ruled that there was insufficient evidence for prosecution, but Monica was sacked from Stevenage New Town.

The Indian government and people held Monica in the highest regard and she chose to move there. The Russians gave her the Stalin birthday prize, which comprised a gold medal, a diploma and 100,000 roubles. This was about £9,000. Monica entrusted me with the care of it and, with the advice of Hoare and Co, it turned into quite a sum. She passed her time writing and teaching. I have one of Monica's letters from 1965 in which she describes the situation in Madras. She was living "in a beautiful flat, just within sight of the Bay of Bengal, and with Russians and Americans as my nearest friendly neighbours. In fact, I should think I must be the most completely non-aligned person left in this country."

John Foster Dulles, falling deeper into his fantasies of wiping out Communism, urged that action be taken to change the government of China. Taiwan was already being used as an American war base and, in return, the Americans offered to help Chiang Kai-Shek in any action against the Communist regime. Chiang announced his willingness to wage a full-scale war, given sufficient arms, and it was reported in London that his troops had been sighted in Siam, heading for the border with China. Jack Dribbon, Secretary of the British-China Friendship Association, set up a campaign round the slogan "NO WAR WITH CHINA!" Churchill was no sooner installed as prime minister than he declared his support for American policy in the Far East and we feared that more British lads would be sent to die in conflicts that had nothing to do with our country.

I remember attending a reception at the Chinese Embassy in Portland Place on the anniversary of the day in 1949 when Mao Tse-Tung set up his government in Peking. This may have been during the Korean War, but I cannot say with certainty. Barbara Castle and her husband Ted were at the embassy. She asked me:

"Surely you are not going on with all this stuff? Haven't you had enough? It has cost you enough already, being mixed up with the Russians and now the Chinese. I have to come because the whips gave me the job. Can't you excuse yourself from this, make your peace and get back into the party?"

The greatest controversy of the Korean War began in February 1952, when the Americans used bacteriological weapons. It was argued that the Americans could not possibly have dropped bombs containing germs for they were our cousins, they were almost British, and it was unthinkable that an ally of ours could do such a thing. Yet Porton Down was a byword for germ warfare experiments. A direct action group at once staged a small protest demonstration outside the research station on the edge of Salisbury Plain. Once, on a feast day at Bryanston, a royal personage came by helicopter to grace the occasion. It was known that the helicopter had stopped at Porton on the way, and the schoolboys greeted it with a giant poster :"KEEP YOUR BEASTLY GERMS AWAY FROM US". The school was not pleased, but the story goes to show that even children knew that we were breeding small and mischievous germs at Porton Down.

Fifty people died of the plague, which had been absent from Korea for more than 400 years. It was also three months "out of season". Carriers of plague have historically been rat fleas, but here the insects were found to be human fleas. Nine cholera deaths were reported, although this disease was thought to have been eradicated four years earlier. Epidemics broke out in that part of Manchuria bordering North Korea. Spiders, flies and other insects were found near sites of epidemics, and often near American propaganda leaflets and the empty containers in which they had landed. When it was discovered that these insects were of types not native to Korea, the North Koreans and the Chinese promptly accused the US of waging germ warfare. The Americans first denied that there were any epidemics, then blamed them on hygienic deficiencies. On 3rd April, American military authorities denied that the canisters used for leaflet bombs could have carried germs, yet two days later a General Bullene testified before a sub-committee of the House of Representatives:

"The means of delivering germs to enemy territory are simple and involve equipment of a type with which we are now already well stocked – such as containers used currently for dropping propaganda leaflets."

The North Koreans obtained confessions from US airmen who had been shot down and captured, but the authors were under pressure. However accurate we now know them to have been, they were not thought "reliable" because of the possibility of brainwashing. Many of the allied prisoners were found to have been inoculated against plague, cholera and yellow fever; they were insured against the danger of infecting themselves. After spending a month in China and scrutinising all possible evidence, Dean Hewlett Johnson joined the protests against germ warfare. This resulted in a *Times'* leader on 10th July, which considered the possibility of prosecuting him for heresy but ruled against it. The newspaper described his "offence" as "rendered both more odious and more harmful by the position of trust in which he is unfortunately entrenched".

The International Association of Democratic Lawyers set up an investigative committee. It was flattering to be invited along by Jack Gaster, but there was some reason for not going and I declined. I truly forget the reason but hope that it was not cowardice, although it could be said that the Korean War was yet another of the wars I dodged. The IADL were fully satisfied that the Americans were at fault, but the gravest charges America had to face were those made by an international scientific commission set up by the World Peace Council. Six scientists of unimpeachable reputation came from England, France, Sweden, Brazil, Italy and the Soviet Union. The British member was Dr Joseph Needham, a world-renowned expert in Oriental medical matters who had been based at the British Embassy in Chungking as scientific attaché during the last war. He was later to become Master of Gonville and Caius College, Cambridge. The scientific commission went to North Korea and Manchuria to examine and to test the evidence and spent two and a half months in assessing it. Their 700-page report concluded that the Americans had undoubtedly used germ warfare, but that it seemed to be experimental work developing techniques pioneered by Japanese scientists during the last war.

At Harbin, Manchuria, the Japanese had experimented with disease germs on Chinese prisoners. America and Japan were the only great powers who refused to ratify the Geneva Convention of 1925 that banned the use of poisonous gases and bacteriological agents as weapons. The Americans took the most important of the Harbin scientists and shielded them from prosecution. Lesser members of staff who had fallen into Russian hands were tried and convicted of war crimes. Russia asked that the US should prosecute the three leaders they held, namely General Shiro Ishii, Massajo Kitano and Jiro Wakamatsu. The Chinese also called for the scientists to be tried for mass murder but again the request was rejected as mere Communist propaganda. Towards the end of 1951, Ishii, Kitano and Wakamatsu had reportedly been transferred to South Korea by their American employers.

Confirmation of our reading of the situation came in 1976, when a Japanese television programme documented their wartime development of a bomb filled with diseased insects. 3,000 Chinese prisoners died during experiments at the prisoner-of- war camp near Harbin and eleven Chinese cities had been bombed with the same germs to test their potency. Details of these attacks had been given to Winston Churchill, who reported them to the Pacific War Council in July 1942. A decade later we took the facts of germ warfare in Korea and gave them the widest publicity that we could engineer, hoping to stop the killing. Although the evidence was overwhelming, few would believe us. Churchill and his advisors knew that America had hired the Japanese scientists and they knew exactly what kinds of murder they were capable of. Germ warfare was probably the dirtiest offence in the history of the United States, but the British government was a willing accessory.

When the Koreans and the Chinese first claimed to be victims of germ warfare, they proposed that the issue be investigated by an impartial commission that should include scientists. America rejected this and proposed instead an investigation by the International Committee of the Red Cross. The ICRC consisted of twenty-five Swiss citizens: a self-appointed group of rich men who nominated their successors. In November 1951, the ICRC had refused to consider American atrocities in Korea, claiming that they had no power to investigate violations of international law. When the Americans asked for assistance, they were at once ready. No one on the left saw them as neutral.

The World Peace Council, wishing to examine the neutrality and the fitness to adjudicate of ICRC members, called on André Bonnard, Professor of Greek at the University of Lausanne and Chairman of the Swiss Peace Movement. Bonnard put together such biographical material as he could from *Who's Who* and similar biographical and financial reference works and set off for Berlin to attend the next meeting of the WPC. Bonnard was forcibly searched at Zurich airport and his file was confiscated. It was said to contain incriminating documents that portrayed the Red Cross as "an instrument of political warfare". According to Bonnard, they were the sorts of things one would find in any public library. Fifty-five papers were seized and the rest were laboriously photographed, the whole affair taking more than two and a half hours. Professor Bonnard abandoned his journey and returned to Lausanne, shocked that pacifists should be so treated in a country with a tradition of wanting peace.

The Swiss authorities announced that Bonnard had been caught on his way to help the work of the "Communist peace group". He would therefore be charged with passing information to a foreign organisation and endangering the security of the State. I went to Lausanne in 1953 to give evidence for Bonnard, but could say little more than that the international peace movement was broadly based and it was quite untrue to characterise it as controlled by the Soviet Union or any other country, although they bore a great part of the expense.

The Americans eventually realised that they could not win in Korea and agreed an armistice at Panmunjom in July 1953. To the best of my knowledge, a formal peace treaty was never signed.

CHAPTER TWENTY-THREE

New Zealand Trip 1951

IN AUGUST 1951, I made my first trip back to New Zealand since coming to Oxford in 1928. I bought a ticket and a half, choosing as travelling companion that child who was oldest but under ten, which proved to be Thomas, our number three, a flaxen-haired giant aged nine. In the attempt to expose Attlee and Bevin as servants of the Cold War, making the UK subservient to America, I had not noticed the same conflict going on in the Pacific. The Americans were then drawing up the defence treaty that was to become the SEATO accord. They were determined to bind New Zealand and Australia to their control as tightly as Britain was by NATO. New Zealand's Prime Minister Sidney Holland was so proud of taking directions from America that he invited John Foster Dulles and US Minister Scotten to attend a cabinet meeting. At the Commonwealth Prime Ministers' Conference in London, Holland boasted that America "was giving assistance to the free world with unparalleled generosity – New Zealand would stick with her through thick and thin and through right and wrong". Holland might have understood the difference between thick and thin, but I doubt that he could tell the difference between right and wrong.

Jessie Street and the British Peace Committee told its sister organisations in India, Australia and New Zealand that I was coming. Each outlined a series of meetings, but the Indian tour came to nothing. J G Growther, head of the BPC, had tried to enter India and Ceylon on a lecture tour and been so obstructed that it seemed undesirable to repeat his experience. A tour of Australia was more inviting. James Healy, General Secretary of the Australian Waterside Workers' Federation, was a member of the World Peace Council and had been elected with me at the foundation congress in Paris. He gave me introductions to his "cobbers" in Sydney.

New Zealand was then in a very sorry state. The Waterside Workers' Union (dockers) were out for 151 days, the longest period known in any labour stoppage in the Southern Hemisphere. The stoppage had been comparatively disastrous but nobly supported: 8,000 watersiders were backed by 40,000 other workers, most notably seamen, miners, drivers, and the men from the freezing works or abattoirs. New Zealand lost £100 million through the disruption of trade. It began as a lock-out by the employers, but Sid Holland declared the lock-out a strike. Having established a state of emergency he deregistered the waterside workers without so much as a charge or a trial – they were just struck off. He imposed measures that were as repressive as any I have known in any independent commonwealth country. Holland's supporters brought in an American mercenary, General Chennault, with four Curtiss commando transports crewed by Americans to fly goods across Cook Strait to dodge the strike. Their real master was Chiang Kai-Shek and they had flown munitions for the Kuomintang. The one wholesome feature of the dispute was that the Federated Farmers did not send in their members as armed and mounted strike-breakers as they had done at Wellington in 1913.

The Emergency Regulations revived interest in civil liberties and Winston Rhodes, a professor at Canterbury University College and manager of a progressive bookshop in Christchurch, wrote asking for help in forming a broadly based civil liberties organisation. A small group already operated from Auckland, but with a very limited remit. Rhodes suggested "a small private gathering of trade union, political, and professional people" for a thorough discussion of the subject. I certainly tried to help while in New Zealand, but cannot say whether anything enduring came of it.

I wrote to Walter Nash, newly-elected Labour leader, sounding him out on the chances of setting up a broad civil liberties movement on the lines of the National Council in London. He answered that if it were practicable, he would try to arrange something. However, "I am doubtful of any extra organisation, preferring rather to extend the investigations and activities of the Labour Movement to achieve this purpose." In the UK, we have found that although the working classes give willing support for human rights through the Labour Party and the unions, most supporters are drawn from the middle classes. Nash was preparing for a general election in September and warned that he might be difficult to find. The parting comment that it would be "a great pleasure" to meet again gave the assurance that my expulsion from the UK Labour Party had not prejudiced him against me.

In those days, the flight to Auckland meant a five-day trip, with overnight stops at Cairo, Karachi, Singapore and Darwin, and several other stops during the day. Our plane was an old-fashioned American Constellation with a triple tail and a beautiful curve in the body. The first persons we came across whom we knew were Sir Raymond Evershed, who had led me in the Gold Clause case and was now a chancery judge, and his wife Joan, going out to some important lawyers' conference in Sydney. Also on the plane was the architect and town planner William Holford, who told me that he was going to try and sell our surplus pre-fabs to Australia, although whether on behalf of the government or for a private concern, I don't now remember. This mission to Australia, and his early advancement in the honours' roll, suggested that he was not engaged in forwarding any particularly advanced social ideas.

At Cairo, we stayed at the historic Shepherds Hotel. In Singapore, it was Raffles. In Karachi we stayed in airmen's quarters next door to a great hangar built for the unhappy airship the R-101, in a group of bungalows round a central dining hall. This stop was made entertaining, especially for Tom, by a troupe of conjurors and magicians. The Labour Lord Chancellor William Jowitt and his wife came on at Karachi. They were greeted in a most cheerful and friendly manner by the Australians, and with deference and propriety by the English. Viscount Jowitt took his seat immediately in front of the Eversheds, who had been placed in the second row. The front seats had been reserved for the Jowitts all the way out from England. They were by no means the best seats in the plane, but that wasn't the point. There being no first class, protocol dictated that the Jowitts be seated at the front.

Tom Dewey, Governor of New York State, boarded at Djakarta. He was at the end of a highly publicised Asian tour in which he announced the Republican thesis that America's prime task in the coming years was to fight Communism in every corner of South-east Asia. When the Chinese entered the Korean War, they drove the Americans back to their starting point. This was perhaps America's first major setback in military affairs since Custer's last stand. Dewey and his protégé John Foster Dulles took the view that they should try somewhere else. The French were by then hopelessly involved in Vietnam in the most bitter war, but it was three years before their defeat at Dien Bien Phu opened the way for the Americans to carry out the Dulles and Dewey policy based on Saigon.

Dewey was a dapper little chap with a smart British subaltern's moustache from the First World War, and four obvious gangsters to protect him. They insisted that Dewey must have the front seat because only there could he be protected. The pilot was eventually persuaded that the Lord Chancellor must give way to Dewey as a matter of comity on a British plane to show respect for so distinguished a foreigner. It was a matter of protocol that the governor of an American state should take precedence over the Lord Chancellor of Great Britain. So it went on for some time until finally, to our shame, Jowitt was persuaded that he must move from his seat. Then other people were moved around so that the four hoodlums might be stationed in aisle seats and spread down the plane: each to cover the other, and all to cover Dewey.

At Darwin, the first Australian landing point, the plane was boarded by a man whose duty it was to disinfest us from Indonesian vermin. He was sunburnt and was dressed in the shortest of shorts and the barest vest, which was little more than two strings of cloth. He was very thin and tall, with a scholarly stoop of the kind you get through carrying heavy bales of wool. He sprayed with a flit gun, squirting a fine mist over everybody and everything, and into all the corners. When he was spraying over Dewey, right in the front, an Australian voice called from the back, "Give him an extra squirt, mate," which summed up the view of everybody and gave general pleasure.

When we got off at Darwin and were waiting for a bus to take us to our hotel for the night, journalists crowded round Dewey. On Australian soil, he began churning out his horrible gospel of world war, and I thought it was almost as bad as doing it on New Zealand soil. I was only just beginning to get work again after three years of heavy infighting with Ernie Bevin, who supported every idea of Dewey and every evil action of Dulles. So I pushed through the crowd and pressed in my questions on the line that since America had taken such a battering in Korea and lost so many lives and brought such disgrace on Britain by dragging her in, was it sensible to go around rooting for further South-east Asian adventures?

Dewey's buddies had wit enough, but only just, to realise that this was a hostile approach and one of them came across and presented me with his own hostile approach. He began to feel my body and to put his hands under my arm and on my crutch. I asked him whether this was normal Australian procedure and whether he was an Australian. Irrespective of the answers, I would not stand for it and I began to frisk him. I put my right hand firmly inside his jacket under his arm, and my left hand on his stomach and began to move it towards his crutch, while at the same time protecting my own crutch with some care. He only broke off contact when nearby Australians gathered round the bodyguards. The police then moved in, not wishing to allow Dewey's guards too much action.

We made a daylight flight across the Australian desert to Kingsford Smith Aerodrome, named after the great Australian aeronaut. When we reached Sydney that afternoon, there were rival gatherings. For Tom Dewey, there was a deputation headed by the acting Governor General, Sir Kenneth Whistler Street, husband to Jessie Street. Sir Kenneth was acting Governor General through being Lieutenant-Governor and Chief Justice of New South Wales. In any capacity, he would have been expected to meet our Lord Chancellor, who was instead met by a handful of the leading Sydney lawyers.

I was flattered to be greeted by what seemed to be the united trade union movement of New South Wales and of the Australian Left generally, including Mr Sharky, Secretary of the Australian Communist Party.

The lawyers were too polite for what followed, but the other two groups held press conferences on the site. After very short introductions and greetings and a few questions, I proposed that we should all go and join Dewey's conference. We arrived in ample time to hear one rather doubting journalist ask Mr Dewey how it was that he managed to identify Communists everywhere he went, and particularly under the bed. Did he ask them, or did they wear badges on their jackets? To this, Dewey answered that you didn't need to ask them; they were everywhere, you knew they were there. The general theme was that the Communists would take over South-east Asia and we must fight them in every corner of those lands.

We then went off in convoy to the Waterside Workers' office where I had put before me several projects. One was that I should defend Jock Barnes, President of the New Zealand Waterside Workers' Union, currently immured in Auckland's Mt Eden jail for criminal defamation of a policeman. (The Australians had given magnificent support to the NZWWU and a number of Australian union leaders were prosecuted for hindering trade with New Zealand.) Another proposition was that I should come back from New Zealand in due course and help fight for a "no" in the nationwide referendum that was meant to declare the Communist Party of Australia unconstitutional and illegal. Dr Herbert Evatt, the leader of the Australian Labor Party, had set up a campaign to defeat the referendum. This was a very attractive project and I agreed to join in.

After a great celebration supper, came the night flight to Auckland by twin-engined flying boat. Dawn brought thunder, and lightning going round and round with the propeller tips. On arrival at Auckland, our baggage was searched. I was then reading Tolstoy's *War and Peace*, which was taken from me. It is right to report that I was treated in some official quarters with grave suspicion because of the publicity about the peace movement, and *War and Peace* by a Russian author was almost too much for them, even though I still had a New Zealand passport. After two hours and long argument, and consultation with the chief librarian of Auckland, the book was returned and Tom and I were released into the arms of our family. Daisy, Bill, Deed and the whole team had come to the airport to meet us at some quite early hour, though it was in the depths of winter. Deed was in general practice. Her husband Dudley ran a dairy farm, and Tom and I were to stay there for a while.

On the day we landed in Auckland, I went to meet Jock Barnes. I had been admitted a barrister and solicitor of the Supreme Court of New Zealand in 1928 but had not paid my dues for the last twenty-three years and had never argued a case before any New Zealand court, although I had appeared in London in a number of Privy Council cases from there. I soon found myself re-enrolled and at least paid up for the current year. Patrick McGavin was the lawyer who instructed me. The appeal was set for 5th September, and Barnes was released on bail. This was to be my only trial in New Zealand.

Prime Minister Holland had determined to break the trade unions by dragging down living standards and fighting the forty-hour week. There was no opposition from the Federation of Labour, for the trade union movement was under the most reactionary rule. Vice-president was the notoriously corrupt Fintan Patrick Walsh (employer, investor, farm owner, rack-renter). He was also President of the Seamen's Union, but there were more in his union that hated him than that loved him. No wonder the Watersiders and their supporters left the FoL and set up a rival Trades Union Congress.

There was another reason for Holland's hatred of the union. He wanted to join in the Malayan war and the waterside workers had banned all shipments: "Not a son or a gun for Malaya, the dirty war!" The union had accordingly been marked for immediate destruction. Holland got the ship-owners to stage a confrontation by locking-out the watersiders for their refusal of overtime. The government intervened with an ultimatum that men must accept overtime whenever it was offered, and the union answered with a forty-hour week. Holland declared a State of Emergency, saying: "Any individual…who stood in the way of or limited the country's preparations for defence…was a traitor to the country and should be treated accordingly." The governor-general declared the Emergency while the men made themselves available at the wharf gates for a forty-hour week.

Receivers were sent in and union funds seized, officials were arrested, the military acted as strike breakers and picketing was banned. The emergency rules were of the strictest character. Trial by jury was ended; arrest could be without warrant; it was a crime to aid or abet strikers in any way; and the penalty for a breach of these rules was a £100 fine or three months' hard labour, or both. The court could admit evidence even if it would not be admissible in other proceedings. If the police thought that one man might influence another to offend, then his presence was an offence and, according to the rules, "it is immaterial whether or not the evidence established that any particular person was intended or likely to be influenced as aforesaid". All views in favour of the strike were banned from the newspapers. Thousands of the best workers in the dominion had been shut out with no source of support except charity, and donations for strikers were prohibited. Every honest person gave the utmost that he could to sustain the families although, in theory, one could be prosecuted for giving a sandwich to a hungry child, if its father were a watersider.

So vicious were the right wing that, when the strike ended and the dockers returned, the employers drew up a blacklist of strikers and took on new labour. Jock Barnes was forced to leave the wharves. When I next came home to New Zealand, he was a master drainlayer and busy contractor for local authorities. Trade union connections and his fame or notoriety through the strike had provided a useful introduction to local authorities under Labour influence. One of the worst aspects of the Emergency Regulations was that they had been drafted by the Labour government under Peter Fraser, before they lost the election of 1949. Fraser's death in December 1950 let Walter Nash in as leader of the party. Nash was unsure of his position with the watersiders. He said, "We are not for the waterside workers and we are not against them." When he was the one who could have given them real leadership, it was disappointing. He was a true Christian Socialist: sombre, austere, conscientious and free from vanity of any sort. My impression is that he wasn't a man who easily made friends.

I saw him at the New Zealand House of Parliament in August. The strike was over and he was busy with the general election due on 1st September. Holland and his National Party won again and this, I think, on the strength of having denounced the strike as a Communist plot. The country was told that there were Soviet agents in the Watersiders Union, although there was not a single Communist on the executive committee or serving as a paid official. There was no basis for the "red scare", and the failure of Nash to commit the Labour Party to the strikers harmed them and lost him the election. Nash was no better in 1951 for the watersiders than Neil Kinnock was in 1984/5 for the NUM. The Social Democrat always seems to throw away the essentials of his beliefs and policy for the sake of getting elected; then he is "too honest" to introduce his deep-seated wishes into legislation. Any government that follows this pattern is likely only to serve one term as its activists become disillusioned and fail to "bring out the vote" for the next election, many of its natural supporters join the Fireside Party in despair and the floating voters float back to their more usual lack of interest.

I took some part in the general election, at least by speaking at meetings that were usually of a radical character and on the fringe of the official party election programme. These meetings in the main cities and other towns in between aroused great interest so that the debate and question-and-answer sessions often went on until midnight. The main theme was that the United States was responsible for the Korean War and the loss of British and Australasian lives. Although the State of Emergency had been lifted, I did wonder whether my arguments for peace might not be seen as standing in the way of New Zealand's "preparations for defence". After all, I still held a New Zealand passport.

It was difficult to make contact with lawyers I had known, most of whom were pretty scared. I suppose the general tenor of colonial life was so reactionary that it was not surprising that they kept their distance. At a Nelson College rugby match, I came across Wilfred Airey and Geoff Rixtrott. It was the first time we had met in twenty-four years. I stood beside them for perhaps half an hour and failed to get either one to turn even to look at me. They would do no more than mutter a few commonplace words. Then the headmaster H V Searle spotted me and invited me into the presidential box so that I was relieved of them both. Later I called on the Secretary of the Treasury (an old school friend who had not changed) and found that Wilfred was his personal assistant or secretary. As we were in private, Wilfred behaved to some extent normally. Yet the town hall meetings were friendly and exciting. Anyone with the slightest understanding of the forces really at work in the world, and everyone who was at all inclined to socialism, pressed their greetings on me. Outstanding amongst them were the university dons and those who ran progressive bookshops or political clubs. New Zealand had a gallant and struggling peace movement with only one full-time worker, yet had managed to send a delegate to the WPC's inaugural conference.

One of the best moments was speaking at a packed Auckland Town Hall with Jock Barnes while he was out on bail before the appeal. Our topic was "Can Peace be Maintained?" It was for a speech at the town hall on 20th May that Jock had been arrested. He told an audience of 4,000 what he had seen two days previously, when a police line attacked a large group of waterside workers:

> "They did not tell you of the old man on crutches who was knocked over and given a kick for good measure by the most vicious constable I have ever seen – 326 was his number – and they did not tell you about the women who were skittled, the children who were knocked over; and further up the road when Drennan was knocked over, one of our members, Dick Richards by name, went to pick him up, and about eight of them knocked Richards over and 326 put the boot in again for good measure."

The alleged assaults on Alec Drennan and Dick Richards were of little interest; Drennan was a Communist and both were waterside workers. But the claim that a policeman had kicked Mr Esther, an eighty-one-year-old cripple, could not be allowed to pass. PC 326 (Robert James Edwards) would have to be cleared or dismissed. Barnes was tried for criminal defamation before a magistrate. He denied the charge, was convicted and awarded two months' prison with hard labour.

The appeal took the form of a retrial before a High Court judge, Mr Justice Finlay. We relied upon three grounds: that what Barnes said was true; that Barnes believed it was true; that there was no danger of any breach of the peace, and that absence of intent was an excuse under Section 236 of the appropriate act. I probably made some pawky joke referring to the numbers 236 and 326. The judge decided that he could not believe Barnes and, as a result, could not believe the independent witnesses who supported him. The more normal approach would have been to consider the witnesses as supporting one another. It was a good appeal and we should have won.

Mr Esther was "absolutely confident" that he had not been kicked, but he had suffered a blow to the head and had not been examined by a doctor. In ninety per cent of head injury cases, the victim doesn't know what happened. Under cross-examination, PC Edwards admitted that he had been badly affected by the strain of serving throughout the stoppage; his nerves had been upset "to a certain extent". Barnes claimed that the young constable had lost control; after kicking Mr Esther, he had assaulted Richards, tried to punch Barnes and generally "gone berserk". Barnes had been so shocked by this behaviour that he had felt a public duty to make it known.

Jock Barnes was a genuine fighter for his men. If he had withdrawn his allegation against PC 326, the case would almost certainly have been dropped. It may have been sheer stubborn stupidity on Barnes' part to stick to his allegation, or it may have been courage and integrity. I believe it was the latter. I believed Barnes because of the detail of the case, and because of his previous good character and well-known attitude towards the police. A main prosecution witness was PC Edwards' father, Senior-Sergeant Frederick Edwards, who admitted that Barnes had prefaced his remarks at the meeting by praising the general conduct of the police. I asked him if the police had ever had trouble with Barnes. The answer was: "To my knowledge they have never had grounds for complaints against Barnes before this case."

The libel laws were originally brought in to stop duelling. By law, there was no criminality in libel unless it endangered the public peace. Mr Justice Finlay said, "There was the gravest likelihood of a breach in view of the nature of the meeting, its size and atmosphere." This was after hearing Senior-Sergeant Edwards tell the court that the police had not even considered stopping the meeting because there was no sign of any likelihood of a breach of the peace. The appeal was dismissed because the judge convinced himself that PC Edwards could not have kicked anyone, and Barnes could not have thought that he did. Jock Barnes went back to prison to complete his sentence.

I was due to spend two weeks in Australia working on the referendum debate so Tom set off to make the trip home alone. He arrived a day late for school and told us that he made the excuse of pretending that he missed his plane in Sydney. It obviously made the right impression. The federal government of Bob Menzies was trying to outlaw Communism. The Communist Party Dissolution Act, passed by parliament in October 1950, was declared unconstitutional by the high court. Undaunted, the government arranged a referendum, asking voters for permission to alter the constitution so that the Communist Party and any groups regarded as "Communist fronts" would be dissolved, and Communists barred from trade union office and from employment by any Commonwealth authority. There would be no real right of appeal, and "Communist was to be given the broadest possible definition". In parliament, members of the government speculated on which clergymen and Labour MPs might be declared Communists.

Civil liberties groups claimed that since the definition of a Communist included "a person who supports or advocates the objectives, policies, teaching, principles, or practices of Communism", it could easily include one who advocated any of the policies favoured by the Communist Party. As these included world peace, free education, price control, sexual equality and the abolition of racial discrimination, anyone who was not profoundly conservative might find himself being punished for his beliefs. The entire Australian left closed ranks against the Menzies government.

We held meetings every day for ten days on end in places as far apart as Brisbane, Adelaide and Perth, and everywhere between. In the morning, there would be a debate at a factory gate or dockyard or similar gathering point, and two at lunchtime, with a town hall meeting in the evening. It was in the days when television had not displaced public meetings over matters of general interest. The Jewish Council wanted an hour on what was happening in Germany, and there were requests from the Australian Russian Society and the Sydney Council to Combat Fascism. I spoke to anyone who would have me. The visit continued long enough to see the voting over and the defeat of the Tory referendum.

Dr Herbert Evatt, leader of the Australian Labour Party, had been full of confidence that the referendum would go his way. He was a big, comfortably built, jovial chap and a KC Pritt introduced us when Evatt had come over to argue a case at the Privy Council. Pritt was much given to entertaining and his Temple flat was a scene of merriment. There he introduced Evatt to a group of fellow barristers including Geoffrey Bing and myself. Because we were with Pritt, he assumed that we were as far on the left as you could go without joining the Communists. He studied us and said, with a twinkle in his eye, "I know. You're pure and democratic and progressive."

He was a great cricket fan. In the Temple, I had the pleasure of inviting Evatt to meet Learie Constantine, the barrister who had captained the West Indies and then gone to the Lords as a West Indian representative. They discussed a match Constantine had played some years previously, debating almost every ball, over after over, as if they'd seen it just the day before. It was extraordinary. On my last night in Australia I spent three hours with Dr Evatt. He was satisfied that the referendum vote was a big set-back against the development of Fascism in Australia; that was what we were fighting against in New Zealand, too.

CHAPTER TWENTY-FOUR

Stalinism

BEING A friend to Russia wasn't easy. During the period of the First Inventors, the Soviet Union foolishly claimed that most of the ordinary devices that simplify modern life had been invented by Russians: the bicycle, typewriter, telephone, the first powered flight – everything was a Russian first. Many countries could claim that they had an early specimen of these originals, and very little imagination is needed to turn that specimen into the original. But in the Soviet Union there was a spate of claims, each allegedly proven by some apparent authority.

Trofim Lysenko was an extreme extension of this showing off. In agriculture, new developments were called for because collectivisation had caused a substantial reduction in food crops. The study of plant genetics was then flourishing and Russia made its contribution through the work of Nikolai Ivanovich Vavilov. He set out to trace the world origins of the main agricultural crops in the hope of finding original stock from which modern breeding processes might provide more useful growths than had evolved through hundreds of centuries of casual development. Shortly after the Nazi invasion of Russia, Stalin called on Vavilov to reduce the time taken to develop higher yielding varieties to only five years. Vavilov protested, which gave Lysenko his chance. Lysenko claimed that all could be done in just three years. This assertion launched him on an ocean of scientific publicity supported by all the propaganda that the Soviet government could arouse. Vavilov was arrested and charged with sabotage and with spying for England, tried and given a death sentence. Although this was commuted, he died in prison.

At one point, Lysenko was said to have established strains of cotton-seed that would yield coloured cotton. The theory was that if you dyed enough cotton on the plant, the plant would succumb and yield colour-bearing seed. Peter and Anne Gregory, with whom I had finally patched up our disagreement over Morelands and Bart Hall, were trained scientific farmers and followed all these supposed developments with surprise. It seemed to us in England, or more precisely in the lawyers' group, that science was having to respond to Stalin's whim. Our Russian contacts expected us to believe it all. I discussed it with Dudley Collard, amongst others. We agreed that it sounded like nonsense, but we ought to take further advice.

Margo Heinemann advised us to ask Des Bernal. He was a crystall-ographer and polymath, one of Churchill's wartime think-tank, generally regarded as the "all wise", hence the nickname "Sage" Bernal. In 1945, he had challenged me with the enquiry "Do you know enough to be an MP?" I said, "Well, I don't know very much. I've got three degrees, but how much should one know?" He replied, "I think you ought to know the main events throughout the world any time in the last 3,000 years as well as have a smattering of all the sciences." I countered, "How do you square yourself with that?" He thought about it, then answered, "I feel all right about the sciences, but I'm not so strong on the north-east corner of the Black Sea in the Sixth Century BC."

Bernal agreed that Lysenko's claims were nonsense, but from the depth of his crystal world would not claim to be an expert. He urged that we all go to J B S Haldane. There we were received by Mrs Haldane and a great profusion of Burmese cats in their house near Highgate. Beautiful house and cats but oh, the smell. We had sent on the material in advance and Haldane already knew all that we did. He pronounced solemnly that "it was all a load of balls". Then we held a conclave: should we tell the world that Lysenko was nonsense and so take the side of those who would rather have bombed the Russians than have joined them as allies? We suffered Lysenko in silence.

I met Lysenko once, when he was at the height of his supposed distinction, in the cowshed of a dairy farm near Moscow. I tried to have a sociable talk with him. He explained that he was concerned with the butterfat yield and he hoped that by crossing big milk-yielders with big butterfat producers, he would be able to obtain both characteristics in one cow. I pointed out that we had been trying to achieve this in England ever since the discovery of the Channel Islands, and I was sure that Russian farmers had done the same for centuries. I suggested that he was dealing entirely with inherited characteristics. It was pretty impertinent on my part to raise such a discussion with him, but as I spoke no Russian, neither of us really understood the other.

I hadn't believed that Russia staged show trials in the 1930s. Pritt and Dudley Collard wrote books exonerating the Soviet Union. Pritt had been there and seen for himself that it simply wasn't true. In the 1950s, there was no longer room for doubt. My friend Otto Sling was accused of being a traitor to his country. His wife Marian was also arrested and their little boys were shunted from one children's home to another until she was released without charge two years later. I had known Otto since the summer of 1940, when he first came to London. We had both cared for Jack Brent, who lingered on until 1951 and died while I was back in New Zealand. Otto and I lodged together for a good part of the war and I knew that he was the truest patriot. When the Czech Army returned home under the aegis of the Red Army, Otto was installed in the civilian job of Party Secretary of Brno. In October 1945, Otto and Jiri Hajek came to London as delegates to our youth congress. In 1948, Janet and I were able to return the visit after a lawyers' conference in Prague and we rejoiced in the success that seemed to be coming to all of Otto's actions in industry and social affairs.

After Yugoslavia's refusal to follow orders, any form of Communism not exactly conforming to the Russian model was seen as Titoist treason. Stalin had convinced himself that Eastern Europe was threatened by a Nationalist and Titoist conspiracy run from Czechoslovakia, under the guidance of Anglo-American imperialists. Beria was sent in to find a suitable scapegoat. In Hungary, Laszlo Rajk was tortured to name his co-conspirators. Rakosi, Hungarian party leader, wrote to President Gottwald demanding arrests. Sling was on the list. At first, it seemed that Otto had been chosen to play the role of chief conspirator. He was accused of plotting to oust Rudolf Slansky, General Secretary of the Czechoslovak Communist Party. Zionism was later added to the list of conspiratorial elements. Otto was Jewish, but so was Slansky.

By the time the case came to court, Slansky found himself on trial beside Sling, along with twelve other prominent and devoted Communists. The basis of the charge against Otto seemed to be that he had passed the war in the UK, where he had come under the evil spell of that "past master in deceit and provocation, Konni Zilliacus, one of the most experienced agents of the British Intelligence Service". Poor Zilly was supposed to have run spy networks throughout the People's Democracies and to have sought the return of capitalism in its Titoist variant. Zilly was "directly responsible for Yugoslavia's defection to the warmongering West".

Zilly's father had founded an underground revolutionary party in Finland in 1904 and was involved in activities against Tsarist Russia. Zilly himself had served as an intelligence officer in the British Military Mission to Siberia from 1917–19, but no one could seriously believe that he was other than the most dedicated of Socialists. As early as 1932, Hugh Dalton had recorded in his political diary hearing "a strange tale of allegations that Zilly is a Bolshevik agent", yet he spent the war years in the Ministry of Information, and the Labour party gladly chose him as candidate for Gateshead in the 1945 election. We had spent four and a half years in the closest contact, polishing up our angry javelins together and hurling them at the Cold War and Ernie Bevin, its bloody midwife. Zilly said, "I didn't do it really, you know," and I did know.

With Otto I had shared even closer acquaintance and was convinced that there was no circumstance of his life in London that gave the slightest opportunity for any of the intrigue and treason that he was persuaded to admit before his trial. No one had better proof to support the innocence of Zilly and of Otto. Stalin must have been mistaken and ill-advised to have allowed such a charge to be set up and I could put him right. I decided to go at once to Prague and offer myself as a witness, carrying the great knowledge of Otto's wartime activities in England, and supported by such goodwill as I had gained throughout Eastern Europe.

I went first to the Czech embassy and asked for a visa to go to the trial, and even asked that it be adjourned until I could get there. This was refused. It was no use trying any of the debris of the Labour leadership for support. They had rejected me and were indifferent to what was happening in Eastern Europe; or rather their attitude was that the worse things were, the more it justified their attitude of studied indifference. From 1948 I had been in and out of Prague several times and knew people there and felt at home with the city and its telephones and trains. Why should I not go through Hungary even without a visa, or apply for one in Budapest? It was harum-scarum stuff and full of wild ideas. I approached Harry Pollitt but he declined to help, saying:

"I've heard of you. I'm told you are ambitious, arrogant and conceited. You think you can get anything you want and always know how to go about it. Well, I was the same. All politicians are the same. The Czechs know better than we do what's happening in their country. They and their movement have suffered more than you or I ever will suffer and they must be left to decide these matters for themselves. Go and try if you want to, but I can't help."

I didn't go. Otto was held for two years before being brought to trial. The "confession" was drawn from him through interrogation sessions of up to twenty hours a day. He was told that by taking all the blame on himself, he would help to unite the party. To admit that he had been suborned in London by British/American military intelligence, and that he alone was responsible for any Czech plot to oppose Stalin would withdraw the fire from everyone else. His sacrifice would protect the men and women who had been in exile during the Hitler occupation, including those who, like Slansky, had actually been in Moscow.

The trial, which lasted a week, was carefully managed. The Czech press coined a new term, "Slingism", to describe Otto's subversive techniques. He was described as a man "who all through his miserable life remained a capitalist; a man completely alien to the working class and to the entire people". The fourteen defendants had learnt their roles by heart and Otto is recorded to have said, "I am justly an object of contempt and deserve the maximum and the hardest punishment." He had been a stout, strongly built fellow but two years of physical and mental torture left him emaciated. The clothes in which he had been arrested no longer fitted and in the courtroom his trousers slipped down.

The prosecutor addressed the Supreme Court:

"Citizen Judges, in the name of our nations, whose happiness and liberty these traitors tried to undermine, in the name of the peace against which they conspired in such a loathsome way, I demand the sentence of death for all the accused. May your sentence of death hit them like an iron fist, without any pity. May your sentence be a fire, burning out this treacherous growth to its roots. Your sentence should ring like a bell through our glorious fatherland, a signal for new victories."

Eleven of the defendants were executed; the others received life sentences. Otto was hanged in Prague on 3rd December, 1952 and no one suffered a more grievous injustice. We later learnt that from the gallows he cried out, "Long live the Communist Party of Czechoslovakia!" It was all a horrible tragedy and he was officially "rehabilitated" in 1963.

In March 1953, I attended Stalin's funeral for the World Peace Council. J D Bernal came to St John's Wood on a Saturday morning and said, "You've got to be on the plane at noon. The ticket's waiting for you. It's in my name but I can't go. They're expecting you." It was necessary to change planes somewhere in Switzerland, where I was meant to collect a Soviet visa. I searched everywhere but couldn't see anyone, so continued on to Moscow without it. When I arrived at Moscow airport late at night, I was met by Ekaterina Furtseva, the lady Minister of Culture. She was to take me straight to the Hall of Columns, the trade union building, where Stalin was lying in state. While coming into town, she said that she wanted me to understand what an extraordinary occasion this was for the Soviet people. It was more than the death of their leader, it represented a complete change in the life of the people.

Looking back, I think that she must have been giving me credit for a much greater understanding of Stalin's position than I had. I now believe that she was trying to press the point that it was the end of a dreadful tyranny and that his death was a mercy for the Soviet Union. Then she added, "All our leaders are there, standing beside him. You and many other persons will be invited to file past." This was the last few hours of the lying-in-state, and it was all very ordered. Among those standing beside Stalin's open coffin was Beria. I looked at them both and not even then had I learned enough to blame them for the murder of Otto Sling. Before the year was out, Beria would be taken from the Kremlin at gunpoint and executed. Stalin was interred in the Lenin mausoleum. On the day of the funeral, Red Square was packed. The British contingent (many of whom were diplomats and soldiers) stood on a raised stand, each vying with the others to say what mighty funerals they'd seen. I had chanced to be in France at the time of the funeral of Marechal Foch and saw the seven cardinals of France, all in scarlet, accompanied by many massed bands. Stalin was deified throughout the Communist world; we now expected a mighty pomp to outdo them all. First came the gun-carriage with the coffin, then a dozen officers carrying his medals on velvet cushions, then thirty or so family members, and a handful of generals in full military array. It was the simplest funeral one could imagine, in the circumstances. This was the first chance that his successors had to express, even in most guarded form, that Stalin was not as we had thought.

It was not for some years that we learned the part that Stalin and his associates played in the murder of Sling. Marian was our main source. Even then, I could not accept that this showed the true character of Stalin. I must have been World Stalin Lover No 1. When Krushchev denounced him in February 1956, I still wouldn't accept it. I reasoned, "If there is conspiracy in Moscow, this is it: a conspiracy to rob Stalin of his just fame as saviour of the world from the Nazis." The correct conclusion is probably that he would have had a greater and quicker success had he not behaved as a barbaric despot in his own country and in other parts.

It was clear to any visitor that the Soviet Union was less than perfect, but I preferred to dwell on the more positive aspects of their society. On my first visit to Russia I had been told:

> "If you leave unaltered the standard of living of your people, then in the next five years you will find that we have almost caught up. On the other hand if only you, with the great skill of your people and your tradition of industrial work, were to start to plan your life so that everyone could have the benefit, then in a moment you could go ahead so fast that Russia would again look like a backward country."

By the early 1950s, there had been enormous improvements and it was no longer possible to say that Russian workers were worse off than their colleagues in the West. The Russian paid less than five per cent of his wages in rent. In England, the figure was nearer twenty per cent. In the USSR, social security was free, since neither worker nor employer made any direct contribution. And the difference in standards of cultural life was striking. The ballet, the opera, the orchestra: the arts were for all people, not only for the rich. From 1945 onwards, my main thought was to prevent the nuclear war threatened by Churchill, Dulles and their backers. It seemed to me that if only the Russian people could be allowed to live in peace, they would soon be the wealthiest people in the world, and that was ample reason why they should give so much to the movement for world peace.

One could find something to condemn in any country. No nation had the monopoly on virtue and I could not understand why the sins of the Communist world should be singled out while we ignored our own. McCarthyism was a peculiarly ugly phenomenon and America was busily exporting it to the West, yet there was little open condemnation in the papers. A notable exception was the report in August 1951 that President Truman had appealed for a stop to intimidation by Senator McCarthy and his supporters:

> "These slander-mongers are trying to get us so hysterical that no one will stand up to them for fear of being called a Communist. Scare-mongers and hate-mongers have created such a wave of fear and uncertainty that their attacks upon our civil liberties go almost unchallenged. Many people are growing frightened – and frightened people don't protest."

Even the President of the United States felt powerless before the evil of McCarthyism. The witch-hunts continued to dislocate professional life in America. In time, they led to McCarthy's disgrace, but only after an unnecessary degree of suffering.

I have a copy of what must be one of the few McCarthy documents that came into being in the UK: Subversive Activities Control Board Docket no 104-53. It was the examination of Dr Hewlett Johnson, the Dean of Canterbury, for the Attorney General of the USA. The National Council of American-Soviet Friendship asked permission of the Subversive Activities Control Board to take the deposition of the Dean on the subject of his visits to America in 1945 and 1948. I appeared for the respondent, the National Council; Elwyn Jones, QC, & Mr Dick Freeman were for the witness. All were instructed by Robert K George, Sussex solicitor and member of the executive committee of the NCCL. The deposition was taken before the US vice-consul at the embassy at Grosvenor Square on 29th September 1954.

We understood that McCarthy's legendary young hatchet-men, attorneys Roy Cohn and David Schine, were to come but instead it was Troy B Conner, Junior, from the Department of Justice. He proposed that both sides should agree that we had "a continuing objection to all questions asked". However, we were there to ask questions and I suspected that he had his own list of questions ready. Attorney Conner boasted that all their hearings were public because the object was to publicise the Communist conspiracy, yet we found that their practice was to hold hearings in camera because they liked to be able to judge, before releasing material, whether or not it would help them. Accordingly, they usually adopted some formula to cover themselves. On this occasion Conner stated that "the reason the press could not be admitted to this particular hearing is because of the lack of facilities in the physical building here" but that he would have no objection to the transcript being made public.

I took the Dean through the main points of his career. He had taken a BSc degree, then a theological degree, intending to become a missionary engineer in Central Africa. Since his offer was not accepted, he had stayed in England. Ramsay MacDonald appointed him a Dean, of Manchester, then of Canterbury. He became interested in the Soviet Union during the First World War. After an initial visit in 1937, the Dean wrote a best-selling book called *The Socialist Sixth of the World*. By 1954, it had gone through twenty-two editions, with a million copies sold in America alone.

He explained his political attitudes in the following way:

> "I was by conviction a Socialist by my engineering experience and wanted a planned economy rather than chaos. By my Christian experience I wanted a society where all were under an obligation to work and where the community was under an obligation to all its members to give to each according to their need. ... All I am interested in is the fundamental definition of Communism by Marx, 'From each according to his ability to each according to his need'. ... I believe that that is fundamentally Christian."

In 1943, the Dean was appointed to the editorial board of the *Daily Worker*. With A T D'eye he set up a fund for the relief of Stalingrad and raised more than a million pounds. Towards the end of the war, he was invited to the Soviet Union for three months. In 1954, at the time of the hearing, Hewlett Johnson was President of the British-Soviet Friendship Society and a recipient of the Stalin Peace Prize.

In September 1945, he accepted an invitation from Corliss Lamont, university professor and Chairman of the National Council of American-Soviet Friendship, to speak at Madison Square Gardens to commemorate the founding of the Soviet Union. Since transport was difficult, the Foreign Office granted him special facilities for the crossing and Ernie Bevin provided a cordial letter of introduction to the American government. In New York, the Dean was met by the chief of police, on behalf of the mayor. In Washington there was a grand reception with leading senators, and a later meeting with the president himself. Next came Madison Square Garden, with Dean Acheson as one of many distinguished speakers and a message from General Eisenhower. The Dean spoke at Washington DC, New York City, Chicago & Boston, and it is difficult to imagine a series of events and a tone of welcome that could show a warmer friendliness.

Within three years, all had changed. The Dean was asked to make another tour of American cities in November 1948. At first, he was refused a visa, and there were many appeals by worthy bodies of citizens before it was granted. The Dean praised "the Soviet Union's successes and her moral qualities" for trying to give education and food to all; for demanding work for all; for her treatment of minorities; and for increased productive capacity. At the same time, he severely criticised both America and Britain for not turning over their atomic secrets to the Soviet Union, for he wanted atomic energy to be placed under international control. So far as the Dean knew, the invitations were in no way connected with the American Communist Party, but a witness allegedly told Senator McCarthy's Subversive Activities Control Board that the visits had been organised by the Communist Party for "the Dean was a great asset to the Communists of the world". You had only to have your name given to the board to lose your job in Hollywood, or the New York Bar or many places in between.

At the taking of the deposition in London, the Dean was confronted with a list of names and asked to recall the receptions or events at which they may have been present. "Do you recall meeting…?" He recalled few of the names except Helen Keller and President Truman:

"I am afraid I cannot remember at all. When I am rapidly introduced to people, a group of them, I cannot carry their names in my mind for years or even for days. … You see, year after year I am speaking to so many groups in so many places that it is quite difficult for me to recall any specific occasion."

He was asked if he had ever been a member of the Communist Party, the Communist International or a part of the world Communist Movement. (To which the answers were: "Never", "Never", and "Not in the slightest".) He "would have been very hesitant in accepting any invitation at all" from the Communist Party. "I was interested in speaking, not in the organisations, nor in the names of the personalities I met." Of his visit to New York the Dean told us: "I had three or four detectives sleeping outside my room at the hotel every night; whether to protect me from the United States or whether to protect the United States from me, I have never discovered."

Hewlett Johnson was bald on top, with a collar of white hair that stuck out all round. He was perhaps an inch taller than my six feet-three inches. In 1955, we went on a motoring holiday in a huge Humber Super Snipe: the Dean, his wife and two daughters, and Janet, Barney and me. It was very cramped. We visited the church at Beauvais where the arch to the west of the crossing was intended to lead straight into the nave but had not been completed. The Dean declared that this was meant to be the tallest nave in Christendom. Barney, aged eleven, spoke up: "Sir, I understood that you were meant to be the tallest knave in Christendom." It was exceptional for parsons to take an active part in politics; their position was usually seen as squarely but passively in the mid-ranks of Conservatism. How could the ruling classes go to prayer unless the Church of England were there respectfully to receive them? It followed that to Conservatives, including masters in expensive schools for little boys, the Dean of Canterbury would be regarded as a traitor to class and country.

The Dean had a house in Harlech, high up and with a wide view. The south-west wind came unobstructed up St George's Channel and, when it blew, it creamed the whole bay. The house struck a pose on the cliff-top and well represented its owner at points in his winding-up in the innumerable speeches I heard him make about Russia. The Dean was not averse to using his hands and arms as aids to declamation and I have seen him, arms stretched full sideways, head up and eyes closed in ecstasy, and then the head toppling forward uncontrolled as though from the last spear thrust – the quietus. He was undoubtedly theatrical. Hewlett wore the noblest and most colourful raiment that custom and the occasion allowed and the sacristy could provide. He was a figure larger than life, who glowed with blessing at home in his own cathedral. His reputation as a preacher of socialism and as the apostle of what he understood to be the heroes of the Soviet Union made him beloved by Britain's Socialists.

CHAPTER TWENTY-FIVE

Friendship Societies

ALTHOUGH I had connections of one sort or another with many friendship groups, my main concerns were the British-Soviet Friendship Society and the Society for Cultural Relations with the USSR. During the 1950s, I served as Chairman of the BSFS and President of the SCR. Our friendship groups had been set up with the active support of the Soviet Union and the other East European countries to present them in the warmest possible light. To us, these were bustling, democratic, co-operative economies with successful industries, a high standard of education and of living, riotously joyful people, and a peasantry so protected and preserved and so influential that William Morris would have been pleased. In the light of what we now learn from those countries themselves, it seems that our information was incorrect; I can only say that we did our best.

These groups promoted exchange visits and cultural tours and encouraged contacts in education, the sciences and the arts. The Friendship Society in Moscow would tell the BSFS or the SCR what institutions or professions were asking for a visitor, and often would name some leading person whom they would like to meet. If we told the Foreign Office who would be going to Moscow, the British Embassy invariably invited them to a reception or other function. The FO was generally helpful to us. Yet constant difficulties with the Home Office over reciprocal visits meant that we had to wait weeks to know whether X the scientist or Y the novelist would be allowed in, at which port of entry the government would prefer him to arrive, and whether they would mind if we took him to meet his fellow scientist at Cambridge, his fellow novelist in Hampstead.

With visitors from Moscow, the Friendship Society would provide the names and ask whether certain institutions would receive them. We would immediately forward the invitation. We know that quite a number of the prospective hosts consulted any government department with which they were normally in touch and in no case that we heard of were they discouraged from accepting. We took this as meaning that the inviters were reputable institutions and that the guests were deemed suitable. In whichever direction visitors were passing, the Russians usually paid. Travel was by Aeroflot so could always be provided free. We did our best to pay for accommodation and travel within the UK, but often the Friendship Society repaid us the full amount through their embassy. It was probably this that made the British government suspicious of us. The Russians wouldn't be paying unless they were getting some real advantage but, in my opinion, the only advantage gained was that influential Britons saw Russia, and influential Russians saw Britain. They were men and women prominent in one calling or another and we were at pains to ship them about the country.

In theory, they were coming to meet people, but their needs were always the same: a comfortable lodging, a shopping expedition, to walk at large in the crowded London streets, to visit their embassy and send messages home, and to see the opera or the ballet. Only then would they want to meet the scientists, writers, designers or athletes or whoever were their local counterparts. The pattern was almost invariable. Then came further shopping expeditions and visits with their newly made friends. They also met a wide range of our own membership, most of whom spoke some Russian.

If ever our guests showed any interest in the House of Commons, as naturally every delegate to the Supreme Soviet did, there were Labour and Tory members most willing to entertain them. The rarest thing was a Liberal, perhaps because there were not many of them in the House. All visitors to London wanted to see Scotland, and vice versa. If there were any government-controlled institutions that interested the guests, we would immediately ask and were given all possible co-operation. At middle levels of contact with Soviet authorities one sometimes found a churlish attitude, an inflexibility, and the official side in Moscow did not hesitate to complain if anything went wrong; yet for the general course of the visits there was nothing but satisfaction. I do not see how we could have done better except with more money to provide luxurious lodging in big hotels.

When the egregious Christopher Mayhew (now Lord Mayhew) engaged in a campaign to discredit our well-established friendship organisations, several newspapers took up his bogus complaint. The misled editors clearly had no idea of how much we had achieved. They showed that they had only the faintest idea of their subject and of what Mayhew wanted them to interfere with. One editor wrote:

> "There can be no free intercourse, no real mingling of minds, so long as our Russian visitors are roped off from the real life of this country by Communist-controlled bodies such as the British-Soviet Friendship Society and the Society for Cultural Relations with the USSR. What does he know of England who only Platts-Mills knows – or the Very Rev Hewlett Johnson?"

I had come to England at the age of twenty-one with a burning interest to find out all I could about Britain and had been doing this ever since. I practised my trade in all the main towns of England and south Wales and, believing that I knew England at least as well as most native-born, I thought Mayhew and his tame editors were bloody impertinent.

Major Mayhew went into parliament in 1945 after a distinguished and varied war experience. He made himself known to Zilly and other obvious left-wingers and we got the impression that he was sympathetic towards our point of view. Mayhew had been educated at Haileybury, as was Attlee, and he was immediately selected for preferment as junior to Herbert Morrison in the Home Office. Next year he was promoted to the similar job with Ernie Bevin in the Foreign Office. Mayhew appeared to maintain friendship with many on the left and talked with us freely in the various common rooms. We really believed that through his influence Bevin would be persuaded to a progressive point of view; for example, that he might adopt a friendly attitude towards Eastern Europe. We were profoundly wrong for Mayhew went on to run the Information Research Department, a secret intelligence group which hired East European émigrés to write anti-Communist materials. The CIA put up most of the money for their subversive work.

As exchange tours increased in number and intensity, the Western intelligence services realised that this was too good a field to omit. There sprang up a group of "front" friendship societies, well-financed and supported by America but based in the UK and sponsored by our government. If I headed one group, Fitzroy Maclean might be president of the rival show. The front groups were largely taken over by Tories, whereas we tended to think of ourselves as Labour enterprises. If we saw the government groups as centres of hostile intervention against the regimes, so they saw us as fifth-columnists, ready to provide bridgeheads in our back yards for invasion by Russians, Yugoslavs, Czechs, Poles and so forth. The government groups had greater success than we did for, it was thought, they introduced wreckers into Communist countries. As the Communists supported our side, so they tried to sabotage the other. Thus Guy Burgess became Mayhew's personal assistant. As his organisation introduced an interventionist or saboteur into Eastern Europe, Burgess gave every detail to Moscow and, in due course, the saboteur was arrested and executed.

If Ernie Bevin's crude hostility to the Soviet Union and its protégés was obvious to all, his greater excesses were kept a close secret. Only when Kim Philby defected did we come to know that Bevin had authorised the British security services to collect, train and equip bands of émigrés and to infiltrate them back into their former homelands in the hope that they would ultimately "set the Soviet Union ablaze". A great deal of British intervention was thwarted by the presence of Kim Philby amongst its guiding lights. In ordinary language, his acts were plainly treasonable. In practice, they saved us from exposure to the world as being engaged in the most stupid and evil escapades. The effect of these hostile actions had a disastrous effect on Stalin's fears and gave him further exercise in his arbitrary methods of resolving them. It is possible that Mayhew was so knowledgeable about paranoia and informed about Stalin's weaknesses that he was trying to provoke Stalin into a frenzy. He may even have succeeded.

Mayhew furthered his own private Cold War against our friendship groups by getting the British Council to set up a Soviet Relations Committee with him as its boss. He used this position to persuade the Soviet authorities that their delegations and their superb artists "were likely to be cold-shouldered by their British equivalents and ignored by the media" unless they dealt through him. He was so obstructive of all normal friendly relations that Soviet officials appealed to the Foreign Office to get rid of him. Their failure was a further example of his success.

The BSFS brought over the Moscow Circus. The performing bears were one of the best features. They did most things that a team of strong, intelligent little boys would do. They danced and played games with all that was usual: with hoops and tubs and boxes, and with clubs to swing. They formed a dozen different bear pyramids and finally made themselves into a great pile that collapsed and the bears ran away as though roaring with bear laughter. They were tremendously popular with the public and we were all looking forward to the return visit. Haringey Arena seemed to suit them well. The publicity was out, the expenses were incurred (an enormous sum) and we were all agog. When they cancelled a few days before arrival date, we attributed it to normal Russian temperament: no conception of time, no notion of capitalist programmes. We wrote long, complaining, lugubrious letters to various officials and were quite unaware that Christopher's slick stiletto had done its work.

In the early 'fifties, I tried to get Gilbert Harding to take part in some BSFS festival about the Soviet Union. It was one of our annual gatherings where we could assure him of an audience of several thousand. He offered to get Harry Secombe to sing for us, but Harding's major-domo heard what was going on and at once ordered him to withdraw from the whole idea, as he did. The major-domo explained that an involvement with us would do Harding's standing with the BBC no good at all and he owed nothing to the Russians that he couldn't repay in many other ways. Even so, we scored some notable achievements. It was the BSFS that first brought to the UK the great violinist David Oistrakh in November 1953. Mstislav Rostropovich and his wife Galina Vishnevskaya came as guests of the SCR in March 1956. Rostropovich's concert at the Royal Festival Hall was a triumph. When we had established a routine of presentation and the Russians were sending performers who were certain box-office successes, the impresarios moved in. They approached the artists in Moscow, paid them handsomely and took an even grander cut for themselves. We were too slow to hit on this and so lost an income that would have made our societies rich. When Igor Oistrakh returned to the UK in 1957, the tour was organised by Victor Hochhauser.

In April 1956, Nikita Khrushchev and Marshal Bulganin came to London. The papers called them "Khrush & Bulge" and the visit was a great success. The Soviet Ambassador held a reception for 1,500 at Claridges Hotel and it seemed that the Russians were entertaining the whole world. At the time, my sons Tim and Tom were regular companions to two of the Gaitskell daughters. At the reception, Hugh and his wife came to me and Janet and said, "Ought we not to shake hands with the amount that our children are seeing of one another?" We duly did so and I was then able to introduce them to Charlie Chaplin, who was a fellow guest. When Dean Hewlett Johnson came and asked whether he could join in the handshaking, the Gaitskells quickly moved away and found other companions.

While Khrushchev was here, I was approached by a London solicitor asking that for a fee I should try to arrange the emigration of an elderly Romanian couple. They were sister and brother-in-law to a titled British lady, widow of a prominent industrialist. Lady H was herself of Romanian origin and wanted her "only living relatives" to come to her in London. They had spent the past seven years trying to get exit visas. Lady H had convinced herself that if she could contact Bulganin and Khrushchev, they might direct the Romanian government to release her relatives. It was an absurd idea. The couple had a valid reason for wishing to emigrate, but if I were to involve myself with them, would this not be confirming the insulting stories put about by Mayhew and his sort? I was so obsessed with the virtues and achievements of the East European countries that I could not believe that anyone was willing to run away from them.

However, for Jewish people the position was somewhat different. There was a long and bitter history of anti-Semitism to be overcome and progress was slow. I had often visited Eastern Europe since 1945 and in the first few years, there was always one common experience. In each country one family was allotted the task of accompanying and guiding our journeys and those families were almost invariably Jewish. They were highly educated, they worked in publishing, higher education or government and had generations of local connections. Many new ideas were bubbling up; above all, in the way in which ordinary people were taking part in running the country.

Now their views had changed. anti-Semitism, which seemed to have disappeared, was on the move again. For example, in Romania the seemingly benign and democratic regime of Gheorghiu Gheorghiu-Dej was giving way to changes that eventually made possible the bloody tyranny of the Ceaucescus. Each Jewish family in turn explained to us that everything had changed. After all that they had told us, and after all the remarkable things that had happened, they could not expect us to understand, but they could no longer go on. Israel called and they were answering with a regretful "Yes".

The solicitor asked that I travel to Bucharest, meet the relevant officials and use whatever influence I might still possess to intercede for Lady H. I did so, but it was an impossible task. I could no longer offer the small inducements an MP has at hand, such as introductions to junior ministers over matters of trade. Negotiations dragged on until it became clear that our only possibility was to offer cash for the purchase of the live body. I knew that any Communist would take this as an insult. To avoid causing offence, the most delicate manoeuvring was called for. It was only on the second trip to Bucharest that the officials could make me understand that the price I was offering was a bit low. One Romanian Minister had developed this "sale of bodies on the hoof", as it came to be called, and was plying a busy trade with an émigré from a flat in Park Lane. He was charging five times as much as we were offering to pay. It is now known that between East and West Germany a similar trade went on right up to the toppling of the Berlin Wall, and in terms of millions of pounds.

Soon afterwards the Israelis invaded Egypt, at the request of the British and French governments, to supply a pretext for the Anglo-French occupation of the Suez Canal zone. This was to punish Nasser for his nationalisation of the canal and for his refusal to join the American-organised Baghdad Pact. At about the same time, Soviet troops occupied Hungary. The BSFS had organised a grand series of forty concerts by Soviet artists for British-Soviet Friendship Month, but we had to cancel the lot. Many people who had given support or shown friendliness to the Soviet Union looked for an excuse to withdraw to a less exposed position. Our friendship societies and cultural groups lost a large proportion of the membership, as did groups such as the World Peace Council and the British Peace Committee, which were seen as pro-Soviet.

My withdrawal from the WPC was not of that character. I felt that I had played a useful part on the council. I had gone on several delegations to governments and attended world conferences. I had done my share of drafting, writing, appealing and supporting. At a meeting of the BPC a bright young man came forward whom we wanted to send to the WPC to represent Britain. There was ample room for two of us, but it seemed that for me to withdraw was the simplest way of introducing him. I proposed that course and it was accepted. There was no demur, no question, no complaint. I dropped out. To the best of my recollection, no one suggested that there was any sinking ship in the offing and there was no mention of the greater rodent ratus ratus. Probably the others thought that I had been of no use at all and it didn't matter a scrap whether or not I continued with either group.

Through talking too much in attempted justification of my attitudes, I contracted a chronic sore throat that became so severe that I could barely speak. This was the greatest suffering I ever underwent through misguided political activity. It carried me to a consultant on throats, whose remedy was a little linctus and then total rest. "My advice is to shut up until you're cured. If your case is very bad, we may be saved from you for the rest of your life. If it's not so bad, you may be cured before you die." The other advice he gave was that the patient make some dramatic change in his or her way of life. "If you live in London, move to the country. If you've never driven a motor car or a motorbike, or bestrode a horse, then take it up." And so forth.

After family consultation, we decided to leave London and, in 1957, we moved to Harrock House in East Sussex, within two hours' drive of the Temple. This was a beautiful William and Mary country house with a magnolia in the recess. It had been built in 1694 by the Rector of Buxted on the site of an earlier rectory dating from the sixteenth century, parts of which still survived. The house, once moated, came with a chain of fishponds, a tennis court, a ha-ha and a ten-feet yew hedge. There were also some seventy-five acres of farmland and woods but, in spite of this, the council proposed to re-rate it as a dwelling house. After contentious correspondence, an inspector came out to see for himself. It was a hot dry day. I was on a tractor in shorts and farm boots and a cloud of dust. He said, "Farm or dwelling house? I suppose you win." Thus the house was rated as a farm and was exempted from payment. We'd had no warning of the visit and it was chance that he didn't find me in bowler hat and umbrella, making for or just back from the Temple. For eight years I did four hours a day travelling from Buxted to London, save for the rarest bit of tractoring.

Many barristers take to the gentlemanly pastime of farming, but you need to put in a manager. If the man is smart enough to make a profit, then he is also smart enough to know what to do with it. On the other hand, every barrister farmer must have taken advantage from the tax laws. So long as you farm seriously and make substantial losses, they all go down to your benefit and you gain over rates, food supply, fuel, telephone, transport

44 May 1948: A flier for the meeting of support called by the local party at Finsbury Town Hall.

45 May 1948: The overflow crowd that couldn't get in.

LET THE PEOPLE JUDGE...

JOHN PLATTS-MILLS, M.P.

Speaks

FINSBURY TOWN HALL
(Rosebery Avenue)

Thursday, May 13th,
7.30 p.m.

Chairman: D. N. PRITT, K.C., M.P.

ADMISSION FREE   DOORS OPEN 7 p.m.

46 May 1948: Speaking at the meeting at Finsbury Town Hall.

47 May 1948: The full house.

48 May 1948: Speaking to the crowd outside.

49 Spring 1950: Janet with five sons at Cavendish Avenue.

50 August 1951: With Pat McGavin (left) and Jock Barnes outside the New Zealand Supreme Court.

51 Harrock House. Our home from 1957 to 1964.

52 1955: *Entertaining the Bolshoi Ballet for the Society for Cultural Relations. Prima ballerina Ulanova at the centre.*

53 1962: *Leaving Cloisters shortly after the Court of Appeal had called us "The Kremlin".*

54 *July 1961: Presenting Yuri Gagarin with a suitcase, "to help his further travels" after he had become the first man in space.*

<u>Opposite</u>

55 1964: *In full-bottomed wig, jabot, knee breeches and buckled shoes on being made a Queen's Counsel ("taking silk")*

56 *August 1964: Being greeted by Jane Jagan on arrival at British Guyana*

57 *June 1981: At one of the many politico/legal conferences*

CONFÉRENCE
INTERNATIONALE
DES JURISTES

"CONTRE LES MENACES
DE GUERRE, POUR LES INITIATIVES
EN FAVEUR DE LA PAIX
ET DE LA DÉTENTE"

MOSCOU, LE 19-20 JUIN 1981

58, 59, 60, June 1977: On the Grunwick picket line. Top: With Ian Mikardo.

Above & right

*61 & 62 June 1977: On the
Grunwick picket line.*

*63 July 1993: "I think I'll
have the potato if it's hot."*

*64 Showing my Leander
socks off on the re-built
cutter* Marigold. *Photo by
Maggie Makepeace.*

65 Early 1980s: Travelling to Chelmsford to defend a drugs case, this time with success, I think.

66 May 1998: With the Emperor of Japan at a State Banquet at the Guild Hall.

and a dozen other minor expenses. Besides, there is nothing better for children than to be brought up on a farm. If you amass a large acreage when the price is low and then sell, you're a rich man, at least for a time. I never had wit enough to make big money at the Bar. There was that very lucky start, but after taking up the Soviet cause the big solicitors were gone in a flash. That I was captured by my own propaganda showed the excellence of the propaganda, and perhaps the weakness of my own discernment. If I reached six figures of income in a year, that was infrequently.

Our neighbour at the grand estate of Buxted Park was Mrs Nellie Ionides, daughter of one of the founders of the Shell Oil Company. Her world-famous collection of Battersea china attracted the Queen Mother, who was quite a frequent visitor to Buxted and expected on each occasion to have presented to her that piece which had most attracted her attention. After the regal visitor had indicated which item might be the next one in her sights, Mrs Ionides would sometimes take the chosen piece and hide it away so that confusion would reign on the next occasion. This process began a little to inhibit the exactions. The village did not want the collection to be vitiated by constant gifts and sent a deputation to Mrs Ionides laying some sort of emotional and parochial claim to the china and urging that it should not be given away. We were all very proud that the Queen Mother should visit the village, but if gifts were to go on as the price of the visits, then the visits should be curtailed. When Mrs Ionides died, the park was sold and the collection went to the Victoria and Albert.

Harrock was the loveliest family house we ever had and was much used for great occasions such as outings by members of friendship societies, with or without visiting delegations from Russia and Eastern Europe. By using trestle tables, we could take a hundred people at a sitting, and the gardens and lawns were perfect for picnics. We twice had a thousand or more out of doors: the entire corps of the Bolshoi Ballet and their supporters, and the Eastbourne division of the Transport and General Workers' Union. I was a member of the T&G, but no one really knew what branch I could attend since our part of Sussex was a blank for factories and rather weak in trade unions. A T&G officer who worked at the district head office in Eastbourne lived near by. The union set up a branch for the two of us and we held regular monthly meetings at his place or at mine. We tried to keep up with current business but it really was too much for us.

To our rescue came the new chicken factory that was to carry the name "Buxted Chickens" throughout the land. They imported from America the process of the broiler chicken, with every farmer being urged to keep them in broiler houses so that the chickens would be edible at a very young age. The birds were then shipped to the Buxted Chicken Factory, where they were put through at some unbelievable rate. The system was so remarkable that visitors outnumbered the workers, but there were sufficient staff to call for a branch of the union. My fellow member and I were not chicken workers, but we did qualify as clerical. Accordingly, we arranged a clerical section of the chicken factory branch and merged with them.

For a time, a rather anomalous group of the T & G met at the Station Hotel in Uckfield, under the leadership of Ted Miller. He and I were sent as delegates to the monthly divisional meeting at Brighton. There was also the difficult job of trying to keep alive the other vestiges of unions to have someone for inter-union activities. Each month Ted and I attended meetings of the Uckfield Trades Council and, at Eastbourne, the Federation of Trades Councils. It was possible to raise points about the ordinary life of the district. For example, such things as a dangerous corner or offensive effluent, the need for seating in a public park, or a train regularly late or wantonly withdrawn. Wherever possible, we would father these issues onto some more appropriate union.

I pictured Harrock House as a sort of rehabilitation centre for worthy trade unionists and politicals and offered to take people in need of rest and care. There were usually two or three at a time, but occasionally up to a dozen. Janet would be left alone with complete strangers, expected to feed and entertain them while I went up to London each day. After a time, a Swiss couple came to look after us. They were ideal for the job, for both loved cooking and domestic work and both liked gardening. When I presented them with a selection of outsiders surplus to the family, they left. Janet had to cope alone.

The crunch came when she was on top of the roof, three stories up, clearing leaves from a roof valley and wondering whether running Harrock was to be her job for the rest of her life. A mark of the disaster I made of Harrock is that we have not a single picture that Janet painted there. The remedy was to buy the adjacent New House Farm with its 300 acres and eight dwellings. We built ourselves a new home, but the property had originally been named "New House" after a house built there in the time of King John and later rebuilt by Ralph Olive, the iron master and gunsmith. We bought the farm from an evangelical named Mr Fegan, who ran it as Fegan's Farm, Mr Fegan's Homes and the Band of Hope Incorporated. We converted the house into flats and then sold both flats and farm in the late 'seventies.

Chapter Twenty-six

1950s' Law

AFTER WORKMAN'S Compensation had been ended by the Attlee government, I went with David Croom-Johnson from one county court to another throughout the kingdom, winding up the last surviving cases. These were usually from spinal injuries which, like the resulting cases, lingered on for years. I was for the workman, through W H Thompsons. David, then a young barrister but now retired from the Court of Appeal, invariably appeared for insured employers through half-a-dozen different solicitors. We usually managed to settle the cases and generally got on well together, although I had fallen out with his father, who was a judge. That began at Birmingham in a case about hire purchase and tractors. Croom said, "You think I am an idiot." I replied, "No, my lord. I would never think such a thing. I would have chosen a shorter word." It was an unwise statement for there was only one word that served as the final denunciation that a barrister or gentleman could utter against another, and that had four letters. Our standing squabble ran for years.

At Salisbury Assizes, Croom sent his clerk to say, "The judge wishes to make friends." I thought about this, then replied, "Well, let us see how he behaves." I was to appear before him in what was known as the Marl Pit Murder. A teenage girl became pregnant by a young soldier. She was good-looking, even elegant in a country way. She was also vain and ambitious. In particular, she wanted another lover as soon as could be and the baby was an impediment. When the babe was a year old, she wrapped it in many sheets of newspaper tied tightly with string and threw it in a nearby marl pit. The parcel sank enough for the baby to drown, but floated enough still to be seen some weeks later by a passing stranger.

The puzzle was that she had kept and cared for the babe until the day by which the killing would cease to be infanticide, with its option of a lighter sentence, and would become full murder with a compulsory death sentence. She kept it one day beyond the "kill before" date, almost as if she were a suicidal lawyer. Her defence did not attempt the one explanation which would have made sense of her behaviour – namely, that she had heard something about the year and a day point but misunderstood it; she came to believe that the law would give her a reward for keeping the baby for over a year. The difficulty was that this would have exposed her behaviour as even more deliberate and wilful than it was already seen to be. In fact, as was shown by the mother of the accused, she had looked after the child very well and had taken normal enjoyment from nurturing it.

Croom-Johnson fought for every point that might establish that the baby was under one year. Could the midwife and her diary entry be wrong? Could the mother telling the priest at the christening have been mistaken? How could the doctor be certain, and what of the Deputy Acting Registrar of Births, Marriages and Deaths? All were certain of the date, and the girl was exposed as a mean, greedy, calculating little creature. The whole law of infanticide is based on the possibility of postnatal depression. This was considered but rejected by the jury, who had no difficulty in concluding that she was a bad girl; they convicted her of murder. The judge cried openly and duly sentenced her to death. He rather stumbled from the Bench. The officer with me from the DPP said that the judge was quite wrong to distress himself like that because the Home Secretary would certainly not let her hang. That was my opinion too.

However the judge at once sent for counsel and, still with evident tears, required me to ring the Home Office and demand that she should not hang. I pointed out that it was after five-thirty and the Home Office would have all gone home. Only a duty officer would be there and he would be having a quiet drink, perhaps with the home secretary's PPS. "But ring him up. Please ring him up. I beg you to do your best." So I rang the duty officer. He asked what the DPP's man thought of it and what I thought, then said that I could tell the old man with complete confidence that the Home Secretary would never let her hang. "Would she soon be told that?" I asked, and received the assurance that the prison governor would be authorised to tell her at their first interview, but that they couldn't reasonably take any such steps at this time of night. I reported all this; there were more tears and great relief. The judge's compassion was outstanding and I congratulated him upon it, as did other counsel present and the officers of the court. We all shook hands with him. Peace was declared and we were friends as he had wished.

Another of the judge's redeeming features was humour. I remember a case in which I appeared against two juniors, Michael Havers and David Croom-Johnson, who were for different defendants. In Father Croom-Johnson's chambers before the trial, he said, "Mr Platts-Mills, I think I ought to tell you that I am a close friend of the father of one of your opponents." By that, he meant Lord Havers.

My most notable – and most litigious – client of the 1950s was probably George Dawson. Between us, Claud Allen and I did more than a hundred cases for him in the high court. Before the war, George had sold lorries. The buyers took them on hire purchase from one of the usual HP companies. The process is well known in the motor trade and takes this form: the dealer introduces the prospective buyer to the finance company which, if satisfied, takes a deposit from the buyer and pays the dealer the full price for the vehicle. The HP company now owns the vehicle and lets it out on HP to the intended buyer. The latter pays his monthly charges for a few years until he owns the vehicle. George was unfortunate in that many of his buyers failed to keep their part of the bargain. They didn't pay, and they also allowed their vehicles to fall into disrepair. The HP companies sued the buyers and often lost their money completely.

They then joined together in bringing proceedings against George, alleging that he had conspired with the buyers to sell defective cars and to obtain for himself the price that would have prevailed if the vehicles had been in good order. There was a big trial for conspiracy and fraud in 1937-38, which lingered on at Bow Street for some months and then went to the Old Bailey. George's counsel were two of the most notable in the history of the Old Bailey: Norman Birkett, KC, leading G D "Khaki" Roberts. They got him off. In 1951 George was back in the courts, and I appearing for him, and it was at once in the papers. On the following day, at lunch in the Inner Temple Hall, Norman and Khaki came in together. Each put an arm round my shoulders. "We see you are appearing for our dear George, the nicest client we ever had. Please give him our love." George Dawson well deserved this accolade.

He had the most beautiful wife in London, a Russian princess, and an even more beautiful daughter. He first came to me through Jasper Addis, although I am not sure whether he was then working as a solicitor. A typical short case would have him coming to our chambers and meeting his solicitor there, declaring that he was too busy to meet the solicitor before. He would produce a writ claiming £150,000 for money lent. "I gave him two Rollers and a steamroller." We would reply, "That will not do. Where is the evidence?" "He gave me a signed paper." We would not be satisfied with this and George and the solicitor would go off by cab to collect the paper that he said would be in a waistcoat on a chair on the third floor of his house in Berkeley Square. They would be back in an hour flourishing a slip of paper reading: "Thanks for the second Roller. Now we are square." (Signed Jed.)

George dealt only in large sums or large and valuable items. One such commodity was concentrated orange juice, which had formed part of the wartime ration for children. In 1954, the Ministry of Food still had half a million gallons of the stuff, for which they had paid £800,000. George bought this off them for £12,000. To store the juice, he obtained a farm with large barns and a small airfield with hangars. The rest was stored in barrels in the open fields. Then the juice began to leak; wherever it was stored, it leaked out. George sold it and pawned it and gave it away. How he ever made any money out of the juice, I never quite followed, but he did. It is just possible that sometimes he sold a load of juice that had already been pawned. Disputes arose and there were inspections of the commodity and gum-boots were needed to see how it had leaked into the fields. The orange juice concentrate led to several trials and appeals; one ran for nine weeks and produced seventy-eight witnesses.

His first million was made with characteristic panache. America flooded Europe with heavy equipment for tidying up after the war. There were lifters, dumpers, bulldozers and cranes galore. The American makers didn't want them back to flood their home market and insisted that they be sold in Europe. They were arranged in parks, neatly fenced off and guarded, and put up for sale by catalogue. No inspections were allowed. George hired the pilot of a light aeroplane to fly him over the fence and so was able to check the mileage and age of the vehicles. When they were arrested, George and the pilot said that they were very sorry but had run out of fuel just over the vehicle park. Their plane was found to be very short of fuel, but containing several crates of champagne. These were a useful introduction to the man in charge, and George improved upon this gambit in ways that I did not try to understand. He attended auctions with knowledge denied to other bidders and so bought the best. On several occasions, he bid for second-hand machines at the appropriate prices but found on delivery that all his wares were brand new and worth many times the price paid. It was not the American Army that supplied the vehicles with which the French and Belgians helped rebuild their countries but George Dawson, and he made millions out of it.

One result was that he spent a lot of money in the South of France. He had a large boat that would be called by critics a gin palace. It was said to have the longest bar of any boat on the Mediterranean. When I was off to the South of France on holiday, George urged that I go to a particular hotel in Monte Carlo, seek out the head waiter and ask for £100 on George's behalf. There was some incident I was told to remind him of, to establish good faith. I found the right man and he did as was expected. He told me that he really owed George several thousands. George was the most generous party giver they had had on the Riviera since the war and his parties were talked about for years. The hotel supplied George's vessel with drinks and he confirmed what we had heard in London, that the ratio of drinkable stores to diesel oil was 10:1. The ship was known to have put to sea, but only to have voyaged from Cannes to Nice to Monte Carlo and no further, and then only on fine days so as not to spill anything.

The National Council for Civil Liberties was another regular client. My experience was that any action taken up or launched by them stood a somewhat better chance in the courts. Many of the cases were brought to me by Bob George, the Sussex solicitor. In the 1950s, the NCCL ran an outstandingly successful campaign to expose the unfair treatment of mental defectives, most of whom were little better than slaves. Apart from individual legal cases, public meetings were held and a national conference was convened. A booklet entitled "50,000 Outside the Law" exposed both the illegality and inhumanity of this exploitation of labour and the Victorian attitudes to inmates of hospitals. Three major legal cases (Pritchard, Garrett and Rutty) led to a Royal Commission set up by order of the prime minister in 1955, and the resultant hearings and official report. The culmination of the campaign was the passing of the Mental Health Act in 1959. Kathleen Rutty had gained the support of the NCCL to bring proceedings and applied for habeas corpus. Miss Rutty had received little education but was in no sense subnormal. She set out her life history in a clear, elegant, and certainly educated fashion. This oddity results from the character of an affidavit, which the draftsman sets out on behalf of the person who is to swear it, in his best essay English and without any of the formalities and clichés and "aforesaids" that one finds in pleadings. I have known several Treasury Devils, as they were then called (junior counsel who do the non-chancery civil work of the Crown) comment upon the cultivated manner in which entirely illiterate young women gave their life story.

In 1927, an inter-departmental committee had set out the view that institutions housing mental defectives should be self-supporting and that sufficient "high-grade" defectives should be available in the institutions to carry out the work. They gave no definition of "high-grade" defectives as lord chief Justice Goddard, doing his best in Miss Rutty's case, found:

> "one who nowadays is described as a borderline high grade mental defective, whatever that may mean. These people, I gather, are those whom no one except psychiatrists would recognise as mentally defective, and that there is room for a difference of opinion among the latter is shown by the affidavits in this case."

The institutions procured magistrates to certify sufficient females as mentally defective to satisfy their needs for domestic servants. One popular method was certifying as "morally defective" women who gave birth to illegitimate children. They could then be indefinitely detained and put to work for as little as two shillings a week. Another tactic was to take a child who had grown up in care and state that she was not mentally fit to live in society. The Matron of St Michael's Hospital told the magistrates that during the three years Kathleen Rutty had worked as a domestic in the hospital, she was "entirely unsatisfactory, being lazy, inefficient and difficult to control". Neither the matron nor the magistrate noticed that these were not very suitable qualities for a person that they were condemning to a lifetime of service as a domestic in a realm where diligence, efficiency and self-control were essential; the devotion of a nun was called for, not the erratic behaviour of a defective.

The main source of supply for these thousands of young women was the orphanages. Miss Rutty was typical. At the age of three months she was taken to a Poor Law orphanage; from three to fifteen she was at a home for girls; from the age of five she attended ordinary Essex schools as a normal schoolgirl and no one suggested that she was mentally defective. After the age of fifteen, she was a resident domestic worker at the same home. While still in the care of the county council and living and working at St Michael's under their direction, Miss Rutty was detained by officers of a mental institution and taken into custody under a "place of safety" order. Six months later, at the age of seventeen, she was taken before a magistrate who duly found that she was a defective fit to be dealt with under the Mental Deficiency Acts 1913-1927 by reason of her being "found neglected, abandoned, or without visible means of support, or cruelly treated". These are defined in the Act as being alternative grounds and to some extent they are inconsistent with each other. So indifferent to the facts were the authorities when she was first certified that they did not bother to consider which, if any, might apply but lumped them all in.

This was a complete pretence because Miss Rutty was living at the home in the custody and under the care of the county council while going about her duties quite normally. In addition, she had kept most of her meagre wages in the Post Office Savings Bank. My recollection was that the matron had taken Miss Rutty to the mayor's parlour and left her sitting in the waiting room. She went into the mayor's room and then both came out to where Rutty sat. "I am so sorry," said the mayor, "to find you here neglected." This was his one chance of judging, as he had to do, that she was both defective and neglected. The Divisional Court had no difficulty in concluding that there was no ground for the finding of neglect. There was equally no ground for the finding of defect, but it was not necessary to establish this. There was no legal ground for holding Miss Rutty and she was released. The false statements made by the authorities were routine and conventional in such cases and the NCCL uncovered a great wrong.

After the threat that many more actions would follow, the eventual outcome was that over 5,000 such women were released. The Attorney General, Reggie Manningham Buller, told me that as many as 10,000 young women came under the Rutty decision. The Home Office had found families and homes for half; for the others, they had done their best but failed to find any resting place other than the institutions in which they were housed. He didn't want to make a statutory provision for locking up these 5,000 women without the NCCL fully understanding the position and preferably agreeing to it. Would I please explain this to them? The Home Office would, if the NCCL wished it, show us the case papers, or samples thereof. The NCCL examined a number of the files that the Home Office had selected as typical. We were prepared to accept their word, but when they had already proffered files for examination, it was only courtesy to look at them.

The hidden argument in the British attitude to mental deficiency that led to the Act of 1913 and gave arbitrary powers of detention was that if women defectives were allowed to be free, the next generation would be swamped with subnormal babies. The best disproof of this proposition is that it was not so from the last Ice Age to 1913, nor is it so today. The other disproof is that orphans from any class are not more inclined to produce defective children than are the daughters of established families.

Of all those I have fought, I think that the Rutty case gives me the most satisfaction in having secured a just freedom for the greatest number of people in the shortest time.

William Bunting was one of our NCCL "regulars" and brought us a whole series of trials. He was an ex-mining engineer who worked hard at what would now be called the ecology of local moors and common land in Yorkshire and became an expert in some aspects of insect life. For example, he was the only person who had bred in a temperate zone the tropical cockroach which is so damaging to several harvests, including banana crops. Met privately and in person and one at a time, we probably all know that cockroaches are quite loveable creatures and comparatively harmless. I dare say what they do after dark, in numbers, is different.

Mr Bunting came into conflict with the Thorne Rural District Council, which was, he thought, not sufficiently protecting the rights of the public in the moorlands and commons. He was a goad to the council and they sought an opportunity to harm him if they could. He was served notice to quit his council house on the ground that it was infested with vermin. In fact, the cockroaches were kept in conditions such that they could never make contact with the ordinary life of the neighbourhood. They were in great glass containers, in tropical conditions, and were well fed and cared for. They were as unlike cockroaches loose in one's house as the zoo animal is to the wild one. He took proceedings to reject the notice to quit.

It was found that he was in correspondence with many learned societies and universities, both in the United Kingdom and overseas. In addition, he sold cockroaches for experimental and for breeding purposes. His distinguished academic supporters established that the creatures were not in any sense vermin. The only trouble was that some of the witnesses disclosed that they bought cockroaches from him. The next step by the council was to move to eject him on the ground that he conducted a business from his house. There was at least more sense in this contention and quite a serious legal point to argue.

The learned societies in the United Kingdom, mobilised by the NCCL, sprang to Bunting's aid. There were several injunctions obtained and then set aside, and innumerable applications to judges. One such application involved the Court of Appeal during the long vacation time when a single judge was sitting. The hearing was to be in open court and I was required to go to Kings Lynn armed with a sheet of printed paper announcing the sitting, and with a hammer and a tack to affix the notice on the outside of the door of the Town Hall where Raymond Evershed, LJ, sat as the Court of Appeal in vacation. There must have been at least half-a-dozen *ex parte* injunctions granted: some to restrain Bunting, right at the beginning, from keeping beetles, and others to restrain the council from "moving" and "carrying" various things on various committees. At one stage, the council, in defiance of an injunction, put the heated cages of the cockroaches onto the street at night and some of them died. The action reached a frenzy. It came on before Mr Justice Hugh Imber Perriam Hallett in May 1956. He was generally known as having been President of the Junior Imperial League, or Imps, the youth wing of the Conservative Party. He went on holding this prestigious position until long past being a junior and earned himself a rich reward in the early 1930s through a special inflow of briefs from Conservative solicitors, urged on by party headquarters. He was a very able counsel and judge, but a bigoted politician. When it came to the left, he could not retain a shadow of common-sense. His imperialism was undeniable and it was from this point of view that he had judged my conduct in the House of Commons. I think at that time he came to hate me.

At the very start of Bunting's case, Hallett discovered that the NCCL was involved. He thought that this was the extreme Left, the Communist Party itself, a cloak for Moscow. From that moment he took an attitude of violent hostility to the plaintiff and to all concerned with him, although I must admit that on reading our letter from the NCCL he said, "Well, they seem to write quite a civil letter." (This was said without a trace of humour.) During counsel's opening the judge began to abuse the plaintiff to such an extent that when we adjourned, I sent an urgent letter to the General Council of the Bar, seeking advice on how to continue. The Secretary, Mr Boulton, consulted the chairman and replied:

"His advice is that you should carry on with the case as though nothing had occurred but to make arrangements, possibly at your own expense, for a shorthand writer to take down everything which is said. It may be that you can arrange this with the shorthand writer who will be in court in any event. When the case is concluded I should be glad if you would let me know and inform me of any further remarks made by the Judge which are in the same category as those to which you have already drawn attention."

Hallett continued his abuse of the plaintiff, and then of counsel as well for being so bold as to represent him. This reached a peak when Bunting went into the witness box and asked to affirm rather than to swear. Hallett commented, "And no morals, either." This plainly meant that he had already decided the man was a liar from the correspondence, without hearing any evidence of the facts. Hallett declared that the pleadings showed the plaintiff to be "evasive" and a "slippery customer". I said that I had settled the pleadings and I didn't think they disclosed any such thing. I stated quite emphatically that he was not of that character. "Indeed, as Your Lordship is indulging in what he regards as plain speaking, I would say that Bunting is a man of as good a character as any High Court judge." Hallett called Bunting a "trouble-making agitator", utterly unreasonable and wanting to manufacture a grievance and said that his evidence had been delivered in a shuffling, evasive and truculent way. And when Bunting was being cross-examined, the judge said to John Busse QC, who was leading for the defendants, "I know the difficulty because he doesn't answer questions straight and you can't tell what he means."

Hallett said to me, "You are conducting this case at public expense simply for advertisement. You are not addressing this court but an outside audience." I then warned him that I was fortunate in having one member of the audience and that was the official shorthand writer. For a moment I feared I had gone too far and that he would order the man to leave the court or to close his notebook. As Tom Denning said when presiding in the final appeal, "The summoning of the shorthand writer was the declaration of war." Hallett told me, "I like to be able to trust counsel. I am sorry I cannot trust you." He let fly at me in most bitter fashion: "I have had it before, and I dread the thought of having you appear before me."

Other choice passages about myself were: "Counsel has sought to misrepresent the evidence and has made reckless statements—"; "You have sought to mislead the witness—"; "You have deliberately put material evidence into the mouth of a witness—"; "Counsel has insulted the Court—"; and, to one of the defence witnesses, "Be careful he doesn't trap you—". John Busse was appalled at the judge's behaviour and tried to persuade him to moderate it. A well-known counsel later reported that the judge's excesses were such that it was almost as though he had said, "Have you given up living with your black mistress yet?" In response to one offensive sally, I actually used the words: "I beg your Lordship, I implore your Lordship not to behave in this manner any further. It will bring the whole case and yourself into the gravest disrepute."

The evidence showed the entirely arbitrary and unjust attitude of various council committees and councillors towards the plaintiff, and there was no getting round this evidence except for the judge's pretence that he did not believe a word the plaintiff said. He rejected assertions that were supported by contemporaneous letters and acknowledged by the council. My recollection is that he even rejected the part of the story that showed the turning out and partial destruction of the collection of cockroaches. Hallett said this did not happen, even though the local newspaper reporter was summoned from his bed and saw it himself and described it to his readers. After finding for the council, Hallett expressed the hope that their not asking for costs might convince Bunting, who "seemed to suffer from an undue sense of his own importance", that there was no vindictiveness on the part of the council. I assured the court that my client bore no ill-will towards them, to which Hallett replied, "I should have thought he was bursting with ill-will."

Before the appeal, Hallett sent his clerk, a big soldierly fellow, begging me not to go on with it. He apologised for the way his judge had behaved. In the Court of Appeal, Denning at first tried to defend Hallett for his obvious abuse of position in the opening by suggesting that there must have been some extreme provocation from counsel in the earlier part of the case that justified or at least explained the judge's attitude. The explanation was, of course, that there would have been no record of the judge's misconduct had it not been for the previous abuses which had led to my summoning the shorthand writer. The Court of Appeal ordered a new hearing for Bunting's case and the matter was settled on terms that were to the advantage of the plaintiff. Settlement did not include a provision that he should cease to harry the local authorities and thirty years later he was still raising substantial challenges to their misuse of the moorlands.

The Court of Appeal also had another case on appeal from Hallett. This involved a compensation claim resulting from a coal-mining death. Hallett had asked so many questions that he had rendered counsel's task all but impossible. Here, too, the appeal was allowed. The two cases combined had a strengthening effect and gave the court and the Lord Chancellor the opportunity of presenting the complaint against Hallett publicly as being that he asked too many questions, rather than that he was a bigot. After the Court of Appeal hearings Reggie Manningham Buller, as Leader of the Bar, obtained from Hallett a personal written apology to the Bar as a whole and a separate one to myself. The Lord Chancellor Viscount Kilmuir realised that Hallett could not go on as a trial judge and asked him whether he would be willing to accept promotion to the Court of Appeal. The members of that court to a man declined to have Hallett as a fellow judge so he retired from the Bench. It is the only case that I know of where a High Court Judge has resigned because of his own misconduct.

Another legal controversy arose in 1960, when I was asked to present stolen documents to the Court of Appeal. I was not at the time aware of their true provenance. Harold "Bill" Auten invented a rotary device for stamping out plastic doilies. When it became obvious that a fortune could be made from this, Colonel and Mrs Rayner, who had loaned Auten money, claimed rights in his firm and in 1956 had him prosecuted for fraud. The judge at the Old Bailey ruled that there was no case to answer and stopped the trial. Colonel Rayner's sister-in-law was a cousin of the wife of Rab Butler; both women were members of the Courtauld family, famed for its textile interests. Butler's appointment as Home Secretary the following year convinced Auten that he had personally intervened with the DPP and forced them to prosecute against their better judgement. The explanation we heard was that the Rayners wanted the doily-making process for the benefit of the Courtaulds. Auten brought proceedings in the Civil Courts against Rayner and his wife, with Detective-Sergeant

Bolongaro of the Metropolitan and City Fraud Department as their fellow conspirator, claiming damages for conspiracy to cheat and injure him, for malicious prosecution and false imprisonment, malicious institution of civil proceedings, and injurious falsehoods. He also sought damages against his own accountants for conspiracy to cheat him and for breach of professional duty.

In January 1960 Glyn-Jones began the trial of the case without a jury. On the evening of the first day, we both turned up at Peggy and Kenneth Diplock's party at the Inner Temple Hall. Glyn-Jones said to me, "I like your case." By the end of the forty-one-day trial he had become most hostile and criticised all Auten's supporters, including his witnesses. We had asked for discovery of the records of the DPP's office showing what authority had been given and by whom for Auten to be prosecuted. The Attorney-General, Reggie Manningham-Buller, appeared and claimed crown privilege, insisting that it was a matter of public policy that such papers were not disclosed. Auten saw this as yet another improper interference by the Home Secretary. The judge set aside our subpoena and we lost the case.

Auten lodged an appeal, but before this could be heard he appeared at Chambers with a great quantity of papers he claimed to have received in the mail. There were approximately 600 documents, and from a wide range of sources including solicitors' offices in Lincoln's Inn and Twickenham; the firm of accountants; the country house of Brigadier Rayner, the colonel's brother: and the Scotland Yard office of Detective-Sergeant Bolongaro, as well as his private house. Auten also supplied us with Colonel Rayner's diary for 1954 and a wealth of his private correspondence. The colonel was a prodigious writer and these letters supplied many of the details we had lacked. We were confident of success.

By now Auten was nearly bankrupt. The Rayners, Bolongaro and the accountants asked the court for security that Auten would pay their costs if he should lose the appeal. While their Lordships were considering this point I sought leave to introduce our new evidence, which had come to Auten "anonymously through the post". The envelopes alleged to have carried them were produced and scrutinised through a magnifying glass. Everyone asked, "Who could have stolen these documents? Who had a motive?" I assured the court that they could only have come from a defendant with conscience enough to want to see justice done; it was not a convincing argument. There was much debate over the admissibility of the new documents before it was agreed that they could, for the moment, be heard, leaving the question of admissibility to be decided later.

When I produced the brief of William Stabb, the junior who had supported Bolongaro's silk, there was a real outcry. Could counsel for one side make use of a brief prepared for and belonging to the opposing side? It was thought to be the first time that any such thing had happened in the Court of Appeal. Counsel for the accountants urged the court not to encourage "jungle warfare of this kind". Lord Justice Sellers, who was not convinced of the anonymity of Auten's "benefactor", told me, "I find it staggering that something that belonged to Mr Stabb is now produced by you." He later spoke of our having introduced "commando methods' into the peaceful sphere of litigation. In the end, the court recognised the rule that documents from any source, if relevant, are admissible even though they have been stolen. However, in this case, their lordships rejected Auten's new evidence and ruled that the appeal could only proceed if he put up £9,000 security of costs. And that was the end of the appeal.

Auten told me afterwards that he had stolen the documents. He had acquired and mastered a set of skeleton keys and added to that the skill of a cat burglar. So equipped, even Scotland Yard was no problem. He had entered on some spurious excuse late in the afternoon, found an unlocked cupboard in the corridor and hidden until the quiet hours. He then found the document he required and let himself out with this trophy. It was no trouble to replace it after photographing it at home. He had been to Rayner's country house as a visitor and knew that there were creaky floors. He learned the art of going extremely slowly and feeling every board with increasing weight until a soundless one was found. At a point outside Rayner's bedroom, he had risked his torch and it shone straight into the face of a fierce-looking hound. The dog was so astonished at the sudden light that it looked frightened and sunk back into its basket and never troubled him. Auten was thus able to help himself to papers from a cabinet in the bedroom. These were the two most daring burglaries and, compared with them, the other sources were easy.

CHAPTER TWENTY-SEVEN

Taking Silk

EAST BERLIN was a convenient staging post for any part of the world served by East German and Soviet airlines. This was important because the International Association of Democratic Lawyers demanded that visits abroad should be made to various countries to put our points of view, and they offered free tickets by Aeroflot or by Interflug, the East German airline. Sometimes the flights were uneconomic in that one would travel to East Berlin before heading west to Chile or to Washington DC. As a result, I was often in Berlin. It might be a week for a conference, or just a day's stop-over en route – for example, to Mozambique or Angola. East German lawyers were always hospitable and I was shown much that was going on.

One complaint of the East Germans was that West Berlin was operated as a show place to try and lure all that could be extracted from the east. Their shops were packed with the finest goods that Europe could offer. All their factories were working hard and paying good wages, and on visiting West Berlin, I found the railway packed from early morning with East German workers. Food prices in the West were much higher, which meant that later trains were packed with peasant women carrying swags of food to sell. I understood that the market hours near the West Berlin stations were so arranged that younger people going to work wouldn't be embarrassed by the sight of old women hawking their East German food supplies. West Berlin was bleeding the East and the only remedy that the Russians could see was to divide the city. The Berlin Wall was erected in August 1961 and I saw it as a purely defensive measure. What I did not realise – or, if I did, do not now remember – is that there was also a substantial brain drain as East German intellectuals, fearful of being swallowed up by the Russians, took their families and fled to the West.

I could not understand fear of Communism. In Poland a chambermaid once whispered to my companion, "Things are terrible here. You don't know how bad it is." It was unsettling, but we agreed that our visits to Eastern Europe had never disclosed anything to justify such comments. There were undoubtedly privileged groups with access to hard currency stores, special schools and clinics, but these unusual preferments were always fully explained. At the Black Sea resorts, one found holiday homes in the form of palatial villas and each major trade union had its sumptuous palace-home at Sochi. One had the picture of thousands of miners having an idyllic holiday. In fact, as each union had enormous numbers to cater for, there can have been not more than a tiny fraction who had this advantage.

Amongst the monster palaces of Sochi were many one-family homes discreetly guarded with trees and gates, armed men and even dogs. These belonged to the apparatchiks, the party officials. It was a little disconcerting to find so marked a difference between one small group and the rest of the people and we couldn't help wondering why, with a popular regime, they felt the need to be so well guarded. Even so, I did not see the deep weaknesses in the system that led to its eventual collapse. It may have been wilful self-blindness because all about me people were pointing them out. To my mind, Communism meant progress. Communists were the protectors of organised labour; they would necessarily be involved in industrial issues and it was senseless to fear contact with them.

At the start of the 1960s, the Chinese workers in Singapore had begun to organise and to realise their own strength. In industry after industry they formed unions or joined existing ones and pressed for improvement in conditions and in pay. The government applied intense political pressure against the unions, their leadership and the rank and file. On the radio, Prime Minister Lee Kuan Yew denounced them as traitors to their country, guilty of treason; they were tools of Russia, Communist-inspired vermin; all were Chinese and so were clearly under orders from the new China. At the end of 1961, when Lee's diatribes were repeated in the *Straits Times*, a prominent lawyer sought leave to issue a writ of attachment for contempt against the Prime Minister and the publishers of the newspaper.

Finally, it came the turn of the shop-workers. At Robinson's department store in Raffles Place, thirty pickets were arrested for obstruction. Among them were two union officers. After the men had appeared in the magistrates' court but before the actual trial, Lee made reference to strikers in terms that plainly referred to these particular men and he described the investigation of the case as if they were already convicted. These radio speeches were collected into book form, with all the abusive statements about the strikers repeated, and released a few days before the case was to come on for trial. The book was published by the government printers and given away free on the most generous scale. It must have cost the taxpayers tens of thousands of pounds. When a person is charged with an offence and is going to be tried, then it is the plainest contempt of court to announce publicly that you believe him to be guilty. For the head of state to do so was quite unthinkable, and more particularly when he was a barrister who had been in Pritt's Chambers after being called to the Bar in London. It was a grave threat to constitutional liberties; it was also unsporting, being the equivalent of kicking an opponent while he is down.

The Business Houses Employees' Union summoned me from London. I arrived on 26th January to find that the government had abandoned the case against the strikers. The union still wanted advice on other legal matters and I was keen to get involved in the contempt of court proceedings against Lee. Admission to the Singapore Bar normally takes many months but can be shortened in the right circumstances. I had all the necessary certificates and testimonials and was confident of success, but learned that no exception could be made for me. As the case in which I was meant to advise had fallen through, I was ordered to leave at once by the Controller of Immigration. By this stage, I was staying with Dennis and Maggie Murphy in their large house that was entirely free of glass. The wind blew straight through: by day, the sea breeze blew in and by night, the land breeze blew out. Dennis had been called as a barrister in the Inner Temple on the same night as I was and had known Brian MacKenna and me very well from those days. After an active war in the RAF in the Far East, he had settled in Singapore and was now a busy and successful solicitor. He had found me settling in to the Raffles Hotel and insisted on taking me home.

Maggie was a great figure in local society and she knew where the chief justice had his daily swim before breakfast. We went there and after doing our lengths, the CJ and I sat together in the sun with our toes in the water and discussed affairs. The story got out that we were swimming together and the prime minister summoned me to his House of Commons. He knew that I had been instructed by the union to get him locked up for contempt of court, but it was a most cordial meeting. We took tea and discussed a number of mutual friends at the Bar; to several of them he sent warm greetings, and particularly to Pritt. Then he said that he was declaring me *persona non grata* and I must leave the country within twenty-four hours. I got him to sign a copy of the offending book for me and left Singapore on the 31st. As Lee's counsel expressed it, the whole thing had miscarried only because Lee turned me out before I could turn him in.

The case against the Robinson strikers was at once resumed. The two union leaders got three months' imprisonment for "voluntarily causing hurt". Lee then instituted the Internal Security Act, which let him keep opponents imprisoned without trial and without charge by the imposition of two-year detention orders, renewable an unlimited number of times. We called this "Operation Cold Store" because it was a form of living death. Lee Kuan Yew had outstanding success with making Singapore profitable. It is a rich community, clean and tidy and well conducted, and an enormous number of ships use the port. Nevertheless, his rule was arbitrary to a savage degree and he well deserved the title of dictator.

In November 1963, I was briefed to appear for Rudolph Truello Fenton, boyfriend to Christine Keeler, a young showgirl and prostitute. Keeler was at the time being pursued by the press for a number of unfortunate alliances. John Lewis, the Labour MP who made a fortune from the rubber industry and tried to impress us all with his lavish parties, was widely thought to be corrupt. He was never more than one step ahead of the Fraud Squad and after he lost his seat in 1951, the party refused to have him back. He conceived a hatred for Dr Stephen Ward and found his chance of revenge through Keeler's involvement with Ward, a Russian Captain named Ivanov, and John Profumo, Secretary of State for War in Macmillan's government. Lewis told George Wigg, hoping to bring down the Tories and ingratiate himself with the Labour Party. He also told the police that Ward ran a call-girl service. Lewis was close to bankruptcy when he died in 1969, and few can have missed him.

On the day that Profumo was forced out of the cabinet a Jamaican jazz singer named "Lucky" Gordon went on trial at the Old Bailey for assaulting Keeler. He was sentenced to three years' imprisonment but the conviction was quashed on appeal. Keeler had told the court that there were only two witnesses to the alleged assault: a young prostitute friend and her "housekeeper". In fact, there were also two male witnesses: both were married, and both were black. Rudolph Fenton had a large family and a wife due to have major surgery on the following day, and Clarence Camacchio was on bail awaiting trial on a charge of pimping. Neither man wished to draw himself to the attention of the police.

At the Old Bailey Fenton, Keeler and the two other women were charged with conspiracy to obstruct the course of justice during Gordon's trial. The women were also accused of perjury. At the pre-trial hearing, Keeler's counsel Jeremy Hutchinson, QC, estimated that the trial might take up to fourteen sitting days, or three weeks. When the trial opened, I moved to quash the indictment on the grounds that the conspiracy charges were couched in such general terms that they could not be fairly understood by the accused or the jury. In fact, they were almost meaningless. Jeremy Hutchinson supported the submission, saying,

> "these indictments for conspiracy…are gradually eroding what one had regarded for years as the individual's rights in this country. It is a very serious matter to hold that citizens have an obligation and a duty so ill-defined as this which, if not fulfilled, makes them guilty of a criminal offence."

It had never previously been thought of as a criminal offence if an individual failed to tell a policeman whether or not someone was present at the scene of a crime. Our judge, Sir Anthony Hawke, the Recorder of London, ruled the indictment perfectly acceptable and said it must stand.

The press had been hounding Keeler and all connected with her. Everyone was interested in the case. She really was a most beautiful girl, slim and elegant in keeping, and probably no one in court except her companions in the dock had seen her before. At twenty, she had no previous convictions and we all knew that a guilty plea would win a lenient sentence. Besides, such a beauty could not possibly be sent to the tumbrels. Accordingly, on the following day, the women changed their pleas to guilty of perjury, and the prosecution accepted pleas of not guilty to the other conspiracy charges. Hutchinson told the court about Profumo and Ward speaking of the latter as if he were wholly evil: Keeler had fallen under his domination and had been used to procure drugs from coloured men.

Hutchinson asked the judge to "bring this long, public and private struggle to a quiet, dignified, and unemotional end. There are many who want to see Miss Keeler brought down." They had the satisfaction of seeing her sentenced to nine months in Holloway. Ward, whipping boy for all the evils of the Profumo episode, was driven into suicide.

My client was to be tried separately, since the others had pleaded guilty. After the luncheon adjournment, the jury was sworn in. Fenton expressed some unhappiness over the composition of the jury, every one of whom was white. I tried to get a coloured juror but the judge said that race was no cause for challenge. Fenton was only the latest on Christine Keeler's list of black lovers. The Recorder noted that she had been under pressure at the time of the offence through her need to prevent it coming out that she had been associating with other coloured men. Race was very much at issue in these trials. When the court resumed, Fenton changed his plea to guilty of conspiracy to obstruct the course of justice. He thought of it as protecting his sick wife and his young family. Fenton was bound over for three years.

I wonder whether all these years later we are more grown up. Leading politicians can still come to disaster if their private lives are not kept cosily tucked away. We had seen Macmillan's government almost brought down by the Profumo affair. Perhaps any excuse is good enough to get rid of such an anachronism as a Tory government, but there would have been no credit to anyone if it had come about in this way. It was said that it was not for the shortcomings of Profumo's private life but for lying to the House that he was upended. Perhaps he should have told the House, "Thank you for the kind enquiry but, for the sake of discouraging any such questions in the future, I do not propose to answer."

I made a second attempt at the Old Bailey to get a coloured juror, in 1965 when defending a black man accused of murdering his wife. This was at the time when a defendant still had seven challenges to jurors as of right, when it was not necessary to show any reason for the rejection. Accordingly, I announced an intention to use my challenges in the hope that at least one of the reserve jurors would prove to be of African or West Indian origin. The jury bailiff checked and found that there was no one black or coloured on the reserve list. The judge was not willing to adjourn the case until a more acceptable juryman could be found and so my client yielded. Publicity about the composition of juries brought a letter from Edward Wooll, Recorder of Carlisle from 1929-63 and one of the great figures at the Bar. He approved my attempts to make the jury more representative. In the Newgate Calendar he had found that "in the reputedly barbarous days of Charles II there was a regulation entitling any foreigner indicted at the Old Bailey to have half of the jury composed of foreigners". This was to counter xenophobia. Although Britain's ethnic minorities would not wish to be treated as foreigners, "trial by one's peers requires us to recognise that racism can distort criminal trials if the jurors are racially prejudiced". Black defendants still commonly find themselves appearing before all-white juries.

In between these two cases, in the first months of 1964, I was approached in Pump Court by G R F Morris who had recruited me for Cyril Harvey during the war. He accosted me with the phrase, "My dear John, last week when I was dining with Hubert he said that Reggie had talked to him about it and they were both of the opinion that this state of affairs could not go on." I said, "Of course not," but then enquired deferentially what it was that could not go on? It became apparent that Hubert was Hubert Parker, the Lord Chief Justice, and Reggie was Manningham Buller, now Lord Chancellor. They had decided that I was to take silk, whatever I thought about it. My clerk must ring the LCJ's clerk and arrange for me to go across to see him, and he would arrange that I should go to Westminster and see the LC. Quite contrary to the practice of lining up all your supporters and references, I was simply to write a note saying "Dear Lord Chancellor, I beg to apply for Silk". I followed instructions. Reggie withdrew from the Woolsack in full regalia and entertained me in his grand apartments to tea and to egg and cress sandwiches. We each put our feet up on a pile of books, demolished our share of the equal stacks of sandwiches and we talked about the law for an hour. At the beginning he said, "You're going to take Silk this year, and I don't care what you say."

I knew each of them by their first names because Parker, while yet a junior, had represented the government at the Birched Boy enquiry in Hereford. Reggie Manningham Buller had in 1932 inherited the Conservative Party's common law junior work, which meant that he was a sort of deputy to the Treasury Junior. Virtually every day he crossed from the tunnel that leads from Essex Court into the Strand and so to the Law Courts, the same route that I trod with my pupil master, and on that route inevitably came to know Reggie. He was a big lumbering fellow, eighteen stone or more. He was in parliament when I got there and gave a bit of friendly support when I was in trouble: not publicly like Quintin Hogg, but with a drink or two at the Bar and talks in the library. Reggie became solicitor-general in 1951 and then lasted eleven or twelve years both as solicitor and attorney. Rayner Goddard, LCJ, hung on to his position longer than he should have with the purpose, it was said, of making sure that Reggie did not inherit it. He said that Reggie was too stupid for any such job. I never saw Reggie in action but had no reason to suppose that he couldn't do the work as well as most. However, towards the end of his time, Goddard adopted a different tone. "Reggie was very good, he had always given their Lordships real help; he was more than competent and was absolutely safe." Somebody had successfully got at Rayner and the whole tide of feeling against Reggie was turned. In due course, in the early 'sixties, he became lord chancellor.

I first applied for silk in about 1954, to Gavin Simonds. I had been led by him on the instruction of Linklaters when Simonds was the leading figure at the Chancery Bar, and in two or three Privy Council cases. He refused me. In 1956, when I was back to a full weight of business and the Lord Chancellor was Lord Kilmuir, David Patrick Maxwell Fyfe, whom I knew well, I again applied. Again I was refused. After about seven applications, I abandoned the idea and decided that I would have to be the everlasting junior. As a last resort, I had gone the rounds of each of the Law Lords, visiting some of them in their homes, some in their miserable little offices in the House of Lords, and some in their Benchers' rooms at the Temple. I had obtained the backing of every one of them, but even that was not enough for Kilmuir. At each of my eight applications I had undergone the most baleful forebodings as to what would happen to my practice and as to how the family would be kept alive.

In those days, you did not know whether you would have silk until it was published in *The Times* the day before Good Friday. Khaki Roberts had given me all his gear: coat, waistcoat, robes and a pair of knee breeches with metal buckles. The latter were quite unfit to be worn, but the rest lasted me for many years. I think a couple of feet or so were taken off the broad back of the great coat. Then, as now, counsel went to the House of Lords with certain members of the family and paraded in full-bottomed wig and court dress with silk stockings and buckled shoes before the lord chancellor, who read some oath of loyalty. Counsel read some appropriate piece in reply, then all went to the law courts and paraded through each of the high courts where judges were sitting.

Each judge called the newcomer within the Bar by reading his (or her) name and saying, "Having been called as one of her Majesty's Counsel learned in the Law, will you now take your place within the Bar accordingly." Counsel then moved from the side of the court into the front row where silks sit, and bowed rather ceremonially to the judge. Then, turning round, bowed to either side and behind, and sat down. The presiding judge then asked, "Mr...do you move?" Counsel, having no motion to move, rose and bowed again, meaning "No, thank you, my Lord" and moved only in that he moved his body out of the front row to leave space for the next newcomer and went off to pass through the next court. Today there are so many new Queen's Counsel that the newcomer is allotted just half-a-dozen or so courts through which he or she shall process. I was the second oldest by some years of the thirty who took silk on that day and remain the only one who is not dead or a judge.

My clerk at the time was James Bothwell, the most comfortable and obliging and happy person that anyone ever had the good fortune to work with. He died in St Barts at quite a young age, but bequeathed to us his widow Maureen as office manager. The effect of taking silk on my practice was accidental but remarkable. On that very first morning, James received two enquiries about instructions to do cases overseas. One was to India, the other was to Uganda; only the latter enquiry came to maturity. That meant a trip to Kampala to defend members of the Youth Wing of Milton Obote's party for their excesses in abducting William Buse, editor of the local English-language paper. This was done as a reprisal against the conduct of the leading white people who had, with the editor apparently supporting them, engaged in a celebration of an ironic and offensive character to mark the forthcoming independence of neighbouring Kenya. I was told that, to the fury of the Ugandans, invitations to the "end of the white man's burden" party were carried in cleft sticks by messengers in loin-cloths, and guests wore full colonial rig or African robes. The principal organisers were deported and the British government tendered an apology.

Members of the Youth Wing abducted Buse and carried him to the neighbouring market place, where they forced him to carry a stick of matoke. Matoke is green banana ready for boiling and each stick weighs about a hundredweight. He was then driven to the local police station and handed in for further punishment. The story of their behaviour had, however, preceded them and the police released the editor and captured his abductors. In due course, they were tried for false imprisonment and common assault. I was there to conduct the appeal and to get them off. The sentences imposed might have been appropriate if Mr Buse had been subjected to violence, but were excessive for a few minutes of public embarrassment. The magistrate had referred to Buse as transparently honest and obviously found it difficult to approach the case dispassionately.

My first visit was to the prison to suggest that the appellants admit that they were in the wrong and apologise; in return, the prosecution would agree not to oppose reduction of sentence. They agreed. Then it was off to Entebbe to meet the minister of justice and the attorney-general, who approved of the suggested compromise and thought that the prime minister and the cabinet would be very pleased with the idea. The only opposition came from the DPP, who was certain that the judges would not give way on the sentence. Although the convictions were maintained, my recollection is that the sentences were reduced so that the appellants were at once released. Jayantilal Shah, my instructing solicitor, had a large mixed practise in Kampala, being both advocate and solicitor. Although of Indian origin, he had acted as personal legal advisor to Milton Obote himself and to a number of ministers of state, for some of whom I later appeared in litigation. That did not save Shah in 1972 when there was a sort of pogrom in East Africa lead by Idi Amin and he became one of 10,000 stateless Ugandan Asians.

Another case that came to me shortly after taking silk was an appeal for one of the Great Train Robbers. The notoriety attracted by the impudence of the robbery led to the imposition of stiff sentences. The original case was tried at Aylesbury and was very much a circuit affair. The railway track where the robbery occurred was in the Oxford Circuit, as was the Buckinghamshire farm where the prospective robbers lay in hiding beforehand and at which they went to ground afterwards. With twenty defendants, there were plenty of briefs going. At one stage Mr Ellis Lincoln, a solicitor of considerable ability and skill, had so many briefs and was due to make so much money out of the prosecution that barristers joked that he must have arranged the actual robbery. This was an entirely friendly joke with no suggestion of malice in it – more particularly because there was actually a solicitor amongst the accused, on trial for conspiracy.

One of the men found guilty of conspiracy to rob the mail train was Tommy Wisbey, a bookmaker from South London. Wisbey's fingerprints and a palm print had been found in the bathroom at Leatherslade Farm, yet he claimed that he had only visited the farm once. A friend had invited him to go for a drive in the country with a man named "Ronnie", who had to deliver a load of food to a remote farmhouse. On going inside to use the bathroom, Wisbey had been jostled and put his hand out to save himself. Despite this ingenious excuse, he was found guilty. Wisbey did not have a bad criminal record and the trial judge admitted that in normal circumstances this would have qualified him for corrective training. The importance of the case ruled out leniency and Wisbey was sentenced to a total of thirty years' imprisonment. After the trial, Wisbey told his solicitor that although his silk had conducted the case with great ability, he would like to change. Mr Lincoln had to look round for other counsel to lead the appeal and he offered me the brief. I had done all manner of civil litigation of the Queen's Bench character in every sort of court, but knew little about criminal law.

Plainly, there were two degrees of wickedness here: robbery, and conspiracy to plan the robbery. Very often, the overriding conspiracy is more evil than the act itself, but here it was generally agreed that the being on the siding and engaging in the robbery with violence was the more serious matter. Wisbey was treated as "in the know" and part of the conspiracy. From the evidence, it was clear no one of those at the farm could be proved to have been at the siding and all the defendants should have been acquitted of the robbery. Accordingly, the prosecutor and the judge between them agreed that proof of presence at the farm was *prima facie* proof of being in the robbery, and this secured the convictions. My argument was that no one should be held to be in the robbery itself unless it had been proved that he was at the railway track where the assaults took place. The Court of Criminal Appeal threw out the argument that the evidential gap was too great. Mr Justice Fenton Atkinson said that since the farm was undoubtedly the base from which the robbers operated, it was inconceivable that they would have permitted anyone not involved to wander round the house, therefore Wisbey's sentence must stand.

In any case where the site itself is relevant, I have always made the practice of having an inspection of the scene of the events. I caused Mr Ellis Lincoln to take me to Leatherslade Farm and to the scene of the robbery. It looked to me as though my client really had gone solely to accompany a deliveryman and I was surprised when he admitted at the trial that he had been given the job of cleaning up evidence. Lincoln was of the opinion that no counsel at the trial had visited the farm, and he gave that as the explanation for his insisting that I represent client after client of his. For a while, Lincoln had all the villains of London to represent in every manner of offence from violence and armed robberies to crafty and elaborate large-scale frauds amongst small-time swindlers and notable executives. He carried me into the London Criminal trade and I have never left it. So it continued through the Richardson "Black Box" torture trial, the Krays in front of Melford Stephenson and again before Fred Lawton, the trial of Fred Sewell, who killed one policeman and wounded another, then a series of terrorist trials and on to the drug-smuggling world.

Before these excitements came the ninety-one-day hearing of In the Estate of Fuld (Deceased). This was, in the mid-1960s, the longest probate suit in English legal history. Peter Fuld was head of a German telecommunications firm but had settled in London to escape from his mother, a possessive, dominating woman. When he died of a brain tumour in 1962, Fuld left a fortune of six million pounds. More than a dozen claimants, including Fuld's mother, girlfriend and ex-wife, appeared in court to challenge the will and all were represented by silks. It was a crowded court, with barristers and solicitors by the dozen and witnesses flown in from around the world. At one stage, the costs were estimated at £1,000 per hour. Fuld's estate took the unusual precaution of insuring the life of the judge, Leslie Scarman, particularly over the long vacation until judgement should be delivered.

My client, Dr Hermann Tarnesby, was Fuld's doctor and psychiatrist. He produced three codicils to the will, each leaving him a percentage of a portion of the estate. These codicils had been made while Fuld was ill in mind and body. Mr Justice Scarman rejected my client's evidence as unreliable and said, "If any man has ever stood convicted by his own utterances of being all things to all men, it is Dr Tarnesby." He added, "Darkness and suspicion are common features in will cases. The truth too often is the secret of the dead or the dishonest." Philip Hartley, Fuld's executor, solicitor and close friend, had the services of two silks, Roger Parker and Hugh Griffiths. In January, they offered my client several thousand pounds to settle. In June, this was upped to more than £80,000 but we refused even to discuss it. In October, we were awarded nothing. Finally, on appeal, Tarnesby lost everything and was ordered to reimburse the Fuld Estate twenty per cent of their legal costs. He estimated that it would take him about eighty-five years to clear the £150,000 debt and said, "I shall have to give up smoking."

It seemed that Hugh Griffiths' main job was to look unceasingly at my client, Dr Tarnesby. It was not that he often glanced at him; Hugh sat turned towards us and all the time he stared at Tarnesby without blinking. We never found an answer to this. Even when Robert Sebrook joined as an extra junior, our team hadn't manpower enough to spare someone to "stand and stare". One of their juniors was John Mortimer, whose role in court was to take the main note for their case. Hugh later told us that John had once asked him to take the note because he had not yet done a radio script to be broadcast that evening. Hugh said it was an early shot at Rumpole of the Bailey. We thought that John was really on the team to give a sort of legal authority to their case, for his father was the author of *Mortimer on Probate*, the leading textbook on probate practice.

As a pupil, I took my lunch in the crypt at the high court, where a handy little tea-room ensured that you could be fed very quickly. Sammy, my pupil master, always went there because he could get something to eat while still fitting in two or three one-thirty summonses in the Bear Garden. In the years of his blindness, when still practising, Clifford Mortimer appeared there regularly at lunch with his wife and I sat with them and came to know them. We all rejoiced in John's later successes in the criminal courts, not to mention his triumphs in writing.

CHAPTER TWENTY-EIGHT

British Guiana

WHEN FORBES Burnham, on the instructions of the CIA, burned down the commercial centre of Georgetown, British Guiana, I doubt whether I had ever heard of the fellow. Dr Cheddi Jagan was different; I knew of him as a Socialist politician facing an uphill battle. Both the NCCL and the Haldane had dealings with him and, through them, I'd heard of Cheddi and admired his work.

When Jack Gaster came to me in August 1964, proffering a return plane ticket and saying that Cheddi needed help, I put off all other cases and went. Jack, son of a chief rabbi, was a left-wing solicitor and I respected him greatly. He may even have been a founder-member of the Haldane, for I had known him since I joined it. If Jack wanted me to do this job, I knew that it must be important: there were plenty of good counsel in British Guiana and he wouldn't get a better one in the UK. However, the effect on the court of bringing counsel from London has always carried a bonus in the colonies.

Janet agreed to come and we stayed with Sase Narain, the senior solicitor instructing me. Sase was a leader of Indian cultural activities for the country and had been Speaker of Parliament for Cheddi. Janet brought her painting gear and it wasn't long before she went off to the local park and settled down to paint. Painters usually take no notice when someone looks over their shoulder at the work, but Janet was a visitor and so this time she looked up. Seeing a friendly black face, she smiled at him. In a moment he snatched her handbag from the ground and ran. With one leg shorter than the other, he proved to be very halt: it was a long stride followed by a short. Janet, made bold by his incapacity, shouted and chased after. He splashed through a pool and by the time Janet had run round it, he was gone among the trees.

It hadn't occurred to us, or to our hosts, that we might become involved in anything unpleasant. The Africans and the Indians were fighting each other but the whites weren't involved, so why should they bother us? It had seemed most unlikely that any of the disturbances would come near to the court or to Sase's home, although we knew that there was much violence in the country and the newspapers were full of alarming headlines. From a paper published by Burnham himself: "PNC vigilance saves country – Had it not been for the vigilance of the People's National Congress, British Guiana would have been safely delivered by Dr Jagan into the bloody hands of his masters across the seas."

The case was an inquest. In Demerara County on 21st May, two cane cutters had been killed by a policeman attached to the special branch of the riot squad. I was to appear on behalf of the bereaved families. There had been industrial unrest among sugar workers, all of whom were Indian, and a group of armed policemen had lain in wait near their township. In the bright moonlight, three Indians came walking along the public road, laughing and relaxed. They carried nothing in their hands. Constable Braithwaite, who was of African origin, jumped up and shot one of the men in the head. He then shot another in the thigh, causing a wound so severe that the man bled to death. Indian policemen testified that they saw no cause whatever for firing upon the workers, who were doing nothing aggressive or threatening. The cutters were in their own village, which the policeman was meant to be guarding; they were unarmed and a fair distance away. It was plain racial murder.

The infamous Forbes Burnham appeared as counsel for Braithwaite. At this time, Burnham was himself in trouble with the police. During raids on his house, his office and the headquarters of the PNC, caches of ammunition had been found. Burnham, who thought he was above the workings of the law, refused to surrender it to the police. I was curious to see how he would behave in the courtroom; it was a most unattractive performance. Burnham sat near the jury and leered at them at every opportunity, leaning his elbow on their table like an American trial attorney. He sneered at those witnesses who were against his client and infused into the proceedings every bit of racial prejudice that he could. In short, he made a fine art of bringing disgrace on the calling of barrister. I reproved him for these offences, inviting him not to behave in so boorish a fashion and the coroner took up this complaint.

The case was drawn out by long adjournments at the request of Burnham's team. This is a device often turned to by home counsel to make it awkward for a visitor, and even to force him out of the case. The only useful reply is to make sure the next date can't be advanced, then take the days off at the client's expense on scenic trips through the territory. I have seen many of the beauty spots of the colonies during such adjournments forced by opponents who intended to drive me back to the UK. When my part in this particular case was finished, I returned to London. I have an idea that the jury didn't agree and the coroner was to give the verdict. It is possible that he adjourned it indefinitely. A barrister is often in more than one case at a time and if he is absent when judgement is given, it is quite possible that he will never hear the result. I remember being in that case, but don't remember what happened. – "Of course you don't remember. You never knew." So it was with the Demerera inquest.

British Guiana had a population of only 600,000, and almost all living on a narrow coastal strip that skirted the dense rainforests of the interior. The country was so wet that many of the houses stood on stilts, even in the capital. The Dutch had applied their skill to make the coast lands habitable and almost every stream had dykes along the banks and a movable dam near its outfall to the sea. Dr Fenton Ramsahoye, Cheddi's Attorney-General, took me on a tour of polder land on the coast and introduced me to families of mixed African and Amerindian descent who claimed to have served the earlier dams for five or six generations. They were wedded to the dykes and dams, and the survival of the country depended on their devotion. These mixed families were the only people of Amerindian descent Janet and I met. Almost all of the Amerindians lived in the high country, where their lives were run by missionaries who loathed Cheddi and his politics. We saw the occasional Amerindian in Georgetown, invariably looking very depressed, and including the only beggar we encountered.

Most of our expeditions were educational in nature, for Cheddi liked his guests to know the whole country. His invitation that I take the flying boat from Georgetown to the Kaieteur ("Old Man") Falls was as much to show how successful he had been in persuading crews to form mixed racial groups – we had Indian and African co-pilots – as it was to show off the country's splendours. There are said to be diamonds at the foot of these falls, where the Potaro River drops 741 feet, but also piranhas to guard them. Anywhere on the water within a mile above the falls was a danger zone and I felt in great peril on the Potaro, though it was not the piranhas that worried me so much as the flow of the river towards them. Cheddi had helped the rice growers to procure the latest giant combine harvesters, which were shipped far inland up the rivers Essequibo, Demerara, Berbice and Courantyne, lesser sisters of the Orinoco and the Amazon. Janet and I had the experience of going up river in a motorised canoe and seeing a mammoth combine harvester making the same journey on heavy Dutch barges towed by three or four canoes with outboard motors.

Cheddi's wife matched him in enthusiasm when discussing the life and economics of rice growing and in an inspection of the crops and machinery. A small, elegant American, Janet was as intelligent as Cheddi and as eager for the welfare of her adopted country. We found her to be most careful and considerate. On a river trip, she would arrange for some local rice farmer to give us lunch, but would also pack us a picnic "just in case". Janet's maiden name was Rosenberg. Her family had come from central Europe and this ancestry gave Churchill and Eden the chance of introducing a slight anti-Semitic note into their dealings with British Guiana. We saw no reason to suppose that she was the source of her husband's political ideas, but she certainly didn't hold him back. Although Janet Jagan played her own part as a cabinet minister, probably her greatest contribution was to sustain Cheddi when Burnham turned against him.

The colony was settled with African slaves, brought in to work the sugar plantations. When slavery was ended by British Act of Parliament, these slaves were the last to be liberated. Most left the plantations at once and refused to work in the countryside. Plantation-owners then brought out men and women from India as indentured labourers, the indenture being a written contract of employment. In Africa, Asians settled in the towns as merchants and professionals, but it was just the opposite in the Caribbean, where they became country dwellers, sugar workers and, more recently, rice growers. The Africans, having resolved never again to work at the menial tasks of the countryside, stayed in town and became factory workers, professionals and civil servants. In time, Indian families began to send their brightest children to university to be trained for the civil service or the professions – jobs the Africans thought should be theirs alone.

In 1950, Cheddi and Janet had, with Forbes Burnham, launched the People's Progressive Party, a new party promising to reform the primitive and miserable life of the people. In 1953 the PPP won eighteen seats out of twenty-two contested and set about the promised reforms: education to be brought under government control; universal adult suffrage without property qualification; fair rent restrictions; provision of medical care for the poor; social security and workmen's compensation; holidays with pay. Cheddi's proposals were quite general throughout Europe and North America but were still denounced as revolutionary by Churchill, who insisted on speaking of the massively popular government as "the faction in power". Within four months, he caused the Queen to suspend the constitution of the colony "to prevent Communist subversion" and to dismiss Jagan and his ministers from office. British forces were landed ostensibly to prevent disorder but they had a different and obvious purpose: namely, to crush any popular demonstration caused by the Governor's suspending the constitution.

Knowing that these events were to be debated at Westminster, Jagan and Burnham wished to come to London to brief the Labour Party. The governments of Trinidad, Barbados, Jamaica and the United States refused them entry, even in transit, so that all airlines refused to carry them except KLM, who would have had to go through Surinam. The Dutch government would allow them only in transit, and the KLM flight meant an overnight stop. It is difficult to imagine a more complicated inter-governmental conspiracy to set aside the ordinary laws so as to thwart the movements of leaders of a friendly government. Having turned the PPP out of office, it was necessary to show how dangerous they were. A state of emergency was declared and the leaders of the PPP were detained without charge or trial. The Labour Party has generally been more liberal and humane in opposition than in power, but Attlee was no more cordial to the needs of British Guiana than was Churchill. In office, Labour accepted the US whip direct; in opposition, they accepted it indirectly through Oliver Lyttelton, Secretary of State for the Colonies.

The prime object of American policy was to stamp out Communism, and that meant trying to obstruct every policy and purpose of Jagan's government. They knew that no argument or inducement would turn Jagan from his course, but they soon discovered that Burnham was by no means committed in principal or loyalty. Patrick Gordon-Walker had headed a parliamentary delegation to the colony and noted that Forbes Burnham was unusually susceptible to flattery and bribery. These weaknesses were exploited to the full. The British government promised free elections, which Burnham would surely win, provided that he broke away from Jagan and set up a rival political party for the Africans. The CIA took Gordon-Walker's advice and became paymasters for the schism. Burnham did as he was told but Jagan's party won convincingly in 1957 because the Africans had not been persuaded that the split was advantageous to them or to the country. Cheddi went on with a sensible development programme, whose main aims were road-building and the provision of land for small farmers. He took a particular interest in the rice industry and saw production double in just three years.

Attempts to oust the government by a divide-and-rule policy having failed, the British turned to gerrymandering. At the 1960 Constitutional Conference, Cheddi had proposed a three-man electoral boundaries commission: one Ghanaian, one Indian, and one Briton. Instead the Tories invoked the services of the egregious High Court Judge Hugh Imber Perriam Hallett (retired after the Bunting cockroaches case) and appointed him as sole boundary commissioner. Hallett so arranged the constituencies that the ones with mainly Indian voters were much bigger, and consequently fewer; those with mainly African voters were smaller. For example, nine seats won by Jagan in one county had an average of 17,639 voters. Three seats won by the opposition averaged 12,109. With fair division, Cheddi could have had two more seats in that county alone. In spite of Hallett's worst efforts, Cheddi won comfortably at the 1961 elections.

"Black Friday" came on 16th February 1962: Forbes Burnham and D'Aguiar, head of the tiny, right-wing United Force party, led the African workers of Georgetown into rioting and assassination and arson. Mobs closed down the electricity plant and the city's water supply. They destroyed a great swathe of the commercial heart of the capital, with fifty-six buildings gutted and another eighty-seven damaged by fire. The bill came to more than $30 million. A police superintendent and four civilians were killed, five policemen and nearly a hundred Indians were wounded. On the first day of the riots, the governor of the colony, Sir Richard Luyt, asked Burnham to moderate the crowds, to urge them to go home. Burnham refused. The Commonwealth Commission into the disturbances later described his attitude as "callous and remorseless". Luyt came from South

Africa. He was a very successful Rhodes Scholar of a few years after me, then entered the British Colonial Service. It was customary for visiting counsel to make a courtesy call on such representatives of the Crown, and not the less so when we were both Rhodes Scholars. Luyt entertained me with great courtesy and seemed properly reserved in the contest between Jagan and Burnham.

Burnham's party, the People's National Congress, then set out to show that the country would be ungovernable under Jagan. On 1st April 1963, they set up a terrorist gang under the leadership of Claude Graham, formerly Deputy Superintendent of Police. This PNC "security force" wanted good, disciplined men. Since theft of arms and ammunition was essential, ex-soldiers were preferred. Main functions of the force were to be the gathering of useful information; the screening of party members and employees; protection of PNC leaders; the organisation of sabotage squads; and the training of members in the use of small arms which would be needed if civil war broke out. The group was financed by an American attorney named Gerald D O'Keefe. In the same month, a general strike was called. The AFL-CIO provided the funds to keep it running. At first, this was costing them about $30,000-$50,000 per week; by the end of the strike, it was nearer $130,000.

To prevent "another Cuba" in their own backyard, the Americans would put up any amount of money. The CIA's annual budget was not normally published but the figure for 1950 was stated as $97 million. In truth, they had unlimited funds with which to corrupt or overthrow governments and they used it with a strong hand. Director of the CIA from 1952 to 1962 was Allen Welsh Dulles, younger brother to John Foster Dulles. The Dulles brothers worked together in applying secret service techniques to any government that showed signs of being on the left. It is reckoned that they ordered and executed a hundred major coups around the world. To explain this, the displacing of a small government could be a major catch, whereas the unseating of one politician would not amount to a coup unless he were highly influential. The count shows that they were hard at work.

From the start, the PNC gang was infiltrated by Special Branch agents. These were Africans, shocked by the brutality of Burnham and his associates. They sat in on conspiratorial meetings and faithfully recorded every detail of the resulting criminal acts. At a meeting in May at Congress Place, PNC headquarters, Burnham agreed that explosives should be used on all government ministries and selected government buildings. Richest target was the Rice Marketing Board with a value of nearly $10,000,000. The plotters intended to destroy the whole industry and all existing stocks, and to prevent the government's sale of foreign goods imported in exchange for the rice. At the first attempt, the vital fuse went out and seventy-nine sticks of gelignite were found under the wharf where a Russian ship was standing waiting to be laden. A second attempt a month later caused considerable damage.

At the request of Cheddi's government, the TUC sent a representative to study the situation. Norman Willis then a very junior figure in the trade union movement but carrying all its authority went to Georgetown. He imperilled his own career and played a most courageous part. When Willis announced his intention to report back that Jagan was in the right and the trade union movement, under the influence of Burnham, was wrong, the PNC took action to persuade Willis that he had made a mistake. African rioters became so violent that the police had to use tear gas. In the middle of this campaign, Burnham sent an ultimatum to Jagan, calling on him to resign within forty-eight hours or face full-scale war. The Africans had already gone some way towards this by beating up the occupants of Indian-owned shops. There was no instance of any black woman or child being raped, killed or burned, although this was the fate of many women and children of Indian origin. A new intensity was added by bombing the homes of Indians. Fortunately, the bombs were home-made and amateurish so that although most exploded, damage was often minimal. They served to engender terror and caused severe injuries, but no one was blown up.

All this may seem beyond belief but official reports give an account of a score of explosions in the summer of 1963. Apart from governmental department buildings, targets included cinemas, private houses, an aqueduct, wharves and their installations. Attempts at blowing up Russian and Cuban cargo ships were among the least successful. Dr Ptolemy Reid, later to become Minister of Home Affairs for Burnham, hosted a planning meeting on 26th August in his own home. He agreed to the suggestion that every man in the group should have a gun and, the agent noted: "He mentioned that when the Cuban ship arrives they would have to blast it up because they did not want any Communist goods to come into the country and they would make an example to show results to the American people."

When the Ministry of Home Affairs was attacked, a police dog followed the bomber's trail and caught him in the yard of Clarke and Martin, Burnham's law firm, where he worked as a watchman. His hands smelt of gelignite and he was arrested and charged with the offence. The intentions of Burnham and his supporters were plainly murderous. The police had detailed records of the daily activities of the whole gang and Superintendent Britton, the African CID man who compiled the reports, recommended a conspiracy charge against twenty-five of the fifty named culprits. Instead, Britton found himself relegated to the uniformed branch as a punishment and the undercover agents were withdrawn. The bombing campaign only stopped because Burnham was warned that the police were going to expose him. The reports were suppressed, and especially were kept from the Minister of Home Affairs, Janet Jagan, who first learned of their existence when a sympathetic police officer secretly passed her a copy the following August.

The bombing started up again in June 1964, but this time there were many victims. The dead included a mother and two children in their own home, two teenagers in a parlour, two adults and two children in a restaurant, four women in a cinema. In August, the police caught Emanuel Fairbain, otherwise known as Batson, in possession of ten sticks of gelignite, five detonators, two watches attached to batteries with wire, fourteen lengths of fuse wire, a .22 pistol, a .38 revolver, shotgun cartridges and many rounds of pistol and rifle ammunition. He also worked for Forbes Burnham's law firm and admitted being a member of the PNC gang. He confessed that he had been involved in the simultaneous bombings of Freedom House (PPP headquarters) and Gimpex (the commercial arm of the PPP by which they raised funds), which killed two and left many badly injured. The bomb at Freedom House went off as it was being removed, otherwise the death toll would have been high, and it would have included Mrs Jagan. After Fairbain's arrest, there were no more bombings of Indian-owned premises in the city.

The Director of Public Prosecutions is supposed to be an impartial officer; it was not so in British Guiana. Fairbain had detailed knowledge of many other Georgetown bombings and admitted this in three statements that were given to the DPP, who failed to act "because the statements had gone missing". A warrant was sworn for the arrest of Clive Wilson, but this was "lost" before it could be executed. Wilson was at the time employed by Mrs Sheila Burnham, wife to Forbes. Detonators were found in the yard of Dr Ptolemy Reid but the DPP refused to prosecute. In one statement, Fairbain told police that Claude Graham, leader of the PNC force, had two bombs at his house in the country; these were later detonated by the army. Graham had been tried for involvement in the bombing of the Ministry of Health but was acquitted. If political matters were involved, no African could be convicted in any of the main towns and everyone knew it.

Fairbain was hospitalised. PNC lawyers claimed that this was because he had been beaten by the police. They called Fairbain a hero and got an African organisation to honour him with an award. On 17th August, Mr Peter Owen, Commissioner of Police for the colony, put out the following press release:

"The police are conducting enquiries into over one hundred murders. These include twenty-two committed in Georgetown and in which women were bombed in shops and a cinema and children burned in their beds. Enquiries so far have revealed that there exists an organised thuggery which is centrally directed. A great effort is being made to bring those responsible for the deaths to justice but it is in the public interest that law-abiding citizens should know now what they and the Police are faced with in this country today.

It is therefore in the interest of everyone concerned to come forward and assist the Police in bringing those responsible to Justice and at the same time to ensure that these dastardly murders be put to an end.

As regards 'Fairbain' wrongly called Batson in certain quarters, he is recovering in the Mercy Hospital and is under Police guard for security reasons. How he came by his injuries is the subject of a separate inquiry but since private legal action has been initiated the matter is *sub judice* and further comment would be improper at this stage."

Although Owen had omitted Burnham's name, he was at once forced to withdraw the statement and it was never published. The PNC lawyers brought *habeas corpus* proceedings for Fairbain to be produced to the court. Owen then informed the Supreme Court that "Mr Forbes Burnham's mainly negro People's National Congress has a terrorist gang responsible for a series of crimes such as murder, arson, causing explosions to buildings and subversive and criminal activities". Police inquiries would be hindered if Fairbain was allowed to contact his lawyers. (Predictably, Fairbain's trial resulted in acquittal.)

I was given two copies of this report and found it as startling a story of mass banditry as I had ever read. My wife had to return home before my part in the Demerara inquest was ended. She reluctantly agreed to take one copy with her and I posted the other. Janet's had to pass through US customs at New York and, being apprehensive that its contents would cause trouble if found, she took surreptitious steps to shuffle the bag containing it from the New York-incoming pile into the transit pile for London, where it would escape attention. In London we made sixty copies and posted most of them to Guyanaian addresses obtained from the local telephone directory. I later learnt that after about twenty had been delivered, the rest were destroyed by PNC workers in the postal service. I hawked copies of the report round Whitehall and Westminster but failed to arouse interest in anyone of sufficient importance.

Probably the worst offender was Tony Greenwood (later Baron Rossendale), Secretary of State for the Colonies. We had supposed that when the report of Burnham's evils came into his hands, he would face up to it frankly. Instead, he announced that the reports were of questionable validity and declined to take the matter further. Tony's father, Arthur Greenwood, was one of the old stalwarts of the Parliamentary Labour Party. Arthur was quite a dominating figure: tall and slightly bent as though from much looking down on people. He had a booming voice and the most protruding eyes that I know except for those of the Druse leader, Walid Jumblatt. Tony came in at a by-election in 1946 and immediately took up a position slightly to the left. He became friends with the younger members of Zilly's lot but soon announced that he could not go on with our acquaintance. His father had warned that if he wanted to get on in parliament he must choose associates closer to the right. Tony was perfectly frank about his decision. After all, he had not committed himself to the left by any strident gesture.

Cheddi came to London in October 1964, on his way to and from the Zambian Independence celebrations, certain that he could win the support of the leaders of the Labour Party. He confided, "I am still hoping for a Labour victory and in spite of the doubts of my colleagues, I am looking forward to the Labour government intervening in some way." Harold Wilson did come to power, but he had no sympathy for Cheddi. The December election was held as planned. The PPP had the biggest vote and the largest number of seats; in normal circumstances, Jagan would have been asked to form a government. Instead the governor called on Burnham, who at once formed a coalition with D'Aguiar's United Force, although throughout the election Burnham had said that he would never join with the party he had previously denounced as Fascist.

Tony Greenwood had dismissed the two Security Branch reports as worthless. He visited British Guiana after Burnham had wrongfully been put into power and gave a picture of harmony and calm. In fact, Greenwood implied that the restoration of peace was thanks to the new coalition government. Of course, the bombings stopped once the PNC gained power, but that the bombers should be praised for this was too much for Cheddi. As he told Greenwood in an open letter, "There is no violence because the authors of violence are now in positions of authority." The violence in the colony had been used by the British government as an excuse to delay independence. When Burnham put a stop to the bombings, he was rewarded by being granted the prestige of being presented as the leader who "won" liberation for his country.

Chief of Police for Georgetown was a Scotsman, Senior Superintendent Andrew McGill Smith, MBE. He had once tried to enter PNC Headquarters to make an arrest and been stopped by Burnham, who threatened the police officer who came to McGill Smith's assistance that when the PNC came to power, he (Burnham) would personally hang the officer up by his thumbs. Burnham was a bully as well as a demagogue. McGill Smith was one of the officers involved in the arrest and detention of Fairbain. All had been suspended from duty and subjected to harassment and death threats. The DPP now proved more than willing to prosecute. Jock McGill Smith and ten other officers were charged with inflicting grievous bodily harm on Fairbain (or Batson) while he was in police custody. The PNC so incited the people of Georgetown that the trial had to be moved to New Amsterdam. Even there, PNC activists mobbed the courtroom. The judge was P A Cummings, formerly Minister of Labour, Health and Housing and closely connected with Burnham. Near the end of the trial, when it seemed probable that the police officers would be acquitted, Cummings adjourned the case for a day saying that he had "urgent business in Georgetown", where he was seen to visit Burnham. The judge then ordered a retrial.

Just before the second trial, Janet Jagan wrote to me with a full account of the judge's double-dealings:

"We know that a secret security report on all of this, heavily implicating the Judge, has been made to the Governor. At this stage, it appears that Burnham has now demanded that ... the Commissioner of Police must leave even though his contract will not finish before three months. As far as we know now, the Governor is suppressing this and is allowing Burnham his wishes. This, too, is part of the whole general political picture here, where the British have evidently made up their minds to give Burnham at every level what he wants, as long as he maintains the status quo in British Guiana

"The police officers so charged now go before another trial next week. What will happen is anybody's guess, but they are being thrown to the wolves. The Commissioner of Police, who is heavily involved, as whatever they did, they followed instructions, has washed his hands of it. He had once agreed to give evidence on behalf of his officers, but refused to attend court when called. There is also another nasty bit on the control Burnham exercises on the courts. A magistrate who dealt with the firearms case against Burnham last year and dismissed the case is the magistrate who heard the case against the police officers and threw it over to the Supreme Court. It is common gossip (and evidently true) that he would be paid off for this, and he has now become a judge.

"The courts of justice have been perverted to vehicles of Burnham. The office of the DPP has no meaning, since it is used at Burnham's directions and the judiciary are political arms of the government. The next stage is not hard to anticipate. Do you think there is anything that can be done? I am sure that at least one of the defendants (an Englishman at that) is prepared to make a complete exposure of the whole business.

"P.S. There is a strong possibility that if the British Government had been willing to recognise the authenticity of the Security Report, the whole elections might have had to be called off, for Burnham was directly involved in the activities; Batson, for that matter, was employed at his legal chambers as a watchman, when he was picked up. That is why Batson and any of the PNC men had to be absolved of the charges, for if they were found guilty, his implication would have been greater. If the police had done their duty and kept Batson and the other terrorists listed in the Report under surveillance, the death of 21 persons could have been avoided."

As had been rumoured, Sir Richard Luyt helped to eject the commissioner of police. He went to Owen with the message, "Burnham wants you out". Owen replied, "You mean just like that?" "Yes." The governor offered to send a cable to the colonial office to clarify the situation, but Owen left before the expiry of his contract. Jock McGill Smith also left early, as soon as he was acquitted by the jury. He was the man Janet Jagan had referred to as "an Englishman". I visited McGill Smith in Hampshire, just into the hills north of Portsmouth, taking a copy of the Special Branch reports. He confirmed every detail and expressed a willingness to discuss the matter with MPs or any other interested persons. Apart from a few on the Left, no one was interested.

Newspapers supportive of the PNC had consistently run stories attacking the government. The last straw was a front-page article alleging that the PPP sent activists to Cuba and the USSR for terrorist training. Cheddi and seven other former ministers sued for libel, with each claiming damages of $100,000. In September 1965, the case reached the Supreme Court and I went back to assist Cheddi. The defence claimed their statements were "fair comment on a matter of public interest", whereas we felt that an additional twenty-nine publications of that comment proved malice. At this point, the new prime minister invited me to a party in honour of visiting British MPs, including the Tory silk, Ian Percival. I felt that I could hardly refuse. The party was held at the official residence at the Botanic Gardens. Most of the guests were men, all in cool white suits, although some brought their wives. One guest, Sir Lionel Luckoo, was a leading silk and also a main racehorse owner of the Caribbean who shipped his string and his jockeys up and down the islands as the meetings summoned them. Two men of Indian origin and one African (a man of great distinction at the Bar) had been in Cheddi's government and were now in Burnham's. I knew them well and could have spent the evening talking with them.

However, Burnham was an attentive host busy with introductions. Here I was being introduced to a number of men whose names I recognised from the superintendent's report. A criminal barrister is often in the company of murderers and gangsters, but in the way of duty and usually when his companions are behind bars. If there had been reason to believe that Burnham would introduce me to such men, I would have found an excuse for not going. Once there, it would have caused an incident to leave in anger. To have expressed my views would have invited a direction to leave the country within twenty-four hours, and I had a job to do for a client. So I made polite conversation about their country, knowing that they would never be brought to trial for their crimes and that they were at the time being protected by Harold Wilson's government. I was almost glad for the moment that I had been expelled from the Labour Party, which could only remain respectable in the mind of the British electorate because such events, thousands of miles away, were concealed from public attention.

No one of the men I was introduced to could know that I had come across their names before; even Burnham wouldn't have known that I had read the report. My memory was then very sharp and I couldn't help associating the names with their various outrages. "What did it feel like to plant a bomb in the cinema, knowing it would be crowded when the bomb went off?" was the question I wanted to ask, instead of "Will Clive Lloyd captain West Indies next season?" and "Did you enjoy setting fire to a house when a young family was asleep there?" instead of "Have you seen the new dykes at Kitty?" Other dictators have come to power by devious and violent means and with the help of unworthy men. They usually are at pains to distance themselves from such companions. Here was Burnham with his henchmen about him. The explanation was that he was so much a part of them and their violence that he felt no shame in their company.

Cheddi Jagan survived the murderous scheming of the CIA, won the 1992 election and was proudly reinstated as President of the Co-operative Republic of Guyana, as the country is now known. Although rich in natural resources, the PNC's corruption and mismanagement had ruined the economy; per capita income was lower than that of Haiti. Cheddi promised that the PPP would not dominate the cabinet: "We will take only fifty per cent of ministries." He wanted a government balanced by race and class since only a government with the broadest of bases could hope to solve the country's problems. Now Cheddi is dead, Forbes Burnham is dead but a form of democracy appears to limp on.

When Cheddi first took office, Jack Kelshall, a solicitor from Trinidad, saw it as the start of democracy in the Caribbean and offered himself as a legal aide-de-camp. The Kelshall family was a distinguished feature of the legal scene in Trinidad. Grandfather was a Methodist missionary held in esteem throughout the West Indies; father combined a solicitor's practice with twenty years on the Legislative Council and five years on the Executive Council. During the war Jack was ADC to the Governor of Trinidad and Tobago, and then a squadron leader in the Royal Canadian Air Force. He returned to build up one of the largest practices in the island. Through Cheddi, I met Jack and was soon accepting cases from him.

On one visit, Jack took me to see his place in Barbados, where he had done much of his sailing. Jack was almost as famous for designing and building cruising boats as he was in the law. He was invited to join the Royal Cruising Club, a rare honour for overseas yachtsmen, and he flew his blue ensign with great pride. On the beach of St John we met Anthony Eden, who was living nearby at Villa Nova with his wife Clarissa. It was well on in the afternoon and they invited us to tea. We stayed until supper and late evening. I behaved in a manner unbecoming a guest by challenging Eden for having adopted almost a Nazi attitude to Janet Jagan as a Jew. He excused himself from any responsibility for taking advantage of Mrs Jagan's position. "That was probably the misguided effort of the local man in the Department" was the sort of answer he gave. But, he insisted, if Jagan had come to power when Labour were in, Attlee and his government would have been just as severe. This was probably true.

The Oilfield Workers' Trade Union of Trinidad and Tobago, under the guidance of George Weekes, was the leading industrial power in the area. They needed Jack as their lawyer for a series of cases with a strong political flavour and I had the luck to be one of their counsel. Oil was Trinidad's highest-paid industry and to shackle the workers in their demand for more pay, Prime Minister Dr Eric Williams caused the Industrial Stabilisation Act to be passed in 1965. This Act denied unions the right to bargain freely and to strike in support of their demands. Infringement of any part of the agreement between workers and employers could result in cancellation of the union and imprisonment of its officers for up to six months. The severity of the penalties went against the territory's constitution, which guaranteed freedom of association. The Industrial Stabilisation Act was plainly undemocratic. It was also badly drawn and contained many obvious errors. There was every chance of getting it overturned.

I advised the Oilfield Workers TU to get a legal opinion on the constitutional validity of the Act from Solly Bernstein, head of my chambers. Solly spent his time in the Privy Council and was undoubtedly an expert on constitutional law. He produced twenty pages of learning and authority that was pretty conclusive in our favour. He invited me to adopt it and as he had never taken silk, although years senior to me, I initialled the opinion, as silks do, and he signed after my initials. One of the Trinidad papers published the whole of our opinion, and I believe that all published some of it. It was also put out as a pamphlet. Members of the OWTU then brought an action against the oil company Texaco Trinidad Incorporated, the Minister of Labour and the Attorney-General, challenging that the ISA violated the territory's constitution.

My arrival at Piarco Airport on 26th August for the trial was a grand affair. I was met by the leaders of the union and a hundred or so oilfield workers, singing their best fighting songs; the Vice-president of the Bar Association, who promised a more formal welcome at a cocktail party; and representatives of all the local press. The General Council of the Bar quickly admitted me to the Bar of Trinidad and Tobago and then entertained me to dinner. Several judges came, including Mr Justice Corbin, who was to be the trial judge. We had a week before the case could be heard and throughout that time, the press followed and reported every movement. The two Conservative papers made a lively exposure of my past. Their readers were informed that the New Zealand Law Society had refused to permit me to practise in my own country; that I had falsely pretended to have appeared for the leader of the Waterside Workers' Union; that an ammonia bomb was thrown at me when I was addressing the Communist League of Democracy in London – a party that I was confident had never existed and whose like I had never heard of. At the invitation of the Bar Council, I refuted the most abusive of the libels and thought that was the end of the matter.

The UK had recently passed legislation designed to restrict immigration rights. It was clearly racist and I had denounced it as such, yet at least one of the newspapers behaved as if I was personally responsible for the "notorious and repugnant Commonwealth Immigration Act". I was berated for the position of the Maoris in New Zealand society and for the fact that citizens of the West Indies could not emigrate to the Antipodes. As Chairman of the British-Soviet Friendship Society, I was ordered to justify Russia's attitude to America and told that I ought to go and advise the USSR on the Indo-Pakistani problem. At the very least, I should return to the UK to help (or to interfere) with their own labour relations problems. Another objection was to the importation of foreign counsel. One editorial asked why the union had not filed the writ in its own name "if the much touted opinion of the eminent and perspicacious English QC is so exceptionally brilliant and infallible?"

To cap it all, I was accused of plotting to oust the prime minister. At the time even members of Dr Williams's own party, the People's National Movement, grumbled about the ISA. Dr Rudranath Capildeo, who led the Democratic Labour Party, the main parliamentary opposition, had kept pretty quiet about the Act. While we were waiting for the case to come on, he publicly pledged his party's support for the OWTU. Dr Capildeo proved to be a thoughtful and intelligent man. It was obvious that if he could only unite the opposition groups, the trade unions and assorted liberal intellectuals, then his party must surely win the next general election. Over a luncheon meeting, several of us pointed this out to him. The *Trinidad Guardian* interpreted it as a conspiratorial gathering and reported that I and others had "offered to make Capildeo Prime Minister". The whole thing was absurd.

The OWTU's case was of the gravest national interest, but there was still a month of the long vacation to run. I tried to persuade the Supreme

Court that the fate of the oil industry was at stake and so our case should be heard immediately. The judge ruled that it was not vacation business. It was just an ordinary case and should keep its place in the list, which meant trial beginning on 5th November and two months to fill in. Before returning to England, I spent four weeks shuttling between Trinidad and British Guiana. George Weekes planned a busy schedule for me, including lectures on the ISA to the Trades Union Congress, the General Council of the OWTU, their shop stewards and numerous branches of the union. It was necessary to tell the oilfield workers what the case was about since they were paying for it. Some malicious person sent the worst of the newspaper cuttings to the Inner Temple and complained that I was holding public meetings and giving interviews on the matter in which I had been professionally instructed. I had even permitted my photo to be taken. Our Bar takes a dim view of all such behaviour and I was required to disprove the allegations.

When the case came to court on 5th November, it was decided that the Minister of Labour and the Texaco Trinidad company had been wrongly included in the writ. The OWTU had to pay their costs for having caused them to be cited as defendants. Sole remaining defendant was the Attorney-General, George Richards, QC, who represented himself. We succeeded in getting the Act declared unconstitutional. The leader of the Oilworkers Union went on to more direct political involvement and, as Senator Weekes, played a part in governing his country.

CHAPTER TWENTY-NINE

Iraq and Tunisia

IN IRAQ in February 1963 the Ba'athist Party staged a coup d'état. It was rumoured that as many as 100,000 of their opponents were arrested, and all were at risk of torture. No one could verify the figures but it was abundantly clear that hundreds had been executed without trial in the first few weeks, and still the executions continued. Some prisoners were punished by solitary confinement. Conversely, as many as a hundred might be crammed into a smallish room and kept in suffocating conditions for months. There were nightly raids by the self-styled 'National Guard', the armed wing of the Ba'athists. Under the infamous Communiqué No 13, these guards were authorised to arrest and even to kill anyone suspected of being a Communist. Some two thousand Iraqis were then studying in Britain. They helped found the British Committee for the Defence of Human Rights in Iraq and set about publicising whatever information they could procure.

The people of Iraq had long suffered under dictatorships and no one involved with the International Association of Democratic Lawyers could help but be aware of their cruel history. After a coup in 1952, 180 members of the Chamber of Advocates were arrested in Baghdad. They had been in correspondence with the IADL and we did what little we could to help them. General Kassem had come to power in July 1958 through a coup that overthrew the dictatorship of Nuri Said and the corrupt King Faisal in favour of a supposedly democratic republic. For the first tine, trades unions and other democratic organisations were made legal and, from January 1960, political parties were allowed, with the exception of the Communist Party. However, no elections were held and Kassem did not permit any real political activity. Then the terror and oppression had begun.

Thousands of Communists and Democrats were arrested and imprisoned, and many were executed. In an attempt to play one group off against another, Kassem set on a war against the Kurds. The Kassemites and the Ba'athists who ousted them were agreed on the necessity for persecuting the Communists and the Kurds.

In the spring of 1963, the IADL set up a commission of inquiry, of which Joe Nordmann and I were members, with the intention of sending a delegation to Iraq. Arrangements became progressively slower and when the European delegates failed to get visas, our trip had to be cancelled. I had more luck with the Iraqi officials, then set about finding a couple of Labour MPs to travel with. It was just a matter of waiting for their visas to come through. While we were waiting, the Iraqi consul summoned me to his embassy and read out a cable from the government. It would not be convenient for the minister of justice to receive me at the moment. However, their new ambassador had just arrived in London and wanted to meet me; as he was a judge and also a member of the English Bar, he would no doubt be able to satisfy all my enquiries. My departure must be postponed. In October I was informed that the visit was, at least for the moment, officially disapproved and my visa was finally withdrawn.

Bertrand Russell had just set up a Peace Foundation in his own name. Sponsors included Queen Elisabeth of the Belgians, Haile Selassie, Prime Ministers Kaunda and Jawaharlal Nehru, and Presidents Ayub Khan, Nkrumah, Nyerere, and Leopold Senghor, so it was high-powered stuff. Perhaps Russell could make some kind of impact on the Iraqi situation. I wrote and sought his advice. He replied, "I agree with all you say. I am utterly appalled by what is happening in Iraq and have been trying everything to help stop the brutality." He sponsored a great conference on Iraq with delegates drawn from around the world, but the Iraqis were impervious to public opinion. I had some contact with the Peace Foundation from tine to time and know that they later performed work of similar value for many other causes.

November brought another coup. The new regime denounced the crimes of its predecessors and promised the release of all political prisoners, yet within weeks military courts began handing out prison sentences to Communists. The Labour MP and lawyer Leslie Hale then arrived in the country. He interviewed a number of officials and even spoke to two women prisoners. On his return, Leslie reported the widespread conviction that the Ba'athists had come to power through the intervention of the CIA. He discounted these claims, which seemed to be based primarily on the speed and efficiency with which the coup had been carried out. I had passed on to Leslie all of the background material I had amassed. He later told me that although many of the claims had seemed extravagant, almost everything had turned out to be correct or, at least, it "certainly approximated to the truth". He had been told that as many as 160,000 were arrested in the aftermath of the February coup.

Leslie's report went into horrific detail. For example:

> "Specific allegations of brutal torture were made even against Ministers, and the worst part about the allegations, which seemed to be substantiated, was that torture was used as a form of evening's entertainment by camp commanders and people in a position of power who invited friends to witness it. One common method was to send for a prisoner and tell him that he was about to be released and while he was rejoicing at his fortune start to beat him up and indulge in perversion and abominable brutality. It was widely believed that two of the Ministers dismissed from the Cabinet, and now living abroad, had participated in this sort of thing. ... a person of the highest repute alleged a case in which instruments were used to torture a man by tearing off his ears and bruising the nostrils and who was finally deliberately blinded by having both eyes gouged out. I cannot establish this story. I repeat it because it was given to me by a witness whose word would normally carry weight."

It was not until September 1966 that I finally managed to reach Baghdad. The International Union of Students wanted someone to try to get student leaders and women professors and lawyers out of detention. It shows something for the progressive character of the democratic forces that there were women high in the professions in a Muslim country. I was told that the visit could be quite dangerous and it would be unwise to go alone. Indeed, those who were asking me insisted that I must take a couple of Labour MPs and tell them all about the dangers. I approached Arnold Gregory and David Kerr, and to my relief they were both most willing. One of us was Jewish but we had no difficulty in calling ourselves Church of England for the necessary visa application forms, for no Jewish person would have been allowed in.

In Baghdad we put up at the biggest hotel and were given a first-floor suite with three bedrooms, a sitting room and dining room. A feature of the bathroom was that it was plain brick and sloped in to the middle where there was a drainage hole. This was before John Calvert modernised the city's sewerage system, and out of our drain came continuously an effluvia, a noxious fetidity, a reeking stink. We complained and asked to be moved, but it was a feature common to all of the bathrooms. We stuffed it with shirt tails and soap, but all in vain. We had to stay at the hotel because it was there that we were to receive instructions. Discreet messages came under our door: please to walk on such a side of such a street at such an hour precisely. We did, and a young man, an old woman, a messenger walked close and asked us to follow to the school round the corner, to the doctor's surgery along the road, to places that were known to be "safe houses". There we were given names and addresses of people and prisons, and suggestions of which minister we should write to and which reference we could properly use.

It was quite obvious that the discretion and even cunning of our informants was based on justified terror. For our own protection, we had been advised to make the fullest use of the British diplomatic services in Baghdad. It wasn't just that we signed "the book" and presented ourselves to take tea with His Excellency and attended the Embassy Garden Party. At the Iraqi government reception for our delegation, we talked loudly of our "friends": "Are there any messages from the BRITISH EMBASSY?" "How do I ring up the BRITISH EMBASSY?" and so forth. In general, we let our presence and our purpose be as widely known as possible, without ever disclosing our contacts. At an early stage, we were told that we ought to see how the police really behaved and we should walk at a particular place. We did so, and found a small procession of young men coming towards us with a banner quite unintelligible to us. Policemen were following. Suddenly the police attacked the procession with batons and there was a running battle in our presence, which included savage blows from the police and plenty of running blood. No one of us would have provoked such an exhibition for the sake of proving how genuine we were.

We secured appointments with Ministers for Justice and for Prisons, for Home Affairs and Foreign Affairs. They were told how gravely

Westminster regarded the arbitrary conduct of the government, but we showed how anxious we were that relations should be restored as soon as possible to their usual harmony. We demanded to be taken to prisons where people were kept without charge and without trial. No minister asked us why the ambassador had not raised any of these points or why the cultural attaché had not asked to inspect the prisons. The contribution of the attaché was to take us south to the site of the Hanging Gardens of Babylon, although that was very unexciting, and to show us the depths of the Souk of Baghdad, which made up for it, and the extraordinary wriggling chasms made by the Tigris and the Euphrates. Mesopotamia, the space between the two rivers, had been occupied by New Zealand soldiers in the First World War; now we crossed it several times.

At meetings with ministers, we asked about certain legal cases. Among them were Selim Al-Fakhri who, with approximately 300 others, had been in custody without trial since 1964 on charges of plotting to overthrow the government. They, along with many hundreds of others, were kept in the brutality and degradation of Nugrat Al-Salman, the "Castle of Death", a remote fortress in the middle of the southern desert where temperatures climbed to 130 in the summer and fell to below freezing in winter. We were assured variously that Al-Fakhri and his colleagues had already been tried, would soon be tried, and – by another authority – that the character of their offences rendered a trial unnecessary. I remember that Al-Fakhri issued an appeal for help immediately before his "final trial" a year later, but what became of him I cannot say.

One of the most tragic cases we brought up was that of the three Al-Saffar sisters, held in the prison known as the "Palace of the End". One threw herself to her death after the killing of her husband. Another, Narjis, was suspended from the ceiling and subjected to prolonged torture, although obviously pregnant. She was not allowed to feed her eighteen-month-old daughter, and her two sons, aged sixteen and fourteen, were tortured in front of her until the elder boy went mad and was killed. The guards then executed her husband. The third sister, Radhiya, no doubt underwent similar treatment. When we returned home, the Deputy Prime Minister and Minister of the Interior wrote to inform us that Narjis and Radhiya Al-Saffar had been released. Since the authorities had denied that they also imprisoned children, we could do no more than hope that the surviving Al-Saffar offspring had been set free.

My next involvement with the Muslim world came almost exactly two years later. In August 1968 Pritt wrote to ask if I would go to Tunis "for expenses only" either to defend a large group of Tunisian students in trouble with their government, or at least to be present as an IADL observer. Joe Nordmann thought some civil liberties issue was bound to occur. Tom had just finished his five years at St Thomas's medical school. He had passed well enough and needed a holiday, so we borrowed Janet's Triumph car to drive along the North Coast of Africa. It was a three-door machine in which the back seats lay down level with the boot; with the addition of a mattress, two could sleep in it. On 20th August we took the four a.m. boat from Newhaven to France and by nine a.m. we were heading for Paris. Over the radio came news that Russian troops had entered Prague. There was detail of the number of tanks in Wenceslas Square, of citizens swarming over the tanks and arguing with the crews, of one man's being crushed under a tank, of crowds everywhere – to resist or complain or approve.

We could not believe a word of it. Just such a prank had been played by Orson Welles in casting *The War of the Worlds* as an invasion of America by Martians. Here was a hoax of world proportions on an Orsonian scale. When the radio bulletins kept on longer than was called for by a joke, we began to worry. In Paris we made straight for Joe Nordmann's office. He said that it was all too true. The governing body of the French Communist Party had met already that morning, had condemned the action, had sent a strong denunciation to Moscow and a message of support to Prague. My association with Russia had already given me more than enough trouble and we set off for the south as fast as could be to distance ourselves from still more.

We crossed the Dordogne at Bordeaux, passed Biarritz into Spain and paid homage at Guernica. A dozen small fishing ports were famous for the resistance of the Asturian miners backing the fishermen, and from Geoffrey Bing's having taken "the last boat" out of each of them as Franco advanced. But we hadn't time for a universal paying of respects and made directly for Gibraltar. On to Casablanca, where I took ill and Ali U. Ata put me up in the big hotel. Ali was the main person responsible for the work of the Moroccan Communist Party from 1945 until they were declared illegal. I think that he may be there still, as Secretary General of the Partie Populaire et Social, the party of light, sympathy, progress and socialism. I had come to the aid of the party in its earlier incarnation, when Ali's urgent appeal for assistance had been passed on through Pritt, who had every sympathy but very little time.

The Moroccan Communist Party had succeeded in ousting the French and, in keeping with the general world mood, had established the country as a constitutional monarchy. It was on this basis that they invited the king back from wherever he had been riding out the storms. He accepted their proposal and returned in 1955. Four years later, Mohammed V declared the Communist Party to be unconstitutional. The party began legal proceedings to challenge this and lawyers were summoned from various lands to make submissions on the subject. In the courts of Casablanca gathered all the might of the North African Bar, from Egypt to Morocco, with back-up support from Rome, Beirut, Paris, Brussels and London. The courts were all French-speaking and advocates were expected to present their submissions in that language. I had tried and managed this before in more than one jurisdiction: for example, in the International Commercial Courts of Bucharest and Sofia, a similar court in Belgrade, and in the first Court de Cassation in Paris.

Certain rather solemn advocates of French origin made their submissions on behalf of the king, explaining that if he were a constitutional monarch (which he wasn't), his was a constitution of a special character which entitled him to say "Heads Off!" to any person or party. There was obvious scope for making jokes at the expense of these grandees and, after argument one way and another, I was set up to conduct a rearguard action against them. I appeared in wig and gown, but put on the wig only to be able to take it off for coolness. Armed with a French Professor of Law from the University of Casablanca, my feeblest sallies were turned into the raciest Maroc French. It was decided that as the judges laughed at my legalistic jokes, I could go on with them. I tried to assert that Britain was the very model of a modern constitutional monarchy and could thus be looked to for guidance, and we had not outlawed the Communist Party. M Rolin, from the Free University of Brussels, made the same claim on behalf of Belgium. The Communists won hands down by a unanimous decision.

The statutes of the Moroccan Communist Party included the assertion that His Majesty Mohammed V was and is the legitimate sovereign and declared the party's support for "working towards a full constitutional monarchy". That was the problem: the king preferred autocracy. He took his case to the Senior Court of Appeal at Rabat, where the decision was reversed. I was meant to go but found myself detained in the London courts. The Moroccan Communist Party then appealed to the Supreme Court to reverse the reversal. The appeal was not heard until 1964, when it was quickly dismissed. The Communists were as neat as the king in adapting themselves to change. They held a congress at which, on the first day, with much talk and presentation of foreign delegates, they dissolved themselves. The visiting delegates went on their way. The next day, happening to have all their own delegates present, a new party was formed under a different name. They held a recruiting campaign amongst themselves and all joined up, then talked for another two days about their policy. (Or so I was told at the time.)

It was a pleasure to meet Ali Ata again and we reminisced while Tom went on to Marrakech. Tom came back for me when cured and we drove through Algeria and Tunisia, keeping about fifty miles inland where the finest Roman remains seemed to be placed. In the foothills of the Atlas Mountains we came upon a soldier in a truck, who had run into and killed three cows. This was three-quarters of the entire stock of an old man in a white hooded cloak, who sat on the ground weeping. The driver was telling him that it was his own fault for having cows at all and was about to go on his way when we joined in. It ended with the three carcasses and their proprietor in the truck on the way to the nearest abattoir and, in the owner's pocket, the truck's identification number, driver's name and number.

It was flaming hot in Tunis. While we advocates introduced ourselves, tried to meet the clients and manoeuvred for position, there came to us an American newspaper reporter named Tania Matthews. In no time Tania had several of us lodged at Sidi-bu-Said, where she presided over a sort of caravanserai establishment with a ring of small houses built round a large central courtyard. It was but a stone's throw from the scene of the Battle of Zama, described in the encyclopaedia as, after Waterloo, militarily the most decisive battle in world history. It decided for the following sixteen hundred years whether it would be Italy or Carthage that ruled the Mediterranean and so ruled the known world. We were made welcome by the American Embassy and by Mr Ambassador Russell, who proved to be a world authority on the Battle of Zama.

In the year 202 BC, Hannibal of Carthage, having defeated every military array brought against him, crossed the Alps with his elephants and moved south. It seemed likely that he would conquer Rome itself. After two years ravaging Italy and failing to conquer Rome Hannibal withdrew to Carthage where Scipio brought him to battle just by Tania's back door and there destroyed his forces. If it had not been so, then the descendants of Queen Dido of Carthage would have occupied Germania and Hispania, divided Gaul into three parts, settled England, and followed Alexander the Great down into Africa and even into Asia. We soon had the ambassador out in the field explaining the disposition of the forces, where Hannibal's elephants were lined up, where were the Roman trumpets that scared them, and how the Romans opened a way in their ranks so that the elephants charged through in a harmless fashion and were bombarded with stinging darts in their behinds as they passed, and what happened to the cavalry on either side. The precise knowledge and exuberance of detail with which the ambassador garnished his story and the eagerness with which he tramped us over the battle site were such that no one of us could ever forget it.

He regaled us with the story of the obliteration of Carthage under the slogan "Delenda est Carthago", a cry espoused by Cato the Elder, who had taken part in the campaign of Zama, and of how Virgil in the Aeneid described the experiences of the travel-weary Aeneas and his rowing crew when they reached Carthage and when Dido decided that this was the very chap to be father of her children and the renewer of the race which was, according to her views, destined to dominate the world. There followed the high drama of the seduction of Aeneas. The Aeneid proved to be the first best-seller in history. Tom and I found the site of Carthage, with no traces of a Punic city but with many Roman ruins. We swam in the entrance to the ancient harbour and there, in the middle of the channel leading out to the Gulf of Tunis and no more than three feet deep, Tom picked up the unmistakable foot of an ancient Greek amphora. To have walked in the footsteps of Hannibal's elephants at Zama and to have paddled in the entrance to the harbour of ancient Carthage gives a possible excuse for remembering them. Tom drove the car home through Sicily and Italy while I flew off to London to obtain the support of the Bar Council and then straight back to Tunis to settle in for the trial.

In June 1967, thousands of young Tunisians rioted, sacking the British and US Embassies and setting fire to the main Tunis synagogue. This was just after the start of the Six Day War between Israel and the Arab countries, which sent Arab youth on to the streets just as the Vietnamese War mobilised their Western counterparts. Sentences were unreasonably severe. One of the demonstrators, a young theology student named Mohammed Ben Jennet who was partially crippled by polio, received twenty years' forced labour for inciting the crowds. Ben Jennet's friends were outraged and brought the whole university out on strike. Teachers joined with students and the demonstrations went on for days. This was in March 1968. Again, there were many hundreds of arrests.

They were tried six months later in a court of state security set up especially for the occasion. From across North Africa advocates of the greatest prominence and skill gathered in Tunis. Then came the most extraordinary feature of the case: Habib Bourguiba, ruler of Tunisia, ordered the arrest of every Arab lawyer who accepted a defence brief. One example was Nabil el-Hillali, a leading Egyptian defender whose father had been the unchallenged lion of the Cairo Bar for many years as well as being one of the wealthiest men in Egypt. The son had devoted his professional life to defending every cause that was worthwhile in terms of human rights and the development of progressive ideas. Several of the French lawyers were refused admittance to the courtroom and one, a M Materi, was arrested and told that he would only be released if he agreed to abandon his clients. Other lawyers were from Italy, Senegal and Switzerland; I think the Genevan was there as an observer for Amnesty International. The case became a bit ridiculous with 60 counsel for 134 students and lecturers, with 30 defendants being tried in absentia. The trial ran for eight consecutive days, commencing at eight a.m. and sometimes going on until ten-thirty p.m. It was most uncomfortable.

The charges all centred round conspiracy: plotting to overthrow the government, with the intention of eventually establishing a dictatorship; endangering the internal security of the state; endangering the external security of the state (a capital charge); along with various offences against Bourguiba and government members. It was rather like the Great Train Robbery: a number had been on the site and a number were in the court, but were they the same ones? There was a total lack of evidence of any plot and no co-ordinated defence to the general conspiracy charge, only separate defences for each individual. When defendants were kept away from their counsel and were not permitted to hear each other's cases, it could hardly have been otherwise. The president of the court excelled himself by issuing a formal instruction that we were to have no communication with the defendants or with any of their family members. Furthermore, we must not by word or by gesture indicate that we had any point of view about the trial or its conduct.

Since the other advocates had been brought up under the influence of the Code Napoleon, I was asked to introduce a common law element into the debate. At one point it seemed as though I were expected to argue that it was routine in common law jurisdictions for students to attack foreign embassies. How else to account for the noisiness thought to be usual in London on boat race night? And what of the extraordinary exhibitions that accompanied college football matches in America? However, these were not my arguments. The President of the court had asked that pleadings should be "brief and useful" but we found that any useful submission, however brief, would be brushed aside with the comment, "That can be dealt with on the appeal". (When the trial ended, we learned that appeals would not be permitted.) The only advocate allowed fully to develop his case was a Frenchman defending one of his fellow countrymen.

The main offences seemed to be holding illegal meetings and demonstrations; writing, printing and distributing "revolutionary tracts" (any leaflet critical of the regime and its policies); and spreading falsehoods. One man was charged because a single leaflet was found in his home. He said, "But I read and rejected it. I've played no part in politics." Any law that forbids the right of association is unconstitutional. We argued this and the president conceded that no one could be punished for an opinion. That should have been the end of the case. However, the procurator countered that every Communist subscribes to the idea that the state must be overthrown, therefore you need only be a Communist to be found guilty of conspiracy. The defendants were variously grouped as Communists, Maoists or Ba'athists, thus firmly in the thrall of foreign interests.

The President asked each defendant: "Do you believe in religion?" In a Muslim country, this was an embarrassing and rather dangerous question to ask of someone with Left sympathies. It was an obvious attempt to expose them as atheists and revolutionaries. He pointed out that the majority of students received state bursaries; clearly, they were also ingrates. Defendants were regularly shouted down by the President. One man entered to the cry, "You lie! You have made a false statement," and

the statement was duly altered. Many of the defendants claimed to have
been tortured by the police, but any attempt to retract statements on the
grounds that they had been made under torture brought the threat of
additional charges of defaming the police. One fellow was said to have
been ordered to dig his own grave – he must have been the only defendant
relieved to be in court.

The whole case was grotesquely exaggerated, with maximum sentences
running to fourteen years. Never was so powerful a hammer used to crush
so modest a nut. Forty of the Tunisians were adopted by Amnesty
International as Prisoners of Conscience. Upon completion of sentence,
anyone regarded as an intellectual was ordered to sign the barra, which
was both a denunciation of the crime and a promise not to re-offend. To
add a new penalty or condition when a man has already served his sentence
is contrary to any of the accepted practices in criminal proceedings. No
additional penalty should be levied unless it had been imposed at the time
of sentencing. The Arabic Lawyers Federation declared the barra to be
illegal, though it was very flattering that lawyers should be included
amongst the intellectuals.

CHAPTER THIRTY

Vietnam and Guinea

WHEN THE French were forced out of Vietnam after their defeat at Dien Bien Phu, the Geneva Conference stipulated that a general election should be held in July 1956. In his book *Mandate for Change*, General Eisenhower admitted that "had elections been held ... possibly 80 per cent of the population would have voted for the Communist Ho Chi Minh". The Americans got in first by staging rigged elections that installed Ngo Dinh Diem as President of the southern half of the country. Diem's brother Nhu was given control of the secret police. Although the Geneva accords banned reprisals against collaborators, the new regime terrorised all who had supported the war of liberation against the French and soon had anything up to 100,000 political prisoners. The united liberation movement refused to surrender and American troops went to war against that part of the country not under the control of the Diems. The Vietnam War continued for many years.

By the mid-1960s, the Americans were responsible for so many iniquities that a great part of the world rose up in protest against them. In November 1965, Barbara Haq, Secretary of the British Council for Peace in Vietnam, arranged a series of deputations to ministers of the British government, sending groups of doctors, scientists, writers, and so forth. Barristers seemed a good bet, for it was clear to any lawyer that the American action in Vietnam violated traditional practice in international law. Eleven American legal experts, including professors of international law at Princeton, Harvard and Chicago universities, had already published their unanimous opinion that the American intervention broke that law. Because foreign involvement in a civil war is illegal, America was breaching not only the Geneva accords but also the Charter of the United Nations. The actions of their forces in Vietnam were also in violation of the US

Constitution, for America had not declared war. Fenner Brockway was responsible for putting together a comparable document from representative British lawyers. It seemed a promising tactic.

In the summer of 1966, the newspapers reported Bertrand Russell's intention to set up a War Crimes Tribunal to prosecute the Americans for their brutality in Vietnam. It was to be organised on the same lines as the Nuremberg War Crimes Tribunal. This was welcome but surprising news, for Russell had opposed the suggestion of a trial to investigate crimes committed in Suez and Hungary in 1956, on the grounds that it would not be possible to find judges of sufficient impartiality. In 1958, he send a curt note to the Stockholm Peace Congress berating their pro-Communist stance and finishing: "I cannot regard your organisation as impartial, and I must therefore sever all connection with it." Had the severity of the situation in Vietnam made impartiality a lesser concern?

The Haldane Society welcomed the proposed tribunal but feared that it would make little impact on public opinion in the UK: no Briton had been suggested for the tribunal, and there were to be no lawyers and no judges. Fenner Brockway shared our concern and tried to persuade Russell to reconsider. When this failed, he asked me to work on the possibility of setting up an international commission of eminent jurists, who would hear all the evidence and then place an indictment before a panel of renowned judges. This was meant not to rival Russell's group but to strengthen and support it. In the end, the Haldane backed down and I was instructed to help Russell collect as many prominent persons as possible for his own tribunal. It was not easy to get through to Russell, for he was busy completing the second volume of his autobiography and all contact was through Ralph Schoenman, his young American assistant.

In mid-December I was meant to leave for a two-weeks' tour of North Vietnam, as guest of the Vietnam Bar Association. It was made clear that if I went alone, the mission would do little good to the North Vietnamese cause in England and much harm to my own. Emlyn Hooson, a Liberal MP, QC and a member of the Bar Council, agreed to come. We hoped to extend the fortnight's tour to include Saigon. Arrangements were well ahead, but I wanted Russell's advice on the mission. This provided another reason to contact him. (As sometimes happens, when it was time to leave for Hanoi I was caught up in a case and quite unable to free myself. Whether or not Hooson managed to go on his own, I do not now recall.)

Russell was a firm and demanding host in the sense that he answered my request to be allowed to call on him: "Yes, catch the train at Marylebone tomorrow morning and you can have seven hours. We travel first class." On the long journey to Plas Penrhyn in Merionethshire we talked about the many people that he expected to draw in. They were all personally known to him and he reeled off names and sometimes addresses from memory, although he was then well into his nineties. His current (and fourth) wife Edith was an attractive and quiet woman who took only the slightest part in the talk, and then only when Russell asked for her recollection of one possible delegate or another. She produced a splendid lunch from a hamper after Birmingham. I already knew Dora, Russell's second wife, who was for a short time a leading figure in the peace movement. Dora had a strong figure and moved briskly in her sturdy suit like a uniform. Her son Roddy was a conscientious objector in 1952 and volunteered to do his national service in the coal mines under the Bevin scheme. He was pulling out pit props when the roof caved in and left him paralysed for life. He died at fifty, after twenty-seven years in a wheelchair.

In Wellington we had known of Bertrand Russell as a leader of radical opinion, but I first became interested in him when he spoke at Oxford in Michaelmas Term 1928. So far as I now remember, the lecture seemed to be a disappointingly boyish potion of free love and free thought. I did not follow his doings again until the end of the Second World War, when he declared himself violently and recklessly anti-Soviet. He saw the Poles and Russians as looting and ravaging the East Zone of Germany to the point of slaughtering half its population. The *New Statesman* received a broadside from Russell to this effect, which Kingsley Martin was expected to publish. Kingsley appealed to me as a witness to refute Russell's outburst. Another of Russell's ideas was that America should take advantage of her nuclear monopoly by setting up a world government which would bomb any other nation that threatened to acquire nuclear weaponry. My feeling that he was just a silly old man lasted until October 1960 when he started the Committee of 100 to encourage mass civil disobedience in the cause of peace. Several thousands sat in Trafalgar Square with him. When three of my sons needed rescuing after a night in Bow Street Station, having been picked up in the square, I realised that, for the young at least, he had an appeal. Barney, being under sixteen, was sent home the night before and I had to appear with him at Walton Street Juvenile Court. It angered him even more that he couldn't appear by himself.

The International War Crimes Tribunal on Vietnam was set up in November 1966, although the first hearings didn't begin until six months later. At first, Russell wanted the tribunal to convene in Switzerland but the government refused to let them into the country. France was second choice until the French government objected and the hotel cancelled the bookings. Stockholm proved to be more tolerant and the hearings began in May in the Folkets Hus (the People's House) with Jean-Paul Sartre as executive chairman. The fifteen men and women of the tribunal included Simone de Beauvoir, former leader of the Yugoslav Partisans Vladimir Dedijer, and Pietro Nenni's political ally Lelio Basso. Lawrence Daly, Secretary of the Scottish NUM, and the historian Isaac Deutscher had promised to come and represent Britain but for some reason failed to appear.

At the opening session Sartre read a speech from Russell:

"The world is numbed by the arrogant brutality of the United States government. In a fever of frustration over the humiliating defeat inflicted on her occupying army in South Vietnam, the United States, in hysteria and hate, boasts of its intent, and its intent is evil. Crimes, barbarous crimes, are reported daily from Vietnam. They are crimes of an aggressor, an occupier, a tormentor. Our task is to display this truth to the people of the world. Our duty is to investigate every fact, so that every fact serves to arouse passionate resistance. In Vietnam we have done what Hitler did in Europe. We shall suffer the degradation of Nazi Germany unless we act."

Scores of witnesses and their interpreters came from Vietnam. They described the effects of saturation bombing of civilian areas, injuries caused by napalm, incendiary and fragmentation bombs, the torture of prisoners, and many of the same evils encountered in the American campaign against North Korea. New refinements were the creation of village concentration camps, which the Americans called "strategic hamlets", and the use of deadly defoliants such as Agent Orange. This information was confirmed by American deserters, many of whom had taken shelter in Scandinavia and Canada. Russell still attacked the Russians, but now it was for their inadequate level of support for national liberation movements. He wanted direct Russian intervention in Vietnam. Until then, he had been an implacable opponent of nationalism, correctly seeing it as the greatest danger to world peace. During the First World War he had worked with the No Conscription Fellowship and served six months in Brixton Prison. It was an extraordinary turnaround.

There was ample evidence to warrant the unanimous verdict of guilty against the USA provided that one ignored stories to the contrary. Although the War Crimes Tribunal took the form of a court of law, it set itself the task of establishing American wrong-doing and not of enquiring whether or not there was any. This was one of the minor inequities for which the convenors of the hearing were responsible. At first, Russell had hoped to try all misdeeds in Vietnam. Well into the preparation of the evidence, it was apparent that newspapers and television were carrying only stories of the success and nobility of the US side, with nothing from North Vietnam to counterbalance it. The only chance of providing a balance was to put out propaganda for the North that was as biased and as bigoted as that promoted by the other side. It was a deliberate decision to reject impartiality.

Russell did not expect a balanced judgement from the Stockholm tribunal. He wanted a favourable result, a judgement upholding the North and condemning the Americans, and a stern judgement at that.

In February 1968, the newspapers published a photograph of the South Vietnamese General Nguyen Ngoc Loan executing with a pistol a young man in the street. The debate was whether or not the general was guilty of murder. I had a letter published in *The Times* arguing that, according to the Geneva Convention for Prisoners of War, he was undoubtedly a murderer. Under Article 4 of this convention, if the victim was a member of the armed forces, then he was entitled to unconditional protection however he was dressed and whatever subterfuge or disguise he might have adopted. If he was merely a civilian, unarmed and with his hands bound, then not even the chief of police was entitled to execute him without trial.

From Hampstead came an extraordinary letter, signed by a retired brigadier:

"During 16 years on active service I cannot count the number of times that I saw summary executions, starting off in Shanghai where prisoners were executed in public for the benefit of tourists in 1937."

He described how in Burma American pilots

"used to drop the trussed up prisoners from the aircraft out on Jap held towns... . There was no torture that I saw — only summary execution which is quite normal in war."

In Holland in 1945, his troops overran a camp of girl prisoners from Warsaw. The girls singled out the cruel warders and "about 50 German guards, men and women, were summarily shot by the Poles. There was no cruelty and the rest went free."

As for the execution of captured Gestapo officers and their helpers in Norway,

"it was part of the game of war if you lost... . Both in the Far East and Europe I was considered soft by the men under my command...as I let so many people go.

"There is a silly and effeminate atmosphere abroad in Britain today (encouraged by the BBC for left wing ends) about war and death. But it will always be with us. So let us face it manfully and decisively without any unnecessary cruelty and suffering. If you are a Christian you do not fear death. And we cannot always have a Judge Advocate General or lawyer in tow. They are usually in comfortable billets wining and dining and uttering platitudes well out of harm's way... . So don't be too pontifical."

The brigadier signed his name, but it was a name that could not be found in the Army List. This letter, whether genuine or not, strengthened my determination to fight such attitudes.

Our many notable allies in the fight for peace included New York lawyers Will Standard and Leonard Boudin. They were very different men. Will was mature and grey, a bit austere, and a leader amongst commercial and shipping attorneys in Manhattan. New York invested a lot of money in other people's ships and Will could nail a writ to a mast in any commercial language and in any part of the world and establish a bottomry bond overnight. He travelled widely on goodwill missions and was a great entertainer. Leonard Boudin was a most successful advocate and, by brilliant work, he won civil rights cases of the greatest importance. In 1958, he argued Rockwell Kent v John Foster Dulles, in which the Supreme Court upheld the constitutional right of an American citizen to travel freely, without hindrance from the state. That was passed by five votes to four. The dissenting opinion on the case was written by Tom Campbell Clark, whose son Ramsey Clark was Attorney General to John Kennedy, then went on to become one of the outstanding radicals of American life.

Leonard Boudin also defended Daniel Ellsberg, who distributed what became known as the Pentagon Papers; the Berrigan Brothers, Catholic priests who preached against the Vietnamese War and, by invading official premises and destroying files, tried to make the draft unworkable; and Dr Benjamin Spock, who did and said everything right about children and about peace. All that Leonard did was treated as a lesson by his daughter Kathy. After graduating from university, she joined the Weathermen, a group so extreme that even killing your opponents was allowed. Nothing learned from her father justified the lengths to which she went. In 1970, she emerged from a friend's house in Greenwich Village, stripped of her clothes by a bomb factory explosion that killed three of her colleagues and gutted the house. She disappeared. I wrote to Leonard and offered a safe place in rural Sussex, although I'm sure that Janet would not have wanted to entertain a terrorist. The offer was not taken up, since Kathy was determined to stay close to home to continue her work. She was captured eleven years later, after an armed raid on a bank security van. I tried to do in peace work what Leonard did and I had been active since 1950. It is a relief that none of my six children misunderstood me as much as Kathy misunderstood her father.

Since the League of Nations debating tour in 1931, I had not really visited the United States. Over the years, I had changed planes in New York several times on trips to the Caribbean and to British Guiana, but had not left the airport. In 1967, I was invited to New York to address the National Lawyers' Guild on modern developments in English law, especially in relation to civil rights. A visa was necessary so I applied. The process would take about half an hour, it seemed. The application form required confirmation that I was neither lunatic nor criminal, neither homosexual nor suffering from any venereal disease, and that I had no connections with Communists or any Communist-affiliated group. I duly signed. Within five minutes, the clerk came back with a really formidable catechism. I was to list every Communist country I had been to, and state when and why and with whom; to name every club, organisation or society I had ever belonged to, with dates and places and any office held. It was twice as demanding as the Labour Party's questioning of a returning black sheep.

I left out fifty-seven varieties of boating, boxing, rugby and similar clubs but offered the British-Soviet Friendship Society, of which I was chairman for ten years, and a few similar bodies. It then took only three minutes for the decision that I was banned from the United States, and seemingly forever. I explained that these friendship organisations were not linked in any way to the Communist Party. "Ahhh, that's nothing," came the reply. "In the eyes of the State Department they are Communist inspired." The bar could be waived by a senior immigration official at Frankfurt-on-Main. After all, he had for years been dealing with possible ex-Nazis. By the 1960s, any connection with Communists was a much graver business than past connection with Nazis. I applied to Frankfurt-on-Main, at first by telephone and then in a long written submission, but without success. By then the National Lawyers' Guild conference was over. We tried to arrange a speech by wireless direct into the conference room. They had risen early for lunch and the hall caretaker was entertained to twenty minutes of unintelligible hisses, crackles and pops.

If the Americans thought themselves skilled in keeping out unwanted visitors, they were the merest amateurs compared with the immigration officers of Guinea. One fine morning in August 1967, when heavy harvest boots were the order of the day and shouted adjurations to the sons to get themselves ready by the time the dew had dried, Noel Henwood rang from the KLM offices at Schiphol Airport and demanded that I fly that afternoon to Conakry. The question "Where is Conakry?" brought the response that it was the capital of the Independent Democratic Fighting Peoples Republic of Guinea, as everybody knows. Well, I did not know and declared that I did not intend to go there. Further enquiry produced the information that Guinea claimed to be the most Marxist state in all Africa, and that KLM would pay a handsome fee for an attempt to rescue four of their ground staff who were being held under house arrest. I was not in Conakry that night but in Amsterdam to meet the parents of the detained men and to help draft a petition for their release and repatriation. KLM provided a written submission, offering to establish a number of scholarships relating to the airline and tourism industries, with two additional scholarships for medicine and engineering. In addition, they would arrange cultural exchanges between Holland and Guinea.

Next call was to Paris because, however free and democratic and fighting and republican the state might be, they would not grant entry without a visa. Guinea had no office in Paris or anywhere else within reach, but it was rumoured that Mali had an office and would issue a visa on behalf of Guinea. The rumour was of little value as they would not offer one to me, despite my claimed acquaintance with the Attorney General of Guinea (whom I had recently met in Paris) and much encouragement from Joe Nordmann of the IADL. It took many weeks to arrange a Guinean visa, but they offered an alternative: if I flew to Conakry, I would be given forty-eight hours' permission to land and could apply for a visa there. I set off at once and arrived in Conakry at four a.m. There followed ten hours of argument and manoeuvre. I mentioned that I had come to see their head of state and Kwame Nkrumah, ex-President of Ghana who was then exiled in Guinea. This information was rewarded an hour later with a visit from two gentlemen on Nkrumah's staff. I told them of my mission and showed a letter of introduction to Kwame from Pat Sloan. Pat was a good friend, a former Secretary of the BSFS and editor of *Soviet Weekly*, whose heart had been broken by Khrushchev's revelations about Stalin. Now he was staunch in support of African socialism and highly regarded. The Ghanaians would see Nkrumah at eight a.m. and promised that they would do their best to persuade him to intervene on my behalf. I spread myself in comfort to await their return.

When they failed to reappear, an approach to a man who seemed to be commissar for the airport brought the welcome news: "It has all been arranged. Bring your bag and come with me." He took me out to a taxi but before there was time to get in, a fellow in a blue uniform rushed out and grabbed my luggage, shouting, "Not in the taxi but over here." Mr Blue Uniform hurried me through the lounge crowded with passengers about to board a UTA flight to Paris, handed my passport to the airline staff and, unwisely, he disappeared. I had no sooner got my luggage back and retrieved the passport than he reappeared, shouting, "Onto plane, no visa, finished here, not have such people here, produce ticket!" I had by then discovered that there was no exit without a visa. My uniformed friend became distinctly agitated, but sat down with a little persuasion. I asked him if he was interested in politics. "Oui, oui." Poor chap. I poured the whole of my political record over him. He came up gasping for breath and left for town to see his chief. I saw off the UTA flight and watched hour after hour of heavy rain.

It was dry when he came back and put me into a small Russian car. A great quantity of fish was emptied out of the boot and shared out all round, then my bags went in. There was a crisis of energy in the state. No car batteries would work and vehicles had to be pushed or bump-started. I joined in with such enthusiasm that it gained the active approval of the commissar, and I think this may have helped persuade them that after our visit to the Sûreté, I should be permitted into the city rather than being taken back to the airport. To the head of the Sûreté, I proffered my letters of introduction from Pat Sloan and from Joe Nordmann and made formal application for entry and exit visas. They produced a magistrate and it all looked most promising. At two p.m. I was taken to a big hotel and left there in a state of exhaustion. Later in the afternoon, a smartly dressed fellow came along on a motor bike to say that the chief of protocol for the president had rung and would ring again. It was the very news I wanted to hear, but delivered so unconvincingly that I could not believe him.

Early next morning I set out to find such Dutch people as were at liberty. One of the KLM representatives told me that she had been received most cordially by the head of state, Sekou Touré, with warm protestations of friendship for the Dutch people and for KLM, but he would not release the families. Touré insisted that the Dutch government approach Felix Houphouet-Boigny, who owned and ran the Ivory Coast a short distance further south-east, and demand from him their release. The two men were great rivals and had been so for many years. While Touré was proposing to take the more popular and Communist course in his country, Houphouet-Boigny embarked on strident capitalism. The Ivory Coast was already advanced in agriculture and had immense American backing, whereas Touré depended on present development of mineral resources and the capitalist world was not going to offer him investment.

In February, a trawler from the Ivory Coast was found close to the shores of Guinea with a large and well-armed crew. Most of the crew were Ghanaians and it was believed that Houphouet-Boigny had sent them to kidnap Nkrumah. The boat was impounded and the crew were taken prisoner. Guinea was already holding François Kamano, former director of the Ivorian Compensation Court, whom they had arrested in 1965 on charges of plotting against the state. The Ivorians' chance of revenge came in June when a KLM plane carrying the Guinean delegation to the United Nations home from New York landed in Abidjan, capital of the Ivory Coast. Members of the delegation were seized and imprisoned. Arsene Assouan Usher, the Ivorian Minister of Foreign Affairs, announced that the men were still "in transit" and enjoying a comfortable stay in residential quarters under "the rules of reciprocity". Plainly, said Touré, this was a primitive act of hostage- taking quite unworthy of us great modern nations and could be met only by an act of reciprocity. He then caused four KLM employees to be placed under house arrest on the grounds that KLM had conspired with the Ivory Coast to snatch his diplomats.

My job was to get the Dutch hostages liberated. Now I was told that Touré would not free them unless the Ivorians first handed back his diplomats. Houphouet-Boigny would not release the diplomats until Kamano and the trawler were returned. I had heard only the basic facts when I was more or less imprisoned in the hotel. A number of young men took turns at minding me in my room; they even handed on a book of short stories at the changing of the guard. The more senior of them apologised for the want of hospitality and stressed that it was not surveillance, it was simply that they had not wanted me to feel isolated. There ensued daily arguments with various bureaucrats over the lack of a visa. Nkrumah's chef de protocol promised that if I would only return to England and re-apply, he would support the application and the visa would come within the week. Although the position between the two presidents was very delicate, he would personally raise the question of my situation. After five days of argument, I was turned out of the country and sent back to Europe.

While in Africa, I had chanced upon a postcard of a game warden. He was in short scarlet trousers, all torn out at the knees, and had on an equally ragged bright blue shirt. His gun pointed straight at the camera whereas a long line of jungle paths stretched into the distance behind, leaving him vulnerable to any lion that might saunter along the track. He seemed to be in just the position and political state of myself and of Arthur Irvine. Arthur came into parliament at a by-election in 1947 and unwisely let himself be known as a lefty. Although he was of great ability, he went on for years representing Liverpool, Edge Hill, with never a chance of any promotion or appointment, save that he took silk quite early and was going well in his profession. Politically, he seemed to have got nowhere. The card went off by post, carrying the note that there were several people like this connected with British politics and every little rabbit that passed had taken a nip out of their scarlet trousers and had become national heroes by waving their booty.

When I returned to London, I learned that Arthur had achieved his knighthood and was Solicitor General and covered with glory. Upon landing, my first phone call was to the new SG, and then to present myself to him and ask eagerly for his guidance as to whom to approach at the Foreign Office to ask about Guinea. He gave valuable and immediate advice, and I then felt brave enough to ask him to do no more than look at the postcard when it arrived, but not to read what was on the back. I followed his advice with gratitude and heard no more about my inapposite message. In the opinion of the FO, nobody had a greater influence in the area than "Big" Bill Tubman, ruler of Liberia, the state between Guinea and the Ivory Coast. He alone had prestige and authority enough to be able to take his two neighbours and knock their heads together and get them to see sense. Mr Tubman was the longest reigning Head of State in Africa and as arbitrary a ruler as any of them. So successful had he been in winning elections in his earlier days that all possible opponents had abandoned the impertinence even of allowing themselves to be put up, and a number of them were no longer alive.

Where was Tubman now? He was in a new, specially built site on the Stanley Heights overlooking the Congo, where the heads of state of the Organisation of African Unity were having a summit meeting at Kinshasa, capital of the Congo. There was still no word on my visa for Guinea, bit it was easy enough to get the equivalent document from the Congo representative in London. Before leaving England, I sought Fanner Brockway's advice. He said that I must send a cable in his name to Touré and Nkrumah, saying that I was a life-long opponent of imperialism and could be completely trusted and "please grant him a visa". On 13th

September it was off to Kinshasa. By the time I arrived, KLM had organised the support of the British and the Dutch Embassies and of the Papal Nuncio and they somehow got me an appointment with Bill Tubman for that very afternoon and the first secretary took me in a British Embassy car to the forbidden city, where we were stopped by four separate groups of militia in different helmets, uniforms and insignia. The Liberian Chargé d'Affaires came, to our rejoicing, but even he could get us no further than the security office until Bill Tubman came to the rescue.

The "big" part of Tubman's name was based on his dimensions as well as his distinction as a ruler. He was perhaps five foot-one inch high and may well have been five foot-one inch in circumference at the widest point. Tubman insisted that we should go and overlook the river so that he could point out where Brazzaville lay on the opposite shore and so we might understand the character of the water hyacinths that came flooding down the stream. We were told that over a century ago some Anglican missionary had brought in this plant so as to have a reminder of home. He planted it at the head waters of the Congo and it flourished as few things can have flourished before. It breaks off and is washed down in enormous patches. It constitutes a main obstacle to easy passage on the river. When a patch exceeds an acre in size, it is said that watchers from higher up will report by telegraph or telephone to the navigation controllers lower down.

Mr Tubman and I got on quite well. If he were to act in any way that was critical of his two neighbours, he wanted it to be with the full authority of the OAU. The heads of state had discussed the matter in their morning session after U Thant threatened to place the dispute on the agenda of the UN General Assembly, and he was optimistic that there would soon be a result. He told us of Houphouet-Boigny's claim that the trawler had been driven into Guinean territorial waters by bad weather and Touré's response that the weather had been fine. "So what can I do with these contradictions?" After the seizing of the diplomats, Houphouet-Boigny told Tubman, "Sekou only understands this kind of talk." Tubman had ordered them to give up the hostages but each responded, "I know I'm wrong, bit I cannot satisfy my own people if I let them go." Tubman had on several occasions tried to set up meetings with his neighbours to arrange an exchange of prisoners but all such arrangements had fallen through, due to a catalogue of mishaps and family health problems. He said, "Follow me to Monrovia and I will show you what I will do."

KLM's plight was known to all the airlines on the coast so I was free to travel on any of them. My roundabout route to Monrovia, capital of Liberia, required that I change planes at Cotonou in Dahomey and at Abidjan. On the plane to Cotonou, I had the good fortune to sit next to Arsene Assouan Usher, Minister of Foreign Affairs for the Ivory Coast, who told me that the basic principle of the exchange was all agreed. The only difficulty was that Touré wanted his diplomats freed a few days before the fishermen in recognition of their superior social and political status, a condition Houphouet-Boigny opposed. In Abidjan, the acting head of state granted me thirty-five minutes with the detained diplomats. Lansana Beavogui, Foreign Minister of Guinea, and M Marof, Permanent Representative at the UN, were being kept in a villa with a student and another man whose large family included quite young children, all of whom had come to visit. Beavogui wrote out a note for Touré and told us that although their health was all right, morale was not too good. Both ministers urged me to see their head of state in person and to get President Tubman to send me with his emissary. The Guinean visa was now in sight.

All and sundry brought their personal and public problems to the executive mansion in Monrovia, where Tubman held his daily morning receptions. These were regulated by Mrs Padmore, a strong and rather bossy woman who seemed to run his diplomatic and political affairs. Mrs Padmore allotted people their time as "I give you two minutes only" and if the suppliant exceeded the allocation, she went in to the reception place and wheeled out the deviant by the arm. I saw her bring someone out by the ear. She was a most extraordinary power in the land. Mrs Padmore gave us forty minutes with the president. He arranged to see the Guinean Chargé d'Affaires at two p.m. "Those people are very long-winded. Come back at three and I'll tell you what he said." The Chargé claimed that he was not permitted to issue a visa without express authority from Conakry, irrespective of circumstances. So we devised a cable for Touré, telling him that I would come bearing messages from Beavogui. All the next day the Chargé was pestered for the visa.

On the following day, it was learned from the US Embassy, through the Dutch Chargé d'Affaires, that Touré had that morning released his share of the hostages. If the KLM employees had been freed, there was no point in my staying. I retired to England. Two days later a message came from Monrovia: "Visa waiting. Letter still held." The Dutchmen had not been freed after all, so it was back to Monrovia, via Amsterdam, Madrid, Lagos and Abidjan. According to the latest news, although the trawler had left Conakry with its crew, Kamano was still waiting for transport home. Houphouet-Boigny would not release anyone until the Ivorians were in his hands or with Tubman. In Monrovia I collected the highly prized visa and met up with General Goodrich, who was going for Tubman to get Kamano. They would probably not return until the following day, which meant that the Dutchmen could be got on board their aeroplane for home. At Conakry, we were met by the Chief of Protocol for Foreign Affairs and it was explained that Kamano might have left in the trawler on Friday, might have gone by air on Saturday, might be hiding in Conakry, but he had certainly left his hotel. My assistance was not needed and I came home. Four days later I received a telex from Lufthansa saying that the KLM employees, now released, had much appreciated the courtesy.

CHAPTER THIRTY-ONE

South Africa

IN JOHANNESBURG in July 1967 the South African Intelligence Service arrested one Edmund Trinka, supposedly a Canadian visitor. Their complaint was that he had photographed police buildings. In September it was announced that he was Yuri Loginov, a KGB spy from Moscow. It was widely reported that he had revealed names of his fellow Soviet agents throughout the western world; he was "singing like a canary" and soon there would be many arrests. I took no particular notice of either event.

In January 1968, I was invited to lunch at the Soviet Embassy in London. Since the war I had been a fairly regular visitor at receptions and the like, but an invitation to a private meal was unusual. I was met by a cultural attaché, who entertained me throughout lunch with general talk about world affairs but gave no indication of any particular purpose. It would have been discourteous to ask bluntly, "Why am I here?" The answer came only when I was taken downstairs to a darkened room, heavily shrouded with curtains as though sound-proofed. My host told me about Loginov. So far as they knew, he was just a businessman in no way connected with Soviet government affairs. Would I please go to South Africa at their expense and find out what I could about him?

The idea was surprising. I had never been to South Africa and didn't see how I could possibly help. He said that lawyers were the best people for finding things out, and I was well accustomed to getting around the world. I would go as a lawyer to get information from fellow lawyers. There was to be no fee, but the Russians would cover all expenses. If they had said, "He's one of our spies", I wouldn't have gone near them, him or South Africa and I'm sure they knew that.

Some cover was needed for the visit. I arranged with the Rev John Collins that he would send me to make enquiries on his behalf. He was a canon of St Paul's Cathedral and was very active in a number of progressive movements. He saw that radical changes were necessary to bring about social justice and he wasn't frightened by the prospect, as most people are. His great achievement was the Defence and Aid Fund, which had its first beginnings in 1956. As much as £2 million had been sent for the defence of blacks suffering under apartheid in South Africa. There was a genuine need to find out about the money, and this gave an excuse to go to the main cities.

One of our neighbours in Sussex, a Quaker, gave an introduction to a relative in Johannesburg. He put me up and introduced me to the first of the lawyers. Within three days, I had quite a number of appointments. There were many sets of chambers in neighbouring buildings, with Rex Welsh's chambers in the middle. We met frequently and he proposed that it would be better if the barristers called on me out of business hours; I should stay with him and the barristers would visit in the evening. Rex represented gold and diamond interests and took a leading role at the local Bar but, so far as promotion was concerned, his prospects were blighted because of his declared opposition to apartheid.

I lodged with his family for some time and was given many introductions by his wife Anne, who was deep in every liberal activity. Winnie Mandela, whose husband was on Robben Island, twice visited. She clearly had the fullest sympathy of the white liberals. She once came to lunch with Rex and me at the restaurant of Stuttafords, a grand department store in Johannesburg. When Winnie sat down, a ripple went round the room. The head waiter came and spoke confidentially to Rex. Our host burst out laughing and roared, "Winnie Mandela? She's not black, she's white!" She was duly served.

Another of the Welsh's friends was Helen Suzman, the one very liberal woman Member of Parliament. With extraordinary courage and charm, she had withstood an unending battering of hatred from the great majority of whites. On one occasion she brought Albertina Sisulu, the great heroine of the ANC, to visit at the Welsh's. Helen Suzman and Anne Welsh took me to gatherings of the Black Sash movement: white women who devoted themselves to helping blacks. One example of their work was the finding of black students who could take advantage of education overseas, particularly in Britain. I was given the chance to meet various local parsons, including the Dean ffrench-Beytagh who, it might be said, paved the way for Archbishop Tutu. One needed no restraint in dealing with the Dean. He was a large, jolly figure in monk's habit and sandals, and was as courageously against the current regime as anyone in public could be.

Through personal introductions, I was put up in the same friendly fashion by barristers' families in Durban and Cape Town. I was taken to a number of courts and saw cases being fought ranging from petty offences about carrying passes, tried in the Magistrates' Court, to graver charges in the higher courts and on appeal. At considerable risk to themselves, lawyers had provided notable service in support of blacks being persecuted in the courts and it was easy to establish that the £2 million had been properly spent in normal legal fees and costs. I doubt whether any lawyer knew of my ulterior purpose.

I had read Alan Paton's *Cry, the Beloved Country*, which spread an understanding and an abhorrence of apartheid round the world. Any trip to Durban required a visit to him as a pilgrimage. I rang him at his home in Kloof, where the land begins to rise west of Durban. It was a large, cold house and he lived there with no family as his wife had died in the previous year and their two sons were grown up. I was asked to lunch: a good local fish, stuffed, with corn on the cob and mangoes. Edward Paget, the retired Archbishop of Central Africa, and Father Guinness came to tea. I really felt that I knew the latter, for he was born and schooled near to where I was brought up so that we shared nearly a common boyhood. It was a good visit.

Sir Richard Luyt, Governor of British Guiana in 1964, had come back to the University of Cape Town as vice-chancellor and principal. The medical school was Groote Schuur (the "Great Barn") and there Christiaan Barnard first showed how to change men's hearts, one for another. I had an introduction to Barnard and was able to call on both men on the same campus. Barnard had time off that morning and showed me his surgery. It was almost "This was the scalpel with which I did it". The world had a high opinion of him and rightly so; I'm not sure that he hadn't an equally high opinion of himself. South Africa became too small; he severed ties with his homeland and was to be found in expensive clinics in Switzerland.

I had lunch with Luyt, who seemed quite at home in the academic world and was obviously glad to be out of the colonial service. He spoke freely of his days in British Guiana. Even though he was governor of a British colony, the CIA were after him all the time with proposals and pressure to denigrate Cheddi Jagan, the premier, and to advance Forbes Burnham. He told me that previous governors had been badgered in the same way. His personal experience showed that direct interference had been going on ever since Jagan first came in to power; that at first it was devoted to luring Burnham away from the PPP and then, if possible, to destroying Jagan. Cheddi is lucky to have survived.

The main problem remained: Loginov. Two Johannesburg women gave the utmost help. They hunted out every reference to Loginov for some months past. The results ranged from simply tracing his whereabouts to the most lurid disclosures of Russian spying activities. For example, in the previous November the *Star of Johannesburg* had published a police report listing the kinds of information the KGB had set Loginov to discover. They wanted details on how blacks could get into and out of the country, and what documents would be required. What were the borders with Botswana and Lesotho like? Was secret landing possible on the Indian Ocean coast south of Durban? What was the strength and influence of the ANC? Was there any organised resistance to the South African regime, and what could be done to foment disturbances? They wished to know about the main American and British establishments and the chances of penetrating them. In short, they painted a picture of valiant, stalwart South Africa defending western interests against the Soviet-backed ANC.

Loginov was being held in the local prison at Pretoria, in the maximum-security section. We were told that in the next cell was Bram Fischer, the outstanding barrister of Johannesburg. He had established that position before the Privy Council in London, where I met him with Pritt. Bram's opposition to apartheid had landed him with a life sentence. Pretoria Prison was by no means a simple place in which to find your way about. There were three separate prisons, each with its own complex of buildings. I found the right one but was sent away. I went again with Joel Carlson, Bram's solicitor, with no better result. Even Carlson wasn't allowed to see his client.

How to get a number of questions and answers to Bram and, through him, to Loginov? Bram's son and daughter visited him as often as allowed, and I was to be there for three weeks. I met them at Witswatersrand University. I think that he was reading law and she was working in the law library. Between us, we devised a course of conversation. It was all done with great discretion. I was told that Loginov was not a spy, had not pretended he was, and there was no foundation to stories that he had talked. He had given no names for he knew no names to give.

When I came back to London I reported to the Soviet Embassy and, in the same dark and muffled room, dictated my story into their machine. A year later I read in *The Times* that Loginov had been handed to the Russians in exchange for eleven Western spies detained in East Germany. According to the *Sunday Times* of Johannesburg, there was a sweetener:

> "South Africa will acquire vital military equipment and goods which she was unable to obtain otherwise. South Africa will be able to acquire complicated secret weapons for her role in the free world's defence."

Major Loginov must have really puzzled the Russians. He had proved himself a competent spy and was trusted. Yet within weeks of his arrest in South Africa, it was claimed that he had betrayed KGB contacts in twenty-three countries. He appeared to have given his captors great quantities of material. What the Russians did not know was that in April 1961, in Italy on his first Western assignment, Loginov thought he had been detected, panicked and fled to the American embassy in Helsinki. The CIA had promptly recruited or "turned" him. The detailed "confessions" produced by the South Africans were really six years of accumulated debriefings from the CIA, Loginov's true employers.

The double-agent had been betrayed back to his original masters on the orders of James Jesus Angleton, the Chief of CIA Counter-intelligence. Angleton was plainly paranoid. Amongst other obsessions, he was convinced that Harold Wilson was a Soviet agent: a belief that was responsible for Harold being persecuted throughout his premiership. Loginov's dealings with the CIA were disclosed to the world by Tom Mangold in his book, *Cold Warrior*, published in 1991. The Russians were probably unaware of Loginov's connections with the CIA until 1988 and it has been suggested that he was sent to work in Gorky as an English teacher. Did the great liberalisation of Russia come in time for him?

A real spy must become hardened by his or her experiences. I found my slight and amateur excursions into the field of espionage very embarrassing. In South Africa, I dealt with people on a number of different levels. My immediate hosts had no idea of what I was up to. Rex Welsh was in court or chambers five days a week. My intriguing, aided by members of the family, took place after he had left. At night we dined well and roistered from then on till bed. In general, he treated me as if I were a guest of the rest of the family, and left my entertainment to them. The second group were those that had to be dealt with in a minor hand of spycraft. Then there were the official persons, mainly lawyers and ministers of state and of the church, to whom I was a foreign lawyer wanting to learn all about their system of law and justice and their social life. This was true, and usually applies to any country I visit.

The more distinguished and august these persons might be, the more certain that I could not hint at what I was doing in their country. If I had been there simply as a visiting lawyer, there would have been no hesitation in raising some interesting points of comparison in our respective relations with blacks in South Africa or in Britain, or with the Maori in New Zealand. As it was, I did not feel I could even suggest a position opposed to apartheid. I saw how the lives of the opponents of apartheid were made difficult and, in some cases, intolerable. For those who could emigrate, it took great courage to stay in the country and go on with the battle in the face of all the obstacles. I felt awkward about keeping quiet, as if I was cheating them. It was an absurd position, justified only by the real feeling of hatred I had for the system.

With fellow lawyers, the conflict of feelings was even more intense. In Cape Town, D P de Villiers, Chairman of the local Bar, took me to lunch at the famous Heer 17 Club, the home territory of the founding Boer families. Likewise, in Pretoria it was the Pretoria Club, the stamping ground, it was suggested, of the Voortrekkers themselves. There I heard the question, "Why does Pretoria have the widest streets in the world?" and the answer, "Because you cannot back oxen, and the streets were built wide enough to turn eighteen span of oxen drawing one wagon." Mr Hoexter, one of the leading prosecutors, gave me a splendid lunch at the Pretoria Club, and it was through him that I met Mr Pelser, Minister of Justice and Prisons, who was a solicitor. Mr Pelser gave me an hour of his time and I was lucky to get his attention. We discussed British/South African relations and legal matters, but without touching on anything controversial. He was most kindly and informative and seemed a thoroughly decent fellow. Mr Pelser must have felt rather upset the following year when he learnt of the real reasons for my visit.

Soon after returning to London, I received a summons from Joe Slovo, South African barrister turned revolutionary, who played a substantial part in the organisational work of the African National Congress. Joe was living in the basement flat of a small house near Camden Town Junction. I was invited to supper. He was a large, comfortable laughing sort of chap and immediately made me at home. Ruth First was busy in the kitchen, and Joe and I sat at the living-room table, sharing it with his daughters while they did their homework. Joe was a Communist and told me that he had learned of my first South African journey from "a friend at the Soviet Embassy". Joe said that he and Robert Resha (an ANC leader who had joined the youth movement and come up through the ranks) wanted me to return, this time on behalf of the ANC. I was to renew my acquaintance with Winnie Mandela and try to form a judgement as to whether or not she was reliable. Could they trust her reports of recent political activity? They wanted me to stop at Lusaka on the way and take any different or additional instructions from Oliver Tambo. I think Joe produced £100 for expenses and I chimed in with a free ticket left over from KLM when they had requited me with a lump sum of fares.

In late April, I went to Lusaka, where I was met by Cynthia Zukas. Her husband took me to a small house to the south of the city, which must have been quite near to the place where Chitepo, leader of ZANU, was assassinated. I had two meetings with Oliver Tambo and Tennison Makilwane, one of his aides, who confirmed Joe Slovo's request and added another task. I was to take instructions to six of their main workers: four in Swaziland, one in Lesotho, and to Albertina Sisulu in Soweto. I was given three books by little-known writers. The books provided the basis for a very simple code. The correspondents had only to name the page and give the number of the word on that page; without the book it meant nothing, with the book the message was instantly revealed.

For the others, there was a bottle of secret liquid that amounted to invisible ink for writing letters. But how to answer any authority who might enquire about the contents of the bottle? What if I were required to drink it? I did, in fact, have a precautionary sniff and decided to pretend it was a distasteful gargle for my throat. As it was not thought desirable to carry the list of names and addresses, I memorised them and which address each book and message related to. I was terrified that I would muddle the addresses or forget them, and tried various mnemonics.

Eventually I devised a system for inserting the addresses, each in its own book, by referring to various letters and words in a secretive way. The purpose of all this was to enable correspondents to report the movement of young recruits who had been enlisted in South Africa and were being sent north for training. It seems that many thousands travelled northward heralded and guided by messages of this sort and it may have played a small part in encouraging the ANC with their proper and successful war against Pretoria.

Being in Lusaka, I called on Edward Shamwana, one of my most successful pupils, who had become a friend. He was the first African to practise as a lawyer in Zambia and was both barrister and solicitor, as the local Bar requires. He already held several responsible posts on official boards and was President Kaunda's personal legal adviser. I telephoned Edward and he came to lunch at the hotel. In the evening he drove me round Lusaka and took me home to supper, introducing me to his four boys and his Cornish wife Stella, of whom I was to see much more when Edward was later tried for treason.

Both Joe and Oliver thought that it was worth taking precautions about arriving in Johannesburg. To come by an international flight from one of the front-line states always aroused attention. To arrive from Rhodesia was the best course. I flew to Livingstone by Zambia Air, then went by bus to Victoria Falls. The Zambesi River is a mile wide at that point and the whole of it falls 350 feet. Its local name translates as "the smoke that thunders"; the head of water was so great and the spray so dense that the falls themselves were not visible. I remembered Freddie Bird's story of how he had travelled up from South Africa to see the falls, taking three weeks with ox wagons and bearers. He had changed for dinner every night and had his brandy and cigar. When he reached within five miles, he saw the spray above the falls, knew that was all that could be seen, turned around and went back. At Moorlands it had seemed an implausible story.

I crossed the bridge into Rhodesia on foot, then flew Rhodesia Air to Bulawayo and on to Johannesburg. The immigration officials took no notice of me. I had conjured up a superficial excuse for going that in South Africa might be thought respectable. It was devised by Noel Henwood, a black business friend, who gave me introductions to financiers in Durban. The idea was to carry a letter from him with proposals for some joint working between Durban and London. This mission was dutifully carried through, but I have no idea whether anything came of it. I suppose they realised that I knew nothing whatever about money.

I had been invited to stay with a young lawyer and his family, met on the first trip. He was much involved in liberal politics, and tennis. He and his wife were strongly opposed to the system under which they lived but took full advantage of it. There was the conventionally "necessary" staff at home, a gardener to keep the tennis court in order, and a driver to take the master to work. He was a busy barrister; not a tycoon in any sense, but had a standard of living well above his British peers. They were wonderful hosts and were typical of all South African hospitality, but it was all based on extreme exploitation. A busy family with the most liberal views and full hostility to the regime would find it virtually impossible to avoid conforming with the living standard of their neighbours.

South African whites have a higher standard of living than one would find, grade for grade, in any other country, and this had been built on the bodies of the blacks. Even many of the poorer whites have servants. A man with quite a routine job might have a big house, a swimming pool, and domestic staff. I drove with a "whites only" taxi driver – that is to say, his cab was on hire only to whites. He told me that he and his wife had three servants, and a chauffeur for their private car. When they went to their seaside cottage, the chauffeur would first take the family, then go back to fetch the staff. It seemed preposterous but was plainly true.

Johannesburg was a crowded black town by day, but after seven p.m. not a black was on the streets. From the surrounding dormitories came a tide of men and women by train from early morning. The measure for the timing of the arrival of trains was how soon the streets leading from the stations could disgorge their burden. There was a two-hour flood in the morning and an ebb at night. There were, of course, night workers: the printers, bakers, caretakers, et cetera, but they were at pains not to be seen out after hours lest it attract trouble from the police. How night workers reached the outgoing trains against the incoming morning tide was never clear. The trains could carry their numbers only by having them riding on every possible surface inside and out. Passengers rode on top and on the running boards and on the buffers between carriages. In the winter it was cold, and the buffers were always dangerous.

White South Africa was up-to-date, but the black areas were in a different age. It was the same with Lesotho, a landlocked independent part of the Commonwealth. I tried to phone Dr Makotoko of Leribe, my first contact. The first call was at eight-thirty a.m. After several reminders, our local exchange rang at ten-thirty to say that Leribe office had informed them that they were closing early. At eleven, they rang to say that Leribe wished to apologise; they had in fact been closed all day. Please try again tomorrow. This was most helpful, but I was meant to be there tomorrow. Maseru, Lesotho's main town, is the highest land in South Africa and is so far from where the wet south-west wind passes the coast that it arrives quite dried out. The land is all red-brown mountains joined by dust except in the rainy season, when deep ravines pour turgid red wine. Its wealth is wool and diamonds. As you fly in, there is no tree in sight, but one sees signs that after the wet season a good crop of Indian corn ripens quickly. I stopped at the first lawyer's office to ask about the system of land tenure. They told me it was tribal with a top-soil of Roman Dutch law. The lawyers were extremely courteous, as indeed was everyone in that land.

The only motion during the heat of the day was a countryman coming to town on his pony. He wore a red blanket and a broad, plain cone-shaped hat proof against rain, dust and sun. He jogged from the distant haze to where trees and fences began on the outskirts of town. Such men wore masks against the dust. There is a storm called the Free State Rainstorm that comes at the peak of the dry season. It begins with a black smudge no bigger than a man's fist on the southern horizon; it grows, both along the arch of the earth and over the heavens, until the sun is blotted out and the whole sky is covered by mighty black clouds. It looks like the father of all thunderstorms, but when it falls it covers the whole land with dry red-brown dust.

The rest of the landscape was an asphalt road running three-quarters of a mile down the centre of Maseru. There was an enormous Catholic cathedral at the bottom end of the road. It was not a no-account backwater of a place: it had a king, now Mashoeshoe II, a prime minister, and a parliament with opposition parties and elections. But it was a puppet government, giving considerable support to the policies of the republic that surrounded it. They had no choice. It was a surprise to learn that the longest established and most successful trader was Baron Fraser of Lonsdale, who controlled most general stores throughout Lesotho. He was blinded at the Somme but had gone on to become a barrister, being called to the Bar at the Inner Temple in 1932, as I was. As Sir Ian Fraser, he had been in our parliament for many years, including 1945-51, although on the Tory side.

Then it was on to Swaziland, which is the loveliest corner of South Africa: rich and lush, even approaching winter. A Johannesburg silk had arranged for a local senator to meet me at the airport. The senator took me home and even lent me his car. The problem was to find the ANC contacts without involving my host. I thought the barrister would be the easiest, but not at ten a.m. when courts should be just starting, so plumped for the doctor and found him finishing morning surgery. What was my ailment, where did I feel it? I began to explain that there was nothing wrong with me, but that I had heard of him and wished the pleasure of meeting him. He excused himself as there was a patient who was seriously ill and he had promised to visit immediately after surgery. Could I come after evening hours?

I tried the barrister. He was in chambers and it was easy enough to introduce myself as a visiting London barrister interested in the legal system. Then followed what to me was an entertaining skirmish. I had no guarantee that he was interested in my problem. What if he had changed sides and would at once call the police? Could the whole project be in jeopardy? I had thought this over in advance and planned certain cautious approaches. Swaziland was not a front-line state but an inland stepping-stone to the frontline, nearly 300 miles from South Africa's northern border. What measure was there of South African control or interference? Did he follow South African politics, local politics, the local parliament and city council? Was there any opposition and, if so, how active was it? I tried to give him a chance of showing where he stood, and of seeing what my position was, and shortly it was clear enough on both sides.

He was quite willing to take his book; he knew the other three contacts in Swaziland and made appointments with them in the most discreet manner. It was all arranged so successfully that I met each intended writer and co-conspirator and passed on the messages and materials. The contacts seemed well chosen and thoroughly reliable and their work has prospered. To a schoolteacher, I had to take £30 in rands. He was recruiting. I was to tell him that his reports had been received and he was to go on as at present. A professional man who had had £4,000 some time ago was to begin to use it now for appropriate purposes. The ANC wanted to know whether Radio Tanzania was readily heard at eight-thirty each second night on the 19 metre wave band. I found no one who listened to it at all and asked some to try.

One of the most important jobs I'd been given by Oliver Tambo was to set up a more sophisticated communications code and new contact addresses with Albertina Sisulu, who was still running her crowded clinic in Soweto. It was forbidden for any white man, or indeed for anyone else who didn't live there, to go into Soweto without official permission, so I asked Winnie how to get leave. She telephoned the Rand *Daily Mail* and asked for a young woman reporter, who came at once to Winnie's office with a car labelled Rand *Daily Mail* and a uniformed driver, and they took me to the clinic. It was equally illegal for the driver, the reporter and for Winnie in arranging it as it was for me, but I could not judge that Winnie had any bad motive in this. Perhaps it was bravado, or sheer over-enthusiasm rather than carelessness.

Albertina was a big, powerful woman, utterly calm and self-possessed, never hurrying. I felt completely at home with her from our first meeting, so there was no fencing and skirmishing to establish confidence. Winnie had been involved in a number of incidents that had led to her being generally regarded as unreliable, and it was clear that the suspicion of the leaders abroad was fully shared by those that remained behind. Albertina thought the ANC leadership already knew the details of Winnie's behaviour, but wanted to be sure. Winnie had belonged to three different groups. In turn, all the other members were arrested and detained, but she was let free to start again. The police seemed to want her to remain as a centre for a new group to form so that they, too, could be arrested. She was as the large blue light contraptions in some food shops that attract the flies and then kill them. The question arose: was she knowingly working with the police, or were the police, by planting spies among her people and not arresting her, making it seem to onlookers as though she were? This was the problem I had to try to settle for myself and for those abroad.

The intrigue between the different groups and the police was so complicated that I hadn't a chance of understanding it. Albertina told me about a young man in Winnie's current group who had, on his own admission, been sent in by the Special Branch. It was not clear to me whether he was working for the police against Albertina, or helping her against Winnie. A similar complication arose with John Mavuso and his group. He, apparently, was a most effective worker for the ANC and the police were really worried about him. They were determined to destroy his work, and were not sure to what extent Albertina was involved with it. It was Byzantine.

I approached Winnie avowedly to ask what she thought could be done towards getting her husband released from Robben Island. We discussed what legal process and appeals had already been tried, what more was open and whether he might at least be brought to a mainland prison, but she had very little hope. Winnie told me that she was working with a man who was an agent for various things such as tourist trips to the gold mines, the game reserve or more general travel, and buying and selling real estate. I visited her office several times and heard negotiations going through; she dealt with the callers in a skilled and authoritative manner. She appeared to earn good money and dressed lavishly. For example, in May 1968, it was fairly cold in Johannesburg and she wore what I thought were quite expensive furs. She was a very attractive young woman and when we went out to lunch, everybody in the restaurant looked at her.

The outcome was that I couldn't tell whether or not she was reliable. Was she devoted to the cause of defending her fellow blacks against the tyrannies of apartheid, or was she utterly reckless and simply having a good time? Was she adventurous rather than serious? I had no idea. I returned to London and, on reporting back to the ANC, left them no wiser than before. Now, thirty years later, the whole world is perhaps equally confused.

In September 1969, I received formal notification that the Minister of the Interior had in my case withdrawn the exemption enjoyed by citizens of the United Kingdom which permitted them to enter South Africa without an entry visa. If I wished to go again, I would not be allowed in without first obtaining a visa. The implication was that such permission would be denied. It was sent in the name of Mr Pelser, with whom I had sat and talked as if with a friend. I understand that Peter Hain had a similar letter. I wrote expressing surprise and wondering whether there might not have been some mistake. I had gone as a visitor to various parts of the country and greatly enjoyed all that I had seen. I had made friends there and hoped that I might have another visit. But no, there was no mistake. So I asked could I call at the South African Embassy in London to discuss it? I put on my tidy suit and not imperial but Commonwealth manner and went to plead with the relevant official. I reminded him that as members of the Commonwealth we had had much else than wealth in common; of our long sporting ties and, after all, I had seen Van Herden score a try against the All Blacks in 1925 at Wellington. The All Blacks won, but I didn't remind him of that. In short, what really was wrong?

He seemed to be convinced by my story and said that he would tell me frankly what had happened. Winnie Mandela had been arrested and one question she was asked was: "What were you doing seeing Platts-Mills last year?" Winnie was talking her way out of trouble and thought it sensible to blame something on what her government might regard as a left-wing trouble maker. She told them, "He asked me whether I would lead the ANC in armed revolt. Whether, if he gave me enough money, I could get the arms myself, or whether I would like him to import them for the ANC. How much money would I need?" I told him that we had just talked about her husband's imprisonment. He did not seem convinced and the order was not rescinded. I do not accept that Winnie said any such things but, if she had, it is not difficult to understand when one considers the particular hardships of her days in interrogation by the South African Special Branch. The sustained ill-treatment over many years may help account for the later tragedies associated with her behaviour.

My spirits went up or down as Nelson Mandela scored a point with the apartheid South African government or lost a handful of his men to Inkatha. From the time when the ANC were first established as the leading force calling for democracy in South Africa, Chief Mangosuthu Buthelezi stood against them. For this he was well paid by the government. His followers were given such concessions as freedom to bear arms in the form of the traditional Zulu weapons, and they were turned into a band of paid murderers. Many ANC supporters were killed, yet the police used their powers against the ANC and not against the Inkatha movement.

I rejoiced with most of the rest of the world when Nelson Mandela was released and was elected to power, and, as a member of the International Association of Democratic Lawyers (IADL), took the opportunity of visiting his country in April 1999. He sponsored our meeting, shook hands with all the delegates, and when I was introduced he embraced me.

CHAPTER THIRTY-TWO

Krays

CHARLES RICHARDSON ran a small empire of crime from the office of his scrap metal yard in Peckham, South London. He and his gang specialised in "firm" fraud. They set up firms which bought freely but modestly from a wide group of wholesalers on credit, sold at slight profit and paid immediately, as agreed. After a number of transactions, they placed giant orders with each supplier, sold off the resulting mountain of goods and disappeared. If someone owed Richardson money, he would be invited to a "discussion". Here he would be seized, stripped and tied up, then beaten or tortured. It was said that, as debt collector, Richardson presided at his own mock court and even wore a black robe. He awarded such penalties as beatings with wooden sticks or iron bars, the extraction of teeth and the stubbing out of cigarettes on bare flesh.

My client was Roy Hall, youngest of the gang. According to the prosecution, it was his job to attach crocodile clips to sensitive parts of the bare and unresisting body. The clips were on long leads to a black box and he turned the handle to generate an electric current. The victims were convulsed with electric shocks while Hall roared with laughter. It was rather a horrible case. Evidence about the "black box" played a major part in the trial, although the defendants denied its very existence. The police said that they had been unable to find the box itself, but the prosecution brought into court a black box with a handle and leads. It is usual that exhibits, once proved, are only kept in court if necessary. The police put their black box in as an exhibit and tried to leave it in different parts of the court where the jury could see it.

Several of the tortured men came into the witness box. Two of the accused turned Queen's Evidence, and one, the eldest, described going to Charles Richardson's office and nearly fainting at the scene. One of the debtors was naked and bound with ropes; his head was so swollen that his eyes had almost closed up, and blood was everywhere. One creditor of the Richardsons visited to collect his money and claimed to have received the full treatment, with the added refinement that Richardson took a knife and stabbed his left foot to the floor. I called an eminent Harley Street surgeon who proved that the scars on top of and on the sole of the foot could not have been made by a knife stuck right through. The bone structure was such that it could not have happened. "It would be approaching miraculous." The prosecution's answer was, "In your experience as a surgeon, have you found that sometimes miracles do happen?" – "Yes."

A de-registered doctor was available to tend the wounds so that victims would not be tempted to go to their own doctor or to a hospital. For a long period, threats of further attention were enough to prevent them from going to the police, but eventually the excesses of the torturers were such that injured men came into the hand of the authorities. One man had been scorched all over and used for stubbing out cigarettes. He had then suffered a fractured skull and wounds needing twenty stitches. The police found bloodstains on the scene and wanted a sample from him for comparison. The man was so horrified that he ran from the hospital, still in his pyjamas.

The police vetted the list of potential jurors, and defence counsel also raised objections. Between us, we went through 101 jurors before twelve were selected.

A fleet of motorcycles and vans of police Special Patrol Group men accompanied the Black Maria with the accused from prison each day. This was meant to suggest to the jury that the gang were so bad that at any moment an armed force might try to liberate them. Throughout the trial, the cavalcade with flashing blue lights and headlamps and screaming sirens was given free passage through London. Late in the trial, Mr Justice Lawton was told that the elderly mother of a juror had been visited by two men. They told her that they knew one son was on the jury and another had his own business, and warned that "there had better be a disagreement" on the jury. The judge then said that two earlier approaches to jurors had also been reported to him, and that before the trial began, there had been attempts to influence potential witnesses. (For the latter offence, five people were sent to jail with sentences from two years to six months.)

Mr Geoffrey Crispin, QC, who was leading for Charles Richardson, responded by expressing the "horror and amazement of all the defendants that it could be suggested that such behaviour could come from them". Were they not all in custody for months past? Such approaches, Crispin suggested, could have been made only by a person hostile to the accused, with the object of creating prejudice against them. It was most unexpected and interesting to have Mr Crispin in this trial. He was unchallenged leader of the divorce Bar – the Family Division – and since his pupil days, had not been in a criminal court. He was brought in for his notable skill as a cross-examiner. It was just at the time when the big, "fashionable" divorce, with names and publicity, was running out of steam and leading counsel were asking their clerks, "Can't you get me a decent brief in some big crime and let me try my hand at that?" In this way, several outstanding non-criminal counsel turned up at the Old Bailey. Usually they would not last more than one trial, finding that the work was not exciting or sufficiently well paid, or that their recollection of the law of evidence was a bit rusty.

It does not require a lively imagination to see how an accused can influence a juror by threatening him or his family, or by bribing him to find not guilty. Each member of the jury was escorted from home to court and back again in the evening, and had a telephone "hotline" direct to the police station for emergencies. I have been in several cases where it has been suggested that tentative approaches have been made to jurors and where they have asked for and received protection. A cautious juror and judge might be wise to interpret any casual conversation as suspicious. The warning given by judges to juries has been greatly sharpened in these last years. "Do not discuss the case with anyone outside your own number; not with members of your family; not at your club; over the weekend; and with fellow jurors only when you are gathered together as jurors in your own quarters."

In an earlier case at the Old Bailey, the prosecutor approached me as I entered the building. "I have done a dreadful thing. I picked up one of our jurors in Fleet Street. I was stationary beside the kerb and thought I recognised him as a press man who was regularly in our court and offered him a lift. On the way, I asked whether he was enjoying the case and what he thought were the chances." We were in our third week and no one wanted to start again. We gathered supporting counsel and saw the judge in his room. He was a conservative fellow and decided to let the case go on, but all were to keep a watchful eye for any sign of upset or reaction in the jury. There was none. I don't remember the verdict, but certainly there has not been added to the usual warning, "and don't allow counsel – particularly the prosecutor – to talk to you in private about the case".

The trial took place at the Old Bailey from April to June 1967 and went on for forty-two days, making it one of the longest trials in British criminal history. There were nine accused with twenty-two different charges ranging over robbery with violence, demanding with menaces, and grievous bodily harm. The judge summed up the case for four days and the jury was out for nine and a half hours. Charles Richardson was sentenced to twenty-five years, and the lesser members of his gang in proportion. My client Roy Hall was shown to have been under the domination of the Richardsons since he was a schoolboy and Mr Justice Lawton treated him as "in some ways, a tragic character". He was a pale, timid, round-faced little chap, so ineffectual that he could be put upon by the superior villain. He had, however, been barbarously perverted and the relish with which it appeared he had joined in the tortures was rewarded with a ten-year sentence.

Frankie Fraser was one of the defendants. In trying to pull out the teeth of a victim with ordinary pliers, Fraser succeeded only in tearing out part of the gums. He was the gang's hard man and, it was said, the most feared criminal in London. In 1956, he had joined in a razor attack on Jack Spot, self-proclaimed Head of the London Underworld, which left Spot with 180 stitches in his face. He was so erratic and extreme that he was known as "Mad Frankie". The mere suggestion of reputable behaviour was anathema to him, so that in 1959 he sued for libel after a newspaper reported that he had co-operated with police enquiries. I later appeared for Fraser when he was brought to London for an Old Bailey trial on a charge of assaulting a prison officer. Such cases are normally dealt with by the governor or by the prison visitors. This was the only such case I have known being brought to London. It was said that Fraser's reputation was such that they would not dare try him in the prison, though he seemed an ordinary enough fellow. He gave every expression of enjoying his trip to London, and arranged for two visitors to come to see him. I had tea with him in his cell. At the time, I was well-known to the Old Bailey cell keepers because I would visit my client every day.

In the Richardson case, the sentences were widely regarded as on the high side. Many a murderer gets life but ends up serving less than ten years. Torture was new to the English scene, as was sustained gang activity, and the aim was to stamp out both. It was also seen as a trial run for the Kray twins, who were more violent and more powerful. The Kray gang also ran Long Firm frauds, but were perhaps better known for offering very expensive "protection" for highly profitable businesses such as night clubs. The territories of the two gangs were divided by the Thames. I had never heard of Ronnie and Reggie Kray as criminals until the brief was delivered, although my wife knew all about them from the newspapers. I had, however, had a much earlier experience with them through Bob Boothby and Tom Driberg. In the early 'sixties, I was approached by a man well placed in the Conservative Party, and a supporter of Sir Winston Churchill. He knew that I had done several rather notorious fraud trials, and he also knew of my personal association with Churchill. I was not expected to respond to the request he would make through any regard for the Conservative Party, but he hoped that I still had some respect for Churchill's reputation; both were now threatened.

Lord Boothby was the nearest thing to a lefty in the Conservatives. He was willing to do something against Franco in the Spanish Civil War, provided it were on an unobtrusive scale, and was inclined to be liberal on social issues. But he was best known as a long-standing ally of Churchill. I was told that men named "The Krays" were trying to make use of Bob in fund-raising and similar charitable activities in the West End. Others, well-known and glamorous, were already involved. Some show-business people are drawn to notorious characters by the hint of danger and the excitement of risk. With Boothby, there was a little of this, for he was something of a showman and tended to make headlines for himself. For the twins, there was the reciprocal urge for the publicity that he could give. I was told that they were constantly pressing him to attend. It was most undesirable, but what could be done?

Someone must go and talk to the Krays in their own language. (By that, of course, I mean strong journalese, rather than anything else.) Tom Driberg, long experienced with Lord Beaverbrook and later with Reynold's *News on Sunday*, seemed just the person to go and urge the Krays to lay off Bob. He did and succeeded, but found himself caught in the same net. He took Bob's place. For some years, Tom was on my conscience. It was a great comfort to learn, as I did later, that he had been well in with the Krays before I mentioned Bob to him. For the twins, it was an advantage to have one or two allies in parliament. Once, when Ronnie was in custody on remand and couldn't get bail, Bob came to his aid by raising the subject in parliament.

The Krays were arrested in May 1968. Their trial, which was heard by Mr Justice Melford Stevenson and a jury at the Old Bailey, began the following January and ran for thirty-eight days, setting a record for the longest murder trial in British history. The twins, their brother Charlie and eight other defendants were charged with various offences, but mainly for the murder of two men, Cornell and McVitie. The allegation was that, in March 1966, Ronnie Kray killed George Cornell in the bar of an East End pub. A witness would testify that Ronnie had shot Cornell in the forehead at point-blank range, then walked out. Jack "the Hat" McVitie was said to have been stabbed to death by Reggie Kray in a basement flat in Stoke Newington seven months later. The body was never found. McVitie had gone about in the clubs that were "protected" by the Krays, waving a gun and shouting abuse of the twins. He claimed that he was better than the Krays and would kill them.

The point about joining cases in the same trial is that they should be offences allegedly committed by the same person and with a common system. Here the police joined two murders. There was no obvious system in the killings and no common feature in the two victims other than that they were gangsters. The prosecution founded themselves on one phrase – "I've done mine, you do yours" – as providing the link. With these words, Ronnie was said to have goaded Reggie into killing McVitie. I protested that it was a misjoinder. It was quite understandable that the prosecutor should offer to try two separate murders at once, for both were weak and this was his best chance of obtaining convictions. In such a trial, it is inevitable that prejudice will spill over from one allegation to the other. It was wrong and Melford should have resisted it.

Melford wanted the eleven prisoners each to have a number hanging round his neck so that we could identify them. I opposed this on the ground that it was bad enough to be a prisoner without the added indignity of being numbered like cattle at market. I told Melford that I had known many factories go on strike for less than that. The next morning the men appeared in the dock with numbers round their necks. As soon as the judge was settled, Ronnie took his number off with a flourish and threw it down. The others followed his lead except for Tony Barry, who was very much the odd one out. He was not a member of the Firm but a night-club owner. The prosecution was obviously uncertain as to whether or not he should even be in the dock. His counsel, Barry Hudson, played on this to the full. When Melford ordered the prisoners to be taken down and have their labels replaced, Barry Hudson quickly drew his attention: ˜"My client has his number on, my lord. May he remain?" "Yes, of course he can!"

In the cells a prison officer tried to put a number on Ronnie, who threatened to kill him. Ronnie sent a written note to the judge saying, "Get stuffed." The air was becoming a bit charged and it seemed the best remedy was to make a joke of it all. There were twice as many counsel as accused and I suggested that we should be numbered so that the accused and witnesses could identify us; Melford should be No 1. No one was numbered. I made a show of mock deference and said I had been asked by one of the accused, on behalf of than all, to say how very much they appreciated the dispensation the court had granted. Melford joined in the pretence and said, "That is a great relief to me."

As in the Richardson case, the police used the device of the flamboyant cavalcade carrying prisoners to court to build up fear. They vetted the jury to get one likely to be on the side of the prosecution and gave the jurors protection against imaginary interference or threats of bribery or violence. The conduct of the police was aimed at influencing the jury rather than protecting them and it was unfair to press upon jurors that they were in personal danger. So determined were the prosecution to bring the maximum prejudice that they caused John Dickson, who was charged only in connection with a third alleged murder, to be brought before Melford in our courtroom for sentencing at the end of the first day. He pleaded guilty to aiding and abetting the escape of Frank "the Mad Axeman" Mitchell from Dartmoor by harbouring him. All this was immediately published in the papers, making it clear that the Krays would face a third murder charge in due course. When the jurors for the Cornell and McVitie murders had been selected, I expected Melford to instruct them not to take any notice of what they might have read in yesterday's papers, thus sending them scurrying to find out what it was. He spared us that excess.

The murder of George Cornell was dealt with first. He was an East-Ender but had given his services to the Richardsons. During their trial, his name often came up and he appeared to be a most violent criminal. Cornell was drinking in the Blind Beggar, one of the Krays' home pubs, when he was shot with a pistol. The scene of the killing became known as the Luger and Lime Bar. All the neighbourhood knew that Ronnie had done it to repay the killing of Richard Hart, one of the Krays' men, who was shot the night before in Catford. Cornell was also guilty of vulgar abuse, for he had called Ronnie a "fat poof", which Ronnie thought was inaccurate on at least one count.

Ronnie and Reggie were identical twins so that one might expect there to be some marked interchange of behaviour and influences. Before the trial started, all the information we had from family and solicitors was that Ronnie was the boss. It may be that there was a defence open to Reggie on the lines that Ronnie, the dominant one, was mentally ill, and that anything Reggie did was under duress. Paul Wrightson and I, with our juniors and solicitors, had a consultation: Should Paul run this defence? We could get psychiatrists to examine the twins, ask the prosecution to hold their own enquiry, and pool the results. I believe the decision was made by Reggie, namely that they were equally responsible and that he would not allow any defence that put more blame on his twin. It was agreed to accept Reggie's decision. Little was then known about the psychological relationship between identical twins. If we had had the benefit of recent research, we might have pressed rather harder.

I went with our defence team to see the Blind Beggar. We already had a statement of the evidence that Mrs X, the barmaid, would give, and we got someone to stand in her alleged position behind the bar while others played the killer and the victim. It all depended on what she saw, and that was determined by precisely where she stood. I suggested that judge and jury should inspect the pub before hearing Mrs X. Melford pointed out that the whole court would then have to attend. If the Krays were taken back to the East End, might not their supporters attempt a rescue? He asked whether the prisoners would agree not to go to the inspection, and counsel were despatched down to the cells to find out. One barrister came back to ask the judge a question, but Melford ruled that he could not answer except in the presence of all the accused and their counsel. All had to be fetched back into court, the question was read out and answered, and we retired again. We then tried to exchange information in the cell corridors, but this only led to confusion. Each client wanted to know what the others thought, so again back into court. A further question was raised with the same result, and by lunch-time little progress had been made. Could we continue these discussions over the lunch break, "the short adjournment"? Prison regulations prevail downstairs and nothing is allowed to disturb the prisoners' lunch. The judge ruled no inspection of the pub.

The barmaid was so frightened that at the inquest she denied having seen a thing. Now Mrs X gripped the edge of her witness box as if looking for any support she could get. With her denial on oath, and her failure to pick Ronnie at an identification parade, I was bound to make the most of her present clear recollection of the whole scene and kept at her with some vigour. How did she account for this plain contradiction? Was not the first statement the truth? Had she often had the experience of a simple story on one day and a different story on the next? On and on it went. The police had persuaded Mrs X to give up her job at the Blind Beggar and take her family to a house in a remote part of the country and start a new life. We had heard that she was eventually given the house. Of course, we wanted to know about her family and about the conditions of the gift. Did she refuse to tell her story until she had inspected the house? We made the best possible use of the suggestion that this was the price of her evidence, but the greater likelihood was that Mrs X could dare to tell the truth only when she felt secure.

With the exception of Mrs X and a very few others, the main witnesses for the prosecution were themselves such villains that if the alleged murders had been tried separately there would have been a good chance of getting the Krays acquitted. Normally, when a prosecutor is going to rely on such witnesses as these to establish his case, he tells the jury in advance what sort of fellows they are. Here he did not do so. One explanation is that there was little to choose between the Krays and their principal accusers, many of whom should have stood in the dock. Another is that, since the full history of each witness was known to the defence, it was for us to decide the extent to which we wanted that information disclosed to the jury. As a rule, it helps the defence that their traducers are people of bad character. However, if there are many of them, all bad and all acquaintances of the defendants, then the balance turns; the jury think the defendants, too, must be bad and so will find them guilty of anything that is alleged.

The joining of the Cornell and McVitie cases brought so many villains together, and all hostile, that the balance surely turned. By the end of the Mitchell trial, twenty-eight acknowledged criminals had been called as witnesses for the Crown.

John ("Scotch Jack") Dickson was a driver for the Krays and had driven Ronnie to the Blind Beggar for the shooting of Cornell. Accordingly, he might have been treated as an accessory to the first murder. Instead, he was a prosecution witness. It was to prepare him for this role that the trial was interrupted in its first day so that he could plead guilty to harbouring Mitchell and be sentenced and effectively discharged. Now his evidence lasted two days and Melford required the prosecution to treat him as a hostile witness, saying, "You cannot believe a word that this unsavoury character has said." This meant that the prosecution had to elicit from Dickson his own bad character and acknowledge it as part of their case.

The star witness to the McVitie killing was Ronnie Hart. He was a big, handsome chap, an ex-sailor, who liked the excitement of being seen about with his cousins, the Krays. He was in the box three days, a good part of which was spent in exploring his own part in their affairs. Hart provided the only evidence that could justify linking the Cornell and McVitie cases. It was his story that Ronnie had incited Reggie to kill: "I've done mine, you do yours." This was exactly what the prosecution needed. The difficulty with this story was that, according to the defendants, Hart was indeed there; he was holding McVitie in a tight grip, urging, "Go on, Reg, do him!" Hart now attributed to Ronnie Kray the very words that he had used himself. When challenged that his evidence was dishonest and given to save his own skin, Hart gave the particularly sanctimonious reply: "Not to save my skin, but because I thought it right." After his cousins had been locked away, he admitted to the newspapers that he had lied in the Old Bailey. It was reported that his sense of shame led him to make several attempts at suicide.

Sir Lionel Thompson appeared as counsel for Connie Whitehead, accused of helping to dispose of McVitie's corpse. Sir Lionel is the 5th Baronet and had a distinguished war record in the RAF and the Royal Navy. Melford was plainly a little jealous but felt that, spurred on by Sir Lionel's elegant suits and display of gold, he could take the risk of making fun of him. Melford descended to that crudest and most offensive of all forms of humour, making jokes about his name. "Oh, Mr Thomas. Yes, it's your turn now. What do you want to say?" Melford had already showed his willingness to be offensive at our expense. The other leaders expected me to try and keep him in some sort of order. There were whispered instructions: "Tell Melford to behave himself. Don't let him get away with it." Some of the whispers were strong enough to reach the judge and he braced himself for the assault. I said, "My Lord, at the Bar we know, and address, my Learned Friend as Sir Lionel." Then – "Sir Thompson, is it? Well, Sir Thompson, what have you to say?" I had to step in again. "No, my Lord, it is not anything but Sir Lionel, and the Bar would appreciate it if you would adopt the usual form of address." Melford sulked and abandoned any form of address to him.

Leonard "Nipper" Read, the police inspector chiefly responsible for bringing the Krays to trial, gave evidence in court. The twins saw the trials as a set-up, and as the result of an order from on high to "get the Krays". The police had failed so often that they would now resort to any device to defeat them and, according to Ronnie, Mr Read had raised it to the status of a personal vendetta. In 1965, the twins were tried for demanding money with menaces from the Hideaway Club in Soho. They held a party to celebrate their acquittal. Mr Read stood outside the club (renamed the El Morocco) to see who was on the guest list and someone invited him in. He went, was introduced to the Krays and allegedly had a drink with them. I was able to put to Mr Read in cross-examination (meaning I had firm information) that before leaving the club he had proposed a toast, "To the next time". This was the only part he denied. To the Krays, it was plainly a threat.

An accused does not have to give evidence in his trial. If he refrains, however, he does so at his peril for the judge may invite the jury to infer from his silence that he has something to hide. The same inference may be drawn from silence at the police station when first arrested. This is a recent change. The rule was that no one could comment on his silence unless the defence made some reference to his position that "let in" the mention of his absence from the witness box. There is a well-known line of speech by defence counsel based on Lord Devlin, when he was counsel at the Old Bailey, saying that the law requires no man to answer a charge of wrong-doing made against him: "Let him have his say, let him do his worst. I will bide my time. If he makes a case against me, I will take advice and consider whether I, too, will go into the witness box or whether I should ignore him." In my opening speech for the defence I said to the jury, "The defendant will tell you." Melford was delighted with this because it committed me to putting Ronnie into the witness box. Melford exclaimed to the jury, "Do you hear that, members of the jury? Learned counsel has given you the assurance that his client Ronald Kray will be going into the witness box as his first witness. Now that will be interesting. He will give us his own personal explanation of all these events." Or words to that purpose.

There followed a protracted argument as to whether my words meant what the judge said. "They were spoken in an unguarded moment." "Counsel is deemed not to have an unguarded tongue," et cetera. The jury was spared this debate. At a later stage in the discussion, the judge suggested that I should take five minutes to ask my client whether he really wished to give evidence. Ronnie then shouted, "Sir, I will go in the box," and the matter was settled. I called Ronnie and took him through his story. He insisted that he hadn't shot George Cornell and gave various examples of friendly acts towards Cornell and his family. Shortly before the killing, Ronnie had tried to get him a job and had sent chocolates to his ailing son in hospital. (This may seem improbable but I saw during the trial several acts of generosity from Ronnie.) Neither he nor Reggie had taken any part in the killing of McVitie. Ronnie Hart was the killer and the police were protecting him by using him as one of their main witnesses.

For his first witness Ronnie wished to call Frankie Fraser. Fraser was then serving fifteen years for his exploits with the Richardson gang and knew nothing of the facts of our present case. He was wanted as a character witness to prove Ronnie's high standing. I urged that we should not call him at all for any purpose. Ronnie might see Fraser as an excellent person – and he might even be one – but coming from jail and with his present convictions, the jury could not possibly be expected to believe him. It led to a long argument. I was persuaded that it was probably the last decision on such a topic that Ronnie would ever take and could not make the slightest difference to the outcome of his trial. I did not want to go so far as refusing to call the witness or of withdrawing from the trial, and Fraser was called. He told the court that Ronnie was a good bloke. The prosecution then put to Fraser with meticulous care the long tale of his own previous convictions, in which it was disclosed that he had twice been certified as insane. Upon leaving the witness box and courtroom, he waved and yelled, "Good luck," but it would have taken a powerful streak of luck to make up for the harm that he had done.

Ronnie was found guilty of shooting Cornell, and Reggie of aiding and abetting him. Reggie was found guilty of stabbing McVitie, with Ronnie abetting. Melford awarded them each a life sentence and recommended that they should serve a minimum of thirty years. Freddie Foreman and Charlie Kray each got ten years for helping to dispose of the body of McVitie. Everyone liked Charlie, the twins' elder brother, who cared for them but found it all a bit beyond him. After the trial, Ronnie wished Ivan Lawrence, my junior, the best of luck in his attempt to get into parliament. This was in the expressed hope that Ivan would go on to become home secretary and give them an early release. Ivan is now a QC and an MP. He sketched all those involved in the trial and gave me a copy of the composite picture of forty-four caricatures, the two best being the grotesque one of himself, and the majestic Melford.

Another especial souvenir is one of Ronnie's oil paintings of a country cottage, whether seen in a dream or nightmare, which he very kindly gave me. It is painted in the harshest colours which I call Kray colours, as in Burnt Kray, Earth Kray or Ultra Kray. The lawyer has no real inducement to impress the client. It doesn't matter what he thinks of the lawyer, so long as he trusts him. But the client, in such a desperate situation, is generally on his best behaviour. He wants the lawyers to work at their hardest and thinks that this can only be achieved if they have been favourably impressed. Most clients are polite and well behaved with their lawyers. The Krays did not differ from other clients in a similar position, but went perhaps beyond them in being unusually considerate.

During the trial, I became quite closely acquainted with Ronnie. In his personal affairs, he seemed most thoughtful and gentle, and he was full of warm feelings for anyone who gave him any help. To a lady who offered to give evidence in our favour on a minor point, "Please send a telegram saying how grateful I am." "A lady down the road" was very kind to his mother. "Please send her a bunch of violets from me." There were many occasions for showing appreciation as people came forward, offering to testify in his favour on one point or another. Ronnie responded in the most generous fashion and always with scrupulous attention to the

March 1969: the leading actors in the Kray Trial drawn by Ivan Lawrence QC.

detail as, "please put some ribbon round the chocolates", and attention to payment.

I did not really come to know Reggie at the time of the trial, but had every reason to think that he had the same basic character, for the influence of their mother Violet was both strong and benign. During the last two years before his death, I saw Reggie on four occasions at Waylands Prison near Thetford in Norfolk. He had done thirty-two years in jail; beyond even the term recommended by the malign Melford. I have several times written to the prison department and to the MP for that part of Norfolk in which is the jail and in which lived Mr Kray and his wife. No answer from either. Manners in the neighbourhood of Westminster are not what they used to be. However, Reggie, having been diagnosed with cancer, spent the last few months of his life in hospital rather than prison. If that was the work of the home secretary or of his MP and not simply a means of transferring the costs of his care to the NHS then perhaps their manners can be overlooked.

Ronnie's warm response was not always appreciated. A woman gave evidence that the twins had often drunk in her East End pub. They had always behaved very well, had paid for their drinks and treated her with courtesy and respect. Apart from this, she had no contact with them. In view of the overwhelmingly hostile stories coming from the Old Bailey, she had agreed to come to court, as she put it, "to do my duty in seeing that they had a fair trial". Ronnie at once wrote thanking her, and on the same day came a phone call from Violet Kray, inviting her to come to tea and to accept some flowers. The witness was upset by this: how would it look to the police "if I were seen coming from their home with a bouquet"? The response to Mrs Kray's invitation was a special delivery letter saying please, please never contact me again. She also wrote to me and explained that her evidence had caused a terrible family row. She had not known at the time that her niece's husband was a personal friend of Inspector Read. I reported this sad tale to Ronnie, who was deeply upset. He asked me to apologise at once and to say how much he regretted having been the cause of such unpleasantness at home.

In some quarters, Nipper Read was dubbed "a good party man". He threw a party for the jurors and for the policemen and women who had been their guards and escorts to and from court. This was by way of thanking them for their co-operation in bringing about the convictions.

Had the twins been acquitted, and had they invited the judge and jurors to a celebration party with them, it would have been equally seemly an event. I understand that the jurors had an excellent dinner with the police. A bouquet from Mrs Kray to a defence witness would have been a trifling thing by comparison.

The second Kray murder trial, for the death of Frank "the Mad Axeman" Mitchell, came before Fred Lawton at the Old Bailey. This was six weeks after the Cornell and McVitie case. Lawton began by asking how the defence proposed to overcome the problem that every juror must know of the two existing convictions. I suggested we try to find a jury that had never heard of the Krays and he agreed to assist in every sensible means to that end. A jury was empanelled in the usual way but not sworn. Then each juror was shown a large sheet of press headlines from the previous trial and asked whether he knew what those headlines were about. If the answer was "of course, the murder trial", then he was at once discharged.

Some observers thought that the decision to allow cross-examination of each potential juror was without precedent bit it was well within the rules. Challenge "for cause" has always been allowed, although you may not engage in a fishing expedition to see whether there is cause for objection. The practice is, I think, to tell the judge your ground for objection and to obtain consent to ask about it, as, "I believe Mr A to be a cousin of the main prosecution witness." – "Very well. Ask him about that." The selection process gave the assurance that our jurors were people who were normally so engrossed with their own affairs that they didn't notice what was going on in the world about them, or were so stupid that they didn't understand or remember very much at all.

Much of the evidence showed that Ronnie was friendly towards Frank Mitchell and solicitous for his welfare. The Krays had arranged for him the most extraordinary life on Dartmoor. He went out on a working party with his fellow convicts but would not be called on for any work. He would spend the morning walking or lying in the sun or drinking at a pub. He made friends with Dartmoor ponies and sometimes rode them bareback about the moor. The twins provided him with plenty of money and occasionally he took a taxi into town to do some shopping for himself and other prisoners. After a good lunch and a snooze, he would be ready to go back to Princetown. It was the strangest prison regime that had ever been.

The main prosecution witness was Albert Donaghue, Mitchell's bodyguard or "minder". Donaghue was a big, strong fellow but had a slight limp, which was attributed to an argument settled by a bullet. Donaghue had himself been charged with the murder. It was only shortly before the start of the second trial that the prosecution dropped the charge and decided to use him as a witness. He admitted "minding" Mitchell and so far as the police were concerned, he was the last person to see Mitchell alive. According to their other witnesses, Donaghue came to the flat and took Mitchell out to the van. Shots were heard, and neither Mitchell nor his corpse were ever seen again. The defence said Donaghue was the killer, but he put the blame on Freddie Foreman and one Alf Gerard, allegedly hired by Reggie.

The twins had sent a car to bring Mitchell to London from Dartmoor, partly through sympathy for him and partly for reasons of prestige to show that they could do anything. The prosecution claimed that they had got rid of Mitchell after ten days as an expensive and demanding nuisance. There really was no evidence that the Krays had murdered Mitchell and, in this particular case, I genuinely believed them to be innocent. Fred Lawton ruled that there was no sufficient case against Ronnie and Charlie Kray, and left the jury the simple issue – did they believe Donaghue? They did not. Reggie was acquitted of having arranged Mitchell's murder and was convicted only of conspiring to break Mitchell out of Dartmoor.

The lawyer does not have to believe in the innocence of his or her client. Indeed, the lawyer should be indifferent to that issue and must try to remain quite neutral. If the client declares to you that he is guilty, you can't put him in the witness box to swear he is innocent. But he may still plead not guilty and you can still get him off. The rules of behaviour provide amply for this. The jury doesn't know of the man's admission to his own lawyer and the prosecutor may fail to prove his case. He may miss an essential point, although this is rare, or the evidence may be lacking.

During the first trial, in reply to submissions or questions from the defence, Melford Stevenson used words to the effect that the case would certainly go to a higher court where the defence submission could be dealt with. He meant that we were certain to be convicted. He later said that there were only two correct statements made by the twins throughout the trial. These were: that he was hopelessly prejudiced against them, and that the prosecutor was a "fat slob". The latter was rather unkind as the prosecutor presented a long and difficult case with exemplary fairness and was as well turned out as a barrister should be. Melford displayed the degree of venom that would be expected from any high court judge faced with the Kray twins. Lawton behaved with scrupulous fairness and that, in my opinion, was the main reason for the acquittal in the Mitchell case. My summary of the first Kray trial is that if Melford had not insisted on trying two murders at the same time, both Ronnie and Reggie might well have got off.

We took the case to the Court of Appeal on the point of improper joinder of two different murders. They produced the answer that "public interest" required the connection. Ivan Lawrence then took the case to the House of Lords. He summed up the argument by saying that what the Court of Appeal must have meant by "public interest" was "Everyone knows that the men are guilty and it is in the public interest that they be found so; and how can that be made more certain than by a joint trial of the two murders". Lord Donovan answered by gesture and demeanour, although not in words, "Lawrence, my boy, you've hit the nail right on the head!" Lord Diplock greeted the argument by going off to sleep.

The most recent explanation that went about at the Bar of the sharp and superficially rather bitter relations between Melford and me was that at Eton I was his fag and he beat me unreasonably because I burned his toast and didn't butter it hot. The main trouble with this story is that Melford never got nearer to Eton than Dulwich in South East London, and I was never nearer during school years than the Mungatukituki Grammar. This is a non-existent Maori name used by me for any place of rare delight such as Nelson College. Melford was, in fact, very bright. He delighted in making quick rejoinders to any unusual situation in court, and enjoyed them even more when they were at the expense of his opponent (at the Bar) or later of the parties or the counsel appearing before him. He tried to present a forbidding or even fierce appearance and reputation. It was consistent with this that he adopted the name Truncheons for his house at Winchelsea.

He was a most comfortable person to get on with. In the late 1950s, I was yet a junior and most nights would find me working at chambers. On one such occasion, I crossed the quadrangle as Benchers emerged from their door after dinner and came upon Melford leaning on the arm of Lloyd Jones, that most charming and gentle of Welsh judges. We passed close

"Would you clarify that last point again, you fat slob!"

enough for Melford to tap my brief case and say, "I'll bet there's vodka in there!" I was able to tap his stomach and to retort, "And gin in there!" With such boyish pleasantries was begun my closer acquaintance with Melford. My last appearance before him was at Chelmsford, where the seats were banked up as in a university lecture theatre. I appeared to be asleep after lunch and Stephen Walsh, my junior, was sitting behind and slightly above. Stephen looked down at me and up at Melford, then raised his eyebrows as though saying, "Shall I wake up the old stupid?" Melford pursed his lips, frowned and shook his head ever so slightly as though saying "Don't wake him, for heaven's sake. He's much less trouble asleep." I was quite conscious of it all, through partly closed eyes.

CHAPTER THIRTY-THREE

Kodak and Return to the Labour Party

CONWAY AND Roberts v Kodak was a strange case that had its origins in a dispute over workers' rights. Kodak, subsidiary of the US parent company Eastman-Kodak, was in principle opposed to the union movement and permitted only an in-house union, their Workers' Representative Council. Godfrey Conway and Ken Roberts had been employed by Kodak, respectively for seventeen and twenty-three years, in processes connected with the making of photographic films. The men were staunch union activists and they enrolled over fifteen per cent of the workers in their factory in the appropriate TUC-affiliated body. This was the Association of Cinematograph, Television and Allied Technicians, of which Roberts had served as vice-president. As might be expected, their efforts attracted considerable animosity from the management.

The genuine trade union organised international gatherings such as film festivals and visits to foreign factories. On one such visit in East Germany, Conway went to an Agfa factory and saw there an unusual device in the manufacture of films. He reported it to the management of Kodak and received an award of £100 for introducing a new idea. The management tried to persuade him to go again to the same factory for further observations but he disliked the idea of industrial espionage and declined their offer. Kodak then hired a German named Dr Soupert to try to persuade the two men to join in such activity. Soupert displayed great ingenuity but failed to obtain their co-operation. He then accused the men of having sold secrets of Kodak production methods such as details of emulsions, wetting agents and so forth to the East German film industry in return for payment largely in German marks. Conway and Roberts were summarily dismissed in December 1964 for alleged misconduct, on the grounds that they were about to be arrested for conspiring to injure the interests of their employer.

At the Central Criminal Court in February 1965, they were prosecuted on charges under the Prevention of Corruption Act 1906. Two Kodak representatives and two men from British intelligence attended court. Soupert claimed to have given the defendants a questionnaire on Kodak's work. The answers had come back to him on a roll of film, but no one could produce the film in question. Soupert claimed that he had come to England for a meeting on a particular date and "proved" this by showing the appropriate passport stamp. MI5 agents, introduced to the court as Mr A and Mr B, backed up his story. We were told of a number of secret meetings where the defendants had handed Soupert parcels. I have been in several spying cases but have not heard of one where the authorities did not at some point pounce and arrest the accused red-handed. The defendants' story was that Soupert, using the alias Dr Stevens, had promised handsome rewards if Conway and Roberts could procure East German secrets for the Belgian firm he claimed to represent.

After Soupert had given evidence, he was recalled to the witness stand where he was obliged to admit having lied to the court. The passport stamp was a forgery, arranged for him by the British secret services. When his evidence had been discredited on all major points, the prosecution conceded that Soupert was, in fact, a commercial spy. Jeremy Hutchinson, QC, for the defendants, produced in court a copy of a letter drawn up by Kodak's solicitors and setting out the terms of a contract which guaranteed Soupert £5,080 for testifying against the defendants, with a bonus for securing a conviction. The Kodak management insisted that the contract had been made with the full agreement of the Director of Public Prosecutions.

Soupert worked for the East German security service but had allegedly been "turned" by the Belgian Sûreté to work as a double agent. Fearful that a court appearance in England would, at the very least, cost him his government pension, he had persuaded Kodak to pay compensation for the loss of pension rights. If the defendants were convicted, he meant to sell his story to the British newspapers. Neither defendant gave evidence in court for the judge ruled that there was no case to answer. The jury brought back verdicts of not guilty on all counts. Soupert was not charged for perjury and was allowed to leave the country. The widespread belief that this case had been brought with official connivance and in furtherance of Kodak's anti-union policy was not discouraged by their dismissal of the chairman of their own trade union branch for his temerity in having attended court on the last day of the trial.

The Kodak management informed the local employment exchange of the reasons for dismissing Conway and Roberts, which meant that they were denied unemployment benefit. Although highly skilled, they had no real chance of working again at their respective trades. Leaving aside the damaging effect of a prosecution for industrial espionage, the film business is fiercely competitive and it is not the practice to take on employees who have left rival firms. Mr Ronald Shulman, their junior counsel, advised Conway and Roberts to issue a civil writ claiming damages for wrongful dismissal and this was done immediately before the start of the criminal trial at the Old Bailey. I did not see anything of the case until some years later, and before I came into it there were several amendments. The statement of claims was altered and the amount of damages claimed was greatly increased. They now asked for their wages to date, pension rights and for the appropriate sum in termination or redundancy pay.

Kodak launched a counterclaim for damages. Apart from the addition of an accusation against Roberts for conversion (theft) of goods, including two terylene work hats, and packets of used film-paper and a broken and rusty torch taken with the approval of his immediate superior, Kodak adopted exactly the allegation made against Conway and Roberts in their Old Bailey trial. There were set out page after page of details of secrets alleged to have been stolen from Kodak and delivered to Soupert and his associates for delivery to East Germany. Although Soupert and the MI5 men had failed to satisfy the Old Bailey jury, they were to be wheeled out again as witnesses in the civil courts. Looking back, I am not sure why Conway and Roberts did not sue the management of Kodak for malicious prosecution. The conduct of Kodak in adopting all the evidence of Soupert as the basis of their defence, as well as for their counter-claim for damages, seemed a pretty strong indication that they were behind the abortive prosecution.

Our case was decided by the Court of Appeal in May 1969 with Lord Justice Harold Otto Danckwerts presiding. Dancky went to Balliol in 1906. From the time he reached the Court of Appeal in 1961, he thought that he should be elected an honorary fellow of the college and he let that be known, using every channel that was open to him. With any other college, the Court of Appeal would have been good enough. With some others, it was enough to fly over a mountain, or run a mile or marry a certain heiress. When Christopher Hill became Master of Balliol, the pressure increased. Danckwerts thought that the new master was so much junior to his predecessors that he might very well yield and persuade the fellows to agree. I was already quite closely acquainted with Christopher and when we met at the Usborne Dinner (a November occasion arranged in London by Tommy Usborne for Balliol men of his time) Christopher set me the task of going to Danckwerts and explaining how greatly the college loved him, how his loyalty was a shining emblem for all to regard, but although the college was indebted to him to an inestimable degree, it was not proposed that he should be a fellow.

"When you are promoted to the House of Lords, it will be considered; the college expects that to happen at any time." The last point in the argument was my own addition but was put with Christopher Hill's consent. It was supported by the fact that Dancky could have had no idea as to how close I stood to the Lord Chancellor of the day, or to recent Attorneys General or Home Secretaries. In 1978, Danckwerts died and, on Christopher's instructions, I attended his funeral and then a memorial service in Lincoln's Inn, representing Balliol. There followed a little speech to the widow about the mutual love between Dancky and the college, and this time an assurance that there would be no portrait in Balliol Hall.

At the Court of Appeal, we asked for trial by jury. This was not permitted. Their lordships dismissed our claim as bogus; they saw it as "vexatious, oppressive and an abuse of the process of the Court", brought not for justice but simply to harass Kodak. Lord Justice Fenton Atkinson condemned Conway and Roberts for idleness claiming that they had "apparently been content to remain unemployed, sending their wives out to work to earn some money, while still maintaining or maybe being maintained in an outward appearance of reasonable affluence". I had not met my junior counsel before – he turned up in the civil claim and it was unfortunate that about this time Mr Shulman seemed to have found himself in possession of a large sum of another person's money. He left England for Brazil and never returned. I lacked his assistance in explaining his pleadings to their lordships and it caused me no end of trouble. Conway and Roberts lodged libel suits against those unwise enough to repeat the allegations of industrial espionage and, in time, received "substantial" payments for damages from the editors of several right-wing newspapers, the author of a book on spying and a Tory MP. They had all preferred to believe a self-confessed liar from the East German Secret police rather than two Englishmen of the "wrong" class.

German politics were my next big involvement in 1969. At the time, right-wing extremism in the Federal Republic was on the rise. The National Democratic Party was doing rather well in provincial elections and in one district of the Rhineland Palatinate they got fifteen per cent of the votes. When they had gained representation in seven of West Germany's ten state parliaments, they decided to contest the federal election and we feared that the NDP might find a place in the Bundestag. Its policies in some respects echoed those of Hitler and a number of court verdicts labelled the party as neo-nazi. At every public rally protestors were threatened and sometimes attacked by party "orderlies": thugs wearing helmets and armed with hammers and iron bars. They had no hesitation in using these weapons. After one meeting in Frankfurt, they beat a young protester over the head and smashed in all of his teeth. The police commissioner called it "sadism and blood lust, the like of which was previously only seen in horror films".

The West German government, sympathetic to the far right, publicly rejected such criticisms of the NDP. In July, two months before the Federal elections were due to be held, Chancellor Kiesinger and the Speaker of the Bonn Parliament both denied any connection between the NDP and neo-nazism. At the time, the British government was trying to organise a Bonn-London axis. As the *Morning Star* put it: "We whitewash Kiesinger, Kiesinger whitewashes the NDP, and the NDP whitewashes Hitler." Several of us tried to draw the attention of the British public to the possible dangers to Germany and to the world posed by the resurgence of neo-nazism. We began by sending out a letter to many hundreds of sensible and influential people summarising the facts and inviting them to a meeting at the Waldorf Hotel. Three German speakers were promised: a vicar and professor of theology, a chairman of young liberals, and a lady leader of the engineering union. The meeting was crowded and we thought it a great success.

As chairman of our early doings, Humphrey Berkeley gave us a splendid respectability and, if the new German party had not soon disappeared, would have been a great strength. He was a former Tory MP who gave his time to works based on Tory headquarters and was, I believe, directed by them to seek out and keep an eye on our activities. I cannot believe that it was any of my doing that shortly after we had worked together he resigned from the Tories and later fought an election for Labour. My main activity was the bringing together of a group of people of extraordinary quality to lead the protest. Elizabeth Harley Williams, a friend from the Temple, was recruited as office manager and she joined in visits to the intended sponsors. First among them was Dame Sybil Thorndyke. I met her in the late 1940s at the Canterbury Deanery, the Red House, home of the Hewlett Johnsons, and at once fell in love with her. Fortunately, Janet did too, as did some millions more on other occasions. The only act of homage we could pay was to see her in *Arsenic and Old Lace* at the Vaudeville and we went twice. The Dean had led the dame into pro-Soviet activities at the very beginning of the forming of Friendship Societies and she remained willing to give her name and her voice well into her mature years.

Dame Sybil was to be found in Chelsea. When we went to visit, I recognised the block of flats as one to which I had been summoned in 1930 by a bevy of women writers. They assumed that, being from New Zealand and from Karori, I would necessarily have known Katherine Mansfield. Sybil suggested Peggy Ashcroft, who at first agreed, but when we had a list of eight, she asked to be left out. Her feeling was that Dame Sybil was so great a star that it was bathos to have her also. I countered that we had two left bishops from London. Peggy's riposte was, "If you had the archbishop, you wouldn't want a bishop as well." It was Sybil who suggested our bishops, Mervyn Stockwood of Southwark and Trevor Huddleston of Stepney. The obvious introduction was Stanley Evans, Southwark's progressive-minded canon. First we heard Mervyn preach in his little cathedral, then followed him to the beautiful Bishop's House in Tooting Bec at the other end of his diocese. Huddleston was more difficult; he was still winding up affairs from his time in Africa and was not easy to trace. Eventually we found that Dean ffrench-Beytagh, late of Johannesburg, was preaching at Lewes parish church. Elizabeth and I went to a service and at coffee afterwards he gave us the lead to Huddleston.

One of the most enthusiastic responses came from Arnold Wesker, then at the height of his popularity. Within the month, he was talking of writing a play dealing with neo-nazism. Trade unions were represented only by Hugh Scanlon, then the leading figure in the Engineers' Union and a man who gave the trade union movement a high profile in many good causes. From the educational world we had Robert Birley, Headmaster of Eton from 1949 to 1963, who was full of support for the cause and qualified himself for the job by disclosing that in the late 1920s he had tried to get a publisher to produce an unexpurgated translation of *Mein Kampf*. This would have given England a clear picture of the character of the Nazis ten years earlier. After Eton, Birley spent three years as Visiting Professor of Education at Witwatersrand University. When we first met, he had just returned from a tour of South Africa in search of blacks to qualify for further education in the UK. One of his outstanding choices was Simon Dabi Kumalo of Port Elizabeth, turned out of school for having criticised the government's policy towards blacks and not allowed into Fort Hare, the Xhosa University. Birley got him into Atlantic College in Wales. Then Simon honoured us by coming first to Balliol and then into my chambers and he has since prospered at the Common Law Bar. He is a young man of great ability and was a real loss to South Africa.

I suppose that Pritt's reply was the most stimulating. Pritt had written a book on the problem, *Unrepentant Aggressors*, and demanded that we should not regard the NDP as the sole danger but should look to "the whole aggressive revanchist policy of the West German government and ruling class". He warned of the presence of Nazis in every government department but particularly in education, the diplomatic service and the army, and of the rise of militarism and the demand for nuclear weapons. Pritt spoke from actual knowledge of the turn of events, for he had spent some time in Germany taking part in the defence of democrats against persecution in the courts. As before, Nazis were thought preferable to Communists. My knowledge of events came from the ordinary newspapers, but my attention was called to them by friends writing from East Berlin. Now that the two Germanies have been reunited, there has come some indication that the East German government went to the trouble and expense of stimulating pro-nazi activity in West Germany so that there might be something to complain about. If this is so, then they were active in rich soil.

In the UK, the Labour Party still preferred the right to the left and 1969 marked the twenty-first anniversary of my expulsion. I decided to make yet another determined effort to get back in. My first attempt had been in 1952 with a letter to Jim Callaghan, among others, asking for support. I publish Jim's reply not for what it says but rather for what it reveals:

Dear John,

I am sorry that I shall not be able to support you when you apply for re-admission to the Party. I have quite firm views about this. The place for a Communist is in the Communist Party and I have no desire to see an affiliation or a link between the two. The Labour Party is a democratic party – the Communist Party is not. How then can I support the admission of a Communist into the Labour Party?

With love and regret,

Yours ever,

Jim

He had been on our tour of Russia in 1946 and knew that I was no more a Communist than he was. Jim had ambitions, like all of us, and he was firmly moving to the right. Here was his chance of demonstrating it. Jim was a dear but, when required, quite ruthless. At the time, I think that George Isaacs was chairman of the committee that made recommendations about who might be admitted to the party. Isaacs was somewhat to the right of Genghis Khan and I gave up trying.

In 1963, Fenner Brockway asked Harold Wilson to get me back, but Harold replied that, as party leader, he was above all that. Frank Cousins invited Harold and me to drink with him in Smith Square. As Secretary of the TGWU, Frank was the most powerful figure in the trades union movement. In my presence, he asked Harold for some action. This time the answer was, "Do it yourself, Frank." In the following year, quite a number of MPs offered assistance, including George Pargiter, who tried his luck with George Brown. General Secretary of the Party was Len Williams, who seemed friendly enough and strong enough to make an effort and I approached him myself. Len's response was to send me a list of proscribed organisations. On it were at least fifteen organisations that I had belonged to, and half-a-dozen that I had played some part in setting up. I had left many of them on becoming an MP, and all except three by 1956. The exceptions were the British-Soviet Friendship Society, the League for Democracy in Greece and the Labour Research Department. The LRD had the most skilled and devoted researchers in the Labour movement but my only connection was to receive their literature. I resigned from them all and reported back to Len, only to learn that it was still not good enough. I asked for reasons and received the following explanation: "It is not the custom of the NEC to give reasons for its decision not to re-admit individuals into membership of the Labour Party".

It took two years to raise steam again, but the answer was that in view of my attachment to the League for Democracy in Greece until 1964, my re-admission could not be recommended. The League for Democracy in Greece was respectable enough. It was founded in opposition to Churchill's war in Greece when he was determined to suppress the partisans and to install the Greek king from his safe hiding in England and in Egypt. The partisans were under strong Communist influence but had been our allies in the Balkans and were as deserving of our friendship and help as were the Yugoslavs with Tito. The League was run by Betty Ambatielos, English wife of Tony Ambatielos, who had organised some thousands of Greek sailors during the Second World War and persuaded them to run British ships through all the war zones. President was Sir Compton Mackenzie, with Pritt as Chairman. Vice-Presidents included Gordon Schaffer, a famous journalist, the Reverend Donald Soper, Willie Gallacher and myself.

Ray Gunter ran the committee that made recommendations about who was fit for Labour Party membership. For me, he had cast a sombre gloom over its affairs. When he retired, Joe Gormley took his place and I was in with a chance. Joe was a miner; not actually from South Yorkshire, but from Lancashire, which was near enough. In 1969, he invited me to an interview at Transport House with just the two of us. Over tea and cake, he announced that I really must get back this time. By the end of the year, I had. I at once began canvassing for a parliamentary nomination for Labour. I applied to a number of constituencies in the south-east but none would have me. The most common reason for rejection was my age.

At the Bar you can go on as long as you please and it had not occurred to me that the party would regard a sixty-three-year-old as unfit for useful service. Lawyers have a definite advantage in standing for parliament, being skilled at persuasive argument. Voters sometimes think that they will be better at framing or interpreting the laws, but it is a specious argument for professionals are employed to do this. Besides, there will always be lawyers enough to tell their colleagues what the legislation means.

CHAPTER THIRTY-FOUR

Ulster and Prison Reform

I HAVE no difficulty whatever in taking sides over Ulster. It is wrong that part of Ireland is forcibly linked with England and the hope should be that all Ireland will be re-united. I have never heard a coherent defence of the rights of Britain to maintain an army in Ulster in support of the "loyalist" majority and against the Catholic minority and, whatever Cromwell may have thought, we have no right to be there. It should not be necessary to state that I am completely opposed to bombings, shootings and any other terrorist violence, but when the French engaged in similar tactics against the occupying Nazis, it was not called terrorism. What might have happened in Britain if the Nazis had crossed the Channel and occupied us? Is it possible that we could have reached the levels of heroism shown by the Dutch or Norwegians in the Second World War? Yet, for the sake of understanding the work of our own army, we are obliged to ignore historical parallels and to regard the Catholics as "disloyal".

I have done several defences of IRA members, but this was not to encourage their work. It was simply because under the "cab-rank rule" a barrister is treated as a professional who must be on hire to defend anyone who seeks legal assistance. It is not for the Bar to deny a legal defence to anyone obliged to appear before the courts. My first IRA case concerned an unsuccessful raid on an arms factory in Dagenham. This was in May 1969, before British troops went to Belfast and before the IRA campaign of violence in England. The gang wore combat jackets, stocking masks and peaked caps as they burst in demanding guns. The elderly watchman said, "You do not get guns," and set his Alsatian on them. He grappled with a raider but was struck violently on the head. The safe contained 1,868 new automatic sub-machineguns and much ammunition but the gang failed to open it and ran away empty-handed. The case was tried at the

Old Bailey four months later, when two men were charged with making an armed raid on the factory and assaulting a watchman with the object of stealing machineguns.

My client was Patrick O'Sullivan, a young man from County Cork who had once worked in the factory. O'Sullivan belonged to the IRA and his co-defendant, Connor Lynch, to Sinn Fein, of which the IRA is the military wing. The defendants were so ingenuous that they did not even attempt to conceal the fact of their membership. My client said that he had come to England at the request of Sinn Fein to conduct a political and economics course for young Irishmen in Essex and denied that he had ever been asked to carry out a military function. Lynch was the organiser of the course O'Sullivan had come to conduct. He, too, claimed to have had no contact with military affairs. O'Sullivan told the court that in recent times the whole concept of the IRA had changed. "I have found that the majority of members have been excellent individuals – very responsible, very sincere." Once British troops were withdrawn, the IRA intended to change the political system on both sides of the border. The defendants recognised that power would not be handed over on a plate: "There is no doubt that in the future weapons will be needed.... We must be ready." Plainly, the Dagenham arms would have been most useful. Even so, they denied taking part in the raid. Both men were found guilty and received seven-year sentences.

Mass internment began in August 1971, two years after the British Army entered Ulster. 342 men were interned on the first day and nearly 1,600 in the first three months, and all liable to be held indefinitely. They were subject to what the army called "interrogation in depth", in which a suspect was kept barefoot and hooded, leaning on his fingertips spread-eagled against a wall, and without food, drink or sleep. Sometimes a loud, throbbing sound was played. One man had forty-three-and-a-half hours of such treatment with questions interspersed. It was psychological torture, illegal by our law, and Gerald Gardiner had no hesitation in calling it "brutality" in his report on British conduct in Northern Ireland. With the aid of doctors and lawyers, Amnesty International set up a tribunal to enquire into the interrogations and their finding was that men had been kicked and beaten by soldiers and threatened with guns. As should have been anticipated, the combined effect of internment and torture – which is what it really amounted to – led to a great increase in bombing, killing and rioting. We were insisting that the Catholics of Ulster were our fellow citizens, but we welcomed them into our happy band with barbarous treatment. It is surprising that they have ever forgiven us to the point of joining the present Ulster assembly although it is a pity that we have been brought to the present pass by Tony Blair's determination not to allow Mo Mowlem to get any credit for the settlement and his lack of judgement in nominating Peter Mandelsen to carry it through: a job at which he has so far significantly failed through his apparent fear of offending the protestant politicians. This is the position as I write and one can still hope for an outcome that will bring credit to all.

My next contact with the IRA came in June 1972, through the Hackney Arms Trial. A Mr John Parker met Irishmen who were raising funds for needy Ulster Catholics and he helped them set up a shop in Hackney for selling second-hand clothes and toys. They thought that they were going to deal with clothing, but Parker was an agent of the Special Branch and he was intent on gun-running. A Sea Cadet building in Kent was broken into and eleven rifles adapted solely for drill and a number of bayonets were stolen. Parker offered the rifles to the Irishmen, who refused them. He had also obtained three pistols that were in good condition. This arms collection was then hidden away in a flat above the charity shop. The men objected and asked Parker to remove them. He agreed, but before this could happen, a group of twenty police appeared and arrested them. There was no sign of Mr Parker.

In this case, no crime of any sort had been contemplated by the Irish and probably none was committed. Arms were on the premises, but only through the secretive acts of Mr Parker. It was the plainest case of entrapment by an agent provocateur. The three pistols were supplied to Parker by Special Branch and had been in their possession at least since 1969, when they had appeared in evidence at Birmingham Law Courts. Every crucial element against all the accused depended on Parker except only for the case against Martin Crawford. He was arrested in Northern Ireland and there made a very long confession that implicated the others. It was offered against him at the Old Bailey, when all were charged with conspiracy to possess firearms. Crawford, who was just twenty years old, disowned his confession and told the court that he had been interrogated for four days by the RUC Special Branch at the army barracks in Belfast. They had punched him repeatedly and thrust a loaded pistol into his mouth to intimidate him. The judge held that the resulting statement had been obtained by psychological torture and so was inadmissible, and Crawford was discharged from the trial at an early stage.

From the beginning of committal proceedings, the police gave the defendants the public status of dangerous armed terrorists, surrounding the court building with guards and dogs. They also rigged the jury to exclude anyone of whose politics they did not approve. I appeared for two of the six defendants and was able to cross-examine a Special Branch officer about their "pricking the list", which had led to the "standing by for the Crown" of six jurors, which was quite exceptional. The officer reluctantly explained that information from various police sources was noted against names in the jury lists. This was to enable the prosecutor to challenge jurors whom the police thought might be unfavourable. I pressed him to find the grounds of objection.

Self: Did they include such things as belonging to the Labour Party?

Judge: There is no question of any political party being listed against any name. Where is this leading?

Self: I intend to show that this whole case has been engineered by the Special Branch through a man, Parker, to plant these guns on my clients.
          (Continuing cross-examination):
          Your objection had *nothing* to do with politics?

Officer: I didn't say "nothing to do with politics". The word "object" that I put against these jurors signified doubt about their political activities and their criminal activities.

Self: It is the right of the defence to have a jury that is not picked by the Special Branch.

Officer: I was asked to take these steps, sir.

The learned judge, Mr Justice Bean, was trying to introduce a new law of evidence that would excuse prosecution witnesses from answering questions on the ground of "delicacy". Fortunately, the law of evidence sustains the coarse and the earthy rather than the delicate. The government was unwilling to produce Parker or the other Special Branch officer who had acted with him. The outcome was that, rather than have questions about the service answered in court, Sir Peter Rawlinson, the Attorney General, Sir Norman Skelhorn, Director of Public Prosecutions, and Mr Brian Leary, the Prosecutor, decided that the case should be abandoned. It was obvious that the defence was scoring some points, but it never occurred to anyone on our side that the government was so sensitive about the Special Branch and its obliquity that they would actually throw in the towel. When our clients were discharged at the request of the prosecutor, everyone, from judge to public gallery, was astounded.

Another Special Branch informer was Kenneth Joseph Lennon. On Good Friday 1974, he was executed in a ditch in a Surrey wood. The question that has never been solved was, who did it? Lennon's history was that he was born in Newry but had settled in Luton. He became active in left politics and trade union work, collecting a group of fellows who were to become known as the Luton 5. As they skirmished with preparation for various money-raising criminal adventures, at each stage Lennon was in touch with the police. Three of the group were arrested while lying in wait although, from the reports, it seems that they themselves were unsure of their target. The trial judge was quite clear as to what they were aiming for, and that was ten years' jail apiece. After the trial of the Luton 5, Patrick O'Brien, aged eighteen, was anxious to try and get his comrades out of jail. Lennon, on Special Branch advice, encouraged him. He and O'Brien were arrested when making a preliminary survey of one of the prisons. They were charged with conspiracy to effect an escape. At their trial, the police had the utmost difficulty in making sure that Lennon got off. They gave false evidence that he had a good character – meaning no previous convictions – and falsely reversed the roles of the Luton 5. Lennon was acquitted, but O'Brien got three years.

Lennon's role as an agent provocateur was now fully exposed to every interested onlooker, including the IRA, yet he was not given the protection that he needed. Even his paltry wages of £20 per month were withheld by Special Branch to keep him close. Lennon made a detailed statement to the NCCL complaining that he had been forced to become a spy and an agent provocateur. He had encouraged fellow-Irishmen in crimes, then betrayed them and escaped free himself. The police were forcing him to continue in this work and were denying him protection. Two days later, Lennon was found with three bullets in the head. He was identifiable only by his fingerprints. The NCCL published Lennon's statement and it appeared in all the newspapers. The Home Office held an inquiry, lasting seven months, but I don't think that their findings were ever published. At any rate, the murder file was still open in November when I represented Lennon's family at the inquest. I wanted a Special Branch representative on the witness stand to give us the facts of Lennon's fatal connection with the department. The coroner and the police raised every possible obstruction and the question still remains: was it execution by the IRA or by Special Branch?

Special Branch has long maintained a band of informers and spies. In general, they are badly treated. Kenneth Lennon and John Parker were very different men. Parker had been an informer for twenty years, Lennon for a few months and then only reluctantly. Parker bore a weight of serious convictions, whereas Lennon's offences were trivial and long ago. Both, however, ended their service with the Special Branch in similar manner. Each was discarded, was dropped, without protection or reward. After public exposure, each was left penniless and then evicted. Parker was living rough when I last heard of him. Lennon was executed by a person or persons unknown and the balance of his pitiful wages was denied his widow, although she was a chronic invalid and the sole support of their young daughter. I hope it is not idle to repeat that the job of the police is to stop crime, to expose and help punish it; to preserve order. It is not their job to stimulate and encourage crime. To set on a man who provokes it and who hopes then to avoid capture and punishment is the very denial of the policeman s job. In no circumstances should it be allowed or encouraged. There should be no defence to the policeman who acts as an agent provocateur and, as a deterrent, parliament should consider adopting a criminal offence comparable with the American entrapment or provocation.

At one stage and another, the IRA has used many different weapons of assault in London. We have sustained bombs by bicycle, by car, parcel, book, letter and carrier-bag. We have had throw bombs, the "come-on" bomb (a little explosion followed by a big one when the rescuers have gathered), and varieties of triggering machinery. At times, the IRA gave warnings of such length as to enable the threatened area to be cleared, but not quite time for the device to be found and defused. Shortening the time would cause even more confusion and terror. With all these, the IRA showed great ingenuity, great courage and great evil. It is to the credit of the police in their various branches that at each phase they have subdued the bombers and defeated them. Yet it could be seen as unfortunate that at the height of the IRA campaign, when there seemed to be as many bombs exploding as firecrackers on Guy Fawkes Day, police policy should have been aimed at the provocation of more unlawful actions.

The closest I ever came to an IRA bomb was in March 1973, when the Provisionals carried out their threat to bring the war to the civilians of mainland Britain. Four substantial car bombs were placed in London. Two were defused; the third injured sixty-one people in Great Scotland Yard; the biggest was outside the Old Bailey, where 162 were injured. I was in the Robing Room on the top floor when it was announced over the loudspeaker that a car standing opposite the main door was believed to contain a bomb. Others hurried to the front and looked out the windows to see what was happening. Showing my usual courage, I retired at once to the lavatories, which are at the back of the building, and stayed there. I believe that James Crespi, a regular Old Bailey practitioner, went into the street to see. Shortly thereafter came a blast that shook the building – perhaps only three to four on the Richter scale, but enough to break many windows. James was badly cut by flying glass but was a walking wounded to St Bart's hospital next door.

Another barrister, Brian Higgs, was wounded on the top of his skull and on the inner side of one wrist just below the thumb. Blood spurted out of the cuts in a fountain going up an inch at each heartbeat. Anxious assistants caused him to sit and then to lie down. The spurts continued. I have, since I first learned of him, had the greatest respect for William Harvey who invented the circulation of the blood, but feel from my own experience that he may have laid too little emphasis on gravity as an aid to circulation. I helped the injured man to stand up and the head leak stopped. I raised Brian's hand above his head and the wrist stopped and he was cured. After two minutes, he lowered his arm and it was stable. He then sat down and all was in order. There was just the mopping up left. This was probably the only occasion when I have been any use in anyone else's suffering.

Early in 1974, substantial bombs went off at Madame Tussaud's, at the Boat Show and at the Chelsea home of a major-general. Two others failed to explode. Three months later, twenty or more tiny fire-bombs, made in cigarette packets filled with burnable mixture, battery and wrist watch, went off or were otherwise found in shops in Uxbridge, Welwyn Garden City and London. Both sets of attacks were attributed to a group who became known as the Uxbridge Eight. In 1975 my client Cornelius McFadden, aged twenty, and seven others went on trial at the Old Bailey before Melford Stevenson. The case started twice. After the first day, a juror realised that one of the parties involved was not exactly a stranger. Melford told the court that a juror had been "somewhat compromised", which was a good enough formula for what we had all learnt. The case had to begin again with a new jury.

After a bombing, the police would generally go to the airport and pick up the first few Irishmen waiting for the Irish plane. At a certain stage, it seemed there were no such young people at the airport and it was realised that the wrong-doers had merged with the local population. The Bomb Squad became convinced that the IRA had gone back to their old practice of using Irishmen long settled in London as their operatives. These "sleepers", now awakened for their turn of duty, were very much harder to catch. The two large bombs that failed to go off were dismantled. The evidence against my client, apart from his being young and Irish, was one plain fingerprint on a timing mechanism. This was identified by the fingerprint officer as having the necessary number of features identical with those on McFadden's fingerprint as taken officially on his arrest. The evidence of McFadden was that he had never in his life touched the inside of a clock and certainly had not touched this particular one. It therefore became the duty of counsel to suggest to the jury any manner in which the fingerprint could have reached this position without McFadden's guilt.

A fingerprint is a succession of ridges and valleys formed of grease and sweaty substances exuded by the skin and deposited onto a surface as the finger touches it. A fingerprint expert told me that prints were preserved by lifting them off a shiny surface with a special type of sellotape. That sellotape "lift" can then be transferred to another shiny surface as though it were the same original finger pressing down again. In court, I put this information to the police fingerprint expert, without giving any indication that it was about to be demonstrated. He was very doubtful. No mark could really be seen by an untrained eye unless it were dusted by a skilled person, and then experience was needed to make anything of it. He insisted that a print could not be reproduced. I had with me sellotape and a small sheet of plate glass, plus the fine aluminium powder, soft brush and duster. I placed a print upon the glass sheet, then lifted that one and successfully reproduced it. The print can be repeated as often as the strength of grease, oil or wax in the lift will allow. Mine was greatly strengthened by unobtrusively wiping a thumb down the side of the nose and so borrowing more grease from that source. The lift was then powdered up and it shone like a diamond.

My client had pleaded not guilty, knowing that he had never handled a partly dismantled clock, but we had been forced to admit that the fingerprint on the bomb's timer was his. After seeing the demonstration in court, McFadden now realised that an expert could easily have lifted his print from a beer glass. He told the court that he had a pint regularly at a local bar, and always from a clean glass; the barman was a great one for polishing up the glasses. Defence counsel does not have to believe in a defence or even to suggest to the jury that "that's the way it happened". It is enough that counsel suggests the question: "Is it possible that you could think that that's the way it might have happened?" Two other defence silks supported the suggestion of the possibility of planting fingerprints.

Melford affected to be outraged. He expressed total disbelief in the possibility of police perfidy and sentenced each defendant to twenty years' imprisonment. Melford complained of our "mud-slinging defence" and the "recklessly flinging of wild accusations". He told the taxing officer that in consequence, our fees should be cut. This meant that the fees of our juniors and instructing solicitors were also cut. It was all widely reported, as were Melford's criticisms of defence counsel. Although he had implied that we were guilty of professional misconduct, Melford declined to make a formal complaint. In due course, the Bar Council considered the point and decided that he had no right to make such an order about our taxation and that the conduct of counsel in challenging the police, as we had done, was entirely permissible. The Court of Appeal confirmed the view of the Bar Council and all fees were paid in full. They also halved the sentences for two of the defendants, but not for my young client.

The arrest of the Uxbridge unit did not end the bombings. Others were already in action and there were many explosions in the summer of 1974. Kevin Dunphy, a bricklayer from Kilkenny, was another contributor to the campaign. He was seen meeting members of the Uxbridge team but police failed to trace his home address until late August. In that period,

Dunphy twice stole a car and planted it as a heavy car bomb in a car-park at Heathrow. The first demolished ten cars and damaged forty-nine. It was mid-morning on a Sunday at holiday time and the airport was crowded, but he had given ample warning. In the second, only part of the charge detonated so that there was little damage. Inside was a car-park ticket with Dunphy's fingerprints. Dunphy's own car was found to contain a tin of incendiary mixture and a twenty-four-hour time switch. It also carried everything necessary for a miniature field hospital, including surgical instruments and blood plasma, in case the bomb-makers scored an own goal, as sometimes happened.

Dunphy is the only client I have had who has "stood mute of malice". That is to say, he declined to plead or to utter a word throughout the trial. Not guilty pleas were entered. Fortunately he wasn't mute below stairs so that his counsel were fully instructed and, one hopes, his best points were made for him. Only after sentencing did he speak. Then it was to remind the court that he had phoned warnings "to give the police a chance to clear the area". It was because his bombings had been accompanied by warnings and no loss of life that he received the comparatively modest sentence of twelve and a half years. He further distinguished himself by apologising from the dock to the owners of the cars he had converted into bombs. After the apologies came a fierce clenched fist salute to Mr Justice Swanwick, who had called him "an able and willing lieutenant". Dunphy also read out a statement:

> "What I did was in retaliation for acts of terror carried out by your army in Northern Ireland. My countrymen will fight, and it is my belief that this country will bear the brunt of that fight if she does not give Ireland her complete freedom."

I think the last of my IRA defences was that of James Gerard "Spotter" Murphy, who was tried with Anthony Cunningham at the Old Bailey for conspiring to cause explosions and discharge firearms between December 1974 and April 1976. They were said to have been errand boys for the bombers involved in the Balcombe Street Siege. After the siege, police searched a flat in Stoke Newington and found a bomb factory, an Army List, the *Civil Service Year Book* for 1974, and a copy of the *Anarchists' Cookbook*. The latter contained simple rules for making bombs and bore

Cunningham's fingerprints. My client, Murphy, was a messenger for a government department and his prints were found on the Civil Service book. He admitted having given a copy to some man whom he would not identify.

The cardinal piece of evidence admitted against my client was a letter (Exhibit 1) addressed "Dear Jo" and signed "Graine", asking Jo to recruit Spotter Murphy for a terrorist campaign in Ireland. This letter was found in a Kensington house where bombs were being made, but it was not shown that Murphy had any connection with that house. The letter showed that there were two conspiracies – namely, one in London where bombs were being made in several places; and one in Ireland, whence came Graine's letter and where Spotter's help was needed. The legal argument: was Exhibit 1 admissible at all? There was no Graine or Jo in the case. If it were admissible, did it prove only that there were these conspiracies, or did it also prove that Murphy was a party to one or both of them? A writes to B, unknown to C, and says, "Please get C to come and commit a crime with me." Why is C implicated? Here it was not even proved that C, Mr Murphy, knew of Jo or Graine or of the Kensington address. This argument failed before the trial judge, who sentenced the two men to ten years imprisonment for their role in what he called a conspiracy so wicked that it was almost beyond the powers of the court to devise adequate punishment.

The Court of Appeal rejected our argument that the conspiracy had not been proved. The next step was to return to the Court of Appeal to ask leave to take the case to the House of Lords. At that stage, the intended appellant formulates a question summarising the point of law that the Lords will be invited to answer. The Lord Chief Justice greeted me by saying, "Surely the only matter here is the form of the question for their Lordships? Why have you not agreed a form?" I explained that I had put my proposed question to the prosecution and was waiting for them to agree it. The chief asked why my draft was not good enough for the prosecutor, who answered that he had nothing against the question, but did not want to agree any form at all. When the court adjourned, there was no suggestion that they wanted any argument and I was sure that the opinion which I had put forward was conclusive and had been accepted. We came back, having agreed the form. The court announced, "We think there is no case here for further appeal." They had changed their minds and ruled out an appeal without hearing any argument. It was a frustrating experience, not least for my client.

The Balcombe Street Siege came about when a fugitive IRA gang burst into a Marylebone flat and held the terrified occupants hostage for six days. The team received life sentences with a recommended minimum of thirty years' imprisonment. They later confessed to having carried out the pub bombings for which the Guildford Four were to spend fifteen years in prison. Forensic evidence backed their claims, but the courts refused to free the four already convicted and sentenced. One of the Guildford Four, Paul Hill, played an important role in the Hull Prison riot of September 1976. I was already well established as a busybody willing to interfere without much excuse in the internal affairs of everybody else, so it was no great surprise when the national prisoners' movement, PROP (Preservation of the Rights of Prisoners) asked me to chair a public inquiry into the riot. Amongst the committee members were Monsignor Bruce Kent, then Chairman of War on Want, and Albie Sachs, a former captive of the South African regime but then a law lecturer at Southampton University and now an appeal court judge in South Africa.

A number of prisoners who had finished their time since the events came willingly to testify. Other evidence was given by family members, solicitors and voluntary workers, but mostly we relied on the testimony of Hull prisoners who had since been transferred to other prisons where they were being kept in solitary confinement as punishment. About thirty smuggled out signed statements on little scraps of paper – sometimes even on toilet paper. There was no possibility of collaboration in the writing of these statements since the men had been split up immediately after the riot, yet each told essentially the same story. We wrote to the prison officers named in the statements, inviting them to attend the inquiry and offering anonymity, but the Home Office and the Prison Officers' Association ordered them not to co-operate. Extreme cases of prison unrest have always begun with severe attacks by warders on men put in their care. There is amongst prison staff a sadistic and a racist element and the POA invariably protects such men. Prison officers are not allowed to go on strike. Consequently, when they have grievances over loss of income from cuts in overtime, the standard remedy is to harass the prisoners, fomenting the kind of dissatisfaction guaranteed to lead to some kind of demonstration. Overtime is then restored.

This was the unstable situation at Hull Prison immediately before the riot. When a rumour went round to the effect that Martin Clifford, a prisoner in the segregation unit, had been badly beaten by four prison officers, a large group of prisoners milled around, demanding that at least one of their number be allowed to see Clifford and to report back on his condition. This was refused. Someone in the segregation unit shouted out confirmation of the assault on Clifford and the riot began. Some 180 prisoners took to the roof, which gave them access to other wings of the prison. They smashed in cell doors to free as many prisoners as possible and brought out the wounded Clifford. His mother attended the PROP inquiry and said, "I have been told that when Martin was beaten up it was just a blood bath. He was left just in a crumpled state on the floor." Martin had told her that one of his assailants was a medical officer. It was a shocking declaration.

The next provocation came when prisoners found files containing reports on each man, his presumed sexual inclinations, and so forth. Much of the detail was inaccurate and it was felt that the files showed a certain viciousness of spirit. As one prisoner reported, the mood changed from shocked disbelief to a quiet fury. They then began to wreck the prison, causing approximately £750,000 worth of damage. Paul Hill's file was particularly worrying. It said that he was moody and unco-operative and must be treated with strict discipline at all times. He was alleged to have spoken of a willingness to take hostages, and there was the warning that he might kill. His girlfriend, the mother of his child, was named in the file with the comment **This relationship must be ended** underlined in red. But what had most shocked and frightened him was a note that he was totally suicidal. "The reason I worry over this is why should they say this knowing it to be untrue?" The inference was that someone in authority might fake his suicide.

Surrender came on the fourth day, when hunger and boredom drove the prisoners down from the roof. That night they were kept awake as officers "roamed like little armies around the landings, banging doors and screaming". During the early morning slop-out, the men were kicked and punched. Their food and drink were polluted by urine as were the floors of the bare cells. Officers smashed up the prisoners' belongings in retaliation for the damage to Home Office property. Then, at breakfast time, the men were forced to run the gauntlet of prison officers lining the corridors, who pummelled them with truncheons and fists and boots. It was clear that black and Irish prisoners were the worst treated. We were told that the boxer John Conteh's brother got "a hell of a hiding". The Irishmen were forced onto their hands and knees and ordered to crawl along singing "God Save the Queen"; all were beaten for refusing. One prisoner told how he had seen Paul Hill being pulled downstairs by his shoulder-length hair, "helped by full-blooded kicks to his stomach, chest and back", while the officer shouted, "Another fucking bomber". Hill was actually thrown down the last few stairs.

Jake Prescott was assaulted with the words, "Gun and bomb merchant. Don't mark his face". "Back they came with Jake, bruised, dishevelled, shaken, roaring like a demon." I had met Prescott in August 1971 when he was on remand in Brixton awaiting trial for membership of the Angry Brigade, an anarchist group which carried out a series of bombings on targets as diverse as the Miss World contest and the Department of Employment. Before he came up for trial, six other members of the "brigade" were arrested and it was widely agreed that the case would have to be postponed until the following January. Legal etiquette required that I accept other work in the meantime. Prescott's co-defendant at once pressed for their trial to be brought forward, which had the effect of forcing me out of the defence team. *Time Out* magazine alleged that I had dropped Prescott in favour of a longer (hence more lucrative) case, which was quite untrue. I went to Brixton prison to make peace. We shook hands and agreed that there should be no hard feelings. His original sentence was fifteen years but involvement in the Hull disturbances meant the loss of eight months' privileges and 700 days' remission (equivalent to an additional two years' imprisonment). I was sorry to find him in such difficulties.

In his book, *Stolen Years: Before and After Guildford*, Paul Hill admitted that the rumour of Clifford's assault had been wrong. When the prisoners finally got through to the segregation unit, they found him unharmed so they blacked his eye and marched him out to show the others: "Look what the bastards did to him!" If the assistant governor had allowed the deputation to see Clifford when the rumours first started, the riot could have been postponed, but probably not for long. It was generally agreed that the riot could not be attributed to a single cause and although the alleged assault on Clifford was the spark that ignited the flame, the fire had been set by the increasing severity of the prison regime and the arrogance of some of the prison officers. Confirmation of this came in 1977 when twelve officers and an assistant governor were tried for assault, theft and destruction of prisoner's personal effects. Eight were convicted but received suspended sentences.

In general, our prisons are barbaric institutions. Cells made for one are habitually used for two or even three, leading to indignities, humiliations and bullying. Sanitary arrangements are abominable. Jerry pots in a jointly occupied cell are horrible and the resulting slopping out justifies the strongest adjectives. If a man is to have the chance to think for himself, or to learn to think for himself, then he needs the possibility of being alone. He should have freedom of association at set times, but he must always have his own cell. Evil as these places are, they have no effect in frightening men away and recidivism is the order of the day. The building of new prisons "to ease overcrowding" would simply induce magistrates and judges to imprison more. It is time to acknowledge that the prison system has failed and should in large part be abolished.

The first remedy is to slash the number who are ordered into prison. We should end remands in custody save in extreme cases. Prisoners in for non-payment of debts should be released and the existing prison population could be halved by reducing all current sentences. The alternative to prison must be community service, administered with flare and with vision. The community is not served well by stone-breaking unless it is by a skilled stone-breaker. The service required is that at which the convicted man is most skilled, for the community is entitled to his best work. Let the architect join the team planning the new public building; let the doctor cure other prisoners. Above all, let the more skilled tradesmen and the professionals run classes for those restricted in capacity or movement. At the moment, one of the worst things is the almost complete absence of any serious attempt to raise the level of understanding of the prisoners or to educate them. "Every prisoner an eager reader" should be the slogan. Those convicted and jailed should also have to submit to lectures from people who had succeeded greatly in life, such as former prime ministers, retired cabinet Ministers and business tycoons. They would be a notable crew of lecturers, and I would also include every Balliol man over eighty. If all that did not keep errant man from folly, then nothing would.

I have approached four lords chancellor almost at the moment of their inception to press upon them the need to abolish the prison system. All have politely said no. Quintin Hogg roared with delight at the suggestion and was ingenious in devising new adaptations of community service. Gerald Gardiner, as the first Quaker on the Woolsack, saw it as his overriding duty to ensure that Sidney Silverman's doughty blows against the death sentence were so strengthened that never again ... but he thought my idea might be fathered upon the next LC, Frederick Elwyn Jones, who felt that it wasn't his province. The fourth was Reggie Manningham-Buller, Lord Dilhorne, who contributed the notion of approaching a man through his hobbies. Let the pigeon fancier become an expert, a racer or breeder; let the postage stamp collector be apprenticed to a stamp shop; and so forth. He suggested that the inveterate car thief, who is destined to be driver to the getaway crew of a robbery, should at once be overwhelmed by the mechanics of driving and set to master the highest skills. His lot should be to drive an ambulance, a fire engine or a squad car, where all his daring and his new skills could be used to the full. Reggie had a dovecote with 200 nest boxes and he would talk to the pigeons as you would to honey bees. That and the wilful destruction of game birds were his best skills and, if guilty and convicted, he felt he could teach his fellow convicts about these things – especially if it would keep him out of jail.

CHAPTER THIRTY-FIVE

Sewell and Murders

IN THE 1970S, I had a good run of murder trials. There was even a "cop-killer" – Freddie Sewell, a South London car dealer who owned several houses and led a flash life, although he was almost illiterate. The extra money came from armed robbery, for he led a gang who specialised in robbing jewellers' shops. They were successful until Blackpool in August 1971, when it all went wrong. A fireman saw the raid and intervened, causing the robbers to run out, jewellery scattering across the pavement. Sewell, carrying a shotgun as well as a briefcase full of jewellery, couldn't open the door of the getaway car. As he wrestled with the handle, he was hit by a brush thrown by a window cleaner. He got into the car just as it was driving off and a furious chase ensued. Sewell's men rammed one police car to put it out of action, then used a revolver to shoot the driver of another, missing his heart by a bare half-inch. While trying to reach their second getaway car, they were cornered and rammed. One of the gang disappeared into the crowd but the other four fled with police officers in pursuit. Sewell fired, shooting a constable in the groin. Three made off in a butcher's van but crashed it. They climbed out to find a constable, an inspector and Superintendent Gerald Richardson, Head of Blackpool Police, confronting them. Sewell waved his gun, ordering them to back off, then ran into a narrow alley. Richardson followed and was shot and killed.

Because of the seriousness of the trial, the prosecution case was opened by the Attorney-General, Sir Peter Rawlinson, who then handed over to Godfrey Heilpern, QC. Sewell insisted that he had not had any intention of using the gun. He claimed that Richardson's death was an accident, but we had to admit manslaughter because it was grotesque negligence to carry a loaded gun and to run and point it. Sewell's story was that as he retreated backward, Richardson had got a grip round his neck. They had both gone down, with Richardson on top. The gun stuck in Richardson's body and went off as they hit the ground. Sewell then dragged the gun free from the dead body lying above him and, as he did so, it had again gone off. Our ballistics expert was Dr Brian Shaw from Nottingham. He took us to a narrow side alley and showed us how, as Sewell went to the ground, one bullet had gone over the top of a small van almost vertical and had landed seventy feet away quite unblemished. It bore the markings or "fingerprints" of that gun and could only have been the bullet that passed through Richardson and was so impeded in its flight that it went only a short distance into the air. Dr Shaw made experiments with bags of meat packed in plastic and showed that, so long as a bullet did not strike a bone, it could be greatly slowed down without damage.

According to the police statements, there was no witness to this final onset between the two men. However, Richardson's deputy, who was now Superintendent Eddie Gray and newly appointed Head of Blackpool Police, presented himself to the court as an eyewitness. Senior police officers are usually staid and undemonstrative men. Gray presented his evidence with such astonishing theatricality that even the judge commented on his "imagining himself to be some Shakespearean actor" and warned the jury not to let themselves be prejudiced against the policeman's evidence through a natural disapproval of the way in which he presented it. The gist of Gray's evidence was that he and Richardson had ducked behind their car as Sewell waved his gun and retreated, and then Richardson had pursued him across the road, arguing and cajoling and trying to persuade Sewell to give up his gun. Gray had followed closely. There was no challenge to the courage of Richardson or of Gray. The only trouble was that in each of the previous statements made to one officer or another, and the last one to the appropriate solicitor in preparation for the trial, Gray's view of the final encounter had been blocked by a van.

In cross-examining Superintendent Gray, I put each of the first three statements to him in succession. The fourth statement, made especially for the trial and to a careful and highly experienced solicitor, was reserved to the last. I do not remember thinking consciously that there must be some break in the drama to get the utmost effect from the last one but, instead of going straight to number four, made some feeble joke. The whole court sighed with relief and looked about itself, the jury roared with laughter and the judge smiled. Godfrey Heilpern, leading for the prosecution, said to Ivor Taylor, his first junior, "My God, look what he's done. It's pure Shakespeare. It's a gravedigger scene and nothing less." When the jury was summoned back to the horror of that fourth statement, which again failed to mention witnessing the killing, the jury seemed to be gripped by it. We could not be guilty of murder on this. There was still the evidence of Sewell and of the ballistic man to come.

Sewell was interrogated by Heilpern, whose manner of cross-examination was like the boxing stance of Muhammad Ali. He danced most delicately round his topic, then struck with paralysing force. He wove a net round his victim, poked and prodded him with cunning thrusts, and then at the end was bound to strike him dead. When this final blow was due, counsel for the defence was very conscious of that most fearful intention and the need to deflect it. It was not Shakespearean dramatic skill, it was pure Old Bailey knockabout to bust open the cross-examiner's plan and spoil the effect entirely. I rose to my feet. Did I understand counsel to think that such and such had been said by the witness? Surely it was something slightly different? I was certain that I had a note, and my junior had a note. Could we not consult them because if it were other than as counsel appeared to believe, then the last question was not appropriate?

Prosecuting counsel was outraged and said so. The learned judge said, "No, we must find the truth," and busily consulted his notes; others did the same, and the interruption proved to be unjustified. The cross-examination was resumed but the whole spell had been broken and poor Godfrey Heilpern, due to become a high court judge, as we thought, at any time, was not used to the rough and tumble of the Old Bailey, which I assume I was hired to bring to Manchester. He and the judge could save their case of murder and avoid the verdict of manslaughter only by mauling and defaming our poor ballistics expert so that no one ought to attach the slightest importance to whatever he had said. That was the final line of the prosecution and it succeeded. Sewell was sentenced to life, with a recommendation that he serve not less than thirty years.

The Sewell case had another aspect. As usual with a red judge (a high court judge) on assize, there came on the Bench with him the High Sheriff of the County, Simon Towneley. He was in the most glorious apparel of scarlet and gold, with royal blue breeches. In due course, he invited the judge and, in turn, several of the counsel to lunch. He was a cellist and I was in the happy position of being able to boast that I knew Mstislav Rostropovich. The high sheriff invited me to accompany him to Burnley with a string quartet which was coming from London to play there in the following week. After court, we met the bearded players at Piccadilly Station. My host was still in his court gear and with one voice they cried, "The bandsman's uniform!" The high sheriff had a great car that bore a pennant with the Plantagenet leopards, for he claimed some Plantagenet descent. (It was also the Lancaster flag.) We travelled over the Pennines to his ancestral home at Dyneley and I learned the whole history of his family, who had shown intense loyalty to Charles Edward Stuart, the Old Pretender.

In the summer of 1982, I had a solemn memorial meeting with a group of distinguished occupants of Parkhurst Prison on the Isle of Wight. I had gone with the solicitor for a whole day's consultation with Mr Herring, the client of the day, to begin at ten a.m. To be in good time, I'd spent the night at Ryde. The morning passed with my feet up in some uncomfortable waiting room, with an explanation that detectives of importance from several parts of England were there to interview my client and would I please mind waiting? I have often wondered what it would be like to shout and blow out one's cheeks and pull rank. The latter is a phrase I have never managed to use in all my life before. I have always been too shy and have never held a rank except as barrister, and so with the right to be heard in certain quarters. I waited until lunch in the prison officers' mess, and all afternoon until four, when I was given three hours in which to compress the day's work.

At seven p.m. the governor arrived with his necessary cortège and issued the invitation. It was realised I had endured a long and disappointing day; would I care to stay and take dinner in the prison? I was not in court next day. There was no reason to hurry back to London, and "prison governors I have known" are interesting men and women. It was most kind of him and I would accept. "Oh, it's not me. I'm not your host. It's some friends of yours who have prepared a spread. They are inviting you, and the feast is just ready." So I stayed to supper. The hosts were Reggie Kray, Charles Richardson, Mr Herring and Freddie Sewell. Freddie was the chef. It seemed that he had impressed the hospital cook and gained his support. The menu began with avocado salad and sherry. They said this was minced advocate, which was what they liked to see – especially if he were for the prosecution. Then came the finest pair of birds on the island. It wasn't for me to point out that they were a bit ahead of time and really were last year's produce that had been frozen. They were real enough, with redcurrant and game chips and all else. For pudding there was some iced confection and with it all, two bottles of excellent wine.

We had a whole open ward in the prison hospital to ourselves. The hosts were dressed in tracksuits and trainers, all seeming brand new and shiny, as though they were modelling the latest. The talk was about their athletic prowess. They played half-a-dozen games, but body-building was the order of the day. All were engaged in gardening, and one kept songbirds in his cell. It was obvious that there was very great freedom within the walls, but the walls themselves were impregnable. It was the first time I had seen Charles Richardson and Reggie Kray since their respective appeals. There was no sign of the well-known enmity that previously existed between the Krays and the Richardsons, and I enjoyed meeting them.

I also visited Ronnie Kray in prison on the Isle of Wight, and in Broadmoor. Life was quieter and more gentle in the hospital. Ronnie was permitted to wear his own clothes, took full advantage of this and dressed immaculately. I last saw him in December 1991. We met in a large room that was all decked up for Christmas. It was used as a theatre by the patients and had a stage at one side. Staff members sat about, but none were within hearing of the talk. Ronnie bought us hot drinks from a machine. He was no longer heavy-set. He was slim, taking plenty of exercise and retaining a strong handshake. The prescribed drugs seemed to keep Ronnie calm and serene, and he was very conscious of the need to take them for the rest of his life. His greatest wish was that Reggie should be out of prison. The Krays were locked up thirty-two years ago. Ronnie has died under duress and Reggie appears to have been only released to die.

It is widely thought that a prisoner released from a life sentence is "free", but such a prisoner is released only "on licence" and this carries strict conditions. He is supervised by a probation officer, who must approve any living- or work-place, and can be recalled to continue his sentence for a slight departure from proper conduct. He runs the danger that any hostile person may provoke an incident that could take him back to prison. To my mind, the strangest of murderers are those who have already served one sentence and been discharged, then come up for trial charged with a recent murder. I have had three. In response to the question, "You know what a life-term is like. Why did you do it again?" one client replied, "I owed him from last time. He was the one who shopped me and took all the money." It was then proved that "he" had come saying, "I didn't shop you. I am the one who saved all the loot and protected your share with interest, and have come to arrange to give it to you." The passion for revenge had quite overwhelmed my client's obvious self-interest, but this is a most unusual response. The time of the Krays has passed and Reggie should have been released some years before his death.

Charles Richardson made money and retained it, invested in legitimate businesses and was thought to be a millionaire. In spite of that, he was defended on legal aid. By the end of the trial, knowledge of his affairs was greater and he was ordered to pay many thousands towards the costs of the prosecution. Eddie Richardson and Frankie Fraser were treated with the same understanding but my client Roy Hall was on legal aid all the way. The Kray firm was bigger and ruled a wider territory but did not amass any great fortune. The twins were defended on legal aid and on conviction were not called upon to contribute any part of the costs. In my experience, the majority of big criminals are defended on legal aid. In civil cases there is a fund built up in great part from the successes gained by aided clients. This was the basis devised by Gerald Gardiner when, acting for the Haldane Society, he first set out the principles of legal aid. With criminal cases this is not so. They draw on a fund controlled by the Lord Chancellor's Department and dispensed by magistrates and other judges. Almost all criminal charges begin before the magistrates so that applications are made to them in the first case.

I am not sure that jurors are ever conscious of whether legal aid is involved in the cases they try. If they were to ask the judge, he would answer that it is a matter of the highest privilege and he could never ask that question himself. In fact, the judge has the right to look at the outside of counsel's brief to see whether it is marked with a fee or "Legal Aid". He may look inside only at counsel's invitation. Even without considering legal aid, the expense of a trial that goes on for months increases the pressure on a jury. The parade of barristers with their showy attire and manners (and all presumed to be expensive), the obvious distinction and learning of the expert witnesses and the scores of lay witnesses mean that to acquit would be to waste public money, court time and police effort. These factors should be borne in mind when considering the extraordinary miscarriages of justice that have sometimes occurred in gang trials.

In my experience, most people who are prosecuted by the police are guilty and there is no surprise in the standard question: "Have you ever got a murderer off whom you know to be guilty?" The answer is 'Yes", and it can happen quite properly. Your client tells you, "I done it, but they can't prove it." What he has told you is secret. It is the subject of "absolute privilege" and cannot be disclosed. However, knowing that, I must then explain to the client that I cannot allow him to go into the witness box and swear that he didn't do it. If he were to insist upon this course, he would first have to dismiss his lawyers or they would withdraw after telling the judge (in private) the reason. This would lead to a commotion most harmful to the client. The judge would find a formula: "Circumstances have arisen between Mr Doneit, the accused, and his counsel which make it impossible for counsel to go on. It is in no sense the fault of counsel, and I have to say in the most grave manner to Mr Doneit that if he is to persist..." et cetera. The client is allowed to plead not guilty and if his assessment is correct and they can't prove it, the judge rules at half-time that the prosecution has not made out their case. Mr Doneit is acquitted. Failing this, you may decline to call evidence – except, perhaps, as to what a good character your client has – and then you argue it out with the jury.

The case of Lizzie Thompson was different. It was the plainest example of an innocent person being found guilty when every feature of the case pointed to that being a perverse verdict by a perverse jury. In Portsmouth in November 1971, Peter Stanswood was found dead in the passenger seat of his own car. He had been stabbed seven times and the knife was still embedded in the body. The police conducted 20,000 interviews and took 2,500 statements but no one was arrested until three and a half years later, when they charged Stanswood's widow, known as Heather Pridham, and Ken Fromant, a gas fitter. Natural gas had just been introduced to Portsmouth. The gasmen had to be found lodgings, and lodging seemed to mean full home comforts wherever possible. Some of the resulting relations were quite stable, but there were frequent changes and for a time the normal sexual restraints were rather in abeyance. Mrs Pridham confessed to the police that Fromant was only one of her dozen lovers, but it was his blood that was found on the murder weapon.

Peter Stanswood was locally christened "Casanova" and this name for him was adopted by the press during the trial. He had fathered three illegitimate children upon three different mothers and showed every indication of wishing to add his wife's friend Mrs Thompson to his credits. He pursued her relentlessly. She resisted all his approaches, and none of them could possibly be a reason for murder. For his wife, every such action – and there were many with other women – could lead to profound dislike and she was reported to have said that she hated him. Mrs Pridham had been given the cruellest reason for hatred only a few days before the murder. Her husband sent her away to stay with Mrs Thompson on the excuse that he was going to make the house unliveable with building repairs. On her return there was no sign of any such repairs having been done, but every sign in the kitchen and, of the grossest sort, in the bedroom, of Stanswood having entertained one of his mistresses.

After Mrs Pridham and Fromant were charged, she told the police that some months after the murder Lizzie Thompson had confessed that she was the murderer. The police made a thorough investigation and declared that there was no case against Mrs Thompson. There was also insufficient evidence to prosecute Mrs Pridham, and Fromant would stand trial alone. Mrs Pridham then rewrote her statement, putting all the blame onto her friend. It was an absurd situation. The only evidence against Mrs Thompson came from the woman who had thereby shifted herself from prime suspect to chief prosecution witness. The story of the alleged confession first surfaced seven weeks after Mrs Pridham's own arrest, and only after she had been interviewed by or given statements to the police on more than fifty occasions. There was no motive for Mrs Thompson to murder Stanswood and she had a well-supported alibi for the occasion; Mrs Pridham's alibi was as worthless as her assortment of statements.

I appeared with Mr Ian Peddie for Lizzie Thompson. We confidently expected an acquittal but she and Fromant were convicted and given life sentences. The appeal was heard in March 1977 but it was impossible. A verdict cannot be overturned simply because the jury has made a foolish decision, and no one could fault the judge's summing up. The Court of Appeal rejected our arguments and we had no grounds for appealing to the House of Lords. Nevertheless, Lizzie's MP took the case to the Home Secretary, who refused to reopen it. A petition was then lodged with the

Home Office. We presented the case in person to Leon Brittan but got nowhere. To the great grief of her young family, she served ten years. If I have said about any other case that it was my greatest disaster as an attempted defence, then I was wrong.

The first brief I ever saw was on the mantelpiece of Graham-Dixon in his cramming chambers. It was delivered in the 1890s to Bodkin, a junior on the Western Circuit, marked £2.4.6d (two guineas, plus half a crown for the clerk) for counsel to travel to Dorchester to prosecute a corpse-lifter at the Assizes. Bodkin, by the 1930s, was Director of Public Prosecutions. There was no sign on the brief of any papers having been delivered; there was no statement of witnesses; it was as simple as the modern instructions "to meet the client at court and to advise upon the course of action to be taken and to take it". On this brief, the only other record was written on the back in counsel's handwriting: "I done it for science." It was obviously the defence of the accused. The trial of that case before a jury would have taken little over one hour from the opening address to the summing up.

Murder trials were equally curt. When I was called to the Inner Temple in 1932, there were stories in every circuit town of the length of a murder trial: "We 'did' four murders in a day" or "I remember three in a morning". Such murder trials were usually based on pleas of guilty, but seldom did a plea of not guilty take more than a day. The longest in my experience was the Torso Murder Trial. When it opened in November 1976, we were told to expect a maximum of eight weeks. At its close seven months later, the proceedings had cost the taxpayer more than half a million pounds and set a record as the longest at the Old Bailey. The seven defendants faced 12 charges, 134 witnesses, 108 exhibits and 716 pages of depositions or statements. Even the judge's summing-up occupied twelve days. There was no real evidence and no reason for any convictions. That four of the defendants were found guilty was generally attributed to a feeling on the part of the jury that if all of the defendants were released, the money and the combined efforts of police and counsel would have gone to waste.

At the outset, the prosecution warned the jury that they would find "no shortage of horror, appalling cruelty and sheer evil" in the case. Pieces of a dismembered body had been found washed up at different parts of the tidal Thames from the Isle of Dogs to Rainham in Essex, mostly by little boys and birdwatchers. Even without the missing head and hands, forensic experts identified the body as that of Billy Moseley, who had a rare blood group and an even more unusual skin disease. The second body was that of Micky Cornwall, a bank robber, who had been shot in the head and buried in the woods near Hatfield in Hertfordshire eleven months later. The two victims were friends and members of the criminal fraternity of North London, but there were no other links between the two crimes. The prosecution tried to gloss over this obvious misjoinder by insisting that Moseley had also been shot through the head, although the head in question had not been found. They had no murder weapons, no material witnesses and no obvious motive but made up for the defect by offering to the court a broad selection of obscure and incoherent motives. These murders might have been the result of an old grudge or the quick-tempered reaction to an insult. Or was it the evils of sadism, or thieves fighting to get hold of a fabulous hoard of stolen jewels?

The favourite prosecution theory related to an affair Moseley was thought to have conducted with the wife of a convicted prisoner named Ronnie Fright. By the time Fright got out, Moseley was himself in prison. Within days of Moseley's release in September 1974 he was killed and dismembered, allegedly by Ronnie Fright and friends as punishment for the offence. They had later killed Micky Cornwall for trying to find out what had become of his old friend. The core of the theory was that the man who seduced a prisoner's wife so offended the criminal community that it became a killing matter. In fact, the prosecution had simply constructed their own idea of a moral code for the underworld and patched onto it whatever bits of gossip their informers could produce. The defendants – Reg Dudley and his daughter Kathy, Bob Maynard and four of their colleagues – were mostly small-time criminals but the press got hold of the idea that they belonged to a ruthless gang of hired killers with an involvement in multi-million pound jewellery thefts. They were portrayed as such desperately evil characters that the jury was intimidated into asking for special police protection and seats out of the public gaze.

Once a story had been constructed to account for the killings, the search began for evidence to back it up. None could be found and the prosecution case was based almost exclusively on "verbals". These are oral confessions said to have been made to police officers or to fellow prisoners in jail. They are an open invitation to dishonest people on both sides: the one to invent unreal confessions, the other to deny real ones. The prosecution leaned heavily upon the testimony of "grasses". The grass is a prisoner who is put into the cell of a remand prisoner with the instruction to find out about his crime. The grass knows perfectly well that he will only be rewarded if he brings back material that helps to secure a conviction. One such individual told the court that Ronnie Fright had confessed to him, but the defence produced two fellow prisoners who were certain that the grass had perjured himself. The most surprising witness for the defence was the assistant governor of the prison in question, who confirmed that the police had asked for permission to put a well-known grass into Fright's cell. A man of the old school, the assistant governor had turned them down. It was courageous of him to come to court.

My client was George Spencer, a friendly young chap whose father-in-law was a vicar. Spencer sometimes did a bit of driving for Dudley and it was for this reason that he had come under suspicion. According to the police, Spencer had denied any direct involvement in either murder but admitted to being present at the killing of Moseley and later clearing out the dead man's flat. Spencer's name did not come up in evidence for many weeks. Criminal work is scarcely law at all and I was still not really used to it. I spent weeks with practically nothing to do except to prepare an argument saying that confessions made to the police should not be allowed as evidence against the man who made them unless there was corroboration of what he was saying. In these days, every court, both civil and criminal, accepts what a man says against himself as the best possible evidence unless there is some extraordinary misunderstanding involved. Yet the policeman can tell us that for every notorious murder, there are several applicants claiming "I did it". I also spent an inordinate amount of time trying to make points of law simply to keep the court awake.

George Spencer's solicitors worked very hard for him. They made the fullest possible investigation and produced Frank Happer, a young robber who had been a fellow prisoner. His story was that the police had approached him in jail and told him they would arrange for him to be put in with Spencer. If he would then report that Spencer confessed to him and give evidence to that effect in court, they would see that his release was greatly speeded up. Happer was duly put in with Spencer and told him the full story. He gave evidence of this at the Old Bailey. The prosecution thought to discredit him by asking, "Who do you suggest is the policeman who put this ridiculous proposal to you?" To our very great surprise, Happer looked round and said with delight, "Why, that's him sitting over there." He pointed to a man seated with some lawyers. There was no reason for any of us to think that the fellow would actually be present in court. I had no power to ask the man his identity and asked the judge if he would find out. He did and the gentleman stood up and admitted that he was a plainclothes policeman. The jury had no difficulty in believing Happer.

The main prosecution evidence came from Anthony Wild who was, we suggested, not a natural grass; he was a planted and cultivated grass, neatly trimmed and shaped. The police had given him his story in advance and he had merely embellished it in his inimitable way. He told the court that my client was one of the mugs, "just a grave-digger", but that three of the defendants had boasted to him of their part in the murders. He said that Dudley had put Moseley's severed head into a paper bag and shown it to the proprietor of a Brighton pub, who had nearly died of shock. It was suggested that the head had then been thrown into the sea. Prompted by Wild's allegations, a fisherman reported that he had almost caught it in his net but had lost the trophy. When last seen, it was floating away on the waves.

Wild was in every way a most unsatisfactory character. He had previously turned Queen's Evidence in armed robbery cases and his criminal record was far worse than that of anyone in the dock. Wild commenced with outlandish boasting of his own sexual excesses, saying that he could bring 500 women to court to testify that he was not a homosexual. He then moved on to an apologetic explanation that armed robbery was a subconscious attempt to regain his manhood. When rebuked for his appalling conduct in the witness box, Wild responded: "Yes, yes, I'm a mad, egotistical homosexual terrorist who wants to fit up these innocent people. Write it down." One of the counsel for the defence was told to "Get stuffed!" and we were collectively dismissed as "sweaty wigs". Confronted with such a bizarre individual, we asked for permission to bring a psychiatrist into court to comment on Wild's behaviour but this was not permitted.

Another interesting feature of the trial was a difference of opinion between two specialist medical consultants called for the Crown. There was no real evidence as to how Moseley had died. A renowned forensic pathologist from Guys gave the benign view that hatched, irregular marks round one shin were due to the nibblings of rats as the leg lay on the river mud at low tide. The prosecution were not satisfied with that report and called another expert of equal distinction from the London Hospital, who said that the marks were made by a metal clamp used to hold the offended leg while the toe-nails were pulled out. The foot had also been burned on the sole by a gas flame. There was argument over whether or not the victim would have died of shock during this torture. This second theory seemed the more likely. The only trouble was that the prosecution, having allowed themselves to propound the first, could be presented to the jury as wayward and uncertain when they presented an alternative. Moreover, the rat nibbles left much greater scope for variety in the manner of the killing.

Four of the defendants were convicted; three were acquitted, including my client, Spencer. Some weeks after the case had ended, Moseley's head, fresh from someone's freezer, was found in a public lavatory in North Islington. He had not been shot in the head. It made no difference to the appeal and one of the convicted men is still in prison as I write. The understanding is that the Home Office would not sanction their early release as long as they continued to insist on their innocence.

CHAPTER THIRTY-SIX

Aden and North Africa

WHERE IT is feared that a trial involving human rights may be less than fair, interested groups will usually try to send an observer. With some countries, simply writing on the visa application that you wish to attend court may be enough to bring proceedings up to standard. In September 1971, Amnesty International sent me off to North Africa to attend treason trials in Cairo and in Khartoum. The first involved Ali Sabri, alleged ring-leader of a plot to overthrow the Egyptian government. President Anwar Sadat wanted to merge Egypt with Libya, Syria and Sudan into one Arab Socialist Union. Vice-President Sabri opposed the plan and resigned, taking almost half the cabinet with him. Sadat had them all charged with high treason. In effect, a small majority of the government put the rest of the government in jail. It was a close parallel to the position of the Labour Party leader, Hugh Gaitskell, when he said that he would fight, fight and fight again to reverse the decisions of the party conference.

The total of those under arrest was brought to ninety-one by an assortment of "co-conspirators". The first group to be tried were the purged political leadership and by the time I got to Cairo the trial had already been on for a fortnight. Since the constitution provided expressly for ministers to be tried by a court of a dozen persons, of whom six must be judges, the three-man "revolutionary courts" had no legal basis. At the opening session, the defendants had put this challenge and lost. From all accounts, the court was following normal Egyptian criminal procedure with defence counsel able to call witnesses and to cross-examine, although the public and the press were kept out. I called at the British Embassy to see what help they might offer, but was told by the Chargé d'Affaires that the Egyptian government had specifically requested the embassy not to interfere with the course and the conduct of the trial. In consequence, the ambassador was most anxious not to appear to be supporting my visit, so there could be neither introductions nor assistance.

Cairo was the home of Nabil el-Hillali, whom I had first met in Tunis in 1968 when he stood in the dock with the students he had tried to defend. I called on Nabil and was taken to meet at least twenty of the defence lawyers. He also introduced me to Loutfi el Kholi, editor of a radical monthly newspaper, who had been in jail eleven times. On the last occasion, his wife was in jail with him. The editor praised Amnesty and spoke warmly of the support they had provided. He was an intelligent and entertaining man, and very well connected. When I told him that I hoped to meet the Minister of the Interior, he made a single phone call and the ministerial car at once came to collect me. I had an hour and a half with the minister, who had been a policeman all his life, and was cultured and sensitive as such men often are. In the evening I went to the National Assembly building to meet the Speaker of Parliament, Mr Hafez Badawi, who was also President of the first Revolutionary Tribunal. Badawi had been a village teacher and qualified as a lawyer by taking evening classes. He became first an MP and then a minister, but still saw himself as primarily a lawyer. He urged me to attend court next morning and said that I might go as often as I wished. Of course, I could meet his fellow judges, the prosecution, the prisoners and defence counsel.

On the following day a high court judge called at the hotel and took me to Heliopolis, a fashionable Cairo suburb where the tribunal sat in a makeshift court in the old Heliopolis Hotel. The outside of the hotel was heavily policed but inside there were virtually no guards. The prisoners sat in a very large, iron-fenced dock, and each had his own personal bodyguard. There were no handcuffs and the guards appeared to be unarmed. The prisoners looked reasonably well and they seemed comfortable enough, talking freely with their guards and sometimes laughing. The defence speech I heard was based in large part on acceptance of the facts and denial that they established any crime. It was clear from all my discussions that a number of defendants on the periphery of the trial would not be found guilty by any court in the world.

Later in the day I called on Mohamed Hassanein Heykal, editor of the newspaper *Al-Ahram*, at his office in a grand new building obviously designed to impress. Heykal was regarded as the mastermind behind Egyptian affairs. He was not only the main intellectual supporter of Sadat but just possibly the main rival and proved to be as remarkable as his reputation had suggested. I found him seated behind an enormous desk surrounded by papers. He was quite small and reasonably round, and his behaviour was rather curious. He smoked one cigar after another, stubbing out each before it was more than one-part finished. They seemed good cigars, but for him alone. I had hoped to meet the prisoners and the president. This idea was supported by almost everyone I met, but the one exception was Heykal. He thought that an insistence upon visiting the prisoners would imply criticism of the conditions in which they were held. Similarly, he thought that a visit to the president would "open the door too wide" for others who might come to Egypt to criticise. He was very much opposed and the outcome was that I did not see either the president or the prisoners. I thought this showed where the real power lay.

Heykal told me that he was very much in favour of Amnesty International expressing its views strongly in Egypt because they coincided with the views of the head of state. President Sadat wanted his new government to be active in establishing the rule of law in all its departments and having this recognised internationally. When Amnesty applied for leave to send an observer and for a visa, he had supported it. When the application was refused and the English Bar Council wrote on my behalf, he had personally intervened and insisted that the visa be granted. He wanted Egypt to have an Amnesty group and we discussed the notion that some Egyptian personality in the Sciences or the Arts or Letters might be found who would agree to act as a sponsor. Back at the hotel, I received a phone call from a former judge and diplomat asking to be put in contact with Amnesty's International Secretariat. He was hoping to join a national adoption group, if such a thing was set up.

On the following night, I was taken to Abdul Salem el Zayatt, Secretary-General of the Arab Socialist Union, Egypt's sole political organisation. He, too, expressed support for Amnesty, particularly as Sadat had that day issued public instructions to his new cabinet, stressing the sovereignty of the law and the necessity of ensuring "the safety of both the individual and the people, and the preservation of the people's rights". He insisted that I should call a press conference at the Hilton, at the expense of his organisation, and say what I thought of the trial. This proposition was entirely without strings so it seemed quite practicable. At the conference, I explained Amnesty's interest in the trial. I gave the government credit for the fact that policemen had been withdrawn from the university campuses and for releasing political detainees in great numbers.

I then contrasted the present condition of the defendants at the treason trial with the unhappy situation after their arrest, pointing out that the arrests and interrogations had not been carried out in accordance with the law; that the prisoners should have had access to their lawyers all along, rather than just immediately before the trial; they should have been allowed to see their relatives once a week; and I criticised the barrage of newspaper and radio condemnation of the prisoners, which in England would have been regarded as contempt of court. Next morning all Egyptian newspapers carried the same story: I had praised everything, and any criticism was carefully omitted. It was an unbalanced report of the press conference, but no one could deny that the defendants were being fully and fairly represented. Their lawyers had made that plain enough. The men were now being well looked after, with regular visits from family members and from legal counsel.

The situation in Sudan was very much worse. The Secretary-General of the Sudanese Communist Party was accused of subversion and of having waged war against the state. Many thousands of trade unionists, farmers, doctors, lawyers and intellectuals had been arrested and tortured. Amnesty adopted a number of them as prisoners of conscience and was agitating for fair and open trials. I was meant to continue on to Khartoum to act as observer but the necessary visa, applied for in London, had not yet been given. Each day in Cairo I went to the Sudanese Embassy and enquired about progress. On the very day I had intended to leave, the consul invited me to apply direct to him. I did so in writing, saying that I meant to investigate for Amnesty the conduct of the political trials. The consul took the paper from me and in a highly English voice said, "For heaven's sake, scrub all that out. I will do it." He then said, "That will be £2," and asked for my passport. The two-week visa was at once inserted. I boldly set off for the border, full of confidence, but was turned away. There was nothing for it but to go home and report my failure.

The background to the trials was that in July Sudanese soldiers calling themselves the Free Officers' Group overthrew the President, Jaafar al-Numeiri, the Sudanese Hitler. Their leader, Lieutenant-Colonel Babiker al-Nur Osman, had been in England for treatment of a kidney complaint and he set off to fly back with one of his aides. BOAC flight 045 was a

VC-10 carrying more than a hundred passengers on a routine flight to Nairobi via Rome and Khartoum. As the plane entered Libyan airspace, their Civil Aviation Authority informed the captain that Khartoum Airport was closed. He must land at Benghazi or be shot down. As the outcome showed, this was on the orders of Gaddafi, who had allied himself with Numeiri. The captain declined, saying that he would instead return to Rome. Malta air traffic control centre agreed to his request and the plane turned 180 degrees north. Soon afterwards, and most probably through the intervention of the British government, Malta rescinded permission. The aeroplane was then at many thousands of feet and flying very fast. The captain consulted BOAC, who consulted the Foreign Office, and the message came back: "Obey the Libyan orders." He dumped as much fuel as possible, then landed.

Al-Nur, newly declared President of Sudan, and his aide were taken off at Benghazi and rushed under guard to Khartoum where a counter-coup, inspired by the capture of the liberal leaders, freed Numeiri. Within days of the forced landing, the two men had been tried, convicted and executed by firing squad. It was rumoured that the trial had been staged three times because Numeiri refused to accept any sentence other than death. The widow, Mrs Khansa al-Nur, sought legal advice on a projected action against BOAC. Today such a case would have had every bias in its favour. At the time, there was only an outside chance of success but it was plainly an action well worth fighting, even if only to expose the conduct of Gaddafi and Numeiri. The terms of the flight contract did not allow of abandoning a passenger at an unplanned stopping place and leaving him to the mercy of bandits. BOAC and the Foreign Office knew perfectly well that the Libyans meant to take improper advantage of the person newly declared president. If he had reached Khartoum as planned, it is probable that Numeiri would never have been restored to power. Money was collected for the essential legal costs. Then, on different advice, the whole thing was abandoned. It was a great disappointment.

Numeiri had himself come to power through a military coup in May 1969 and was well established as one of the great butchers of Northern Africa. (The reputation of his close friend Colonel Muammar al-Gaddafi, Chairman of Libya's Revolutionary Command Council, has since taken its own course.) Numeiri's supporters believed that the officers' coup had been organised in concert with the Iraqi Ba'ath Party and, on the day of the BOAC hijack, an Iraqi plane bound for Khartoum exploded in the skies over Saudi Arabia. On board was a delegation of prominent Ba'athists, prematurely offering their congratulations on the success of the coup. Jordanian sources said it was shot down by a jet fighter of unidentifiable origin. It was thought that the Communist Party of Sudan – the biggest and easily the strongest in the Middle East – had also had a hand in the planning of the coup. Al-Nur was pro-Communist and he would have kept Sudan out of the proposed Arab Socialist Union. One reason for the great popularity of the Communists in Sudan was their respect for the Islamic faith; all party meetings commenced with readings from the Koran. After he had been restored to power, one of Numeiri's first speeches contained the following passage:

"I hope every member of the armed forces and every member of the people will be with us against every renegade who belongs to the Communist Party. Arrest them, or immediately notify the nearest police or army point, because these Communists are traitors."

In January 1972, Martin Ennals, Secretary-General of Amnesty, advised another attempt at Sudan. This time it was to investigate the conditions of political detainees – who were said to be allowed only one small piece of bread and a single glass of water per day – and to check on the judicial system. It was known that two judges had been interned, including the chief justice. Martin sent a cable to Numeiri, introducing me and requesting government co-operation with the mission. The president was informed that his "personal reception" of me "would be most appreciated". On the way out, I was to stop at Cairo to discuss the formation of an Egyptian national section. Again, the Sudanese refused to let me in. Janet came and after a few days in Cairo we flew to Luxor to see something of the historical glories of Egypt – at our own expense, of course.

In the Cairo trial, Ali Sabri had been sentenced to death for high treason. This was later commuted to twenty-five years' imprisonment with hard labour. He was repeatedly offered immediate release if he would only write a formal letter of apology to the president, but he always declined. After ten years of offer and refusal, he became desperately ill. Sadat relented, and only then was Sabri freed.

In May 1975, Martin Ennals sent me back to Arab lands. This time it was with Katrina Mortimer, a young researcher on the Middle East, on a mission to the governments of the two Yemens: the Yemen Arab Republic in the north and the People's Democratic Republic in the south. We were to introduce them to Amnesty's ideas on human rights and ask to inspect their prison systems. The last leg of the journey to Sanaa, capital of the Yemen Arab Republic, was made in an ancient Dakota. The Pakistani pilot was most welcoming and he insisted that I should fly his plane. It was well over 100 degrees in Aden and, as we battled up towards the middle of Arabia, it got hotter. I'd forgotten that you could let in some fresh air by sliding open the front windows a bit. I hadn't flown since leaving the Oxford University Air Squadron. It was one thing to fly straight ahead, but when the pilot suggested that I should also land the plane, I declined.

The journey out from London had been made slow and tedious by long hours of sitting in waiting rooms in the stifling heat. We were both suffering from exhaustion by the time we reached our hotel and found that the rooms were up fifty-nine steep, very high steps. Katrina was feverish and so we removed ourselves to the best hotel, where our rooms proved to be sixty-six steps up. Since it was a Sunday, we ventured out for a short stroll to inspect Sanaa. The two Yemens suffer from a severe shortage of water, and no sign of the oil that has so enriched their neighbours. Here the common feature of all life was dust and dirt. On our return to the hotel, Katrina was too weak even to attempt the climb back upstairs. A phone call to the British Embassy brought a land rover to carry her away to the care of the ambassador's wife. I set off for a leisurely stroll to the famous castle on the rock overlooking the town and came back at midday to find the foreign minister waiting for me with the president's political and legal advisers. We had a big six-course lunch while I told them about Amnesty and opened the possibility of their country's ratification of the UN covenants on civil, political and other rights. They were most friendly and all spoke well of Amnesty's work in Aden in the 1960s.

At six p.m. it was off to meet the prime minister on the top floor of his palace, which had the rare luxury of a lift. His government was trying to combat infant mortality rates of fifty per cent, illiteracy rates of ninety per cent and a life-expectancy of less than forty years. The one bright spot was a reported improvement in human rights. To inspect the prisons we needed the approval of the Minister of the Interior, who behaved for all the world like a Sandhurst product but whose connection with army college had been four years at a military instruction centre in Moscow. He produced for us the head of the prison service, a formal chap with a smart moustache and silver-rimmed spectacles, who agreed with the minister that we could see as many prisons as we wanted. Three central prisons were selected: the Citadel, where most political prisoners were held, and the Al Rada', each holding perhaps 300 men, and the one women's prison with some thirty prisoners. The day after the palace reception, Radio Sanaa announced that the republic was to ratify the UN convention against torture. Two days after that, the Minister of Foreign Affairs told us that the necessary orders had already been given to their Permanent Delegate to the UN. We were charmed by the warmth and sincerity of their response and it was a great disappointment that they failed to ratify the convention until 1991, after the unification of the two Yemens and following a visit from the Secretary-General of Amnesty in November 1990.

The first prison we visited was surrounded by mud walls perhaps twenty feet wide. Into the lower part of the walls were built dingy caverns in which the prisoners lived. The crudest possible wicket gate, with a wooden bar across to hold it shut, led into a little mud hut where the guards slept. The rags that acted as their mattresses lay underfoot throughout the day. The sentry room had a whole wall of manacles, iron anklets and chains waiting to be hammered onto the legs and hands of prisoners. These devices were not for punishment or to make a hardship but simply to stop prisoners from leaving the unlocked prison. In the middle of the floor sat a large granite slab that was the base for hammering on the links and also for prising them off. While we were there, the anklets were struck off a sixteen-year-old boy who was being discharged from the prison after ten days. The guards were not in uniform but wore the usual local clothing of shirt and jacket with a sort of kilted skirt that came below the knee, with bare legs or shoes with short socks. They were all armed to the teeth. In a country where every man is free to carry knives and loaded rifles, one of the worst deprivations of the prisoner was that he could not carry arms. It was such a hostile comment on the citizen's freedom and manliness that it was a great punishment in itself.

To make room for our inspection, the prisoners had been ordered into their sleeping quarters. Men sat round the edge of the rooms, crammed in side by side. Lying down, they would surely have covered the whole floor. There were no beds, just a small gathering of rags that each man accumulated around him. The only prisoners outside were the insane, who chattered to themselves, and a few invalids. The Red Cross provided a cupboard of medicines and a nurse came in each day to administer these to the sick. Medical care was available to only a limited extent in the country, so the prisoner's lot was superior to that of his fellow citizens in this respect, as it was in the provision of water. In each of these prisons, a big tap was left constantly pouring water so that the men could drink from it and bathe in it. Since we saw no provision of any kind to occupy the time of the prisoners, it was fortunate that visitors were allowed in every day. In fact being in prison was something of a family affair, rather like a nineteenth century English debtors' prison. Visitors would bring in food to feed the man and his friends, then tidy up and carry the necessary cooking gear home with them. The standard prison meal consisted of brown beans boiled in a sort of soup, but the cooking area was adjacent to the lavatories, which were no more than holes in the ground. The smell from the lavatories affected the whole compound.

Many of the prisoners had appeared before a Koranic court. They had been found guilty but did not know the term of their sentence. The probable explanation was that they had been condemned to life imprisonment but had a good chance that the period would be heavily reduced after five years. It seemed quite normal for men to be allowed to go home on parole during the ordinary course of their sentence. In the next jail we met a pair of well-to-do young men who had been involved in a political assassination. We noticed them first when, while passing the small hut they had to themselves, Katrina cried out, "Look, there's a man with a book!" Their place was spick and span, considering the surroundings. They had mattresses and bedding, washing and cooking gear, as well as a small library and were trying to persuade the authorities to let them teach other prisoners.

The women's prison consisted of a small compound with two sleeping huts. For the duration of our visit, the prisoners were sent into their dens, one of which was locked. The lady in charge wore no veil and was obviously tough enough to overpower all the prisoners together if she had to. The second-in-command was the only other woman in the jail who was not covered from head to foot. She wore a short skirt and tights and a blouse, had an attractive necklace and many bangles. She was a prostitute. Her husband divorced her after he had been jailed for living on her immoral earnings. She had no known sentence and it seemed that she would stay there until she could get herself another husband. The chances of that happening seemed slim indeed. In the meantime, she had become a "trusty", being a bit educated, and was put in charge of one of the groups. She held the key that unlocked the sleeping den and disclosed a really horrible smelling place, with those poor, unhappy girls clamouring to be let out to get some air. Her behaviour towards the other prisoners was the most inhumane of anything we saw.

We had in mind the standard minimum conditions for the conduct of prisons as laid down by the World Health Organisation but soon realised that these were quite unrealistic for the foreseeable future. If they were realised, the prisons would be filled to overcrowding because the living conditions of the prisoners would be so much higher than that of the bulk of the population at large. In contrast, it would have been almost an affront to remind their southern neighbours, the People's Democratic Republic of the Yemen, of the minimum requirements for they were well in advance of them. The main feature shared by the two prison systems was a humaneness, an easy-going and comfortable relationship between jailors and jailed that was entirely unexpected and stemmed from the Moslem way of life and the teaching of the Koran. Both north and south based the prison structure on a lot of open space where prisoners were free to go and to talk and meet at all times when they were not engaged in anything specific. Most of the prisoners we saw lived in unlocked dormitories with a minimum of regulations. Apart from these general likenesses, though, the difference between the two systems was profound.

The south was under British subjection for 140 years. For all the officially and publicly expressed distaste for the British past, the new People's Democratic Republic had benefited from inheriting all the paraphernalia of a state organised by the civil service. However, since independence in 1967, hundreds of people had reportedly been executed or imprisoned without trial. The legal system had failed and there was no longer the right to a legal defence nor any right of appeal. Cubans trained the militia and other security forces, with East Germans running internal security. Nearly everyone with British connections had been dismissed from office and many had emigrated. Each ministry made its own decrees, which often conflicted with the interests of other ministries, but the country as a whole was moving steadily towards women's emancipation, agrarian reform, the abolition of illiteracy, and the raising of living standards.

On arrival at Aden, capital of the People's Democratic Republic, Katrina and I were met by the head of the prison service, who carried a large pistol under his shirt. As he was also head of immigration, he saw us through customs and the like. We were taken direct to the museum of the history of the revolution, which covered a very short period. The first rooms were devoted to various items such as guns captured from the British, but then we came to a room which honoured that great revolutionary occasion, the day of the nationalisation of the soft drink industry, which included Pepsi and Coca Cola. Countries under Soviet influence seem to attribute great virtue to soft drinks. We then had an hour and a half with the head of state at his own home. We had come rather hesitantly to ask that he give up the practice of cutting off people's limbs as legal penalties. The president declared that this sort of thing had long been abandoned and that it would be no difficulty for his state to adhere to the UN convention. We showed the president half-a-dozen lists of people said to be missing, disappeared or executed and he replied that these matters had all been considered in anticipation of our arrival. Directions had been given that we were at liberty to ask any questions we liked, and all questions would be answered. He suggested that we go next day to the Al Mansura prison on the outskirts of Aden, where all the records were kept, and we could stay and work with the minister in charge of prisons for as long as we liked until we were satisfied on all points.

We arrived at the prison at nine-thirty a.m. and stayed a full eight hours. The entrance and guardhouse were modelled on a modern British prison, with double metal gates leading into an outer covered yard, then through further gates that clanged impressively. Beyond the open yard of the main prison lay the bright, white-washed walls of the administrative offices. There were enough locks and keys about to show that there would be no need for manacles or balls and chains. We were introduced to the officers, then taken on an hour's tour of inspection. The prisoners lived in large, open, airy dormitories. Most of these were occupied by half-a-dozen or so inhabitants who were off sick or had some other reason to be excused work or study. The dormitories we inspected were clean, with mattresses and blankets tidy in military style. Each living place had a television set. We saw representatives from each dormitory carry back food from the main kitchen and it was my impression that prisoners ate in their rooms. Enormous cauldrons of soup and mutton stew with vegetables were brewed up for dinner and we ate our share of the food in the governor's office, picking out of communal pots with our fingers. Food in the jail was so well done and in such plentiful supply that it was difficult to imagine that anyone would want to put his friends and relatives to the trouble of bringing in further rations.

The prison workshops had several hundred men at work on various labour-intensive activities such as the spinning and weaving of wool to make webbing for upholstered furniture. Dozens were busy learning the furniture maker's trade. The prisoners worked under skilled tuition in workshops that seemed clean and bright and fresh, particularly when compared with what is common in British prisons. One prisoner had a studio to himself, where he designed and painted large-scale revolutionary paintings of a crude sort with slogans galore. Others were making similar honorific designs of carved wood stuck on wooden backgrounds. Subjects were well-known buildings in the republic or symbolic pieces representing aspects of national life. It was impossible to avoid being presented with a number of these plaques; all were duly packed and carried home.

The prison uniform for convicted men was a pair of white below-knee-length shorts and a white open-necked jacket, worn with a cotton, peaked cap. It was ideal for cleanliness, tidiness and cool. Two orderlies in white coats manned the medical centre. We saw one inmate with shrunken arms and both hands missing. He seemed to be well into his fifties, and we learnt that he had lost his hands as a young man in Saudi Arabia as punishment for two separate thefts. He had not been able to do any work since, and we thought it likely that he had done none before his conviction. There was a real contrast with our young companion from the Foreign Office, who had lost his own leg while on a demonstration against the British and had been rescued and largely restored by a British hospital. He had twice been to Roehampton for the planning and fitting of an excellent artificial leg and was soon due to go again for adjustments.

We brought out the lists and ploughed through them, name after name, as Mr Ali, the head of the prison service, and his assistants went through their records. From a list of Amnesty-adopted prisoners, it emerged that a dozen or more were in Al Mansura. We were invited to meet them all: alone, if we preferred, or in the presence of prison authorities. When we found that one of the prisoners spoke excellent English, having been three years at Hull University and two years at St John's College, Oxford, reading law, we chose private meetings. Mr Ali tearfully embraced the man, for they had served together in the army under the British and then on the central committee of the party until the younger man had fallen out over some matter of principle and been awarded fifteen years in prison. Six of the group were political detainees who had been held for varying lengths of time. Even those without any chance of trial foresaw the prospect of release at a certain stage. They wore ordinary Yemeni clothes and none complained about their treatment or of any cruelty or torture. The general level of good relations between guards and prisoners was impressive, as were the high standards and excellent facilities of the prison. Above all, we were delighted by the glad co-operation from everyone we met. We were invariably given the utmost assistance.

While in Aden we took the opportunity of having a look around. Aden claimed a great nautical history. It was said that Alexander the Great gave the place its name as being potentially the harbour of the south corresponding to Athens. The fishermen claimed that in their dhows they had traded with the Malabar Coast of India before the domestication of the camel and that they had made the passage of the Red Sea before the caravan routes were established. They had carried the thousands of pounds' weight of cloves and spices from the South-west Indian coast that the ancient Romans had used to buy off the Goths and the Vandals when they first invaded Rome, the only land journey being from the top of the Red Sea to Alexandria. The fishing in Aden was superb, and the fish likewise. Lobster lunches at a swimming resort were memorable, but they were also notable for the fact that the Russians isolated themselves and sat at their separate tables while the rest of the world mixed freely.

Katrina stayed behind to conduct more interviews and to inspect other facilities. I left for London via Cairo by Egypt Air. The Suez Canal was soon to re-open and when the flight was delayed and even my seat was in doubt; it was obvious that notables were making the journey. Into the VIP lounge at Aden came an Egyptian general or brigadier. I served as batman while he shaved and changed, helping to swathe him in layer after layer, then dusted his shiny white shoes and gave his buttons and badges a bit of a touch up, turning him out as resplendent as the sun. He took it all in good part and joked about his role as courier and companion to the distinguished personalities who would be going from Aden to the opening of the canal. Compared with him, the guests looked very dowdy and humdrum. They were civilian dignitaries and heads of the armed forces, but all in sombre green jackets cut in the Chinese style, buttoned high up in front. They bore no medals, but I am sure that this was not for want of courage in their recent battles against the British but as reflecting the modest style of the day.

Cairo airport was unapproachable and we joined the stack of aircraft circling above it. For miles around one could see streams of tanks and other military vehicles passing in all directions.

When we were safely back in London, Martin Ennals said that he should have reminded us in advance that they had an unwritten rule: no sex on an Amnesty mission. I pointed out that it was a bit late to mention it, and that Katrina might have said something. But, with responsible campaigners, no such rule was needed.

CHAPTER THIRTY-SEVEN

Shrewsbury Pickets and Chile

THE TRIAL of the Shrewsbury pickets is the only case I know of where the government has ordered a prosecution in defiance of the advice of senior police and prosecution authorities. Ted Heath's government had suffered various setbacks at the hands of the shipbuilders, dockers and miners and he was determined that building workers should not have comparable success. The Shrewsbury trial, which came after the first national strike ever held by building workers, was an attempt to even up the balance. On 6th September 1972 some 200 men visited eight sites in Shrewsbury and Telford to canvass for their unions and to try to persuade workers to join the strike. Because the sites were small and scattered and the unions, in consequence, poorly organised, they used the flying picket strategy pioneered by the miners. There were a few disturbances but the police, who accompanied them to the sites, saw no grounds for intervening and no arrests were made. The building contractors complained to their federation, who complained to the Tory MPs, and they to the home secretary. The two forces involved, North Wales and West Mercia, questioned some 800 witnesses before deciding that proceedings could not be brought as it was not possible to identify wrong-doers. The home secretary, in defiance of the advice he had received, ordered the police to bring proceedings and in February 1973, thirty-one men were arrested, of whom twenty-four were eventually prosecuted.

There were several trials of the pickets, beginning at Mold. David Turner-Samuels QC from our chambers was the leading counsel there and I came in for Des Warren at Shrewsbury. At Mold, the main charges of affray, intimidation and damage to property failed, resulting in many acquittals. Counsel for the defence had challenged a juror whose trade was listed as "building contractor". I believe that for five hundred years the occupation of each person in the jury list has been put against the name. In the interval before trial at Shrewsbury, Quintin Hogg as Lord Chancellor decreed that henceforth occupations should not appear against names in the list. If I may speak lightly of so grave a matter, for all we knew our jury list could have been fixed so that every juror was a contractor. The prosecutor also added the charge of conspiracy, which is, as a rule, easier to prove than the corresponding substantive charges that had already failed with the other defendants. To justify the change in attitude, they had to invent the story that the remaining defendants were the ringleaders, although in a normal case the chief wrong-doers are prosecuted first. On the day in question, no union officers were present and the police acknowledged that the actions of the men seemed to be spontaneous. There were no "ringleaders".

Des Warren and Eric Tomlinson went regularly to the action committee meetings at Chester and were the only two of the twenty-four who had experience in trade union matters. Warren was extremely conscientious so that if a resolution were passed that might be interpreted as putting an obligation on him, he would do his very best to carry it out in full. A few years earlier he had been blacklisted by employers and had to work under an assumed name. This showed him to be a most courageous fellow. On trial at Shrewsbury with Warren and Tomlinson were John Carpenter, John McKinsie Jones, Ken O'Shea and John Llywarch. Our judge was Sir Hugh Mais. He had been active in the ecclesiastical courts, then a county court judge, and was now newly upgraded to the high court. Mr Justice Mais was the ideal choice for a trial of active trade unionists for he showed a deep dislike for them all and clearly had no real understanding of the trade union movement. The construction industry is the most dangerous that we have. In 1991, 150 men died on construction sites — a quarter of all workplace fatalities — and many thousands were seriously injured. To this, one can add breaches of the safety rules, hostility to trade unionism, use of the blacklist to harm militants, and absence of even the most basic facilities such as dinner-huts, lavatories and wash-places.

In this industry, a system called "the Lump" or labour-only subcontracting prevails. The lump-worker is treated as a subcontractor letting himself out on hire for labour only. He is not paid wages but a sum calculated on the basis of wages. It is a costly business for which he needs premises (his house), staff (his wife), electricity and gas, transport, telephone and an accountant to verify the expenses. All of these come off the lump-sum he is paid for his contract with the result that the net income shown to the authorities is brought below the taxable level. If he were an employed worker, he and his boss would both contribute to his tax and National Insurance. As it is, other taxpayers must pay more to make up the difference. The Lump is a fraud on the Revenue and on Social Security and on all those who contribute to them. It is also accompanied by a steady increase in the proportion of accidents and a steep decline in the number of apprentices and of men in the building trades unions. Objection to this practice was officially adopted by the TGWU in one of its more progressive phases under Jack Jones and by the newly-founded Union of Construction Allied Trades and Technicians (UCATT).

On the day of the Shrewsbury/Telford visits, at each site the pickets spoke to the site agent or the foreman and asked permission to speak to the men. At two sites, the workers agreed to back the strike, and at a third the employers had already accepted the union demand. They were not so successful elsewhere. In one case, the workers were ordered to leave the site and hurry off rather than stay and hear the argument. As the only way of speaking to them, the pickets hurried after, which gave the superficial appearance that the pickets were chasing the workers off. We had evidence of bricks being thrown from scaffolding, and on one site a lumper produced a shotgun and pointed it at the pickets. They snatched the shotgun, broke it open to make sure it was unloaded and later gave it to the police. I cross-examined a constable about the gun and asked, "Did you not think 'My God, what an explosive thing to have on a building site where pickets were?'" The judge interrupted to assert that so long as he had a licence he could take the gun wherever he liked. This is not strictly correct but one can imagine the attitude of His Lordship if a picket had turned up with a shotgun and aimed it at a lumper. He would probably have been charged with attempted murder. It was ample proof of the political character of the trial. A charge of unlawful assembly was included in the indictment, and it was said that this had been ordered by the attorney general.

Another charge was conspiracy to interfere with the lawful employment of building workers. As the Lump was in defiance of Building Regulations, I argued that it was not lawful. We took our expert building engineer with the prosecution's engineer to the eight sites involved. In spite of the fact that it was months after the events complained of, on each site there still remained substantial breaches of the Building Regulations. Some scaffolding wobbled when shaken, lacking handrails and toe-boards, diagonal pieces and adequate ties to the building. There was no proper lunch place or shelter for rest and insufficient testing of the quality of work. The judge insisted that the Lump was irrelevant, for the employers were not on trial, and the quality of the work was of no concern. If the latter were found to be bad, surely, he argued, it would only show that the accused and their mates were poor workmen. He declined to believe that bad conditions of work could affect the quality, and when I insisted that they did, he sulked. I have not before seen a judge sulk. In spite of that, relations between Bench and Bar remained normal and in every other way there was total courtesy on both sides in the courtroom. The judge had counsel to lunch and to supper at his lodging; we had him to dine in mess.

One of our more distinguished counsel was Tom Rhys-Roberts. He carried more weight that most and we had to arrange a front-row seat which was expanded to twice the width and depth of the normal one. His car, a large Bentley, had a specially broadened and strengthened driver's seat. His father really did know Lloyd George; Tom told us that they had been partners in the law firm that made the money to enable Lloyd George to go to London and seek his (and the nation's) fortune. One of Tom's contributions to the trial was that he would occasionally invite all counsel, including the prosecution, to a feast at a convenient hotel. It was based upon some delicacy such as venison or wild swan or hare from his family estate in Wales. The meat was hung to the point where it dropped from the hook and each feast was presided over by Mrs Rhys-Roberts, a British Olympic hockey player and as elegant and slim as Tom was gigantic. They made jolly hosts. The trial proved to be a long one, but for us it was shortened by these interludes.

A main reason for the length of the trial was the contradictory character of the evidence. The police found themselves in difficulty because, with rare exceptions, they did not claim to have seen any violent conduct or damage being done. They had heard the sound of material breaking or been told by fellow officers that someone else had seen violence. At Brookside, the sixth site visited that day, Warren spoke to the workers and persuaded them to join the strike. Chief Superintendent Meredith was so impressed that he shook hands with Warren and congratulated him on the meeting and on the conduct of the pickets generally. In cross-examination I reminded Meredith of this. He answered, "Yes, I did go to Warren and shake his hand, as one would with any member of the criminal fraternity." Whether he meant that this was his hopeful approach to receiving a bribe or that he expected a few stolen diamonds to fall from the cuff of any building worker was not clear. When I suggested it was an absurdity, he said that he had not really shaken hands with Warren. He had merely put out a hand to detain him. Another typical corruption of the evidence was an attempt to prove that Warren had threatened to commit arson. On one site, he addressed the men in the rough cabin that served as a canteen and he criticised them for putting up with so wretched a building. A number of witnesses supported his story that what he had said was "Look at this cabin. It's filthy. It's only fit to have a match put to it."

The prosecution was also alleging affray. For this, they need only show that witnesses were fearful that persons in their sight were likely to attack them. Maurice Drake, the Prosecutor, relied upon a continuous affray that covered all the sites, bridging any that came between, and where there was no threat of violence. We were supposed to imagine that a flood of pickets had gained such momentum that they could not stop themselves even where their point of view had already won the day. Yet the police were present on seven of the eight sites. If they had wanted more help to control the pickets they could have obtained it at once. We were told that the police were so heavily outnumbered that they could only have made arrests by using gross violence. This was all in flat contradiction of the evidence that no policeman had seen any arrestable offence. Although the crime of affray is very easy to prove, the evidence was so weak that reliance could not be placed upon it, hence the use of conspiracy charges to bolster the affrays. Conspiracy was an ancient common-law offence of agreeing to do an unlawful act or to use unlawful means to achieve a lawful purpose. It was given new vigour in the mid-nineteenth century in an attempt by government to control trade union activities and today is relied upon as a scourge for the IRA and in the battle against drug barons.

It is the rarest thing to have direct evidence of a clandestine meeting to plot events. Once the events have taken place, and if they show a series of wrongful acts, it is easy enough to infer that they were agreed in advance.

Mr Drake told the jury, quite correctly, that to establish conspiracy he need not prove that there was a meeting or a decision of the wrong-doers. It was enough to show that the illegal events complained of had a common pattern and were done by men acting together. From this, a conspiratorial agreement could be inferred. "A nod or a wink" would do, and you don't even need an independent witness to prove the nod or wink. In company law, the same sort of rule has been applied to a directors' meeting. Two men pass on the platform of a railway station. Some such exchange as "Is that all right?" – "Yes, that will do" was held to constitute a decision at a meeting. When I reminded the jury in a final speech that the six men had never been together until the picketing at Shrewsbury and Telford and had not all known each other, the judge interrupted, "You know very well, Mr Platts-Mills, that for conspiracy they never have to meet and they never have to know each other."

Judges know or imagine that the evil or, as it is now called, the criminality of an event is greatly increased by a conspiratorial meeting and agreement between wrong-doers beforehand. At common law, the penalty for conspiracy was unlimited, and now by statute it is bad enough. Common sense tells us that every acting together by two criminals necessarily involves an agreement, even if it is come to only at the moment of action. Every such agreement has all the elements of conspiracy, but whether a charge of conspiracy is added, with its ease of proof and further penalty, is at the whim of the prosecutor. As an offence, it is totally unsatisfactory and should be reconsidered by the various bodies that review such things. If a crime has been committed, let us call it by its name and prosecute – and defend – for it. This case was brought only on the insistence of the cabinet and it was an impertinence that it was brought at all for, in my opinion, no offence was shown by the evidence. If there were to be charges, they were fit only for the magistrates' court.

Throughout the trial, I had thought that the defendants would all get off. The evidence was poor and the jury was sensible. Towards the end, it seemed possible that with the judge's hostility and the over-vigorous presentation of the defence, we might have brought on our own conviction. Even so, there could be only a fine at the worst. The jury quickly disposed of most of the lesser counts but found it difficult to reach a decision on the conspiracy charge. They were held in a hotel overnight before finding three of the accused guilty of conspiracy. In mitigation, I raised with the

Assistant Chief Constable of West Mercia, who came as a witness to give the antecedents of the men, the confidential report that his force had given to the DPP. This gave the police opinion that such violence as had arisen on certain sites was both spontaneous and episodic. Both prosecutor and judge objected. They argued that the law of exclusion of documents as privileged on the ground of public interest applied to all parts of court proceedings, while I argued that it did not apply to the stage after verdict. I did not manage to get this point before the Court of Appeal or into the reports, although something like it appeared before Mr Justice Wood in 1988, when he maintained the privilege.

Before sentencing, two of the defendants asked to speak. Des Warren told the judge that seasoned convicts he'd met in jail had warned him that a speech would probably increase his sentence. Mr Justice Mais wanted to know what Warren thought of that advice: he was determined to have his say. Warren then set to work on the Tory government, the employers and the trial as a whole, and denounced all as being inspired by politics of an unsavoury character; theirs was the conspiracy. The judge tried to stop him but Des rejected every effort. He argued that if governments were to interfere against workers every time the employers complained, there could be no free negotiations between trade unionists and the bosses. Every strike could be treated as an attempt to wreck the economy. He compared this to the indifference of employers toward safety laws, which was the direct cause of many deaths, and reluctance to prosecute guilty employers.

Eric Tomlinson was very vocal, and almost eloquent. He compared the security at the time of their arrest with that accorded the Great Train Robbers and the Krays. "Locked in a police van, with police in vehicles in front and police in cars behind, police motor cycle escorts, police with Alsatian dogs.... Are those the methods used for an ordinary criminal case? I think not." Counsel, judge and jury had a similar experience, for ground-floor windows and doors near the courthouse entrance were all boarded up and remained like that throughout the two and a half months of the trial, and the police cordon far exceeded the honour party that accompanies the trumpeters at the opening of assizes. The idea can only have been to suggest to the jury that the accused and their friends were uncontrolled hooligans likely at any moment to hurl stones at every piece of glass in sight, or stink bombs at the judge and jury.

The judge sentenced Carpenter, O'Shea and Llywarch to nine months, suspended for two years. McKinsie Jones and Tomlinson were sentenced to prison: nine months and two years respectively. At this point, the foreman of the jury shouted, "I'm leaving this court." We all turned to look and there he was, forcing his way out past the crowded knees in the jury box. He shouted, "It's disgraceful," and kept on shouting until he disappeared through the jury door. Another juror followed, showing his anger by slamming the door of the jury box. Everyone was astounded. I had never seen the like, and I don't think any of us had. Mr Justice Mais tried to salvage the situation by saying, "Well, we don't really need them any more, do we? Let the jury be discharged." This neat rescue operation did credit to his presence of mind, since it was a very public attack on him. The sentencing stopped because he was plainly hoping that the jurors would come back. When the two men returned, rather sheepishly, they heard Warren sentenced to three years' prison. Outside court, the distressed foreman told the wives of the defendants what had happened. The jury wanted none of the accused to go to prison, but one juror claimed to know the law and had insisted that this could not possibly be the outcome. They were eight/four for nearly twenty-four hours. Finally, two gave way on the basis of the argument, "You can't keep us here forever." The jury bailiff confirmed a lot of this to counsel. The foreman had stood firm throughout against the conspiracy charge and was crying as he spoke to the wives.

The defendants had done no wrong, and the act of agreeing to do no wrong was the "conspiracy" for which they were tried and convicted. We appealed and convictions for affray were set aside, but we made no progress with conspiracy. Intimidation is tri-able only in the magistrates' court and not by indictment at the Crown Court and the maximum sentence is three months. For conspiring to intimidate, Warren had been sentenced to three years. The Court of Appeal accepted that this sentence was not really based on the personal conduct of the accused but was mainly deterrent in the face of a crisis over picketing. They added views about the joinder of conspiracy with the substantive offence: if the charge of doing the act itself, the intimidation, would not give sufficient penalty, then by all means add conspiracy and up the ante by twelve times. In effect, the Court of Appeal said to the prosecution and judge, take your own course. If it is against trade unionists, we will support any excess that you may care to indulge. If you can obtain a conviction for conspiracy as well as for the actual offence, the defendant will then pay both the proper penalty for the substantive offence, and another sentence twelve times as much.

In sentencing, the judge had called Des Warren vicious and arrogant. These were perverse judgements upon qualities that I would have called determination and courage, and both exercised on behalf of his fellow workers. Warren proved to be the most uncomfortable prisoner that ever occupied a cell. He had a copy of the Prison Regulations and the Prison Rules and the Appendix to Rules. On dozens of occasions, he was charged with prison offences and each time he lost remission, although his behaviour had been correct by the book. When Labour came into power in March 1974 Roy Jenkins was Home Secretary. His first job should have been to let the Shrewsbury Three out of jail and to pardon them. His own father had suffered from the same sort of prejudiced judgement and had gone to jail for nine months for picketing offences in 1926. Jenkins let the building workers serve out their time. His reasoning seemed to be that the trade unions were too strong and were likely to dominate the Labour Party. He thought that the most suitable Labour leaders should come from the claret and chips department.

In August 1974, the International Union of Students, through the National Union of Students, sent me off to see what was happening in Chile. One of the worst tragedies of the decade was the dictatorship of the Chilean junta that saw thousands of leftists and democrats tortured to death. This was triggered off by the assassination of the Socialist President Salvadore Allende, during a military coup led by General Augusto Pinochet. Chile used to be a stable democracy. In the 150 years prior to 1973, the country had only once been under an extended dictatorship and that was from 1927 to 1931. Since then, the military had kept out of politics, until the CIA chose to bring them back. Pinochet's coup was the culmination of three years of intensive destabilisation in which the Americans manipulated the politics and economy of Chile in an effort to foment anti-Communism. It was the same old story, as replayed in other lands and in other decades. Washington approved of free and democratic elections as long as no Marxist was permitted to win.

They slipped up in November 1970 when Allende came to power at the head of a Popular Unity coalition. Allende's leadership polarised the country. All were either for or against, and nothing could keep those on either side from expressing their beliefs and acting upon them. The three years of Allende's office were the richest forcing bed for democratic activity. It all came to an end on the 11th September 1973 when the Moneda Palace came under attack by tanks and aircraft. Within days of the coup, at least a thousand of the government's supporters had been killed. At first mutilated bodies were heaped up on the roadside or thrown into the Mapocho River, which flows through the middle of Santiago. Later, thousands disappeared into mass graves. An International Commission of Inquiry into the Crimes of the Military Junta in Chile was set up by sympathetic parties, including Joe Nordmann of the IADL, Ramesh Chandra, Secretary-General of the World Peace Council, and Alexander Berkov, a Soviet expert in constitutional law. The Chilean delegation to the first session included Hortensia and Isabel Allende, respectively widow and daughter to the president. There was no shortage of atrocities to report, only a shortage of ideas on how to combat this new and murderous regime.

The junta's published Declaration of Principles averred that Marxism denied the fundamental values of civilisation. "In politics or morality, just as in mathematics, the denial of a negative implies an affirmative. Anti-Marxism implies, therefore, the positive affirmation of the freedom and dignity of the human being." General Pinochet had told the world that he would eliminate all Marxist ideas from Chile forever. Since socialism has a natural attraction for the young, this required the re-education of the best of Chilean youth. The armed forces were sent in to occupy every university and every school. University rectors were replaced by military men, teachers and students were interrogated about their political beliefs and all were treated like prisoners when on campus. A great many were arrested and tortured, and some were killed. By the time I was sent to enquire into the situation, some 300 left-wing students were still detained without charge and most had been held for sixteen months.

Although life seemed outwardly calm, the country was in a state of suppressed terror. The military behaved as if they were occupying an enemy territory; given the level of support for Allende, perhaps this was not surprising. I met many students but a greater number of ex-students, for the junta had expelled thousands from the campuses. Over 75,000 were forced out in fifteen months and there was no right of appeal. The brightest young people were being denied education and forced to take what jobs they could, such as manual work or hawking goods on the street. To avoid the attention of the military, it was essential to have a job, an identity card and short hair. Anything less was regarded as proof of subversion and invited the attentions of DINA, the notorious intelligence investigations department. It was believed that Walter Rauf, a Nazi who had killed thousands of Jews during the last war, was helping DINA and rumour suggested that he had been appointed director of the service.

An almost military discipline appeared in the schools. The Minister of Education, Admiral Castro, had spent years as the Director of the Naval Academy. I got an appointment with him and was told of his success in streamlining the curriculum. This seemed to mean removing anything that might refer to, or even hint at, Marxism. Sociology, economics, journalism, psychology, philosophy and history were dangerous territory. The junta was trying to brainwash an entire generation so they would have no social or political ideas except those of the extreme right. Studies disapproved of by the junta lost so many professors that classes could not be held. The East Campus of the University of Chile at Santiago lost more than 2,000 academic staff, and dismissed teachers were not permitted to apply for posts anywhere else. Sporting activities were divided into "healthy" and "unhealthy". The former were encouraged, while the latter were discouraged. "Unhealthy" distractions included thinking and all forms of self-defence such as judo. From junior levels, every subject bore a coating of nationalism and jingoism. All students over the age of fifteen were made to study the new subject "National Security", which sought to persuade the pupil that even thinking about a political idea was subversive and potentially as dangerous to the state as an enemy invasion.

While I was in Santiago, a mass arrest took place in the northern part of the city. A shanty-town area was circled by armed police and air force men and at four a.m. they drove out every male over fifteen to have his papers inspected. Two houses caught fire during the search and burnt down, but this was said to be coincidental. The men, numbering some 300, were marched to the local stadium. Every man who could prove his employment was sent home by midday. The rest were divided into two groups. Those who were young and apparently healthy were immediately and forcibly recruited into the military services; the others were carted off to prison. I had a first-hand account of the incident from one who was detained and released, and the whole operation was widely reported in the national press. I was told that such raids were a common occurrence in the poorer quarters.

One of the worst things I saw was a woman who had been branded on the thigh with a hammer and sickle as big as my hand. Her husband was imprisoned as a Communist. In the early hours of one morning in May, three men armed with machine-guns broke down her door and demanded to know who were her husband's friends. In front of her young children, she was raped by each of the men and told that she would be killed if she told anyone what had happened. The visit was repeated in every detail a week later, although with three different soldiers. In July they brought an electric soldering iron and branded her with the Communist emblem. Now she had been to a solicitor and was attempting to take her case to the courts. Lawyers who tried to help such people put their own lives at risk from the security services. Eight months after my visit, Fernando Ostornol and Graciela Alvarez, two lawyers who worked unstintingly to defend others and were of the greatest assistance to me, were put into Tres Alamos torture camp. Ostornol was meant to be in the defence team for Luis Corvalan, leader of the Chilean Communist Party, who was himself held in Tres Alamos.

Political prisoners were tried by military tribunals where they were not permitted to question or to challenge the prosecution story, nor to cross-examine prosecution witnesses, nor to call witnesses of their own. There was no publicity and no right of appeal. Sentences were far more severe than would apply in the ordinary courts, and any sentence could be revised at will by the chief of the regional state of siege. I was told of one trial in which a lawyer protested that his client's statements were all extracted by torture. The lawyer was removed from the court, reported to the Bar Council and reprimanded by the College of Advocates. The Supreme Court could have insisted on the right to oversee the military tribunals – and this was what the lawyers I met all wanted – but the judges had not the courage. I thought that they should instead be fighting for the abolition of military trials for civilians. If this could be stopped, the ordinary appeals machinery would provide sufficient safeguards against unduly harsh sentences in the normal courts. I met the President of the Supreme Court and it was clear that nothing could put courage into him. It was equally obvious that he would soon have to be succeeded by his deputy, Jose Maria Eyzaguirre, who happened to be a friend of Fernando Ostornol.

On the day of the coup, the junta decreed a "State of War" for the whole country. This allowed them to run Chile as if it were genuinely at war, although the declared enemies were the supporters of Allende. These were not only the people who voted for him in the 1970 elections, but the forty-six per cent of the electorate who voted for the Popular Unity government at the elections held in March 1973. When I met the Minister of the Interior, General Cesar Benavides, I asked him about this fictional "State of War". He asked his legal adviser to explain the concept, which was that the pretence of a state of war permitted the doubling of penalties. To facilitate the conviction of Allende's supporters, the military tribunals ruled that the declaration of a state of war could be antedated to 1969, to the point at which it was first seen that Allende was likely to succeed in the presidential election of 1970. It was thus established that a state of war had existed in 1969, although no one had been aware of it.

The whole leadership was convinced that immense quantities of arms had been secretly imported under the Allende regime. Caches of these weapons were supposedly hidden away, waiting for the Communists to stage a counter-coup. The President of the Supreme Court said that these caches were sufficient to arm twenty brigades. The difficulty of finding them he attributed to the fact that those who had hidden them had since fled the country, or were themselves in hiding, or had committed suicide. When faced with the same question, General Benavides claimed that the intelligence services had already found double that amount of arms. When asked whether the men in hiding had tanks, the minister expressed some doubt. When asked whether they had warplanes, he thought they had not. It was only when the questioner asked whether they had warships that he realised that the whole proposition about hidden arms was being ridiculed. General Benavides confirmed that they were still searching for the arms. He told me, "We have only found fifteen to twenty per cent of what we know is there." The obsession with these weapons was a main reason for the persecution of the Left. People were tortured on the supposition that if they had supported Allende, they must know of hidden arms and they died under torture for their inability to supply the locations of these non-existent arsenals.

In a series of trials, the military junta successfully accused the elected government of rebellion against them, as the armed services, on the basis that since the five parties of the left were Marxist, they must of necessity be enemies of the state. They were seditious because, as Marxists, they did not recognise any fatherland. (The tribunal did not deal with the question of whether Christianity recognised a fatherland.) They decided that Marxism had a juridical quality; it was seditious. Yet defence lawyers were prevented from discussing Marxism on the ground that the court was not there to discuss political questions. A group of air-force officials were tried from May until August for passing secrets to the Enemy of the State, meaning President Allende. I think that the most remarkable assertion made at their trial was that the treasonable conduct of the elected government was as grave as that of any treason in recorded history. The defendants were compared with Dreyfus, Tukachevsky, the Rosenbergs and the Bay of Pigs. This overlooked the fact that Dreyfus was later vindicated as completely innocent, that Tukachevsky was the victim of one of Stalin's greatest frame-ups and that the Rosenbergs were executed to discredit Soviet science. What the tribunal thought of the Bay of Pigs as an example of treason it was impossible to imagine.

CHAPTER THIRTY-EIGHT

1976: Three Commonwealth Capital Cases

JANET AND I were visiting Antigua in the Windward Islands in March 1976 when there came a summons from the journal *Liberation* that I must go at once to the neighbouring island of Dominica and extract from the noose the neck of Desmond Trotter. On the flimsiest of evidence, he had been convicted of the murder of a white American tourist during the carnival in February 1974. The young man had an excellent alibi. He was confined to his house several miles away with bronchitis and severe asthma, for which he had a medical certificate, and a woman police constable had seen him on his veranda in pyjamas around the time of the shooting. Two men in my chambers were appearing for him in the Privy Council, but if the appeal failed he would be hanged. No local resident seemed to have observed the incident, but two Antiguan girls on holiday in Dominica came forward as witnesses. Since the trial, they had sworn affidavits declaring their statements to be false and attributing them to police pressure and offers of financial reward from the same source.

Why was Trotter set up for the murder? He was an eighteen-year-old civil servant and a noisy critic of the government. He had joined the Rastafarians, with their back-to-the-land movement, and belonged to a group of young mostly unemployed people who worked hard at bringing wasteland into cultivation. As squatters, they were reviled as a dangerous Communistic influence and almost every incident of violence and theft was attributed to them. The Rastafarians were also known as "dreads" for their distinctive hairstyle of long, thick, matted pigtails known as dreadlocks. These were sometimes smeared with mud to signify humility and a direct contact with the earth. Eight months after the murder of the

American tourist, the Parliament of Dominica passed the "Dread Act" which outlawed the wearing of locks. It also provided that any wearer of such locks found in someone else's home could be shot on sight without fear of legal reprisals. It was the most monstrous law imaginable and it was to the great credit of the Home Secretary, Mr Isiah Thomas, that it was suspended within the year.

Whom could I approach in Dominica? The governor of the island was Sir Louis Cools-Lartigue, whose son Joey was one of my former pupils. The father had once come to Sunday lunch and dozed in the window-seat in the long room at Harrock House. I rang up and asked how is Joey? He is well and practising law in Canada. I was invited to visit and went next morning to Roseau, the capital, by the island-hopper, a small plane that takes in every possible airstrip in the islands. The next morning I was installed in the Fort Young Hotel, converted from a real fort built in 1770, and rang the governor to announce my arrival. He said that it had all been a misunderstanding. It wasn't his son Joey who had been my pupil but his nephew Joey, who was now dead. He himself was not the Cools-Lartigue who had come to Sunday lunch and slept on the window seat; that was his brother Alexander, who was also dead. But I was expected at Government House for lunch just the same, and his wife looked forward to meeting me.

Lady Cools-Lartigue was a real expert on French wines and had as splendid a cellar as was possible in the Caribbean. This was to be a real feast. There was a sort of local caviar – pink and lumpy, over-salted, but plainly associated with fish. There was "mountain chicken" (frogs' legs) and "mountain angels" (snails) and legs of "mountain quail". Then hors d'oeuvres of supreme of delight, which was thin slices of eel cut from the part by the tail, and baked mountain banana – a very small plantain, but lots of it. At that stage, the real eating began. There was fish and rich lobster and poultry of two sorts, with sorbet in between courses. Then it was back to the mountains for "mountain goat", which was real goat, although the only mountain it had seen was the mountain of garbage collected from the city of Roseau. Next came pudding and fruit accompanied by the sweetest sauterne, second only to Chateau d'Yquem. Every other dish or course in the itinerary through the mountains and the sea was accompanied by a new wine.

By the end of the meal, it was getting a bit late and we were all tight.

I at last raised the subject of Desmond Trotter. The whole atmosphere changed completely. The governor said, "Oh, I am glad you have raised that question. Of course he has got to die. No one of us is safe here while he is about. He has got to hang. If I could, I would shoot him at once. I can't do that, but he is a most dangerous young fellow." I said, "Well, actually, I've come to get him out," and the atmosphere changed again. I pointed out that there really was no evidence against Trotter since the two Antiguans had retracted their statements. They were plainly imported for the job, their supposed identification of Trotter was a farce, and the good name of justice in Dominica was at stake. Sir Louis was much moved by this and, reminded of some of the bare facts that supported the brief for a reprieve, promised that so far as his position would allow, he would urge the case for remitting the death penalty.

Patrick John, the Prime Minister, was determined to go ahead with the execution but he was out of the country. For the moment, the acting Prime Minister was Isaiah Thomas, the Home Secretary, who favoured a reprieve. Here was our chance. The governor rang Mr Thomas and arranged for me to see him. He added, "You'd better try and give him something that he can later show to the prime minister as, for example, some big submission and apology by Trotter." I went to the prison hoping to persuade Desmond to make an assertion of deep regret for all the trouble that he had caused to the Dominican authorities, coupled with a promise to lead the most useful, moderate and proper life. I urged the inclusion of an open address to the young people of the island, calling on them to reject violence, but Desmond objected on two grounds: it carried the suggestion that he was putting himself forward as a leader whereas there could be no leaders in a movement where all are equal, and he was so averse to violence that he could not bring himself even to use the word. We talked for an hour and a half and I was impressed by his modesty and integrity. He wrote a letter, but it was not the letter we had hoped for.

Rastafarian comes from Ras Tafari, one of the names of Haile Selassie. The Rastafarians called for modesty, truth, friendliness and hard collective work, and these were very much the superficial poses adopted by the late dictator of Ethiopia. I discussed with Desmond the fact that Selassie was a ruthless and greedy exploiter. He said that he was aware of these things, but was undeterred. "DesTrot" had by now become something of a hero for blacks around the world. Messages of protest poured in from the UK, the United States, Canada, Western Europe and various parts of the Caribbean. Three or four weeks later, Desmond's reprieve was announced by the prime minister himself "in his capacity as temporary chairman of a prerogative of mercy campaign". Desmond settled down in jail, nominally for life. What none could foresee was Hurricane David that struck the island three years later, destroying a large part of Roseau including the Fort Young Hotel and the prison. It took Desmond a shorter time to act than it took for the warders to react; he disappeared into the night, never to be seen at the prison again. I had supper with him in London some time afterwards, when he was the guest of the solicitor Mr Michael Seifert.

Two other cases involving capital punishment cropped up in the summer of 1976. Although August is the start of the barristers' season for taking it easy, the long vacation from the English Bar means that you are more readily available for cases overseas. In late July, Ken Harwood, the clerk at Cloisters, was asked to send an advocate to Lusaka to try to save the necks of three ZANLA officers on trial for the assassination of their leader, Herbert Chitepo, who had been blown up by a car bomb sixteen months previously. ZANLA was the armed wing of ZANU, the most militant of the revolutionary groups fighting against the white leadership of Rhodesia. The three defendants were Josiah Tongogara, ZANLA's Chief of Defence, who oversaw all military operations; Joseph Chimurenga, a top provincial commander; and Sadat Kufamazuba, a young bodyguard to Chitepo who had himself been badly injured in the explosion. Since their arrest, the three defendants had been kept incommunicado and it was widely rumoured that they had been tortured by the Zambian police. The first choice as defence counsel had been bullied and intimidated into backing down and it was thought that the second choice would benefit from foreign support. I accepted the case and at once began studying background material supplied by their friends in London and by Amnesty International who, because of the allegations of torture, had agreed to help with the cost of sending over a barrister.

Ken cabled Eddie Shamwana in Lusaka for the date of the hearing and for advice on how to arrange a visa and call to the local Bar. Eddie had been a pupil in chambers and was now President of the Law Association for Zambia, so we thought there wouldn't be any difficulty in getting a temporary practising certificate. Even so, in an acutely political case it is always useful to have the best possible introduction to the head of state. Dr Kenneth Kaunda I had first met with Fenner Brockway at some Commonwealth occasion in London many years before, but not in a manner that warranted saying I knew him. By good chance, Sir Seewosagur Ramgoolam, Prime Minister of Mauritius, was in London. Dr Ram was an old and dear friend; a doctor of medicine, who had been the leader of every move towards independence in Mauritius over the last forty years and was shortly to be its first home-born governor-general. As head of the Organisation of African Unity for the year, he had recently played host to Kaunda. Dr Ram offered a letter of introduction to Kaunda and backed this up with a cable sent via the Zambian High Commission.

While waiting for the trial to come on, Ken received an urgent appeal: "Off to Dacca in Bangladesh and rescue a Dutch boy from the noose." I had several former pupils in the area and plenty of contacts. Was there any chance of doing both cases? From the available information, each was sufficiently serious and the threats to the accused men so outspoken that it called for advice from the highest quarters. As always happens, the Foreign Office knew a great deal about the events leading up to the proposed trials and had firm ideas as to what was the likely outcome. In each case, they could see only one possible hope and that was to nobble the respective head of state. The approach to Kaunda was well in hand, but Major-General Ziaur Rahman of Bangladesh I had not even heard of. Neither of these colossi could be reached because both were shut up in Colombo at the summit meeting of the non-aligned countries.

Over a hundred grandees with their supporting legions had gone to Sri Lanka and, as a result, the whole country was barred to foreigners until the distinguished visitors and their supporters had left. No visas were being issued and no one was being let in except their own returning diplomats, yet I would have to be there by the following evening or else it was too late. Mauritius was a non-aligned country and the High Commissioner, Sir Lecraz Teelock, suggested that I should go to Colombo as special adviser in International Sea Law to Dr Earn, who was in Colombo not only as representative of Mauritius but as Chairman of the OAU, so commanding his full share of distinction in the gathering. A main topic of the conference was "The Indian Ocean – an ocean of peace". It was agreed that I should advise, if necessary, on the important question of the dimensions of the Indian Ocean: the top, the bottom, the North, the South, et cetera. In fact, no occasion for advice arose.

The conference was nearing its end and I was squeezed onto the first plane the next morning. I had no visa and no ticket, only a receipt for having paid the fare. The one condition laid down by British Airways was that if they were forced to bring me away at once, I would be responsible for any extra fare. The plane had been crowded when we set off for Bahrain; from there on to Colombo we were four passengers only. I had no promise of a visa, but only the confidence that Dr Ram would do his best. He had indeed, for there at the airport and at the foot of the plane steps was a stout lady looking for all the world like Prime Minister Bandaranaika, but in fact her representative, accompanied by two attendant brigadiers. It was all tea and smiles and then into the minister's car with banners flying. At the Lanka Oberoi hotel, where eighty or more heads of state were housed, I was given a suite next door to Dr Ram. Nobody else could have responded so promptly and so successfully. By lunchtime I was fellow guest with a number of Sri Lankan ministers and at five p.m. was admitted to the conference hall and heard Dr Kaunda make his speech. I quote one of the final passages, where he was approaching his peroration and addressing the Arab woman who was chairing the session:

> "Madame Chairman, my Lords, Ladies and Gentlemen, your Holinesses, Eminences and Excellencies, Kings and Queens, Princes and Princesses, Brothers and Sisters, Comrades: Let the struggle go on. Let it be waged with the utmost ferocity, the battle against hunger, disease and superstition. In all other realms let there be peace, above all in our beloved Indian Ocean."

Kaunda had earlier said that the armed struggle must go on in Zimbabwe (Rhodesia) and must be intensified, but it seemed that he was treating this as entirely an internal affair and in no way inconsistent with universal peace.

Security was so strict that there was no getting into or out of the hotel save with a special pass and your own car, both of which I lacked. The only way was to hitchhike in the personal vehicle of a head of state; it was fortunate that there were so many about. That evening Dr Ram took me to a party given by Marshal Tito, the senior of all the heads of state, in honour of the conference. It was aboard an old British warship moored in Colombo harbour, which had been given to the newly independent Sri Lanka because it was unfit to sail. There Dr Ram introduced me to Kenneth Kaunda and to Major-General Ziaur Rahman. The first proved to be somewhat intractable and said the matter could wait until I came to his country. I was free to come and defend whomever I liked, so long as he was not expected to pay. The second was more accommodating. We were both booked on a commercial flight next morning to Bangkok and he suggested that I should then travel by his private plane on to Dacca. I was not to say too much about it, but just get on the aircraft. On the trip from Colombo there was no chance of a private talk with Ziaur, who sat rather in state in the first-class compartment, although as compensation I did get to know Mr Michael Aubrey, Master of Oundle School, a most pleasant travelling companion.

At Bangkok, there stood on the tarmac the shiniest new aeroplane ever seen; it was labelled Bangladesh Biman, the new national logo. I was urged to get on board as quickly as possible up the back stairs. I ran across the tarmac without a word of tickets or passes, and also without my luggage, which followed on the next day, lacking only my gold watch and chain, which I had foolishly brought with me and even more foolishly left in the bag. For the rest of the journey I sat with the major-general, who looked most distinguished. He was slim and trim with a tight-buttoned beautiful bright blue blazer with golden buttons and a wasp waist, and he sat as though at attention on his horse; a Bengal Lancer if ever there were one. I told him of the high regard in which the whole of Britain held the Bengal Lancers, being quite unaware that he had recently disbanded the tank regiment and arrested nearly half its strength. He made no mention of this and we came, quite naturally, to talk of his own military experiences and of his taking over his country. Next it was the wider question of the amity of nations, and especially the flow of contracts between England and Bangladesh, and above all between Holland and Bangladesh. When we were scarcely halfway on our journey, it was agreed that, for the sake of amity, the young Dutchman would be home by Christmas, whatever the outcome of the trial, but I must promise to keep this secret and let the trial proceed.

The supposed wrong-doer, Dr Peter Custers, had taken a degree in International Law at Leyden University and had then gone to Washington

DC to do research in international affairs. In 1973, his university had allotted him the practical task of spending three months in Bangladesh helping to implement the government's programme for making the peasants more independent. A main part of the programme was aimed at increasing literacy above its then rate of only twenty per cent. Custers mastered the Bengali language and stayed on as a development aid worker. Under the pseudonym Revo Conti, short for Revoluzione Continua, he became a regular correspondent for De Volkskrant and De Groene Amsterdammer, two reputable newspapers. Custers lived a simple life amongst the very poorest people and, in some ways, he took the problems of his new friends too much to heart. According to the police, Custers came to agree with the peasants that the best way of making them more independent was to arm them with guns and teach them how to shoot. This was obviously a practical idea but it did not appeal to the authorities and in December 1975 he and others were seized and charged with unspecified "anti-state activities".

I arrived in Dacca on 20th August and met Custer's parents and his uncle, who had come from Holland to attend the trial. We got permission to visit in prison and found him thin almost to the point of emaciation and with a poor, straggly beard. The uncle was a physician and we soon learned that the young man had suffered a broken wrist that would require an operation to re-set properly and several injuries to the back and the front of his head. Throughout his time in prison, Custers had been denied access to legal advice. Just before our arrival, this was changed and he now had two barristers, a team of husband and wife. We had several meetings with our client and helped him to prepare a statement, explaining his conduct and apologising if he should have committed any wrong. The sixteen co-accused had an element of treason in the case made against them; this could not apply to the Dutchman, who owed no allegiance to the State of Bangladesh. One part of our argument was that it was equally unfair on Custers and on the Bengalis that he and they should be tried together. The charge against Custers had been changed to "conspiring to overthrow the government through violent means". He told us that he did not wish to claim that the case made against him was not a genuine one, only that his motives may have been misunderstood.

Before the trial began, there was a hearing by the military tribunal and a civilian magistrate to decide whether I could appear as advocate. The law provided that nobody could practise in any court unless he were enrolled in the list of advocates. This argument was taken from the appropriate volume of Halsbury's Laws. Halsbury dominates all British-origin jurisdictions as the code of Justinian of the fourth century dominated the known world for a thousand years, or the code of Napoleon in the nineteenth century. The authorities in Halsbury make it clear that the word practice must be taken in its ordinary sense to mean 'to carry on, or do, habitually or constantly; to make a practice of; to act habitually". It was decided that as there was no sign of my coming again for a further case I could not be considered to be practising in their courts. It was therefore agreed that I was not there to practise but merely to appear before them. If it would help me, they would rule that I must never again appear before them. I had my permission and the case was on.

We were told that Custers' trial would be under conditions of martial law before a tribunal of two army officers and a civilian. All defence counsel would be sworn to the strictest secrecy, never to divulge a word of what happened in court. At the first sitting, we pleaded for a public hearing and for the press to be granted access. That was it. The relatives were told that they could not attend at all, the diplomat sent by the Dutch government as an observer was also banned, and the trial was suspended. The local barristers expected a considerable delay and asked me to come back on or about 4th October to resume preparations for the trial, so on 26th August I set off for Lusaka. A few days later, the Court of Appeal of Bangladesh ruled that I was not entitled to appear before the tribunal. However, on 7th September the press was informed that Custers would be expelled from the country as soon as the trial had ended. Since Ziaur Rahman clearly meant to keep his word, there was no point in even trying to return.

On 20th September, the trial was suddenly ended. The defendants read out their statements and defence counsel made their final pleas – all in the absence of the president of the court who had, it was rumoured, gone off to collect the verdicts and sentences from the head of state. These were handed down on his return with no indication of which accusations and allegations had been accepted or rejected by the tribunal. Seven of the defendants, including Custers, were convicted and sentenced to fourteen years' imprisonment (described as "transportation"), another seven were acquitted, and the remaining three were released. None were to be executed.

Three days later the government announced that Custers would be deported immediately "as a gesture of goodwill" for the Muslim festival of the Eid. He did not have to wait until Christmas after all.

The flight across Asia and down the coast of Africa needed five changes and a merciful night-stop at Bombay. Eddie Shamwana came to the airport at Lusaka and took me home to stay with his family. Eddie was widely regarded as the most influential man in Zambia, of those not active in political life. One ambassador said, "He may play golf at State House whenever he wishes, and is the only one who can refuse when he wants to." President Kaunda was away for most of the three weeks of my visit, so there was no chance of presenting my letter of introduction, and all attempts at reaching him through one or other minister failed. At the British High Commission I met Ted Rowland, the visiting Minister of State, and Stephen Miles, the High Commissioner, to ask their opinion of the Tongogara case – what would they like to see come of it, and what did they expect? Their main concern was that no one should think that they had any point of view at all and they insisted that a casual visiting barrister must not pretend to speak for the British government, as though he conceivably might. This was thrice repeated in fifteen minutes. They insisted that the liberation of Zimbabwe was a matter of peaceful negotiation only, and that the ceasefire should be maintained at all costs. It was a courageous but irrelevant point of view.

The view of my clients was that the peace negotiations were aimed at giving the illegal Smith regime another ten years of security. The explanation was that through breaking off contact with South Africa, Zambia was suffering grave economic effects. The Zambians had to pay for airfreighting heavy copper-mining machinery instead of having it shipped by train from South Africa at a fraction of the cost. Now Kaunda wished to make peace and had agreed with the South African government that, as the term of restoring this commercial contact, he would force ZANU to give up their guerrilla warfare against the Rhodesian state. ZANU's National Chairman, Herbert Chitepo, opposed Kaunda's negotiations with Vorster and Smith on the grounds that a forced ceasefire was tantamount to surrender. Zambia's official party newspaper, owned by Lonrho, warned that ZANU would be destroyed if it didn't toe the line. Almost at once, an armed mutiny broke out within the ranks and approximately sixty guerrillas were killed before the rebellion collapsed.

The Zambians exploited differences over tribal affiliations, educational level, and whether the guerrillas were pro-Chinese or pro-Russian to weaken ZANU's capacity to resist the policy of détente.

I went to see the place where Herbert Chitepo died. He had got into his Volkswagen beetle, parked in a carport beside his miserable little house, had just started to back it out, and boom. There was some sort of crater still in the road, now only a minute little dent. We inspected the wreckage of the car, cut in two by the force of the explosion. The official supposition was that the three defendants had killed Chitepo through tribal jealousy. However, the other ZANU leaders were convinced that Chitepo was killed for his opposition to Kaunda's policy of détente. The murder had been preceded by rumours that Chitepo was about to be either arrested or deported. A number of guerrillas had been abducted or assassinated in Lusaka by South African agents, and the only people who would stand to benefit from Chitepo's death were the white minority regimes and the Zambian state. Nothing coming from Zambia could have pleased them so much as the heads of these leaders of Rhodesian independence severed and delivered up on a silver dish. After Chitepo's funeral, nearly 1,300 ZANIJ fighters were detained by the government, putting an end to the guerrilla war. This was in March 1975. In December, on the insistence of Tanzania and Mozambique, all except fifty-seven were freed, the remainder being held on suspicion of having assassinated their leader.

Kaunda then set up a Special International Commission of Inquiry to investigate the circumstances of the assassination, but really to clear Zambia's name. Their report was completed and published in March 1976. The Commission was international only in name: the chairman, secretary and chief inquisitor were all Zambians and Zambian authorities chose all the witnesses. In the main, these were members of the rebel group who had staged a bloody mutiny and had themselves threatened the life of Chitepo. The greatest enemies of the ZANU leadership accused them in their absence, and no cross-examination was permitted. It was no better than a secret inquisition. The published report declared that the assassination had been ordered by the entire ZANU Supreme Council and the Military High Command. All were now to be put on trial for their lives. According to Eddie Shamwana, the detainees were being held only "for their own safety as they might be killed by their fellow guerrillas if they were released". Eddie was a friend, but it was not a convincing argument. The detainees appealed for help to the OAU, the International Commission of Jurists in the Hague, to the UN Human Rights Commission and to Amnesty International.

Our three clients were in Lusaka Central Prison, regarded as the worst jail in the country. They had not been permitted visitors or legal advice. We were told that we could not see them without a note from a commissioner or assistant commissioner at Police Force Headquarters. Senior Assistant Commissioner Dickson Mupundu said that he could not give such a note unless we produced a personal letter of introduction from the attorney general or the director of public prosecutions, countersigned personally by the home minister. Mupundu's best efforts to delay and to inconvenience the getting-leave to see our clients were defeated by the DPP's sending a senior officer direct to the prison to introduce us. After that, we were free to go at any time. Josiah Tongogara and Sadat Kufamazuba shared an eight-foot by five-foot cell with three other prisoners. They slept on the floor without bedding of any kind. I spent twelve hours in prison with the accused over five days, and many further hours at court and we went through all aspects of their case.

In particular, I took a full statement of the precise treatment that the bodyguard Kufamazuba had undergone. He had been pulled out of the wreckage of the car with serious burns and shock. On the day after Chitepo's funeral, he was taken from hospital and placed in solitary confinement in jail. Kufamazuba was tortured for two and a half months until he agreed to sign a "confession" that he had helped to place the bomb in the car. One of our main submissions was that this statement had been extracted under torture when he was still suffering from injuries received in the explosion, and that stitches closing an arm wound were pulled out as part of that torture. Dickson Mupundu was generally regarded as most efficient in obtaining statements from reluctant witnesses. Beating of a straightforward kind had become fairly routine in hostile interrogations. I was told that at first victims had been taken to remote farms for "treatment", then obscure houses in towns were selected. Now the beating was done almost openly at force headquarters.

Tongogara told us that at his first interrogation Mupundu had said, "The only thing I want from you is to say yes or no to this statement I have here, that you, Tongo, murdered Chitepo and you directed the murder." Tongogara was then beaten with broken chairs and heavy rubber pipes, and tortured with electrical shocks and the insertion of small sharp pieces of wood under his fingernails. He couldn't remember how many times he had collapsed. Interrogations usually lasted seventy-two hours, although a session lasting a whole week was not uncommon. After one such three-day session, Mupundu had forced Tongogara to sign a confession that he had not even read. Tongogara had given the Chitepo Commission a full account of his ill-treatment but was not believed. The government of Zambia had decided that he and the ZANU collective leadership were guilty and there seemed no reason for confidence that the high court would be any more just.

There proved to be no up-to-date provision for reciprocal dealing with the English Bar. I would not be allowed to address the court but it was agreed that I might sit with the defence team to consult and advise at every stage. We had two very young lawyers named Mundia Sikatana and Pierce Annfield and it was agreed that Pierce should act as spokesman for the team. The trial began on 6th September before a single high court judge. There was no opening of the case by the prosecutor, just straight into the calling of witnesses. The principal witness for the prosecution was Cornelius Sanyanga, Secretary of Lonrho (Zambia) Ltd, summoned to convince us that ZANU was torn with racial strife. "There were many rumours spread of tribalism, but I am not quite sure that I could give evidence of any experiences myself." This dishonest tittle-tattle went on for the whole of the day. Then we had the admission of statements by the defendants. We challenged Kufumazuba's confession as having been obtained under duress and disclosed the names of the senior policemen who had taken part in the beatings. This opened a trial within a trial to test the admissibility of the statement.

In evidence, Mupundu said that Kufamazuba could not have been beaten and certainly not for periods of more than twenty-four hours at a time because of an absolute rule that no prisoner could be absent from the prison where he was lodged for more than twenty-four hours. When taxed that the prisoner had been taken to police headquarters by Mupundu himself and for four days, he retorted, "But that is impossible because we have not any sleeping accommodation." Ten days after the start of the trial, the judge summoned us to his chambers and announced that he wished to be away for a few days. The prosecutor then disclosed that he would like to have the remainder of the fortnight free and the trial was adjourned for a month. I returned to London. We resumed on the 18th October and on the 20th the judge bravely dismissed all charges on the grounds that prison records had been tampered with and that Kufumazuba's statement had not been given freely and voluntarily. He said, "My conclusion would indicate beyond doubt that Accused 3 was a victim of unfair and improper conduct on the part of the police authorities," and he instructed the DPP to commence criminal proceedings against the police. On Kaunda's orders, no action was taken.

We learned that Machel and Nyerere had put considerable pressure on Kaunda to stop the trial and to send the remaining ZANU detainees to Tanzania or to Mozambique, but that the acquittal of our defendants was mainly the responsibility of Robert Mugabe, who was in urgent need of Tongogara's negotiating skills at the Geneva conference. Tongogara was a brilliant strategist, eloquent and well-mannered. He was widely regarded as the key figure in bringing about a settlement at the Lancaster House conference at the end of 1979. It is most sad that he did not survive to continue his active work, for he died a few days later when his car crashed into the back of a truck in Mozambique. Foul play was suspected, but it appears to have been a genuine accident. After Zimbabwe gained Independence in April 1980, senior officers of the Rhodesian Special Branch volunteered the information that Tongogara had been innocent of Chitepo's death, although none was willing to say who had been responsible. In 1987 Ken Flower, who led Rhodesia's external intelligence unit for seventeen years, published his reminiscences, *An Intelligence Chief on Record*, from which the following quotes are taken:

> "The Zambian Special Branch who investigated the assassination were not interested in ZANU's version of events; they prepared their own statements and tortured those in detention to obtain false confessions. Tongogara, in particular, was handled with the utmost brutality. At one stage it was reported that his back had been broken under interrogation, which persuaded me to take the unusual step of sending a personal message to the Head of Zambian Special Branch, expressing regret and suggesting that our disinformation had gone far enough. There was no reply, indicating that he was unaware of the convention between Intelligence Services that on the rare occasions when one Head

speaks to another on an issue such as this it is most likely to be the truth, no matter what one's juniors are required to do when practising deception. In the circumstances, Mugabe could not be blamed for later labelling Chitepo's death as 'an act done through or by direct participation of the Zambian government'."

By the time the Chitepo Commission had issued their report, it was clear that Zimbabwean independence would come very quickly. When Ken Flower learned that the ZANLA High Command and ZANU's Supreme Council would be indicted for the murder, he told Kaunda's lawyer that the findings of the Commission were worthless and that Tongogara had nothing to do with the assassination. "Chitepo was dead and Tongogara had suffered enough, so surely Rhodesia could afford to be magnanimous." Kaunda felt that Zambia could not afford magnanimity and Tongogara and his comrades would have been executed were it not for the insistence of the leaders of the other front-line states, and especially Robert Mugabe.

CHAPTER THIRTY-NINE

Establishment Attitudes; Arrest in Czechoslovakia

I WAS elected a Bencher of the Inner Temple in 1970, which was rather sooner after silk than most Benchers. Frank Soskice was always a little ashamed of having turned me out of chambers in 1953 for attending Stalin's funeral and he persuaded Gordon Wilmer to support him in getting me elected. The Bar looks to Benchers of the various Inns with quite undeserved respect. Members of the Inn and all its servants address one as "Master" and there are bows and counter-bows. We give ourselves quite considerable privileges in return for governing the affairs of the Inn. We pay "commons" as termly contributions to culinary affairs, like battels at college. So many dinners are then free and the remainder of the nights during dining term are very reasonably priced. There is as much wine as we care to drink, and that is virtually free. In return, one must keep up a certain decorum.

When John Mortimer, now Sir John, was put forward as a Bencher of the Inner Temple, the first he knew of it was in a letter from the treasurer for the year, Reggie Manningham-Buller, then Lord Dilhorne and ex-Lord Chancellor, saying that the suggestion of his name for election had led to certain members of the Bench raising grave objection and saying that they would vote against him and would, if necessary, blackball him. Would he not prefer to save embarrassment to himself, to the Inn, and to the Bench as a whole, by causing his name to be withdrawn? I am sure that this was the only occasion in John's life when he appeared as a lame dog, but he brought the letter to me. We agreed that the course for him to take was to fight this out. We discovered that the objection was because someone thought that it was not possible to have as a member of the Bench a man whose wife, after their divorce, had described intimate scenes of their personal life, as Penelope Mortimer had done in *The Pumpkin Eater*. He stood his ground and his name was duly announced.

Within a week he had signed a letter to *The Times*, as the only lawyer with a group of people from different professions, commenting upon the law that said that it was a crime to approach a soldier and express a view about whether he should fight in a particular war or not. They had in mind, of course, the position of a young Irishman asked to go and fight against his own countrymen in Ireland. This was a comment on the Incitement to Disaffection Act of 1934. At once, the critical Benchers changed their point of view. "We cannot have a traitor on the Bench."

This was an even stronger ground on which the aspirant could fight. After all, in 1912, F E Smith and Edward Carson had declared publicly and with the greatest vehemence that a young Irish soldier need not obey his lawful orders if they involved his going to fight in Ireland against his fellow countrymen. Each later went to the House of Lords as lawyer, and each became Treasurer of his Inn. This was suggested to the liberal members of the Inner Temple Bench, who were enough to carry the day, if needed, and with one voice they cried, "But you cannot rely upon Smith and Carson. Those villains may have been Treasurers, but from quite different Inns: one from Grays Inn and one from the Middle Temple. Find someone from the Inner Temple who made the same outcry and then you are getting somewhere."

By chance, there appeared the story of Jack Seeley. His father had a large estate in the Isle of Wight, but the money flowed from Anthracite coals in the Monmouth area. Jack had come down from Oxford in 1894 and gone to the Bar at the Inner Temple, where he built up a workable practice. In 1900, when it seemed that Her Majesty might lose the South African war, he joined with others in forming the CIV, or City Imperial Volunteers. This was like a group of feudal levies. Young men volunteered with their whole personal team in attendance. Jack Seeley had horses and outriders, farriers, grooms, stablemen and batmen. Similar supporting teams came from business and the semi-professions of the city fringes. They held great parades in London, then went off to South Africa.

Jack Seeley first became noted when, at some crossing or other, the Boers captured several of his personal waggons. Two were filled with champagne! The Boers made fun of this throughout the world. Seeley decided that he must take a graver attitude, and he resolved that he and his team would kill every sharp-shooter or sniper who fired a shot within their hearing. When the warning shot was heard, his team would disappear from the line of march, and by evening had so surrounded the sniper that he had spent all his ammunition, had shot not a single person, and was unarmed as they closed in upon him. Seeley would eventually ride him down with a sabre or with a lance and kill him by hand. When he could claim twenty such victims without a single loss, he created history by being treated as the bravest man in South Africa and by being the first British officer to cite himself for the Victoria Cross. He did this by the stratagem of citing his own batman for the award with the phrase "He followed me wherever I went".

Seeley entered parliament in the Liberal landslide of 1905. In 1910, he was made Minister of War in honour and recognition of his own warlike accomplishments. In 1912, he was sacked for having signed a note which mirrored Smith and Carson's view. In 1933, Seeley became Lord Mottistone and for all the years since the war he had been known as an extremely brave man. Seeley's story was appropriate enough to spread around amongst the Benchers, and it so took aback the ultra-hard-right members that there was not a single dissenting vote nor a single blackball. John Mortimer became a Bencher in 1975, and an extremely popular one.

One of the pleasures of being a Bencher is the taking of Sunday lunch at the Inn during term time. To this feast come the master and the reader, our two parsons, with their spouses and all the Benchers and families who have been to church. This makes a most enjoyable gathering and the pleasure is not diminished by teasing the preacher on his sermon. The Temple Church is crowded, the choir is glorious, and you sit close under the pulpit. For me, it is not a question of belief; it is positive knowledge that there is no God. If I be wrong in this, then a most humble apology will be called for, with the plea in mitigation that a clearer explanation at the time would have been helpful. I do not think of myself as irreligious for I have a deep sense of reverence. I revere so much that it is not reasonable to start listing. Beauty in many forms has me, figuratively, on my knees with delight. Women are wonderful beyond compare and there are a number to whom I have been devoted without necessarily ever daring to say so.

Religious ideas were not possible until the brain of man had so developed that it could work them out for itself. As man's intelligence grew and he had more experience at explaining his thoughts, so his God developed from a log of wood with carvings to a golden calf and thence to the Glorious Conception that we have today. Man created God in his own image and continues to do so, and it is a wonderful achievement. Man has no soul save what he has thought of for himself, or others have thought of for him. He will be remembered, if at all, according to anything done of renown, for then others will write of it. Otherwise, nothing will live on after him except in the memory of those who survive. "Earth to earth, ashes to ashes, dust to dust." The memory of earth or ashes or dust is three or four generations at most. But if you are a conformer by nature – or like to appear so – then you go to church. I was for many years a trustee of the Vestry of St Dunstan's, Fleet Street, and I still attend communion at Oxford on the Saturday afternoon of the annual Balliol Society dinner.

I am also a member of the Leander Club, the Worshipful Company of Ironmongers and the Athenaeum. I did not apply to join the Leander, nor was I asked to join. It was thought that the attraction of swaggering in Leander pink among oarsmen on boating occasions was such that no one could refuse. There is a rule that if you have rowed in the trials of either Oxford or Cambridge and the secretary of your boat club puts forward your name, then you are in. You are simply told that you are a member. Then came the Ironmongers, one of the great historic City Livery Companies. In 1936, I shared a room in chambers with Brother Whiteside of the Ironmongers. In addition to that, he was clerk to some nineteen other companies, each of which existed mainly through a large tin box with its name on the outside and its rolls, scrolls and charters inside, and all minded by Brother Whiteside. The members came together only in a hall borrowed from one of the greater companies. Whiteside put me up for the Ironmongers. He had an especial right because his son was killed in the First World War and he could fill his son's place with another choice. I was moved by the somewhat honorific position in which he had placed me and knew nothing of any political flavour that might attach to membership. This was just before my marriage and before joining the Labour Party. Now I am almost the oldest in call of the liverymen of the company, and the only one of such standing that hasn't been promoted into the higher realms of cityhood. Five of my sons are Ironmongers and Freemen of the City.

The Athenaeum is the premier club and I have greatly enjoyed it – not the less because it provides parking space. I believe there are various bigwigs who are at once made members of the club on assuming office, as for example, certain royal appointments, the Keeper of the Queen's Musick and the like, archbishops, presidents of this and that. One evening, friends took me to dine at the Reform Club. I was just leaving to collect my car from the Athenaeum when three Lords Justices accosted me and asked what I was doing at their club. I explained and they said with one voice, "No Court of Appeal judge has been a member of the Athenaeum since Kenneth Diplock achieved it." I told them that I could get them all in if they liked, but only for a drink. I first visited the club in the 1930s. After our wedding, Janet and I kept up friendship with Bishop Bell of Chichester. He was strongly anti-Nazi and I believe he even entered into debate in the *New Statesman* as to whether Hitler would attack Poland and Russia, or would lead off at France. Kingsley Martin wanted him to write more positively in the *New Statesman* and I was asked to introduce them to one another. The Bishop, as a member, had us to the Athenaeum on several occasions and I was impressed by the convenience of the club for such gatherings. I decided that if ever there should come a chance to be a member, I would take it.

I had to wait another thirty years until the two members who composed the club's Commission for the Fine Arts, renowned in their respective spheres, decided to get me in. They had both been at art school with Janet, and were both junior to her. They greatly admired her work but realised that she would not now be likely to be elected to the Royal Academy, her career having been hampered by an excess of children and a complete lack of any help from me. They would propose me for the Athenaeum in honour of Janet. I heard of this only when they reported that questions had been raised as to whether I was not a Communist. They had answered without hesitation that undoubtedly I was not, but had asked whether there was a rule about this. Had not the Soviet Ambassador Maisky been elected a member, and possibly he was a party member?

It is a most curious position, belonging to and making use of institutions that are more appropriate to a retired Tory minister or colonel than to a worn-out colonial leftie. Members of the Bar are generally conservative.

In the 1970s, it was so unusual for barristers to accept cases that criticised the police that I'm sure there were those who thought that my purpose was to embarrass or even to undermine the police, rather than to help my clients. It certainly wasn't so, but the mistake is understandable. This reputation as a police-basher, added to a continuing involvement in issues on the left, meant that a certain notoriety continued, though there is no longer the slightest trace of the hostility of the past. Those who were once so angry have mellowed with the years. I remember coming into the Robing Room at the Old Bailey in the early 1950s and being greeted by a rather senior member of the prosecuting team, "You can't expect to come in here and be treated like an ordinary decent person. No one here will have any truck with your ideas." Later we became close friends and he began calling me "Johnnie". He was the only person who habitually addressed me by that name.

At the institutions I frequent, the dinner table is a standard meeting point and above and during the meal comes the talk. I am usually seated with men of quite mature years, but often not known to me. The older men used to say, "But weren't you the fellow who was hanged and put in the oven and beheaded? What happened? Remind me of it." Now the recollection of people of my age is even more remote and the comment on meeting is no more than "I remember the name. Wasn't there something...? Was it in parliament? I don't remember. He seems quite an ordinary sort of fellow." That is the stage it has reached; "an ordinary sort of fellow" and, I hope, a fair enough judgement. Younger people know nothing of that distant past and are quite content to be chided about their own actions or lack of action. They are, as a rule, so busy answering about their thoughts and opinions that they seldom reach the stage of a cross-interrogation.

What little criticism I have encountered in recent years has invariably come from someone whose thinking remained stuck in the past. When the Unity Theatre burned down to a shell in 1975, the building was under-insured and we were offered only £30,000 for the land. A trust was formed to exploit the site and since I had gone on the first Unity Theatre Trust when it was set up in the 1960s, I was invited to join. Edith Summerskill urged the other trustees to reject me, saying that I would be "the kiss of death" to their plans. It was an absurd exaggeration and treated as such. I didn't resign and the board decided not to have Edith as a trustee, even though she was offering and nominated and waving a £5 note. One of the other trustees was a chartered accountant. He took a guiding hand with our finances and thanks to his advice, the fund has greatly increased to something approaching £500,000. Other trustees have included the actors Alfie Bass and Bill Owen and Alan Bush, the Socialist composer. At a normal trust meeting we treat ourselves to a "crust to eat and a wee refreshment" and even that slight indulgence has the sponsorship of ASLEF, on whose premises we meet, and of one of ASLEF's professional officers, Ena MacMillan. We believe at times that we are seeing the throes of the rebirth of Unity and sometimes we picture ourselves as again being the owners of a great theatre.

When I started at the Bar in 1932, every barrister, with the rarest exception, wore a high collar and bow tie as ordinary professional dress. Perhaps there were half-a-dozen south of the Strand who wore turn-down collars, as all do now. Two exceptions were Lord Justice Scrutton and my own pupil-master Sammy, who both wore their stiff turn-down collars with their white bibs, even in court. Gerald Gardiner and D N Pritt were always in plain suit, but it was exceptional to find anyone else so attired. Today not five per cent wear routine black and pinstripes. I persevere with the old style because of ample supplies of striped trousers in my wardrobe and want of another suit fit to wear. That is probably the usual reason why old men keep to old styles.

There was some surprise expressed when I turned up on the picket line at Grunwick in black jacket and waistcoat, fancy pants, bowler and rolled umbrella. The Haldane Society had agreed to lend their support to the pickets and I stopped by on my way to court in the morning, wearing my ordinary working gear. At least twenty Haldane members were already there, but isolated from the main group of pickets and penned in by the police. Jack Dromey, who was Chairman of the NCCL and Secretary of the local Trades Council, was on the strike committee for the factory. He thrust a megaphone into my hand and said, "You have a go." It seemed to me that the appropriate line would be, "Who would picket for the police if they went on strike?" Why, who else but the Haldane Society? We would be there to picket for them. The police roared with laughter. I added a few jokes, then spoke seriously about the exploitation of the Asian women, with a few actionable slanders about the proprietor, George Ward, whose treatment of his workers was a source of delight to the Tories. In fact, he was lauded as a national hero.

This battle over union power started in August 1976 when the Grunwick workforce, mostly Asian women, came out on strike for the right to have union representation in negotiations with the management. They were poorly paid and greatly exploited. When they all joined APEX, Ward dismissed them. The women picketed for forty-four weeks – timidly, quietly, and ineffectually. Then all the Left joined in to help. There's no battle of that kind that isn't worth fighting. Even when you lose, they pay a dividend in knowledge and experience. The mass picket began in mid-June 1977 and at once degenerated into violence. The trouble was that the police over-reacted and they harassed, struck and arrested pickets who were doing no more than exercising their lawful rights. I had just finished my little speech to the pickets and the police when the chief superintendent came up to me and said, "Excuse me, sir. Would you mind very much just stepping over that wall and getting behind that tree? I think there may be some trouble." He was right, but I was safely out of harm's way. I doubt that the officer would have shown the same concern for my welfare had it not been for my attire, still regarded as an establishment "uniform".

When Janet and I put our farm on the market a few days after this, it was reported in the William Hickey column as "Scourge of the gentry asks £300,000 for his acres". I was described as "one of our cuddly old Lefties recently seen among the chanting multitude in the Grunwick picket line" and "that strangest of birds, the wealthy Socialist". They said that I had made a fortune from the Bar. Unfortunately, this was quite untrue. I was paid 80 guineas in my pupil year, and 400 guineas in my first year after that. These were treated as records among those of my call, but were soon eclipsed by others who were not beguiled into the byroads of the law. I have never made much money, and what little I did have was spent on school fees for the six sons or lost through bad investments. The greatest disaster came through the purchase of six blocks of flats in Pembroke Dock. They were a "mares' nest". I'm not sure what a mare's nest is, but it was difficult to get them properly managed or controlled, to get the rent collected and damages repaired. Local amateurs tried, local professionals tried, the longest occupying tenant tried. I had the flats for years and always at a loss. By the time I finally got rid of them, I believe they were so wrecked that they were thought fit only for the most needy. The local authority would resort to them for desperate cases. It took me a very long time to get out of debt.

The left-wing reputation didn't prevent me from being arrested in Prague just before Christmas 1979, but it did help to get me freed pretty quickly. I have often been followed and rather scared in strange countries, but this was the only time I was ever arrested. In October six members of VONS (the Committee for the Defence of Persons Unjustly Prosecuted, an offshoot of Charter 77) were charged with trying to bring disrepute to Czechoslovakia abroad. This was for publicly monitoring their government's compliance with the human rights provisions of the Helsinki agreement. Sentences ranged from two to five years' imprisonment. I was chairman of a London support committee that arranged for Peter Archer, who had just ceased to be Labour Solicitor General, to attend the trial. He was willing, but we were unable to get him a visa. When it came to the appeal in December, the committee decided that it was my turn to try. This would be an openly anti-Soviet gesture, and the only one I had ever made. I thought of Otto Sling; I owed it to him to go. I wrote a letter to the Czech Ambassador asking for a visa to attend the trial and sent it by messenger. Someone at the embassy read it and said, "If I act on this letter you'll never get the visa. Simply go to the consular office and ask for a visitor's visa." I took my passport and it was granted at once. But wasn't there a danger that once in Prague some official might say, "So, you pretended to be a tourist and concealed the fact that you were coming to spy into our internal affairs?"

I arrived in Prague the day before the trial and went straight to the British Embassy to find out whether the ambassador was offering any support to the appellants. He greeted me in most cordial fashion and disclosed that every West European embassy in Prague was to send a representative to the trial. They were to meet at the court and all hoped to get in, or at least to be able to say that they had been refused entry. He contacted the Czech Foreign Office and informed them that I wished to call on the judge of appeal before the case was heard. I was introduced to the British minister and it was arranged that we should meet at the court at seven-thirty the next morning. At the end of our interview the ambassador complained that I had not remembered him; he had for two years running been part of the cricket team of fathers against sons at Dane Court. I, having five little boys there, had been captain of the father's crew for four years on end. This appointment was not as a recognition of prowess but for long service. On the last occasion, we were soundly beaten by the boys, but I had the satisfaction of bowling out Mark, no 6, with a Yorker.

Other lawyers had come from Austria, France and Belgium. I met several at breakfast the next day and we travelled together to the Supreme Court at the Prague-Pankrac Palace of Justice. It was here that Otto had been tried and condemned, and this reinforced my determination. I got into the entry lobby by protestation of a possible appointment with Dr Jarmila Dojcarova, the Appeal Court judge who would be hearing the case. A helpful messenger carried notes to her and I was invited to stay until the end of the session when the judge might be able to spare time for me. After an hour's wait, it seemed more sensible to go back outside and join the families and colleagues of the chartists, the diplomats having already left. Amongst the crowd in the street, I saw Jiri Hajek, a founder of Charter 77 and one of their first spokesmen. He had previously come to London as Czech Ambassador, then served as Minister for Education and Foreign Secretary to Dubcek in the spring of 1968. Since the Russian occupation, he was much out of favour. We all retired to a small cafe opposite the court to take a late breakfast and made our plans, including that I was to stay with Jiri. He had a house in the suburbs, left to him by his father, but he had no job. He had no chance of a job in any realm: not as a don at the university, where he had been before, nor as the lowest clerk in the most humble position. He had also lost the pension awarded to him for his wartime resistance work.

Representing Amnesty International was Hans Goldmann, a young Austrian lawyer. We decided to go in search of the Minister of Justice, Dr Jan Nemec. I had met him on a number of occasions, for he had spent many years as general secretary of the Czech-Soviet friendship association. We wanted an introduction to the judge and an instruction that we be admitted to the court. We were not permitted to see Nemec, but were told to return to the Supreme Court building where we would meet the head of the Bar Council, Dr Josef Ondrej, who had offices there. Dr Ondrej was an active member of the International Association of Democratic Lawyers, of which I was then vice-president, and through which we had become friends. We were given a paper from the ministry with the name and address of Dr Ondrej written in Czech. At the Supreme Court building, Mr Goldmann showed the paper and insisted that we really were now guests of the minister and of the chairman of the Bar Council.

This got us back into the entry lobby, where we were politely requested to wait. It was now 12.30 and we waited with some confidence.

A few minutes later two smart young men in trench coats burst into the building, accompanied by perhaps a dozen armed police. We were informed that we were under arrest and ordered to accompany them. The unoffending (as we thought) lawyers were dragged and hurried out of the building into separate cars and we were then driven to Central Police Headquarters in Bartholomew Street. During the car journey, only the plainclothes man spoke to me. He indicated that none but an idiot would go about without his passport, and anyone who behaved so stupidly deserved to be arrested. As my passport had been taken by the hotel clerk when I had registered the previous day, I asked that we pass the hotel so as to collect it. This was refused; why should anyone believe such a foolish story as that a hotel would keep someone's passport?

The situation was not made easier by the fact that once at the station, everyone pretended not to speak English. I was kept in a room with a most dour and uncommunicative young man. He wouldn't answer in any offered tongue and affected to be mute. After a while I realised that the pennants on his wall were all of Czech football clubs. I asked him which club he supported and how the Czechs would get on in the World Cup. In the best English he asked, "Will Chelsea buy Kevin Keegan from Hamburg?" I revealed sufficient ignorance about English football to enable him to score several goals and me a few own-goals on the topic. After that we got on quite well and I was even allowed to put my feet up and have a sleep. I foolishly suggested that this short rest should be taken after lunch, but he countered that that did not apply because I hadn't had any.

Then I was taken to meet a senior questioner who, through an interpreter, asked, "Have you been in Czechoslovakia before?" I presented him with nearly an hour's worth on the Haldane Society petition over the Runciman betrayal of 1938, the setting up of Czech escape routes, the Czech Friendship Club and several more incidents presented in a way most favourable to myself. After I stopped, he retired. About quarter of an hour later he came back with a much older man, whom the interpreter introduced as head of their Special Branch. This fellow looked for all the world like a mature English civil servant. He spoke excellent English and seemed to be dressed in his best Saville Row suit. He bestowed upon me an encomium, adding that it was acknowledged that I was a valued friend of Czechoslovakia and most worthy and even noble in my relations with the Czech people, but it was thought in some quarters that I might have been misused by evil-minded persons. He offered a profound apology for my arrest and a cup of coffee, both of which I accepted. It was understood that my return flight was arranged for the next morning, and he wished me a comfortable evening. I was warmly thanked and discharged with a blessing.

As I was going out the front door, I saw that a young man came into the outer passage, as it were from some side room. He was dressed for the street with a sort of trench coat, and a hat pulled down over his nose. When I got into the main street he offered to exchange some money. He could give five times the official rate and cash was immediately available. I had no intention of falling into so easy a trap, thanked him profusely but declined, then continued down the street. On pausing to look into a shop window, I noticed that he was doing the same a little further back. Seeing the doors of a tram about to close, I hurried across the road and jumped on board. He followed. I got off immediately at the next stop and moved round in front of the carriage. I looked carefully to see that he didn't get off and just as the tram clanged its bell to move forward, I got out of its way on the other side and never saw him again.

Then to the restaurant in Wenceslas Square where the leaders of Charter 77 were due to meet for a late lunch. It was now well after three p.m. and many had left, but Jiri Hajek and Zdena Tominova were still there with a few others. Mrs Tominova was the wife of Julius Tomin, the philosophy professor who had been detained outside the courtroom that morning. Hajek had a permanent following of three plainclothes men, and one or more popped in and out of the restaurant to make sure that he was still there. We arranged a meeting point for the evening and then, immediately after one of the surveillance visits, Jiri went off to make some telephone calls. One of his guardians looked in again, and then came real excitement. A plainclothes officer came with a number of armed and uniformed men and proceeded to arrest me. Three of them I recognised from the Supreme Court. Mrs Tominova abused them roundly in Czech and explained what nincompoops they were for not knowing that I was a distinguished supporter of their country. I had just come from a most friendly interview with the head of the Czech police service, with the utmost courtesy and every expression of appreciation and thanks, and now they were making fools of themselves by their unprovoked behaviour. They would be in great trouble if they took me back to the police station. She did all this in a loud voice, standing up so that everyone in the restaurant saw what was going on. An oral battle ensued in which a number of those who sat at the tables took part.

The senior policeman ordered her arrest in an absurdly theatrical display. She refused to go but eventually yielded to their demand with such bad grace and resentment that it took them ten minutes to secure her exit. Two officers went to the back of the restaurant to collect the coats, leaving only the youngest policeman to guard me. When he began to move towards his colleagues, a waiter who had throughout the incident shouted abuse of the police in French, summoned me to a side exit and pushed me out into what seemed like the shop next door and I was away. A trip down an escalator into the basement of the neighbouring shop and out the side door and upstairs into another building and out another side door, to confuse things a bit more, and I was back to my hotel. In the evening, I had dinner with Jiri in some local cafe, then home to his wife and family for a comfortable and, I hope, comforting visit. I was on the plane next morning and regret that I have not seen him since.

Professor Tomin remained in custody for many days. He had been turned out of his Chair at Charles University because of his support for Charter 77 but continued to hold philosophy seminars for current and ex-pupils in his own flat. Because he was in trouble with the government, his attempt to maintain contact with students at the university was frowned upon, although his seminars involved the most non-contentious discussions about classical philosophy from the Greeks onwards, without ever being so up-to-date as to touch upon Marxism. In January 1980, he appealed to some English universities for support and a number of Balliol philosophy dons began the practice of going in turn to Prague and taking part in his Wednesday talks. Visitors were constantly under surveillance and when the Master of Balliol, Dr Anthony Kenny, himself turned up to attend the first discussion meeting after the professor's release, the place was raided and the master arrested. He suffered the indignity of being taken straight to the frontier, for which the explanation may have been that he had not played in the fathers' cricket team with the British Ambassador.

My nephew Edward Irving was an undergraduate at Balliol, and with Stephen Lukes, a philosophy don, we arranged that Tomin and his wife should be invited to Oxford and given at least temporary residence at Balliol. This duly happened, to fairly universal satisfaction. Several years later he was still in residence; the college had not quite expected this. When he subsequently appeared as barman at a Swindon pub with the title "visiting philosopher", his photo was in all the English papers. And what of the six dissidents whose appeal we had tried to attend? Otka Bednarova is retired, Vaclav Benda and Dana Nemcova went into Parliament, Petr Uhl became Director of the Czech Press Agency, Jiri Dienstbier was made Secretary for Foreign Affairs and Vaclav Havel, the Head of State.

CHAPTER FORTY

Zambian Justice; Denning and other Denizens of Law

PUPILS ARE a feature of bar life. For at least twenty years I had four at a time, which meant that they received scant instruction. The only way of making up for the fact that you had too many pupils was to insist that they should all be in constant attention at every conference and court attendance, and should at least glance at every set of papers that the pupilmaster saw. Each pupil would be given the chance of concentrating on one set of papers at a time and of doing them thoroughly, by which I mean preparing notes, settling the pleadings, and so on. I discovered that the real requirement of a pupil was that he or she should take pep-pills or amphetamines to keep up. I discovered these by chance because one pupil was taking them already and they seemed most effective. I must add that this was years before they became illegal.

I used to ask pupils what they wanted to do and then to encourage them in that direction. Whether it was criminal or civil work, advocacy or paper work, I always tried to provide what was wanted. From one Indian pupil, Mihir Sen, the answer came: "I wish to swim the Channel." It was midwinter but I took Sen to the Serpentine to prepare. We both plunged in. I gasped and spluttered and plunged straight out. He went a hundred yards up the lake with a solemn, steady but rather slow trudgen stroke, a kick to each arm beat – not the most economic stroke for a twenty-five-mile swim. For our next visit, we had obtained the lanolin that channel swimmers use to keep out the cold. I smeared it over Sen's body, at which the lake keeper and one or two perverse swimmers who actually seemed to like the cold protested vigorously at the soiling of their water. I explained that he was a potential Channel swimmer, the first for all Asia. Sen was already well up the lake and going strong. He was forgiven and invited to come again. Having introduced him to English waters, my job was done. When the summer came, he went into training. He got himself a boat and an attendant boatman and swam ever greater distances. On the attempt, he gave up after fourteen hours, having made only a little progress. When being hoisted out, he said, "I feel a fool for having tried." *The Times* wrote him up as the first honest Channel swimmer.

Sen finished his year in chambers, married a nice English girl and went off to set up in India. Three years later, he was back again with a moustache, a fearsome beard and heavier by a couple of stone. He now looked the part. Sen took the swim in his stride and in due course was presented with the medal of the Channel Swimmers' Association at India House by Lord Freybar. As his former pupil-master I was bidden to attend, and no one ever was so proud of his pupil. I was still on the list established by Krishna Menon and went as the guest of Vijayalakshmi Pandit, the sister of Nehru and aunt of Indira Gandhi. She has been described as the most decorative high commissioner that ever came to England from anywhere. Sen later swam every appropriate water in the world, including the Straits of Gibraltar, the Hellespont and Dardanelles, the Straits of the Bosporus, the Panama Canal, and many miles along the East India coast. He became a successful lawyer in Calcutta, winning a wide reputation as one who worked for civil rights and for the neighbouring Bengalis.

A couple of dozen of my pupils have become judges, attorneys-general or leading politicians in one Commonwealth nation or another. Probably none climbed so high or had so cruel a fall as Eddie Shamwana, who was pupil to Claude Allen in my chambers. The trial of Tongogara was only the first of several cases in Zambia and I was always made very much at home by Eddie and his wife Stella. Eddie had built up a busy practice in Lusaka and was, at one time or another, Leader of the Zambian Bar, Chairman of the Bar Council and High Court Commissioner. It was rumoured that President Kaunda intended to make him the next Chief Justice. Then Stella wrote to ask if I would return to Lusaka to defend Eddie if, as seemed likely, he was committed for trial for high treason. Mundia Sikatana, one of the young lawyers in Tongogara's defence team, had gone to the police and warned them that a coup was being plotted. A secret army was being assembled and immediate action must be taken to forestall the plotters. Soon afterwards, Kaunda announced the arrest of those Sikatana claimed as his co-conspirators. Amongst them were the Commander of the Air Force, two army majors, a former governor of the Bank of Zambia, a couple of politicians, several top businessmen and Eddie Shamwana. That was in October 1980.

At first, the defendants were held in a prison in Lusaka. It was overcrowded, but at least the wives could carry in food and clean clothes daily. Kaunda had promised that the conspirators would be tried within a fortnight but when the DPP saw how little evidence was available, preparations for trial slowed to a snail's pace. After six months, the prisoners tried to put a petition before parliament. This impudence was punished by transferring them to a far worse prison some 300 miles away. Eddie's application for a writ of Habeas Corpus was rejected, as was an appeal to the Supreme Court. The next step was to seek redress under the Constitution of Zambia; again he lost. In passing judgement on a writ of habeas corpus filed by one of the other defendants, the judge had actually said that the president had the power and the right to detain anyone at any time, even if they were innocent, and there was nothing the courts could do to overrule Kaunda, even if there were provisions under the constitution.

In November 1981, it seemed that the trial was about to start so I hurried off to Lusaka. There was very little happening, and certainly nothing for me to do, so I was home for Christmas. The prosecution had resorted to the common tactic of trying to shake off unwanted defenders by a series of contrived adjournments that made it difficult and expensive for overseas counsel to come and go and come back again. By January, the case had moved into rather horrid areas. All manner of inconvenience was heaped on the wives of the defendants. The most beastly circular letters were sent anonymously from a non-existent address to important people thought to be supporting the defence. Eddie's fellow lawyers got up petitions in his support and were themselves arrested. Stella was constantly harassed about her husband's financial affairs so that she had to be trotting about the courts trying to get dishonest people stopped from trying to enforce bogus claims. It all seemed to be an attempt to counter some good publicity that the defence had scored before Christmas. There was some indication that the source of it all was the office of the attorney general.

The trial was being held before a judge with a dozen lay assistants, each specially chosen by the prosecution. The Attorney General, Mr Gibson

Chigaga, said that the trial would probably last twenty-four months, and the rate of progress while I was there suggested that it was quite possible. Mr Chigaga, who was also the Minister of Legal Affairs, had chosen to act as prosecutor. No attorney general had previously prosecuted a criminal case in Zambia and the defence made a formal objection to Chigaga's leading the prosecution. There were serious grounds for objection: as attorney general, he had been involved in the investigations; it was known that the case was being discussed in the cabinet of which he was a member; it was probable that the defence would call him as a witness. The DPP called the defence motion "premature, frivolous and vexatious". It was not, but it may as well have been, for the judge held that although the attorney general's decision to prosecute was unprecedented, it was up to Chigaga to decide for himself if his behaviour might be unethical.

This was a case of enormous complexity and the utmost gravity. Evidence was offered in the form of many pages of statements of intended witnesses, much of it simply hearsay. A preliminary investigation would have stripped away all of this unfair and inadmissible evidence, but the attorney general had decided that such an investigation was unnecessary. Corroboration, meaning evidence from an independent source, was missing, although it was mandatory under the Treason Act. Certainly, the prosecution spared no effort to produce corroborative evidence. They called over 130 witnesses and spent some months in doing it. They investigated every conceivable aspect of Eddie's blameless life, but the case against him rested almost entirely on the uncorroborated evidence of the air force commander, who had turned Queen's Evidence and was now star witness for the state. His place as a defendant had been taken by Mundia Sikatana. Sikatana had only volunteered the information on the assurance of a presidential pardon. In front of witnesses, Kaunda had thanked him and promised that he would neither be prosecuted nor asked to testify in court. Ten months after the arrests, Kaunda wrote a personal letter to the terrified lawyer, confirming the original agreement but insisting that he now give evidence in person. This was backed up by a note from the attorney general to the same effect.

As soon as the trial began, Sikatana produced the pardon. The attorney general conceded that Kaunda had pledged to pardon Sikatana, but said that the president had since broken the agreement by failing to pardon him. Therefore, all that Sikatana could show the court was a broken promise. On that basis, the poor man had to stand trial for his life with those he had implicated. After two months, I left the case. All we had really done was argue procedural matters, trying to establish the form that the trial would take. Much remained unsettled but there seemed no part for me to play at the moment, so I returned to England for a murder defence at Reading. The treason trial dragged on and on. Two of the defendants contracted tuberculosis, which was rife in the prison. One developed a spinal form of the disease and had to be hospitalised. It was agreed that he might be tried separately, if he were to recover, and the case against the others continued. When the prosecution finally closed their case in August 1982, Sikatana and three others were acquitted. Eight of the remaining defendants were convicted of treason; one received a sentence of ten years and seven were sentenced to death, Eddie among them. The sentences were commuted to life imprisonment after protests from legal colleagues and from Amnesty International. In 1990, a series of violent riots forced Kaunda to make certain political reforms. Eddie and his friends were freed.

At the time of Eddie's arrest, I was a member of the International Commission of Inquiry into the Crimes of the Racist and Apartheid Regimes in Southern Africa. This had been set up by the Afro-Asian Peoples' Solidarity Organisation to help eradicate colonialism by publicising the cruelty of the racist governments in the area and to encourage independence for Namibia. I was put onto the commission by the Haldane Society. The first session was chaired by Sean McBride, holder of the Nobel and Lenin Peace Prizes and a former UN Commissioner for Namibia. Our meetings were usually held in Luanda, Angola, which meant that we always had sheaves of papers in Portuguese, along with the English translations. This came in rather useful for the 1980 arbitration sessions of the Lonrho case against Shell and BP, in which we must have been presented with over 100,000 pages of documents, many of them from Mozambique and in Portuguese. It wasn't too hard pretending to speak the language. Besides, politics and the law have so many "international" words that once you know the "ifs" and "ands", the rest tends to follow.

Lonrho was suing Shell and BP for £116 million in damages for sanction-breaking against Ian Smith's Rhodesia. The case started in 1977 when Lonrho lodged a claim in the high court against twenty-six other oil companies and three former executives of Shell and BP, claiming that they had breached the contract which committed them to supplying oil to Rhodesia only through a pipeline owned by Lonrho's Mozambique subsidiary. The contract agreed between Shell, BP and Lonrho provided that any dispute be resolved by arbitration. The case against the other defendants went on hold while the arbitrators tried to decide whether or not Shell and BP had conspired together. The arbitrators were Sir Harry Fisher, retired from the high court Bench and holding a position as head of an Oxford college, and Dr Jorge Mota, a Portuguese lawyer of great distinction, who could explain Portuguese law and history and practices. Lord Cross of Chelsea was the umpire. They had begun dealing with preliminary matters in June. When I came in, they had already taken over the first floor of the Piccadilly Hotel, where each party had a suite.

Throughout the summer, Bob Alexander, leading for our opponents, made perhaps one or two interventions a week. Each time he would have a note and would begin by saying, "I have only eight points to make" or "sixteen points to make" or, sometimes, "only three". Then he would go through them all. Eventually we referred the case back to the high court for a ruling on certain legal questions and the judge found for the oil companies on each point. David Altaras, one of my juniors from chambers, met Bob at lunch in Middle Temple Hall and reported him as saying, with his hands cupped together in the form of notes although he hadn't any, "My dear David, I have only three points to make. First, we were so glad to have you and dear John join with us for the long vacation. And second, dear John need not worry about his holiday in New Zealand because we are bound to win in the Court of Appeal and then there will be no chance of your going to the House of Lords and the case will be over." After a pause David said, "And what was the third point, Bob?" "Oh yes, the third point. How much we enjoyed having you in the case." The case was argued in the Court of Appeal, although not by me, and their Lordships unanimously agreed that Lonrho had no legal basis for proceeding with the damages claim.

It was said that Bob Alexander had a fee of a quarter of a million for the first day, although his fee in a later case was supposed to have been even greater. In a good year, he probably does better than I have done in a lifetime. My brief was for £45,000, and it remains my biggest ever fee. The barrister who had had twelve weeks to prepare dropped out on the Friday before the arbitration was to open. Solicitors for Lonrho asked

Michael, our junior clerk, whether I could be ready to lead off on Monday. He replied, "Well, he's just an Old Bailey hack. He has never had more than the night before to prepare anything. He can certainly do it over a weekend." I inherited a team of four juniors and brought in one extra, David Altaras, then opened the case for eight weeks.

At the time, Michael was just standing in for Ken Harwood, my chief clerk from 1968 to 1985. Ken was most successful at his job and portly in proportion. He had an endless supply of good stories and he shouted and laughed at the same time. When we were in need of more clerking, Michael arrived. He was tall and elegant, a trifle acerbic and aloof. If Michael were busy, you could talk to him for three minutes before he appeared to take any notice and then he could answer as though he had been following all the time. Was he not a C B Fry Exhibitioner from his school? This award made him the Rhodes Scholar of Commercial Road. If all our Rhodes Scholars were as bright as he, they would justify the expectations of their founder and every one of them would be PM of his respective country. When Ken retired through ill-health, Michael took over as chief clerk. Although clerks have only a first name, Michael made it known that he thought that he should be addressed as Mr Martin. That project was not really achieved in full.

Barristers are often accused of taking an unreasonable interest in their own financial welfare; we invariably try to step to one side and put the blame on our broad-shouldered clerks. All clerks have as a necessary quality the determination to earn a lot of money for themselves and a little for their barristers on the way. They do not begin with that idea. Their entry is as quite young men by family connection or introduction. If they survive it is because they show the qualities that are needed. Senior clerks are ruthless in sorting them out and in rejecting those who they feel will not succeed. They do the same with the barristers, both young and old, when in their opinion it is called for. It was my second clerk, Frederick, who used the phrase, "the barrister is a bird of passage to be plucked in passing".

When Denning started at the Bar, his clerk became famous for two phrases. The first was: "Young gentlemen who hope to succeed at the Bar should never be seen carrying papers. They must let it be understood that they know everything", which was why Tom's clerks always carried his papers. The second was: "Mr Denning, sir, young gentlemen who hope to succeed at the Bar must speak with a deep rich voice, not with a high-pitched squeaky voice." Denning followed this advice and the high squeaky sound he had made when he first appeared in the Temple was replaced by the rich sort of brogue he attributes to Whitchurch, his Hampshire birthplace. I had a run of cases with Denning, and there was even an early case where he was a junior. That was at Bristol where Berrymans, the London solicitors, were defending a shopkeeper who had sold a Harris Tweed coat to lady who contracted dermatitis. It is fair to say that Harris Tweed, in its manufacture, has as unhappy a start as anything that could be imagined. In its early stages, it has a rather intimate life with the crofters of Harris and with their goats and sheep. It is permeated by smells that never leave it. After that, it is so washed and boiled and scraped and scoured that with any lesser cloth there would be no particle left. The tweed retains its known strength and coarseness and savour, but it is inconceivable that a particle of anything except this rare bouquet could remain.

Berrymans briefed the son of the family, Monty Berryman, as a junior to come "special" off the circuit. They also briefed Walter Monckton to lead. A stranger could not appear on the circuit at assizes unless he were paid a special fee and had in his team a junior who was a member of the circuit. I had this job and the case was fought against a local junior, who appeared for the plaintiff. We won before Mr Justice Charles, who held that the cause of the dermatitis was some idiosyncratic tendency inherent in the plaintiff herself and could in no way be attributed to the character of the tweed. Mr Justice Charles was no doubt a great judge, but not great enough. His decision was of precious little use as an authority in any other court. We wished to have it decided by the Court of Appeal, and for that purpose it would need to be argued by some outstanding person so that we could obtain a judgement after due consideration of all possible arguments. The underwriters could not afford silk, so we were to provide the plaintiff with a distinguished leader. I was told to find the outstanding common law junior of the day and persuade him to take the brief against us.

The test today of who is outstanding would probably be: who is paid the biggest fees. In those days the only test could be, who has been asked by the publishers to edit the latest edition of *Smith's Leading Cases*, or of *Bullen and Leake on Civil Pleadings*. Denning was known to have edited both and so clearly took pride of place. I explained the case and he agreed to present the argument for the plaintiff but he had to withdraw in the week before the appeal came on. A successor was quickly found when John William Morris, who later became Lord Morris of Borth-y-Gest, agreed to take the case. We won again and had our Court of Appeal judgement that you can't recover damages because of your own peculiarity of bodily make-up and you can't recover cash from Crofters' Handwoven Harris Tweed. However, for a moment it could be said that Denning was in the case as a junior.

D N Pritt once said of Tom Denning that he was like a babe in a pram; you fed him some facts and he puked out this wonderful law. Shortly after this comment, I was waiting my turn in the Divisional Court before Denning and Mr Justice Hodson. Doughty, who was then Chairman of the Bar Council, was reading and arguing about a document. Pritt was sitting beside him, but not involved in the case. Pritt whispered over his shoulder to his junior that "Doughty on a document must be a bit like Pritt on a horse". There was a certain amount of amusement in court and I found myself at the centre of it. Mr Justice Hodson summoned me to attend in his room and asked why I had laughed at Tom Denning, who was his close friend. I was able to explain that the learned judge was in no sense the cause of the laughter. Pritt was a very sharp fellow, renowned for his "pritticisms".

When we held a chambers party in the Inner Temple Hall., Denning wrote a letter of a very friendly character which I dare to reproduce:

"My dear John,

I do wish I could have come to your party on 26 Nov.

Pritt was indeed a great figure – he led me often – he gave me my red bag – and I admired him much.

And I have also had the most sincere regard for you all watching your good purposes over the years. It is indeed one of the best of Chambers – and I send you all my very best wishes for continued success and happiness.

Yours very sincerely

Tom Denning"

As Master of the Rolls, Lord Denning became an institution in the law courts and, for tourists, a rather more sophisticated attraction than the Tower of London and the Changing of the Guard. Every lawyer who had been brought up on the English system (that is, America and the former colonies) finding himself in London, wanted to go to Denning's court. It was crowded at all times. If you had any luck or time, you would certainly hear him speak for he talked quite a lot, though very politely. On interlocutory days he would hear a dozen cases in the morning and pass judgement on them all. The visitor could go home and say, "I have actually heard him speak." The speech, like as not, would run as follows:

> "This is a case where the plaintiff should have known better and his counsel, too, and probably did. That's why he loses his case and has to pay the costs. If he were allowed to see the documents he asks for, et cetera, it would be an abuse of our process as we've known it for a century. Now, who's next?"

Denning was eighty-three when he retired. The question was asked, had he become mentally infirm? Many of his earlier decisions were garlanded for their brilliance and grace, but more recent ones were often over-ruled. When for a short time he was in the House of Lords, he so regularly differed from the majority that they demanded that he should be restored to the Court of Appeal where they could help to put him right; hence his many years as Master of the Rolls in that court. This makes it all the more surprising that he should have mentioned the case of the Weitzman brothers as the one case where he'd been over-ruled as the result of a legal nicety. In 1978, when the Birmingham Six asked that the police officers responsible for their interrogations should be tried for assault, Denning refused. If the police had been guilty of perjury and of violence, it would open "such an appalling vista that every sensible person in the land would say 'It cannot be right that these actions should go any further'." As is widely known, Denning later said that it was better to ignore injustices uncovered by television rather than cast doubt on the reputation of British justice. In effect, it was better that the innocent should be imprisoned or even hanged than that the public lose confidence in the law. He seemed incapable of understanding the damage caused by such absurd and cruel statements.

He had a reputation as representing "the ordinary man", but that was really only so if it was a case against the trade unions. It was for this consistent hostility to the unions that the Haldane Society passed a resolution at the 1981 AGM calling for Denning's resignation. Denning had several times asserted that he would not retire, saying, "I have every Christian virtue except retirement," and I believe that he was quite upset by the resolution. Our 1982 AGM came just days after the publication of his latest book, which included a statement about black members of London juries that was flagrantly and viciously racist. He said that blacks were so unreliable that you couldn't trust them with any serious decision and we should abandon juries rather than continue allowing blacks to take part in them. He had clearly gone too far. The book was at once recalled by the publisher and a leading article in *The Times* echoed our call that Denning be made to retire. Within a few months he was back at Whitchurch for good.

Discrimination against blacks and against women, and for that matter, against Jews is widespread at the Bar, but with the exception of Denning, no barrister or judge would ever express such a view in public. No Christian should have racist feelings, and certainly no Socialist. The anti-apartheid movement and similar groups have made considerable advances in the UK. Things have changed so much that evil-minded people have to set up movements such as the National Front to keep racism going. Growing up in New Zealand, I never saw any evidence of racism. Brother Bill and I exchanged holiday visits with the Pomare children and we never thought of Maoris as anything other than friends and companions. When I returned home in 1951, I asked Bill about New Zealand's economic problems. He replied, "It is all the fault of the Maoris and the Pacific Islanders. Look, they're lazy. They just sleep in the sun." It was as idiotic as any answer given by Moseley in his day, but there was no reasoning with Bill. On each of my visits home, the only disappointment has been in seeing the increase in racism amongst the whites.

When Denning said that he still had a firm belief in trial by jury, he meant the juries of his youth: middle-aged, middle-class and white. He didn't really want "ordinary people" to be represented unless they fell into those categories. He said that he only objected to the method of selection, for "random juries" might result in "random justice". As a junior, I accepted the conventional view that one should challenge any man who looked like a retired major or better, or carried the *Financial Times*. There were other equally flimsy and stupid grounds. I used such challenges to show the client that I was on his side. I would stand by the dock and discuss the appearance of jurors with him and make my challenges from there. As a silk, I would get my junior to go through the same process; it would give him or her the idea of showing off to the jury without too much fuss. I have since come to believe that you can't tell by looking at a person whether he will make a good juror or not, whether he will be merciful or severe. Jurors are best taken as they come. A genuine cross-section of one's fellow citizens is likely to include a few rather dotty ones as well as a few wise ones, but in my experience the wise ones are likely to guide the others.

Juries will usually deal sensibly with even the strangest evidence. In one case we heard how a young man ran downstairs from his flat into the street with the steel tip of a crossbow bolt sticking out of his back and the feathers in front. The bolt was through his heart. He was crying, "Look what he's done." The "he" was my client – a dealer in drugs who sold to the supposed victim. My client had not introduced him to drugs since the young man was established in the habit before they had met, and indeed divided up his purchase and sold on at a profit. A policeman showed the jury how the crossbow worked and even offered a bolt up to the bow when it was slack. He then discharged the wound-up bow without a missile, and it went off with a powerful bang and clatter. The young man had survived and gave evidence that my client had shot him, but he failed to convince the jury. We discovered that he had twice previously tried to commit suicide, and often wound up his crossbow and had target practice in his flat. There was just room to get the loaded bow pointing the wrong way round between his chest and outstretched hands. Either he shot himself deliberately, or it went off by accident when he was playing the reckless fool.

The importance of a jury is not only as a means of trial that is believed by the public to be fair, but as an opportunity for jurors to exercise a constitutional function of high significance. They judge their fellow men. At elections, we all do something similar, but then we are one in millions; as jurors, one voice can carry the day. All this century the jury has preserved the balance of justice in Britain, but throughout the latter part of it, authority in one form or another has weakened their power to say not guilty. I have by chance been in a number of cases where the government developed and perfected their practice of interfering with jury selection. The Home Office is naturally reluctant to discuss these things but has admitted that guidelines on jury vetting were formulated in 1948 – the year in which Attlee, on Washington's instructions, began the witchhunt amongst civil servants. If civil servants were to suffer positive vetting, why not jurors? The Richardson torture trial was the first case where jury vetting became generally known and it is rumoured that the jurors for the 1969 Kray trials were pre-selected by the Crown. If this were so, it was done with great skill for the defence lawyers were quite unaware of it.

It is understandable that if the police see men get off whom they firmly believe to be guilty, their frustration can lead them to exceptional measures. In the 1960s, there was public concern about gangland killings and the government had to assert themselves. The trials and resultant sentences were intended to put an end to gangland terror in London and so great was the effort and expense put into these trials that the Crown could not risk the wrong verdict. It was widely believed that the Richardsons and the Krays had on several occasions avoided conviction by nobbling juries. One corrupted voice, one dishonest vote and they were free. They could scarcely complain if their own tactics were used against them, but society as a whole must protest for any such behaviour is against the interests of us all. When the Crown realised that juries were being interfered with, they adopted countervailing measures: juries were segregated more thoroughly when out of court; were lectured and hectored by the judge with greater severity; and the majority verdict was introduced so that one bribed or intimidated juror would not destroy a case. The last of these measures has proved the most effective.

I have the greatest confidence in juries. They almost always produce some member who is interested in any specialist subject that may arise. In several cases, I've had a juror produce a slide rule and begin his calculations before the expert similarly equipped came into the box and I have seen jurors raise crucial questions which counsel had overlooked. I had one Old Bailey trial in which four defendants were charged with fraud related to DHSS and housing benefits and obtaining mortgages by deception.

The alleged frauds involved hundreds of thousands of pounds and the trial itself cost £4 million. To cope with the mass of evidence, the jury was provided with computer terminals. Two of the jurors had furnished themselves with calculators and were busy following totals and comparisons and making their own checks on the sums. I laid a trap for them by suggesting figures for the amount or percentage of security held by the lenders very much less than it actually was. The two jurymen communicated with the foreman that they had a point and he at once raised it with the judge. I appeared to check my own calculations, then found and acknowledged my error. I have not often had a jury so openly and expressly in agreement at so early a stage with a point vital for the defence and had never before used so plain a trick to get them on my side.

Two other jury members — one Indian and the other a black lady — were so genuinely independent and correct in their attitudes that they were both anxious to show that they could not adopt any kind of prejudice in favour of the defendants, all of whom were coloured. For this purpose, they were unable to repress some slight indications of hostility. It was a classic example of inverted racism. Even so, it became clear that we would get off and I pointed this out to Femi Adelaja, the main defendant. The effect on Femi was most curious. He was something of a hero amongst his peers in Croydon. He had borrowed more money and owed more money than anyone he knew. He had more charges of fraud brought against him than anyone he had ever heard of, and confidently expected the case to run for a record time. He was certain that the longest sentence would be imposed on him, rather than on any of the co-defendants. The shock of hearing that he was going to be acquitted was so great that he died the next day. I arrived at the Old Bailey the following morning and was met at the door by ambulance men. They were carrying out a stretcher with a blanket covering the whole body and face of the occupant. Either the person had a bad head cold or he was dead. They put the stretcher into the ambulance and went off in the direction of Barts. Inside the courthouse I was met by a shocked Debbie King and Anesta Weekes and others from our team. Femi had just a moment before had a heart attack and died in their presence.

We took the day off while the prosecution considered their position. The defence also reconsidered. Until then, the co-defendants had adopted a rather hesitant course, not actually supporting Femi but standing close enough to take advantage of every favourable point that might emerge and lately edging somewhat closer. With Femi out of the way, a new path was open. He was now completely guilty in every way of each offence, while they were equally and fully innocent. The trial dragged on for another three months before the jury cleared one defendant of all charges and the other two defendants of some charges. After nine days' deliberation they had not reached agreement on the others. The prosecution decided not to proceed and the judge entered not guilty verdicts for everyone. He thanked the jury, saying that their devotion to duty had reinforced his deep belief in the jury system and expressed the hope that no other jury would "ever again be faced by a trial like the one that has just finished". It was a jinxed case. Apart from Femi, the original judge, a junior barrister, two witnesses and a juror died. It was thought that the juror committed suicide, for he was found dead in his own home over the weekend under strange circumstances. There was talk of curses, and we would all look around the courtroom and wonder who would be the next to go.

CHAPTER FORTY-ONE

Lebanon; The Miners' Strike

AT THE end of the Second World War, I played a trifling part in trying to protect a shipload of Jewish refugee children when the Royal Navy sought to intercept them in the Channel and have them returned to Germany. In my argument, I referred to them as "these hapless kids" and was interrupted by Mr Justice Jenkins: "Mr Platts-Mills, let us preserve the usual court standards. You will be calling them 'nippers' soon." I think that in spite of technical problems, we ended up with the judge granting Habeas Corpus to the unidentified children. All the liberal world welcomed the establishment of Israel after the war. Janet and I had friends who joined kibbutzim, and in parliament I did my bit in pressing Ernie Bevin to recognise the new state. The economic achievements of Israel were the occasion for general rejoicing and I later saw for myself how the deserts had been turned into gardens and plantations, as well as the growth of real industrial power in Haifa. The sole disappointment was the total failure of the Jews to help the Arab Israelis to master and enjoy the same skills.

There followed a number of warlike actions such as the Six Day War and the pre-emptive strike of 1967. In some of these, Israel was plainly defending herself, but thanks to American money the Israeli army was soon powerful enough to establish a momentum of its own and by the 1980s newspaper reports were full of barbaric attacks on Palestinians. It seemed impossible to establish a compromise between the two pre-requisites for peace in the area: Israel's right to exist and fair treatment for the Palestinians. In June 1982, Israel invaded the Lebanon, intending to destroy the Palestine Liberation Organisation by killing as many Palestinians as possible – or so it appeared. The UN Security Council at once demanded the immediate and unconditional withdrawal of all Israeli troops, but invasion is regarded as the right of the powerful and the troops stayed.

In the occupied territories, all Palestinian males from sixteen to sixty were taken into detention camps. Fourteen refugee camps and thirty-two villages came under attack. Large parts of the ancient cities of Tyre, Saida (Sidon) and the capital city, Beirut, were destroyed, and Beirut was besieged.

As soon as we heard of the invasion, it was clear that there would be some form of international enquiry and it seemed sensible to start gathering and evaluating evidence as soon as possible. The most likely candidates for such an enquiry were those who had been engaged in similar ventures dealing with comparable illegalities in other lands. We needed, and got, people of the calibre of Dorothy Crowfoot Hodgkin, Oxford scientist and the only Englishwoman to win a Nobel Prize; the Bishop of Stockholm; Nikis Theodorakis, the Greek composer and MP; Field-Marshal Francisco da Costa Comes, former President of Portugal; judges from the Supreme Courts of India and Sri Lanka; and such experts in international and constitutional law as Paulette Pierson-Mathy of Belgium and Dr Alexander Berkov of the Soviet Union. I was in London, which was central to all, and took the initiative by ringing round a few, who rang others. I ran up a very large telephone and telegram bill but didn't worry because it was all on credit. (I have for many years adopted the attitude that anything that could be had on credit was worth getting and would, some day, be paid for.)

It was agreed to convene in Nicosia because Cyprus was fairly close to Lebanon and witnesses could be brought straight from the front lines and from the hospitals. Besides, the local city council enjoyed being at the heart of world events and we were certain that they would give us some support. Nicosia also had the advantage of being home to Ellie Mozora, a very knowledgeable young woman who loved organising conferences and such like things. Ellie proved to be a power in her own country. She knew everyone and everything and she got the government and the council to provide accommodation and meeting places, entertainment and local transport. Many good people wanted to attend, and the cause was so worthy that the East German airline contributed free tickets for anyone travelling from or through any city to which they had scheduled services.

We had no Israeli on the commission, and we excluded any person of Arab origin lest it be thought that we were less than impartial. This was foolishness because our name – the International Commission of Inquiry into Crimes of the Israeli Government and Army in Lebanon – made it clear from the start that there was no possibility of impartiality. We were convened to establish what we were already convinced was the truth: namely, that Israel had made an unjustified and ruthless war in Lebanon. It was expected that leading articles in various papers would denounce us for shooting at the hare before we had even sighted him, but there was no such criticism; the English-speaking world paid us not the slightest attention. Another reason for excluding Arabs was the fuss occasioned by an open letter to President Reagan, published in *The Times* on 24th July 1981 and signed by 219 people, including four dozen MPs, six MEPs, five lords, ten general secretaries of trade unions, professors, university lecturers and such renowned radicals as Barbara Castle, Lord Jenkins of Putney, the Bishop of Edinburgh, the Very Reverend Lord Macleod of Fuinary, Past Moderator of the Church of Scotland, and myself. This reasoned and moderate critique of Reagan's foreign policy was ignored, once it became known that the advert had been paid for with Arab money.

The Greek Cypriots proved to be most generous hosts and we were welcomed by representatives of the government and innumerable local organisations, every one of whom expressed sympathy for the Lebanese and the Palestinians by comparing their situation with "the big 1974 crime of double betrayal – the Fascist coup and the Turkish invasion in our island". The Greeks told us that hosting an investigation into the Israeli invasion of Lebanon would serve to remind the world that Cyprus was itself a victim of injustice, and that the Greek Cypriots were also "refugees in their own country". In mid-August 1982, the siege of Beirut was at its height and the evidence we heard was of the grimmest character. Witnesses included Scandinavian medical teams, some of whose workers came direct from the battlefield, and experts on military matters and on the latest Israeli weaponry. We demanded an immediate Israeli withdrawal from Lebanon and the release of all PoWs; an international trial for war crimes; guarantees for the repair of damage and full reparations; and the provision of urgent medical aid. Each group of doctors was set the task of getting supplies from their home country. From this, several hundred tons of material were shipped into Lebanon, including a few ambulances and a mobile hospital or two.

I had no sooner returned to London than Francis Khoo wrote to tell me that his wife Dr Swee Chai Ang was in Lebanon with the British medical contingent. The couple had fled from Singapore in 1977 when threatened with imprisonment for an involvement in the Students Christian Movement and I had known them for several years. In London Khoo worked part-time for Medical and Scientific Aid for Vietnam while studying to qualify as a UK solicitor and Swee Chai worked at St Thomas's in Westminster. On learning that Christian Aid needed an orthopaedic surgeon to serve in Gaza hospital for three months, she had resigned her post and left for Beirut, although the city was under constant fire. Swee Chai was tiny and enchanting and inspired. Now she was working in the heart of the twin camps of Sabra and Chatila, caring for the poorer Lebanese as well as the Palestinian refugees who lived in the camps. She had spotted me in Nicosia while attending the hearings, but I had failed to notice her.

By September, thousands of Lebanese and Palestinians had been killed. The PLO fighters agreed to leave Beirut if the Americans would protect their women and children. Philip Habib, Reagan's personal representative, promised to guarantee the safety of the civilians left behind in the camps, then had the marines withdrawn two weeks before the agreed date. On the next day the President-elect Bashir Gemayel was crushed to death in a massive explosion. The Fourth Geneva Convention requires an occupying authority to uphold the law so that the civilian population is protected, yet the Israeli military sealed off the refugee camps and let in the Lebanese rightist militiamen, the Christian Phalangists, knowing that they wanted revenge for the death of Gemayel. The Israelis even provided illumination at night by sending flares into the sky above the camps. Swee Chai was in Sabra and Chatila when the massacres of 16-18th September began. Israeli soldiers removed the foreign staff from the hospital and so she had escaped the forty hours of killing in which an estimated 2,400 died.

In November, we held an inquiry in Athens to assess and quantify medical needs. We had fifty-eight delegates from seventeen countries and heard evidence from doctors and other medical personnel, as well as lawyers and journalists. Apart from the camps, residential areas of Beirut had come under attack from the air, sea and land. The Israelis were using fragmentation, vacuum, cluster and phosphorus bombs, all banned by international conventions. The city was so thoroughly besieged that such basic supplies as water, food, electricity and even blood plasma had been cut off. I found it hard to understand how the Jewish people, who had themselves suffered grievous injustices, could allow Israel to behave so cruelly. At the end of the year, Paulette Pierson-Mathy and I spent several days in Israel. The foreign minister was abroad but his deputy was good enough to see us. We also met representatives of 1,400 soldiers who had served in Lebanon but had since signed a document that they would not return. I was struck by the numbers of uniformed soldiers one saw everywhere, and always armed. We went to a museum to see the most fascinating record of the diaspora, of 2,000 years of history. Soldiers were also studying in the museum, going past in small groups, and still with their automatic weapons. It was terrifying to see so many people walking around armed and I was reminded of certain central African countries where there is a surplus of rifles.

In February 1983, the Commission reconvened at Geneva to consider evidence about the refugee camps, and more particularly the massacres at Sabra and Chatila. We considered films and photographs from the camps and listened to eyewitness reports from more than twenty experts. One suggestion was that we should try to institute legal proceedings against identifiable Israeli officers and men who had been individually guilty of wrongs, but nothing came of this. In violation of Security Council resolutions, the Israelis had remained in Lebanon and were still illegally occupying an important part of the country, although a resistance movement was growing up to confront them. Beirut was falling apart, and yet nothing was being done to prevent further tragedies.

Suddenly I, too, began to disintegrate. One quiet morning in June whilst putting some point to the Privy Council I began to feel exceptionally tired. As the morning wore on, I realised that I would not last out. I tried every possible dodge to finish the argument but one or another of their Lordships had a question to raise. At 12.40 I was unable to go on and in despair said, "Would your Lordships care to rise for the short adjournment now?" with a distinct accent on the last word. The presiding judge said, "Well, why not? We've had a good morning's work. We'll rise now." As the last member of the court withdrew behind the curtain, I collapsed into the arms of my junior, the stalwart Edward Irving, Janet's nephew, who lowered me gently to the floor. Before the month was out, I had a pacemaker installed at Northwick Park Hospital. My son Tom had earned us much goodwill at Northwick Park, where he had taken his first steps as a consultant. I was not only on NHS but NHS with laurels. That was a temporary pacemaker and, in August, I was summoned back to receive the latest long-life American model, which is supposed to see me out.

Then came the replacement of a bad left arthritic hip. Our dear friend Lippman Kessell was an outstanding orthopaedic surgeon. "Lippy" said that with any luck I would have four years still to live, so they might as well be lived in comfort. He had long since stopped operating but he knew a good surgeon at Northwick Park and I was soon back in the theatre. It's just a routine operation these days and I had the other hip done a few years later. (Janet did rather better, having one hip done five times.) The next operation began with the quietest evening known to man. I was invited to supper with the Sussex branch of the Oxford Society at a girl's school in Burgess Hill. We were to meet and sup at six p.m. on a Friday evening and then be lectured on the "History of museums of the history of science in Oxford". The whole function was over by nine. The guests were all dazed with their half-glass of nondescript white wine and set off for home in as calm a condition as one could hope. By nine-twenty I was writhing with pain and strong enough only to stop the car at the railway station and persuade two nice young people to ring for an ambulance.

There is nothing more to report until five days later, except the plain recollection – without sight or feeling – of the sound of a voice saying, "You don't want to live, do you?" I answered, "Yes," with a certain desperation. The voice came again, "So you don't want to live?" to which I answered, "No". "Which is it, yes or no?" During the last question, the middle fingers of my two hands were locked together and something or someone was struggling to tear them apart. The next thing I knew it was Wednesday afternoon and a gentle voice was saying, "Now you must be very good and very polite, for your wife has been waiting all these days." I was sure I had been nothing but polite to everyone, but Sister said that immediately after the operation on Saturday morning there had been a great row. Surprising conversations had taken place, "and the things you said!"

I had suffered an aortic aneurysm. There was a succession of pieces of extreme good luck and a miracle or two. Where in the wilds of Sussex do you find a team capable of a rescue operation in the face of the one per cent chance that arises when an aneurysm in the aorta bursts? Where do you find the surgeon who has that day come back from a holiday in Germany and who will be ready for business with the First Division at six a.m. on a Saturday? I soon learnt that a life-support machine is not accepted very happily by the lucky but prostrate survivor. It cannot be guaranteed to breathe at the rhythm the body is accustomed to, nor with the amount of air required, and makes no allowance for the occasional yawn or any of the other oddities of normal breathing. This last operation left me quite exhausted and for many months I was able to sleep at any time of day, in bed or out, indoors or out. For two months, all food tasted the same, like boiled cotton wool. That was in the midst of the richest soft fruit season we had had for years. To a greedy self-indulgent person who loves food, it was a hardship and I dropped a stone and a half. The administering of twenty pints of strangers' blood and the loss of one's own no doubt played a part.

I was just beginning to recover when the great miners' strike began. This was on 12th March 1984, after the National Coal Board (the NCB) announced that twenty pits were to be closed and 20,000 miners would lose their jobs. Workers in the power unions know that their best chance comes from a strike in the late autumn or early winter. Arthur Scargill, President of the National Union of Mineworkers, was much criticised for calling a strike at the worst possible time, but he had no real alternative. Delaying action until the autumn would have seen the mines long since closed down and a closed pit isn't put into cold storage, it is destroyed. The shaft is filled and the pit-head machinery demolished. It is inconceivable that such a pit would ever be reopened and, once closed, the coal is lost to the nation forever. One of the main demands of the NUM has been for a policy of no pit closures unless stocks are exhausted. Many, if not all, pits are uneconomic at some stage but there is always a possibility that they will become economic propositions at some later time.

I feel strongly that we must make the fullest possible use of our coal reserves, which should last for some hundreds of years, because our oil supply is more limited and time is needed before we can place any reliance on the energy produced from nuclear fuels. Nuclear power is curious stuff. Through one channel, it is gone in a whiff – and much else gone with it; in another way, its validity goes on and on. There may come a day when we are so much in control of nature and of ourselves that nuclear power is safe and workable. In the meantime, it would be a sensible idea if this period were to be treated as one in which we provide for every possible experiment in the development of alternative resources. If our coal industry is maintained, then we have a long respite, a shield within which we could take advantage of the best that man can develop. I truly believe that to close pits currently in production is an act of sabotage of the future of the country. This is understood by our partners in the European Community; in 1984, we were the only coal-producing nation not to have import barriers on coal. Foreign coal is cheap because it is massively subsidised.

Margaret Thatcher turned Britain into a neat little lower-grade power with highly developed secondary industries such as the export of biscuits, whisky and clothing. There was to be complete freedom for financiers and small enterprises, and equally complete freedom for millions of unemployed to starve and to diminish daily in their morale and in their contribution to the welfare of mankind. Mrs Thatcher set out to destroy the trade unions, the most powerful and representative organisation of the working class, and to attack the miners was to attack trade unionism itself. She determined to break the brow of the NUM and to do this, she was willing to end Britain's coal-mining industry. Preparations for the 1984 confrontation were worked out well in advance. The law was changed to cut social security payments to the families of strikers and coal stocks were built up in every area. In 1983, the government brought in Ian MacGregor to run the NCB. As chairman of British Steel, he had butchered that industry, cutting the workforce by more than half. It was obvious that the miners were next for the slaughter-house and few were surprised when the union was forced into calling a strike.

The strike was to be run on an area-by-area basis, starting from Yorkshire. Before neighbouring counties had the chance to ballot their members on whether or not to join, Yorkshire miners were there, at the collieries, urging a united front. Nottinghamshire, which became the heartland of opposition to the strike, had a long tradition of Conservatism – or moderation, as they would explain it. A pit lad in Yorkshire Main in 1944 soon noticed the hostility between Yorkshire and Nottingham miners. The talk went back to 1926 and the great miners' strike, when Nottingham betrayed the whole industry. The few Nottingham men working at Yorkshire Main in my time were sometimes treated with real contempt. "I see bloody Notts is still here." Even forty years later, attempts to get Nottingham miners out on strike were fore-doomed. With the Yorkshiremen determined to bring them out by confrontation, striking pickets were soon locked in battle with working miners and with the police, who were sent in their thousands to protect the scabs.

The Haldane Society set up a full-time permanent office in Ollerton, Nottinghamshire, where many thousands of pickets were arrested. Barristers and solicitors alike took statements and helped miners to work out their defences and witnesses. Had it not been for the intervention of the Haldane, hardly any of the striking miners would have been defended in court. There were few local solicitors, and these only at a distance from the mining villages. No man went undefended if we could help it. Legal aid was obtained wherever possible; if not, then the service was given freely. It was reminiscent of the Poor Man's Lawyer scheme, or the idealistic young American lawyers from the Northern states who helped the Southern blacks get their civil and voting rights in the 1960s.

Highways were illegally obstructed by police road-blocks. Cars were stopped, the occupants were questioned and if they were going anywhere near a pit or pit village, they were turned back. When miners tried to walk past the road-blocks, they were arrested for "obstructing the police in the execution of their duty". The police were, in the ordinary meaning of the words, obstructing the miners. The police acted on the pretext that they "apprehended a breach of the peace". Possibly the reasoning was that wherever the miners might go, the police would set upon them and there would be a breach of the peace, so it might as well be got over with. Had the Haldane been able to spare anyone, we should have brought proceedings for obstruction of the highway and at least fought it out before the magistrates. Civil liberties were blown to the wind. In parliament, Roy Jenkins, in one of his more restrained moods, said that ministers were reducing the country to a "second rate police state", and this was true.

I don't know if anyone can say exactly how much the Tories spent on defeating the miners but the figure of 8,000 million pounds has been suggested. Certainly, all the strength of the government, police and media was brought to bear to smash them in a campaign of violence and abuse. The television companies and the press used every trick to engender public hostility, playing up stories of intimidation and even of death threats against working miners but giving little coverage to the acquittals that followed when the cases eventually reached court. The slightest attack on scabs was reported, but little was said about the fearful onslaught on the pickets. There were cases of strikers being threatened or attacked by working miners, but the intimidation and victimisation of strikers and their families was consistently ignored, as was police violence on picket lines.

Policemen were brought from every corner of the kingdom. They turned up in full riot gear expecting violence, and, in some cases, they provoked it. Riot is a very grave offence carrying a maximum penalty of life imprisonment. Defendants accused of rioting at Mansfield in May came to trial long after the strike had ended. The trial lasted fifty-seven days, then the jury took ten minutes to acquit; it was their way of saying that the police were at fault. In June, ninety-five pickets were arrested during a ten-hour "riot" at Orgreave coking plant near Sheffield. In a test case, fifteen were tried for unlawful assembly and riot. All were found not guilty after a trial that lasted forty-eight days and cost a half-million pounds, and at which the prosecution had eventually to admit that they could offer no evidence. The police threw in their hand and abandoned prosecutions against the other eighty. In June 1991, the South Yorkshire police agreed to pay compensation of £425,000 plus costs to thirty-nine of the Orgreave pickets in settlement of their claim for wrongful arrest, malicious prosecution, false imprisonment and assault. The police asked for a no-publicity clause and the settlement was itself an admission that it was they and not the pickets who had rioted.

Because our political beliefs were somewhat similar, Arthur Scargill and I were co-sponsors of a number of worthy causes, but I did not get to know him until November 1980, when a court case took me to Wakefield and I hurried across to Barnsley. We spent an hour or so in conversation and I found him to be quick and intelligent. The exciting "triple alliance" between workers of the mining, steel and railway industries had been launched in Scotland and South Wales and there seemed a possibility that the unions of the north-east might be able to join in a work-in to keep the Consett steel works running. Consett, with its own supplies of coal and iron ore, was the ideal testing point. If they could succeed in re-establishing the industry at Consett, there would be hope for Yorkshire and South Wales. It seemed to me that Arthur was the only person with the drive and initiative and sufficient standing to unite and lead the workers of the three industries in the north-east. I wanted to add my voice to those who were trying to persuade him. If he thought it was presumption on my part – a barrister coming from London to offer unsolicited advice on the running of his union and, indeed, on his future career – he gave no sign of it. Even when I lectured him on his manner of public speaking, he still took me to lunch. I admired the vigour and flow of his speeches, although his single gesture of stabbing down with his right forefinger with each staccato phrase detracted from the strength of his speeches.

Two months later I made a return visit to Yorkshire Main. Ian Ferguson, NUM branch secretary, organised the visit and got together six of the chaps with whom I had worked. We inspected the site and went up the tower to see the winding gear, which was now enclosed, with the winding man sitting in great comfort on his throne. Then we reminisced about the names of some of those from the past and shed a tear over a pint in the Welfare. I had kept up union membership throughout my time in parliament. Jack Squires, branch secretary when I was in the pit, agreed that he would pay my subs and I should pay him back a year at a time. When I was turned out of the party, he let the membership lapse. I complained and tried to continue, but without success. At that time, the union leadership was very much dominated by the right, and this was particularly true of the Yorkshire area. This right-wing domination continued until the advent of Arthur Scargill. In 1981, I asked for permission to rejoin the union on the grounds that once a member, always a member. The NUM does not cut adrift unemployed or retired miners; they are permitted to stay on in the union, but are not asked to pay contributions. The NUM very kindly took me back.

A united front and the promise of backing from other unions had brought the NUM victory in previous clashes with the government. In return, the miners had been quick to show solidarity whenever other, weaker unions were in dispute. Miners had strengthened the nurses' picket lines in 1982 and played an important role at Grunwick. Now they received scant support. The Seamen's Union refused to shift coal and the dockers and railwaymen also gave some kind of assistance but many others, such as the EETPU, the electricians union, and the EPEA, which represented electrical power engineers, helped to keep the power stations running. One of the tactical errors of the NUM was its failure to seek the support of the TUC and other unions until rather late in the day. The strike led to a new alignment of progressive forces as those even nominally on the left were forced to declare themselves for or against the NUM. Neil Kinnock, being more influenced by middle-class opinion than by the Labour rank and file, reacted as if the strike was a personal embarrassment, but from Labour constituency parties there was strong support for the miners.

In the autumn, the high court declared the strike unofficial and illegal on the grounds that no national ballot had been called. Arthur refused to accept this and was fined £1,000 for contempt of court; the NUM was fined £200,000.

When they declined to pay, the union's assets were sequestrated, then taken over by a court-appointed receiver. It was a time of great hardship for mining families. The wives set up support groups and took their turn on the picket line. They ran soup kitchens and distributed food and clothing sent in by members of other trade unions and those who were simply compassionate. Donations of all kinds came from overseas. One of the great features of trade-union life is international solidarity and there is little of which we are more proud than to have helped overseas. It is a right and a duty to assist fellow workers, and to do so without reference to race, creed or national borders. I tried to get money for Yorkshire Main, collecting modest donations from friends and colleagues. At Cloisters, we raised £51.50, which was made up to £100 at the AGM of British Soviet Friendship Houses, a voluntary society that promotes Anglo-Soviet links. Our Labour branch at Ringmer also gave money directly to Yorkshire Main, but the Lewes constituency party politely said that if I didn't mind, they would prefer to send their donation to the General Fund.

CHAPTER FORTY-TWO

Gadaffi; Lebanon

IN THE summer of 1984, Tony Gilbert of Liberation invited me to join him on a visit to Libya. Diplomatic relations with Britain had been broken off in April when Yvonne Fletcher, a young policewoman, was shot dead in St James' Square. It was just outside where Nancy Astor used to live and, more significantly, immediately against the bureau of the Libyan People's Republic, the Jamahiriya. At the time, the offices were besieged by a noisy demonstration organised by opponents of the Jamahiriya and the Libyan explanation was that the shot was fired by a person who had, in the general confusion, just walked in off the street. The more likely explanation was that the bullet had been fired by a member of staff. The Libyan leader, Colonel Muammar al-Gaddafi, had previously angered the British government by expressing support for the IRA and by supplying them with arms or the money for arms. When the Libyans announced plans to celebrate the fifteenth anniversary of Gaddafi's revolution by hosting an international conference, Tony saw British attendance as a way of breaking the diplomatic deadlock and re-establishing contact.

The provisional list was fifteen-strong and was headed by six Labour MPs, including MEPs Richard Balfe and Alf Lomas. The press was to be represented by BBC researcher Haydn Shaughnessy, *The Times'* diarist Martin Fletcher and Ian Mather of the *Observer*, while Christopher Strachan and I provided the legal contingent. The satirical magazine *Private Eye* described me as coming "from the tomb in Highgate Cemetery" but it was Ron Brown, who had earlier visited Afghanistan and claimed to have seen no Russian tanks, who attracted most of the criticism. Libya was then, as now, a thoroughly disreputable country in the eyes of British officialdom and, through the media, the British public. Our proposed visit brought a predictable reaction from Conservatives who wished to continue the ostracism of Libya and from sections of the press, who called it disgraceful, deplorable and an insult to the memory of WPC Fletcher. Much was made of the timing, the fact that it was so soon after the St James's Square shooting.

Yet the severing of connections had brought its own share of suffering. Contracts with the Jamahiriya provided employment for several thousand British workers in Libya and in Britain. As Ron Brown pointed out, there was no sense in our government seeking to penalise Libya by punishing our own companies and workers. Full diplomatic and consular relations were needed. Approximately nine thousand Britons were then living in Libya. Six had been taken into custody, although no charges had been preferred, and others were said to be under house arrest. Whitehall saw this as an act of hostage-taking in reprisal for the way in which Libyan nationals had been treated after the killing of the young policewoman. Relatives of the detainees, angry that negotiations had not yet begun for their release, approached each of the delegates asking for help. I was to enquire about Malcolm Anderson, a young welder from Wallsend, and Alan Russell, a fifty-year-old who had taught English to oil refinery workers. Russell's chief offence seemed to have been too frequent visits to the British Embassy, where he practised for the English Madrigal Group.

Our delegation was received by Colonel Gaddafi in his Bedouin tent at the Aziziya barracks in Tripoli. The Minister of Foreign Affairs and the Minister of Justice were also present. We put forward the idea that if the present British government would not re-establish normal relations, then we should try to bypass the breakdown. The suggestion was to set up a joint commission with representatives of our three main political parties and a few specialists and, if possible, Foreign Office representatives. Libya would match this with an equivalent team. Gaddafi offered a joint investigation to be held on neutral territory; he invited our government to send judges to attend the inquiry being held in Libya; and agreed to send three Libyan high court judges as observers to any London inquiry.

Dr Ali Treiki, the Foreign Minister, told us that they had suggested one or two impartial countries to provide a forum for hearing evidence from both sides, but this had been refused. The British press was reporting rumours that four Libyans had been executed for the shooting, but Dr

"Please Colonel! I beg you to be careful — these men are obviously mad!"

Treiki told us that the investigation was still going on. He thought that Leon Brittan, our Home Secretary, was a Zionist and so not a person who could be entrusted with any enquiry into what had happened at St James's Square. I knew Leon Brittan personally. We belonged to the same Inn of Court and I knew that he was of the most upright character. I told Dr Treiki that he was quite wrong and insisted that Brittan really could be depended upon to behave fairly. Dr Treiki remained unconvinced, but other members of the delegation were amused, for it is not often that I defend a Tory minister.

Every Libyan we met was aware of the virulence of the propaganda against them and realised that anyone who took up the Libyan cause would be defamed without restraint. The Minister for Justice greeted us by saying, "It is wonderful that you have come in spite of the hostile propaganda." He complained that the UK harboured criminals ("counter revolutionary terrorists") and gave an example of twelve men wanted for crimes in Libya. They seemed to be based in England and the leader of the gang had gone in and out quite freely. The Minister assured us that Libya co-operated with Interpol and followed the procedure that they laid down for pursuing criminals, and yet nothing was done. The UK office of Interpol replied to the Libyan branch by telegram. A copy of this was sent to Israel, presumably by the General Secretariat in Paris, which "surprised and shocked" the Libyans. Why should an international police body send to their worst enemy information concerning Libyan criminals? Was it an invitation to the Israelis to make use of them, or was it part of a general service to Mossad, the Israeli intelligence agency? These were questions that we couldn't hope to answer.

There was more to come. He complained that CIA agents were encouraged to spread reports harmful to Libya and asked that the British press should be restrained from reckless reporting. Then he expressed concern about the welfare of Libyan students in the UK who were, he said, harassed and abused. If they came home for a conference, we wouldn't have them back again. It seemed a bit odd that they should want their students back for conferences and it was just the sort of thing that would arouse suspicion in official eyes. Foreign Office representatives might have pointed out the problems in each of these points: the supposed criminals, if sent back, might be in danger of injustice; the CIA reports were worth considering – what if they were accurate?; our press reports may have been correct; some of the students were thought to have been sent to spy on dissidents and émigrés. I didn't raise any of these suggestions with our hosts.

As part of the anniversary celebrations, some of our group went to inspect new settlements and a giant steel mill. Others went to the water spectacle some hundreds of miles into the desert. From the Koran came the text, "water is the origin of life". We sat in state for a while amidst an enormous gathering, including a great number of ambassadors. Bands played while men marched and chanted, causing the fine sand to rise to the heavens. Horsemen rode by, as gaily caparisoned as their Arab steeds. An engineer made a speech, but no sign of the head of state. Then we were invited to hurry across 400 metres to the scene of the inauguration. Thousands ran, and the ambassadors stumbled and hobbled. Suddenly, out of nowhere, came Gaddafi in colonel's battledress and flowing Arab headgear. He has a youthful figure and a powerful head. He seemed to float along, surrounded and borne up by the shouts and obvious devotion of a throng of supporters. In fact, he was on a low motor-driven platform. The horses and men stood still and the dust miraculously settled. The uproar subsided and the sun went down with the sound. Then the lights went on, the speaker was in place, and we were just beside him.

There followed a quiet factual talk, each essential figure or detail greeted by roars of approval. Then he moved a few feet and pressed the button. Moses struck a rock with his staff and water gushed forth, but his success was poor compared with ours that evening. Water streamed from the very heart of the desert itself and shot up a hundred feet. As the lights shone upon the water, hundreds of young men and women ran into the falling spray. The bands played and the horses galloped, again the dust rose, the leader floated away again with a fast steady movement above the shoulders of the crowd as though spirit-borne. There was not a gun in sight, and only a great triumph. The water had been found at some depth by British engineers. We were given supper by those working on the site and they told us the story of their discovery of the water and the deep drilling to bring it up, and explained how the capping and releasing had been done.

Tripoli is a harbour city and on another occasion we were taken to a parade at the sea front. A thousand uniformed and armed young women marched along the broad esplanade, followed by several different military detachments including a camel corps and a cavalry unit on white steeds with scarlet tassels as part of their get-up. Then came the naval display. There were, I think, sixteen small vessels, all highly manoeuvrable. They came from the high seas in line ahead at some speed. They would almost strike our waterfront and then peel off, odd and even, to right and to left, with a great swish of bow waves coming at us. They came back four abreast, and then eight abreast, and finally all in a line. Next came their dolphin games. They criss-crossed, did figures of eight, gambolled and cavorted. In fact, they did everything short of bumping and sinking. I haven't seen the like before or since.

We got our chance to meet the British detainees when five of them were brought to a public meeting. The detainees, who sat on the platform in a full hall, read out their statements and then joined in a session of questions and answers conducted by one of our MPs. The men had enjoyed working in Libya and even saw themselves as coming back to it after they had been home. That they were "in the grip of political events" was pointed out by Alan Russell, one of the two I was specially asked to look for. I thought that the men were very reasonable. Afterwards, we were told that some would be pardoned and released and allowed to go home with us. This was to be as a gesture of respect for our delegation, for humanitarian reasons, and because the Libyans were anxious for any kind of contact with Westminster. The following day most of the delegates went home, taking two of the detainees. Then we learnt that Mrs Thatcher had made a new statement saying that their release was not due to our delegation but to her hard line against Libya. She would not permit the resumption of diplomatic relations. I know that we would have brought home a third detainee, had it not been for her churlish boasting.

The NUM was still defying Mrs Thatcher, and I took the opportunity of explaining privately to our hosts how the miners' strike had come about and suggested that it was a worthy cause for international solidarity. No one asked me to do this; it was entirely my own idea. When money was so urgently needed to relieve the suffering of mining families, I really don't think it matters where the money comes from – although I doubt that anything came in response to my request. In October, Arthur Scargill sent the NUM Chief Executive, Roger Windsor, to Tripoli to ask Gaddafi for aid. The newspapers got hold of the story the following month and expressed righteous indignation, if not outrage. Some talked of treason but I thought that Windsor's trip was an excellent idea, and ours likewise.

The miners' strike was now eight months old and money had to be raised somewhere. It was rumoured that Gaddafi had at one stage proposed to give the miners some millions of pounds, so he was an obvious target.

I discussed the position with Fawzeya Makhlouf, a clinical and research worker in psychology whom I had known since the early 1960s and who was for many years my adviser on Arab affairs. Fawzeya was much concerned with the fate of political prisoners in Egypt and Sudan and had been present in 1961 in the Temple at the founding meeting of Amnesty International. For plain ability, she is the most outstanding woman that I know. If the UN had some intractable problem that was not entirely technical, she would be a fit person to consult. Fawzeya can produce a relative or close friend in a responsible position in every Arab capital and is fluent in many languages. She had just succeeded in convincing me that Arabs should be brought onto the International Commission of Inquiry into Israeli Crimes in Lebanon, for without their involvement we would have neither influence nor credibility. We were considering a visit to the Middle East and to the North African coast to drum up financial support and to seek representation for the next full meeting of the Commission, to be held in Bonn in March 1985, and it was agreed that we would combine this with money-raising for the NUM. It seemed unwise to go straight back to Gaddafi. Better to try the idea amongst Middle East and Arab trade unions so that the story might spread along the coast and perhaps arouse some idea of emulation. We would start by mapping out who was who on the chart of trade unionists, navigate towards them for support, and then address Gaddafi to test his proposition.

Fawzeya remained a member of the PNUP, the Egyptian equivalent of our Labour Party, and possessed a bounty of information and acquaintances throughout the region. In 1979, she was invited to give a paper on Egypt to the Middle East committee of the Labour NEC. At that meeting, a decision was taken to form closer links between the Labour Party and the PNUP. They invited the chairman to London to discuss matters and Fawzeya was then appointed the co-ordinator between the two parties. A month later, the Labour government fell. Amongst the activities Fawzeya devised was a seminar on the Middle East, held at the House of Commons in 1980. She brought over politicians, trade unionists, journalists; Libyans, Kuwaitis, Lebanese, Syrians and Egyptians. It was partly through Fawzeya's tireless work that the Labour Party conference voted in 1982 to support a Palestinian independent sovereign state. After the conference, the Jordanian Ambassador asked Fawzeya to write a report on how to approach the Labour Party to improve mutual understanding. He wanted to present this to the Arab Ambassadors' Meeting in London, in the hope that they would fund her proposals.

In my opinion, the only Arab nations that find favour with the Tory government are those ruled by reactionary and feudalistic regimes. The others are treated with contempt, unless there is the prospect of making money at their expense. They are fit to exploit, but that is all. The CBI and large industrialists make plenty of money from their contacts with the Arabs and are not accused of treachery, but let anyone on the left try to establish links and they are at once pilloried. So long as our government seeks to maintain hatred of the Arab world while milking it, there can be no interest in building links at any lower level. I thought that Arab contracts should go to firms in British Socialist constituencies and that wherever possible each contract should include a training provision so that British workers might pass on their skills to their Arab colleagues. Some machinery must be set up to avoid this present one-sided exploitation, establishing links at all levels of society: between British trade unionists and their counterparts, between doctors, lawyers, and so forth.

In November 1984, I wrote to Arthur Scargill with a new proposal for getting financial assistance. I suggested that the NUM's International Department set up a small Middle East Committee to liaise with the Arab trade unions and, in particular, with the Egyptian unions, whose leadership I knew well. The Arabs are notably generous in supporting worthy causes and it seemed likely that they would be willing to help the British miners. Also, I reminded him that the parliamentary parties each had a Middle East Council. That of the Labour Party seemed to have lapsed, but could be revived to strengthen Socialist links. I explained that I had been working for two years with the Commission on Israel and so had wide connections in the Middle East. In particular, I had met Arab trade unionists and the lawyers' trade union, who defended their comrades throughout those lands. As a result, there were good prospects for fund-raising. Arthur was very keen on the idea. Fawzeya and I arranged a programme of visits to London embassies and to the Prague headquarters of the World Federation of Trade Unions to collect introductions to ease our way round the Middle East. We could scarcely go about asking for money without the written approval of the NUM, so Arthur agreed to write a formal letter of authorisation.

Before we could take things any further, I had to go to Nicosia for a routine meeting of the Secretariat of the Commission. Following reports from Lebanese and PLO representatives, Sasha Berkov suggested that three of us (Paulette Pierson-Mathy, Mikko Lohikoski, the Finnish journalist who served as our liaison officer, and myself) should continue on to Lebanon to make preparations for evidence which would be brought to Bonn. On 4th December we flew to Beirut and put up at the Beau Rivage hotel. Our principal adviser and guide was the secretary of the local Communist Party, who took us from north to south so we could interview the heads of each of the groups that had taken part in the resistance to the Israelis. We found that we were then expected to meet the leadership of all the other significant groups in the land, including President Gemayel, brother of the Gemayel whose assassination had triggered off massacres at the Sabra and Chatila camps; President of the National Assembly Hussein Husseini; Prime Minister Rashid Karami; Mr Nabih Berri, President for the South and head of the Amal faction; and Walid Jumblatt, leader of the Druse militia, whom we met in his romantic palace in the Shuf Mountains.

We found the home of each political leader heavily protected by sandbags and armed men, and some even by tanks. Walid Jumblatt was safe behind miles of mountain roads with armed checkpoints to give warning in both directions. The journey to his feudal seat at Moukhtara gave us our first certain proof that the Israelis were blockading the south. They had closed the coast road (a straight, fast, modern route) and insisted that all traffic should go through the mountains and across the bridge at Bater. The road varied between steep slopes and precipice, at some points hundreds of feet straight down. The crossing was opened an hour after sunrise and closed an hour before sunset. We saw forty lorries laden with citrus for Beirut left waiting two days or more at the first of their checkpoints. This was at a high altitude with winter coming on and no shelter. The occupation aimed at reducing the south from riches to comparative beggary.

Walid Jumblatt's stronghold was a medieval dream of a fairy palace. Clouds and mist had closed in so that we couldn't see far, but the palace was splendid from any view. On one side, the walls must have stood fifty feet high unbroken before a window appeared. Inside was modern elegance, with plenty of silk and embroideries. The owner of the castle was tall and lean, with a powerful head rather like an eagle. At one o'clock, as we were showing signs of leaving, Walid pressed us to stay for lunch: a magnificent spread with silver and fine linen, and Lebanese food and vodka. Then the French Embassy arrived in strength and it became apparent what role we were expected to play. The ambassador had come with his wife and back-up team to persuade Walid to give up his objections to the occupying of the coast road by the Lebanese army. To the French, it was simply a means of enabling the army to occupy the south as the Israelis withdrew; to the Druse, it was a dangerous step in the civil war against them. Walid thought the official army was inspired by the Christian Phalangists and saw their thirty or more checkpoints along the road as giving an assurance that his people would never have access to the Mediterranean.

We were there to show the ambassador that it was all so obvious that any stranger could understand. Out came a great map perhaps four metres by three, and it was plain that even the smallest roads from the Shuf mountains were to be faced with armed checkpoints. "But you are in the Cabinet," said the ambassador. "If you are worried about the composition of the army, why not change it?" Walid had his own characteristic answer: "I could change it, but only by shooting 2,000 officers." At lunch, it was not possible to question Walid about Lebanese affairs. He held the floor with questions, and his interests were wide and detailed. What was happening to the miners' strike? What sort of man was Scargill? Was Mrs Thatcher's popularity as high as ever? Were the unemployment statistics still rising? He took a small plate of nuts and a glass of vodka and left the table before we had finished eating. He did not tell us that he was going to a public meeting at a village open-air winter fête in a snowstorm to appeal for more recruits. He was truly an extraordinary man.

We then spent three days in Sidon, lodging with Mustapha Saad. He was the leader of the Shia Moslems, who form the majority in South Lebanon. The situation under Israeli occupation was grave and we marvelled at the courage and determination of the resistance. While inspecting a refugee camp, I began to feel very sick and faint. After a day's rest and sleep in the Saad sitting room, it was clear that the pacemaker was playing up. Saad took me to a distinguished physician, Dr Nassif Bassila, who ordered an immediate return to England. Thanks to his authority, on 13th December I was taken by Lebanese Red Cross ambulance over the mountains and through the Israeli lines. The ambulance was full almost to the roof with stores of all kinds and there was not enough room for me to climb on top of the load. The only way was for me to be laid flat and to be shuffled in feet first, with my face almost touching the roof. I pressed hard down to make a little space for myself and then travelled with my hands braced against the roof to deal with the bumps in the road. We returned safely to Beirut and I was soon back at Northwick Park, where all was put right.

A few weeks later, the block in which Mustapha Saad lived came under murderous attack and was badly damaged by a bomb blast. Saad was very much a force for unity and the bombing was believed to be in retribution from the Israeli forces, then beginning their withdrawal. He suffered brain damage and was close to death when the Americans flew him to Massachusetts General Hospital for treatment. Mustapha never fully recovered. His wife was blinded in one eye and their daughter – a beautiful little girl with the liveliest manner – was killed.

It was not until the New Year that I could get back to the problems of the miners. On 4th January 1985, Arthur wrote our necessary letter of authorisation:

Following our conversation, I am writing to ask if it is possible for you to use your influence, both nationally and internationally, to secure substantial financial aid for the National Union of Mineworkers whose members have been on strike for over ten months.

The miners' dispute in Britain is now the longest in the history of British Trade Unionism. We have witnessed the most incredible hardship and unprecedented State interference and repression, with the massive involvement of a national police riot force, the extensive misuse of the judicial system and the denial of basic social security benefits to the families of striking miners.

During the course of the dispute, over 9000 people have been arrested, 4000 have been injured – some very seriously – 4 people have been killed on picket lines and a further 6 people killed in incidents associated with the strike.

The Union is facing the gravest financial crisis in its history and has been hijacked by the British Law Courts and its funds and assets sequestrated. The three elected Trustees of the Union, including myself, have been sacked by the judiciary and replaced with a Court appointed Receiver in an attempt to smash the strike. Court decisions have been obtained seeking to declare the strike illegal and placing tremendous constraints on the Union's organisation.

We would ask if you could make representations on our behalf, both here and abroad, to secure very substantial aid for the Union. In order that the NUM can survive and maintain its historic struggle against the Government and Coal Board's policies, it is estimated that we require at least £10 – £20 million as quickly as possible.

Donations were to be paid into a Warsaw bank account. Although this was in the name of the Miners Trade Union International, funds could only be withdrawn for the use of the NUM and its members, and only on the specific instructions of the president.

With Arthur's blessing, Fawzeya and I immediately began a series of visits to London embassies, starting with the Syrian Ambassador, Dr Lotf Allah Hayder, a PhD from Moscow University. He greeted us warmly and advised that we contact the Arab League. This was an excellent idea because one of the top officials was El-Akhdar Ibrahimy, who had spent ten years as Algerian Ambassador to London. He happened to be a close friend of Khaled Mohieldine, Chairman of the PNUP, Fawzeya's party in Cairo. The Saudi Ambassador Sheikh Nasser el-Manquour, a powerful man who was the doyen of the Arab Ambassadors in London, suggested that we visit his country to discuss the work of the commission. Our worst failure was in not visiting Saudi Arabia and Kuwait, in spite of the warmest invitations. We ran out of time and both countries had to be omitted from our itinerary. These two were excellent prospects for supporting the work of the commission, although likely to be hostile to Arthur's strike.

In October, on my own initiative, I had been to the Soviet Embassy to speak to Counsellor Alexandrov and to Gennady Fedosov, the Cultural Attaché. It was time to try Fedosov again to explain once more how greatly our miners were suffering and to ask for help from their own trade unionists. Soviet miners had already sent shipments of food and clothing they could ill afford, had provided free holidays for the families of many striking miners, and generally behaved with great compassion.

In mid-January Fawzeya and I went to the WFTU offices in Prague to meet the Secretary, Ibrahim Zahuriah, who was very knowledgeable about Middle Eastern trade unions. We hoped for an introduction to Ahmed Abou Bakr Jalloud, Secretary General of the International Confederation of Arab Trade Unions, who was related to Major Abdul Salam Jalloud, second in charge in Libya. Major Jalloud was a close boyhood friend of Gaddafi. after the revolution Gaddafi made him deputy premier and, it is said, sent him to Chou En Lai to bid for a nuclear bomb. Zahuriah was due to go to Lagos in a few days time, where he would meet Ahmed Jalloud and pave the way. We stayed a few nights at the WFTU hostel, which was of the standard of a good hotel, and everyone asked about the miners. We learned that Danish trade unionists had collected food for the NUM under the slogan "A Chicken for British Miners". The president of the Kuwaiti trade unions told us that he would continue to offer support and to collect funds. I said, "What about 'A Barrel of Oil for British Miners'?", but it brought no response.

We came back to London to await news from Zahuriah and to prepare our tour of the Middle East, for the commission and for the miners. We approached several British trade union leaders to discuss the possibility of introductions to their Arab counterparts. The WFTU had recommended that we try Jim Slater of the Seamen's Union, which had particularly wide international connections. I got in touch with Arthur and reported on progress. His letter had proved invaluable in detailing the position of the NUM and was well received by the various embassies. However, the situation had deteriorated markedly in the meantime. The miners had now been out for nearly a year. In South Wales ninety-eight per cent of the men were still standing firm, but everyone knew that the battle was lost. We decided that it was worth one more effort. The reasoning was that if Gaddafi came up with some millions, the men would be given encouragement and would go on with renewed courage. Arthur agreed to update his letter. The new version showed another 2,000 injured and one more death.

Tony Benn has had a long and honourable interest in the Middle East and is well-regarded there. As he represented a mining constituency, I asked if he would be willing to write in support of our mission. On the 25th February he sent a most helpful letter:

> Thank you for telling me of your trip with Fawzeya Makhlouf (sic) for discussions with political leaders in the Arab World. The fact that both of you, with your great knowledge of the Labour movement, will be having these talks should help to create closer links with parallel movements in the Arab countries.
>
> Your visit is most timely, both from the point of view of the immediate situation, and from the point of view of building links on a longer term basis.
>
> I hope you will be able to convey the thanks of the Mining Communities in Great Britain for the help that has been sent, and report on the continuing problems that are caused by the present situation.
>
> Please let me know the outcome of your talks upon your return.

On the eve of our departure Arthur sent Nell Myers round to the Temple. She was always his intermediary. Nell is an interesting woman: American, with a gentle, self-effacing manner, but tough enough to be the NUM's press officer throughout the strike and, at the same time, Arthur's personal assistant. The NCB then had a full public-relations department and perhaps two dozen PR officers in addition. Nell equalled them all. Each time Arthur has been challenged he insists that he did not "ask" me to visit Libya, he did not "send me". This is quite correct; I offered. I was regularly combining errands in the hope of fitting as much work as possible into a journey, and it seemed sensible to publicise the miners' plight and to try to raise funds for the NUM while travelling through the Middle East. I see nothing shameful about any of this and am only sorry that I was not of more assistance. The miners' strike of

1984-5 was the greatest working-class struggle in modern times. The miners suffered injustice, but although starved back to work, it could be said that they were undefeated for they still refused to accept the government's terms. The fight against pit closures had not been abandoned. A strike that is not "won" need not necessarily be considered a defeat; it can be viewed as another stage in the struggle. I fully believed in Arthur's vision of the miners reuniting behind the NUM and its leadership and becoming strong again.

CHAPTER FORTY-THREE

Learn to Say Jamahariya

ON 27TH February, Fawzeya and I returned to Prague. Head of the
WFTU's Middle East department was Jihad Shamass, whom we had met
at the Tripoli conference and in Lebanon in December. Now he phoned
Damascus and arranged the interview we wanted with Ahmed Jalloud.
Shamass felt that the Libyans would not wish to be seen as the only
ones giving money to the miners. The most impressive voice for them
would be Algiers; a donation from the Algerians would give the best
encouragement to Tripoli. We then moved on to Beirut to begin the round
of talks with Arab leaders. These followed a common pattern. We would
explain the work of the commission and why a broader representation
was needed, particularly from the Arab countries. We talked of Bonn,
and the need for cash and air tickets. Several of the countries were willing
to give tickets for their national airline. In fact, the possibility of making
a donation at minimum expense by giving a few free tickets seemed to
be an added inducement to send delegates. (They were housed by the local
embassy, and this brought several ambassadors and consuls as observers
to the Bonn session.)

We then turned to the miners, asking for financial backing to help the
NUM re-establish itself. I explained that the Warsaw Bank account had
to be held in complete secrecy so that the Tory government could not
seize it. All monies placed in the account would be used immediately, so
urgent was the need. Because the account was under Arthur's direct control,
he could guarantee that donations would be kept secret and, in view of
the current situation, it might well be useful for both sides to avoid publicity.
However, so soon as the donor thought it desirable to publicise the gift,
Arthur would see that it was acknowledged, with the NUM giving the
utmost appreciation. In any case, once the strike was over, they intended

to publish in full the sources of help given to the union. We explained the proposal for Labour Party links and, after showing Arthur's letter, handed over a copy of the Arabic translation. I relayed Arthur's firm promise that, so soon as convenient, he would redeem their help by setting up a section in the NUM's International Department to advance and develop relationships with the trade unions and the Labour/Socialist movements in Arab countries. I fear that none of these promises was fulfilled.

Our hosts did not seem to understand that keeping the pits open would postpone the day when the UK would become even more dependent on Middle East oil for its power supplies and I thought it wiser not to explain this somewhat ironic point. What I found surprising was that although several of the politicians to whom we spoke were substantial businessmen and capitalists, they quite genuinely sided with the men against the NCB. I put this down to their colonial history, whether under the British or the French, which overrode their normal feelings as bosses. It was as if the colonial rulers were now represented by the Coal Board. In addition, news film of police, armoured from top to toe and wading in to attack pickets, had been shown round the world. There was a strong element of plain human sympathy upon which we were entitled to draw.

We were really quite touched by the compassionate response. In Beirut Elias el-Haber of the Seamen's Union gave us a splendid reception. He was most friendly and enthusiastic and undertook to raise support for the miners at Aden and at Baghdad. It was he who got Arthur's letter translated for us.

We then had a meeting with Nabih Berri, followed by lunch with Walid Jumblatt. In the evening, we went to the home of the then Prime Minister Rashid Karami and also met Selim el-Hoss, who succeeded him in the post. Each of these was chief in his own sphere or area, but I had the feeling that the president presided over a slightly different area from that ruled by the prime minister. After only a couple of days in Beirut we went on the short ride to Damascus. The contrast was striking. Damascus was quiet and serene; not a bomb crater nor a torn-down building to be seen and no gunfire in the night. You could drive freely without being stopped at checkpoints by armed men and the roads were not obstructed by military vehicles.

We were at last to meet Ahmed Abou Bakr Jalloud of the International Confederation of Arab Trade Unionists. He remarked on the negative role played by the TUC, which he saw as defending capitalist rule in the world and failing properly to represent the interests of British workers – a point on which we were in agreement. It was a view commonly held by the British left and was based on the general stance of the TUC, which we interpreted as being that unless capitalism were kept going, there would be nothing against which to defend the workers, and so the trade unions would be out of business. Most regimes in the Middle East were reactionary and seemed intent on handing the region over to the big multinational oil companies rather than improving democratic rights and the standard of living of the workers. His organisation had supported the British miners by sending telegrams and writing articles in their monthly bulletins. They had sent $5,000, despite having only a small budget. He said, "It was nothing, but we feel that we have got to fight and support." They saw the miners as part of their own struggle, for "if the miners win, we win".

Similar sentiments were expressed by other trade unionists. Mustapha Issa of the Confederation of Syrian Trade Unions told us that the miners were predominant in their thoughts and they were exploring ways of expressing support. He said that the miners' strike sent a signal to all other trade unions to mobilise, for the whole world faced the same struggle and all national unions should unite. The young lady editor of a weekly newspaper for the Socialist workers' struggle urged us to send her NUM material. Her English was very good and she was as well-informed about British affairs as an LSE student. There had been a London demonstration in support of the miners just before we left and Fawzeya gave a report on it. Although the strike was now in its dying days, this was not generally recognised. We were expected to know the latest developments, for which we relied on the *International Herald Tribune* and occasional trips to our embassy to read the British papers. With a little effort, we appeared quite knowledgeable.

On 5th March we flew to Tripoli. We had no visas and had to talk our way in. I made the utmost of a previous meeting with Colonel Gaddafi and Fawzeya translated it so nicely that we looked a very important pair of delegates. What we were delegates to was not apparent, but we made it abundantly clear that our intentions were of the best. Visas were granted at the airport and we were in, established in the delegates' hotel on the seafront. I was given a notable suite with two bedrooms, a study, kitchenette, butler's pantry and reception room, for it was expected that I would entertain. Fawzeya was some way along the corridor in a small room. In recognition of her languages, she had been entered as translator. Tripoli maintains a great many interpreters and so their status is put lower than it deserves.

On the first visit to Libya, we had met and become friends with Omar Khalifa Al-Hamidi, Gaddafi's chief adviser on Western European matters, and we were soon back under his protective wing. Omar is short and comfortable, a roundish chap unlike the tall aquiline stereotype of the haughty Arab. He wears an ordinary dark European suit, but if there is the slightest hint of business, then he covers it with a simple white robe. In any public place Omar will be seen with one or more young men in attendance as couriers. They come and go, and when they come to a delegate it is always in the most courteous manner. "Omar would like to see you and wonders whether you would be so kind as to.... ." Omar speaks in a low and gentle voice, for the Al-Hamidi approach is all thoughtfulness and consideration. His first concern is for the well-being of his guest the room, the comfort, the provision for any work that has to be done and then about the conference. He wants to know what part you will play. Are you ready for it? What more preparation do you need? Then come the suggestions:

Could you deal with this point or that? When would you like to be called? Won't that be too soon after lunch? and so on. He is a good host and a conference under his aegis tends to run smoothly. It was good to see him again.

Omar introduced us to Bashir Howij, Secretary of the General Producers Union of Libyan Workers, the only trade union permitted in the country. We had two important men almost making it their full-time job to arrange the meeting with Gaddafi and each day we were told that it was being done. On the 8th, it was mistakenly reported that we'd left, so all appointments were cancelled and it was back to square one. Sunday 10th was the most frustrating. We were told that Bashir had fixed it and were promised from minute to minute throughout the day. At ten a.m., it was "within two hours". At noon, "within the hour". At one p.m. "soon", but we knew that everyone has lunch and then a siesta. At five, we tried by telephone but had no luck. At seven it would be "any minute now" so we didn't go to the Soviet reception at the National Fair. At nine, Omar said that he would try again. We had supper and went back and found all was closed down for the night. They say beggars can't be choosers and we were trebly beggars. We had no right to demand a meeting with Gaddafi, we couldn't press our intermediaries too urgently, and our main object was indeed to thrust out a begging bowl.

We couldn't openly express irritation so entertained ourselves by exploiting the resources of the hotel including the cinema, swimming pool and gymnasium. The management made it clear that any entertaining I did would be at their expense and we were kept well supplied with food. There were real delegates in the hotel attending conferences on a variety of topics, so we could always find someone to ask back to the suite. We were free to go about as we chose and there were plenty of free taxis into town. Down near the waterfront we came upon what must be one of the outstanding glories of Tripoli: a Roman arch finely decorated, and a nearby pediment delicately carved with maidens and with warriors and their steeds, and propped up on the ground among blocks of masonry. It would grace any of the world's museums. Shops in the old souk were no more than a niche in the street wall, the proprietor sitting on the floor at the front and no room for anyone else to go in. The poorest streets were piled with rubble, but not a beggar to be seen. As one would expect in a hot climate, the houses were white, flat-topped squares surrounded with greenery. The main shopping streets were rather grand, but everywhere was spoiled with litter.

To foreigners, Colonel Gaddafi is the Libyan head of state. Officially, he is no more than a committee chairman. The description is typical of the man's habit of modest self-derogation and his insistence that he is just one of the people. Yet he is often spoken of in a messianic way, and is certainly so depicted in posters and on postage stamps. The Libyans have an unusual system of government. They say that in the West we only practise democracy at voting time and between elections there is nothing. In Libya every street, block of flats, factory or group of workers has a committee – its own jamahiriya – and each such unit is a People's Congress. Everyone takes an active part in the election of as many committees as the People's Congresses he belongs to: for example, at home and at work. I suppose the reality is that the vigorous or ambitious take the lead while those not inclined to politics take little part. Voting was by show of hands. If conscious of the intimidation that may result from voting in this way, the Libyans I spoke to gave no sign of it.

The Libyan system has to be called an experiment in socialism: so much is supplied free to the people that no other name fits readily. It is said that socialism has failed wherever it has been tried. I have reservations about this, but if socialism has not failed in Libya, it is because the oil money still flows. The system could not function if the oil ran dry. According to the Libyans, to make a profit is to exploit, to deny freedom, so society has been liberated from exploitation and therefore from profit. Food is subsidised and sold below cost price, so markets exist solely for the purpose of distributing goods. Transport permits are issued to suit one's needs and regular users travel free on routine journeys by bus, train or boat. Education is free at all stages and in all schools, including the universities. No one pays rent, or for the provision of medical services. Every worker is part owner of the factory he works for and of its products. No one has servants at home unless too old or otherwise unable to manage without. I think that "unable" was stretched to include those who were too busy to do the housework, but the Libyans clearly despised the soft and self-indulgent life led by the wealthy of Saudi Arabia and Kuwait.

It was clear that some obstacle was blocking our attempts to reach Colonel Gaddafi. Omar and Bashir continued to make valiant efforts on our behalf, but it was all most disheartening. I realised that we would have to use some other approach. Diplomatic relations had not been restored and the British were acting through the Italian ambassador. He was away but his chargé d'affaires said that he would be quite happy to try, but wouldn't our best approach be through the Soviet ambassador? The Russians were on a very friendly footing with Gaddafi. We made an appointment to meet the Soviet ambassador but on arriving at the embassy found that he was too busy to receive us because Premier Konstantin Chernenko had died the previous night. It was hopeless. We spent ten days in Tripoli in the fruitless task of trying to see Gaddafi, then gave up. Fawzeya continued on to Tunis and Egypt while I returned to London on 15th March for a court case. On the following day, I rang Anne Scargill with a summary of the results. Arthur and Nell later came to chambers for a full report. We were all very disappointed.

It was not until several years later that I learned through Fawzeya why we had been so remarkably unsuccessful in Tripoli. Soon after our arrival,

Omar had spoken to her privately. The Libyans were aware of her diplomatic skills and wanted her to set up in London an organisation to forge links between the Arabs and the British. They wanted to be publicly associated with what we all saw as her good deeds. The work would continue as before, but they would be in charge. In return she would be very well paid; they offered funding of several million pounds. Fawzeya is a thoroughly independent woman and made a very strong refusal. I had no idea that all this was going on. If I'd known of their offer, I would have done my best to persuade her to accept.

When people come to Tripoli and ask for financial assistance, they are often at pains to stand a distance away as if afraid or ashamed of their would-be benefactors and the Libyans are sensitive to this. Omar was hurt and offended, there being nothing wrong or disreputable in his proposal. He never spoke to Fawzeya again and our projected meeting with Gaddafi was off, despite all assurances to the contrary. We were kept waiting day after day in the forlorn hope that Fawzeya would give in. For all the months of plotting and manoeuvring, taking expert advice from various quarters and travelling throughout the whole region with, as I thought, good prospects of success, my little mission was rattling along on rails that led nowhere.

The Americans knew of Fawzeya's skills and, in 1983, this sparked a most curious incident. Fawzeya was Head of the Department of Clinical Psychology at the Southend District Health Authority and providing services for the Basildon District Health Authority but after twenty years with the DHSS, her employers treated her in a most disreputable manner. An American nominee from the University of West Michigan at Kalamazoo came with the commendation of his professors to do practical work for his PhD. He offered her two research grants and four well-paid American students each year, all while she remained in her employment. Fawzeya declined these offers because she thought they should go to the departmental budget as she was receiving a salary. At the same time she received a personal invitation from the Dean of the Faculty of Medicine at the King Khaled Hospital, Saud University, Riyadh, to advise on the setting up of a dept of clinical psychology. Fawzeya went to Riyadh on her annual leave, and with the full approval of her district administrator. She was then asked to set up a Department of Psychology and to be its first professor, undertaking the teaching and training of clinical psychologists.

After Fawzeya's return to England written approval was granted by the North Thames Region of the DHSS and by Derek Plumbly, Head of the Desk for Gulf States at the Foreign Office, so that she could combine the Southend and Riyadh posts. Two weeks later this approval was withdrawn without any explanation. The American had gone home, and Fawzeya was suspended. The deputy regional administrator brought in to trigger her dismissal wrote of Fawzeya: "There is no evidence of recent research activity." Three months later the same man wrote: "the Authority is concerned that a district employee was so heavily committed and engaged in research work". I have never been much of a one for the conspiracy theory, but its application might be justified here. Whether it was justified or not was never contested in the one way known to English lawyers. A full-blooded case was brought by the wronged Fawzeya alleging conspiracy, but the DHSS paid many thousands of pounds to settle out of court.

I had enjoyed following Fawzeya's activities in psychological research, for the New Zealand law degree included a short course in the biology of the brain and nervous system and in psychology, which proved useful in the worst compensation cases of head injuries. Fawzeya's research methods showed the patient how to think about himself and then to put information about his complaint into his own words. His conclusions were so guided that he put them into a shape that could be reduced to a mathematical formula susceptible of treatment by computer. En route to the computer, he found himself set out in a group and a diagrammatic system. Many of those who come to the psychologist are accustomed to thinking about themselves; in fact, one of the main problems is that they do it too much. The Makhlouf system used the sufferer's own weakness as a step in the cure.

At the end of March, Fawzeya and I went to Bonn for the third full session of the commission. This time the main purpose was to establish and publicise what had happened during the Israeli occupation of South Lebanon, to investigate the state of families in the camps in the north of the country and in Beirut, and to monitor the Israeli withdrawal. Palestinians had been massacred at Ain el-Helweh in Sidon, and the detention camp at Ansar continued to operate. Apart from hearing evidence, we tried to solicit expert advisers to aid in the reconstruction of Lebanon, should peace ever be re-established. It was difficult to maintain public interest in what was by now an old story and we were eventually forced to the conclusion that there was little we could do in Lebanon except get ourselves into trouble. Even so, the Bonn conference had great potential and if we had put more effort into trying to build on such beginnings, perhaps the competing militias of Beirut would not have resorted to the taking of hostages.

Manchester City Council then invited me to head an independent inquiry into a series of disturbing events that had occurred at the local university in March, while I was touring the Middle East. The Home Secretary, Leon Brittan, had been invited to speak at Manchester University on 1st March by the students' Conservative Association. Mindful that a similar visit by Michael Heseltine in 1984 had been disrupted by demonstrators, the organisers laid out the most careful and scrupulous plans. No one would be admitted without a valid student union card and a ticket for the event. The police and university authorities were consulted at all stages of the planning and were entirely satisfied. Various student groups made it known that they would demonstrate at the front steps, where Mr Brittan would be confronted with a selection of placards protesting against immigration laws, VAT, foreign policy issues and the like. To spare him any possible embarrassment, the executive committee asked that he should enter at the rear of the building. The Conservatives and the police were informed of this change of plan but clearly felt that it was undignified for the holder of one of the highest of Cabinet posts to enter a building by the back door.

On the night of the visit around 500 students gathered outside the Student Union building. A BBC camera crew was also in attendance, filming the good-natured crowd massed on the front steps. Twenty minutes before the home secretary was due to arrive two lines of policemen, totalling about forty men, marched across the road and up to the building. They did not ask the demonstrators to leave. In fact, they made sure that none had the chance to leave because they forced their way up the front steps in a wedge formation while kicking, punching and elbowing to force the students back until they were jammed hard at the top of the stairs, pressed against the closed doors of the building, unable to move and almost unable to breathe. Another mighty push brought the police right up to the doors. They then went sideways, forcing the students back down the steps. It was brutal treatment. Some were trampled underfoot in the crush, some were beaten, and many others were seized and thrown down the steps. A group of ten female students were pushed against an iron railing with such force that it broke under the pressure, dropping them down onto a collection of bicycles and thence to the ground. All sustained some form of injury.

By the time the home secretary arrived, the steps were perfectly clear. He could easily have walked up slowly and sedately, unattended and quite without hindrance. Instead, a large police guard surrounded him and ran up the steps and almost carried him into the building, although no such dramatics were needed. After the speech, Mr Brittan left the building without incident. The police again struck out, hitting students and forcing them out of the building and away from the vicinity. As before, several of those arrested were dragged along the ground, and sometimes by the hair. Many of the students complained about police violence. The BBC film crew and other photographers provided the clearest possible evidence that the police had used excessive force but the police denied this, claiming that there had been no more than "hard pushing".

James Anderton, Chief Constable for Greater Manchester, set up his own secret investigation, but it was obvious that some form of public inquiry was needed. Students who filled in supposedly confidential complaint statements saw these handed to the DPP and used in evidence against them. Of forty students arrested, thirty-three were charged with offences relating to public order such as conduct conducive to a breach of the peace or obstructing the police. Punishments ranged from fines and conditional discharges to one sentence of fourteen days' imprisonment. Manchester City Council then set up its own inquiry. The panel was asked to look into both the visit and its aftermath. We went to Manchester three times and also held three meetings in London. At our public hearings we listened to oral evidence and considered statements submitted through the Students' Union executive. The police declined to co-operate but we had more than 100 photographs and 102 eye witnesses, of whom practically all complained of the aggressive style of policing. Nearly half claimed to have been assaulted and four required hospital treatment.

The principal lecturer in law at Manchester Polytechnic told how he had pleaded with the two senior officers on duty to exercise some control over their men "because they were behaving like animals. It was a perfectly peaceful demonstration until the police moved in." One of the most disturbing claims was that police collar numbers had been obscured to prevent later identification. Even so, fear of disciplinary procedures had led to several incidents in which students had been "so pursued, harried, harassed and beset" by the police that they left the city to seek refuge while waiting to sit their final exams. One of our witnesses had been hospitalised for a serious neck injury after the police had seized her by the hair and thrown her down the steps. When her father complained about this treatment, the girl's house was burgled and statements from witnesses to the assault were removed. After giving evidence to our enquiry she was stopped by two plainclothes policemen who said, "You can just go back and tell them not to take any notice of what you have said because you were lying. If you don't, we'll pay you a little visit in hospital next week." When she came back to us, she was plainly terrified.

Another student who had begun to collect evidence for an independent inquiry was writing a thesis on police technology. His home was broken into and research for the thesis was taken. After this, his car was repeatedly stopped. On one occasion, on the pretext that he might be involved in drugs, he was taken to the station where he was slapped and punched and subjected to the painful indignity of an intimate body search. The police reminded him of the dates of his final exams and warned him that they could, if they chose, arrest him at any time. The university then provided him with "safe accommodation" on campus. One of the members of our inquiry panel had come to us from the Greater London Council police monitoring committee. He kept his own file on the Brittan visit in their office, where it was tampered with at the same time that the Manchester City Council's own police research unit was broken into. That these "coincidences" might have been the work of the Special Branch or some other section of the police was denied as an outrageous slur.

Our report found that although the university had planned the Brittan visit with great care, the police had not made proper arrangements for policing the event. They had used excessive force on the day and had been improperly supervised. The deliberate attempts to frighten and harass key witnesses might have occurred without the prior knowledge of superior officers, but when those officers were made aware of the harassment, they declined to put a stop to it.

In February 1987, three police officers were tried for criminal offences at the demonstration: two were accused of assault, and the third for having given perjured evidence. Another eleven officers were formally warned about the falsification of entries in their notebooks. The Police Complaints Authority acknowledged "errors of judgement on the part of two senior officers and the excessive use of force by relatively few policemen" but found that the majority had acted properly. It was conceded that some officers had not taken into account that they were dealing with young students, many of them female, but "some violence was inevitable". On the whole, the demonstrators had only themselves to blame. "In those cases where the evidence clearly showed that an assault had occurred", the "accidental" obscuring of collar numbers meant that it was not possible to identify the individuals responsible. This report was not released until September 1988, three and a half years after the Brittan visit. They might as well not have bothered.

CHAPTER FORTY-FOUR

Expropriation in Ghana

IN NOVEMBER 1990, I was briefed by a London solicitor to go to Ghana to defend Dr Kwame Safo-Adu on eight charges of misapplication of public property and two of economic sabotage. The brief was preceded by an urgent appeal from Margo Boye-Anawomah, a young Ghanaian at the British Bar, that I should defend her "uncle", the title given to all senior or older men in that nation. There was no money in it, but the doctor was important in any democratic future that Ghana might have. According to the charges, he could face a firing squad. I was expected to think it was just my sort of case.

Dr Safo-Adu was trained at Ghana University and at Kings College in London. He lectured on drugs at Kings and at Ibadan in Nigeria and took an especial interest in the pain-relieving and curative properties of native plants. The doctor saw the possibility of setting up in Ghana a factory of such quality that he could obtain licences from the world-famous druggists to make their products. The factory would be surrounded by extensive herb gardens, from which he would test and market the best of the traditional medicines. It would be near Kumasi, his birthplace in the Ashanti heartland.

The head of state, Flight Lieutenant Jerry John Rawlings, has twice staged coups and it is said that he personally executed the first handful of his political opponents. He certainly had a very lively manner of forwarding his own interests. The Safo-Adu factory opened in October 1989. At the beginning of the following month, Rawlings closed it down. He camped overnight in a tent on the lawn of the factory, then led hundreds of soldiers and armed police in a raid. Terrified neighbours thought it was the start of yet another coup. Rawlings kept the factory for nearly three years with no offer of recompense. I found it abandoned except for a watchman, and with its surrounding gardens a wilderness.

The confiscation of assets was commonplace in Ghana. The best properties were passed on to favourites for a fraction of their true worth. However, in this case, the head of state had other motives. Apart from his position as managing director of Industrial Chemical Laboratories (ICL), Dr Safo-Adu is a prominent supporter of the Ghanaian democratic movement and a former cabinet minister. Since the country gained independence in 1957, it has known only two periods of multi-party politics, totalling just seven years. Dr Safo-Adu served in both of the democratic governments and was twice imprisoned by the military dictatorships that followed. In October 1990, he joined the executive committee of the newly founded Movement for Freedom and Justice. His arrest for "economic crimes" came seven days later.

Colonel Gaddafi financed Rawlings' 1982 coup and it is said that the two were close friends. Although Rawlings was once seen as an idealistic young leader opposed to corruption, one now hears rumours that he is a very rich man. He dislikes doctors and often refers to them as avaricious and unpatriotic parasites. It is true that many have emigrated to the West and there are more Ghanaian doctors in America than in their own country. Developments in Eastern Europe had their effect throughout Africa. There was strong pressure for free elections, which Rawlings found difficult to resist. How best to strike at potential rivals before the contest came? Dr Safo-Adu was an obvious target as the new factory could finance a whole party. But Rawlings sought to deprive the doctor not only of his money, but also of his prestige and even of his life, for every count in the indictment had a statutory element added that allowed of a death penalty.

When you're wanting to go to a country and take part in a case where sharp political issues are involved, such as attempting to put the head of state in jail or saving the head of a political opponent from the noose, there is always the question of whether to apply for a visa on a non-contentious basis ("to visit" or "for business") or whether to face the issue boldly and to challenge the government by saying what you're really after. I have generally stated my purpose openly. This leads to delay, and sometimes even the suggestion from consular authorities that it might help to adopt a less provocative attitude. Margo was coming as junior counsel. We paid extra to obtain visas at twenty-four hours' notice and booked the flight. Five days later, with the trial already underway, no visas. We needed them urgently, but were told: "It depends on Accra. We are waiting to hear from them. Call this afternoon / call tomorrow morning / call this afternoon." And so it went on and on.

I wrote a vexed letter to the head of state: a short essay in support of the proposition that being represented by counsel of your own choice has advantages, however foolish and erroneous the choice. "Are we to understand, in England, Sir, that in your country…? et cetera. I dropped such names as I could. The high commission staff were not pleased with the letter and accepted it with reluctance. If I had known the reputation of Jerry Rawlings, I doubt whether I would have written it, or having written would have dared to go. The leave to grant our visas was there next morning. But there was a caveat: "Of course, it was nothing to do with your letter. We've not yet sent it." They were at pains to make this clear. The person we dealt with had always been polite and correct, but cool. Now it was changed – all warmth and welcome and charm.

Arrival at Accra was in steaming heat and in darkness. We found the doctor waiting outside, his spotless white "cloth" pressed up against the wire netting fence. The cloth is a man's one-piece garment wrapped twice round the waist and over the shoulder, like a Roman patrician's toga and, more particularly, the white toga of the candidates. The doctor lived very near the airport, in an area served by unsurfaced roads. A red trail of dust followed every vehicle, although for years residents had been paying for the main road to be sealed. The houses varied from small bungalows to mansions with enclosed many-flowered gardens and formidable gates. Some houses, like the roads, were half-built and abandoned. The whole was a fair representation of the economy, which had boomed at times but had been in recession for some years.

At Dr Safo-Adu's home, the gates were swung open by a swarm of retainers as if eager to get us safely inside. There were always several young men about, and the place seemed a bit like a fort. This fitted in with the story we heard of a murderous invasion by some of Rawlings' officers that left two dead bodies lying in the front drive near the gates. In 1987, the house was attacked by armed men seeking the doctor, who was absent. A young man alerted the police anti-robbery squad, who arrived to find that a daughter of the family had been taken hostage. In the ensuing gun battle, two of the "robbers" were killed. One turned out to be an army major; the other was a flight-lieutenant in the air force, and also a close friend of Rawlings. A burial with full military honours followed, attended by the head of state.

There was something of a banquet to greet us, with cousins and aunts in their best attire. Traditional Ghanaian dresses have bustles and puffed out shoulders quite exceeding our own Edwardian styles. Later that evening half-a-dozen lawyers came from our defence team and we learned of the state of play. One of our senior counsel, Kwamena Bartels, had himself been arrested in court on the opening day of the trial, to reappear in the dock as the second accused. His main offence was to have come to England to find English lawyers. All defendants were now on bail, despite facing possible death sentences.

The Ghanaian legal system is inherited from colonial days and tries to maintain the highest British standards. As with us, there are some shortcomings but on the whole it is a very effective system. This, however was not entirely satisfactory to the head of state, who set up "people's tribunals" to handle cases of especial interest to the government such as political trials. Lawyers who appear before the tribunals have been ostracised by the Ghanaian Bar. This decision not to recognise the tribunals must have caused them the greatest anxiety and it is a bit hard on defendants, but we were told that by the time an "enemy of the state" is named to appear, he is already beyond help. The tribunals are headed by junior barristers, assisted only by lay members. They are not bound by any rules of evidence, and it has been said that they're quite capable of making up what is lacking. We even heard suggestions that judgements have been written at Osu Castle (the home of the head of state and the seat of government) and delivered to the chairman before the case begins. It must be handy to know what you're working towards.

Margo and I had to obtain the leave of the Bar Council to appear before the tribunal. They gave me no slightest indication that they were blacklisting the tribunals and it was two weeks later that I first learned of this. After fifty-eight years at the English Bar, I had been long enough to be called to the Ghanaian Bar without more ado, but it was still a long and arduous process with several adjournments for the convenience of senior members of the council. Since Margo was of only three years' call, it was decided that although she would not be permitted to address the court, she could sit with counsel, take notes and discuss the case. We presented ourselves and took our places at the Bar.

The trial was held in the Old State House, a well-proportioned building with a notable entrance hall and stairway, but with the tattiest threadbare carpet and plaster peeling off the walls. From its state of decay, we thought it had been built last century. Our courtroom must have been twenty-five feet to thirty feet high. The ceiling had beautiful plaster decorations but these, too, were greatly in need of renewal. Pigeons passed their busy distracting lives in recesses just below the ceiling. Under that had been the air conditioning ducts; their removal left great holes the length of the wall. It had been replaced by old-style colonial cooling – that is, by having the building wide open to the wind. Pairs of glass doors lined two opposite sides of the room and the wind blew in all day from the Atlantic. It was as constant as the Trades Wind in the Caribbean. The pigeons flew from their high roistering place across the courtroom and out the doors. Paperweights were not provided. It seems that in other tribunal cases, no one bothered much about papers. We took the defence seriously and brought in many documents, which meant that we had to find suitable weights. An array of shiny pebbles from the doctor's garden was introduced and counsel's Bench soon resembled the seashore. Eventually the clerk and the Bench began to borrow pebbles.

Even worse than the wind was the noise. The whole of Ghana was preparing for the No-Conference – the meeting of foreign ministers from the Non-aligned Movement, which was of something over one hundred states. The acres of paved courtyard in front of the State House were being polished incessantly by giant machines. In addition, a stand was being erected and pneumatic drills were at it all day. The witnesses hadn't a chance and loudspeakers had to be set up. Any one of us not accustomed to the Ghanaian intonation was at a serious disadvantage and I was constantly whispering to Margo, "What does he say?" This was a contributing factor to the difficulty in which Margo found herself as in loyalty she tried to answer. It also made my presence there pretty well valueless, except as a "foreign observer".

Mr Kwaku Boakye Danquah, chairman of our three-man tribunal, was a junior counsel of three years' call. He had done scarcely any cases as counsel but had been several years as a chairman of tribunals. His second in command was a sergeant in the security police. Number three, on the chairman's left, was a most serene lady; always paying fullest attention but saying nothing, and doing nothing that could draw attention to herself. She was reputedly the aunt of the head of state. The chairman took very full notes. Although his colleagues each had a pad of papers, they seldom raised a pencil to offend them. The sergeant had difficulty in finding a comfortable posture for his arms and took off his jacket so soon as he came in, and his shoes so soon as he sat down. He changed his socks each day, and they became more gay and more brilliant. I had three pairs of Leander pink socks and wore them in response to the sergeant and took my shoes off when he did.

After a few days, Margo came down with a heavy dose of malaria, the main local disease. It exacerbates every problem that arises in these parts of Africa: pregnancies, miscarriages, child and infant deaths, education, length of life, food supply, and general health. We had started taking anti-malaria pills before we set off for Ghana but were attacked by mosquitoes at dawn and at dusk. Margo proved to have a hostile reaction to the pills so that her grief was compounded. Many people are allergic to the main anti-malarials, which are normally produced in tablet form. Dr Safo-Adu put it into capsules so that the drug would be released later and further along the alimentary tract, avoiding the allergic response, but Margo was ill for many days.

Any such illness brought one into contact with the lavatory system. That in the basement of the Old State House was quite deplorable. There were no lights, the doors to the separate cubicles were unhinged or partly hinged, the water supply was fitful; all was unswept and floored with loose rubble. There was no separate provision for women. The tribunal had their private place but the common facilities had to be shared by everybody else: barristers, the accused, the public, reporters and court officers. I had not previously known a courthouse lacking in special arrangements for counsel. It's not that barristers are so special, but when they are showing off that they are different because they have the "right of audience", they must not be undermined by having to pee with the public.

On a day when Margo was feverish and thoroughly ill, the assistant attorney-general came to court. He sat with the prosecution side for a few moments, speaking to the prosecutor. The prosecutor then told the court he had been informed that Margo was not a member of the Ghana Bar and requested that she be moved from the Bar seats. I explained our respective rights and it was agreed that she could sit in the first row of the public seats directly behind defence counsel. We would then still be able to consult. The prosecutor would not permit even this and Margo made the most majestic exit from the courtroom. Although mightily indignant, I think she was glad of the intervention for it sent her home to bed.

The charges against our clients were fatuous; they were quite lacking in reason or sense and this was obvious so soon as the essential material was presented. Hearing the "evidence" repeated by different witnesses only emphasised the lack of support for the allegations. Perhaps after so bold a denunciation I ought to give examples. Eight charges were for intentional misapplication of public property. In 1982 and 1983, Dr Safo-Adu borrowed money from the World Bank and with the full approval of that bank, and of Ghanaian Government representatives, spent it setting up his pharmaceuticals factory. The money did not leave the World Bank except to go direct to the sellers of approved goods, who were in America or in Europe.

"The People" (who were v Safo-Adu and others) argued that this money was public property. Their argument ran: because Ghana is a member of the World Bank, World Bank funds belong to Ghana; and when money is lent, that money still belongs to the lender. These two propositions were put forward by Mr Odoom-Boadu, a senior officer in the National Investment Bank of Ghana, the government bank. When cross-examined, he acknowledged that his propositions were nonsense, and the tribunal agreed. So it was with the alleged misapplication. All the spending was with the approval of, and actually by the World Bank itself, under the direct instruction of the National Investment Bank.

Of the loaned money, 0.74 per cent was, with the approval of the World Bank, spent on balsam concentrate. The government decided that this was an improper import. It was a shampoo and not a drug. The doctor had an excellent library and we produced a paper showing that from Genesis to Shakespeare, balm or balsam was treated as a pain-relieving and curative drug. When Peruvian balsam was discovered by Portuguese adventurers, it became a significant marker in Atlantic trade. The constructing of that paper gave me as great a pleasure as any I have taken from a short essay.

Mr Odoom-Boadu admitted that an important document that he put in as evidence was forged by an employee in his department, although he did not know who had done it. He brought it in without disclosing that it was forged, and his bringing it in with knowledge was as guilty an act as if he had forged it himself. The forgery was of the simplest. Someone had rubbed out two words that did not suit the prosecution and typed in two that did. The erasure was done in so childish a fashion that you could see with the naked eye where the substance of the paper was partly scraped away.

It is difficult to imagine a trial more surrounded with intrigue than was ours. It exceeded anything I've ever encountered before. When we were only halfway through the prosecution case, an intermediary for the chairman made contact. I was asked to approach the British High Commission to see if they would lend their premises as a neutral ground for a meeting between the chairman and one of our defence team. They naturally declined. Instead, we met on a remote part of the coast many miles from any human habitation. Boakye Danquah came alone, and I was with the doctor and his wife. We stood in a coconut grove where the only sound was the gentlest lapping of breakers on the beach, the cry of seabirds and the occasional thump of a ripe coconut as a small team of helmeted but otherwise lightly-clad harvesters moved along at a distance.

The chairman told us that the judgement had already been written for him. Although his orders were clear enough, it was obvious from the evidence that he could not possibly convict. He was determined to acquit all of the defendants, though this course would place him in the gravest physical danger. The protection he wanted was to leave the country so soon as the trial ended, and, for this, he needed practical help. Our side was certain that this would give no difficulty. A route could be found into a neighbouring country. It would be over farmlands that bridged both territories where the border was unmarked and unsupervised. The farmlands began two or three miles into the Ghana side and a car would be waiting half a mile over the border. It was feared that if he stayed in any African country the chairman would be pursued and assassinated. A visa was needed to a distant and more important country. His wife had already been sent to America. If he applied to go there, it might be thought that he planned to try to stay permanently, whereas his real purpose would be to collect his wife and go on to study in Vancouver. However, he would prefer to further his legal work at the London School of Economics. His fear was obviously quite genuine.

The chairman had an interesting history. In a previous trial, he had been offered a very substantial bribe. He reported this to the police, who kept a watch and observed the defendants handing him a parcel. The police at once made arrests.

The chairman produced the parcel, which was found to contain £25,000 in sterling notes. When tried, the defendants claimed that they had given him £75,000. It was not conceivable for him to have disposed of £50,000 between the handing over of the parcel and its surrender to the police. However, the defendants made such a fuss that it all received considerable publicity. In the outcome, it was suggested that the chairman was now, as it were, on parole. If in the Safo-Adu case he were to give the required judgement, then no bribery investigation would take place. By acquitting the defendants he would be doubly endangered, yet he made it clear that a verdict in our favour was not conditional upon a promise of help in getting away. He was a most courageous man.

In court, the chairman took the fullest of notes. His note-taking was probably the most meticulous that I have ever seen. He would often read it out and if in doubt ask for the answer to be repeated. If the witness changed the form even slightly, he conferred with counsel and with his fellow members on the Bench about what the precise answer was. The two lay members of the tribunal played little part, but I thought that the chairman's conduct throughout was of the highest standard. I commented to the prosecution on what a splendid tribunal we had. After the coconut grove event, when I was quite sure how they would find, I praised them even more.

It was so hot in court that people were fairly exhausted after three hours' work, and so no hearing seemed to last longer than that. Sometimes only two sessions a week would be devoted to our case. On Friday the Chairman might say, "Next week we'll have a full week. Let's sit at ten o'clock on Monday morning." For some reason or other, perhaps because counsel did not bother to attend, they would start only at eleven or eleven-thirty, and sit until two. Then they would adjourn till the following Friday — another three hours, and that was the whole week's work done. It soon became plain that the prosecutor Mr Bright Akwetty was stringing it out as long as he could to get rid of me. It was generally thought that our side couldn't lose so long as I was present — not because of any contribution of mine, except that I added an overseas factor that the government was a bit scared of. The prosecution claimed to have more witnesses, but couldn't get them to come. Their case was dying in their arms so they cuddled it tighter and pressed the last bit of life out of it.

The prosecution constantly asked for long adjournments and a typical occasion was in mid-February. Counsel Eisen was for one of the defendants, a bank official, and his notion of defending was to do everything possible to accommodate the prosecution. To demonstrate his independence from the defence, he even sat with prosecuting counsel. On the Wednesday, the prosecutor had run out of witnesses and asked for an adjournment until the following Tuesday. The witness came "from outside Accra". The chairman said, "Why not tomorrow?"

"Because he comes from outside Accra."

"But if that is just outside, he can be here in half-an-hour. Where is he from?"

"From outside Accra. Tuesday, please."

"Well, I'll give until Friday."

"No. Tuesday, please."

Our brother Eisen then took a hand: "He asks for Tuesday. Please give him until next Wednesday."

So Wednesday it was. Almost every time he stood up, he said something similar that made us laugh. Even the chairman smiled politely at the humble subservience of our Brother Eisen.

I often took advantage of these breaks to see a bit of the country. On the way to the Ashanti lands, one sees the skeletons of giant agricultural machines sticking above the scrub, relics of the Attlee government's disastrous Groundnuts Scheme. They reminded me of goldmining dredgers on the West Coast of New Zealand, isolated in a small pool and surrounded for thirty miles in all directions by a sad, dead landscape of small washed boulders. The Portuguese heard of Ghana and of its gold from Arab traders in the fifteenth century They began the "beads and mirrors" trade and gold was the first commodity exchanged. I spent a day at Obuasi, a main centre of the Ashanti gold fields and said to be the deepest mine in the world, as the guest of Sam Jonah on the introduction of my son Jo. I wanted to go down the pit but they said nobody over sixty had ever done so and they were not going to begin with me. This was the only time I've been refused a trip down a mine. As hosts, they made up for this refusal in every other way.

On the next day, I was taken to the Adae Kese. This great festival is held in Kumasi, the home of the Ashanti, who are the most powerful and warlike of the tribes. The King of Ashanti was borne into the large parade ground on a canopied litter all decked with gold and with flowers. Behind him was carried the stool of gold, his ceremonial throne. This needs four strong men as it is solid twenty-four carat and weighs more than a hundredweight, and is worth well over a million pounds. So great is the regard for the stool as the symbol of tribal power that the king sits beside it, not on it. Between times, it is kept in a bank vault and is no doubt insured with Lloyds of London.

There were thirty other main entrants, each under a giant umbrella about twelve feet in diameter in gorgeous colours and with long soft fringes. The umbrellas were all twirling or bobbing up and down as the retinue emphasised the magnificence of their king or queen, and fanned them at the same time. They beat drums or blew trumpets or tooted horns. Few were lower than king or queen, although some had less august titles like paramount chief, or merely chief. Dr Safo-Adu had been MP for this area before becoming a cabinet minister and was resplendent in a many patterned cloth. There were greetings and handshakes and triple brushings of queenly cheeks as we made our own progress halfway round the arena to reach our seats.

The combined military and police band sat fanning themselves for two hours, then gave us five minutes of martial music. It was time for the entry. First came a police car at high speed, blowing its siren. It drove round once and went straight out. Next came five mini buses without passengers. There was speculation that in one the head of state might have been sitting discreetly low, even lying on the floor. They too made a single circuit and out. Then came an armoured troop carrier with soldiers in battle array and guns pointing over the sides in all directions as much as to say: "Take heed! Beware!" And out they went. Again the mini buses with two or three passengers in each, but their purpose could not be made out. They now stood to one side.

At last the moment came. The head of state made his triumphal entry, protruding from the sunroof of a saloon car. His body, it seemed, could barely squeeze through the space and he looked nervous in this awkward stance. When he left the car, it became apparent that the real explanation for his straitened appearance was that his air-force uniform had grown too small for him and needed letting out at the seams. The flight-lieutenant made a tour on foot and gave a thousand salutes with the hand raised to the peak of his air-force cap and then flicked out in the direction of the person greeted, American style. The danger of this is that the person greeted must be at least an arm's length away for his own safety. Rawlings then sat in a royal pavilion to watch the parade.

It was a high spectacle. Massed shield bearers sent their hide shields spinning in the air and caught them, still spinning, on their fingertips. Twenty white-uniformed and helmeted police on twenty latest white Mitsubishi motorbikes, gifts to the state from an interested trading nation. There were marchers with muskets – said to be the original gift of Queen Victoria – and several groups of dancers, including some rather solemn stompers. Big and small drums were hurled spinning in the air. The drumming was unceasing, and the entertainment as varied and at as high a decibel level as the drumming itself.

The festival ended with a big speech by Rawlings. He urged that the Adae Kese should be held every two years instead of five-yearly. This was received with a roar of delight, for everyone except Rawlings knew that it already was biennial. The reception given to his gaffe may well have misled him into misinterpreting the noise that accompanied the rest of his speech. He spoke of turning traditional values into loyalty to the people and the state, and "even to me, the Head of State". He, being of the Ewe tribe, had usurped what the Ashanti saw as their traditional right to rule. They hated him. He must have known this, yet seemed unconcerned. If he had bodyguards there, they were unobtrusive.

At an earlier stage in his dictatorship, Rawlings murdered rivals and even three critical high court judges. At that time, there was terror in the land and Osu Castle, where he lives and whence governmental orders issue, was regarded as a brooding monster controlling all. There have been no political murders for some time and there is nothing approaching terror today, but there is nervousness and hesitation when "the Castle" speaks or is spoken of. The British government, through the Foreign Office, react in the manner most convenient to themselves. The general attitude is that Rawlings is better than he was; he is better than many other African dictators, past and present; he is acceptable. For the Ghanaians, our position is a puzzle. Ghana was the first colony to gain its independence, to become democratic. Democracy faded and bloomed, then faded again. Some British interests draw enormous wealth from its products. And yet our government looks on as though what happens to the Ghanaians is of no interest, and of no importance to the world. How can they? I am afraid their attitude is no worse than that of Creech Jones under Attlee.

The trial dragged on for a year. When it ended, I was back in London but later heard a full account from the main defendants over a celebration dinner with Margo and her parents. The prosecution had realised that their demands and threats had not intimidated the chairman. The case would be judged on its merits and they were bound to lose. In his final speech, Mr Bright Akwetty denounced the tribunal and the defence team as perverts. By this he can only have meant that the tribunal were about to pervert the course of justice by coming to a conclusion contrary to his argument. This contention cannot have helped his case and I don't think it is an argument I would ever advance. The tribunal adjourned for six weeks, then gave judgement on 28th October 1991, the day of St Jude, patron of lost causes.

The court had proposed to assemble in the morning. When the defendants arrived at nine a.m., there was no sign of the tribunal, though the clerk said that all were present. The public filled the hall, and nearly all the men wore the black cloths of mourning. The women wore traditional dresses, and were again mostly in black. The police did not anticipate trouble and had only one senior officer and a constable there, with a dozen prison officers and a prison van waiting outside for the defendants. Seeing the black demonstration, the police took fright and sent for reinforcements so that, by eleven a.m., there were about fifty police present. They then ordered the public to leave the hall, to be searched as they returned, one by one. There was pandemonium. 'This is not South Africa! Dictators!" Hearing this, the chairman came out. He raised his arms and called for quiet. Then the doctor came from his bench at the side of the room to join the chairman and made the same appeal. The crowd became quiet and permitted themselves to be ushered out.

It was learned afterwards, through "the usual channels", that all three members of the tribunal had agreed and signed the judgement some time before it was to be delivered, but that on judgement day one member had suddenly disagreed with many parts of it. Three hours were spent by two persuading the one. At twelve-five, the chairman started to read the judgement and it took, without respite, until six-ten. The first five hours brought the general history of events and a broad outline of the charges. At five p.m. a mighty storm descended upon Accra. The wind rose to a gale, rain came in a deluge, there was thunder and there was lightning. "The heavens themselves blaze forth the death of princes" – *Julius Caesar*, Act II (ii). For the first time during the trial, the doors along the Atlantic side of the State House had to be shut.

The chairman dealt with the thirteen charges in detail. At five-fifty-five he gave the verdicts themselves, with the final reasoning. At six-ten he reached, "And so, Count 13: Not guilty." There had been a sense of surprise as the first not-guilty verdict was given, for the public had prepared for something different. When the last verdict was pronounced, there was an instant of astonished silence, and then uproar. The noise of all the demons broke out. Mourning cloths were thrown aside as men leaped and shouted for joy. Then the crowd moved on the acquitted men, who were hoisted shoulder-high and tossed in the air. Kwamena Bartels found himself standing with others on a bench, one foot somehow caught underneath. As they tried to lift him, the bench with all its burden had to go up as well.

To provide for an immediate trip to prison, the doctor had a good bulging wad of cedis in his hip pocket. Realising that this might be in danger, he reached a hand back to protect the pocket. As he was tossed up and down, he felt another hand firmly move his to one side and the pocket was emptied. He looked down at the upturned faces, each aglow with pleasure, but could not tell which had a special, secret reason for delight. The city of Accra soon learned the result of the trial. Drums were beaten throughout the night and taxis went up and down the main streets, blowing their horns. We ended up with the doctor acquitted, his reputation greatly enhanced, and our brave chairman safe in London. From the Castle came word that 'the People' would appeal against the acquittals, but this was only for show.

The promised "democratic elections" were held at the end of 1992. Rawlings took few risks. He rigged the voting registers so that many who were abroad and should have been excluded found that votes had been improperly returned for them, and all in favour of Rawlings and his men. Many known progressives were removed from the registers, although a substantial part of the democratic front wanted no part in the elections, either by voting or by standing as candidates. They were apprehensive of the results even if they were to lose, for past experience of previous democratic candidates was gruesome. Rawlings had complete confidence in the loyalty of the military forces and didn't bother to control their vote – which, I am told, disclosed a heavy majority against him. Ghana now has a sort of hung parliament. Many of the Members recognise that they didn't win fairly and hesitate to use even the limited powers granted them. The result is that a form of one-man rule continues from the Castle.

CHAPTER FORTY-FIVE

More of Libya; Terry Pattison

IT WAS on my first visit to Tripoli that I met Kate Adie, the BBC war correspondent. She reproved me roundly for going to the country and for giving support to the colonel and his regime by my presence. I asked about the others in our delegation, such as the MPs, and was told that they had a public duty to get about and see the trouble spots of the world, but I had no such responsibility. So I asked, "What about yourself?"

She, too, had a duty. I suppose that's true, for if she hadn't gone to Tripoli she wouldn't have been able to upbraid me. Since then I have noticed Ms Adie's camera-calls in many difficult places. I have equally approved her disregard of danger and the bold expression of her own judgements. It may also be assumed that Ms Adie's judgements are more or less correct. Even so, when it was reported in 1992 that Libyan officials had pleaded with the BBC to spare them from her further attentions, I knew how they felt.

Many people are agreed that Libya should be ostracised. The government and the press have decided that the country and its leadership are "bad" and no one need go to see for him or herself. I disagree. I find the Libyans an enthusiastic and friendly people. Although proud of their country, they are uniquely lacking in ostentation, probably as a result of their colonial experience.

Libya must have been occupied more than any other land in history. The Phoenicians were there in 1000 BC. Then came the Greeks, the Romans, the Vandals. The Ottoman Empire followed and the Turks stayed on until 1911 when the Italians drove them out, killing nearly 4,000 Libyans in the process. During the Second World War the country was fought over from end to end by 1.5 million fighting men, with Rommel and Montgomery as the leading protagonists. Libya was the site of 127 land battles and 3,128 air and sea actions; Tripoli suffered 248 air raids, while, in just three months of 1941, Tobruk took 1,000 Axis air raids. The Libyans' only offence was in being an Italian colony and they had resisted this with the greatest determination.

Anyone who supported the resistance or who failed to endorse the Fascist regime risked imprisonment or exile, with or without their family. The Italians deported thousands of men, women and children, from the youngest babes-in-arms to octogenarians. The deportees were imprisoned on inhospitable islands such as Tremiti and Ustica. Forced to do hard labour on inadequate food supplies and lacking proper medical treatment, most died of pneumonia, pleurisy, malnutrition or the epidemic diseases. Libya has always regarded these punitive deportations as genocidal. Before the First World War, citizens of Ustica wrote angry letters to the national newspapers complaining that exiles had been buried in such shallow graves that stray dogs had been eating the bodies. To this day, the Italians refuse to tell the relatives of exiles when and how they died, or if they somehow survived and have descendants still living in Italy. Because of this history, any liberation movement fighting against an occupying force will find the Libyans on their side. After three thousand years of resisting colonialism, it is hardly surprising that they should wish to support such causes as the Irish and the Palestinians.

My third trip to Libya was in 1986, shortly after the Americans bombed Tripoli and Benghazi. This was nominally as punishment for the bombing of a West Berlin disco that injured 230 and killed three, one of whom was an American serviceman. The Americans at once attributed it to the Libyans, reasoning that as Colonel Gaddafi had committed and claimed responsibility for so many other terrorist acts, he well deserved the blame for this one. It was widely believed that Syrian and/or Lebanese terrorists were the wrongdoers, although after the reunification of the two Germanies, it was reported that the Stasi, the East German secret police, had in fact both planned and executed the attack. Either way, it is a reminder that no nation should be the judge in its own cause.

The approach of the lawyer in such matters should be, "What is the relevant rule that applies, and who is in breach of it?" Some international conflicts are so involved and spread over so long a period that it is not easy to point to a simple cause, nor readily to allot blame. The bombing of Libya was different. It had a beginning, a middle and an end, and in dealing with that single event there was no trouble in deciding who was responsible for breaching the UN Charter by which peoples and governments are bound to keep the peace. Neither Mrs Thatcher nor Sir Geoffrey Howe had the approval of the Security Council for permitting President Reagan to send his F111 bombers from their base at Upper Heyford. I thought that someone ought to apologise to Colonel Gaddafi on behalf of Mrs Thatcher and, if not for her, then for the British people, for we were no part of the killing of the Libyan people and she was. When offered the chance to go and take part in some debate in Tripoli shortly after the bombing, it seemed a most proper and salutary thing to do. Once there, I asked Omar al-Hamidi if I could see Colonel Gaddafi to apologise to him for Mrs Thatcher. Omar brought back the message: meet Gaddafi at his house and he would show me what the American planes had done. So there we met.

It was a squarish city house that had been dive-bombed and suffered a direct hit, reducing it to two storeys. Other bombs had fallen nearby, adding their shockwaves. I couldn't tell whether the pockmarks on the front of the building were made by shrapnel or machine-gun fire. After so determined an attempt to get the occupants, it was hardly surprising that two of Gaddafi's sons were injured and his infant adopted daughter died. We inspected the bedroom where the child was killed and her blood-soaked mattress. Napoleon had made some observation about the undesirability of killing the enemy's general. I couldn't remember quite what he had said, so made up and palmed off on Napoleon the phrase, "Because if you do, he won't be there to surrender his sword to you". The building was left in its bombed condition with slabs of the ceiling hanging down, windows and doors and parts of the walls blown in and floors strewn with rubble as a permanent reminder of the Americans' attitude to peace.

It was perhaps ironic that the next ruin I inspected was that of Yorkshire Main. I returned there in 1988 and found that it had long since been closed down. Acres of the pit area were now covered by a modern housing estate. The mighty stack had gone, as had the tower that contained the winding wheels and all its adjacent structures. Some of the pit offices remained in red brick from the early part of the century, but nothing more save for Pit Pony Field with several years of growth of rough tussock and scrub. An old man passing by told me that the mine had simply been abandoned. The cages and the pit-head structures were cut to pieces or blown up and dropped down the pit. Both shafts were then filled to the top with all the rubble and rubbish that could be found, including the bulk of the slag heap, then it was concreted over. No sign remained of them. It won't be long before the children will be unaware that Yorkshire Main pit stood right alongside the main road in their village. It seemed to me that the British miner would himself soon be extinct, and who would then know of his skills, his great courage and the solidarity of the union?

In August 1989 I received a phone call from Terry Pattinson, who introduced himself as Industrial Editor for the *Daily Mirror* and explained that he was writing a book about the miners' strike of 1984-85. I was delighted to talk to him and offered every possible assistance. He knew that "Arthur" had asked me to raise funds abroad and although Mr Pattinson never said that he was a friend of Arthur Scargill's, I mistakenly assumed that he was and spoke to him quite freely. He phoned several times and I told him what I could recall of the fund-raising, although this was without reference to any records, from unconsidered memory of events five years before. It all seemed quite ordinary until he suddenly began to speak about financial irregularities – specifically, about large sums of money which had been donated for the relief of miners' families but had instead been shuffled from one foreign bank account to another. He was talking about millions of pounds. It was surprising, to say the least.

I have always believed that Arthur put the interests of the miners above other considerations. Even those who disliked him on personal or political grounds had conceded that he was incorruptible. Arthur would have to know what was being said about him. I rang the NUM office in Sheffield but he had already left for Blackpool for the TUC conference, as had Terry Pattinson. On September 6th, Nell Myers rang and in a long discussion I told her all that had happened. She came to London at once and took photocopies of the only letters I could find relating to the strike. Nell assured me that Arthur was grateful for the warning. They knew that the *Mirror* had some kind of investigation afoot, but had not known the precise nature of the allegations. I had already given Mr Pattinson an appointment to do an interview but cancelled it without comment.

It was a full six months before the *Mirror* printed the results of their investigations, in tandem with a television programme, the *Cook Report*.

Every day there were new revelations, and each more startling than the last. The *Sun* jumped in by pretending that I had also spoken to them. On 8th March *The Times* rang me up at home in the country, wanting my opinion on an article which would appear in the *Mirror* the following day. It was all about a trip to Libya and was described as arising from "a remarkable interview". I told them that I had had no interview with the *Mirror*, and it was only when my clerk Michael showed me a copy of the article several days later that I realised that it was based upon Mr Pattinson's phone calls of the previous August, which could quite reasonably be termed an interview. Some sort of enquiry was called for. The NUM contacted the Haldane Society and asked if they could recommend a lawyer suitable for the job. They suggested Gavin Lightman, a QC with a distinguished name at the Bar. I was not acquainted with him and had no part in the selection. However, I was President of the Haldane and also a potential witness. The *Mirror* refused to co-operate and it was suggested that the enquiry would be no more than a whitewash. Not wishing to cast a shadow of suspicion over Mr Lightman's enquiry, I offered to resign from the post of President, but this was rejected.

It is not much use a man's going to the Bar unless he has a fairly good memory, but he must make a particular use of it. The documentation for a legal case may run into many volumes; all have to be carefully studied, for the barrister has to be familiar with every detail of the material. Yet he must be at pains to dismiss from his mind each case as soon as it is over so as to clear the way for the next problem. For example, a barrister doing crime may have a run of armed robberies and it is no use muddling up two cases just because they have some features in common. On the other hand, a past case may be dealt with as an appeal and memory will have to be revived. This means reading all the papers again, when it all floods back, and memory is probably strengthened by the revival. In seventy years at the Bar I have had my full share of cases. They must go into thousands. The one memory aid for the barrister is the taking of notes. We write notes before, during and after meetings, filling our light-blue foolscap notebooks by the score and the hundred. All letters are collated and kept in case of future need, but whereas those that come into the keeping of my clerks are filed carefully away, the more personal documents go into large brown envelopes to be buried in dusty boxes in the loft and may never be seen again.

Owing a certain loyalty to both the NUM and the Haldane, I had a moral obligation to co-operate with the enquiry. While waiting to be summoned, I turned up old diaries, letters and other records to establish on what dates I had visited Russia and Libya. The problem was that I had gone to both countries on a number of occasions. If one visited a country only once, then the visit would no doubt stay fresh and clear and distinct in the memory. If one makes a number of visits to the same place, and each of those visits has common features, then memory of them tends to overlap. Few of my notes could be found, and without them it was impossible to allocate a particular meeting to a particular date. I had visited Libya in August 1984 and in March 1985 but could not, offhand, say on which date I did or did not see Colonel Gaddafi. On both trips I had certainly asked Omar about the chances of getting financial help from their trade unionists. With Russia the situation was rather more complicated. I have had a great many contacts there over the past fifty years. I've been there so often that it is possible for a brief visit to go unrecorded. Were there any visits to Russia at that time? I remembered speaking to embassy officials and telling them of the desperate plight of the British miners and their families and asking for assistance, and I'm sure it was reported in the papers that a million pounds had been donated by Soviet miners.

In June 1990, I was summoned to Gavin Lightman's chambers in Lincoln's Inn. He asked many questions about foreign bank accounts and possible donations to them, including whether or not Ron Brown had also asked for help for the miners. I had no idea whether or not Ron had been involved. I'm afraid that I wasn't much help to Mr Lightman because it was not until some months later that the bundles of contemporary notes on the matter came to light. Another question dealt with the purpose of donations: whether money was intended for hardship purposes, for "the fabric of the union", or for international solidarity.

To my mind, given the suffering amongst the British miners and their families, international solidarity meant money coming from foreign sympathisers for use in Britain. Throughout 1984, the main need was to help families with food, clothing, rent and so forth. Insofar as "the fabric of the union" had any meaning for me, it meant the membership and their wellbeing. By the end of the strike, the position was rather different. Now the question was for the survival of the union itself. A union needs funds to pay for wages and basic administration and, in this case, massive legal expenses.

When the news first came out that Roger Windsor had visited Gaddafi, Norman Willis backed NUM denials, saying that Arthur Scargill had given a categorical assurance that his union had neither sought nor accepted money from Libya's "odious tyranny" and never would. After the publication of the Lightman Report, Norman Willis had rather a blunt exchange of letters with Arthur over the matter. Their exchange included copies of my correspondence with Arthur during the strike. When they reached an impasse Norman Willis circulated the entire correspondence, including my letters, to the General Council of the TUC (the heads of all the largest unions) and to myself. The first I knew of this was when the bundle arrived with the briefest possible covering letter: "I enclose a copy of correspondence I am having with the President of the NUM." Arthur had not taken the elementary step of letting me know what was going on. In reply to Norman, I included the comment:

> "I cannot feel that I am very deeply involved in any dispute that may arise between Libya or Russia and the UK, or between one union and another, or between one individual and another. You will not expect me to take sides or to feel that there is any sort of self-defence that arises."

It was thoroughly unpleasant to find myself in the middle of such a dispute.

Libya is still the international pariah, home of the "odious tyranny" of Gaddafi, as Norman Willis phrased it. Mentioning that I am on the nominating committee for the Muammar Gaddafi Annual Prize for Human Rights tends to leave people rather stunned. This is an award given for genuine and deep-rooted commitment in the struggle for freedom and democracy, as defined by the Libyans. In 1989, the inaugural year, the winner was Nelson Mandela, in 1990 the children of the Intifada. In 1991 the Indians of the Americas. In June 1992, the substantial prize money was awarded for research to halt the spread of AIDS in Africa. The awarding of the prize coincided with a conference on "human rights in the 21st Century" and I returned to Tripoli to present a paper on the subject.

This was a Libya cut off from the outside world by order of the United Nations for refusal to hand over two men suspected of having a connection with the bombing of Pan Am Flight 103, which crashed at Lockerbie in December 1988, killing 270. At first, the West claimed that the Syrians were responsible. The next theory, and the most popular, held that the bombing was set up by the Iranians in retaliation for an incident earlier in the year when the USS *Vincennes* shot down an Iranian Airbus, clearly a civilian plane in a commercial corridor, with the loss of 290 civilians. According to this theory, the revenge bombing was planned in Damascus by Ahmed Jibril's Popular Front for the Liberation of Palestine – General Command, which has spent two decades attacking planes. Iran and Syria were cleared when the West needed their support for the Gulf War coalition against Saddam Hussein.

The Montreal Sabotage Convention of 1971 lays down legal requirements for the prosecution of terrorists who attack commercial aeroplanes. Article 5 of the Convention states that a contracting state must either extradite an alleged offender or prosecute the alleged offender itself. Libya had already begun a full investigation of the complaints against the men with a view to bringing charges. Article 36 Paragraph 2 of the UN Charter requires that members of the Security Council should, in any such dispute, urge that the parties submit the matter for arbitration by any relevant authority and not take steps that lead away from peaceful settlement. Libya had already submitted the issue to the International Court of Justice and was behaving in full accord with her legal duties. Despite this, the UN imposed sanctions, prohibiting arms sales and access by air. If a permanent member of the Security Council forces a resolution to the vote, as the Americans did with Resolution 731 on Libya, they must themselves abstain. The Americans did not abstain; in my opinion, they then coerced the other members of the Security Council to vote in favour. The Security Council should not have lent itself to such misconduct.

Extradition, the sending of a person wanted for crime in another country, comes into operation solely by reason of a treaty. There is no extradition treaty between Libya and the United States or between Libya and the UK. At the same time that Libya was being condemned for refusing to honour an extradition treaty she had not signed, France was pressing Switzerland to refuse the extradition of a French spy the New Zealand authorities believed to have been involved in the bombing of the Greenpeace ship

Rainbow Warrior. New York refuses to extradite IRA fugitives for trial in the UK on the grounds that they would not have fair trials and, after recent decisions by the Court of Appeal, there seems to be some foundation for this opinion. If it is unsafe for Irishmen to be sent to the UK, is it much better for Libyans? America refused to allow two of her pilots to attend a British inquest into their killing of nine of our servicemen in the Gulf War, although they were summoned by a duly appointed coroner and there was nothing to stop them except American Air Force orders. Where is the consistency of action? The rule is universal: we extradite prisoners only on the basis of a treaty. The most the West is entitled to ask of the Libyans is that they should agree to negotiate a treaty to govern future conduct. I believe that the same rule applied in the period BC when Rome began to govern the known world.

The summer of 1992 was a time of flux. Every nation joined in the UN embargo; the Libyans stood alone, isolated and friendless. It was thought that they might now begin to move towards the West, to stabilise the economy and to prevent an oil embargo. There seemed every reason to hope for a change of attitude. If there was a chance for real progress in Libya's relations with the West, it was well worth trying to encourage them towards reforms. They would have to take note of certain valid criticisms from the West, and they should also realise that the advice of Amnesty International could be almost as valuable to them as that of Kate Adie herself. I wanted to say my piece to the conference and to urge the necessity for every country to hold to the provisions of the UN Declaration of Human Rights. However, it would have been a bit out of place to say anything in favour of the United Nations, which had allowed itself to be grievously misused by America and the UK in imposing illegal sanctions, so inconveniencing most of the conference delegates, who were prevented from flying into or out of the country and had to find other ways of travelling.

In the first session of the conference, we heard speeches somewhat in praise of Colonel Gaddafi. A typical effort ended, in translation: "Thank you very much to the Committee, to Libya, to the people of Libya, to Gaddafi, Leader of Man, Hope of Humanity." Others followed in the same vein and I began to doubt the suitability of my effort. So many nations see the very concept of human rights as an additional extra, a mere embellishment of life for the citizens of the rich Western nations, or a weapon that they use to interfere in the private affairs of Third World nations. This is understandable, and those regularly on the receiving end of such criticism generally feel that the West is unfairly setting itself up as the model of perfection, something to emulate. I spoke in praise of the universality of the basic human rights: that human rights belong in all circumstances, to all races, and in all countries. The Socialist countries had recognised rights to education, housing and employment that are sometimes not seen as rights in the West, or are under threat. It would be a tragic waste if the peoples of Eastern Europe were, in their eagerness to obtain such human rights as they felt had been denied to them, to abandon the advantages that they already had. No one system is perfect; we must learn from each other.

All nations make mistakes and we in the West are not immune. At the English Bar, we have constantly in mind the recent disclosure of a series of gross miscarriages of justice which saw prisoners freed after serving up to eighteen years of imprisonment for crimes they did not commit. To my mind, the sole consolation was that they were not subject to death sentences. Because of human fallibility, there should be no death penalty, no torture, no degrading treatment or punishment, no arbitrary arrest or detention. All should be entitled to proper legal representation and access to the courts. Because Amnesty International reports have been somewhat critical of Libya in relation to human rights, I did not name them in my speech. Instead I mentioned "various international organisations that concern themselves with human rights" and urged that however critical they might be, we should be wise to listen to their voices. The speech ended by asking that all countries should honour the UN Declaration of Human Rights. I had half-expected to be set upon for the audacity of the speech, which could be seen as critical of our hosts, but it was warmly received and Omar insisted that I should speak at the final prize-giving ceremony.

My second speech, summarising the history of the Gaddafi prize, was a disaster. The sound system was a highly sophisticated affair with simultaneous translation into a number of languages, but the microphone took a dislike to me and screamed so much that only the latter part of the speech could be clearly heard. Even so, I spoke with such passion that as I stood at the rostrum some underground reservoir of blood on my left shin burst open. This is one of the trials of old age. I was sockless and felt the sandals awash. After a ten-minute panegyric to the excellence of our past prize-winners, much of it inaudible, there was slight and modest applause. When I stepped out from the shelter of the lectern and the left leg of my light summer trousers was seen to be soaked in blood, the audience was rather more vocal.

At the time of the conference, Western journalists were speculating on the chances of another American raid on Libya. I'm sure no one of us thought of ourselves as hostages, but if President Bush had bombed Tripoli he would have had a chance of getting rid of some of the delegates, as well as any of the Gaddafi family that might have been about. A guided tour for delegates took me back to Gaddafi's bombed house. I had not previously seen the main bedroom, which was notable. The round bed (of dark blue) had wide arm-panels set with quite a number of switches. They must have worked the air-conditioning, stereo, television set and so forth, although nothing electronic remained in the room. A round bed and bath would normally be thought to indicate an indulgent lifestyle but the caretaker carefully pointed out that the bedroom was not luxurious, that it was "small for a head of state". Then came the obvious correction that Gaddafi was really only chairman of a committee. I don't think any one of us had forgotten. The house was in much the same state as six years before, except that everything was now coated thick with dust. It must be a problem for the curators – whether to repair and clean and cocoon the place, turning it into a museum, or to leave it in disrepair and let wind and weather do their worst.

Chapter Forty-six

A Touch of Family

JANET CREE put up with me for fifty-six years of married life. We had entered our marriage bargain when I was a junior barrister and Janet a painter and, we hoped, a mother. She kept her implied bargain by producing six sons and about 400 paintings, of which 150 remain within the immediate family. I have written a long and accurate and illuminating passage about each of our children. When the material was first available to be read, I was met by the united sons armed with shredders and dumpers. I was contradicted, challenged, condemned and banned. Six tall sons: each endowed with menacing wit and vigour; each alone capable of silencing so quavering a voice as is offering to speak out; and all six together more than capable. Salman Rushdie's position was comparatively a secure one. I shall content myself with the merest mention of them.

Tim, the eldest, is a perfectionist. He went into forestry and has only to look at an area of growing trees, put a dampened finger into the air and by the time it has dried he will know the necessary figures: so much hard wood, so much semi-soft, and so much soft wood for paper or pit props.

Jonathan, the second, was somewhat precocious. He was a roving trouble-shooter for Lonrho before going on the board of directors and can be relied upon for at least three good new stories a week, with a host of throwaway lines at any moment. One week he was overseeing new housing in Russia and the next, deep in some extraordinary African adventure. He has recently taken early retirement but I wait with baited breath for his next adventure.

Tom is an immunologist and a pioneer of research into the most intimate details of the life of the house-dust mite or the cockroach. When not at home in Virginia, he flies all round the world, lecturing on his subject to gatherings of distinguished doctors.

Barney was the only one not to go to university. He left school at fifteen and soon set himself up as a film producer, having marked success with Bronco Bullfrog and Private Road. His films are highly regarded by intelligent and informed persons, even after he went into Gaelic but were not necessarily box-office bonanzas. He now teaches and proclaims video for all under the slogan "video, vidi, vinci".

Ben took to sculpture, at first in wood and then, when apprenticed to an English sculptor in the foothills of the Carrara Mountains, in marble. On a trip to Amsterdam, he was so moved by the paintings that he largely abandoned wood and stone in favour of oil paint. He is also a self-employed designer of an improved state of nature; he devises woodlands and gardens, then plants them out and tends their development. He uses these new environments as settings for the new generation of carvings cut from standing dead oak trees and thirty feet tall.

Only our youngest, Mark, followed me to the Bar. He is a patent lawyer specialising in the most obscure things like intellectual property rights. He is a busy and successful silk.

They are all entirely different, the one from the other, but I am equally proud of them all. None has been so foolish as to pursue my political interests and inclinations.

I did not keep my side of the marital bargain and dissipated my efforts. Politics accounted not only for the years in parliament but also the Peace Movement, the work of colonial emancipation and the battle for civil liberties all about the Commonwealth and in so many foreign parts. And was my wife pleased with these fancy excursions? Perhaps only one in ten of them was backed with a solicitor waving a fee, and in at least one case I paid the fare myself. Janet really disliked this work. It was not the causes or the people involved but the demands on time and attention. For an artist, the distraction was impossible; for a lawyer, it should have been. If this were not accepted, it threw a heavy and unfair burden of the family on one parent; a one-parent family where two should have been available. Janet's opinion was that if I had taken a full share in family affairs, I would have made acquaintance with my sons instead of meeting them mainly at school on parents' day or sports days. There would also have been many more paintings and a wider recognition of her talent.

Janet died on the eve of her eighty-second birthday, when we had almost given up celebrating such anniversaries and had quite forgotten the possibility of death. The week before there had been a heart attack, followed by a week in bed at Barts. The day after being discharged as recovered, she was back in Barts and three hours of open-heart surgery proved too much. There was a memorial service at the Temple Church and the installing of Janet's ashes in the columbarium, and a retrospective exhibition of her work. I'm still practising at the Bar but have retired as head of chambers. Since my retirement, the conference room at Cloisters has been decorated, hung with Janet's work and named the Cree Room, to the very great pleasure of the whole family. In these very days I have moved to Tooks Court and am to share a room with Michael Mansfield, some-time pupil of mine and now Leader of the Criminal Bar.

Index